lonely planet

W9-CEH-282

Sarah Johnstone &
Tom Masters

London

The Top Five

1 Thames Journey
Take a trip down the river (p94) to the home of time, Greenwich

2 Glorious Architecture
Wander past the ornate, neo-Gothic Houses of Parliament and their clock tower, Big Ben (p134)

3 Top Shops
Browse through the famous Harrods department store (p342)

4 Fascinating Art
Peer into the galleries and out the windows of Tate Modern (p152)

5 Stunning Views
See for miles atop the London Eye (p149)

Contents

Published by Lonely Planet Publications Pty Ltd
ABN 36 005 607 983

Australia Head Office, Locked Bag 1, Footscray,
Victoria 3011, ☎ 03 8379 8000, fax 03 8379 8111,
talk2us@lonelyplanet.com.au

USA 150 Linden St, Oakland, CA 94607,
☎ 510 893 8555, toll free 800 275 8555,
fax 510 893 8572, info@lonelyplanet.com

UK 72–82 Rosebery Ave, Clerkenwell, London,
EC1R 4RW, ☎ 020 7841 9000, fax 020 7841 9001,
go@lonelyplanet.co.uk

© Lonely Planet 2006
Photographs © Neil Setchfield and as listed
(p420), 2006

Printed by SNP Security Printing Pte Ltd, Singapore

The Authors

SARAH JOHNSTONE

Sarah came to London soon after finishing her first university degree and, despite regularly swearing she's leaving, she's still here a decade and a half later, so she reckons the place must have something, after all. As a poverty-stricken student working towards her MSc from the London School of Economics and now as a freelance journalist who has worked for Reuters, *Business Traveller* and a host of other publications, Sarah has seen the capital from many different sides.

She wrote the Introducing London, Architecture, Shopping, Sleeping, Excursions and Directory chapters and contributed to the City Life, Arts, Neighbourhoods, Walking Tours and Eating chapters.

TOM MASTERS

Tom grew up in Buckinghamshire, moving to Bloomsbury at 18 to study Russian literature. He has had 10 London postcodes, although never one beginning with S. Tom has worked abroad in journalism and TV, but London's wonderful public-transport system and cheap rent keep him coming back.

Tom wrote the History, Drinking and Entertainment chapters, as well as the bulk of City Life, Arts and Walking Tours. He also contributed to the Neighbourhoods and Eating chapters.

PHOTOGRAPHER

Welsh-born Neil Setchfield has worked as a full-time travel photographer for the past 15 years. His work has appeared in over 100 newspapers and magazines throughout the world, as well as in food and guide books. In his spare time he drinks beer and laughs a lot – not always at the same time.

Neil is represented by Lonely Planet Images. Many of the images in this guide are available for licensing: www.lonelyplanet images.com.

Introducing London

Some cities are born great; others have greatness thrust upon them. During its long history, London has managed to achieve both. While this sprawling metropolis has grown naturally into a global colossus, in adversity it's always demonstrated its power to endure.

But although it's one of the planet's hardiest perennials – a timeless classic, an evergreen – London also combines such far-reaching tradition with a vibrant modernity, in a way no other place can match. Just picture the wildly successful Tate Modern gallery facing the implacable St Paul's Cathedral across the Millennium Bridge, or conjure up a postcard view of the world's oldest elected parliament through the spokes of the London Eye observation wheel.

The sci-fi City Hall across the River Thames from the medieval Tower of London and the gherkin-shaped 30 St Mary Axe skyscraper watching guard over the Victorian-era Tower Bridge show that a confident 21st-century London has taken a foothold beside the famous old.

The transformation that has propelled the city forward in the past decade is more than just architectural window-dressing, however. Although not far shy of its 2000th birthday, this is the only major European capital that's still growing, fuelled by the continual stream of newcomers who have always made it so great. What's different this time around is that instead of London just winging it with its vibrant nightlife, stimulating culture and youthful energy, many of its long-standing weaknesses are finally being addressed, too.

The warts-and-all city that was deprived of a mayor for 14 years by national government seems to be responding well to renewed central planning since the turn of the century. Plus, with London already gearing up to host the 2012 Olympics – a surprise victory for many – there's added impetus for the authorities to continue sorting out the lousy public transport, congestion and dirty streets.

Meanwhile, by some lucky coincidence, an increasing number of exciting restaurants and chefs have seen this once culinarily challenged city declared by one set of critics (French President Jacques Chirac famously not among them) as the best place in the world to eat. Better-priced hotels also continue to improve the experience for short-term visitors.

Lowdown

Population 7.3 million
Time zone Greenwich Mean Time
3-star double room £150
Coffee in the West End £1.75
Daily Travelcard Zones 1 and 2 £4.70
Pint of lager £2.50
No-no Chatting to a stranger for no particular reason – sadly, they'll usually think you're crazy
Best way to annoy a Londoner Stand on the left-hand side of a tube escalator
Best view From the western side of the Golden Jubilee Bridge – at night
The butt of many jokes 'Hoodies' (teenagers with allegedly criminal intent shielding their faces with hooded tops, and the controversy surrounding them); tackily dressed 'chavs' (p18)

Tourist brochures portray a city of black cabs and red buses, where you can take afternoon tea at the Ritz before swinging by Buckingham Palace en route to a spot of shopping at Harrods. Yet London's everyday reality is quite different. It's a hard-working commercial giant with an economy as large as some of the European Union's smaller states, and that's what makes it such a magnet for creative talent and entrepreneurial skill.

Essential London

- A stroll across **Hampstead Heath** (p194)
- **Houses of Parliament** (p134)
- A ride on the **London Eye** (p149)
- The Great Court of the **British Museum** (p107)
- The view from **Tate Modern** (p152) to **St Paul's** (p110)

As successive waves of immigrants arrive (most recently from Eastern Europe) to join this exhilarating, irrepressible dynamo, a multicultural tapestry has been woven that forms the very fabric of society here. More than one third of Londoners were born outside the country. The city speaks more than 300 languages and some 40 ethnic groups live together here. Sure, events of the past few years have shaken any notions about complete multicultural harmony and thrown up some major challenges. However, it's still difficult to think of another city where different populations so readily intermingle and mix.

Its broad sweep of influences has won London the moniker 'the world in one city', but the place has enormous depth, too. It's certainly not just about headline attractions like Westminster Abbey or the Victoria & Albert Museum, it's also about small, quirky gems like the Wallace Collection and the Old Operating Theatre Museum. Its expansive, manicured royal parks are complemented by noisy, chaotic street markets; it mixes cosy Victorian pubs with chic cocktail bars; and it runs the gamut from clubbing in Clerkenwell and gigging in Brixton to shopping in Shoreditch and highbrow theatre on the South Bank, all with equanimity.

Such contradictions and complexity, coupled with its geographical vastness, might make London seem intimidating initially. However, whether you're here for a couple of days, a few years or a lifetime, the trick is to accept that no-one can ever truly 'know' the collection of villages that comprises this megalopolis and to find yourself a niche. So, breathe in. It's time to begin exploring the many possibilities of this fascinating, ever-changing city that – in no sense of the word – will ever be finished.

SARAH'S TOP LONDON DAY

No matter how many times I do it, I never tire of taking a morning stroll up Parliament Hill on Hampstead Heath, where you can see the skyline from a clear distance and get an overview of the city you're about to dive into. Afterwards I'll head down to Islington for breakfast and the *Guardian*'s Sudoko puzzle at Ottolenghi, before continuing on to Soho for a few museums. Feeling particularly enthusiastic, I'll pop quickly into the Great Court of the British Museum, whiz around the tiny Photographers' Gallery and do a quick perusal of the National Portrait Gallery, either staying for lunch in the Photographers' Gallery café, the restaurant at the top of the NPG or going for fish pie at nearby J Sheekey. In the afternoon I'll cross the river via the Golden Jubilee Bridge, admiring the London Eye and the Houses of Parliament as I go, before turning left along the riverbank for Tate Modern. Here I'll visit the Rothko and Bill Viola rooms, before nursing a coffee on the fourth floor balcony overlooking the Thames. With only a few hours before the shops close, I'll hurry across the Millennium Bridge and head for the streetwear boutiques of Brick Lane, leaving me in a perfect position to move on to the fabulously over-the-top Les Trois Garçons for dinner and a night of drinking at nearby Loungelover.

City Life

City Life

LONDON TODAY

Trying to reconcile the manifold faces of the British capital is, to say the least, a tricky game and the city always seems to be one step ahead of anyone playing it. A visitor expecting to see little more than the pomp and circumstance around Buckingham Palace and the House of Commons will be bewildered by a short stroll north into the West End, London's stern and traditional heartland immediately giving way to its mercurial and chaotic soul. Likewise, people travelling to London in hopes of finding Europe's achingly modern capital of fashion, music and art may be more than a little surprised to see that the cabs are still black, the double-deckers and post boxes are still red and life goes on in the City of London much as it has for the past century. At the risk of sounding like a pimp, it's this very juxtaposition of styles that gives London its vibrancy and its intensity – compare Brixton Market, Belgrave Sq, Whitechapel High St and Camden Town and you'll see exactly what we mean. London's a city that thrives on its ever-changing elusiveness. But what's it like to live here?

Transport remains the biggest bugbear for Londoners and the priority for mayor Ken Livingstone, who in 2003 slapped a £5 tax on private cars entering the city centre (this rose to £8 in 2005). The populace was in an uproar and then, after a few months, begrudgingly patted the mayor on the back as the traffic jams disappeared and the average speed in the centre rose by 10km/h. He has set about integrating the whole of London transport and has also brought much improvement in the bus service, even if this has been at the expense of the capital's beloved Routemaster buses, which have pretty well disappeared from the city streets, replaced by Ken's 'bendy-buses', with none of the retro charm or easy jump-on, jump-off access of their predecessors (see p96).

Getting the creaking Underground system into shape is a much more ambitious project. The weakest link in the system is the confusing line-sharing Circle, District, Metropolitan and Hammersmith & City lines – running on the oldest and most dilapidated track in the capital (the stretch from Baker St to Farringdon was the world's first underground line in the mid-19th century!). Delays and overcrowding are endemic. Overall the tube is fine, even efficient, but remains horrendously overpriced and extremely crowded in rush hour. There's also a lack of coverage, particularly across much of South London. New lines are not being built, meaning that the network has not been able to keep up with the expanding nature of postwar London. The promised East London line extension is under way, bringing the tube to some much needed areas, although there's still considerable bitterness that no effort has been made to bring the tube to Hackney Town, one of the capital's most socially deprived neighbourhoods, and served only by buses and irregular mainline trains.

Almost as important an issue to Londoners is housing. The capital is currently seeing the biggest migration of people *out* of London since WWII, due to a lack of affordable housing. Blue-collar workers like nurses and firemen are being forced out, with some having to commute several hours just to get to work, while an entire generation of young people are finding it impossible to get on the property ladder, because they can't afford anything worth living in without first earning twice as much as they do at present.

But it's not all doom and suburban gloom. There is little or no ghettoisation in London, and the haves live cheek by jowl with the have-nots, with notable exceptions such as Belgravia and Holland Park. Equally, in the very areas such as Hackney, Brixton, Whitechapel and Haringey where ghettoisation has occurred in the past (mainly for poor first- and second-generation immigrants), the cheaper rents have attracted the middle classes, creating extremely diverse communities.

The push outwards to the suburbs has helped to create clusters that are like self-contained minicities, while the demand for central locations has seen the regeneration of many areas and led to impressive urban renewal. London is looking better than ever: the centre is no longer choked by traffic; buildings have been scrubbed up and new ones erected; previously run-down areas like Clerkenwell, Shoreditch and Hoxton have been funked up; the long-neglected South Bank of the Thames has been transformed into a gallery and playground for the city; and a major development of Trafalgar Sq has revealed the magnificent public space that was there all along.

One fairly recent feature of London – and no doubt a measure of its status and appeal – is the number of young Europeans choosing to relocate here (mostly propping up the restaurant, construction and hotel service industry). Frankly, you're as likely to hear Italian, Polish, Spanish or Russian on the streets of central London as you are English.

As sophisticated as they are in some respects, Londoners are also terribly undiscerning in others. So many chain pubs, cafés and restaurants have sprung up over the last decade that it's difficult to tell streets apart. The Starbucks chain is the most recent villain, having swamped the city and doing more than anyone else to turn London into 'Generica', a place where all the urban landscapes look the same. A recent *cause célèbre* involved the residents of smart Primrose Hill fighting the green giant and successfully campaigning for it to abandon plans to open a branch there. Unfortunately, this was the exception rather than the rule.

The spread of the chains continues because a cash-rich and time-poor populace is too busy staying ahead to think ahead. The economy is booming still, although not quite to the degree it was a few years ago. The economic good times have been attributed fairly directly to Chancellor Gordon Brown, Prime Minister Tony Blair's great rival for power (he has the premiership in his sights) and, officially at least, his right-hand man. Amazingly, many Londoners still seem to have a lot of cash to spend on going out, eating out, consumer goods and foreign travel, despite having the highest rents and priciest public transport in Europe.

Londoners also give a damn. Although they'd be more likely to vote somebody out of *Big Brother* than into parliament, there is still a sizable, active corps of radicals ready to take to the streets and challenge the status quo. Between one and two million people marched in 2003 to protest against the imminent US/British-led invasion of Iraq. Protests, rallies and assemblies are part of the fabric of life in this city.

What's amazing is that the capital – ancient and modern, sprawling and compact, angry and indifferent, stolidly English and increasingly multicultural – works quite as well as it does. It is a lesson in life for some and a rite of passage for others. The music of the city will resound in your ears long after you've left.

Hot Conversation Topics

- The Olympics are coming! London won the 2012 bid and now has the daunting task of seeing through its massive development plans for East London. Londoners are both proud and wary at the same time, but not unhappy at the prospect of more tube lines.
- The demise of the beloved Routemaster bus (the double-deckers with the open backs) is a constant lament among Londoners. Ken has replaced them with his derided 'bendy buses' and the capital's residents have yet to fall for them.
- House prices are rising... falling... rising. Every half-percentile nudge up or down sends homeowners or those hoping to get on the property ladder into a frenzy. With some of the most expensive house prices in Europe, can you blame them?
- Is the government-led campaign for 'a culture of respect' going a bit far? Antisocial behaviour orders (ASBOs) have been levied against a retired schoolteacher, a famous peace campaigner, a DJ, a male sunbather and feuding families. Teenagers wearing 'hoodies' (hooded jackets) have been banned by some shopping centres, while the government has proposed bright-orange uniforms for young offenders.
- Londoners love celebrity and, with the recent glut of reality TV shows, there's no reason not to clock their common or garden versions regularly. 'Was that that bloke from *Big Brother*?'
- Did you see the match last night? A conversation you'll hear almost anywhere in a city as football mad as London, and particularly when there's a clash of current titans Arsenal and Chelsea.

CITY CALENDAR

You might imagine that in a country with such a thoroughly derided climate as England, the weather is not much of a topic for conversation, and yet, like their middle-England cousins, Londoners are relentless weather-watchers and every rise or fall of the mercury will provoke smiles or gloom respectively. It's good therefore that London is not a city where fun depends on the weather – as Londoners do, expect overcast skies and rain (even in summer) and then be elated when the sun comes out.

While summer is a great time to visit (and in recent years has seen some very Continental heatwaves), spring and autumn are also great times to come, when the crowds are far thinner and sights less crowded. Winter's all cold, wet and dark, although if you're after outdoor pleasures, you'll have them largely to yourself.

For a full list of events in and around London, look out for Visit London's bimonthly *Events in London* and its *Annual Events* pamphlet. You can also check the website at www.visitlondon.com.

JANUARY

NEW YEAR'S CELEBRATIONS

On 31 December, there's the famous countdown to midnight on Trafalgar Sq – London's biggest bash, but one worth avoiding unless you love crowds. If you can get up the following morning, the mayor of Westminster leads 10,000 musicians and street performers through central London, from Parliament Sq to Berkeley Sq, in the lively London Parade.

INTERNATIONAL BOAT SHOW

Excel, Docklands; www.londonboatshow.net
Early January sees this long-running exhibition of all things aquatic.

LONDON ART FAIR

Business Design Centre, Islington; www.londonartfair .co.uk
Over 100 major galleries participate in this contemporary art fair, now one of the largest in Europe, with thematic exhibitions, special events and the best emerging artists.

CHINESE NEW YEAR

Chinatown; www.chinatown-online.co.uk
In late January/early February, Chinatown fizzes, crackles and pops in this colourful street festival, which includes a Golden Dragon parade and eating and partying aplenty.

FEBRUARY

PANCAKE RACES

Spitalfields Market, Covent Garden & Lincoln's Inn Fields
On Shrove Tuesday, in late February/early March, you can catch pancake races and associated silliness at various venues around town.

MARCH

HEAD OF THE RIVER RACE

Thames, from Mortlake to Putney; www.horr.co.uk
Some 400 crews participate in this colourful annual boat race, held over a 7km course.

LONDON LESBIAN & GAY FILM FESTIVAL

www.llgff.co.uk
This rather low-key event is one of the best of its kind in the world with hundreds of independent gay-themed films from around the globe shown over a fortnight at the National Film Theatre.

APRIL

LONDON MARATHON

Greenwich Park to the Mall; www.london-marathon.co.uk
Some 35,000 masochists cross London in the world's biggest road race.

OXFORD & CAMBRIDGE BOAT RACE

From Putney to Mortlake; www.theboatrace.org
Big crowds line the banks of the Thames for this annual event, where the country's two most famous and historic universities go oar-to-oar and hope they don't sink (again). Dates vary year to year due to the universities' Easter breaks, so check the website.

MAY

ROYAL WINDSOR HORSE SHOW

www.royal-windsor-horse-show.co.uk
Prestigious five-day equestrian event attended by royalty, gentry and country folk and hosted in the Queen's private gardens at Windsor Castle, the only chance to visit them for most people.

CHELSEA FLOWER SHOW
Royal Hospital Chelsea; www.rhs.org.uk
The world's most renowned horticultural show attracts green fingers from near and far.

JUNE
ROYAL ACADEMY SUMMER EXHIBITION
Royal Academy of Arts; www.royalacademy.org.uk
Beginning in June and running through August, this is an annual showcase of works submitted by artists from all over Britain, thankfully distilled to a thousand or so pieces.

BEATING THE RETREAT
Horse Guards Parade, Whitehall
A warm-up for the Queen's birthday, this patriotic evening full of royal pomp and circumstance involves military bands and much beating of drums.

TROOPING THE COLOUR
Horse Guards Parade, Whitehall
The Queen's official birthday (she was born in April but the weather's better in June) is celebrated with much flag-waving, parades, pageantry and noisy flyovers.

ARCHITECTURE WEEK
www.architectureweek.org.uk
Late June is about exploring the city's architecture and urban landscapes with various events across town.

WIMBLEDON LAWN TENNIS CHAMPIONSHIPS
www.wimbledon.org
For two weeks the quiet south London village of Wimbledon is the centre of the sporting universe as the greatest players on earth gather to fight it out for the championship. While it's as much about strawberries, cream and tradition as smashing balls for those in attendance, the rest of the capital is riveted by the women's and men's finals that take place on the final Saturday and Sunday of the tournament.

JULY
CITY OF LONDON FESTIVAL
www.colf.org
Two weeks of top-quality music, dance and theatre held in some of the finest buildings, churches and squares in the financial district.

London Pride parade (below)

PRIDE
www.pridelondon.org
The gay community in all its many fabulous guises paints the town pink in this annual extravaganza, featuring a morning parade, a huge afternoon rally and a ticketed evening event in Finsbury Park (although the location changes).

GREENWICH & DOCKLANDS INTERNATIONAL FESTIVAL
www.festival.org
Every weekend in July you can catch (mostly) free outdoor dance, theatre and music performances on either side of the Thames.

SOHO FESTIVAL
www.thesohosociety.org.uk
All sorts of shenanigans from a waiters race to a spaghetti-eating contest and lots of food stalls at this charity fundraiser.

BBC PROMENADE CONCERTS (THE PROMS)
www.bbc.co.uk/proms
Two months of outstanding classical concerts at various prestigious venues, centred on the Royal Albert Hall in Kensington.

RESPECT FESTIVAL
www.respectfestival.org.uk
A free outdoor music and dance festival (at changing venues), dedicated to promoting antiracism and multiculturalism. There are lots of other activities on offer, but the festival is centred on big-name headline acts.

AUGUST

NOTTING HILL CARNIVAL
www.londoncarnival.co.uk

One of Europe's biggest – and London's most vibrant – outdoor carnival is a celebration of Caribbean London, featuring music, dancing, costumes and a little street crime over the summer Bank Holiday weekend.

GREAT BRITISH BEER FESTIVAL
www.gbbf.org

If you think there's an oxymoron in the name, have your perceptions merrily overturned by joining tens of thousands in downing a wonderful selection of local and international brews at the Olympia Exhibition Centre.

SEPTEMBER

THAMES FESTIVAL
www.thamesfestival.org

Celebrating London's greatest natural asset, the River Thames, this cosmopolitan festival provides fun for all the family with fairs, street theatre, music, food stalls, fireworks, river races and a spectacular Lantern Procession.

GREAT RIVER RACE
From Ham House to the Isle of Dogs; www.greatriver race.co.uk

Barges, dragon boats and Viking longships race 35km to contest these traditional boat championships.

LONDON OPEN HOUSE
www.londonopenhouse.org

One of London's biggest treats. For a weekend in late September the public is invited in to see over 500 heritage buildings throughout the capital that are normally off-limits. A unique

---

London Royalty

The cockney monarchs are the Pearly Kings & Queens, the sparkly spectacles that wear tens of thousands of studded buttons sewn into their clothes. A 19th-century barrow boy by the name of Henry Croft, keen to raise money for the poor, began sewing pearly buttons into his garments to attract attention. Others soon followed pearly suit and a tradition was born. Today's pearlies, often descendants of the originals, work for charities and gather at St Martin-in-the-Fields Church in Trafalgar Sq in early October for their annual festival (www.pearlysociety.co.uk) to sing songs, speak in slang, pose for photographs and slap their thighs a lot.

---

chance that has Londoners and visitors alike heading to their favourite places in droves.

OCTOBER

DANCE UMBRELLA
www.danceumbrella.co.uk

London's annual festival of contemporary dance features five weeks of performances by British and international dance companies at venues across London.

TRAFALGAR DAY PARADE
Trafalgar Sq

Commemorating Nelson's victory over Napoleon, marching bands descend on Trafalgar Sq to lay a wreath at Nelson's Column.

LONDON FILM FESTIVAL
National Film Theatre & various venues; www.lff.org.uk

The city's premier film event attracts big overseas names and is an opportunity to see more than 100 British and international films before their cinema release. There are masterclasses given by world-famous directors and Q&A sessions with moviemakers too.

NOVEMBER

LONDON TO BRIGHTON VETERAN CAR RUN
Serpentine Rd; www.vccofgb.co.uk/lontobri

Pre-1905 vintage cars line up and rev up at dawn in Hyde Park before racing to Brighton.

STATE OPENING OF PARLIAMENT
House of Lords, Westminster

The Queen visits Parliament by state coach amid gun salutes to summon MPs back from their long summer recess.

GUY FAWKES NIGHT (BONFIRE NIGHT)

One of Britain's best-loved traditions, Bonfire Night commemorates Guy Fawkes' foiled attempt to blow up Parliament in 1605. Bonfires and fireworks light up the night on 5 November and effigies of Fawkes are burned, while young kids run around asking for 'a penny for the guy'. Alexander Palace, Clapham Common and Crystal Palace Park are some of the places to see the best fireworks displays.

LORD MAYOR'S SHOW
www.lordmayorsshow.org

In accordance with the Magna Carta of 1215, the newly elected lord mayor of the City of London travels in a state coach from Mansion House to the Royal Courts of Justice to seek their approval. The floats, bands and fireworks that accompany him were added later.

REMEMBRANCE SUNDAY

Cenotaph, Whitehall
The Queen, prime minister and other notables lay wreaths at the Cenotaph to remember those who died in two world wars.

DECEMBER

LIGHTING OF THE CHRISTMAS TREE & LIGHTS

Some celebrity is shipped in to switch on all the festive lights that line Oxford, Regent and Bond Sts, and a huge Norwegian spruce is set up in Trafalgar Sq.

Only in London

Changing of the Quill (☎ 7283 2231; St Andrew Undershaft Church, St Mary Axe; 6 Apr) Every three years (next one in 2008) there is a memorial service to John Stow, the first chronicler of London, who is buried here. A learned address is made to his monument and the lord mayor replaces the quill in its hand, presenting the old one to the child who has written the best essay on London.

Horseman's Sunday (Hyde Park Cres; Sep) A vicar on horseback blesses more than 100 horses outside the Church of St John & St Michael, W2, followed by horse jumping in Kensington Gardens.

Hot Cross Bun Ceremony (Widow's Son Pub, 75 Devons Rd E3; Good Friday) This ceremony commemorates a widow who hung a hot cross bun in a basket for her son, a sailor, who was due to return from sea on Good Friday and had asked her to bake his favourite Easter treat. He never returned but every year on the same date she hung another bun in the unwavering hope that someday he would. When she died and her cottage was demolished, the collection of stale buns passed to a pub that was built on the site, where the tradition continues. Today, sailors make the trip here to pay respects to the widow and have a great time in this Victorian alehouse.

Punch & Judy Festival (Covent Garden Piazza; late Sep/early Oct) In the twilight of summer, puppet fans gather in the tourist heart of London for much Punching and Judying (not to mention crocodiles and policemen) in the very spot the first performance took place.

Swan Upping (3rd week of Jul) Held along stretches of the River Thames, the annual census of the swan population dates from the 12th century, when the Crown claimed ownership of all mute swans, a noble delicacy at the time. By tradition, scarlet uniforms are worn by the Queen's Swan Marker and Swan Uppers, and each boat flies appropriate flags and pennants. 'Upping' means turning the birds upside-down to tag them or check whether their beaks are marked or not. In the 15th century the Crown granted ownership of swans with marked beaks to the Vintners and Dyers companies.

CULTURE

IDENTITY

The typical Londoner is dead, long live the typical Londoner… While you aren't likely to find the pin-stripe suited, bowler-hatted city gent much outside the confines of the Square Mile (or much inside them any more, either), you will see 21st-century Londoners everywhere else. How do they define themselves? Largely by being indefinable. Although the populace is primarily white, more than a quarter of locals are from other ethnic backgrounds and your average tube carriage at rush hour is likely to contain a representative from every continent on earth. London is in a constant state of flux and its population thrives on the racial, social and cultural palimpsest that comes with it being such a cosmopolitan city, making it one of the most exciting places on earth.

Foreigners look surprised if they meet someone who claims to be a Londoner. 'But where are you from originally?' they often ask, and not entirely without grounds; London can often seem to be a place people arrive at, aspire to and live for, but are rarely born in.

Of course, it's easy enough to find Londoners, but the constant flux of the population creates an interesting impression; refugees from every corner of the earth, as much from the small towns of the British regions than from abroad, inevitably colour everyone's experience of the capital. With many people living here for a couple of years before moving, exhausted and financially ruined (but definitely exhilarated) back to somewhere far less demanding, it's truly a challenge to talk about the identity of the capital's millions of inhabitants.

Throughout history, refugees and immigrants arrived in dribs and drabs. Pockets of distinction soon emerged as groups of Irish, Greek, Chinese, Turks and Jews set up home. Then in the 1950s Britain opened the gates and ushered in a huge influx of people from the former colonies of the Empire, particularly from the Indian subcontinent, the West Indies and Africa.

Naturally, the new arrivals clustered together and pretty soon areas took on the colours of their new ethnicity as the settlers sought to preserve their customs and way of life: Sikhs in Southall, Bengalis in Shoreditch, Chinese in Soho, West Indians in Brixton, Africans in Dalston, Irish in Kilburn, Vietnamese in Hackney, Jews in Golders Green and Cypriots, Turks and Kurds in Stoke Newington. The walls came down as successive generations integrated and now the boundaries, where they exist at all, are blurry at best. Londoners these days can be of any colour and follow any creed (or, indeed no creed, as 16% of the city in the last census said they had 'no religion' at all).

Underground Etiquette

Given the vital role it plays in London life, it's natural that the tube should have its own code of customs. Not adhering to the code is how you can annoy Londoners most. Here's your guide on how to fit in.

Don't stop to get your bearings as soon as you get through the turnstiles. Absolutely under no circumstances should you stand still on the left-hand side of the escalator; it's reserved for people far busier than you and others keen to exercise and tone their bottoms. Do move along the platform and don't point at the little furry things running along the lines. When the train pulls in, stand aside until passengers have got off. Under pain of death, do *not* offer your seat to the elderly, disabled, pregnant or faint; instead, you should bury your head in a book and pretend you can't see them. It's fine, even courteous, to leave a newspaper behind in the morning but it's your bloody litter in the evening. Do mind the gap.

Roughly 12 million people live in Greater London, some 7.3 million of them close to the centre. Population is growing by 1.4% per year and the average age is decreasing (36, compared with 38 nationally). London's nonwhite population is the largest of any European city. With an estimated 33 ethnic communities and a staggering 300 languages being spoken, it's no empty boast when the mayor calls London 'a world in one city'.

It's virtually impossible to generalise about a city so big and diverse, but we'll give it our best shot. The most common preconceptions about Londoners being reserved, inhibited and stiflingly polite are total untruths and, while these are all English traits to some degree, the English in London tend to be slightly less timid than their country cousins. Much is made about the silence on the tube, but take any trip late in the evening and that argument will be trounced. It's true that Londoners are polite and love a queue, which are two of the best things about them (particularly when you're seeing the sights), but few who have experienced walking down Oxford St would ever term Londoners 'stiflingly polite': London is one of the most crowded places on the planet. What's more, it often feels like it's on the verge of a breakdown so it's only natural that people should modify their behaviour in order to cope.

Londoners are not necessarily reserved, although like most big-city dwellers, they are dashing around in their own little worlds with things to do and people to see. At the same time, they'd never refuse a request for help and when you do befriend a Londoner you'll have a couch to sleep on any time you want.

They're a tolerant bunch, unfazed by outrageous dress or behaviour. This tolerance generally means only low levels of chauvinism, racism, sexism or any other 'ism' you can think of. The much-publicised racial tensions of northern England haven't existed in London for decades. The annual London Pride in late June/early July is a sparkling celebration of gay culture that passes off without incident, and London's history of absorbing wave after wave of immigrants and refugees speaks for itself.

In a city this big, though, you won't have to look far to see the exact opposite of all we've just said. The image of the English football hooligan still rings true, although gangs of lads and lots of beer are recipes for loutish behaviour in any culture. There are pockets of bigotry all over the capital, but you'll encounter few problems in tourist London as long as you don't get 'lippy' with geezers or 'take liberties' (get too familiar). For much of the year, Monday to Friday is about work, drudge, commuting and TV – Friday night and Saturday are for partying, and Sunday's about hangovers, newspapers, roast lunches and football on the box.

Many Londoners are militant, rail against injustices and join demos, although more again are likely to ponder the same issues quietly over a pint in their local pub.

The only thing they like more than celebrity is the backlash. It's sport to trumpet someone as the next big thing, wait until he's at the point of greatness and then groan 'he used to be good but now he's shite'. They're constantly in pursuit of what's hip, trying to keep ahead of the pack. Discount airlines have changed their lives and weekend breaks in European capitals are their safety valves. They love their music, arts, literature, TV and football. They are first of all Londoners, surprisingly similar inside despite being hugely diverse, united by their magnificent and always-surprising home town.

LIFESTYLE

The pace in London is hard and fast, the price for residing in such a vibrant, teeming city. This capital runs on adrenaline – as well as a goodly amount of coffee, Red Bull and ProPlus. And, with an average age of a comparatively fresh-faced 36, it brims with the energy and enthusiasm of youth. However, if that's the overall picture, London moves to many drumbeats, too. All human life is here or passes through, from wealthy City bankers in Chelsea and trendy creatives in Hoxton, to Brixton crusties and struggling single mothers in Hackney.

Spend any time in this renowned cultural colossus and you will swiftly be seduced by how much there is to do here, how much history and how much variety. It's easy to run yourself off your feet with trips to the cinema, theatre, galleries, bars, restaurants and clubs. This is one of the most invigorating, multiculturally diverse spots on earth, where you can eat any national cuisine, enjoy any musical style or eavesdrop on conversations in nearly 300 languages. 'No city in the world is more internationalised', mayor Ken Livingstone has ventured in the past, and sources as diverse as *Newsweek* magazine and Nelson Mandela – who backed London's bid to win the 2012 Olympics – have recently agreed.

London isn't totally devoid of racism or homophobia, but with locals pretty well having seen it all before, it is one of the most tolerant cities on the planet. After immersing yourself in its constantly moving sea of humanity, you'll find nearly anywhere else on the planet feels a bit like hicksville.

However, while in London, you will inevitably hear a chorus of local complaints, mostly concerning the high cost of living, high property prices and the dilapidated state of the tube.

Canary Wharf Underground station (p178)

This is the world's second most expensive city (after Tokyo) but – mind the gap – only ranks 35 for quality of living. While many newcomers arrive for the job opportunities, maintaining a healthy work/life balance can be tricky. Britons in general put in longer office hours than workers in the rest of Europe (see p29). In addition, London is also hugely competitive, in a peculiarly veiled English way. This is not New York, where flagrant boasting will go unpunished, professionally or socially. It's important not to *look* too thrusting or overly ambitious. (In the recent local version of the hit TV show *The Apprentice,* billionaire entrepreneur Sir Alan Sugar chose a mild-mannered, promising but inexperienced assistant over a much louder, pushy candidate.)

After all those long hours at work, you might not emerge with what you consider sufficient disposable income, either. The Office of National Statistics puts the average London salary at £31,000 a year, compared to £22,000 nationwide, but the National Housing Federation reckons that renting a one-bedroom flat will swallow up 44% of that (after tax). More tellingly, high City salaries of between £60,000 and £200,000 skew that average, meaning that many key workers like nurses, ambulance drivers, teachers and garbage collectors are earning only about £19,000 to £24,000. With the average price of £188,000 for a property, they're finding it too costly to live in the capital and often commute from outside.

Hard work to pay bills can play havoc with your social life. Many young career-minded singletons now find it necessary to enrol with dating agencies or go speed-dating. However, it doesn't have to be this way. You'll quickly be taken with how much office chit-chat revolves around getting 'bladdered', 'hammered' or 'wasted' (drunk) last night, as well as what's in iconoclastic celebrity magazine *Heat* and last night's TV. Londoners have elevated social drinking to an art form, and at less poverty-stricken times of the year (ie not January), twentysomethings particularly are liable to spend more time socialising in their local pub than in the home that's eating up 44% of their budget. That said, social research has recently confirmed a marked increase in the tendency for people to throw dinner parties in their own homes – a combined result of the increased media coverage of food and celebrity chefs on the one hand and a desire to cut costs on the other.

Admittedly, it can take time to get to know people to go out with, or to invite you to a dinner party. Londoners are frequently too cool to acknowledge well-known faces from TV, film or the music business, so sadly don't expect them to acknowledge you too soon! People are sometimes brusque in public, they rarely chat to each other in shops or on the street, and most certainly not on the tube. While newcomers generally find this odd, cold and indifferent, once they've developed their own circle of friends (often through work), many also say they appreciate the privacy this brings.

The distances across the city, and the poor public transport, do mean people tend to find an area and social circle that suits them and stick to it – whether that be indie-music Camden, fashion-conscious Notting Hill, literary Hampstead, cutting-edge Hoxton, or arty, sleazy, gay Soho. There's little dropping around to people's places unexpectedly; in fact, it's virtually unheard of not to call beforehand, and busy schedules mean less spontaneity when it comes to arranging social meetings.

If this all sounds quite formal, however, rest assured that things aren't really that uptight. It might be fast, hassled, congested, expensive and unrelenting, but London is also exciting, buzzing, life-affirming and simply lots of fun. Which is why so many Londoners spend a good deal of time complaining about London, but would never dream of leaving, really.

FOOD

In 2005 French President Jacques Chirac raised some eyebrows when he was overheard saying to his German and Russian opposite numbers that after Finland, Britain is 'the country with the worst food' and then adding for effect that 'one cannot trust people whose cuisine is so bad'. We can't help wondering when Jacques last ate anything in the UK save a royal banquet, but it's safe to say that if he's been let down by the royal household, he may find that real Londoners are eating better than ever.

Indeed, London's culinary catching up and overtaking of its European cousins in the past decade has been nothing short of phenomenal. Time was when London was derided even by Londoners themselves as being a hellish place where overpriced, underperforming restaurants were the only option aside from fish 'n' chips or a takeaway.

Yet in 2005, food bible *Gourmet* magazine singled out London as having the best collection of restaurants in the world, something that is already old news to Londoners. Eating out here, like most things, will usually cost you (although not always), but the food standards now make this a price many people are more than happy to pay.

So what exactly happened to make it all so good? At some point the purveyors of stodge were lined up against the wall, stripped of their pinnies and replaced by a slick and savvy new generation of young chefs. As trailblazing restaurants progressively raised the bar, the competition followed. Fresh, free-range, organic produce replaced unexciting, defrosted (no, really!) and bland ingredients, staff were drilled into professional service and the designers were brought in to create some of the world's coolest and most aesthetically pleasing eating spaces.

As a result, eating out here can be as diverse, stylish and satisfying as anywhere else on the planet and it's no exaggeration to call London a foodie destination. Designer eating is all the rage, with restaurant openings attracting as much glitz and glamour as fashion parades, and every week there seems to be a hot new place where half of London is trying to get a reservation.

That's not to say you can't still get greasy fries, overcooked vegetables and traditional British stodge (particularly in pubs, although this is changing too with the inevitable arrival of a gastropub to a high street near you), but with chefs absorbing the influences of this most cosmopolitan of cultures, you're more likely to get the world on your plate – anything from *agedashi* to *zahtar*. Look hard enough and you'll find some 70 different cuisines, a reflection of London's multicultural wherewithal.

But it's not just dining out that's got Londoners in the mood – food is suddenly interesting, and they're talking about it, being more adventurous in their own kitchens and more discerning when they shop. Farmers markets have sprung up all over the place, tantalising shoppers with fruit and vegetables that taste remarkably like fruit and vegetables did in the days before supermarkets ran the world. The bad press received by the British cow focused minds on the joys of organic produce and there's now a plethora of chemical-free producers, grocers, markets, cafés and restaurants. Suspicion also swelled the ranks of the meat-free brigade, and there are now several gourmet vegetarian dining options.

The bad news, folks, is that all this comes at a price, and the blossoming of the London food scene does not equate to value for money. Unless you're in the know or have a good guide (nudge, nudge) you generally have to dig pretty deep to eat well, although, even then, choosing a restaurant can be a hit-and-miss affair. You could as easily drop £30 on a 'modern European' meal that tastes like it came from a can as spend a fiver on an Indian dish that makes your palate spin and your heart sing (so follow our recommendations in the Eating chapter, p230).

Even much-maligned British cuisine gets an increasingly convincing and visible showcase in some of the fashionable establishments of the moment, which are given over to rediscovering the meaty dishes of centuries past (more pig trotters, Mr Chirac?). Despite this, even the most ambitious Londoners realise that it'll be a while before foreigners flock to the British capital to enjoy gourmet black pudding and jellied eels. But at this rate it's bound to happen one day, surely?

The Top Table

The celebrity chef concept is relatively new to London but, boy, has it taken off. Here are a few to look out for:

- Heston Blumenthal – The creative force behind the 'best restaurant in the world' (**Fat Duck**; p394) is a self-taught chef who developed an obsession with food after a teenage visit to France, and hoarded French cookery books even though he couldn't read the language. While working as a credit controller, he began creating his highly experimental flavour combinations, based on a passionate, scholarly interest in the science of taste and smell (molecular gastronomy, he calls it). Bacon-and-egg ice cream is one of his famous concoctions.
- Gordon Ramsay – The baddest bad boy of the crop and possibly the finest chef London has ever seen. His eponymous Chelsea restaurant has three Michelin stars, but Ramsay is as famous for his temper, tantrums and denigration of fellow chefs as he is for exquisite creations. Before leaving the reality TV show *Hell's Kitchen* to Gary Rhodes and Jean Christophe Novelli, the Ram traumatised several celebrities working under him in his kitchen. Now he's taking strips off local restaurant owners in *Ramsay's Kitchen Nightmares*.
- Jamie Oliver – The kitchen pin-up boy, Oliver wowed food fans with his TV series *The Naked Chef*, so-called because the recipes were pared back and made simple. He lays on the cheeky, Mockney patois too thick but seems to be an all-round top geezer. In 2003 he opened a new restaurant called **Fifteen** (p240), where he took 15 underprivileged youngsters and trained them – in theory at least – as professional chefs to work under him. His latest noteworthy activity has been campaigning for better standards of nutrition in school dinners. That knighthood can't be far off...
- Nigella Lawson – Nobody has done more to get men into cooking than this self-trained TV chef whose voluptuous curves and finger-licking sensuality attract as much attention as what she can do with a rrrrrrrrack of lamb. However, her recent foray into chat show presenting has been a total disaster.

Traditional English Tucker

Although English food has never exactly been welcomed at the world table, it does have its moments, particularly a Sunday lunch of roast beef and Yorkshire pudding or a cornet of fish and chips eaten on the hoof after a few pints down the local.

The best place to sample London soul food is in the pub, where menus feature the likes of bangers and mash (sausages served with mashed potatoes and gravy), Shepherd's pie (a baked dish of minced lamb and onions topped with mashed potatoes), an assortment of pies and the ploughman's lunch (thick slices of bread served with chutney, pickled onions and Cheddar or Cheshire cheese). Old reliables on the dessert tray include bread-and-butter or steamed puddings, sherry trifle and the alarmingly titled 'spotted dick', a steamed suet pudding with raisins.

The most English of dishes, though, is fish 'n' chips: cod (rare these days), plaice or haddock dipped in batter, deep fried and served with chips doused in vinegar and sprinkled with salt. American chains threaten traditional shops but there are still a few gems around, such as the **North Sea Fish Restaurant** (p237) in Bloomsbury and **Masters Super Fish** (p255).

The staple lunch for many Londoners, from the middle of the 19th century until just after WWII, was a pie filled with spiced eel (then abundant in the Thames) and served with mashed potatoes, liquor and a parsley sauce. Nowadays, the pies are usually meat-filled and the eel served smoked or jellied as a side dish. See p259 for the best places to try.

FASHION

Britannia Waives the Rules

In the fickle world of fashion, London's cachet has dropped in recent years, for several reasons. Some of the blame belongs to the domination of the big luxury brands, which largely emanate from Italy. Some of it is attributable to the failing fortunes of London Fashion Week, a bit of a chaotic, amateur event at the best of times. Many British designers, including Alexander McQueen, Stella McCartney, Vivienne Westwood and even avant-garde label Boudicca, now don't show their clothes in London, saying it doesn't garner enough attention. This might be true, with key industry figures like Vogue's Anna Wintour not bothering to turn up in the audience. Finally, the sharp fall of the dollar, which has served to make the pound more expensive, has kept American buyers at bay.

Fortunately, though, the influence of London's designers continues to spread well beyond these shores. The 'British Fashion Pack' still work at, or run, the major Continental fashion houses like Chanel, Givenchy and Chloe, while London, particularly **Central St Martins School of Art & Design** (see opposite), still produces top talent. Meanwhile, regardless of whether they send models down the catwalks here, designers like Alexander McQueen and Matthew Wil-

---

The Rise of the Chav

The origins of the word may be obscure (some believe it is an Romany term for a young lad, others claim it was originally Cheltenham Native, others still claim it's an acronym for Council Housed And Violent), but it's been the buzz word in the UK since 2004 when a media frenzy began, yet to stop. As a result, 'chav' is a catch-all term of abuse for anyone working class who has the audacity to spend lots of money on Burberry, Kappa, Reebok and other labels deemed 'chavvy'. They are identified too by their behaviour (bad), age (under 30), names (Wayne) and their supposed propensity to father children all over the place.

If the term originated as one of abuse for young males with earrings, gold chains, white trainers and Burberry caps, it's become just as much of a term for women too. The greatest 'chavette' icons include former *EastEnders* star Daniella Westbrook, Matt Lucas's teenage mother Vicky Pollard in *Little Britain* and the queen of the chavs, Coleen McLoughlin, football sensation Wayne Rooney's girlfriend. So significant is this trend however that Coleen even graced the pages of *Vogue* magazine in 2005 and chav fashion has seen quite a bit of catwalk action.

At its worst, the word is cruel and discriminating, but that doesn't stop people throwing chav parties or using the word all over the place. If there's one word of current English slang you should know before you arrive in London, this is it. For a thoroughly un-PC glance at chavs in all their wonder, check out www.chavscum.co.uk.

St Martins

Most of the stars of the British fashion industry have passed through the rather shabby doors of St Martins on Charing Cross Rd, the world's most famous fashion college. Founded in 1854, Central St Martins School of Art & Design – to give its rather cumbersome and correct title – began life as a place where cultured young people went to learn to draw and paint. In the 1940s a fashion course was created and within a few decades aspiring designers from around the world were scrambling to get in. Courses are more than 100 times oversubscribed these days and the college has faced some criticism for admitting names over talent (a famous Beatles daughter, to name just one). St Martins' graduate shows – for which Stella had friends Naomi Campbell and Kate Moss model – are one of the highlights of the fashion calendar and are ALWAYS shocking, making huge statements – be they good, bad or ridiculous.

The less-conspicuous Royal College of Art only takes postgraduates and its fashion course is just as old and almost as successful as St Martins. Its alumni are said to provide the backbone of some of the world's most prestigious fashion houses.

liamson retain design studios in London, keeping the rest of the fashion world on its toes and celebrities like Sienna Miller, Keira Knightley and Kate Moss well dressed.

A few year ago labels like Burberry, Mulberry and Pringle led a British heritage rebirth, and this still continues despite unfortunate side effects like 'chav' fashion (see opposite). Originally classic Hooray Henry/Country Weekend style, they've now been adopted by the new 'Gentry Geezer', a strange hybrid of scooter-riding, lager-swilling, golf-playing, football-hooligan, cashed-up-wide-boy and *Lock, Stock and Two Smoking Barrels* types.

Sitting alongside these are the traditional Savile Row boys (named for the Mayfair street traditionally the home of English tailoring), wearing a Gieves and Hawkes high-brake, lean-cut suit and stovepipe pants, just a touch too short to reveal an elastic-ankled 'Church' dealer shoe. Add a cutaway collar and monogrammed business shirt with a full Windsor knot in a silk tie. It's a slightly dapper old London city look, supported by the cream of British movie celebrities, the Primrose Hill dwellers Jude Law and Johnny Lee Miller. This is where you'll see the slick understated statement makers, where labels like Gucci, Prada and Paul Smith fit into place.

The British fashion industry has always been more on the edge of younger, directional stuff, and never really established that very polished 'Gucci Slick'; the London equivalent is the bespoke men's tailoring of Savile Row. London has no history of real couture like Paris or Milan, where tastes in styles and fabrics are much more classic and refined. The market also shapes British fashion to a large extent; customers here are more likely to spend £100 on a few different bargains – hence the boom in outlet malls – while their sisters in Paris and Italy will blow the lot on one piece, which they'll wear regularly and well.

So London fashion has always been about street wear and 'wow', with a few old reliables keeping the frame in place and mingling with hot new designers who are often unpolished through lack of experience, but bursting with talent and creativity.

Of course, the good news for London is that fashion is always cyclical, so if interest has temporarily dwindled, it will be redirected here in a few years. In the meantime, London Fashion Week has found new stars to keep the punters interested. Thrown out of Sloane Sq by irritated neighbours and now relocated to Battersea, it's been commissioning works from the likes of Tracey Emin to help jazz up the stage.

SPORT

England proudly gave the world many of its most popular games, including football, rugby, cricket and tennis. It rankles with the English, however, that the world took many of these sports and became better at them than the creators themselves. Having said that, England is a major world sporting power and London hosts a calendar of prestigious sporting events that would be the envy of any other city in the world. Londoners are generally potty about sport and are fiercely passionate about their teams, although they draw the line when it comes to actually participating. There is no one team in any major sport that represents the whole of London.

Dogs & Gee-Gees

Gambling is something close to the hearts of many Londoners, and even the Queen likes a little flutter every now and again. There's no better way to lose your money than horse racing, traditionally known as 'the sport of kings' and colloquially known as the gee-gees (child-speak for horses). There are several racecourses within a short drive of London if you fancy a day at the track. The flat-racing season lasts from April to September while the National Hunt (over fences) takes place from October to April. The Queen and her entourage turn up for Royal Ascot in June, while Derby Day at Epsom the same month is much more down-to-earth.

Although greyhound racing, the urban cousin of horse racing, was introduced from the US, it seems right at home in London as it combines three local passions: gambling, drinking beer and cheap entertainment. Walthamstow is the most popular place to watch eight dogs chasing a mechanical rabbit, and it's more fun than we'd care to admit.

There is no dedicated sports newspaper, probably because the coverage from the dailies is so good. The *Daily Telegraph,* the *Times* and the *Guardian* all have particularly hefty back pages. The tabloids obviously go for the scandal but they are often the first to break major stories. The *Daily Sport,* by the way, is not a sports paper, unless photographs of glamour models wearing nothing but a pair of Arsenal socks count.

Football

Football was invented in England around the 12th century, when unruly mobs tore each other to shreds in pursuit of some kind of ball. Despite repeated royal bans, the ruffians kept playing until 1863 when the Football Association was founded and the formal rules of the contemporary game were adopted.

You may know this game as 'soccer', but calling it that won't endear you to the natives. (A public-school boy coined the term 'soccer' in the 1880s. It was, and still is, common practice for these privileged chaps to abbreviate words while adding 'er' to the end. When asked if he wanted to play rugger – rugby – the student said he'd rather play soccer, a curious abbreviation of 'association'.) Football is by far the most popular sport in London, which is home to 14 teams playing in every division of the Nationwide League.

The season climaxes in May with the FA Cup final. Traditionally this has been played at Wembley Stadium and it's expected to be back here in 2006 when the stadium reopens (although reports in mid-2005 about a cost blow-out on the rebuilding project raises the possibility of further delays). In the interim, it has been moved to Cardiff's Millennium Stadium. This is the oldest football competition in the world, where, with a good run, amateur teams could get the opportunity to scalp the likes of Manchester United. Such romantic notions are at the cornerstone of the game in general and the reason for its enormous popularity, although the cold harsh realities are a bit different. In 2005 the FA Cup was won by Arsenal, beating Manchester United in a tense last-minute penalty shoot-out.

The most successful London clubs are Chelsea (the 'Blues'), Arsenal (the 'Gunners'), Tottenham Hotspur ('Spurs'), Charlton (the 'Addicks') and Fulham (the 'Cottagers'), all of them in the top league, the Premiership. West Ham – the 'Hammers' – rejoined the Premiership in 2005 after two years out of it. The Gunners and the Hammers are so-called because their original teams were drawn from munitions and ironworkers over a century ago, while Charlton got its nickname after its tradition of treating visiting teams to a fish supper after games – haddock became 'addick' in the local vernacular. Below the Premiership comes the Championship league, formerly called the first division.

For more than a decade Arsenal was the pre-eminent London team, and towards the end of that decade, when it beat Manchester United, it was even the leading English team. However, that dominance has changed, with Chelsea winning the FA Premiership in 2005 (see Chelski Revolution, p206). Chelsea's rise to the top wasn't exactly unexpected, as Russian billionaire Roman Abramovich spent two years pumping £350 million into the team beforehand, but many rival fans have nevertheless been impressed by the speed of the ascent. Chelsea now has its eyes on the FA Cup and the European championships, and much is expected from it in the next few years.

That said, the biggest rivalry within the city remains that between Arsenal and fellow north Londoners Tottenham Hotspur. Arsenal's fans were traditionally Irish and Greek, while Spurs' supporters were predominantly Jewish – the two have loathed each other since 1913 when Arsenal moved into the neighbourhood. Arsenal is due to inaugurate its new Emirates Stadium in summer 2006, having outgrown its long-time home in Highbury. Despite the rivalry, Tottenham cannot really touch Arsenal's current form or reputation as one of the best clubs in the country.

The other local derby is between Chelsea and Fulham, although there's not that much needle involved in this one, because Fulham has only recently become a threat on the pitch. Matches you might want to be wary about attending are those between Championship league Millwall and the much-hated West Ham or even less-despised Crystal Palace. Although much has been done to improve the behaviour of Millwall's 'firm', some nutters and violence are arguably still attached to the team.

Despite having five or six teams in the top flight at all times, London has always played second fiddle to the north of England, the game's real stronghold. Between them, London clubs have only won 14 titles since the league began in 1863, with Arsenal claiming 11 of them. Nevertheless, London is one of *the* greatest cities in Europe if you're a football fan, as some of the world's best players strut their stuff here and there are top games to see every week.

The season runs from mid-August to mid-May, although there are no matches the weekend before international games. However, it's virtually impossible for the casual fan to get a ticket for one of the top matches, and you're better off watching it in the pub, like most ordinary fans that can't afford the outrageous £20 to £60 ticket price. Alternatively, go and see a first-division match and sense the atmosphere that many believe has been lost in the slick, new, family-entertainment Premiership.

English football reached its pinnacle in 1966 when Bobby Moore lifted the World Cup trophy for England at Wembley. (A moment English fans still cannot forget, although it was 40 years ago. The commentator's immortal words from the end of that match –'They think it's all over. It is now.'— having become part of the vernacular.) The national game sank to its deepest low in the 1980s when fans rampaged across the Continent and all English clubs were banned from European competition. This, combined with two stadium disasters that cost the lives of 140 fans, spoiled the general public's appetite for the game.

Football was revolutionised in the early 1990s thanks to billions of pounds in TV money, slick marketing off the pitch and foreign flair on it. Author Nick Hornby set the ball rolling, so to speak, with his brilliant book *Fever Pitch,* the memoirs of a soccer fanatic. It brought credibility back to football, even made it hip, and pretty soon the stands were packed again.

Walthamstow Greyhound Stadium (p328)

TV coverage improved beyond recognition, which was lucky because many ordinary fans were suddenly priced out of the game, an unfortunate by-product of its modernisation.

At many clubs now, fans can't get to see games unless they cough up for an expensive season ticket in the summer. And so a new pub culture has emerged, where drinking pints and watching big games is a regular Sunday afternoon and Monday night pastime (or midweek if your liver's up to it). Most games, at least those featuring the less-glamorous teams, are played on the traditional Saturday afternoon.

English club football has underachieved in Europe (the big prize these days) over the last decade. There have been a few decent runs in competitions, but the only major successes were Manchester United winning the Champions League in 1999 and Liverpool beating AC Milan in 2005 in a thrilling penalty shoot-out. The England national team, under coach Sven-Goran Eriksson, has also promised much but failed to deliver.

Rugby

Two different codes of rugby are played in Britain: rugby union and rugby league. Union is traditionally the privilege of the middle and upper classes, while league is predominantly played and supported by the workers. Predictably, then, London is the heartland of union and has four big teams: Harlequins, Saracens, London Wasps and London Irish. The main competitions are the Zurich Premiership and the terrifically exciting – and relatively new – Heineken Cup, contested by the top clubs in Europe. The season runs from August to May, and games are played Saturday and Sunday afternoons. Union has a big following among women, which has nothing at all to do with the physique of rugby players or the very social nature of the support.

The most important annual international competition is the Six Nations Tournament, which takes place in February/March and is contested by England, Scotland, Wales, Ireland, France and Italy. Each team plays alternate home and away matches, and plays each of the other teams only once during the competition. This is one sport that the English invented and *are* particularly good at; they've wiped the floor with the opposition in this comp over recent years, although they still trail behind the powerhouses of the southern hemisphere. They play at Twickenham in London, hallowed turf of English rugby. Unfortunately, unless you've got connections, it's nigh on impossible to get tickets to the internationals.

Rugby is believed to have originated in 1823 at Rugby School in Warwickshire, England, when a fellow by the name of William Ellis picked up the ball and ran with it during a football match and was chased by the other players.

Rugby league broke away in the 1890s. The rules are similar to union, although it's a bit more like the traditional sport of British Bulldog, where players barge their way through a wall of opponents to reach the other side. The London Broncos are the only team outside northern England, the heartland of the code.

Cricket

During the days of the Empire, the English brought the game of cricket to the colonies, thrashing the pants off 'the natives' while teaching them 'how to be gentlemen'. While the tables have largely turned, and the likes of Australia and India frequently give England a thumping, the national team under Michael Vaughan is in better form than it has been for years.

Sports Without Strain

The English like their sports so much they even invented games they could play down the pub. The late 1980s was the heyday for darts, when entire arenas were turned into bars for major competitions, TV audiences were huge and the best players were household names. Internal divisions somewhat spoiled the sport but it's still shown on Sky Sports.

Snooker is another sport that used to get massive TV audiences, although, on the face of it, you'd be hard-pressed to think of a duller spectacle. But trust us, close and important games can be as tense and exciting as a penalty shoot-out in the World Cup. The game still gets healthy TV audiences, largely down to entertaining players like rapscallion Londoner Ronnie O'Sullivan, the best player in the world.

If you're unfamiliar with the rules and have only seen bits and pieces of the game, you may see cricket as a form of English torture (and if there was ever a case to be made for TV highlights, surely this is it). On the other hand, if you're patient and learn to appreciate the intricacies of the game, you may find it immensely rewarding and think watching every single ball of a five-day test match is a perfectly good use of one's time. What's even more surprising to people who don't know a googly from an Internet search engine is that fans love following the cricket on the radio!

Tests are international matches lasting five days, and are regarded as the purist form of the sport. The one-day game, where each team bats once and faces a limited number of balls, is a fairly recent development – it's TV-friendly, more accessible for the uninitiated, and regarded as totally irrelevant by purists.

The England team tours each year and hosts at least one touring side from the rest of the cricket-playing world (primarily Australia, the Indian subcontinent, South Africa, Zimbabwe and the West Indies). Most keenly contested is the biennial test series against Australia, known as 'the Ashes', which was won by England in 2005 for the first time in nearly two decades. (The name comes from a mock obituary published in the *Times* after a great Australian victory in 1882, which said that the 'body' of English cricket had been cremated and the ashes taken to Australia. The trophy itself is said to contain the burnt bails of the 1882 game.) Tickets for the big tests can still be difficult to come by unless you book in advance.

The teams that make up the main domestic competition in England are drawn from counties (or shires), disproportionately from the 'home counties' (southeast of England, around London). This is known as county cricket and the season lasts from April to September. Some of the world's best cricketers – Shoaib Akhtar, Stephen Fleming, Sanath Jayasuriya, Muttiah Muralitharan, Graeme Smith and Shane Warne among them – regularly come over and play for stints with the county teams.

Some of the original clubs established in the 18th century still survive today, including the famous Marylebone Cricket Club (MCC) based at **Lord's** (p193), the sport's spiritual home, in North London. Lord's is also home to Middlesex, one of London's two county cricket clubs. The **Oval** (p204) is home to the team of the moment, Surrey, and also hosts international fixtures.

Tennis

Wimbledon, that quintessentially English affair – which also happens to be the world's most famous tennis tournament – has been held in SW19 since 1877. In late June/early July, tennis fever grips London as the world's best players congregate for the sport's most prestigious event, and fans descend on Wimbledon for strawberries and cream, bursts of sunshine between the inevitable rain, Cliff Richard singing (if you're particularly unfortunate) and high drama on the increasingly hard, grass courts.

England – as you will gather if you're in London at this time – is desperate for a local winner, something it hasn't been able to celebrate since Fred Perry won in 1936 and Virginia Wade in 1977. During 2005's Wimbledon, former local hopes Tim Henman and Greg Rusedski went out even earlier than usual, but the media found a new idol in the promising 18-year-old Andy Murray. Although he proudly emphasises that he's Scottish, not English, Murray has been warmly embraced as 'British'. The so-called 'Henman Hill' outdoor area with its huge viewing screen has been variously renamed 'Murray Mount' or 'Murray Field'. The media, which always goes totally over the top about local players, realises Murray could be a real talent and – despite the pre-eminence of Switzerland's Roger Federer – expects big things.

For the best seats, you have to enter a public ballot (p328) between August and December of the previous year. If you don't plan so far in advance, you *can* get tickets at the venue during the tournament but the queues are exceedingly long, prices exorbitant and conditions cramped – you may end up thinking that Wimbledon is, ahem, a bit of a racket.

MEDIA

London is in the eye of the British media, an industry comprising some of the best and worst of the world's TV, radio and print media.

Newspapers

The main London newspaper is the fairly right-wing *Evening Standard*, a jingoistic tabloid that comes out in early and late editions throughout the day. Foodies should check out the restaurant reviews of London's most influential critic, Fay Maschler, while style aficionados shouldn't miss Friday's ES magazine, an indispensable guide to the city's cutting edge. *Metro Life* is a useful listings supplement on Thursday.

The *Standard* now has two rival freebies, which litter tube carriages: *Metro* and the *London Line*, which is a young and funky weekly. Both are fairly lightweight, easy-to-digest reads.

National newspapers in England are almost always financially independent of any political party, although their political leanings are easily discerned. Rupert Murdoch is the most influential man in British media and his News Corp owns the *Sun*, the *News of the World*, the *Times* and the *Sunday Times*. The industry is self-regulating, having set up a Press Complaints Commission in 1991 to handle public grievances, although many complain that the PCC is unable to really maintain any level of discipline among the unruly tabloids, being a 'toothless guard dog'.

There are many national daily newspapers, and competition for readers is incredibly stiff; although some papers are printed outside the capital, they are all pretty London-centric. There are two broad categories of newspapers, most commonly distinguished as broadsheets (or 'qualities') and tabloids, although the distinction is becoming more about content than physical size.

Readers of the broadsheets are extremely loyal to their paper and rarely switch from one to another. However at the time of writing, there was a bit of a war on between them to poach new readers with more and superior versions of the number puzzle Sudoku. The *Daily Telegraph* is sometimes considered old-fogeyish, but nonetheless the writing and world coverage are very good. The *Times* is traditionally the newspaper of the establishment and supports the government of the day; it's particularly good for sports. On the left side of the political spectrum, the *Guardian* features lively writing and an extremely progressive agenda, is very strong in its coverage of the arts and has some excellent supplements, particularly Media Guardian, a bible for anyone in the industry. It's also the best paper for white-collar job seeking. Politically correct, the *Independent* has single-issue front pages and rejoices in highlighting stories or issues that other papers have ignored.

The Sunday papers are as important as Sunday mornings in London. Most dailies have Sunday stablemates and predictably the tabloids have bumper editions of trashy gossip, star-struck adulation, fashion extras and mean-spirited diatribes directed at whomever they've decided to hunt for sport on that particular weekend. The qualities have so many sections and supplements that two hands are required to carry even one from the shop. The *Observer,* established in 1791, is the oldest Sunday paper and sister of the *Guardian;* there's a brilliant Sports supplement with the first issue of the month. Even people who normally only buy broadsheets sometimes slip a copy of the best-selling *News of the World* under their arm for some Sunday light relief.

See p412 for a list of the major daily and Sunday newspapers.

See p412 for a list of the major daily and Sunday newspapers.

Magazines

There is an astonishing range of magazines published and consumed here, from celebrity gossip to political heavyweights. Lads' monthlies like *FHM, Loaded* and *Maxim* powered the growth of consumer magazines in the 1990s, as new readers tucked into a regular diet of babes, irreverence and blokeishness.

London loves celebrity and *Heat* is the most popular purveyor of the literary equivalent of junk food. US import *Glamour* is the queen of the women's glossies, having toppled traditional favourite *Cosmopolitan,* which is beginning to look a little wrinkled in comparison with its younger, funkier rival – maybe time for a nip and tuck. *Marie Claire, Elle* and *Vogue* are regarded as the thinking woman's glossies, such as they are.

A slew of style magazines are published here – *i-D, Dazed & Confused* and *Vice* – and all maintain a loyal following.

Political magazines are particularly strong in London. The satirical *Private Eye* (below) has no political bias and takes the mickey out of everyone. You can keep in touch with what's happening internationally with the *Week,* an excellent roundup of the British and foreign press.

Time Out is the listings guide *par excellence* and great for taking the city's pulse with string arts coverage while the *Big Issue,* sold on the streets by the homeless, is not just an honourable project but a damned fine read. London is a publishing hub for magazines and produces hundreds of internationally renowned publications specialising in music, visual arts, literature, sport, architecture and so on. There's a comprehensive list of these in the Directory chapter (p413).

New Media

There's a thriving alternative media scene catering to the many who feel marginalised by the mainstream media, much of which still covers global protests by describing the hairstyles of the 'ecowarriors'. Some sites worth checking out include the outstanding and original

Private Eye Lashes Establishment

'We're married at last...' says Prince Charles in a speech bubble to his mother as he leaves the church with Camilla Parker Bowles, '... and to each other!' replies the Queen frostily. This is a typical cover of London's best-known satirical magazine, *Private Eye,* a barometer of how well you know what's going on politically and culturally in the country.

It was founded in 1961 by a group of clever clogs that included the late comedian and writer Peter Cook and still retains the low-tech, cut-and-paste charm of the original. It specialises in gossip mongering about the misdeeds of public figures and in the giddy lampooning of anyone who takes themselves too seriously. There are lots of running jokes (the Queen is always referred to as Brenda, for example, Tony Blair as the Dear Leader), wicked cartoons and regular features such as an editorial from Lord Gnome, a composite of media magnates. There's also a serious investigative side to the mag and its reports have contributed to the downfall of several high-fliers including Jeffrey Archer and Robert Maxwell.

But that it still exists at all is astonishing. It has regularly been sued by its targets and only remains afloat thanks to the charity of its readers. Its future is looking brighter these days with circulation above 600,000 and at its highest level in a decade. *Private Eye* is now far and away the most popular current affairs magazine in the land. Essential reading, even if you don't follow much more than the cartoons.

Urban 75 (www.urban75.com), the global network of alternative news at Indymedia (http://uk.indymedia.org), the weekly activists' newsletter from SchNews (www.schnews.org.uk) and the video activists Undercurrents (www.undercurrents.org).

Email magazines have taken off here in a big way, largely because they're so good. The Friday Thing (www.thefridaything.co.uk) is a well-written and exceedingly cheeky weekly mag covering news, culture and current affairs. Online gossip sites have also gained notoriety in recent years by knocking spin on its arse and breaking some big stories about celebrities misbehaving. Check out Popbitch (www.popbitch.com) and the satirical technology newsletter Need to Know (www.ntk.net).

Top 10 Books on London Culture & Society

- *18 Folgate Street* – Dennis Severs
- *Guide to Ethnic London* – Ian McAuley
- *London: A Biography* – Peter Ackroyd
- *London, A Social History* – Roy Porter
- *London in the 20th Century: A City and its People* – Jerry White
- *London Perceived* – VS Pritchett
- *London, The Unique City* – Steen Eiler Rasmussen
- *My East End* – Gilda O'Neill
- *Sin City: London in Pursuit of Pleasure* – Giles Emerson
- *Soft City* – Jonathan Raban

Broadcasting

Radio has been hugely popular in London since Arthur Burrows first read the news in the inaugural broadcast in 1922. The BBC is one of the greatest broadcasting corporations in the world and one of the standard bearers of radio and TV journalism and programming (p200). Its independence frequently irks the establishment and it incurred the very significant wrath of the British government in 2003 because of its tenacious probing of the events leading to the US/British/Australian-led invasion of Iraq. When BBC journalist Andrew Gilligan alleged that Tony Blair's then press secretary Alistair Campbell had 'sexed up' a dossier of evidence against the Iraqi regime in order to generate public support for going to war, there was a huge outcry and mutual recriminations between Westminster and White City began. The country's chief weapons expert, Dr David Kelly, committed suicide after being named by the government as the source of the BBC's report, and when the government-appointed Hutton inquiry came down on the BBC as the wrongdoers, almost everybody in the media dismissed it as a whitewash. The BBC's Director General resigned the same day and, chastened, the BBC has since been toeing a far less controversial line when it comes to reporting on the government.

New media ownership laws introduced in 2003 paved the way for major newspaper proprietors to own British terrestrial TV channels, namely Channel Five. There are fears in some quarters of a cultural colonialism with cheap US TV shows swamping the airwaves, although given the slender popularity of brilliant American shows like *The Sopranos* and *The West Wing* in Britain, you'd think it was unlikely that inferior ones would get much attention.

The BBC broadcasts several stations, including BBC 1, 2, 3, 4 and 5, catering to young, mature, classical, arts and talkback audiences respectively. XFM is your best chance of hearing interesting music these days.

Britain still turns out some of the world's best TV programmes, padding out the decent home-grown output with American imports, Australian soaps, inept sitcoms and trashy chat and game shows of its own. There are five regular TV channels. BBC1 and BBC2 are publicly funded by a TV licensing system and, like BBC radio stations, don't carry advertising; ITV, Channel 4 and Channel 5 are commercial channels and do. These regular channels are now competing with the satellite channels of Rupert Murdoch's BSkyB – which offers a variety of channels with less-than-inspiring programmes – and assorted cable channels.

Digital radio and TV are being touted and hyped – the radio offered 36 stations at the last count – but the uptake has been slow so far. Many listeners and viewers feel that the investment in new technology is damaging to the core channels and that the BBC is spreading itself too thinly, trying to chase ratings and compete with the commercial channels rather than concentrating on its public-service responsibilities.

LANGUAGE

English is the country's greatest contribution to the modern world. It is an astonishingly rich language containing an estimated 600,000 uninflected words (compared with, for example, Indonesian's or Malay's 60,000). It's actually a magpie tongue – just as England plundered treasure for its museums, so too the English language dipped into the world's vocabulary, even when it already had several words of the same meaning. Dr Johnson, compiler of the first English dictionary, tried to have the language protected from foreign imports (possibly to reduce his own workload) but failed. As far as English goes, all foreigners are welcome.

English-speakers are spoilt for choice when they go looking for descriptive words such as nouns and adjectives, as you'll discover pretty quickly (fast, swiftly, speedily, rapidly, promptly) by looking in a thesaurus. Some 50 years ago linguists came up with Basic English, a stripped down version with a vocabulary of 850 words, which was all one needed to say just about anything. But where's the fun in that? Shakespeare himself is said to have contributed more than 2000 words, along with hundreds of common idioms such as poisoned chalice, one fell swoop, cold comfort and cruel to be kind.

Be grateful if English is your mother tongue because it's a bitch to learn, and has possibly the most illogical and eccentric approach to spelling and pronunciation of any language. Take the different pronunciation of rough, cough, through, though and bough. Attempts to rationalise English spelling are passionately resisted by people who see themselves as the guardians of proper English and rail against the American decision to drop the 'u' from words such as colour and glamour.

In terms of accent, Standard English or Received Pronunciation (RP) centres on London and, traditionally, was perceived to be that spoken by the upper classes and those educated at public schools. It is by no means the easiest form to understand; in fact, sometimes it's near impossible ('oh, eye nare' apparently means 'yes, I know'). Those 'what talk posh' despair at the perceived butchering of their language by most ordinary Londoners, who speak what's come to be known as 'Estuary English', so called because it's a sort of subcockney that spread along the estuary in postwar London. And so a common language divides the city.

The BBC is considered the arbitrator on the issue, and by comparing the contrived – and frankly hilarious – tone of old newsreels from WWII with today's bulletins, it's obvious that Standard English has gone from posh to a more neutral middle register.

Some say that Estuary English – which can now be heard within a 100-mile radius of the capital – is quickly becoming the standard. Its chief features, according to Stephen Burgen in Lonely Planet's *British phrasebook,* are: rising inflection; constant use of 'innit'; a glottal 'T', rendering the double 'T' in butter almost silent and making 'alright' sound like 'orwhy'; and, in general, a slack-jawed, floppy-tongued way of speaking that knocks the corners off consonants and lets the vowels whine to themselves. The lack of speech rhythm that can result from blowing away your consonants is made good by the insertion of copious quantities of 'fucks' and 'fucking', whose consonants are always given the full nine yards. In London there are many people whose speech is so dependent on the word 'fuck' they are virtually dumbstruck without it.

London's Languages

These days you'll encounter a veritable Babel of some 300 languages being spoken in London, and there are pockets of the capital where English is effectively the second language. Head to Southall if you want to see train station signs in Hindi, head to Gerrard St in Soho for telephone boxes with Chinese instructions, Golders Green or Stamford Hill for shop signs in Hebrew and Kingsland Rd in the East End for *everything* written in Turkish.

But like just about everything in London, the language is constantly changing, absorbing new influences, producing new slang and altering the meaning of words. The city's ethnic communities are only beginning to have an influence and many young Londoners these days are mimicking Caribbean expressions and what they perceive to be hip-hop speak from black urban America.

As England has absorbed wave after wave of immigrants, so too will the insatiable English language continue to take in all comers. Meanwhile, as class distinctions exist, the linguistic battle for London will rage on.

Cockney

The term cockney was originally a derogatory one. Derived from the old English for 'cock's egg', it was used by Shakespeare to describe a fool and later came to be associated with the uneducated working classes of London and the way they spoke. It was a dialect that had remained virtually intact since the 11th century and its typical features were dropped 'ls' (ball/baw), missing consonants (daughter/dau'er), the hard 'th' replaced with a double v (brother/bruvver) and the soft 'th' replaced with a double f (nothing/nuffink). If you're having difficulty hearing the sounds, just think of the quintessential cockney, actor Michael Caine, particularly in the film *Alfie*. This cockney is not all that different from the Estuary English spoken by most Londoners today.

The upper classes, predictably, looked down their noses at the poor and the way they spoke. However, a certain folklore grew up around cockney during the golden era of the music halls at the end of the 19th century. Working-class performers like Albert Chevalier created a folksy version of the East End that middle-class audiences found quaint, un-threatening and entertaining. The image of salt-of-the-earth, cheeky chappies and irrepressible East Enders became widespread. After a while, being and speaking cockney became something to be proud of. Indeed, perhaps inspired by an inverted snobbery, cockney soon came to apply only to those East Enders born within earshot of the church bells of St Mary-le-Bow.

However, cockney is best known for its rhyming slang, which entered the vernacular in the first half of the 19th century. Market traders devised it, possibly, so they could talk to each other privately in public, or street villains perhaps developed it as a code.

Cockney slang replaces common nouns and verbs with rhyming phrases, whereby wife becomes 'trouble and strife' and so on. With familiarity, the actual rhyming word in some phrases gets dropped, so just 'trouble' replaces wife; 'loaf' (of bread) becomes head; 'china' (plate) means mate; 'syrup' (of fig) is a wig; and a butcher's (hook) is a look.

You'll still hear conversations peppered with cockney phrases, although the slang has evolved considerably, and often ridiculously, since its East End origins. You wouldn't Adam and Eve the number of new versions and sometimes even the locals don't have a Danny La Rue what's being said – and that's no word of a porky pie.

Cockney in Common Usage

apples and pears	stairs
artful dodger	lodger
bag/tin of fruit	suit
barnet (fair)	hair
boat race	face
boracic (lint)	skint
brown bread	dead
currant bun	son
dicky bird	a word
dog and bone	phone
ginger beer	queer (gay)
jackanory	story
Mae West	best
mince pies	eyes
Mutt and Jeff	deaf
Pete Tong	wrong (a modern addition)
radio rental	mental
rosy (rosy lea)	tea
tea leaf	thief

ECONOMY & COSTS

The British economy has remained consistently healthy since 1997 under the guidance of 'iron chancellor' Gordon Brown. Admittedly, a slowdown began in 2005, when retail and property sales began a long slide, but as Europe's richest city London is largely capable of weathering such trends. This is a mecca both for those in search of jobs and international corporations drawn by the city's reputation as a financial hub. Its wealth might not be immediately apparent to the visitor passing blocks of high-rise buildings on the way into town, but London beats the likes of Hamburg and Vienna in terms of wealth per head of population. It's just that the financial gap between the haves and have-nots is significantly wider in London than in most cities.

Standard Spends

Pint of Lager £2.50

Financial Times newspaper £1

36-exposure colour film £4

Bus ticket £1.20

Adult football ticket £20 to £40

Three-course meal with wine/beer from £35

Taxi per km 90p

Cinema ticket £9

CD £10 to £15

Admission to a big-name club on a Friday £15

The bad news for visitors is that London is by far the most expensive city in the European Union (EU) and the second most expensive location on the planet. Accommodation and transport costs are particularly high compared with the rest of the EU. These factors, together with higher duty on items such as alcohol and tobacco, are why visitors' credit cards get a flogging in London.

One in eight Britons lives in the capital and they keep pouring in – the population is growing at five times the national average. They're drawn to the big smoke by fatter pay packets as much as the bright lights, as wages are around 20% higher in the capital than elsewhere in Britain. But the extra dough barely covers the increased cost of living according to the Centre for Economics and Business Research, which estimates that Londoners actually have a lower standard of living than their compatriots outside the city. Rents, for example, are as much as 56% more expensive. Going out will set you back more, with drinking at least 5% more costly. On top of that, almost a quarter of all Londoners have to commute 51 minutes or more to get to work each day, more than anywhere else in the country. And people here work hard. While most of Western Europe works 40 hours a week and the French 35, Britain has long had an exemption to the EU's maximum 48-hour week. When the EU recently voted to reimpose the limit in Britain, Blair vowed to fight Brussels on the issue.

Overall property prices have boomed in recent years and even a recent slowdown hasn't made it much easier for first-time buyers to get a foot on the property ladder. So many potential home-buyers can't even get mortgages big enough to let them buy into the *bottom* of the market and are leaving the city in droves. Even without them, though, London remains the proverbial economic powerhouse, and its £162 billion economy makes it the ninth largest in Europe – larger than those of Sweden, Poland, Norway, Austria or Denmark.

Much of this wealth is generated in the square mile known as the City, the original settlement of London, the financial core, and the reason it has survived and prospered over nearly two millennia. It is the most prosperous area in the EU generating more wealth than any other region in the bloc. A quarter of Londoners are employed in business services. Every working day up to 300,000 workers descend on the City, make a million here and there, and then race home in time for tea. At night and weekends the City is deserted.

Some of London's biggest employers are its airports: Heathrow (the world's busiest commercial airport), Gatwick and Stansted together provide some 35,000 jobs. Pockets of industry and manufacturing still exist on the outskirts of town.

The British economy has remained buoyant over the past few years; annual growth is just over 2% and twice the eurozone average, while inflation is steady at around 2% per year. This explains why the British government is in no hurry to ditch its currency, the pound, in favour of the euro. Britain dropped out of the preparations for the European Monetary Union (EMU) in 1998 because its economy was so out of shape, but that humiliation has turned to something of a triumph as a recovered and robust Britain has sprinted past its sluggish euro neighbours.

The City, however, is all set up for the euro, using it in foreign exchange and bond markets.

Playing Footsies

London is Europe's most important financial centre in terms of volume of shares traded. The organisation that actually runs the market is the London Stock Exchange, the most international of the world's stock exchanges. If you ever wondered what the 'footsie' (FTSE 100) is, it's an index that tracks the share price movements of the top 100 companies and is calculated every 15 seconds the market is open.

GOVERNMENT & POLITICS

LOCAL GOVERNMENT

When 12th-century King Richard the Lionheart gave London the right to self-government in exchange for a little pocket money, supporters cheered 'Londoners shall have no king but their mayor'. That's been true for the City of London ever since, but Greater London, where the vast majority of the population lives and works, has had a trickier time of it.

Some form of the Greater London Council (GLC) was going about its business quietly for a few centuries, looking after local interests and acquiescently toeing the national government's line. That all changed when Labour man Ken Livingstone took over as boss of the council in the early 1980s, the same time Margaret Thatcher was prime minister. These two couldn't have been more different and a clash was inevitable. Livingstone campaigned for cheaper public transport in the capital and generally became a thorn in Thatcher's side. She got so fed up with him that in 1986 she abolished the GLC altogether, and London became the only major capital in the world without a self-governing authority. Fourteen years later the Labour government brought back a new version, the Greater London Assembly (GLA), and arranged elections for London's first-ever popularly elected mayor (see opposite).

The 25-member GLA has limited authority over transport, economic development, strategic planning, the environment, the police, fire brigades, civil defence and cultural matters. It is elected from GLA constituencies and by London as a whole. It is not a conventional opposition, but can reject the mayor's budget, form special investigation committees and hold the mayor to public account. It currently comprises nine Conservatives, nine Labour Party members, four Liberal Democrats and three members of the Green Party. It has its headquarters in the futuristic GLA building in Southwark, beside Tower Bridge.

The City of London has its own government in the form of the Corporation of London, headed by the *Lord* Mayor (note that only the City mayor gets to be Lord) and an assortment of oddly named and peculiarly dressed aldermen, beadles and sheriffs. It sits at the Guildhall. These men – and they usually *are* male – are elected by the City of London's freemen and liverymen. Though its government may appear out of time and obsolete in the

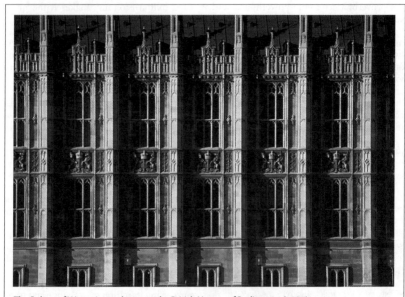

The Palace of Westminster, home to the British Houses of Parliament (p134)

Red Ken

London's first-ever popularly elected mayor is a colourful, charismatic character who has done much to improve London for tourists. As the leader of the Greater London Council (GLC) during the 1980s, 'Red Ken' – as the socialist was once popularly known – went head to head with that most conservative of prime ministers, Margaret Thatcher. He pushed a huge 'Fare's Fair' campaign to reduce the cost of public transport in London, and put a giant counter on the roof of County Hall, which gave updated unemployment figures and was clearly visible from the House of Commons. Thatcher became so infuriated with Livingstone that she scrapped the GLC altogether.

He entered Parliament as an MP and proposed many policies that seemed radical at the time, but which have since been adopted as government policy. His refusal to always toe the party line made him popular with Londoners but earned him the mistrust of the parliamentary Labour Party. He was a hate figure for the right-wing tabloids, and the *Sun* once called him 'the most odious man in Britain', and portrayed him as a freak for his love of newts (Ken's big hobby).

When Labour decided to reinstate the London council as the Greater London Assembly (GLA), popular Livingstone seemed a shoo-in for the job of mayor. However, Tony Blair was determined to halt Livingstone's election bandwagon and, shamelessly rigging the selection process against Livingstone, the Labour Party's nomination went to a Blair loyalist. Crash, bang, wallop...Livingstone resigned from the party and ran as an independent candidate, promising to lock horns with the central government whenever it came to London's best interest. He swept to victory on a tide of popular support in May 2000. Undermining Londoners' fierce independence was perhaps Tony Blair's single biggest mistake in his first term in power.

Livingstone did little in his first year apart from banning pigeons from Trafalgar Sq. With those pesky blighters almost out of the way, and the famous square being given a face-lift, he has since made transport his number-one priority, fighting tooth and nail against the government-proposed, part-privatisation of the Underground (and failing), improving bus services, and introducing the bold, risky yet hugely successful congestion charge in 2003. His most important strategy is the £100 billion London Plan, a planning framework for the city over the next decade, which aims to overhaul London's use of resources and its relationship with the environment. One of its toughest and most contentious challenges is the provision of affordable housing and the mayor's plan to build 15 new skyscrapers by 2013 has been widely derided. Some say the plan will be the capital's biggest make-over since the aftermath of the Great Fire in 1666.

Despite a long-running feud with the influential right-wing London tabloid the *Evening Standard*, which has tried to smear him with charges ranging from corruption to anti-Semitism, Livingstone continues to enjoy a high level of popularity, which is rare for any elected leader in London. His readmission to a mercurial Labour Party (who quickly realised its mistake in ever taking him on as a rival) and subsequent re-election in 2004 confirm that, whatever take you have on London's mayor, he remains one of the most important and talented politicians of his time.

third millennium, the Corporation of London still owns roughly a third of the supremely wealthy 'Square Mile' and has a good record for patronage of the arts.

London is further divided into 33 widely differing boroughs (13 of which are in central London), run by democratically elected councils with significant autonomy. These deal with education and matters such as road sweeping and rubbish collection. The richest borough in terms of per capita income is Richmond in the west; the poorest is Barking in the east.

NATIONAL GOVERNMENT

London is, of course, the seat of the national government. For the record, Britain is a constitutional monarchy with no written constitution and operates under a combination of parliamentary statutes, common law (a body of legal principles based on precedents, often dating back centuries) and convention.

Parliament is made up of the monarch, the House of Commons and the House of Lords. The monarch is essentially a figurehead with no real power, while the House of Commons is where the real power lies. It comprises a national assembly of 659 constituencies (or seats) directly elected every four to five years. The leader of the biggest party in the House of Commons is the prime minister, who appoints a cabinet of 20 or so ministers to run government departments. Prime Minister Tony Blair's Labour Party holds a majority of nearly 70 MPs – much reduced from before the 2005 election – over the Conservative Party. The Conservatives have been in the doldrums now for a decade, and weren't even able to properly capitalise on widespread public dissatisfaction with Blair over his controversial decision to lead Britain into the Iraq war 'shoulder to shoulder' with Bush's America. Therefore Labour still managed to win a historic third term in May 2005, despite Iraq, the failure to find WMD, an inquiry into possibly distorted secret-service intelligence and a general feeling among many voters (especially those who voted in dissident George Galloway instead of Blairite 'babe' Oona King in Bethnal Green and Bow) that 'Bliar' had lied. Notwithstanding calls for Chancellor Gordon Brown to take over the leadership of the Labour Party (and hence become PM), this might not happen until the next election in four to five years' time.

The House of Lords has a little power but these days it's largely limited to delaying legislation – even then, it's only a question of time before it goes to the Queen to be rubber-stamped. For centuries the House of Lords consisted of some 900 'hereditary peers' (whose titles passed from one generation to the next), 25 Church of England bishops and 12 Law Lords (who also act as Britain's highest court). But Tony Blair targeted the Lords with the same zeal with which the mayor went for the Trafalgar Sq pigeons – the similarities possibly end there – and most of the hereditary peers were shuffled out in 1999. Ninety-two of them have been allowed to stay, for the time being. A new system of 'life peerage' was introduced which, critics say, allowed the prime minister to hand out plum jobs to loyal MPs who wouldn't have to go through the bother of getting elected in the future. In the second stage of Lords reform (for which there is no time frame), elected peers will enter the upper house for the first time and hereditary peers will be swept away altogether.

ENVIRONMENT

THE LAND

Greater London comprises 607 sq miles enclosed by the M25 ring road. As well as being essential to the trade upon which London was built, the River Thames divides the city into north and south, a partition that had much more than geographical implications. The Romans designated the southern bank as a seedy London of gaming and debauchery, and for almost two millennia thence, respectable and cultured folk settled on the northern side while the outcasts lived in the insalubrious south. The potential of the South Bank has only been realised in the last decade.

Although London grew from the area known as the City, it doesn't have a single focal point. Its expansion was never really planned; rather, the burgeoning city just consumed outlying settlements. Thus – as any reader of Dickens will appreciate – London today is more a patchwork of villages than a single city. Although the city can feel like a never-ending concrete jungle, there are actually huge swathes of green on its outskirts – take Richmond Park and Hampstead Heath – and large parks such as Regent's and Hyde in the centre.

A Different London Underground

Pressure on space is nothing new to central London – when Victorian engineers were faced with the same problem they decided to build down, digging tunnels, railways and roads and burying rivers beneath the city. So much activity took place down there that a veritable subterranean city exists beneath your feet.

Although the Thames is the only river associated with London now, the city is crisscrossed by many 'lost' waterways that have come to run underground. Fleet St is named after the most famous of all, the Fleet, which rises in Hampstead and empties into the Thames at Blackfriars Bridge. By the 18th century it had become a reeking sewer and was covered up.

Also, the dozen or so bridges spanning the Thames are far outnumbered by the 30-odd tunnels that zigzag beneath its course. After several failed attempts, the first tunnel was opened in 1840 and it later became the Underground's East London line.

If you're interested in what lies beneath your feet, pick up Stephen Smith's *Underground London: Beneath the City Streets*, where, among other things, it's revealed that Queen Boudicca lies beneath Platform 10 at King's Cross (allegedly) and that WWII 'Careless talk costs lives' posters are still plastered over the now unused King William St underground station.

GREEN LONDON

The most serious environmental problem facing the centre of London, the pollution and chronic congestion caused by heavy traffic, has been partially alleviated since 2003 when the Mayor's Congestion Tax was introduced, whereby every car entering the centre had to pay £5 (now £8) for the privilege. There are now 15% to 20% fewer vehicles on central streets, traffic jams are fewer and average speeds have nearly doubled. What's more, it's possible to inhale the air on many streets without it grating on the back of your throat, and London is a much more enjoyable place to stroll around because of it (see also p34).

Recycling has been available in London for many years but mainly in the form of community bins rather than separate household ones, and the mainstream hasn't really been encouraged to go green. Some boroughs are better than others but the London average for recycling household waste is a miserable 9%.

To look at the Thames' murky waters, you'd assume it was another pollution black spot, but below the surface, its health has

Rollerblading in Hyde Park

improved dramatically in recent years and the river is playing an increasingly important role in recreation. By 1962 the combined impact of untreated sewage and industrial pollution had killed off virtually every sign of life in the river, but thanks to a massive cleanup it's now home to some 115 species of fish, including shad, sea lamprey and even salmon (for which special ladders have been built over the weirs). With them have come 10,000 herons, cormorants and other waterfowl that feed on the fish; even otters have been spotted on the river's upper reaches. The reason it still looks so murky in central London is that it is the brackish centre of marine and freshwater zones.

London boasts more parks and open spaces than any city of its size in the world – from the neatly manicured (Holland Park, St James's Park) to the semiwild (Richmond Park, Bushy Park). Between them they provide suitable habitats for a wide range of animals and birds.

The mammal you're most likely to spot on land is the grey squirrel, a North American import that has colonised every big park and decimated the indigenous red population. Hedgehogs also live here, though their numbers are dwindling, perhaps due to the increased use of slug pellets. You probably won't be able to see foxes because of their nocturnal habits but they're here, while Richmond Park hosts badgers as well as herds of red and fallow deer.

Bird-watchers, especially those keen on waterfowl, will love London. There are ducks, pelicans and the Queen's swans in St James's Park, and more ducks and beautiful, chestnut-headed great-crested grebes in Hyde Park's Serpentine. London canals are also happy hunting grounds for spotting waterfowl.

Garden birds, such as long-tailed and great tits, sparrows, robins and blackbirds, roost in all the parks, but some parks attract more interesting migrants. In Holland Park in spring you might glimpse flocks of tiny goldcrests. Kestrels also nest around the Tower of London. The open stretches of the commons in Barnes and Wimbledon also harbour a rich assortment of birds and mammals.

The **London Wildlife Trust** (LWT; ☎ 7261 0447; Harling House, 47-51 Great Suffolk St, London SE1 0BS; www.wildlondon.org.uk) maintains more than 50 nature reserves in the city, which offer the chance to see a range of birds and occasionally small mammals. Battersea Park

Home Economics

The need for additional homes is one of the most pressing issues impacting on the quality of life in London. The capital needs hundreds of thousands of new homes to meet its projected population growth and various schemes have been put in place to try to solve this crisis. There are now special UK government housing grants for key workers, such as nurses, ambulance drivers and so on. Mayor Ken Livingstone's London Plan envisages 23,000 to 30,000 new homes being built, and for developers to gain planning permission for building projects there is now a City Hall requirement that 50% of schemes within each borough are dedicated to affordable housing. (When it came to agreeing on a deal for the Dome and surrounding area, the mayor was reportedly willing to settle for 40%.)

Other projects include the £1.45m Wyndham Rd scheme in Camberwell, South London, where prefab apartments made in Poland will be erected to house key workers cheaply. The mayor has also successfully negotiated more affordable housing in Grand Union Village in Ealing and Imperial Wharf in Hammersmith & Fulham.

Nature Reserve has several nature trails, while the Trent Country Park even boasts a Braille trail through the woodlands. Parts of Hampstead Heath have been designated a Site of Special Scientific Interest for their wealth of natural history.

Green fingers won't want to miss the exotic plants in the exceedingly lovely **Kew Gardens** (p210), while London's parks boast a variety of common or garden trees, shrubs and flowers. Many Londoners also take pride in their private gardens, which range from handkerchief-sized back yards to sprawling mini-estates, some of which open for a few days each summer through the **National Gardens Scheme** (NGS; ☎ 01483-211535; Hatchlands Park, East Clandon, Guildford GU4 7RT; www.ngs.org.uk). Admission usually costs £2, which goes to charity.

URBAN PLANNING & DEVELOPMENT

Central London has been considerably smartened up in recent years, and mayor Ken Livingstone is at the forefront of other bold and imaginative schemes to make the city a more pleasant place to live and visit. Traffic was banished from the north side of Trafalgar Sq, now connected by a new pedestrian plaza that stretches to the National Gallery, itself undergoing massive renovations. Plans are afoot to give seedy Leicester Sq the same treatment and transform it into a clean and sociable European-style plaza, while the ongoing development of the South Bank continues to impress.

But the biggest challenge facing London is how to house its growing population without encroaching on the green belt surrounding the city. Previously run-down central areas like Hoxton and Clerkenwell were dolled up in the 1990s with young populations moving in and converting warehouses. The repopulation of the Docklands continues, but London is quickly running out of space. The mayor has taken measures to address the problem (see Home Economics, above), and in his London Plan he has also built in the protection of green space, although business interests are mobilising to scrap that protection and reduce the 'burden' on developers.

In what is perhaps a sign of things to come, the government is facing an inevitable conflict with environmentalists over the proposed regeneration of the Thames Gateway, the 60km on each side of the Thames from East London to the North Sea. The plan is to build 200,000 homes and provide 300,000 jobs but in an area that contains some of Britain's most valuable wildlife sites and a 25km stretch of shore that is designated as an EU high-priority special protection area. Only time will tell.

We'd Be Lost Without Harry Beck

In 1931 an out-of-work engineering draughtsman, Harry Beck, created the city's most famous icon, the London Underground map (p466). Beck realised existing maps were too impenetrable so he designed one that presented an ordered vision of a chaotic city. Beck was paid five guineas (£5.50) for his revolutionary work, which changed the face of London forever and continues to make the city feel almost navigable for tourists and locals alike.

Arts

Arts

Wherever you come from, whatever art forms you enjoy, you'll find them generously and excitingly represented in London. The English capital has traditionally been the artistic centre of the country and, in many ways, of Europe as a whole, particularly throughout the 20th century, when it's led the way in music, fashion, theatre and literature.

The arts make an important contribution to London's economic success, but it's the feel-good factor they give the local population that's perhaps the most valuable. Hollywood stars queue up to tread the boards of the capital's theatres, while London continues to be the heart of English literature, housing both the most innovative publishers in the country and some of writing's greatest stars. While the dust is still settling after the storm of Britart, a generation of less obviously shocking artists is emerging – not to mention the host of new galleries and museums that have opened in the past five years – ensuring that Londoners are still art crazy.

London's actors and actresses are known the world over, and the British film industry still throws out some notable productions, from Oscar-nominated *Vera Drake* to the comic brilliance of *Shaun of the Dead* and blockbusters such as the Harry Potter and James Bond series. Musically, the city is making a comeback from the post-Britpop torpor that set in around the turn of the millennium, while remaining one of the best places to see live bands anywhere on earth. London is also a capital of comedy, and its dance companies cut a splendid dash across the world stage.

LITERATURE

THE CURRENT SCENE

While London publishing houses are continuing to produce hundreds of new books a year, there has yet to be a movement or grouping of writers to challenge the group of 1980s London novelists who have dominated the scene for years: Martin Amis, Ian McEwan, Salman Rushdie and Julian Barnes, to name just a few. While Amis's last book, *Yellow Dog*, met a critical panning (one particularly scathing review described the work as 'like catching your favourite uncle masturbating in a schoolyard'), he continues to be one of the most popular and successful writers working today, while McEwan continues to receive critical acclaim.

If anything, the current scene is most notable for the wealth of superb children's literature being produced. JK Rowling and Phillip Pulman have between them totally revolutionised the concept of what children's books can be. That's not to say that new voices haven't broken through in the last decade – on the contrary – but no easy-to-identify movement has presented itself either. Indeed, there have been some outstanding new London writers in recent years – from Jonathon Coe and Monica Ali to Jake Arnott and Patrick Neate. The shape of the industry is best exemplified by the 2000 runaway success *White Teeth*, a brilliant debut novel by Zadie Smith about

Top Five Literary Locations

- **Dickens House Museum** (p108), where the most London of authors wrote *Oliver Twist*.
- **221b Baker St** (p190), the address of Sherlock Holmes, although it didn't even exist in Arthur Conan Doyle's day.
- The **Globe** (p153), an exact reconstruction of the theatre where Shakespeare wrote and worked much of his life, is the first place for anyone with a passion for the Bard.
- **Bloomsbury WC1** (p106), where the influential group of writers, artists and intellectuals known as the Bloomsbury Group lived and worked early in the 20th century.
- **Hampstead** (p194), a leafy hilltop suburb that was home to great writers such as John Keats (see p195), HG Wells and DH Lawrence.

Prize Writers

The Booker Prize is the most important literary-fiction prize in Britain. Since its foundation in 1969 it has only been open to Commonwealth and Irish authors, but new sponsors the Man Group insisted that it be opened to US writers by 2004, drawing uproar from sections of the British media. Despite fears that American competition would lead to no British writer ever winning the prize again, the 2004 Booker went to Londoner Alan Hollinghurst for his *The Line of Beauty*. Any well-read Londoner will have an opinion about the Booker Prize – some rubbish it as a self-promotional tool of publishing houses, while others slavishly read not only the winner but any book to make the short list. Either way, few are indifferent to the prize, and the winner is usually highly indicative of contemporary literary trends in Britain.

multiethnic assimilation in north London. This novel propelled Smith, pretty much overnight, from obscurity to being the poster girl for young, hip literary London.

Smith arrived on the scene already represented by a ruthless literary agent who invited publishers to bid for the book on the strength of – not even a full manuscript – a sample of 100 pages. The feeding frenzy that followed has already passed into London legend. Zadie fulfilled all the current criteria: as well as being a bloody good writer she was young, gorgeous and multicultural (ie eminently marketable). Bling. Bling. Bling. Bling. All the lights lit up and Grub St went into orbit. Penguin finally claimed victory when it paid the *unknown* author £250,000 for the *unknown* book.

As it turned out, Penguin's 'hunch' was spot on; *White Teeth* was fresh, original and generally fabulous, and the publisher made a handsome profit from it and from her somewhat less impressive follow-up, *The Autograph Man*, in 2002. But it's the nature of the first book's publication that characterises London's literary scene right now: it's dominated by assorted editors, publishers, agents and booksellers desperately sniffing around for 'the next big thing'. Publishers on a quest for the jackpot are shelling out bigger and bigger advances for new books by unknown authors in the hope that they'll uncover 'the next Zadie Smith'. Which they may just have done.

Once every decade, 20 young British writers are named in the prestigious *Granta* list, which sets the literary agenda for a generation. One of the names in the 2003 dream team, Londoner and Anglo-Bangladeshi Monica Ali, hadn't even been published before she was being trumpeted as one of the most significant British novelists of the day. She met all the criteria and her book, *Brick Lane,* is a winner.

Older, less photogenic authors grumble that literary success is now as much about looks as the quality of the books. Whether a new author is young and gorgeous has much to do with what kind of marketing push each book gets, which, these days, has more bearing on success than what the critics say. Publishers are less likely to give an author the luxury of a couple of books to find their readership, and one can only wonder what masterpieces might never have seen the light of day had the same criteria applied in the 20th century.

In the meantime the media and the marketing folk try to come up with new and marketable trends where none really exist. Some cling anxiously to 'chick lit', although that label is a decade out of date, while one hopeful faction was trying to flog 'granny lit' because there had been a slight increase in the number of books published by over-50s.

As a reaction to the industry's obsession with hip, a couple of editors got together to form a literary movement known as the New Puritans, with a manifesto not dissimilar to the Danish filmmakers' Dogme 95. Their aim was to produce fiction in 'its purest and most immediate form'. The New Puritans banned poetic license, and were widely rubbished, as you might expect.

Whatever the arguments about chasing trends, it has at least reinvigorated the book-publishing industry in Britain. Only a few years ago, British newspapers and literary magazines were lamenting the demise of fiction and drafting its obituary. However, the chairman of the 2004 Man Booker Prize judges announced in his speech at the prize ceremony that 'our overall conclusion has been that contemporary English fiction is in robust health'.

See p326 for details of readings and spoken-word events around the city.

OLD LITERARY LONDON

London is unique in English literature, having constantly been portrayed in countless ways over a period of six centuries, from Chaucer to Monica Ali, making a history of London writing a history of the city itself. London has been the inspiration for such timeless masters as Shakespeare, Dickens, Thackeray, Defoe, Wells, Orwell, Conrad, Greene and Woolf, to name but a few. It's hard to reconcile the bawdy portrayal of the city in the *Canterbury Tales* with Dickens' bleak hellhole in *Oliver Twist*, let alone Defoe's plague-ravaged metropolis with Zadie Smith's multiethnic romp in *White Teeth*. Ever changing, yet somehow eerily consistent – something brilliantly illustrated in Peter Ackroyd's *London: The Biography* – the capital has left its mark on some of the most influential writing in the English language. What follows is a small selection of seminal moments from the history of literature in London – you can get a detailed listing in *Waterstone's Guide to London Writing* (£3.99), available at Waterstone's bookshops everywhere.

The first literary reference to the city comes in Chaucer's *Canterbury Tales,* written between 1387 and 1400, where the pilgrims gather for their trip to Canterbury at the Tabard Inn in Southwark.

William Shakespeare spent most of his life as an actor and playwright in London around the turn of the 16th century, when book publishing was beginning to take off here. He trod the boards of several Southwark theatres and wrote his greatest tragedies – among them *Hamlet, Othello, Macbeth* and *King Lear* – for the original Globe theatre on South Bank. However, though London was his home for most of his life, Shakespeare was an ardent fantasist and set nearly all his plays in foreign or make-believe lands. Even his English historical plays are hardly ever set in the capital; only *Henry IV: Part II* includes a London setting: a tavern called the Boar's Head in Eastcheap.

Daniel Defoe was perhaps the first true London writer, both living in and writing about the city during the early 18th century. Most famous for *Robinson Crusoe* (1720) and *Moll Flanders* (1722), which he wrote while living in Church St in Stoke Newington, Defoe's *Journal of the Plague Year* is nonetheless his most interesting account of London life, documenting the horrors of the Black Death in London during the summer and autumn of 1665, when the author was a child.

Two early-19th-century poets found inspiration here. Keats wrote his *Ode to a Nightingale* while living near Hampstead Heath in 1819 and his *Ode on a Grecian Urn* after inspecting the Portland Vase in the British Museum. Wordsworth visited in 1802 and was inspired to write the poem *On Westminster Bridge*.

Foyle's bookstore (p346)

Grub Street

Grub St was the original name of a London street (now Milton St, located behind the Barbican) inhabited by impoverished writers and literary hacks. In the 18th century, any inferior book or work of literature was known as 'Grubstreet', but these days – and you shouldn't read anything into this – the term seems to be used for the whole London publishing industry. The London publishing world takes itself extremely seriously, and that's why publications such as *Private Eye* (p25) are so refreshing, always on the lookout for individuals or organisations that are getting too big for their boots.

Charles Dickens (1812–70) was the definitive London author. When his father and family were imprisoned for not paying their debts, the 12-year-old Charles was forced to fend for himself on the streets of Victorian London. Although his family were released three months later, those grim months were seared into the boy's memory and provided a font of experiences on which the author would later draw. His novels most closely associated with the city are *Oliver Twist*, with its story of a gang of boy thieves organised by Fagin in Clerkenwell, and *Little Dorrit*, whose heroine was born in the Marshalsea – the same prison where his family were interned. His later *Our Mutual Friend* is a scathing criticism of contemporary London values – both monetary and social – and a spirited attack on the corruption, complacency and superficiality of 'respectable' London. The Old Curiosity Shop, made famous by the book of the same name, can still be seen standing just off Lincoln's Inn today.

Sir Arthur Conan Doyle (1858–1930) portrayed a very different London, and his pipe-smoking, cocaine-snorting sleuth, Sherlock Holmes, came to exemplify a cool and unflappable Englishness the world over. Letters to the mythical hero still arrive at 221b Baker St, where there's now a museum to everyone's favourite Victorian detective.

London at the end of the 19th century is described in a number of books. HG Wells' *The War of the Worlds* captures the sense and mood of the times wonderfully. Somerset Maugham's first novel, *Liza of Lambeth*, was based on his experiences as an intern in the slums of south London, while his *Of Human Bondage,* so English and of its time, provides the most engaging portrait of late-Victorian London we know.

20TH-CENTURY WRITING

Of the Americans writing about London at the end of the 19th century, Henry James, who settled and died here, stands supreme with his *Daisy Miller* and *The Europeans. The People of the Abyss*, by American socialist writer Jack London, is a sensitive portrait of the poverty and despair of life in the East End. And we couldn't forget Mark Twain's *The Innocents Abroad*, in which the inimitable humourist skewers both the Old and the New Worlds. St Louis–born TS Eliot settled in London in 1915, where he published his poem *The Love Song of J Alfred Prufrock* almost immediately and moved on to his groundbreaking epic *The Waste Land.*

The End of the Affair, Graham Greene's novel chronicling a passionate and doomed romance, takes place in and around Clapham Common during WWI, while *The Heat of the Day* is Elizabeth Bowen's sensitive, if melodramatic, account of living through the Blitz.

Between the wars, PG Wodehouse (1881–1975), the most quintessentially British writer of the early 20th century, depicted the London high life with his hilarious lampooning of the English upper classes in the Jeeves stories. Quentin Crisp, the self-proclaimed 'stately homo of England', provided the flipside, recounting what it was like to be openly gay in the sexually repressed London of the 1920s in his ribald and witty memoir, *The Naked Civil Servant.* George Orwell's experiences of living as a beggar in London's East End coloured his book *Down and Out in Paris and London* (1933).

Colin MacInnes described the bohemian, multicultural world of 1950s Notting Hill in *City of Spades* and *Absolute Beginners,* while Doris Lessing captured the political mood of 1960s London in *The Four-Gated City,* the last of her five-book *Children of Violence* series, and provides some of the funniest and most vicious portrayals of 1990s London in *London Observed.* Nick Hornby finds himself the voice of a generation, nostalgic about his days as a young football fan in *Fever Pitch* and obsessive about vinyl in *High Fidelity.*

Before it became fashionable, authors such as Hanif Kureishi explored London from the perspective of ethnic minorities, specifically young Pakistanis in Kureishi's most well-known novels *The Black Album* and *The Buddha of Suburbia* – he also wrote the screenplay for the ground-breaking film *My Beautiful Laundrette*. Author and playwright Caryl Phillips won plaudits for his description of the Caribbean immigrant's experience in *The Final Passage*, while Timothy Mo's *Sour Sweet* is a poignant and funny account of a Chinese family in the 1960s trying to adjust to English life.

The astronomical success of Helen Fielding's *Bridget Jones's Diary* effectively concluded the genre known as 'chick lit', a series of hugely successful books that were, depending on your perspective, about finding Mr Right or about independent, brassy young women finding their voice. Will Self – *enfant terrible* and incisive social commentator – has been the toast of London for the last decade. His *Grey Area* is a superb collection of short stories focusing on skewed and surreal aspects of the city.

Peter Ackroyd is regarded as the quintessential London author and names the city as the love of his life. *London: The Biography* is Ackroyd's inexhaustible paean to the capital, while his most recent book, *The Clerkenwell Tales*, brings to life the 14th-century London of Chaucer.

Recommended Reading

- *Absolute Beginners* (1959; Colin MacInnes) This brilliant novel is a must-read for anyone interested in the youth culture of London during the '50s, particularly the mod scene and the mixed-up culture that existed in post-war London. It's the best piece of literature to come out of this period and infinitely more engaging than the film of the same name.

- *The Adventures of Sherlock Holmes* (1892; Arthur Conan Doyle) The first collection of short stories featuring the snobby sleuth and his trusty sidekick, Dr Watson, this book is for everyone 10 years old and up who likes mystery and captivating tales. Conan Doyle once described London as 'that great cesspool into which all the loungers of the Empire are irresistibly drained'.

- *Brick Lane* (2003; Monica Ali) The most hyped book since Zadie Smith's *White Teeth*, this debut novel tells the story of Nazneen, an Islamic Bangladeshi woman who comes to London after an arranged marriage and initially accepts her circumscribed life, before embarking on her own voyage of self-discovery. The author, herself half-Bangladeshi, writes with wit and gentle irony.

- *The Buddha of Suburbia* (1991; Hanif Kureishi) This winner of the 1990 Whitbread prize is a raunchy, heart-warming, funny and insightful trawl of the hopes and fears of a group of Asian suburbanites in 1970s London, from the preeminent Anglo-Asian voice of his generation. It may feel a little aged compared with the chronicles of multiculturalism that have been all the rage in more recent years, but this one arguably has more punch.

- *The End of the Affair* (1951; Graham Greene) Set in battle-scarred London at the end of WWII, this intensely emotional classic deals with a three-way collision between love of self, love of another and love of God (coloured by the very real tension felt by the author between his Roman Catholic faith and the compulsion of sexual passion).

- *Grey Area* (1994; Will Self) Piercing wit, narrative virtuosity and incisive social commentary characterise the writing of Will Self, who is considered by Londoners to be either the best writer of his generation or a smug, self-indulgent smartarse. In this collection of nine short stories – or 'comic nightmares' – he lays into contemporary London and evokes the most disturbing failings of society.

- *High Fidelity* (2000; Nick Hornby) This extraordinarily successful novel by one of London's most famous scribes tackles the really big questions, at least those pertaining to the lives of 30-something men. Is it possible to share your life with someone whose record collection is incompatible with your own? Quite sad and very funny.

- *The Jeeves Omnibus* (1931; PG Wodehouse) One of the funniest writers in English, Wodehouse sends up the English upper classes with 31 stories about Bertie Wooster and his butler, Jeeves; Bertie lived in exclusive Mayfair and revelled in the London high life.

- *Journal of the Plague Year* (1722; Daniel Defoe) Among the most gripping accounts of natural disaster in the history of literature, Defoe's classic reconstruction of the Great Plague of 1665 scans the streets and alleyways of stricken London to record the extreme suffering of plague victims. At once grisly and movingly compassionate.

- *Last Orders* (1997; Graham Swift) Four friends getting on in years cast their minds back to the East End of wartime London in this beautifully written, understated and bittersweet tale. It was made into an equally charming film starring the ultimate cockney, Michael Caine.

Finally, Iain Sinclair is the bard of Hackney, who, like Ackroyd, has spent his life obsessed with and fascinated by the capital. His acclaimed and ambitious *London Orbital*, a journey on foot around the M25, London's mammoth motorway bypass, is required London reading.

THEATRE

THE CURRENT SCENE

Apologies to Shakespeare's birthplace of Stratford-upon-Avon, but London is really the spiritual home of English theatre, and in recent years it's been at the top of its game. It's no longer such big news when Hollywood stars parachute in to tread the boards in the English capital, although still they come, from hot young stars such as *The Motorcycle Diaries'* Gael Garcia Bernal and A-listers such as *Friends'* David Schwimmer, to Brooke Shields and Val Kilmer. In a city where Dame Judi Dench, Sir Ian McKellen, Simon Callow, Ralph Fiennes and Ewan McGregor all appear in the lengthy roll call of home-grown talent, there are sufficient non–Hollywood related developments to keep the critics interested.

- *The Line of Beauty* (2003; Alan Hollinghurst) A surprise Booker Prize winner in 2004, Hollinghurst's account of high-society homosexuality in Thatcher's London paints a portrait of a divisive period in modern British history and follows on where his first novel, *The Swimming Pool Library*, left off. Both bring west London society into a sharp critical focus and are beautifully written.
- *London Fields* (1989; Martin Amis) By using a constantly shifting narrative voice, Amis makes the reader work damn hard for the prize in this middle-class-fear-of-the-mob epic. Dark and postmodern – Dickens plus swearing and sex, minus compassion, wrote one reviewer – it is a gripping study of London low life.
- *London Observed* (1992; Doris Lessing) A collection of stories from this hugely successful and much-celebrated Iranian-born author, who observes London and its inhabitants with the shrewd and compassionate eye of an artist in 18 sketches of the city.
- *London Orbital* (2002; Iain Sinclair) Sinclair, Hackney's irrepressible voice of dissent, sets off to circumnavigate the capital on foot within the 'acoustic footprints' of the M25, London's massive motorway bypass. Hilarious and insightful, this hard-to-classify classic was recently voted Londoners' favourite book about the capital by *Time Out* readers.
- *London: The Biography* (2000; Peter Ackroyd) Regarded by some as the definitive guide to London, this tome provides a fascinating tapestry of the life and history of the capital, arranged by theme rather than chronologically.
- *The Long Firm* (2000; Jake Arnott) The first – and best – of a London trilogy set in the seedy world of 1960's Soho and featuring walk-on parts from, among others, the Krays and Judy Garland. Brutal but often hilarious reading that was made into a compelling BBC drama series too.
- *Mother London* (2000; Michael Moorcock) This engaging, rambling novel follows three mentally disturbed characters who hear voices from the heart of London, which provides for an episodic romp through the history of the capital from the Blitz to the end of the millennium. The city itself becomes a character, along with its outcasts and marginals, all treated with great compassion by a self-assured author.
- *Mrs Dalloway* (1925; Virginia Woolf) Bloomsbury Group stalwart Virginia Woolf goes full throttle with her stream-of-consciousness style in this story, which follows a day in the life of various people trying to cope in 1923 London. It is beautifully crafted, and as brief as it is exhilarating.
- *The Naked Civil Servant* (1968; Quentin Crisp) A 1976 TV film of this autobiography, starring John Hurt, made Crisp famous and infamous overnight. It's the story of an openly gay man in London in the 1920s, a world of brutality and comedy, told in Crisp's characteristically sarcastic, self-derogatory, bitchy and very funny way.
- *Oliver Twist* (1837; Charles Dickens) Although not necessarily Dickens' best novel – or a good introduction to the author – this moving story of an orphan who runs away to London and falls in with a gang of thieves is beautifully told, with rich, unforgettable characters and a vivid portrayal of Victorian London.
- *Sour Sweet* (1982; Timothy Mo) Nominated for the Booker Prize, this tongue-in-cheek novel follows the fortunes of a Chinese family trying to come to terms with life amongst the 'foreign devils' of London and is a fascinating look at the city through the eyes of an immigrant. Sharp writing and black humour.
- *White Teeth* (2000; Zadie Smith) Zadie Smith's hugely hyped novel is a funny, poignant, big-hearted and affectionate book about friendship and cultural differences, as seen through the eyes of three unassimilated families in north London. It's not quite as dazzling as the critics made out, but nothing could be.

After several terrible years from late 2001, the mainstream West End is back in fine fettle, while the fringe continues to boom (as does English regional theatre). Smaller theatres such as the Almeida and the new Menier Chocolate Factory continue to take admirable risks, but the hottest ticket in town for the serious theatregoer is the National Theatre.

Over at the Old Vic, big-name import Kevin Spacey is generally regarded to have wasted opportunities during his tenure as artistic director – although he won much approval for his threat to throw out audience members who let their mobile phones ring. However, the National's Nicholas Hytner has won universal acclaim for his and his team's programme of newly commissioned plays, resurrected or revamped classics, experimental theatre, and cheap seats. Huge successes here have included new plays from such heavy hitters as Alan Bennett (*The History Boys*, Bennett's first new play for years), Michael Frayn *(Democracy)* and David Mamet *(Edmond,* starring Kenneth Branagh), as well as the discovery of newer playwrights such as Kwame Kwei-Armah *(Elmina's Kitchen).*

There's something for all tastes in London's theatreland, and even the revivified West End juggles the serious with the frivolous. Recent productions have included Friedrich Schiller's *Don Carlos* – an unlikely, but huge, hit from director Michael Grandage – and a rerun of David Mamet's *Oleanna*. At the same time, feel-good musicals such as *Guys and Dolls, The Producers* and *Mary Poppins* have been walking away with not just massive box-office takings but also critical acclaim. The genre-bending *Jerry Springer – the Opera* has continued to stir up controversy on stage and (filmed by BBC TV) on screen.

Several minor trends have been discernible in London theatre recently. There's been an increasing number of European plays (*Don Carlos* and Molière's *Hypochondriac*, to name just two), while, much to the chagrin of the *Guardian*'s clock-watching critic Michael Billington, productions seem to be getting shorter. The line between cinema and theatre has also been blurred, as director Rufus Norris brought a much-applauded version of *Festen* (a Danish Dogme film about incest) to the West End, Stephen Daldry turned *Billy Elliot* into a musical and the *West Wing's* Rob Lowe appeared in a revival of *A Few Good Men*.

Perhaps most notable, and possibly predictable, was the upsurge in political theatre in the wake of the Iraq war. The satire and analysis spread all the way from the fringe – where plays such as *Justifying War*, *The Madness of George Dubya* and *A Weapons Inspector Calls* were on show – to the West End, where *Guantanamo* played.

The liberal-minded Hollywood star Tim Robbins brought a stylised satire on media coverage of the war, *Embedded*, to the Riverside Studios, while respected British playwright David Hare chronicled the build-up to war in *Stuff Happens*. 'What we are finding is that when we do plays about politics the place is really buzzing,' the National's Hytner revealed in 2005, announcing a season in which the theatre would 'take on the world in which we are really living'.

Of course, the greatest English playwright, William Shakespeare, was frequently political himself – Hytner easily turned *Henry V* into an antiwar production recently – and the Bard's towering legacy endures in the capital in two principal forms.

First, the Royal Shakespeare Company constantly stages one or two classics. After years at the Barbican Centre and a few years in the wilderness after ill-advisedly leaving the Barbican, the RSC is now using the Albery Theatre (possibly to be renamed the Noel Coward Theatre) in St Martin's Lane as its main London base.

Secondly, the open-air Globe on the south bank of the Thames attempts to recreate the Elizabethan theatregoing experience. A faithful reconstruction on the site of the original Globe in which Shakespeare worked, the building places audiences unusually close to the actors, and the management is quite happy to let them heckle each other. Since it opened in 1997 the Globe has enjoyed considerable success as a working theatre (as opposed to a mere curiosity). New artistic director Dominic Dromgoole, having taken over the reins at the start of 2006, plans to keep Shakespearean plays at the core of the theatre's programme and at the same time introduce a wider range of European and British classics.

DRAMATIC HISTORY

Very little is known about London theatre before the Elizabethan period, when a series of 'playhouses', including the Globe, were built on the south bank of the Thames and in Shoreditch. Although the playwrights of the time – Shakespeare, Christopher Marlowe *(Dr*

Faustus, Edward II) and Shakespeare's great rival, Ben Johnson *(Volpone, The Alchemist)* – are now considered timeless geniuses, theatre then was more about raucous popular entertainment, where the crowd drank and heckled the actors. As venues for such, the playhouses were promptly shut down by the Puritans after the Civil War in 1642.

Three years after the return of the monarchy in 1660, the first famous Drury Lane Theatre was built and the period of 'restoration theatre' began, under the patronage of the rakish Charles II. Borrowing influences from Italian and French theatre, restoration theatre incorporated drama, including John Dryden's 1677 *All for Love*, and comedy. It's the latter, known for its burlesque humour and sexual explicitness, that most holds the attention of today's audiences. During the restoration period the first female actors appeared on stage (in Elizabethan times men played female roles), and Charles II is recorded as having had an affair with at least one, Nell Gwyn.

Despite the success of John Gay's 1728 *Beggar's Opera*, Oliver Goldsmith's 1773 farce *She Stoops to Conquer* and Richard Sheridan's *The Rivals* and *School for Scandal* at Drury Lane, also in the 1770s, popular music halls would replace serious theatre during the Victorian era. Light comic operetta, as defined by Gilbert and Sullivan *(HMS Pinafore, The Pirates of Penzance, The Mikado* etc), was all the rage. A sea-change was only brought about by the emergence at the end of the 19th century of such compelling playwrights as Oscar Wilde *(An Ideal Husband, The Importance of Being Earnest)* and George Bernard Shaw *(Pygmalion)*.

Comic wits such as Noel Coward *(Private Lives, Brief Encounter)* and earnest dramatists such as Terence Ratigan *(The Winslow Boy, The Browning Version)* and JB Priestley *(An Inspector Calls)* followed. However, it wasn't until the 1950s and 1960s that English drama yet again experienced such a fertile period as the Elizabethan era.

Perfectly encapsulating the social upheaval of the period, John Osborne's *Look Back in Anger* at the Royal Court in 1956 has gone down as generation defining. In the following decade, a rash of new writing appeared, from Harold Pinter's *Homecoming* to Joe Orton's *Loot*, Tom Stoppard's *Rosencrantz and Guildenstern are Dead* and Alan Ayckbourn's *How the Other Half Loves*. During the same period many of today's leading theatre companies were formed, including the National Theatre, under the directorship of Laurence Olivier, in 1963.

Although somewhat eclipsed by the National Theatre in the cyclical world of London theatre, today's Royal Court retains a fine tradition of new writing. In the past decade it's nurtured such talented playwrights as Jez Butterworth *(Mojo, The Night Heron)*, Ayub Khan-Din *(East Is East)*, Conor McPherson *(The Weir, Shining City)* and Joe Penhall *(Dumb Show)*.

For theatre listings, see p329.

For theatre listings, see p329.

Showtime!

Cats might have used up all of its nine lives and been cancelled after more than two decades, but Andrew Lloyd Webber has a new show – *The Woman in White* – and musical theatre sings on in London. If you're a fan, there's still plenty to see, from long-runners *Chicago, Phantom of the Opera* and *Les Misérables* to the likes of *Fame: The Musical* and *Saturday Night Fever*.

Some of the offerings have been little more than a 'greatest hits' collection strung together with a threadbare plot. The Abba musical *Mamma Mia!* and the Queen-fest *We Will Rock You*, for example, will really only appeal to those bands' dedicated followers.

However, recently even the musical has been made respectable, with revered dancer Matthew Bourne choreographing *Mary Poppins*, Mel Brooks bringing the excellent *The Producers* to town, Stephen Daldry helping to rework *Billy Elliot* for the stage, Ewan McGregor appearing in *Guys and Dolls*, and the National Theatre briefly getting in on the act by staging the classic *A Funny Thing Happened on the Way to the Forum*.

Musicals first became popular in London in the 1980s when the Thatcher government cut funding to theatres, which then decided to programme overtly populist shows. The doyen then, as now, was Lloyd Webber *(Phantom of the Opera, Joseph and the Amazing Technicolor Dreamcoat)*, who has since acquired the title Sir. It's been said by some wags that Conservative supporter Lloyd Webber's 1997 threat to leave England permanently in the event of a Labour victory helped propel Tony Blair to power. In the end, however, Lloyd Webber relented and stayed to produce more music for the masses.

MUSIC

Whatever your musical inclination, something in London will strike the right chord. Popular music is perhaps the city's greatest contribution to the world of arts, and after more than four decades at the top, it is still a creative hotbed and a magnet for bands and hopefuls from all over the place. Complementing the homegrown talent is a continuous influx of styles and cultures that keeps the music scene here so fresh. Per head, Britons buy more music than any other nationality – the range is enormous, and we reckon London's still the best place in the world to see live bands. For a list of venues, see p312.

London's prolific output began with the Kinks and their north London songwriter Ray Davies, whose lyrics read like a guide to the city. 'You Really Got Me', 'All Day and All of the Night' and 'Dedicated Follower of Fashion' capture the antiestablishment mood of the '60s brilliantly, while 'Waterloo Sunset' is the ultimate feel-good London song.

Another London band, the Rolling Stones, got their first paying gig at the old Bull & Bush in Richmond in 1963. Originally an R&B outfit, they went on to define rock and roll, and success and teen mayhem quickly followed. Their second single 'I Wanna Be Your Man' came to them via a chance encounter on the street with John Lennon and Paul McCartney, two blokes down from Liverpool, recording in Abbey Rd and on their way to making their band, the Beatles, the biggest the world has ever known. The Stones, no slouches in the fame stakes themselves, released 'Not Fade Away' in 1964, and they're doggedly sticking to their word after 40 years of swaggering, swilling and swearing.

Struggling to be heard above the din was inspirational mod band the Small Faces, formed in 1965 and remembered long afterwards. The Who, from West London, got attention by thrashing guitars on stage and chucking televisions out of hotel windows. The band is remembered for rock operas and hanging around far too long flogging their back catalogue. Jimi Hendrix came to London and took guitar playing to levels not seen before or since. In some ways, the swinging '60s ended in July 1969 when the Stones played a free concert in Hyde Park in front of more than a quarter of a million liberated fans.

A local band called Tyrannosaurus Rex had enjoyed moderate success up to then. In 1970 they changed their name to T Rex, frontman Marc Bolan donned a bit of glitter and the world's first 'glam' band had arrived. Glam encouraged the youth of uptight Britain to come out of the closet and be whatever they wanted to be. Brixton boy and self-proclaimed 'chameleon of pop' David Bowie began to steal the limelight, sealing his international fame with *The Rise and Fall of Ziggy Stardust and the Spiders from Mars* in 1972, one of the best

Crowd at Underworld (p314)

albums of the decade. Roxy Music, incorporating art rock and synth pop, sang 'Love Is the Drug' in 1975.

Meanwhile, a little band called Led Zeppelin formed in London in 1968 and created the roots of heavy metal. Seventeen-year-old Farok Bulsara came to London from India (via Zanzibar) in the '60s and, in 1970, changed his name to Freddie Mercury; the consummate showman formed the band Queen with a few local lads and went on to become one of the greatest rock-and-roll stars of all time. Fleetwood Mac stormed the US as much as Britain; their *Rumours* became the fifth-highest-selling album in history (one behind Cambridge boys Pink Floyd). Bob Marley recorded his *Live* album at the Lyceum Theatre in 1975.

A Musical Journey through London

※ ■ Zebra crossing on Abbey Rd, St John's Wood – the Beatles' most famous album cover

※ ■ Heddon St, Soho – where the cover for *Ziggy Stardust* was photographed

■ 23 Brook St – former home to composers Handel and Hendrix

■ St Martin's College – first Sex Pistols gig

■ Tree on Queen's Ride, Barnes – where Marc Bolan died in his Mini in 1977

■ 6 Denmark Terrace, Muswell Hill – the family home of Ray Davies of the Kinks

Arts – Music

While glam opened the door for British youth, punk came along and kicked the fucking thing down, and set about turning the whole British establishment on its head. The Sex Pistols were the most outrageous of a wave of bands, including the Clash and the Damned, which started playing around London in 1976. The Pistols' first single was, appropriately enough, 'Anarchy in the UK'. 'God Save the Queen' and 'Pretty Vacant' followed and were brilliant. The album *Never Mind the Bollocks Here's the Sex Pistols* was released a year later to critical acclaim.

Fortunately, fellow Londoners the Clash had harnessed the raw anger of the time and worked it into a collar-grabbing brand of political protest that would see them outlast all of their peers. They tread the fine line between being pissed-off punks and great songwriters. The Clash were protesters who raged against racism, social injustice, police brutality and disenfranchisement. The disillusioned generation finally had a plan and a leader; *London Calling* is a spirited call to arms.

The ranting and raving John Lydon (formerly Johnny Rotten) became an embarrassment to a generation weaned on punk, but the reaction to the death of Clash frontman Joe Strummer in late 2002 showed that there was still lots to be proud of.

In 1977 the Jam, punk pioneers *and* mod revivalists, went on tour opening for the Clash (what days!). Lead singer and bristling live performer Paul Weller followed up with a hugely successful solo career.

Out of the ashes of punk came, God knows how, the new wave and new romantics. Guitars were chucked away and replaced with keyboard synthesizers and drum machines. Fashion and image became as important as the music, and it's the seriousness with which the new romantics took themselves that gives the '80s such a bad rap. Overpriced, oversexed and way overdone, '80s London produced such unforgettables as Spandau Ballet, Culture Club, Bananarama, Wham! and Howard Jones' haircut. Wham!'s Georgios Panayiotou shaved his back, changed his name to George Michael and went on to a hugely successful solo career.

Depeche Mode broke new ground in neo-synth pop, while American London adoptee Chrissie Hynde formed the Pretenders and became the first bad-ass rock-and-roll chick; Northern-lads-turned-Londoners the Pet Shop Boys managed to avoid the '80s-pop path to oblivion, redeeming themselves with synth innovation and eventually symphonic spectacle as they performed their own score to Eisenstein's *Battleship Potemkin* on Trafalgar Sq alongside the Dresdner Sinfoniker in September 2004. Neneh Cherry started rapping, and Madness came up with a winning ska-pop combo and featured London in many of their hits and video clips.

But it was all to no avail, because blonde boy-band Bros emerged from South London to top the charts and confirm that the local music scene was really in deep shit. Relief was already coming from up north with the Smiths, and at the end of the decade the Stone Roses and the Happy Mondays broke through with a new sound that had grown out of the recent acid-house raves, with jangly guitars, psychedelic twists and a beat you just couldn't resist. Dance exploded onto the scene, with dilated pupils and Chupa Chups, in 1988's summer of love. A generation was gripped by dance music and a new lexicon had to be learned: techno, electronica, hip-hop, garage, house, trance and so on. Although the E generation that launched the rave/dance culture has grown up and the scene is, well, stagnant at best, London still ranks among the best club cities in the world.

The early 1990s saw the explosion of yet another scene: Britpop, a genre broadly defined as back to (Beatles) basics, familiar old-fashioned three chords and all that jazz, with loads of slang and in-references which, frankly, made it so 'British'. There was a very public battle between two of the biggest bands, Blur from London and Oasis from Manchester, and the public loved the tit-for-tat between the cocky geezers from the capital and the swaggering, belligerent Mancs. For the record, Oasis won the popularity contest, but the more dynamic Blur are ageing better. Weighing in for the London side were the brilliant and erratic Suede (who finally disbanded in 2003) and Elastica, fronted by the punky, poppy Justine Frischmann, not to mention Sheffield defectors to the capital, Jarvis Cocker's Pulp.

Skirting around the edges, doing their own thing without the hullabaloo, were Radiohead (from Oxford, close enough to London), in our opinion one of the best groups in the world. As the Britpop bands and fans became more sophisticated, the genre died around 1997. Groups like Coldplay – who released two superb albums in 2000 and 2002 – are in the same mould but several times better than the over-hyped Britpop stars.

At the beginning of the 21st century it's multicultural London pushing things forward, to bend the words of Mike Skinner (aka the Streets), whose debut album, *Original Pirate Material,* took London by storm in 2002 and whose follow-up *A Grand Don't Come For Free* has seen equal success, with everyday tales from the life of a modern lad. It's a genre-straddling classic from a young white rapper originally from Birmingham and now living in Brixton, a cross-cultural gem that lights the way for London's music scene in the 21st century.

Another London revelation has been Ms Dynamite (aka Niomi McLean-Daley), a young rapper from north London who won the prestigious Mercury Award in 2002 for her outstanding debut album, *A Little Deeper.* Her hard-hitting, finger-wagging lyrics are political and challenging.

London's Asian community has also made a big splash in recent years, with Talvin Singh and Nitin Sawhney fusing dance with traditional Indian music to stunning effect, and Asian Dub Foundation bringing their unique brand of jungle techno and political comment to an ever-widening audience, despite being dropped by the major British record labels.

Pete Doherty has single-handedly renewed interest in guitar music in recent years, first with his punk-rock group, the Libertines, formed with fellow student Carl Barat in a Stoke Newington flat. Their 2002 debut single *What a Waster* made it into the top 40 despite no mainstream radio play, and their first album went platinum. However, despite such huge success, the duo split up after drug-addicted Doherty broke into Barat's Marylebone flat to steal money for heroin. Kicked out, Doherty has gone on to form Babyshambles, who have also enjoyed success, although their musical output is often overshadowed by Doherty's private life (dating Kate Moss) and his continued problems with heroin addiction.

Parallel to the re-explosion of interest in punk rock has been London's exceptional electro scene, which continues to fulminate and produce exceptionally interesting music today, despite many observers predicting it would be a flash in the pan. Stars of the London scene (there's a strong showing from Leeds and Manchester as well) include Atomizer, the DJs who run seminal electrotrash club Nag Nag Nag (see p304).

Top 10 CDs by London Artists

- *Exile on Main Street* – The Rolling Stones
- *A Little Deeper* – Ms Dynamite
- *London Calling* – The Clash
- *Modern Life Is Rubbish* – Blur
- *Rafi's Revenge* – Asian Dub Foundation
- *The Rise and Fall of Ziggy Stardust and the Spiders from Mars* – David Bowie
- *A Rush of Blood to the Head* – Coldplay
- *Silent Alarm* – Bloc Party
- *Something Else* – The Kinks
- *Sound Affects* – The Jam

The London scene has fought its way back from being an overhyped late-90s destination for those seeking cool by association and is again one of the major creative musical hubs on earth. Whether it's home-grown capital talent or refugees from the provinces seeking fame and fortune, London's music scene is throwing up plenty of exciting and ground-breaking music. Current local stars everyone is talking about include Deptford's Athlete, indie hipsters Razorlight, punksters the Paddingtons and New Cross collective Bloc Party, to name just a few.

VISUAL ARTS

THE CURRENT SCENE

After a couple of millennia, the sum total of Britain's contribution to the higher echelons of visual art were the romantic landscape painter JMW Turner (1775–1851), and John Constable (1776–1837), whose skyscapes were a big influence on French Impressionism. Despite its incredibly rich collections, Britain had never led, dominated or even really participated in a particular epoch or style. That all changed in the twilight of the 20th century, when Britart burst onto the scene with its sliced cows, elephant dung and piles of bricks. It's questionable whether the movement will leave a lasting impression, but one thing's for sure: during the 1990s London was the beating heart of the art world.

Britart sprang from a show called Freeze that was staged in a Docklands warehouse in 1988. It was organised by showman Damien Hirst and largely featured his fellow graduates from Goldsmiths College. Influenced by pop culture and punk, this loose movement was soon catapulted to notoriety by the advertising guru Charles Saatchi, who came to dominate the scene like a puppeteer. Indeed, you could almost say he created the genre with his free spending and commissioning. From 1992 he held a series of seven exhibitions entitled Young British Artists (YBAs), which burst onto the national stage with 1997's epoch-making Sensation exhibition at the Royal Academy.

The work was brash, decadent, ironic, easy to grasp and eminently marketable. To shock seemed the impulse, and the artists did just that. Hirst chipped in with a cow sliced into sections and preserved in formaldehyde; flies buzzed around another cow's head and were zapped in his early work *A Thousand Years*. Chris Ofili provoked with the *Holy Virgin Mary*, a black Madonna made partly with elephant poo; the Chapman brothers produced mannequins of children with genitalia on their heads; and Marcus Harvey created a portrait of notorious child-killer Myra Hindley, made entirely with children's hand-prints.

The areas of Shoreditch, Hoxton and Whitechapel – where many artists lived, worked and hung out – became the epicentre of the movement and a rash of galleries moved in. Among these was White Cube, owned by one of the most important patrons of early Britart, Jay Jopling.

The exhibitions sent shockwaves around the world, as sections of society took it in turns to be outraged. Liberals were drawn into defending the works, the media went positively gaga promoting some of the artists like pop stars and Britart became the talk of the world. For the 10 years or so that it rode the wave of this publicity, its defining characteristics were celebrity and shock value. Damien Hirst and Tracey Emin became the inevitable celebrities – people the media knew they could sell to the mainstream.

One critic said the hugely hyped movement was the product of a 'cultural vacuum' and had become like the emperor's new clothes, which everyone was afraid to criticise for fear they'd look stupid. 'Cold, mechanical, conceptual bullshit', was how the culture minister described the nominations for the Turner Prize one year. Hirst finally admitted in 2005 that some of his own work even irritated him.

Tracey Emin went on to become the most famous artist-behaving-badly. She was shortlisted for the Turner Prize with an installation called *My Bed,* her unmade messy bed, strewn with blood-stained underwear and used condoms. For another installation, called *Everyone I Have Ever Slept with 1963–1995,* she sewed the names of all the relevant people on a tent. She was perfect for Britart because she pandered to the public's darkest levels of voyeurism *and* their love of celebrity. When her cat went missing, people tore down the notices she put up and kept them as *objets d'art.*

Top Five Galleries

- **Tate Modern** (p152)
- **National Gallery** (p99)
- **Serpentine Gallery** (p144)
- **Tate Britain** (p135)
- **Courtauld Institute of Art** (p104)

But while the world was focusing on the stars, there were a lot of great artists hammering away on the fringes. A highlight of the era has to be Richard Wilson's iconic installation, *20:50* (1987), which is one of the few Britart works remaining in the **Saatchi Gallery** (p150). It's a room filled waist high with recycled oil, where you walk in and feel you've just been shot out into space. In his most famous work, *24 Hour Psycho*, Scottish video artist Douglas Gordon slowed Alfred Hitchcock's masterpiece down so much it was stripped of its narrative and viewed more like a moving sculpture, while Gary Hume quietly went about his work, the less-fashionable painting. Hume first came to prominence with his *Doors* series of full-size paintings of hospital doors, powerful allegorical descriptions of despair – or just perfect reproductions of doors.

Rachel Whiteread won the Turner Prize in 1993 for *House*, a concrete cast of an East End terrace dwelling that the council controversially knocked down shortly afterwards. In the same week she won £40,000 in the doubly lucrative prize for Worst British Artist of the year, an award set up by former disco funsters KLF, who out-shocked the Britartists by burning £1 million in cash in front of assembled journalists.

That London had embraced modern art was confirmed with the immediate and resounding success of the Tate Modern when it opened in 2000, and again when the Saatchi Gallery relocated to the centre of town in 2003.

This move was perhaps a trifle late. The public's interest with the YBAs was briefly rekindled and the gallery shot into the headlines, after which came long months of apathy.

Then, tragically, in May 2004 the Momart warehouse in East London storing many Saatchi-owned works caught fire. Many seminal Britart works were destroyed, including Tracey Emin's tent.

Today, the Saatchi Gallery has moved on to Continental painting, rather less successfully, and things can become relatively muted within the British art world. The biggest date on the current calendar is now the Turner Prize at the Tate Britain, won in recent years by Grayson Perry, a transvestite potter, and Jeremy Deller, a video artist who freely admits to not being able to draw.

BEFORE BRITART

In comparison, the history of British art before the wild ones of the 1990s is decidedly piecemeal.

It wasn't until the rule of the Tudors that art took off in London at all. The German Hans Holbein the Younger (1497–1543) was court painter to Henry VIII, and one of his finest works, *The Ambassadors* (1533), hangs in the **National Gallery** (p99). A batch of great portrait artists worked at court during the 17th century. Best of them was Anthony Van Dyck (1599–1641), a Belgian who spent the last nine years of his life in

Courtauld Institute of Art (p104) in Somerset House

London and painted some hauntingly beautiful portraits of Charles I, including *Charles I on Horseback* (1638), now in the National Gallery. Charles I was a keen collector and it was during his reign that the Raphael Cartoons, now in the **Victoria & Albert Museum** (p141), came to London.

Local artists began to emerge in the 18th century. Thomas Gainsborough (1727–88) extended portraiture to include the gentry and is regarded as the first great British landscapist, even though most of his landscapes are actually backgrounds. William Hogarth (1697–1764), by contrast, is best known for his moralising serial prints of London lowlife (see p85).

England has a fine tradition of watercolourists, beginning with the poet and engraver William Blake (1757–1827), some of whose romantic paintings and illustrations (he illustrated Milton's *Paradise Lost,* for example) hang in the **Tate Britain** (p135). John Constable (1776–1837) was a much more skilful and important visual artist than Blake. He studied the clouds and skies above Hampstead Heath, sketching hundreds of scenes that he'd later match with subjects in his landscapes.

JMW Turner (1775–1851) represented the very pinnacle of 19th-century British art. Equally at home with oils and watercolours, through innovative use of colour and gradations of light he created a new atmosphere that seemed to capture the wonder, sublimity and terror of nature. His later works – including *Snow Storm – Steam-boat off a Harbour's Mouth* (1842), *Peace – Burial at Sea* (1842) and *Rain, Steam, Speed* (1844), now in the Tate Britain and the National Gallery – were increasingly abstract, and although widely vilified at the time, later inspired the likes of Claude Monet.

The Pre-Raphaelite Brotherhood (1848–54), founded in London, burst briefly onto the scene. Taking their inspiration from the works of the Romantic poets, they ditched the pastel-coloured rusticity of the day in favour of big, bright and bold depictions of medieval legends and female beauty.

Two of Britain's leading 20th-century painters emerged around the same time. In 1945 the tortured, Irish-born painter Francis Bacon (1909–92) caused a stir when he exhibited his *Three Studies for Figures at the Base of a Crucifixion* – now on display at the Tate Britain – and afterwards carried on unsettling the world with his distorted, repulsive and fascinating forms. The chaos in Bacon's studio was almost as legendary as his Picasso-meets-Velazquez-meets–Van Gogh–meets–Gerald Scarfe paintings. He famously worked knee-deep in scraps of paper, paint rags, newspaper cuttings and other general litter. As he was largely homosexual, it was considered a rare find in the art world when a painting of one of his female lovers went on sale in 2004, and he was also in the news when a forgotten triptych of his was found in an Iranian gallery.

Renowned Australian art critic Robert Hughes has described Bacon's contemporary Lucian Freud (1922–) as 'the greatest living realist painter', although YBA Tracey Emin was less than impressed with his recent portrait of her friend, supermodel Kate Moss. From the 1950s the bohemian Freud has concentrated on pale, muted portraits – often nudes, and frequently of friends and family, although he has also painted the Queen. Twice married and

Taking It to the Streets

As you wander around central London, look out for the works of Banksy, England's most celebrated graffiti artist, who uses the streets as the canvas for his beautifully subversive, politically potent stencils and slogans. Straddling street and commercial art, the Bristolian has published two books, staged a gallery show (albeit in a scruffy warehouse in Hackney) and designed the cover of Blur's *Think Tank* album in 2003 – although he remains totally anonymous. He might be the world's most famous stencil artist, but his parents still think he's a humble painter and decorator. It's a thrill just to happening upon Banksy's stuff on the streets, but visit www.banksy.co.uk first so you'll recognise his signature.

In 2004 Banksy installed a three-and-a-half tonne bronze statue, depicting justice as a prostitute, in London's Clerkenwell Green, to protest about the state of the British legal system. However, it was removed soon after. Banksy's latest escapade was placing one of his own works in four of New York's most respected museums, including MoMA and the Metropolitan Museum. All the works were eventually removed, although some went unnoticed for days. Whatever you think of his tactics, Banksy is definitely one of London's most talked about artists today.

Woody ♥ London

It's long been a lament of English cinephiles that their capital city has never had a filmmaker to lovingly put it up on the big screen in the same way that Woody Allen has captured New York. Now it does, and surprisingly it's the original NYC neurotic funny-man himself. UK financing initially lured Allen to London for the recent *Match Point*, a tennis romance starring Scarlett Johansson. But the man whose movies and themes have become virtually synonymous with Manhattan fell in love with London and has decided to stay to do another, as yet unnamed, movie.

Match Point had a British production designer who was careful to avoid clichéd tourist images of Buckingham Palace, Trafalgar Sq and the Palace of Westminster. Instead the film intersperses shots of the Gherkin, the Tate Modern and the Millennium Bridge with shots of the Covent Garden Hotel and Curzon Soho cinema in an attempt to portray London as a contemporary city. St James's Park replaces NYC's Central Park, and the homes of Belgravia also feature. 'I'm sure I shot a certain amount of picture-postcard London, but that wasn't on my mind. I was just trying to do the story,' Allen told *Blueprint* magazine.

The director might be past his heyday, but, if nothing more than as a curiosity, this is one film worth seeing.

rumoured to have up to 40 illegitimate children, Freud's recent self-portrait *The Painter Is Surprised by a Naked Admirer* fuelled a press frenzy, as journalists tried to guess the identity of the naked woman clinging to his leg.

After the initial shock of Bacon and Freud during the 1940s and '50s, pop art perfectly encapsulated the image of London in the swinging '60s. The brilliant David Hockney (1937–) gained a reputation as one of the leading pop artists through his early use of magazine-style images (although he rejected the label). After a move to California, his stuff became increasingly naturalistic as he took inspiration from the sea, the sun, swimmers and swimming pools. Two of his most famous works, *Mr and Mrs Clark and Percy* (1971) and *A Bigger Splash* (1974), are displayed at the Tate Britain.

Gilbert & George were the quintessential English conceptual artists of the 1960s. They, at the very least, paved the way for the shock and celebrity of Britart and were the art as much as the work itself. Despite their long careers, they are still at the heart of the British art world and represented Britain at the 2005 Venice Biennale.

Two British sculptors are particularly noteworthy and have works displayed in the Tate Britain. The abstract, rounded sculptures of Henry Moore (1898–1986) are immediately recognisable to art lovers. Antony Gormley (1950–) is best known for the 22m-high *Angel of the North*, located beside the A1 trunk road near Gateshead in northern England, but he also has a penchant for creating slightly robotic-looking human shapes from welded metal.

CINEMA & TELEVISION

London is the home of TV; it was born and bred here, with John Logie Baird first demonstrating it in Soho to a select group of scientists, and then to the public a few years later. Perhaps more significantly, the world's first public broadcaster, the British Broadcasting Corporation (BBC), began here too and has originated some of the world's most recognised TV formats and personalities.

While the BBC is constantly proving that it can still turn out world-beating TV, when it comes to movies, however, London's enormous pool of talent seems to have found a better outlet in the Hollywood studio system than in any indigenous industry.

Certainly, there have been some individual triumphs, including recent Oscar-nominee *Vera Drake* and futuristic nightmare *28 Days Later,* not to mention '90s smash hits such as *Four Weddings and a Funeral.* However, the renaissance in UK film each gem is supposed to herald always fails to materialise.

Fans often nostalgically refer back to the golden – but honestly rather brief – era of Ealing comedies, when the London-based Ealing Studios turned out a steady stream of hits. Between 1947 and 1955, when the studios were sold to the BBC, they produced enduring classics from *Passport to Pimlico, Kind Hearts and Coronets, Whisky Galore* and *The Man in the White Suit* to *The Lavender Hill Mob* and *The Ladykillers*. This was also the time of legendary filmmakers Michael Powell and Emeric Pressburger, the men behind *The Life and Death of Colonel Blimp* and *The Red Shoes*.

Today, such halcyon days seem far distant, as the industry seems stuck in a rut of romantic comedies (see Richard Curtis's horribly saccharine *Love Actually*), costume dramas (the usual adaptations of classic novels starring Helena Bonham Carter in a corset) and gangster pics, and continues to go through frequent cycles of boom and bust. Producers, directors and actors complain about a lack of adventurousness in those who hold the purse strings, while film investors claim there are not enough scripts worth backing.

A system of public funding through the UK Film Council exists alongside private investment, and although in 2002 it only accounted for a minority of the £570 million spent on film in the UK, some critics object to the scheme. The *Evening Standard*'s late, lamented former film critic Alexander Walker was one of those who suggested that it led to poor projects being made, simply because the money was there.

Meanwhile, well-known English actors such as Ewan McGregor, Ian McKellen, Ralph Fiennes, Jude Law, Liam Neeson, Hugh Grant, Rhys Ifans, Kristen Scott Thomas and Emily Watson spend time working abroad, as do many British directors, such as Tony Scott (*Top Gun, True Romance*), Ridley Scott (*Bladerunner, Alien, Thelma & Louise, Gladiator*), Anthony Minghella (*The English Patient, Cold Mountain*), Michael Winterbottom (*The Claim*) and Sam Mendes (*American Beauty, The Road to Perdition*).

Pilgrim's Progress

Many film locations are obvious, such as Westminster Bridge and Big Ben. Here are a few less obvious places where you can chase the footsteps of your movie heroes. More details are provided in Colin Sorensen's *London on Film: 100 Years of Filmmaking in London*; in *The Worldwide Guide to Movie Locations Presents: London*, by Tony Reeves (www.movie-locations.com); or on Film London's website at www.filmlondon.org.uk.

Borough Market (p350) *Bridget Jones's Diary* was filmed in and around the market, particularly along Bedale St (although the last scene is at the Royal Exchange in Threadneedle St). Park St, in Borough, should also look familiar to fans of *Lock, Stock and Two Smoking Barrels*.

King's Cross Station Platform 4 in King's Cross station now has a plaque commemorating its use as Platform 9¾, from where the Hogwarts Express leaves in the Harry Potter movies.

Leadenhall Market, the City (p114) Also known as Diagon Alley, where aspiring witches and wizards buy their school supplies in *Harry Potter and the Philosopher's Stone*. Harry and Hagrid are seen walking along here, and Harry buys a wand.

London Zoo, Regent's Park (p190) This is where David wakes up one morning in *An American Werewolf in London* (1981) and where Richard E Grant delivers Hamlet's soliloquy to a family of wolves in the final scene of cult classic *Withnail and I* (1987) – although the wolf enclosure has now been moved.

Maryon Park, Woolwich According to Film London, this is one of the most popular movie tourism sites in London, as fans come to see where the tennis match with the invisible ball took place in the cult movie *Blow Up* (1966).

Postman's Park, Smithfield This is where Jude Law and Natalie Portman begin to fall in love in *Closer*. It's a charming little square set back from a quiet street in Smithfield in memory of people who died heroic deaths.

Tavy Bridge Shopping Centre, Thamesmead The subway behind this shopping centre served as the location for a particularly brutal beating of a tramp by Alex and his droogs in Stanley Kubrick's cult movie *A Clockwork Orange* (1971).

Travel Bookshop, Notting Hill (p347) In truth, the bookshop at 13 Blenheim Cres is not the shop that appears in *Notting Hill* (1999), as that was mocked up behind 142 Portobello Rd especially for the film. However, the owners have long been happy to oblige anyone who wants to take a photograph.

Wander along Portobello Rd and Westbourne Park Rd and around Elgin Sq Garden and Hempel Garden Sq for more movie memories.

Although it's not as photogenic as New York, London does appear as a cinematic backdrop more times than you might initially guess. That's been particularly true in recent years. Naturally, the eponymous west London neighbourhood pops up in 1999's *Notting Hill*, the Dickensian back streets of Borough feature in such polar opposites as chick-flick *Bridget Jones's Diary* and Guy Ritchie's gangster romp *Lock, Stock and Two Smoking Barrels*, while Smithfield is given a certain bleak glamour in *Closer*.

The city's combination of historic and ultramodern architecture certainly works to its advantage in this respect. Ang Lee's *Sense and Sensibility*, for example, could retreat to historic Greenwich for its wonderful parkland and neoclassical architecture. Inigo Jones' Queen's House, in particular, features in interior scenes. Merchant Ivory's costume drama *Howard's End* and the biopic *Chaplin* feature the neo-Gothic St Pancras Chambers, while the early 1980s film *The Elephant Man* took advantage of the moody atmosphere around the then-undeveloped Shad Thames (the site of today's Butler's Wharf).

There are some films that Londoners find heart-warming just because they feature ordinary shots of the contemporary city. *Sliding Doors* is quite fun to watch for the shots of the Underground, west London and Primrose Hill. Similarly, 2002's *28 Days Later* has amazing opening scenes of central London and Docklands lying abandoned after a biological attack. Popcorn blockbuster *Mission: Impossible* features Liverpool St railway station, and John Landis' irrepressibly entertaining *An American Werewolf in London* finishes with a mad chase in Piccadilly Circus.

When it comes to televisual output, London plays with a somewhat stronger hand than in film: some 13% of programmes shown during peak viewing times throughout the world still originate in Britain, from *Teletubbies* to *Who Wants to be a Millionaire*. There are five free-to-air national TV stations: BBC1, BBC2 (established 1964), ITV (1955), Channel 4 (1982) and Channel 5 (1997). Even though cable is now available and digital services were introduced in 1998, the BBC derives funding from a system of TV licences paid for by viewers. Ever since the BBC began broadcasts in 1932 (regularly from 1936), there's been a public-service ethic driving British TV. John Reith, the first director-general of the BBC, took quite a paternalistic view of the audience, seeing the role of TV as to inform and educate as much as to entertain, and insisted on quality. There's still a hangover of all this today, although recent years have seen the BBC chase ratings to an extent that many thought was plainly embarrassing, supporting populist, prime-time rubbish over more Reithean pursuits such as documentaries, news and political debate.

A complete history of English TV is obviously not possible here, but anyone familiar with the subject will be aware of an enormously long roll call of classic series, from comedies such as *Fawlty Towers* and *Rising Damp* and cop shows such as *The Sweeney* and *The Professionals* to cult series such as *The Prisoner*, *The Avengers* and *Minder*; from 1970s comedies (*The Good Life*) to heritage offerings in the 1980s (*Brideshead Revisited*), from thrillers (*Edge of Darkness*) to dramas (*The Singing Detective*) – the list could go on endlessly. However, undoubtedly, the two most famous TV serials associ-

Electric Cinema (p300)

Top 10 London Films

- *28 Days Later* (2002) Most famous for its superb scenes of a desolate London, devoid of all human life after zombies take over the world, this modern-day thriller is compulsive viewing as the few London survivors escape the capital and head for safety in the north.
- *Bridget Jones's Diary* (2001) and *Bridget Jones: The Edge of Reason* (2004) Skinny Texan Renee Zellweger piled on the pounds and polished the English accent to play Bridget Jones, the archetypal 30-something London career gal who just can't find a man – until she has to choose between two. The follow-up also features plenty of London.
- *Closer* (2004) Memorable for hearing Julia Roberts saying extremely dirty things, *Closer* is the adaptation of Patrick Marber's play of the same name. Jude Law lives in Smithfield and has fidelity problems. As does everyone else in the disagreeable cast of rogues and nutters. Lots of London, though, including the Aquarium, South Bank, Postman's Park and National Portrait Gallery Restaurant.
- *The Ipcress File* (1965) More London-centric than any of Michael Caine's other 1960s films (including *Get Carter* and the original *The Italian Job*), this moody spy thriller shows off Blackfriars Bridge, the Royal Albert Hall, Marylebone Station, Trafalgar Sq and the Victoria & Albert Museum as they were 40 years ago. A brilliant period piece.
- *The Krays* (1990) Gary and Martin Kemp (from 1980s new-romantic band Spandau Ballet) star in this biopic of the notorious Kray brothers, Ronnie and Reggie, whose gang controlled the East End underworld in the 1950s and '60s. Not on the level of *GoodFellas*, by any means, but decent enough to have you wanting to learn more.
- *The Ladykillers* (1955) In the last great Ealing comedy, Alec Guinness is a criminal mastermind planning a heist. He and his gang, including Peter Sellers and Herbert Lom, rent rooms in King's Cross from a little old lady, who unwittingly foils their scheme.
- *Lock, Stock and Two Smoking Barrels* (1998) Four silly Jack-the-lads (including Nick Moran and Jason Statham) find themselves £500,000 in debt to a scary East End 'ard man when a rigged card game goes wrong. And then they really get out of their depth, in this anarchic, sassy gangster flick by Guy Ritchie (now Mr Madonna).
- *My Beautiful Laundrette* (1985) An interesting vignette from the Thatcher years, *My Beautiful Laundrette* follows outsider Omar (Gordon Warnecke) and his sometime lover Johnny (Daniel Day-Lewis) in their small-time quest to make it big by opening a fabulous neon-lit, music-filled, coin-operated laundry. Of course, Hanif Kureishi's script goes further than that, exploring themes of racism, sexuality, adultery, greed and dignity.
- *Secrets & Lies* (1996) The most popular of Mike Leigh's bleak but funny examinations of the minutiae of working-class British lives, this has Hortense, a successful black optician, go in search of her natural mother. That mother turns out to be Cynthia (Brenda Blethyn in an award-winning role), a rather unbalanced white woman with a troublesome family.
- *Vera Drake* (2005) Bleak, touching and tragic, Mike Leigh's period piece recreates the post-war East End to perfection, following the ill-fated eponymous abortionist who 'helps out' young girls in trouble. Imelda Staunton was nominated for an Oscar for her portrayal of Vera, and rightly so.

ated with London itself are the long-running soap opera *EastEnders* and police drama *The Bill*. Ironically, the first of these is actually filmed at the BBC studios in Elstree, Hertfordshire, although Albert Sq is said to be modelled on Fassett Sq in Dalston. *The Bill* is shot around the East End.

In recent years Britain, like elsewhere, has been in the grip of reality-TV fever. *Big Brother* has made a huge splash, while wannabe pop stars were given the chance to be discovered and moulded in *Pop Idol*, spawning the now huge star Will Young and a few more forgettable sidekicks. Even more popular have been ITV's *I'm a Celebrity Get Me Out of Here!*, where D-list stars annually undergo humiliating and disgusting bush-tucker trials in order to win food in the Australian jungle.

Comedy has always been something that Britain does particularly well. Currently the huge buzz is about the BBC's *Little Britain*, a brilliant, camp and irreverent sketch show starring Matt Lucas and David Walliams, most notable for spawning numerous catch phrases that will perplex nonviewers. Similarly, Ricky Gervais' *The Office*, another BBC smash hit, remains in the forefront of Londoners' minds on a daily basis when they go in to work, David Brent having become an instantly recognisable synonym for an annoying boss.

DANCE

Whether you're into contemporary, classical or crossover, London has the right ballet moves for you. Recently in the throes of renewed *Billy Elliot* fever, thanks to the new musical, the city's up there with New York and Paris as one of the world's great dance capitals and has been the crucible of one of the most significant developments in modern choreographic history. Although it's been more than a decade since classical ballet was mixed with old-fashioned musical and contemporary dance in Matthew Bourne's all-male *Swan Lake*, that piece is still seen as pivotal – a watershed that catapulted dance from the back of the arts pages into the popular global mainstream.

Even today, Bourne's *Swan Lake* still tours the world, while the man himself produces newer pieces, from the Scottish-influenced *Highland Fling* to *The Car Man* (a *West Side Story*–style reworking of Bizet's opera *Carmen*). Having presented his own take on Tchaikovsky in *Nutcracker!,* Bourne crossed over into theatre in 2004, with his superlative *Play Without Words*, a two-part drama told solely through graceful movement. (He's also worked as a choreographer for the West End musical *Mary Poppins*.)

Other leading London-based talents have helped take the dance message to the wider world, with Rafael Bonachela scripting Kylie Minogue's (sadly interrupted) Showgirl tour, and Wayne McGregor working on the latest Harry Potter film.

However, it's not just Bourne, Bonachela and McGregor in the vanguard. The **Place** (p309), in Euston, was where contemporary dance emerged in London in the 1960s, and it's recently been joined by **Laban** (p309) as a place to catch cutting-edge performances. Meanwhile, the revamped **Sadler's Wells** (p309) – the birthplace of English classical ballet in the 19th century – continues to stage an exciting programme of various styles from leading national ballets and international troupes, such as Pina Bausch, Twyla Tharp, Dance Theatre of Harlem and Alvin Ailey.

Old-Fashioned Fun

Ballroom dancing is enjoying something of a bizarre renaissance in the UK, following the unexpected success of BBC TV's *Strictly Come Dancing* programme. Essentially a revamp of a classic ballroom-dancing competition – with lots of glitz and, you guessed it, celebrities – this Saturday night viewing has pulled in as many as 11 million viewers at its peak. (That's one in every six Britons, which is quite an achievement in the digital age.)

Now hosted by appropriately camp comedian Graham Norton, the show's appeal possibly lies in seeing well-known faces such as comedian Julian Clary and singer Aled Jones make absolute fools of themselves and their poor professional partners, although just as many viewers seem genuinely happy to share in the delight of winners such as *EastEnders* star Jill Halfpenny, BBC TV presenter Natasha Kaplinsky and (we're not making this up) the England football team's former goalkeeper, David Seaman, in an 'On Ice' special. Oh, and the frocks are nice.

If you fancy a bit of Baz Luhrmann–inspired *Strictly Ballroom* fun yourself, the BBC website (www.bbc.co.uk/strictly comedancing) has local listings of classes. Reportedly, the number of people taking dance classes has risen by an estimated one-third, and apparently all age groups are doing it.

Get into the Groove

Ballroom dancing aside (see Old-Fashioned Fun, opposite), London offers every other style of dance, from belly danc-ing to tango lessons. Apart from serious professional training at the Place or Laban, there are the following schools, or check weekly listings in *Time Out*.

Cecil Sharp House (Map pp440–1; ☎ 7485 2206; www.efdss.org; 2 Regent's Park Rd NW1) For Morris and other English folk dances.

Danceworks (Map pp444–5; ☎ 7629 6183; www.danceworks.co.uk; 16 Balderton St W1) Bollywood grooves, flamenco, break dancing and much more.

Drill Hall (Map pp448–9; ☎ 7307 5060; www.drillhall.co.uk; 16 Chenies St WC1) Salsa, tango, jive and classical Indian dance.

Pineapple Dance Studios (Map p452; ☎ 7836 4004; www.pineapple.uk.com; 7 Langley St WC2) From ballet to jazz, salsa to hip-hop and more.

Despite a slight flirtation with newly commissioned pieces, including one with a Jimi Hendrix soundtrack, the capital's leading classical-dance troupe, the Royal Ballet, has largely been sticking to the traditional recently. Several back-to-back anniversaries have meant retrospectives devoted to choreographers George Balanchine and Frederick Ashton, as well as to dancers Serge Diaghilev and Dame Ninette de Valois (the latter of whom was the ballet's founder). All the same, the Royal Ballet has made itself more accessible during this period by dropping some ticket prices to £10, as at the National Theatre.

One troupe always worth keeping an eye out for is the innovative Rambert Dance Company. Another is that of former Royal Ballet dancers Michael Nunn and William Levitt. Having made their name, via a Channel 4 TV documentary, as the Ballet Boyz, and then the George Piper Dances, they have most recently teamed up with London-based French superstar Sylvie Guillem to perform works by acclaimed modern choreographer Russell Maliphant. Guillem, still a principal guest artist at the Royal Ballet, is also planning to reach out to London's strong South Asian dance tradition, teaming up with Kathak dance specialist Akram Khan.

The main London dance festival is **Dance Umbrella** (☎ 8741 5881; www.danceumbrella .co.uk). Running for six weeks from late September, it's one of the world's leading dance festivals of its kind. Otherwise, for the latest on what's on, check www.londondance.com. For more information on specific venues and companies, see p309.

SCIENCE & PHILOSOPHY

London has spawned innumerable philosophies and fostered a wealth of scientific discovery over the centuries. Both communism and the theory of evolution, perhaps the single most significant political and scientific theories of the 19th century, can be identified as products of the city. London's progressive nature, its freedom from tyranny and its curiosity about the unknown has inspired foreigner and Londoner alike for centuries.

Karl Marx (1818–83) and his lifelong collaborator, fellow German Friedrich Engels (1820–95), both moved to London for its permissive political climate, and this is where Marx wrote the bible of modern communism, *Das Kapital*, largely in the famous Reading Room of the British Museum.

Charles Darwin (1809–82) lived for more than four decades at Down House in southeast London. Here he wrote the controversial *On the Origin of Species* (1859), in which he used his experiences during a five-year voyage to South America and the Galapagos Islands to develop a theory of evolution by natural selection.

Isaac Newton (1642–1727), who legend tells us promulgated the law of gravity after an apple fell on his head, moved from Cambridge to London in 1701 and was president of the Royal Society of London from 1703. He is buried in Westminster Abbey. Edmund Halley (1656–1742), the scientist who first observed the comet that now bears his name, and James

Bradley (1693–1762), who provided direct evidence that the earth revolves around the sun, were the second and third Astronomers Royal at Greenwich between 1720 and 1762. The chemist and physicist Michael Faraday (1791–1867), a pioneer in electromagnetism and inventor of the electric battery (1812), spent much of his adult life in Islington and is buried in Highgate Cemetery.

Twentieth-century London residents who made a great impact on science include the Scot Alexander Fleming (1881–1955), who discovered penicillin while working as a research immunologist at St Mary's Hospital, Paddington, and John Logie Baird (1888–1946), who invented TV and gave the first public demonstration of the newfangled medium in a room above a Greek St restaurant in Soho in 1925.

In the field of philosophy, London can claim a link to Thomas Hobbes (1588–1679), author of *The Leviathan* and the first thinker since Aristotle to develop a comprehensive theory of nature including human behaviour. He was tutor to the exiled Prince Charles and a great favourite at court when the latter assumed the throne as Charles II in 1660. George Bernard Shaw (1856–1950) and Mahatma Gandhi (1869–1948) studied, thought and wrote in the British Museum Reading Room. Influential thinker, pacifist and Nobel Prize–winner Bertrand Russell (1872–1970) was a lecturer at the London School of Economics at the end of the 19th century and was elected to the Royal Society of London in 1908.

London continues to be more than just a graveyard of ideas and philosophies, however; it remains a centre of worldwide scientific research. Leading research institutions include University College, King's College and Imperial College, all at the cutting edge of medical experimentation, particularly in the field of genetics.

Architecture

Architecture

Architecture is looking up in London, literally, as a city that for centuries hugged the ground closely discovers that the idea of more skyscrapers appeals. That's to say, the idea appeals to some, and the reality has only begun to appear on the skyline. However, the popularity of 30 St Mary Axe – which opened in 2004 – has given the city the confidence to continue planning more heady buildings.

By 2010 London could be home to Europe's tallest building, in the needle shape of the **London Bridge Tower** (see Five Big Ones, p60). And that will be accompanied by a host of other high-rises, from several new towers near the Lloyd's building in the City, to further lofty constructions on the edge of Docklands and at Canary Wharf.

Mayor Ken Livingstone and Deputy Prime Minister John Prescott both favour 'clusters' of high-quality high-rises throughout the capital. The financial districts of the City and Canary Wharf, with the biggest concentration of existing skyscrapers, are obvious candidates for expansion, while Paddington Basin to the west, Elephant and Castle to the south and central Victoria provide further fertile soil.

Several architectural critics are wary of such plans, foreseeing an 'architectural zoo', as each iconic building attempts to upstage the last. Sceptics among the London citizenry also suggest that all this 'reach for the skies' ambition is simple blue-sky dreaming (and recent terrorist attacks might prompt a rethink on some projects).

Despite a millennial makeover in public buildings and spaces – which has improved the city's appearance beyond belief – the capital still needs 400,000 extra private dwellings by 2016 to meet its projected population growth. Its decaying public transport also desperately needs to be improved.

Architects and the authorities haven't entirely ignored these challenges. Affordable homes are being planned around the Millennium Dome and along the Thames Gateway from Stratford to Barking. Meanwhile, an extension of the East London line of the tube to Hackney is in the pipeline.

However, in the few years to July 2005, as London was trying to win the right to host the 2012 Olympic Games, eyes were more focused on wooing the International Olympic Committee with grand schemes for sports stadiums in the Lea River Valley near Stratford.

Having won the right to host the games, London now has to get down to the nitty-gritty of building the Olympic Park (p76) and improving its transport infrastructure – all the while continuing to improve its general urban landscape with great design.

LAYING THE FOUNDATIONS

Unlike some great metropolises such as Paris, London has never been methodically planned; it simply grew like Topsy. Its roots lie in the walled Roman settlement of Londinium, first established in AD 43 on the northern banks of the Thames. However, the Saxons who moved into the area after the decline of the Roman Empire are thought to have found that settlement (roughly on the site of today's City or Square Mile) too small. Instead, they built their communities further up the Thames. In the 7th century an abbey was built on Thorney Island (**Westminster Abbey**; p133) and the royal palace was established at Aldwych. It was only under threat from marauding Danes that the Saxons moved back into the walled city in the 9th century.

Two centuries later the Normans invaded, and soon after William the Conqueror arrived in 1066 the country got its first example of Norman architecture in the shape of the White Tower, now at the heart of the larger **Tower of London** (p118). The next five centuries saw a gradual move through Gothic and Tudor styles, during which the long-term refurbishment of Westminster Abbey from the 13th to the 14th century and the construction of **Hampton Court Palace** (p213) were of outstanding architectural interest.

Skyline Shapes

Londoners have nicknamed their new skyscrapers with such alacrity that one could almost mistake them for Australians in this regard. The most popular (inspired by the building's outline):

The Cheese Grater (Leadenhall Building; see Five Big Ones, p60) The proposed building looks like one apparently.

The Egg (City Hall; p171) Also called the testicle.

The Eye (The London Eye; p149) Its real name, so fair enough.

The Gherkin (30 St Mary Axe; p113) Also referred to as the Swiss Re Tower (after its major tenant), Cockfosters (after its architect, Norman Foster), pickle, missile etc.

The Shard of Glass (London Bridge Tower; see Five Big Ones, p60) The proposed London Bridge Tower is one mother of a splinter you wouldn't want to argue with.

KEEPING UP WITH INIGO JONES

The English were latecomers to the Renaissance, and even then it was one man who was largely responsible for bringing home the artistic ideas that had revolutionised the Continent a hundred years earlier. Take a bow, Inigo Jones (1573–1652). The architect had already been appointed surveyor to Henry, Prince of Wales, in 1610, when he spent a year and a half in Italy. There he became a convert to Palladian Renaissance architecture, a style promoted by the late Andrea Palladio (1508–80) but based on classical Roman style and its notions of mathematically calculated, geometric proportions.

Although Jones is nowadays regarded as one of London's most important designers, at the time his work was often misunderstood. After he returned to England in 1615 and was promoted to the post of surveyor-general to King James I, his new-found obsession with Italianate design soon brought him into conflict with traditionalists. At a time when the public purse strings were very tight, he made a start on the landmark **Queen's House** (p183) in Greenwich and successfully completed the **Banqueting House** (p137) at Whitehall in 1622, before moving on to a piazza at Covent Garden (since rebuilt).

However, by the time Jones began a similar public space in Lincoln's Inn Fields in 1642, the Civil War had broken out. With the seizure of the king's houses by the Puritan-controlled Parliament the following year, he found himself out of a job and, as a loyal monarchist, was forced to flee London. He was rescued from the siege of Basing House in 1645, and died in 1652 without completing any more buildings.

LONDON'S BURNING

In September 1666, as London was still recovering from the plague, a fire broke out in a bakery on Pudding Lane. Four days later, 80% of the city had been burnt to the ground. It was a national disaster, of course, but one in which few lives were lost. Furthermore, it had a few unexpected benefits: it finally cleansed London of the plague, and it created a blank canvas on which Christopher Wren (1632–1723) would build.

Naturally, Wren wasn't the only architect to get the city back on its feet. The priority was to reconstruct as much of the housing stock as possible as quickly as one could, and that was left to property developers. However, Wren was responsible in whole or in part for 51 churches over a period of nearly 50 years. The most influential London architect of all time began as a brilliant physicist and astronomer who merely dabbled in architecture. But in the aftermath of the Great Fire, his childhood friend King Charles II appointed him as a member of the commission to rebuild London.

In fact Wren, like the much-besieged Inigo Jones, was a fan of classicism, although he combined it with Baroque. He drew up a Utopian plan to reconstruct the city along classical lines, replacing the warren of twisting streets and alleyways with broad tree-lined avenues radiating from piazzas or major buildings. The scheme was shelved, however, partly for being too radical and partly because the compulsory purchase of the necessary land wasn't achievable.

Wren's first two plans for **St Paul's Cathedral** (p110), his magnum opus, were similarly thrown back in his face. The main objection both times was that the cathedral's dome was too Roman Catholic and too little like a Protestant steeple. Wren plugged away with substitute proposals, toning down the dome and incorporating a spire. However, the necessary warrant of royal approval allowed for 'ornamental' variations. Craftily, during construction Wren gradually slipped many of his previous ideas in through this loophole. By the time this ruse was uncovered, the dome was too far advanced to change.

St Paul's took 35 years to build and Wren turned 66 before it was completed, but in a full and long life he managed to squeeze in a couple of other enduring London landmarks. His signature is writ large all over the Royal Exchange in the City, the Royal Hospital Chelsea, the **Old Royal Naval College** (p182) and the Drury Lane Theatre. When Wren died in 1723 he was the first person to be buried in St Paul's Cathedral.

With Wren gone, his protégés Nicholas Hawksmoor and James Gibb stepped out of his shadow. Both had worked with the great man, especially since Parliament passed an act in 1711 to build 50 new churches, but now they moved on to their own masterpieces, such as **Christ Church, Spitalfields** (Hawksmoor, 1729; p123) and **St Martin-in-the-Fields** (Gibb, 1726; p101). These two architects' buildings are usually termed English Baroque.

Meanwhile, commercial developers had helped rebuild homes that were lost in the Great Fire. Their exploits are noteworthy for three things. Firstly, many of these developers gave their names to contemporary London streets, such as Storey, Bond and Frith. Secondly, they invented the formula of leasehold when they divided their land into plots and leased them with the proviso that the properties on those plots all be built in a certain style. (Thomas Wriotheseley was the first to do this at Bloomsbury Sq.) Thirdly, they set a precedent in London in which commercial concerns drove the city's architecture. This is a phenomenon that the capital has seen a lot of since.

GEORGIAN MANNERS

By the time the 18th century rolls around, you begin to feel sympathy for Inigo Jones. Though he was treated with suspicion for introducing classicism to Britain, it seems that now the time was ripe for a revival. Neo-Palladianism is still much in evidence in surviving Georgian town houses. Among the greatest exponents of this revived style were Robert Adam and his brothers. Much of their work was demolished by the Victorians, but an excellent example that endures is **Kenwood House** (1773; p195) on Hampstead Heath.

Five Big Ones

Mayor Ken Livingstone has suggested that London needs another 10 to 15 skyscrapers within the next 10 years if it is not to lose its preeminence as a financial capital. However, a poll by the *Evening Standard* newspaper in 2004 found that 46% of Londoners thought that number too high, and Prince Charles has typically waded into the debate, calling tall buildings 'overblown phallic sculptures'. English Heritage initially contested some of the following proposed high-rises on the grounds that they might obstruct 'strategic' views of St Paul's Cathedral, but its fears have been assuaged. Four out of the following five have planning permission, but as they need to be 35% to 50% pre-let to tenants before construction can begin, even some of these might not be erected.

London Bridge Tower (300m; on the site of Southwark Towers SE1; Renzo Piano; £350 million) Luxury Asian hotel group Shangri-La has already signed up as a tenant for this thin, tall glass spike.

Minerva Building (217m; cnr Houndsditch & Botolph St EC3; Sir Nicholas Grimshaw; £350 million) Built by the Eden Project's creators, this will have a slim profile, windows that open and a public restaurant on the top floor.

Heron Tower (183m; 110 Bishopsgate; Kohn Pederson Fox; £425 million) The four façades of this stepped skyscraper will each be different, reflecting the buildings they face.

51 Lime Street (124m; 51 Lime St E1; Lord Foster; £425 million) Construction began in 2005 on this stepped, modestly sized tower, which will have a concave façade facing the Lloyd's building.

Leadenhall Building (224m; 122 Leadenhall St E1; Lord Rogers; £500 million) Not yet given planning permission, this 52-storey tower would be the tallest in the City and face Richard Roger's 1980s Lloyd's building.

Kenwood House (p195)

The Adam brothers' fame has been eclipsed by that of the Regency architects John Nash (1752–1835) and John Soane (1753–1837). 'Once and only once, has a great plan for London, affecting the development of the capital as a whole, been projected and carried to completion,' wrote John Summerson in his book *Georgian London* (Penguin, 1978). The plan to which Summerson refers is that by John Nash to give London a 'spine' by creating **Regent Street** (p98) as a straight north–south axis from St James's Park in the south to the new Regent's Park in the north. This grand scheme also involved the formation of Trafalgar Sq, the development of the Mall and the western end of the Strand, as well as the cutting of Regent's Canal to serve Regent's Park.

Although completed, the plan did involve compromise, as many landowners lining Nash's proposed route refused to sell, and he was forced to opt for a sweeping curve of a street. However, that curve was initially a great success. The Victorians later ripped down some of his buildings, but his legacy remains. Nash worked on Buckingham Palace and left some lovely crescents full of 'Nash terraces' at the entrance to Regent's Park (Park Cres, for example).

Nash's contemporary John Soane was arguably a better architect. However, he lacked the royal patronage that Nash enjoyed and is best remembered today not for a building but for the jaw-dropping collection of *objets d'art* that's assembled in the **Sir John Soane's Museum** (p104). All that's left of his Bank of England on Threadneedle St is a bastardised version of his exterior wall. The **Dulwich Picture Gallery** (p187) is a better example of his work.

'GOTHICK' CITY

The 1830s saw a new direction in architectural fashions. One man in particular, August Welby Northmore Pugin (1812–52), lobbied for change. Sick of classicism and Protestantism, Pugin called in his 1836 pamphlet *Contrasts* for 'a revival of Catholic art'. Two years earlier the Palace of Westminster, or the **Houses of Parliament** (p134), had burnt down, and by the time he published *Contrasts* Pugin was already putting his words into action by acting as assistant and interior designer to architect Charles Barry during the building's reconstruction. The result, which is what you see today, is typical Victorian High Gothic (often spelled

'Gothick'), with perpendicular towers, pointed arches and ornate turrets and interiors. However, it's a very romantic interpretation of medieval architecture, an outpouring of nostalgia for allegedly more innocent times during a fast-gathering industrial age.

Another leading proponent of the Gothic revival was George Gilbert Scott, who was responsible for the anachronistic **Albert Memorial** (p145) in Kensington Gardens, the Foreign Office building in Whitehall, and **St Pancras Chambers** (1874; p192), the hotel at the eponymous railway station. One's admiration for this gingerbread-style masterpiece is tempered somewhat by learning that Gilbert Scott himself once declared it 'possibly too good for its purpose'. Alfred Waterhouse, the creator of the wonderful neo-Gothic building that houses the **Natural History Museum** (p142), was never recorded making such a claim, although his architecture is equally exquisite.

The emphasis on the artisanship and materials necessary to create these elaborate neo-Gothic buildings led to what has become known as the Arts and Crafts movement, of which William Morris (1834–96) was a leading exponent. Pugin himself was more than simply a designer of buildings, and also worked in furniture, stained glass, metal, textiles, tiles and wallpaper. These were the same media in which Morris worked his famously ornate designs. Morris' work can be best enjoyed in the Green Dining Room of the **Victoria & Albert Museum** (p141) and the **William Morris Gallery** (p177).

THE SOUND OF THE SUBURBS

Gothic architecture was only one aspect of the Victorian anticlassical backlash, which in general had a fundamental, lasting impact on London's landscape. Donald Olsen in his book *The Growth of Victorian London* (Penguin, 1976) talks about 'the ambivalent love-hate relationship the Victorians sustained with the London their Georgian parents had bequeathed them'. Essentially romantics and lovers of art, they took exception to the utilitarianism of Georgian and Regency buildings. As students of the classics, they detected a certain inaccuracy in Nash's handling of Roman details in his terraces and were offended by it. Even worse, they considered that Nash's grand plan for London had celebrated London, and as they grappled with the metropolis's congestion, crime and lack of sanitation this was an accolade that they didn't think it deserved.

Top 10 Exteriors

Any list of buildings of this sort will, by nature, be subjective, but here are a few starting points.

- **City Hall** (Foster & Partners, 2002; p171) London's answer to Berlin's Reichstag.
- **Laban** (Herzog & de Meuron, 2002; p309) The façade of semitransparent polycarbonate changes colour according to how it's lit.
- **Lloyd's of London** (Rogers, 1986; p114) Inside-out, with ducts, lifts and stainless-steel features on its façade, Lloyd's makes a great sci-fi backdrop.
- **Oxo Tower Wharf** (Lifschutz & Davidson,1996) The neon-lit windows of this Art Deco tower spell out O-X-O vertically; it's a graphic designer's dream.
- **Palace of Westminster** (Houses of Parliament; Barry & Pugin, 1847; p134) This neo-Gothic masterpiece is an elegant symbol of British democracy.
- **Portcullis House** (Michael Hopkins, 2000; Map pp448–9) The politicians inside don't like it much, but many architects think highly of this new parliamentary building.
- **St Pancras Chambers at St Pancras Station** (George Gilbert Scott, 1874; p192) This giant, curving, red-brick edifice looks more like a medieval palace than the railway hotel it was (and once again will be).
- **St Paul's Cathedral** (Wren, 1697; p110) He had to be sneaky to get it built, but Sir Christopher Wren's dome still lords it over London.
- **30 St Mary Axe** (Foster & Partners, 2003; p113) The gherkin-shaped tower with its black winding stripes has proved an enormous public hit.
- **Tate Modern** (Herzog & de Meuron, 2000; p152) It's the two-storey glass box that's been added to the roof and is lit up at night that creates the extra genius.

So, down came large chunks of Georgian Whitehall, down came John Soane's old criminal law courts and eventually down came many of the original buildings which lined Regent St. Not even the work of Christopher Wren was considered sacred, and many of his churches were demolished, while others had incongruous stained-glass windows added to them.

'If the Regency prized smooth stucco,' writes Olsen, 'the Victorians produced the roughest stone surfaces possible; if the Georgians preferred unobtrusive grey bricks, the Victorians produced the brightest red bricks they could manage; if the Georgians sought restrained, uniform monochrome façades, the Victorians revelled in glazed, polychrome tiles; if the Georgians admired flat cornices topping their buildings, the Victorians sought jagged skylines...for symmetry they substituted asymmetry; for the two-dimensional, the three-dimensional; for the unadorned, the enriched.'

It wasn't only in their architecture that the Victorians rejected 18th-century values, but in the very layout of the city. Rather than planned growth, they were happy to allow the organic growth of the city to reflect their way of living. True, the division of London into various neighbourhoods can be said to have begun in the 17th century, with the creation of St James's, Covent Garden and Bloomsbury. Suburban villas had existed in the 18th century, particularly in Clapham on the south side and in Islington, Hackney and Highgate to the north. However, it was when the railway and the omnibus made commuting possible in the 19th century that the dormitory suburb really took hold. Suburbanisation started closer in, in places such as Kensington, Chelsea and Notting Hill, before spreading to areas such as Wimbledon, Richmond and Highgate.

Ribbon development – rows of houses side by side with party walls – lined the roads out of central London. Contemporary notions of privacy and individualism meant that the house was very much favoured over Continental-style apartments. However, a few did make an appearance in the 1850s.

DICKENSIAN SLUMS

Property developers such as Thomas Cubitt were instrumental in erecting new middle-class housing in Belgravia and Pimlico. However, the 19th century was also the first age during which homes were purpose-built for the working classes. Before that, poorer city dwellers had tended to inhabit the cast-off homes of the rich. Now, with London's population going through a boom – from just under one million at the start of the 19th century to 4.5 million at its end – private property speculators began erecting buildings designed to be affordable for the underprivileged even when new.

The effect this had on building quality is encapsulated in one landlord's instruction to a builder working on 20 hectares of his land in Camden Town to erect 500 third-rate houses, 'or a lesser number of superior rate, so as to be of the same value in 15 years'. This kind of slapdash approach reached its apogee in the East End, where crowded tenements soon turned into crime-ridden slums, or 'rookeries' as they were known.

In the 1860s philanthropic efforts were begun to ease the suffering of the Victorian poor. The philanthropist William Booth founded the Salvation Army and set up the Christian Mission in the East End, and Dr Joseph Barnardo established schools for the underprivileged. Meanwhile, on his death in 1869 businessman George Peabody left half a million pounds for the construction of decent but affordable housing. The Peabody Trust survives today.

Some decades later, architect Ebenezer Howard (1850–1928) also addressed himself to the quality of life in London, deciding the simplest answer was to get out. His plans for green, planned, largely independent cities outside the capital came to fruition in 'new towns' like Welwyn Garden City and Milton Keynes. The great 'traditionalist' architect Edwin Lutyens (1869–1944) also demonstrated a penchant for the rustic. Although Lutyens, from Sussex, mostly built outside London, he did contribute to the countryside-within-a-city development of Hampstead Garden Suburb. (He also designed the Cenotaph in Whitehall, the Reuters Headquarters in Fleet St and Britannic House in Finsbury Sq.)

Top 10 Interiors

- **British Library** (Colin St John Wilson, 1998; p191) This building's fine, vaguely Scandinavian-influenced interior detailing brings out one's inner bookworm.
- **British Museum Great Court** (Foster, 2000; p107) Oops, the colour of the stone doesn't quite match the older walls, but the spectacular glass-and-steel roof infuses the new court with life-affirming light.
- **Courtauld House, Eltham Palace** (1937; p186) The domed, circular entrance hall with its woven carpet and sturdy armchairs is one of London's most memorable interior spaces.
- **Imagination Building** (Herron Associates, 1989; Map pp448–9) The unassuming façade of an Edwardian school hides a dazzling, multipurpose interior.
- **Painted Hall** (James Thornhill interior, 1725; p182) In the Old Royal Naval College, the rich ornateness of James Thornhill's mural-covered ceiling and walls will win over even those with modern tastes.
- **Peterborough Court/former Daily Telegraph building** (Robert Atkinson interior, 1931; Map pp448–9) One of the few examples of 'full-blooded' Art Deco in London, the entrance hall has wiggly black-and-blue flooring, a silver ceiling rose and metal snake handrails refurbished in 2001; peer through the glass curtain wall.
- **St Bartholomew-the-Great** (p124) This gloomy Norman interior is just right for reflection and contemplation, and parts of *Shakespeare in Love* were shot here.
- **St Paul's Cathedral** (Wren, 1697; p110) The newly renovated Wren interior is awe-inspiring.
- **Sir John Soane's Museum** (p104) It's not just the collection of Egyptiana that's quirky; the building also has a glass dome, bringing light to the basement.
- **Tate Modern** (Herzog & de Meuron, 1999; p152) It's the huge Turbine Hall entrance space to this art gallery that has most visitors rapt.

FLIRTING WITH MODERNISM

With so much happening during the 19th century, perhaps it's unsurprising that the 20th century began so quietly. Not many public buildings of note were built during the first decade and a half, apart from **Admiralty Arch** (Aston Webb, 1910; p129) and **County Hall** (Ralph Knott, 1922; p150). In the period between the two world wars English architecture was hardly more creative. Indeed, it was left to visiting architects to inject a bit of life into an otherwise pretty flat scene. Those from Europe, in particular, brought with them the modernist style of architecture, but the monuments they left are on a small scale.

Russian Berthold Lubetkin (1901–90) is perhaps the best remembered, principally because of the penguin pool, with its concrete spiral ramp, at **London Zoo** (p190). One of London's earliest modernist structures when it was built in 1934, the pool is still the object of much affection today – and the penguins the envy of many a child.

However, there were also émigrés from Germany, who spent several years in London before moving on to the United States. Among them was the director of the Bauhaus school, Walter Gropius (1883–1969). He lived in No 15 at the flat, geometric-shaped Isokon apartments in Lawn Rd, Hampstead (Map pp440–1), themselves a famous modernist landmark by the Canadian architect Wells Coates (1893–1958). The Grade I–listed flats, whose other tenants included crime writer Agatha Christie, have been undergoing refurbishment and are now up for sale to private buyers.

RECONSTRUCTION AFTER THE BLITZ

Hitler's bombs during WWII wrought the worst destruction on London since the Great Fire of 1666, and the immediate problem was a chronic shortage of housing. Developers soon rushed to fill the void, erecting tower blocks to provide as many family homes in as short a time as possible. Unsurprisingly, given the haste, many of the resulting buildings were of poor quality, not to mention lacking in aesthetic appeal. Many of those blocks still contribute to London's urban blight today.

In 1951 the government decided to throw a party to cheer up a populace it believed was suffering a kind of collective post-traumatic stress from WWII. The Festival of Britain was a celebration of the modern nation, and of the centenary of 1851's Great Exhibition in

Crystal Palace. All that remains of that patriotic carnival is the **Royal Festival Hall** (1951, Robert Matthew and Leslie Martin; p151) at the South Bank Centre, the first major public building in London in the modernist style. With its curved roof and Portland stone façade (slightly less grimy than concrete), the hall has traditionally been more loved than the buildings that shot up around it, including Denys Lasdun's National Theatre (1976). However, with the entire South Bank Centre undergoing renovation today, there's been renewed interest in its concrete brutalist style. Across town, at the junction of Charing Cross Rd and Oxford St, even the once-vilified modernist Centre Point Tower (Richard Seifert, 1967) has been listed by English Heritage. The BT Tower (formerly the Post Office Tower, Ministry of Public Building and Works, 1964) always enjoyed far more public affection than Centre Point as one of London's most famous landmarks (and also because of the revolving restaurant at its summit that was once open to all). It, too, has now been granted listed status.

POSTMODERNISM & DOCKLANDS

Modernism held sway until the end of the 1970s. Its Utopian ideal of providing housing for the masses in large-scale, conformist redevelopment schemes and its frequent reliance on public-sector funding was very much in keeping with the post-war welfare state. However, as Britain itself experienced a political U-turn with the election of Margaret Thatcher's mould-breaking Conservative Party in 1979, modernist architecture no longer seemed appropriate. In the freewheeling 1980s and early 1990s, a more commercially driven international architecture, postmodernist and hi-tech, began to take hold.

Whatever the criticisms of post-war publicly funded buildings, one could never, looking back at the 1980s and '90s, argue that commercial concerns provide a universally better guarantee of architectural quality. The record there is equally patchy. The utterly unappealing NatWest Tower (Richard Seifert, 1981) still reproachfully skulks over the city skyline as cast-in-concrete proof of that.

Still, there were several successes, including Embankment Place (Terry Farrell, 1990) and most notably Richard Rogers' **Lloyd's of London building** (1986; p114). Rogers was already famous for his collaboration with Italian architect Renzo Piano on the low-level Pompidou Centre in Paris (1977), where the building's exterior consists of a steel skeleton and service elements such as air-conditioning ducts and pipes. Similarly, the hi-tech Lloyd's tower takes many constructional elements that would normally be found inside the building, from ducts and pipes to lifts and concrete-and-stainless-steel winding fire stairs, and places them on the exterior.

No mention of this era would be complete without discussing the reconstruction of Docklands. The Thatcher-approved plan to transform the unused and neglected docks east of Tower Bridge into London's second financial hub was always a controversial one.

Open Wide, Come Inside

It's human nature to be interested in seeing how the other half lives, and if you want to stick your nose inside buildings you wouldn't normally be able to see, September is the time to visit. One weekend that month the charity Open House arranges for owners of about 500 private buildings to throw open their front doors and let in the public free of charge.

Major buildings also participate. The fabulous 'Gherkin' at 30 St Mary Axe was accessible during open-house weekend in 2004, while City Hall, the Lloyd's building, the Foreign Office, Portcullis House, St Pancras Chambers and many more have welcomed the public at this time.

For more details, contact **Open House Architecture** (☎ 0900 160 0061, 60p per min; www.londonopenhouse.org). The charity also runs three-hour, architect-led tours (☎ 7380 0412; adult/student £18.50/13) every Saturday. There's a rolling programme visiting the Square Mile, Bankside, the West End or Docklands.

Another annual event worth keeping an eye out for is **Architecture Week** (☎ 7973 5246; www.architectureweek .org.uk) in June, which has an enticing mix of talks by leading architects, designers and well-known TV design critics, plus events involving actors and bands. It's run as a joint venture between the Royal Institute of British Architects and the Arts Council.

Obscure Objects of Desire

Buckingham Palace Ticket Office (Hopkins, 1994; Map pp448–9) This prefabricated red wooden cabin is erected each year for the crowds that come during August and September; it has a striking, acrylic flyaway roof.

Hammersmith Health Centre (Guy Greenfield, 2000) This curved sliver of a building turns a defensive back to the road, while gazing out onto an internal Japanese garden; it's almost worth getting mildly sick to see it.

London Ark (Ralph Erskine, 1991; Map pp438–9) From the outside of this Hammersmith office building (now occupied by Seagram), everything looks perfectly ship-shape; inside, the nine storeys of offices are open plan.

Lord's Cricket Ground Media Centre (Future Systems, 1999) This aluminium-and-glass pod on stilts has been called a spaceship, a bar of soap and a gigantic alien eye peering down on the cricket field.

Peckham Library (Will Alsop, 1999; p204) Obscure mainly in the sense of its location, this playful, colourful building saw off stiff competition to win Britain's most prestigious architectural prize, the Stirling.

Penguin Pool, London Zoo (Berthold Lubetkin, 1934) Getting to play every day on a spiral concrete ramp that's a modernist icon, the penguins at London Zoo have it better than most captive breeds.

Public Lavatory (CZWG Architects, 1993) On the corner of Westbourne Grove and Colville Rd, Piers Gough and his firm have created their best-known work: a little Art Deco–style masterpiece.

Red Phone Box (Giles Gilbert Scott, 1924) This once-familiar landmark is found only in tourist areas today; its shape and glass-paned sides were inspired by John Soane's tomb for his wife in St Pancras churchyard.

Sainsbury's, Camden Town (Nicholas Grimshaw, 1988) The supermarket chain now has several innovative-looking stores; this early example has an industrial façade vaguely reminiscent of the Pompidou Centre.

Serpentine Gallery Summer Pavilion (p144) Every summer an architect is invited to erect a temporary pavilion next to the gallery; recent takers include Daniel Libeskind and Brazilian colossus Oscar Niemeyer.

The stated intent was to alleviate the congestion of the City. However, people still lived in the area entrusted to the London Docklands Development Corporation (working in tandem first with developers Travelstead, and then with Olympia and York), and the social upheaval created by building skyscrapers and offices was enormous.

The terms offered for the acquisition of land for commercial development were often criticised. That was only part of the controversy, though. For all the pain involved, the new Docklands initially didn't seem to work very well. The main transport link, the Docklands Light Railway, proved unreliable for years, and, on the central Isle of Dogs, Canadian architect Cesar Pelli's obelisk-shaped **Canary Wharf Tower** (officially known as 1 Canada Sq, 1991; p178) was so hard-hit by the recession of the early 1990s that it had to be saved from bankruptcy. The **Museum in Docklands** (p178) chronicles much of this ill-fated history.

Only now, in the early years of the 21st century, is Docklands starting to meet the aspirations its planners had for it. Transport has improved beyond belief, especially with the extension of the Jubilee tube line into the area. Meanwhile, the 244m-high Canary Wharf Tower has reached near total occupancy and no longer stands in less-than-splendid isolation. London's tallest skyscraper is already flanked by the twin-tower HSBC Holdings building and the Citigroup headquarters, while a handful of other towers have begun heading skywards.

THE ROYAL SEAL OF DISAPPROVAL

Even before the riot of multicoloured, Lego-shaped developments began to spread across the Isle of Dogs and Docklands like a postmodern rash, Prince Charles, of all people, proved that the age-old battle between architectural traditionalists and modernisers had not gone away. In a 1984 speech to RIBA the self-proclaimed architecture expert launched a full-frontal attack on contemporary buildings.

The Prince immediately targeted a proposed extension to the **National Gallery** (p99), which he described as 'a monstrous carbuncle on the face of an elegant and much-loved friend'.

(Continued on page 75)

1 *Leicester Square (p102)* 2 *Young diner at a food stall at Portobello Road Market (p350)* 3 *Café culture in Soho* 4 *The Coach & Horses pub (p277) in Soho*

1 Restaurant on Gerrard St in
Chinatown (p103) 2 Friendly chain
restaurant Giraffe (p254) 3 Canary
Wharf Underground station (p178)
4 Columbia Road Flower Market
(p351)

1 *Tower Bridge (p121)* 2 *Imperial War Museum (p148), Lambeth North* 3 *The Tower of London (p118), one of the city's most popular attractions* 4 *The quire and its dazzling mosaic ceiling in St Paul's Cathedral (p110)*

1 Turbine Hall in the Tate Modern
art gallery (p152), Bankside
2 Sculpture in the forecourt of the
Royal Academy of Arts (p131)
3 The Tate Britain (p135), Millbank
4 Relief sculpture in the Courtauld
Institute of Art (p103)

1 Gold statue at the Barbican
(p116) 2 The National Gallery
(p99) 3 Whitechapel Art Gallery
(p174) 4 Mural at the Docklands
commemorating the Cable Street
riots (p179)

THE NATIONAL GALLERY

ADMISSION
TO THE
PERMANENT
COLLECTION
IS FREE

Please give
as much
as you can
to help us
keep it free

1 City Hall (p171), Queen's Walk
2 The media centre at Lord's
Cricket Ground (p193) 3 Millen-
nium Bridge (p152) 4 The Royal
Opera House (p102), Covent
Garden

1 *The Natural History Museum (p142), South Kensington* 2 *Oxo Tower (p251), South Bank* 3 *The Victorian Gothic façade of St Pancras Chambers (p192)* 4 *The British Library (p191)*

1 Cycling over Grand Union Canal, Regent's Park (p189)
2 View over London from St Paul's Cathedral (p110) *3* View from the London Eye (p149) *4* St James's Park (p128)

(Continued from page 66)

However, while he had the stage, he took the opportunity to argue for a more 'humane' architecture and eulogise about city churches, Georgian terraces and green parks.

The effect of the Prince's speech was quite remarkable. Indeed, he seems to have caught the public mood and succeeded in getting the firm Arhends Burton & Koralek fired from the National Gallery project in favour of the partly classical designs of Americans Venturi, Scott Brown and Associates. Another criticised project at Mansion Square House was dropped and a wave of traditionalist buildings was begun.

However, the reaction from many architects was furious. 'Modern architecture is in danger of being obliterated by an indiscriminate wave of nostalgia', Richard Rogers fumed. And according to Kenneth Powell in his book *New London Architecture,* the Prince's crusade against it ultimately gave postmodernism an unintentional boost, with architects such as James Stirling (responsible for the 1985 Clore Gallery extension to the **Tate Britain**; p135), Terry Farrell and a whole range of others willing to champion its cause.

The Tate Britain (p135)

MILLENNIAL CHANGE

The Thatcher years (1979–91) were not kind to London's public schools or hospitals and saw much of the city's low-rent, council-owned housing stock sold off to private owners. Worse, in 1986 the Tories abolished the Greater London Council, which it saw as a power base from which GLC leader Ken Livingstone (now London's mayor) could challenge the government. That left one of the world's largest conurbations without a planning and coordinating authority – which was a disaster for public transport.

In 1992 the Major government took a more positive step with the introduction of the National Lottery, funds from which would be put towards public buildings. Throughout its history, London had never really been a city of *grands projets* on a Parisian scale, but as the new millennium loomed that was about to change. Among the scores of projects underwritten by the lottery-funded Millennium Commission were several of the landmarks that would define London in the 20th century: Tate Modern, the Millennium Bridge and the Millennium Dome.

Tate Modern (Herzog & de Meuron, 2000; p152) was a success beyond perhaps even the architects' wildest dreams. From the disused Bankside Power Station (originally by Sir Giles Gilbert Scott) they fashioned an art gallery that went straight to No 2 in the Top 10 London tourist attractions, and then walked away with international architecture's most prestigious prize, the Pritzker.

The **Millennium Bridge** (Foster, 2000; p152) infamously had a case of the wobbles when it was first opened, but is now generally considered to be a boon to the city. Even the **Millennium Dome** (Rogers; p184), the dunce of the class of 2000, probably through no fault of its Teflon exterior, is about to enjoy a second lease of life as a sporting stadium.

While not a publicly funded millennium project, British Airways' **London Eye** (Marks & Barfield; p149) also appeared on the South Bank in 2000, enjoying immense popularity ever since.

Olympic Heights

When the International Olympics Committee decided on 6 July 2005 to award the 2012 Olympic and Paralympic Games to London, its members chose vision over completed infrastructure. Unlike its main rival, Paris, London had no stadium in place which it proposed to use for the opening and closing ceremonies as well as the athletics. So between now and 2012 it must transform the earmarked 200-hectare site, near Stratford in London's east.

Nine new venues are planned here, many of which will be kept for community use after the games.

The first construction to get off the ground has been the Aquatics Centre, designed by Pritzker prize–winner Zaha Hadid. The other venues will include:

- an 80,000-seat new main stadium
- a 15,000-seat Hockey Centre
- a Velopark, complete with indoor velodrome and outdoor BMX circuit
- the Olympics Village, which will house some 17,000 athletes and will be later converted into 3600 homes. In total, 9000 homes will be created after the games in the Olympic Park area. Many of them will provide low-cost accommodation.
- a state-of-the-art Media Centre.

Meanwhile, transport links are being built to link the site at Stratford with central London in seven minutes.

There's not much to see yet; the Olympic site is still largely a brownfield site in a relatively deprived neighbourhood. However, those with a keen imagination and a desire to see London's vision for the future might enjoy the walking tours of the area that can be downloaded from www.london2012.org (under Olympic Park/Walking Tour).

COMMON GROUND

All this brings us back to where we started, in the London of today. The new City Hall and 30 St Mary Axe have joined the millennium landmarks in opening up new vistas around London's previously much-neglected river. In this most commercially minded city, there's even been a reawakening sense of connectivity and public space – walkways along the South Bank now connect public areas from Butler's Wharf to County Hall.

Norman Foster's 'World Squares for All' pedestrianisation of Trafalgar Sq has done the same thing in the busy West End, giving the plaza a much-needed human touch. And architect Terry Farrell is working on the same principle, with his plans for easy pedestrian links between several of the city's major parks, from Richmond and Greenwich through Hyde and St James's to Regent's Park.

However, while London has found new creativity and impetus in its major public projects, there remain concerns about commercially driven development. Critics such as architect Richard Rogers and the *Observer's* architecture writer, Deyan Sudjic, have expressed concern that many private riverside developments fail to meet good standards of design and drive out everything else.

Community groups have often had to battle against greedy developers in recent years, too. The fact that the Oxo Tower Wharf, for example, has residential apartments as well as shops and restaurants – rather than being solely devoted to offices – represents a success for the Coin St community. Similarly, vociferous opposition to redevelopment around Spitalfields and Smithfield markets have largely kept those great communal institutions in place.

Not all the new developments in London are to everyone's taste, but while the worst excesses can be averted, there's no denying that the massive changes are exciting. At the time of writing, a new national football stadium was set to open soon at Wembley, while the Channel Tunnel extension was scheduled to bring trains from the Continent directly into King's Cross station from 2007. Work has started on the regeneration of the Paddington Basin, as a sort of Canary Wharf around a reconstructed Paddington station, while a much-needed overhaul of Elephant and Castle (a good candidate for the ugliest spot in London) has finally been green-lit. Now, if only they could sort out the tube…

History

History

21ST-CENTURY LONDON

Just one day after the International Olympic Committee announced that London would be the first triple Olympic city in history, London's buoyant mood and extraordinary confidence were shattered when terrorists detonated a series of explosions on the city's public transport. Triumph turned to terror, followed quickly by anger and then defiance. While shaken by events, the resolve of ordinary citizens of the city – both British and foreign – not to allow terrorist attacks to change their way of life truly makes comparisons to the Blitz perfectly valid. London is no stranger to the threat of terrorism (the IRA terror campaign during the '70s, '80s and '90s is still a vivid memory to most Londoners) and despite the very real threat of further attack, in the long run the city is a hard one to keep down.

Re-electing Tony Blair's Labour government with an unheard-of third term in May 2005, and giving controversial Mayor 'Red' Ken Livingstone a second term in 2004, London remains a liberal, left-leaning boom town. The perennial problems of the capital – high housing costs and poor public transport – continue to dominate the political agenda, but the day-to-day life of London continues to be that of creative maelstrom, financial buoyancy and developmental frenzy, something that it's been famous for since the arrival of its first colonisers.

TIME IMMEMORIAL...

ROMAN HOLIDAY

Despite Celtic tribes making the Thames valley their home for around half a million years, a settlement recognisable as London didn't really take shape until the arrival of the Romans. They first visited in the 1st century BC, traded with the Celts and had a browse around. In AD 43 they returned with an army led by Emperor Claudius and decided to stay, establishing the port of Londinium. They built a wooden bridge across the Thames (on the site of today's London Bridge) and used the settlement as a base from which to capture other tribal centres, which at the time provided much bigger prizes. The bridge became the focal point for a network of roads fanning out around the region, and for a few years the settlement prospered from trade.

This growth was nipped in the bud around AD 60 when an army led by Boudicca, queen of the Celtic Iceni tribe based in East Anglia, took violent retribution on the Roman soldiers, who had abused her family and seized their land. The Iceni overran Camulodunum (Colchester) – which had become capital of Roman Britannia – and then turned on Londinium, massacring its inhabitants and razing the settlement. Boudicca was eventually defeated, though (and according to legend is buried under platform 10 of King's Cross Station), and the Romans rebuilt London around Cornhill.

A century later they built a 1.8 mile (3km) defensive wall around the city, fragments of which survive today, most visibly off the aptly named street London Wall. The original gates – Aldgate, Ludgate, Newgate and Bishopsgate – are remembered as place names in contemporary London. Excavations in the City suggest that Londinium, a centre for business and trade although not a fully fledged *colonia* (settlement), was an imposing metropolis whose massive buildings included a basilica, an amphitheatre, a forum and the governor's palace.

By the middle of the 3rd century AD Londinium was home to some 30,000 people of various ethnic groups, and there were temples dedicated to a large number of cults. When

TIMELINE	AD 43	80–90	200
	Romans invade and Londinium is founded	Romans rebuild	Romans build defensive wall around the city

78

Emperor Constantine converted to Christianity in 312 it became the official religion of the entire empire, although remains of the Temple of Mithras survive in the City today, as testament to the city's pagan past.

Overstretched and worn down by ever-increasing barbarian invasions, the Roman Empire fell into decline, as did the city of Londinium. When the embattled Emperor Honorius withdrew the last soldiers in 410, the remaining Romans scarpered and the settlement was reduced to a sparsely populated backwater.

THE SAXONS & THE DANES

Sometime in the 5th century, Saxon settlers began crossing the North Sea and establishing farmsteads and small villages in the south of England. For 200 years at least, they appear to have shown little interest in what remained of Londinium.

'Lundenwic' (London port) gradually grew in importance as trade flourished. When Ethelbert, the Saxon King of Kent, converted to Christianity in the late 6th century, Rome designated Lundenwic as a diocese. Its first bishop, Mellitus, built the original St Paul's Cathedral.

Saxon settlement was predominantly outside the city walls to the west, towards what is now Aldwych and Charing Cross, but the settlement became the victim of its own success when it attracted the Vikings of Denmark, who raided the city in 842 and burned it to the ground 10 years later. Under the leadership of King Alfred the Great of Wessex, the Saxon population fought back, drove the Danes out in 886 and re-established what soon became Lundunburg as the major centre of trade.

Saxon London grew into a prosperous and well-organised town divided into 20 wards, each with its own alderman, and resident colonies of German merchants and French vintners. But the Danes wouldn't let it lie, and Viking raids finally broke the weakening Saxon leadership, which was forced to accept the Danish leader Canute as King of England in 1016. His reign lasted until 1040, during which time London took over from Winchester as capital of England.

With the death of Canute's son Harold in 1042, the throne passed to the Saxon Edward the Confessor, who went on to found an abbey and palace at Westminster on what was then an island at the mouth of the River Tyburn (which now flows underground). When Edward moved his court to Westminster, he established divisions that would – geographically, at least – dominate the future of London. The port became the trading and mercantile centre, what we know as the City, while Westminster became the seat of politics and administration.

THE NORMANS

By the turn of the first millennium, the Vikings – who by this time had trimmed their beards, spoke French and preferred to be known as Normans – controlled much of the north and west of today's France. After the death of Edward the Confessor there was a succession dispute over the English throne. William, the duke of Normandy, mounted a massive invasion of England. In 1066 he defeated his rival, Harold, at the watershed Battle of Hastings, before marching on to London to claim his prize. William the Conqueror was crowned king of England in Westminster Abbey, ensuring the Norman Conquest was complete. William subsequently found himself in control of what was by then the richest and largest city in the kingdom.

Historical Reads

- *London: A Biography* – Peter Ackroyd
- *London at War* – Philip Ziegler
- *London in the Twentieth Century* – Jerry White
- *The Newgate Calender* – Clive Emsley
- *Restoration London, Elizabethan London and Dr Johnson's London* – Liza Picard

312	410	842	852
Emperor Constantine converts to Christianity	Romans pull out of Britain	Vikings raid London	Vikings settle in London

William distrusted 'the fierce populace' of London and built several strongholds, including the White Tower, the core of the Tower of London. Cleverly, he kept the prosperous merchants sweet by confirming the City's independence in exchange for taxes.

MEDIEVAL LONDON

Successive medieval kings were happy to let the City of London keep its independence so long as its merchants continued to finance their wars and building projects. When Richard I (known as 'the Lionheart') needed funds for his crusade, he recognised the City as a self-governing commune, and the appreciative merchants duly coughed up. The City's first mayor, Henry Fitz Aylwin, was elected sometime around 1190. A city built on money and commerce, London would always guard its independence furiously, as Richard's successor, King John, learned the hard way. In 1215 John was forced to cede to the powerful barons, and to curb his excessive demands for pay-offs from the City. Among those pressing him to seal the Magna Carta of 1215 (which effectively diluted royal power) was the by then powerful mayor of the City of London.

Trade and commerce boomed, and the noblemen, barons and bishops built lavish houses for themselves along the prime real estate of the Strand, which connected the City with the Palace of Westminster, the new seat of royal power. The first stone London Bridge was built in 1176, although it was frequently clogged, and most people crossed the river with waterboatmen (who plied their trade until the 18th century). Their touting shouts of 'Oars? Oars?' are said to have confused many a country visitor tempted by more carnal services.

Though fire was a constant threat in the cramped and narrow houses and lanes of 14th-century London, disease caused by unsanitary living conditions and impure drinking water from the Thames was the greatest threat to the burgeoning city. In 1348, rats on ships from Europe brought the Black Death, a bubonic plague that wiped out almost two-thirds of the population (of 100,000) on regular visits over the following decades.

With their numbers subsequently down, there was growing unrest among labourers, for whom violence became a way of life, and rioting was commonplace. In 1381, miscalculating – or just disregarding – the mood of the nation, the king tried to impose a poll tax on everyone in the realm. Tens of thousands of peasants, led by the soldier Wat Tyler and the priest Jack Straw, marched on London to make their feelings known. The archbishop of Canterbury was dragged from the Tower and beheaded, several ministers were murdered, and many buildings were razed before the Peasants' Revolt ran its course. Wat Tyler died at the end of the mayor's blade, while Jack Straw and the other ringleaders were executed at Smithfield. However, there was no more mention of poll tax (until Margaret Thatcher, not heeding the lessons of history, shot herself in the foot by trying to introduce it in the 1980s, with not dissimilar results).

Tower of London (p118)

<table>
</table>

886	1016	1066	1154
King Alfred reclaims London for the Saxons	Danes take London back and Canute is crowned king of England	William I crowned in Westminster Abbey	Henry II of the House of Plantagenet crowned king

London gained wealth and stature under the Houses of Lancaster and York in the 15th century, also the era of the charitable mayor Dick Whittington, immortalised for many children in the fairy tale of his rise to power from poverty. William Caxton set up the first printing press at Westminster in 1476, just in time for the century's greatest episode of political intrigue.

In 1483, 12-year-old Edward V of the House of York reigned for only two months before vanishing with his younger brother into the Tower of London, never to be seen again. Whether or not their uncle Richard III – who just happened to become the next king – murdered the boys has been the subject of much conjecture over the centuries. (In 1674 workers found a chest containing the skeletons of two children near the White Tower, which were assumed to be the princes' remains and were reburied in Innocents' Corner in Westminster Abbey.) Richard III didn't have long to enjoy the hot seat, however, as he was deposed within a couple of years by Henry Tudor, first of the dynasty of that name.

TUDOR LONDON

London became one of the largest and most important cities in Europe during the reign of the Tudors, which coincided with the discovery of the Americas and thriving world trade.

Henry's son and successor, Henry VIII, was the most ostentatious of the clan. Terribly fond of palaces, he had new ones built at Whitehall and St James's, and bullied his lord chancellor, Cardinal Thomas Wolsey, into gifting him Hampton Court.

His most significant contribution, however, was the split with the Catholic Church in 1534 after it refused to annul his marriage to the non-heir-producing Catherine of Aragon. Thumbing his nose at Rome, he made himself the head, no, *supreme* head, of the Church of England and married Anne Boleyn (the second of his six wives). He 'dissolved' London's monasteries and seized the church's vast wealth and property. The face of the medieval city was transformed; much of the land requisitioned for hunting later became Hyde, Regent's and Richmond Parks, while many of the religious houses disappeared, leaving only their names in particular areas, such as Whitefriars and Blackfriars (after the colour of the monks' habits).

Despite his penchant for settling differences with the axe (two of his six wives and Wolsey's replacement as lord chancellor, Thomas More, were beheaded) and his persecution of both Catholics and fellow Protestants that didn't toe the line, Henry VIII remained a popular monarch until his death in 1547.

The reign of Mary I, his daughter by Catherine of Aragon, saw a brief return to Catholicism, during which the queen sanctioned the burning to death of hundreds of Protestants at Smithfield and earned herself the nickname 'Bloody Mary'.

By the time Elizabeth I, Henry VIII's daughter by Anne Boleyn, began her 45-year reign, Catholicism was well on the outer, and hundreds of people who dared to suggest otherwise were carted off to the gallows at **Tyburn** (p146).

ELIZABETHAN LONDON

The 45-year reign (1558–1603) of Queen Elizabeth I is still looked upon as one of the most extraordinary periods in British history, and it was just as significant for London as it was for the rest of the nation. During Elizabeth's reign English literature reached new and still unbeaten heights; religious tolerance rather than persecution became the ethos of the day; Britain became the world's unrivalled naval superpower, having defeated the Spanish Armada; and the city established itself as the premier world trade market with the opening of the Royal Exchange in 1572.

c1190	1348	1397	1534
London's first mayor elected	Black Death arrives in London	Dick Whittington first elected mayor	Henry VIII splits with Catholic Church

London was blooming economically and physically; in the second half of the 16th century the population doubled to 200,000. The first recorded map of London was published in 1558, and John Stow produced *A Survey of London,* the first history of the city, in 1598.

This was also the golden era of English drama, and the works of William Shakespeare, Christopher Marlowe and Ben Jonson packed them in at new playhouses such as the Rose (built in 1587) and the Globe (1599). Both of these were built in Southwark, a notoriously 'naughty place' at the time, teeming with brothels, bawdy taverns and illicit sports such as bear-baiting. Most importantly, they were outside the jurisdiction of the City, which frowned upon and even banned theatre as a waste of time.

When Elizabeth died without an heir in 1603, she was succeeded by her second cousin, who was crowned James I. Although the son of Catholic Mary, Queen of Scots, he was slow to improve conditions for England's Catholics and drew their wrath. He narrowly escaped death when Guy Fawkes' plot to blow up the Houses of Parliament on 5 November 1605 was uncovered. The discovery of the audacious plan is commemorated on this date each year with bonfires, fireworks and the burning of Guy Fawkes effigies throughout Britain.

THE CIVIL WAR

Charles I took to the throne in 1625, and the three-way struggle between the king, the City and Parliament finally came to a head. With the City tiring of increasingly extortionate taxes and Parliament beginning to flex its muscle, the crunch came when Charles tried to arrest five antagonistic MPs who fled to the City, and the country slid into civil war in 1642.

The Puritans, extremist Protestants and the City's expanding merchant class threw their support behind Oliver Cromwell and the Parliamentarians (the Roundheads), who battled against the Royalist troops (the Cavaliers). London was firmly with the Roundheads, and Charles I was defeated in 1646. He was beheaded for treason outside Banqueting House in Whitehall three years later, famously wearing two shirts on the cold morning of his execution so he wouldn't shiver and appear cowardly.

Cromwell ruled the country as a republic for the next 11 years, during which time he banned theatre, dancing, Christmas and just about anything remotely fun. Soon after his death, Parliament decided that the royals weren't so bad after all and restored the exiled Charles II in 1660. It was decided that death wasn't good enough for Cromwell, whose exhumed body was hung, drawn and quartered posthumously at Tyburn, and his rotting head was displayed on a spike at Westminster Hall for two decades. Despite the disdain of his contemporaries, Cromwell is celebrated by a statue outside the Palace of Westminster that was erected in the late 19th century.

PLAGUE & FIRE

Despite the immense wealth that London saw during the reign of the Tudors, the capital remained a crowded and filthy place where most of the population lived below the poverty line. A lack of basic sanitation (urine and faeces were routinely poured into the streets from the slop bucket), dirty water and overcrowding had all contributed to recurrent outbreaks of illnesses and fevers from which few ever recovered. The city had suffered from outbreaks of bubonic plague since the 14th century, but all previous incidences were dwarfed by the Great Plague of 1665.

As the 'sweating sickness' spread, the panicked population retreated behind closed doors, only venturing out for supplies and to dispose of their dead. Previously crowded streets were deserted, the churches and markets were closed, and an eerie silence never before experienced descended on the city. To make matters worse, the mayor believed that dogs and cats were the spreaders of the plague and ordered them all killed, thus in one stroke

1558	1572	1599	1605
First map of London created	The Royal Exchange opens	The Globe theatre opens	Guy Fawkes fails to blow up Parliament

ridding the disease-carrying rats of their natural predators. By the time the winter cold arrested the epidemic, 100,000 people had perished, collected up and thrown into vast 'plague pits', many of which continue to stand empty of buildings today.

The plague finally began to wane in late 1665, leaving the city's population decimated and a general superstition that the deaths had been a punishment from God for London's moral squalor. Just as Londoners breathed a sigh of relief, another disaster struck. The city had for centuries been prone to fire, as nearly all buildings were constructed from wood, but the mother of all blazes broke out on 2 September 1666 in a bakery in Pudding Lane in the City.

It didn't seem like much to begin with – the mayor himself dismissed it as 'something a woman might pisse out' before going back to bed – but the unusual August heat and rising winds fanned the flames, and the fire raged out of control for four days, razing some 80% of London. Only eight people died (officially at least), but most of London's medieval, Tudor and Jacobean architecture was destroyed. The fire was finally stopped at Fetter Lane, on the very edge of the city, by blowing up all the buildings in the inferno's path. It's hard to overstate the scale of the destruction – 89 churches and over 13,000 houses, leaving tens of thousands of people homeless. As a result, many Londoners left for the countryside, or to seek their fortunes in the New World.

RESTORATION

One positive to come out of the inferno was that it created a blank canvas upon which master architect Christopher Wren could build his magnificent churches. His plan for rebuilding the entire city was unfortunately deemed too expensive, and the familiar pattern of streets that had grown up over the centuries since the time of the Romans quickly reappeared (by law, brick and stone designs replaced the old timber-framed, overhanging Tudor houses, to avoid a repeat of 1666; many roads were widened for the same reason). At the same time, Charles II moved to St James's Palace, and the surrounding area was taken over by the gentry, who built the grand squares and town houses of modern-day Mayfair and St James.

By way of memorialising the blaze – and symbolising the restoration and resurgence of the subsequent years – the **Monument** (p115) was erected in 1677 near the site of the fire's outbreak. At the time it was by far the highest structure in the city, visible from everywhere in the capital.

In 1685 some 1500 Huguenot refugees arrived in London, fleeing persecution in Catholic Europe. Many turned their hands to the manufacture of luxury goods such as silks and silverware in and around Spitalfields and Clerkenwell, which were already populated with Irish, Jewish and Italian immigrants and artisans. London was fast becoming one of the world's most cosmopolitan places.

Invasion of the Body Snatchers

During the 18th and 19th centuries, as the understanding of anatomy and surgery advanced, there was a huge shortage of bodies on which doctors and students could experiment. Legally, only the corpses of executed criminals were fair game for the scalpel, but the demand for specimens far outstretched the supply, leading to the rise of the notorious body snatchers, or resurrectionists. Gangs of men would surreptitiously remove recently interred bodies from their graves, replacing everything as they found it, so in many cases the relatives never found out. In fact, though horrific, the practice was not even illegal, as by law the human body was not a possession and thus taking it could not be stealing. The area around St Bart's hospital in the city was notorious for this practice, with entire gangs emptying local graveyards. However, the strong common belief that the human body had to be intact to enter heaven meant that, when body snatchers were discovered, they were often on the receiving end of mob justice and torn to pieces on the streets.

1642	1665	1666	1710
Start of Civil War	Great Plague	Great Fire	Rebuilt St Paul's Cathedral opens

The Glorious (ie bloodless) Revolution in 1688 brought the Dutch king William of Orange to the English throne. He relocated from Whitehall Palace to a new palace in Kensington Gardens, and the surrounding area smartened itself up accordingly. In order to raise finances for his war with France – and as a result of the City's transformation into a centre of finance rather than manufacturing – William III established the Bank of England in 1694.

Despite the setbacks of the preceding decades, London's growth continued unabated, and by 1700 it was Europe's largest city, with 600,000 people. The influx of foreign workers brought expansion to the east and south, while those who could afford it headed to the more salubrious environs of the north and west. London today is still, more or less, divided along these lines.

The crowning glory of the 'Great Rebuilding', Christopher Wren's **St Paul's Cathedral** (p110), opened in 1710 – one of the largest cathedrals in Europe and one of the city's most prominent and visible landmarks to this day.

St Paul's Cathedral (p110)

GEORGIAN LONDON

When Queen Anne died without an heir in 1714, the search began for a Protestant relative (the 1701 Act of Settlement forbade Roman Catholics to occupy the throne). Eventually an heir was found, George of Hanover, the great-grandson of James I. He arrived from Germany, was crowned king of England and never even learned to speak English. Meanwhile, the increasingly literate population got their first newspapers, which began to cluster around Fleet St.

Robert Walpole's Whig Party controlled Parliament during much of George I's reign, and Walpole effectively became Britain's first prime minister. He was presented with 10 Downing St, which has been the official residence of (nearly) every prime minister since.

London grew at a phenomenal pace during this time, and measures were taken to make the city more accessible. When Westminster Bridge opened in 1750 it was only the second spanning of the Thames after London Bridge, first built by the Romans. The old crossing itself was cleared of many of its buildings, and the Roman wall surrounding the City was torn down.

Georgian London saw a great creative surge in music, art and architecture. Court composer George Frederick Handel wrote his *Water Music* (1717) and *Messiah* (1741) while living here, and in 1755 Dr Johnson produced the first English dictionary. Hogarth, Gainsborough and Reynolds were producing some of their finest engravings and paintings, and many of London's most elegant buildings, streets and squares were being erected or laid out by the likes of John Soane and the incomparable John Nash (p61).

All the while, though, London was becoming ever more segregated and lawless. George II himself was relieved of 'purse, watch and buckles' during a stroll through Kensington Gardens. This was the London of artist William Hogarth (see the boxed text, opposite), in which the wealthy built fine new mansions in attractive squares and gathered in fashion-

1751	1837	1837	1884
Bow Street Runners established	Coronation of Queen Victoria	Charles Dickens publishes *Oliver Twist*	Greenwich Mean Time established

able new coffee houses while the poor huddled together in appalling slums and drowned their sorrows with cheap gin.

To curb rising crime, two magistrates established the 'Bow Street Runners' in 1751. This voluntary group – effectively a forerunner to the Metropolitan Police Force (set up in 1829) – was established to challenge the official marshals ('thief-takers') who were suspected (often correctly) of colluding with the criminals themselves.

In 1780 Parliament proposed to lift the law preventing Catholics from buying or inheriting property. One demented MP, Lord George Gordon, led a 'No Popery' demonstration that turned into the Gordon Riots. A mob of 30,000 went on a rampage, attacking Irish labourers, and burning prisons, 'Papishe dens' (chapels) and several law courts. At least 300 people died during the riots, including some who drank themselves to death after breaking into a Holborn distillery. As the century drew to a close, London's population had mushroomed to almost a million.

VICTORIAN LONDON

While the growth and achievements of the previous century were impressive, they paled in comparison with the Victorian era, which began when the 18-year-old Victoria was crowned in 1837. During the Industrial Revolution, when small 'cottage' industries were suddenly overtaken by the advance of the great factories, spurring the creation of the first industrialised society on earth, London became the nerve centre of the largest and richest empire the world has ever known, one that covered a quarter of the world's surface area and ruled more than 500 million people.

New docks in East London were built to facilitate the booming trade with the colonies, and railways began to fan out from the capital. The world's first underground railway opened between Paddington and Farringdon Rd in 1863 and was such a success that other lines quickly followed. Many of London's most famous buildings and landmarks were also built at this time: the **Clock Tower** at the Houses of Parliament (1859; p134), the **Royal Albert Hall** (1871; p145) and the magnificent **Tower Bridge** (1894; p121).

The city, however, heaved under the burden of its vast size, and in 1858 London found itself in the grip of the 'Great Stink', when the population explosion so overtook the city's sanitation facilities that raw sewage seeped in through the floorboards of wealthy merchants' houses. Leading engineer Joseph Bazalgette tackled the problem by creating in the late 1850s an underground network of sewers, which were to become copied around the world. London had truly become the first modern metropolis.

Though the Victorian age is chiefly seen as one of great Imperial power founded on industry, trade and commerce, intellectual achievement in the arts and sciences was enormous. The greatest chronicler of the times was Charles Dickens, whose *Oliver Twist* (1837) and other works explored the themes of poverty, hopelessness and squalor among the working classes. In 1859 Charles Darwin published the immensely controversial *On the Origin of Species* here, a book that still attracts scandal today, despite being the basis for the theory of evolution.

Of Rakes & Harlots: Hogarth's World

William Hogarth (1697–1764) was an artist and engraver who specialised in satire and what these days might be considered heavy-handed moralising on the wages of sin. His plates were so popular in his day that they were pirated, leading Parliament to pass the Hogarth Act of 1735 to protect copyright. They provide invaluable insights into the life – particularly the low variety – of Georgian London. Hogarth's works can be seen in **Sir John Soane's Museum** (p104) in Holborn, **Hogarth's House** (p208) in Chiswick, the **Tate Britain** (p135) and the **National Gallery** (p99).

1901	1908	1915	1922
Queen Victoria dies	London hosts its first Olympic Games	First WWI zeppelin bombs fall on London	BBC's first radio broadcast

Crystal Palace & the Great Exhibition

Queen Victoria's husband, the German-born Prince Albert, organised a huge celebration of global technology in Hyde Park in 1851. The Great Exhibition was held in a 7.5-hectare revolutionary iron-and-glass hothouse, a 'Crystal Palace' designed by gardener and architect Joseph Paxton. So successful was the exhibition – in excess of two million people flocked to see its more than 100,000 exhibits – that Albert arranged for the profits to be ploughed into building two permanent exhibitions, which today house the Science Museum and the Victoria & Albert Museum. The Crystal Palace itself was moved to Sydenham, where it burned down in 1936.

Exactly 10 years after the exhibition the 42-year-old prince died of typhoid, and the queen was so prostrate with grief that she wore mourning clothes until her death in 1901 (largely why she is remembered as a dour curmudgeon).

It was also the era of some of Britain's most capable and progressive prime ministers, most notably William Gladstone (four terms between 1868 and 1894) and Benjamin Disraeli (who served in 1868 and again from 1874 to 1880).

Waves of immigrants, from Chinese to Eastern European, arrived in London during the 19th century, when the population exploded from one million to six million people. This breakneck expansion was not beneficial to all – inner-city slums housed the poor in atrocious conditions of disease and overcrowding, while the affluent expanded out to leafy suburbs, where new and comfortable housing was built. The suburbs of London are still predominantly made up of Victorian terrace housing today.

Queen Victoria – of 'We are not amused' notoriety – lived to celebrate her Diamond Jubilee in 1897, but died four years later aged 81 and was laid to rest in Windsor. Her reign is seen as the climax of Britain's world supremacy, when London was the de-facto capital of the world.

EDWARDIAN LONDON & WWI

Victoria's self-indulgent son Edward, the Prince of Wales, was already 60 by the time he was crowned Edward VII in 1901. London's *belle époque* was marked with the introduction of the first motorised buses, which replaced the horse-drawn versions that had plodded their trade since 1829, and a touch of glamour came in the form of luxury hotels such as the Ritz in 1906 and department stores such as Selfridges in 1909. The Olympics were held at White City in 1908.

What became known as the Great War (WWI) broke out in August 1914, and the first German bombs fell from zeppelins near the Guildhall a year later, killing 39 people. Planes were soon dropping bombs on the capital, killing in all some 650 people (half the national total of civilian casualties). Tragic as these deaths were, however, they were but a drop in the ocean compared with the carnage that the next generation would endure during WWII.

BETWEEN THE WARS

While the young, moneyed set kicked up their heels after the relative hardships of the war, the 'roaring 20s' brought only more hardship for most Londoners, with an economic slump increasing the cost of living.

The population continued to rise, reaching nearly 7.5 million in 1921. The London County Council (LCC) busied itself clearing slums and building new housing estates, while the suburbs encroached ever deeper into the countryside.

Unemployment rose steadily as the world descended into recession. In May 1926 a wage dispute in the coal industry escalated into a nine-day general strike, in which so many

1924	1926	1936	1936
In Soho John Logie Baird demonstrates TV for the first time ever	General strike cripples London	BBC's first TV broadcast	Edward VIII abdicates and George IV made king

workers downed tools that London virtually ground to a halt. The army was called in to maintain order and to keep the city functioning, but the stage was set for more than half a century of industrial strife.

Despite the economic woes, the era brought a wealth of intellectual success. The 1920s were the heyday of the Bloomsbury Group, which counted writer Virginia Woolf and economist John Maynard Keynes in its ranks. The spotlight shifted westwards to Fitzrovia in the following decade, when George Orwell and Dylan Thomas clinked glasses with contemporaries at the Fitzroy Tavern in Charlotte St.

Cinema, TV and radio arrived to change the world, and the British Broadcasting Corporation (BBC) aired its first radio broadcast from the roof of Marconi House in the Strand in 1922, and the first TV programme from Alexandra Palace 14 years later.

The royal family took a knock when Edward VIII abdicated in 1936 to marry a woman who was not only twice divorced but, heaven save us, an American. The same year Oswald Mosley attempted to lead the British Union of Fascists on an anti-Jewish march through the East End but was repelled by a mob of around half a million at the famous Battle of Cable St.

WWII & THE BLITZ

Prime Minister Neville Chamberlain's policy of appeasing Hitler during the 1930s eventually proved misguided as the Führer's lust for expansion could not ultimately be sated. When Germany invaded Poland on 1 September 1939, Britain declared war, having signed a mutual-assistance pact with the Poles a few days beforehand. WWII (1939–45), Europe's darkest hour, had begun.

The first year of WWII was one of anxious waiting for London; although over 600,000 women and children had been evacuated to the countryside, no bombs fell to disturb the blackout. On 7 September 1940 this 'phoney war' came to a swift and brutal end when German planes, the Luftwaffe, dropped hundreds of bombs on the East End, killing 430 people.

The Blitz (from the German 'blitzkrieg' for 'lightning war') lasted for 57 nights, and then continued intermittently until May 1941. The Underground was turned into a giant bomb shelter, although one bomb rolled down the escalator at Bank station and exploded on the platform, killing more than 100 people. Londoners responded with legendary resilience and stoicism throughout. The royal family – still immensely popular and enormously respected – were also to play their role, refusing to leave London during the bombing. Begged to allow her children to leave the capital, Queen Elizabeth (the present monarch's late mother) apparently replied, 'the children could not possibly go without me, I wouldn't leave without the King, and the King won't leave under any circumstances'. The king's younger brother, the Duke of Kent, was killed in active service in 1942, while Buckingham Palace took a direct hit during a bombing raid, prompting the Queen to announce that 'now we can look the East End in the face'. Winston Churchill, prime minister from 1940, orchestrated much of the nation's war strategy from the Cabinet War Rooms deep below Whitehall, and it was from here that he made his stirring wartime speeches.

The city's spirit was tested again in January 1944, when Germany launched pilotless V-1 bombers (known as doodlebugs) over the city. By the time Nazi Germany capitulated in May 1945, up to a third of the East End and the City had been flattened, 32,000 Londoners had been killed and a further 50,000 had been seriously wounded. The scale of the destruction can only really be felt by taking a walk around the City – wherever you can see immediately post-war buildings (many of them monstrous) was somewhere hit by German bombs.

1940–41	1948	1952	1953
London devastated by the Blitz	London hosts its second Olympics	Great Smog	Coronation of Queen Elizabeth II

POST-WAR LONDON

Once the celebrations of VE (Victory in Europe) day had died down, the nation faced the huge toll that the war had taken. In response to the critical housing shortage, the government threw up ugly high-rise residences on bomb sites in Pimlico and the East End. Hosting the 1948 Olympics and the Festival of Britain in 1951 boosted morale. The festival recalled the Great Exhibition of a century earlier but left only the concrete complex of arts buildings, the **South Bank Centre** (p151), as its legacy.

The gloom returned, quite literally, on 6 December 1952 in the form of the Great Smog, the latest disaster to beset the city. A lethal combination of fog, smoke and pollution descended, and some 4000 people died of smog-related illnesses. This led to the 1956 Clean Air Act, which introduced zones to central London where only smokeless fuels could be burned.

Immigrants from around the world – particularly the former British colonies – flocked to post-war London, where a dwindling population had led to labour shortages. The city's character changed forever. However, as the Notting Hill race riots of 1958 attest, despite being officially encouraged to come, new immigrants weren't always welcomed on the streets.

Rationing of most goods ended in 1953, the year Elizabeth II (the current queen) ascended to the throne, and three years before the first red double-deckers appeared on London's streets.

SWINGING LONDON

Some economic prosperity returned in the late 1950s, and Prime Minister Harold Macmillan told Britons they'd 'never had it so good'. London was the place to be during the '60s when the creative energy that had been bottled up in the post-war era was suddenly and spectacularly uncorked. London became the epicentre of cool in fashion and music, and the streets were awash with colour and paved with vitality. The introduction of the pill and the popularisation of drugs such as marijuana and LSD through the hippy movement created a permissive and liberal climate never before experienced, outraging the conservative older generations and delighting the young. Two seminal events were the Beatles recording at Abbey Rd and the Rolling Stones performing free in front of half a million people in Hyde Park. Carnaby St was the most fashionable place on earth, and pop-cultural figures from Twiggy and David Bailey to Marianne Faithfull and Christine Keeler became the icons of a new era.

PUNK LONDON

The party didn't last long, however, and London returned to the doldrums in the harsh economic climate of the 1970s, a decade marked by unemployment and IRA bombs.

But London, ever thriving on adversity, ensured that it was at the centre of the world's attention when suddenly in the mid-1970s a new aesthetic, punk, came vomiting and swearing into sight.

Despite the sexual liberation of the swinging '60s, London had remained a relatively conservative place, and the new generation who had witnessed flower power as kids suddenly took things a step further, horrifying *Daily Mail* readers with strategically placed safety pins, dyed hair, mohawks and foul language. Punk was born – Vivienne Westwood shocked and awed the city with the wares from her clothing shop, Sex, on King's Rd, while the Sex Pistols' alternative national anthem, 'God Save the Queen', released during the national celebrations for Queen Elizabeth's Silver Jubilee in 1977, was more outrageous than anything the '60s could have come up with.

1956	1958	1966	1969
Red double-decker buses hit the streets	Notting Hill race riots	England win World Cup at Wembley	Rolling Stones play free concert at Hyde Park

THE THATCHER YEARS

While the music and fashion scene was in overdrive, torpor had set into Britain's body politic, as demonstrated by the brief and unremarkable Labour premiership of James Callaghan (1976–79), who was seen as weak and in thrall to the all-powerful trade unions, who crippled the UK with strikes in the late '70s, most significantly during the famous 'Winter of Discontent' in 1978–79.

Lloyd's of London building (p114)

Recovery began – at least for the business community – under the iron fist of Margaret Thatcher, the leader of the Conservative Party, who was elected Britain's first female prime minister in 1979. Her monetarist policy created a canyon between rich and poor, while her determination to crush socialism sent unemployment skyrocketing. Her term was marked by rioting and unrest, most famously in Brixton in 1981 and Tottenham in 1985. Hugely popular abroad and largely reviled in her own country by anyone with a social conscience, she is nonetheless one of the most notable prime ministers of recent times.

The Greater London Council, under the leadership of 'Red' Ken Livingstone, proved to be a thorn in Thatcher's side and fought a spirited campaign to bring down the price of public transport. Thatcher responded in 1986 by abolishing the GLC, leaving London as the only European capital without a local government. The GLC wouldn't resurface for another 14 years.

While poorer Londoners suffered under Thatcher's assault on socialism, things had rarely looked better for the suits. Riding on a wave of confidence partly engendered by the deregulation of the Stock Exchange in 1986, London underwent explosive economic growth. New property developers proved to be only marginally more discriminating than the Luftwaffe, though some outstanding modern structures, including the **Lloyd's of London building** (p114), went up amid all the other rubbish.

History – Time Immemorial...

The World in One City

London is made up of immigrants – whether Roman, Viking, Anglo-Saxon, Norman, Huguenot or Jamaican, the city has always assimilated large numbers of ethnically diverse people. While Africans are well documented to have served in the Roman army, they first came to England in significant numbers as slaves in Elizabethan times, although their numbers were relatively tiny. The first truly large influx of foreigners was in the late 17th century, when Huguenots, French Protestant refugees fleeing religious persecution at home, settled in Spitalfields and Soho. Wave upon wave followed. Jews have arrived throughout the past four centuries; their traditional areas have been the East End (particularly Spitalfields and Stamford Hill) and North West London. The last large group of Jews arrived from India as late as the 1960s. During the potato famine in the mid-19th century there was massive migration from Ireland; Londoners with Irish ancestry remain concentrated in Kilburn today. WWII brought Poles, Ukrainians and other Eastern Europeans to London, and today the Poles are a long-established community in Hammersmith and Shepherd's Bush. The single biggest wave of immigration came in the 1950s, when, facing a labour shortage, the government allowed anyone born in a UK colony to have British citizenship. This brought a huge Black population from the Caribbean and a large Asian diaspora from India, Bangladesh and Pakistan. The Black population settled in west London and South London, while the Asians were concentrated in the East End. Other less noticeable waves include Italians to Clerkenwell in the early 20th century, Vietnamese refugees to Hackney in the 1980s and the Iraqi diaspora that has grown in northwest London since the 1990s. Whoever you are, wherever you're from, you'll feel at home in London.

1979	1981	1986	1990
Margaret Thatcher elected prime minister	Brixton sees the worst race riots in London history	Margaret Thatcher abolishes the troublesome Greater London Council	Poll-tax riots in Trafalgar Sq

Like previous booms, the one of the late 1980s proved unsustainable. As unemployment started to rise again and people found themselves living in houses worth much less than what they had paid for them, Thatcher introduced a flat-rate poll tax. Protests all around the country culminated in a 1990 march on Trafalgar Sq that ended in a fully fledged riot, which helped to finally see her off. Thatcher's resignation the same year brought to an end a divisive era in modern British history, and her roundly derided successor, her former Chancellor of the Exchequer, John Major, employed a far more collective form of government, something that was anathema to Thatcher.

THE 1990S

In 1992, to the horror of most Londoners, the Conservatives were elected for a fourth successive term in government, even though the inspiring leadership of Margaret Thatcher was gone. Unfortunately for the party, the economy went into a tailspin shortly thereafter, and Britain was forced to withdraw from the European Exchange Rate Mechanism (ERM), a humiliation from which it was impossible for the government to recover.

To add to the government's troubles, the IRA detonated two huge bombs, one in the City in 1992 and another in the Docklands four years later, killing several people and damaging millions of pounds' worth of property.

Invigorated by its sheer desperation to return to power, the Labour Party, having elected the thoroughly telegenic Tony Blair to lead it, managed to ditch some of the more socialist-sounding clauses in its party credo and reinvent itself as New Labour, finally leading to the single biggest landslide in British history in the May 1997 general election. The Conservatives were atomised throughout the country, and the Blair era had begun.

BLAIR'S LONDON

Most importantly for London, Labour recognised the legitimate demand the city had for local government, and created the London Assembly and the post of mayor. Despite this laudable attempt to give Londoners back the much-needed representation stolen by Margaret Thatcher, Blair quickly discredited himself by attempting to rig the Labour mayoral selection process against New Labour's then *bête noire* Ken Livingstone, former leader of the Greater London Council and, due to his one-time far-left sympathies, best known by his moniker 'Red' Ken. Londoners were incensed at Blair's attempts to parachute his close ally Frank Dobson into the position, and when Ken Livingstone stood as an independent candidate he stormed the contest. However, Livingstone never became the thorn in Blair's side that many predicted. His hugely popular and successful congestion charge has done wonders for the city's traffic flow, and he's now been readmitted to the Labour Party and is looked upon as one of the party's most significant weapons.

However, despite the success of congestion charging, Livingstone's legacy as mayor remains uncertain. The tube was forced by central government (to the horror of Ken, who even took the matter to court) to submit to the controversial Public Private Partnership (PPP) between big business and Transport for London, the results of which are still unclear. Public transport continues to be Londoners' most consistent complaint, with Ken's 'bendy buses' still far from loved, and money for new, much-needed tube lines still not found.

London's successful bagging of the 2012 Olympic Games will mean a vast building program in East London is shortly to roll into action. Most importantly for Londoners, the games will release money for much-promised new transport routes, including the Crossrail scheme that will see the construction of two brand new underground train lines linking London's east to its west.

1997	2000	2003	2005
Labour sweeps to victory	Ken Livingstone elected mayor of the reestablished GLC	London's congestion charge introduced	London wins bid to host 2012 Olympic Games

Neighbourhoods

Neighbourhoods

London can feel like the densest and most impenetrable of cities – a vast and sprawling megalopolis made up of myriad neighbourhoods and lacking any real focus. To make it a little more navigable, we've divided it into 12 hefty portions (see the map, p436). Get your bearings downtown at the frothy and frivolous West End, which is chaotic, colourful and never stands still. It's propelled by a torrent of locals and visitors searching for a good time and is packed with pubs, bars, restaurants, clubs, cinemas and some of the best shopping in the world. At its centre are the neighbourhoods of Soho and Covent Garden, but it also includes the perfectly tousled intellectual pockets of Bloomsbury and Fitzrovia, as well as Holborn and the fading grandeur of the Strand. To one side of the West End lies East Central, which incorporates the commercial heart, simply known as the City, along with perpetually trendy Islington. We've christened it after the areas of Clerkenwell, Hoxton and Shoreditch, London's current centres of cool. On the other side of the West End, west of Regent St, is West Central, home to the traditional seats of parliamentary and royal power, at Westminster and the area around St James's. You can add glitzy Mayfair, chichi Chelsea, haughty Hyde Park and the museumland of Kensington to this exclusive mix. The area around the South Bank is another neighbourhood on the up, and takes in the most central areas south of the river. It has become home to several of London's top attractions in recent years, including the London Eye, the Tate Modern, Borough Market and Shakespeare's Globe.

From here, the neighbourhood names are geographically self-explanatory. The underdeveloped East End is immediately associated with cockney geezers, but these days it's buzzy and multicultural; Docklands is the only part of it that has already seen a fully fledged dramatic revival. Southeast London begins in beautiful Greenwich, a village-like enclave exuding royal, architectural and maritime history, before fanning out into places such as Charlton, Woolwich, Dulwich and Forest Hill. North Central refers to irrepressible Camden, charismatic Marylebone and the well-mannered Regent's Park. Overlooking these – often beyond the reach of the tube – North London is renowned for fashionable villages, heathlands and history. Many of London's showbiz personalities live around Crouch End, Muswell Hill, Highgate and Hampstead (the last has been luring artistic types since the year dot). Notting Hill is the pick of West London, a label largely referring to affluent residential areas, before moving into the infamous backpacking hub Earl's Court, Hammersmith and the BBC's Shepherd's Bush. South London takes us into Brixton, 'the soul of Black Britain', before moving onwards into upwardly mobile Battersea, which has more than a power station and dogs home to recommend it. Little-known areas in Southwest London include Fulham and Putney, which offer many a pastoral delight by the river. Finally, we head Up River, swimming against the current to Richmond Park, Kew Gardens, Hampton Court Palace and the heart of suburbia.

SUGGESTED ITINERARIES
ONE DAY
Most of us see London in a hurry, but one day is pushing it. Start your express tour by rising early to beat the queues at the **London Eye** (p149). After a spin on the big wheel, cross the river for a (brisk) walk around Westminster. Admire **Big Ben** (p134), **Westminster Abbey** (p133) and the **Houses of Parliament** (p134). Just soak up the atmosphere; you don't need to visit the sights. Head to the revamped **Trafalgar Square** (p98) and take a peek down through **Admiralty Arch** (p129) down the Mall to **Buckingham Palace** (p127). If you have time and the inclination, nip into the **National Gallery** (p99) or the more manageable **National Portrait Gallery** (p100). If not, plunge directly into the choked heart of Soho or Covent Garden for lunch (see p232). Reinvigorated, do a bit of window-shopping before catching a bus along the Strand and Fleet St

to **St Paul's Cathedral** (p110). Climb the dome. Once at the Cathedral, you'll find it hard to resist the temptation to walk directly across the **Millennium Bridge** (p152) to the **Tate Modern** (p152). After exploring this world-beating contemporary gallery, head to a traditional-looking or riverside pub. Peruse the weekly listings over your beverage of choice, then go to see a band or a play.

THREE DAYS

Explore the **British Museum** (p107), not forgetting the Great Court. Head west to Hyde Park and Kensington Garden, and take in one of Kensington's 'big three': the **Natural History Museum** (p142), **Science Museum** (p142) or **Victoria & Albert Museum** (p141). Indulge in a little retail therapy, either at **Harrods** (p342) or along King's Rd.

Visit **Tate Britain** (p135), Tate Modern's older sister, and catch a ferry back down the river to **Shakespeare's Globe** (p153). Take a tour and picture the throngs listening to the Bard's words for the first time. Afterwards, stroll along the riverbank to **Tower Bridge** (p121), before heading to the hulking **Tower of London** (p118) for a history lesson. A riverside pub would be nice around now.

Victoria & Albert Museum (p141)

ONE WEEK

If you've got the luxury of a week, you won't need to follow our subjective recommendations above. In whatever order you fancy, fill your week with any of these. Head to magnificent **Somerset House** (p103). Pop back to Westminster or St James's and visit a few sights; the new **Churchill Museum** (p136) will wow you with the wartime PM's oratory. A day out in Greenwich – visiting the **National Maritime Museum** (p181) and the **Royal Observatory** (p180) – will be a day well spent. You don't have to pay the exorbitant admission prices at the palaces and sights of Royal London to get a feel for it. Go for a wander over to **Buckingham** (p127) and **Kensington** (p143) Palaces, and around **St James's Park** (p128) and **Kensington Gardens** (p144). Don't, like most people, forget smaller sights such as **Sir John Soane's Museum** (p104) and the **Wallace Collection** (p190), two outstanding highlights of any trip to this big smoke. The Victorian Valhalla of **Highgate Cemetery** (p195), in north London, is also worth the trip. On the weekend, you're spoilt for choice with markets; choose **Borough** (p350), **Portobello** (p350) or **Spitalfields** (p351).

ORGANISED TOURS

Although many people would rather shoot themselves than submit to the traditional coach-tour option, organised tours can nevertheless provide a decent means of seeing the main sights while allowing you to return to certain areas for more in-depth exploration under your own steam. Similarly, for anyone with very limited time, it is (just about) possible to see the major landmarks of the British capital in one day. A huge variety of companies offer countless wacky options, and with the very good 'jump-on, jump-off' services that allow you to combine group tours with individual exploration, you shouldn't necessarily run a mile at the suggestion, although do proceed with caution.

Air

ADVENTURE BALLOONS
☎ 01252-844222; www.adventureballoons.co.uk; Winchfield Park, Hartley Wintney, Hampshire

Weather permitting, there are flights every weekday morning shortly after dawn from May to August. London fly-overs cost £165. The flight lasts around one hour, but allow four hours including take-off, landing and recovery.

AEROMEGA HELICOPTERS
☎ 01708-688361; www.aeromega.co.uk; ⊖ Debden, then taxi to Stapleford Aerodrome, Essex

Thirty-minute flights over London two Sundays every month for £120 per person. Hire an entire four-seater helicopter for £445.

CABAIR HELICOPTERS
☎ 8953 4411; www.cabair.com; Elstree Aerodrome, Borehamwood, Hertfordshire

Offers the same service as Aeromega at £149 every Sunday, and some Saturdays.

Boat

Travelcard holders (p405) get one-third off all boating fares listed here. In addition to these tours, there are plenty of dinner cruises. Try www.thames-dinner-cruises.co.uk (prices start at £20 per person).

BATEAUX LONDON – CATAMARAN CRUISERS LTD
☎ 7987 1185, 7925 2215; www.bateauxlondon.com; 'Hopper' River Pass adult/child £9/4.50; ☷ every 30min 10am-5.30pm Apr-Oct, 6 times daily 10am-5.30pm Nov-Mar

Services link Embankment, Waterloo (London Eye), Bankside (Tate Modern), Tower and Greenwich Piers, for £3 to £8 (adult) or £1.50 to £6 (child) return. Dinner and party cruises are also offered; see the website.

CIRCULAR CRUISES
☎ 7936 2033; www.crownriver.com; adult/5-15yr/student & senior/family £6.80/3.40/5.80/20; ☷ every 30-40min 11am-7pm Apr-Sep, 11am, 12.20pm, 1.40pm & 3pm Oct-May

Vessels travel east from Westminster Pier to St Katharine's Pier near the Tower of London, calling at London Bridge and Embankment Piers, plus, on weekends in summer, at Festival and Bankside Piers. Fares are cheaper between just two stages (eg Westminster to/from London Bridge costs £5.60/2.80/4.60/16).

CITY CRUISES
☎ 7740 0400; www.citycruises.com; River Red Rover Day Ticket adult/child/family £9/4.50/22; ☷ every 20-40min 10am-6pm

Year-round ferries between Westminster and Greenwich, sometimes requiring a change at Tower Bridge. There are later departures in summer (June to August) and fewer sailings in winter (November to March).

LONDON WATERBUS COMPANY
information ☎ 7482 2660, bookings ☎ 7482 2550; www.londonwaterbus.com; 2 Middle Yard, Camden Lock NW1; adult/child one way £4.80/3.10, return £6.20/4; ☷ 10am-5pm Apr-Oct, 10am-3pm or 4pm Sat & Sun Nov-Mar, services every hr or 30min on Sun Apr-Oct; ⊖ Camden Town

Runs 90-minute trips on Regent's Canal in an enclosed barge between Camden Lock and Little Venice, passing through Regent's Park and London Zoo.

TATE-TO-TATE BOAT
www.tate.org; adult single £4; ☷ every 40min 10am-5.30pm

The Damien Hirst–painted boat not only visits both Tate museums, but stops at the London Eye, plus Blackfriars and Savoy Piers during the week. Discounts are available for Travelcard holders, seniors, students, and children.

THAMES RIVER SERVICES
☎ 7930 4097; www.westminsterpier.co.uk; adult/child/senior/family one way £6.80/3.40/5.60/18.70, return £8.60/4.30/7.10/23.60; ☷ every 30min 10am-4pm or 5pm Apr-Oct

These cruise boats leave Westminster Pier for Greenwich, stopping at the Tower of London. Every second service continues on from Greenwich to the Thames Barrier. The last boats return from Greenwich about 5pm (6pm in summer).

WESTMINSTER PASSENGER SERVICES ASSOCIATION
☎ 7930 2062; www.wpsa.co.uk; Kew adult/child/senior/family one way £10.50/5.25/7/26.25, return £16.50/8.25/11/41.25, journey time 1½hr; Hampton Court adult/child/senior/family one way £13.50/6.75/9/33.75, return $19.50/9.75/13/48.75, journey time 3hr; ☷ 4 daily 10.30am-2pm Apr-Oct

These boats go upriver from Westminster Pier to the Royal Botanic Gardens at Kew and on to Hampton Court Palace. It's possible to get off the boats at Richmond in July and August. While an enjoyable excursion, there's less to see en route compared to the trip east.

Bus

Big Bus Tours (☎ 7233 9533; www.bigbus.co.uk; adult/child/family £20/8/48), **London Pride** (☎ 0170 863 1122; www.londonpride.co.uk; adult/child/family £15/9/50) and **Original London Sightseeing Tour** (☎ 8877 1722; www.theoriginaltour.com; adult/child £16/10) all offer commentary and the chance to get off at each sight and rejoin the tour on a later bus. Tickets are valid for 24 hours.

Specialist

LONDON DUCK TOURS
☎ 7928 3132; www.londonducktours.co.uk; adult/child/concession/family £17.50/12/14/53; ⊖ Westminster
Amphibious craft based on D-Day landing vehicles depart from outside County Hall and cruise the streets of central London before making a dramatic descent into the Thames at Vauxhall.

LONDON OPEN HOUSE
☎ 7267 7644; www.londonopenhouse.org; 39-51 Highgate Rd NW5
Besides the annual weekend event, sometime in September, when more than 500 buildings are open to the public, there are architectural and school-group tours.

BLACK TAXI TOURS OF LONDON
☎ 7935 9363; www.blacktaxitours.co.uk; 2hr for up to 5 passengers £70
Hire your own black cab with a trained tour guide at the wheel (although you are likely to hear equally amusing tales from any other cabbie in the city).

Walking

ASSOCIATION OF PROFESSIONAL TOURIST GUIDES
APTG; ☎ 7403 2962; www.aptg.org.uk
Hire a prestigious blue-badge guide – these guides have studied for two years and passed written exams to do their job.

LONDON WALKS
☎ 7624 3978; www.walks.com; adult/concession £5.50/4.50
A huge array of walks, including Jack the Ripper tours at 7.30pm daily and 3pm Saturday, and Sherlock Holmes Tours at 1.30pm Tuesday & 2.30pm Thursday.

MYSTERY TOURS
☎ 0795 738 8280; www.tourguides.org.uk; adult/concession £5/4
Tour Jack the Ripper's old haunts at 7pm on Wednesday, Friday and Sunday and visit Haunted London at 7pm on Tuesday. Meet outside Aldgate tube station.

THE WEST END

Eating p232-8; Drinking p277-80; Shopping p335-9; Sleeping p356-9

Culturally, socially and physically, this is London's heart and the place where everything happens in the city. First-time visitor, regular or resident, you'll inevitably find yourself walking its animated, glamorous streets for much of your time in the city and, love it or loathe it, knowing the area is essential to experiencing life in the British capital. The West End is a vague

term (any Londoner you meet will give you their own take on which neighbourhoods it does and doesn't include), and its component areas are often startlingly unlike one another.

Undeniably at its centre, historic and bohemian Soho attracts party animals of all persuasions. Its historic alleyways and busy streets include some of the best restaurants, shops, bars and clubs in the capital. On the other side of Shaftesbury Ave this gives way to the bright lights and exotic smells of Chinatown and the squalor of Leicester Sq, the latter being one large tourist trap until you get to magnificent Trafalgar Sq. East of Charing Cross there's shoppers' paradise Covent Garden, while to the north are Bloomsbury and Fitzrovia, two of the city's intellectual villages which, despite the ever greater encroachment of Soho, remain quiet and surprisingly uncommercial oases in the middle of the city. Dominated by a contradictory blend of consumerism and culture, the West End is the perfect place to begin your exploration of London in all its manifold contradictions.

On the Buses

If the red double-decker buses you see on London's streets don't quite resemble those you remember from pictures, there's a simple explanation. The last of the original – and best – red buses was taken out of everyday service in 2005. 'Routemasters' were designed in the 1950s specifically for London's narrow streets, but today's buses come from Sweden and Germany. Whereas the old-fashioned Routemaster had a separate driver's cab, a conductor selling tickets and an open running board at the back – great for catching your bus at the last minute – the new buses only have a driver, whose job is to open and close doors, take passenger fares and, in between all this, navigate the bus through crowded London streets.

Critics of these newer models point out how this slows public transport journeys and complain about the fewer seats. Worst of all, the new buses lack the grace and style of their predecessors. As Jonathan Glancey, the *Guardian*'s architecture critic, describes it in excoriating detail, the newer 'mobile shoeboxes' have 'muddled floorplans, décor designed as if by an underachieving ape let loose with a box of crayons, an ear-splitting engine, hissing air-brakes, sticky, plastic-backed seats, some facing backwards to induce nausea, and lighting swiped from an FBI interrogation room'.

So why did the Routemasters have to make way for this? There were a couple of serious issues. They provided no access for people with disabilities, and two or three people died every year falling off the open running board. Transport bosses say the buses were at the end of their working life. However, Routemaster devotees – and the Routemaster inspires many devotees – asked why the custom British design couldn't have been modified, instead of buying off-the-peg solutions from overseas. Teething troubles, including spontaneous fires, with the new, single-decker 'bendy buses' only fuelled the feeling of discontent.

After the last bus left proper service, two 'heritage routes' were announced, using the Routemasters as a tourist attraction. At the time of writing, the exact routes were yet to be mapped out, so check with **Visit London** (☎ 0870 156 6366, 7234 5800; www.visitlondon.com).

If you wish to do your own little tour on a scheduled bus, try one of the following services:

- No 8 – from Victoria, via Hyde Park Corner and Oxford St to East London
- Nos 9 and 10 – from Hammersmith, through Kensington and Knightsbridge, then down to the Strand (No 9) or to north London (No 10)
- No 19 – from King's Rd, Chelsea, past Hyde Park, through Piccadilly and north through Holborn to Islington and Finsbury Park
- No 24 – from Pimlico and Victoria through Westminster and Trafalgar Sq, straight up through Camden to near Hampstead Heath
- RV1 – from Covent Garden to Tower Bridge, via the Royal Festival Hall, the London Eye, the Tate Modern and the Oxo Tower.

SOHO

The quaint urban village that forms a square between Shaftesbury Ave, Regent St, Oxford St and Charing Cross Rd is London's core. It's known as Soho, an old hunting cry from Tudor times, when the neighbourhood was in the countryside outside the walls of the medieval city and a favoured recreation ground for Henry VIII. Here, despite the inevitable crowds and numerous tourist traps, you'll find some of the city's most exciting restaurants, bars, shops and attractions.

With its many pedestrianised streets, distinctive shops, quaint buildings, atmospheric laneways, fashion credentials, gay magnetism, exuberant cafés, lively boozers and late-night action you'd be forgiven for thinking the place is maintained for the benefit of the tourists (à la Covent Garden). But its irrepressible spirit is largely down to the 5000-strong community that lives here, the thousands of media sorts who work here and the multitudes that come for fun and games after dark. In fact, you get the distinct impression that they couldn't give a damn about the tourists, although they're more than welcome to join in.

Wardour St divides Soho neatly in two halves; high Soho to the east, and low or West Soho opposite. Old Compton St is the de facto main high street and the gayest street in London. The West End's only fruit 'n' veg market is on atmospheric Berwick St. Carnaby St, the epicentre of 1960s fashion, has thoroughly recovered from decades of tourist tack and the surrounding streets are now home to some of Soho's hippest shopping.

The history of Soho has been one of immigration. In the 17th century, after the Great Fire levelled much of the city, residential development began with an influx of Greek and Huguenot refugees. In the 18th century, when the well-to-do moved to Mayfair, they were replaced by more immigrants (particularly Italian and Chinese), artisans and radicals. Writers and artists were soon drawn to the cosmopolitan vibe, and the overcrowded area became a centre for entertainment, with restaurants, taverns and coffee houses springing up.

It got even livelier in the 20th century when another wave of European immigrants settled in, and Soho was a bona fide bohemian enclave for two decades after WWII. Ronnie Scott's famous club on Gerrard St provided Soho's jazz soundtrack from the 1950s, while the likes of Jimi Hendrix, the Rolling Stones and Pink Floyd did their early gigs at the legendary Marquee club, which used to be on Wardour St. Soho had long been known for its seediness but when the hundreds of prostitutes who served the Square Mile were forced off the streets and into shop windows, it became the city's red-light district and a centre for porn, strip joints and bawdy drinking clubs. Gay liberation soon followed, and by the 1980s Soho was the hub of London's gay scene, as it remains today. The neighbourhood has a real sense of community, best absorbed on a weekend morning when Soho is at its most village-like.

DEAN STREET Map p450
Karl Marx and his family lived hand to mouth at 28 Dean St, above **Quo Vadis** restaurant (which has its own colourful history – see p233), from 1851 to 1856. The founder of communism spent his days in the British Library reading room and didn't seem all that interested in earning any money to help his wife raise their family. Three of their children died of pneumonia, but they were eventually saved from the poorhouse by a huge inheritance left to them by Mrs Marx' family, after which they upped sticks and moved to the more salubrious surroundings of Primrose Hill. Today it's a lively street lined with shops, bars and many other consumer outlets that no doubt would have given Marx indigestion.

LONDON TROCADERO Map p450
☎ 0906 888 1100; www.troc.co.uk; 1 Piccadilly Circus W1; admission free; ⏰ 10am-1am; ⊖ Piccadilly Circus
This huge and soulless indoor amusement arcade has six levels of high-tech, high-cost fun for youngsters, along with cinemas, US-themed restaurants and bars for anyone else with nothing better to do (or nowhere else to take shelter from the rain). A Sex Museum in the basement was under construction at the time of writing and expected to be open by 2006. Dubbed a 'reproductive health and sexuality museum', its exact remit is unknown, although given its location in Soho, the smart money is on it being more than a little titillating.

PICCADILLY CIRCUS Map p450
Although this traffic-snarled junction is not the most pleasant place to linger, it's been a popular meeting spot for centuries, and for some reason its giant neon signs always make our hearts go giddy with the excitement of being back in London. The hub was named after the stiff collars ('picadils') that were the sartorial staple of the early 17th century (and were the making of a nearby tailor's fortune).

Today it's best known for a lousy statue, the **Angel of Christian Charity**. Dedicated to the philanthropist and social reformer Lord Shaftesbury, it was derided when unveiled in 1893 and the sculptor skulked into early retirement. Down the years the angel has been mistaken for Eros, the God of Love, and the misnomer has stuck. It's a handy meeting place for tourists, although most Londoners cringe at that notion. The charging **Horses of Helios** statue at the edge of Piccadilly and Haymarket is a much cooler place to convene, apparently.

Running off the circus, Coventry St (possibly the most unpleasantly touristy street in the entire city) leads to the even less attractive Leicester Sq, Shaftesbury Ave to the heart of the West End's theatreland, and Piccadilly itself to the sanctuary of Green Park. Regent St runs north to Oxford St and south to the Britain Visitor Centre, parallel to Haymarket, which passes New Zealand House, the former Carlton Hotel where the Vietnamese revolutionary leader Ho Chi Minh (1890–1969) worked as a waiter in 1913. Have a look down Lower Regent St for a glimpse of glorious Westminster.

Top Five – the West End
- **National Gallery** (p99)
- **Trafalgar Square** (p98)
- **Somerset House** (p103)
- **British Museum** (p107)
- **National Portrait Gallery** (p100)

REGENT STREET Map p450

Regent St is the border separating the hoi polloi of Soho and the high-society residents of Mayfair. It was originally designed by John Nash as a ceremonial route, linking the Prince Regent's long-demolished city dwelling with the 'wilds' of Regent's Park, and was conceived by the architect as a grand thoroughfare that would be the centrepiece of a new grid for this part of town. Alas, it was never to be – too many toes were being stepped on and Nash had to downscale his plan. There are some elegant shop fronts that look older than their 1920s origins (when the street was remodelled) but, as in the rest of London, the chain stores are gradually taking over. Two distinguished retail outlets are **Hamleys** (p336), London's premier toy and game store, and the upmarket department store **Liberty** (p337).

COVENT GARDEN & LEICESTER SQUARE

Covent Garden, the heart of tourist London, was developed about 30 years ago as a respectable alternative to Soho. It is dominated by the piazza that gives the area its name, an elegant and easy-going tourist mecca with boutiques, stalls, pubs and buskers. Sure, it's a tourist trap – Londoners go out of their way to avoid it – but it's a pleasant place to walk around all the same and one of the few parts of London where pedestrians rule over cars. Be aware though, it can get hopelessly overcrowded in summer.

The area around the piazza also features hot spots for street fashion and hip homewares with lots of creative and exciting stores. Neal St is no longer the grooviest strip, although the little roads cutting across it maintain its legendary style. Neal's Yard is a strange and charming little courtyard featuring overpriced vegetarian eateries. Floral St is where swanky designers such as Paul Smith have stores, while a block north on Long Acre you'll find St Martins fashion college (p19), the incubator for some of the world's best designers.

The area took shape in the 17th century when Inigo Jones was asked to convert a vegetable field into a piazza, and it soon became a focal point for London society. Writers such as Pepys, Fielding and Boswell used to saunter down of an evening looking for some action. By Victorian times a bustling fruit and veg market – immortalised in *My Fair Lady* – dominated the piazza. Whether it was the market, the porters or the general hullabaloo, the tone of the neighbourhood was soon lowered. Coffee houses gave way to brothels, and lawlessness became commonplace, leading to the formation of a volunteer police force known as the Bow Street Runners (p85). In 1897 Oscar Wilde was charged with gross indecency in Bow St magistrate's court. The market was relocated in 1974 when the piazza was transformed into what you see today. To one side of the piazza is the Royal Opera House, ruthlessly yet brilliantly rebuilt in the late 1990s to make it one of the world's most superb singing venues.

The area of St Giles – around St Giles High St – had perhaps the worst reputation of any London quarter. It was first known as the site of the leprosy hospital established in 1101, and later had the dubious distinction of being the place were the condemned stopped for a last drink on their way to be executed at Tyburn (see St Giles-in-the-Fields, p103). As if its association with lepers, prisoners and social outcasts wasn't enough, it was within the boundaries of St Giles that the Great Plague of 1665 took hold. In Victorian times it was London's worst slum, oft name-checked by Dickens. Forbidding streets and smacked-out drug users make at least parts of the area feel like things haven't changed much.

TRAFALGAR SQUARE Map p452

In many ways this is the centre of London, where many great rallies and marches take place, where the new year is ushered in by tens of thousands of revellers, and where locals congregate for anything from communal open-air cinema to protesting against the war in Iraq. The great square was neglected over many years, ringed with gnarling traffic and given over to flocks of pigeons that would dive-bomb anyone with a morsel of food on their person. But not any more, oh no.

One of the first things Mayor Ken Livingstone did when he got his gown, comically, was take aim at the pesky pigeons and ban people from feeding them. Once he had reclaimed the square on behalf of the people of London, he embarked on a bold and imaginative scheme to transform it into the kind of space John Nash had intended when he designed it in the early 19th century. Traffic was banished from the northern flank in front of the National Gallery, and a new pedestrian plaza built. The front of the National Gallery itself has been dolled up, with a new façade and entrance hall, and there are plans to expand the summer programme of cultural events to showcase the city's multiculturalism.

The pedestrianisation has made it easier to appreciate not only the square but also the splendid buildings flanking it; the National Gallery, the National Portrait Gallery and the eye-catching church of St Martin-in-the-Fields. The ceremonial **Pall Mall** runs southwest from the top of the square. To the southwest stands **Admiralty Arch** (p129), with the Mall leading to Buckingham Palace beyond it. To the west is **Canada House** (1827), designed by Robert Smirke. The 52m-high **Nelson's Column** (upon which the admiral surveys his fleet of ships to the southwest) has stood in the centre of the square since 1843 and commemorates the admiral's victory over Napoleon off Cape Trafalgar in Spain in 1805. Many visitors, however, seem less interested in this history than clambering on the backs of the lions at Nelson's feet.

Several years back the Mayor tried to erect a statue of Nelson Mandela on the north terrace but a Westminster committee decided, controversially, that it was inappropriate. Apparently a memorial to the revered South African was less palatable than that of George Washington, the man who denied England its colonies in the New World, which also stands in the square, near the National Gallery.

Three of the four plinths located at the square's corners are occupied by notables, including King George IV on horseback, General Charles Napier and Sir Henry Havelock. One, originally intended for a statue of William IV, has largely remained vacant for the past 150 years. Now, however, the Fourth Plinth Project (not, as it initially sounds, a prog-rock group) has determined that works of contemporary art will be erected here, according to a changing rota. At the start of 2006, Thomas Schütte's *Hotel for the Birds* (self-explanatory) will be open for business, but in the summer it's scheduled to be replaced by Marc Quinn's *Alison Lapper Pregnant,* a statue of a Thalidomide-affected woman 'with child'. After that, the commission responsible is accepting proposals. So if you've got any ideas…

NATIONAL GALLERY Map p452
☎ 7747 2885; www.nationalgallery.org.uk; Trafalgar Sq WC2; admission free to permanent exhibits, prices vary for temporary exhibitions; 🕙 10am-6pm Thu-Tue, 10am-9pm Wed; ⊖ Charing Cross; ♿

With more than 2000 Western European paintings on display, the National Gallery is one of the largest galleries in the world. But it's the

The National Gallery (above)

quality of the works, and not the quantity, that impresses most. Almost five million people visit each year, keen to see seminal paintings from every important epoch in the history of art, including works by Giotto, Leonardo da Vinci, Michelangelo, Titian, Velázquez, van Gogh and Renoir, just to name a few. Although it can get ridiculously busy in here, the galleries are spacious, sometimes even sedate, and it's never so bad that you can't appreciate the works (like at some big museums in Continental Europe). That said, weekday mornings and Wednesday evenings (after 6pm) are the best times to visit, as the crowds are small. If you have the time to make multiple visits, focus on one section at a time to fully appreciate the astonishing collection.

The size and layout can be confusing, so make sure you pick up a free gallery plan at the entrance. To see the art in chronological order, start with the relatively modern Sainsbury Wing on the gallery's western side, which houses paintings from 1260 to 1510. This is where you'll also find the Micro gallery, a dozen computer terminals on which you can explore the pictorial database, find the location of your favourite works or create your own personalised tour. In the 16 rooms of the Sainsbury Wing, you can explore the Renaissance through paintings by Giotto, Leonardo da Vinci, Botticelli, Raphael and Titian, among others.

The High Renaissance (1510–1600) is covered in the West Wing, where Michelangelo, Titian, Correggio, El Greco and Bronzino hold court, while Rubens, Rembrandt and Caravaggio can be found in the North Wing (1600–1700). The most crowded part of the gallery – and for good reason – is likely to be the East Wing (1700–1900) and particularly the many works of the impressionists and postimpressionists, including van Gogh, Gauguin, Cézanne, Monet, Degas and Renoir. Although it hardly stands out in such exalted company, the impressive display featuring 18th-century British landscape artists Gainsborough, Constable and Turner is also well worth checking out.

Temporary exhibitions – for which you normally have to pay, and often even book in advance – go on show in the basement of the Sainsbury Wing and are often outstanding.

The highlights listed in the boxed text (right) include many of the most important works, but if you want to immerse yourself in this pool of riches rather than just skim across the surface, borrow a themed or comprehen-

National Gallery Highlights

- *Pentecost* – Giotto
- *Virgin and Child with St Anne and St John the Baptist* – Leonardo da Vinci
- *Arnolfini Wedding* – van Eyck
- *Venus and Mars* – Botticelli
- *The Ansidei Madonna* – Raphael
- *The Madonna of the Pinks* – Raphael
- *Le Chapeau de Paille* – Rubens
- *Charles I* – Van Dyck
- *Bacchus and Ariadne* – Titian
- *The Entombment* – Michelangelo
- *Rokeby Venus* – Velásquez
- *The Supper at Emmaus* – Caravaggio
- *Bathers* – Cézanne
- *Sunflowers* – van Gogh
- *The Water Lily Pond* – Monet
- *Miss La La* – Degas
- *The Hay-Wain* – Constable
- *The Fighting Temeraire* – Turner

sive audioguide (£4 donation recommended) from the Central Hall. Free one-hour introductory **guided tours** leave from the information desk in the Sainsbury Wing daily at 11.30am and 2.30pm, with an extra tour at 6.30pm on Wednesday. There are also special trails and activity sheets for children.

The handy Gallery Café is in the basement of the West Wing and the fine restaurant Crivelli's Garden is on the 1st floor of the Sainsbury Wing.

NATIONAL PORTRAIT GALLERY
Map p452

☎ 7306 0055; www.npg.org.uk; St Martin's Pl WC2; admission free, prices vary for temporary exhibitions; ☒ 10am-6pm, to 9pm Thu & Fri; ☻ Charing Cross/ Leicester Sq; ☒

One hundred and fifty years old in 2006, the National Portrait Gallery is a fantastic institution that puts faces to names over the last five centuries of British history. Despite being more about history than art, it's a thoroughly modern museum with an exciting and playful approach to its potentially rather fusty remit.

The gallery houses a primary collection of some 10,000 works, which are regularly rotated. The pictures are displayed in chronological order from top to bottom. An elevator whizzes you up from the entrance hall to the top floor, where the early Tudors line the walls of an Elizabethan-style Long Room. Among them is the museum's first acquisition, the famous 'Chandos' portrait of Shakespeare. Despite the recent discovery that the Royal Shakespeare Company's Flower portrait of the Bard was a 19th-century forgery, the National Portrait Gallery still believes this one to have been painted during Shakespeare's lifetime. Tests are still ongoing, however, and the topic remains in the limelight, with 'Searching for Shakespeare' – the first time ever that the six 'contender' portraits of the man have been displayed together – an integral part of the gallery's 150th anniversary year.

Beyond the Bard look out for the cravat-wearing Duke of Monmouth, the 14th illegitimate son of Charles II. Soon after the Catholic James II beheaded the duke in 1685, somebody remembered that, as a royal personage, the duke should have had a portrait. The Royal Surgeon was summoned to stitch the duke's head back on and he was propped up in front of a painter who had 24 hours to capture the essence of his subject before it 'went off'.

On the 1st floor you'll find portraits of the current royal family, many of which, particularly the more recent ones, are laughably bad. However, you might be lucky and see one of the two portraits of the Queen made by Andy Warhol.

The ground floor will be of most interest to tourists, focusing as it does on contemporary figures we're more likely to be familiar with, and using a variety of media, including sculpture and photography. The only problem down here is that the artists seem to be getting ideas above their station, and some of the works say more about them than the subject. Among the most popular of these is Sam Taylor-Wood's *David*, a video-portrait of David Beckham asleep after football training. (There's often a throng of women dreamily milling around this area of the gallery for some reason.)

Audioguides (a £3 donation is suggested) highlight some 200 portraits and allow you to hear the voices of some of the people portrayed. The Portrait Café and bookshop are in the basement and the **Portrait restaurant** (p235) is on the top floor, offering some superb views towards Westminster.

On a traffic island outside the entrance to the National Portrait Gallery is a **statue of Edith Cavell** (1865–1915), a British nurse who helped Allied soldiers escape from Brussels during WWI and was consequently executed by the Germans.

ST MARTIN-IN-THE-FIELDS Map p452

☎ 7766 1100, for brass-rubbing ☎ 7930 9306, for concert box office ☎ 7839 8362; www.stmartin-in-the-fields.org; Trafalgar Sq WC2; admission free; ☺ 8am-6.30pm, brass-rubbing centre 10am-6pm Mon-Sat, noon-6pm Sun (pay for materials); ⊖ Charing Cross

The 'royal parish church' is a delightful fusion of classical and Baroque styles that was completed by James Gibbs (1682–1754) in 1726. Its wedding-cake spire is enchantingly floodlit at night and looks particularly fetching since the redevelopment of the square. The churchyard, now home to a fairly tacky souvenir stall, contains the graves of 18th-century artists Reynolds and Hogarth.

The pleasant if unremarkable interior has been the site of many royal baptisms, while the crypt is famous for its café. But perhaps the biggest draw at this acoustically gifted church, where Handel and Mozart once jammed, is the calendar of classical concerts. There are free lunchtime recitals by students Monday, Tuesday and Friday at 1.05pm and candlelit performances at 7.30pm throughout the year (£6 to £20).

COVENT GARDEN Map p452

London's first planned square is now the exclusive reserve of tourists who flock here to shop in the quaint old arcades, be entertained by buskers, pay through the nose at outdoor cafés and bars, and occasionally have their pockets picked. On its western flank is **St Paul's Church** (☎ 7836 5221; www.actorschurch.org; Bedford St WC2; admission free; ☺ 8.30am-5.30pm Mon-Fri, 9am-1pm Sun). The Earl of Bedford, the man who had commissioned Inigo Jones to design the piazza, asked for the simplest possible church, basically no more than a barn. The architect responded by producing 'the handsomest barn in England'. It has long been regarded as the actors' church for its associations with the theatre, and contains memorials to the likes of Charlie Chaplin and Vivien Leigh. The first Punch and Judy show took place in front of it in 1662.

LONDON'S TRANSPORT MUSEUM
Map p452

☎ 7379 6344; www.ltmuseum.co.uk; Covent Garden Piazza WC2; adult/child/concession £5.95/2.50/4.50; ☺ 10am-6pm Sat-Thu, 11am-6pm Fri; ⊖ Covent Garden; ♿

Tucked into a corner of Covent Garden, this unexpected delight explores how London made the transition from streets choked with horse-drawn carriages to streets choked with horse-powered cars. It conserves and explains the city's transport heritage and is full of displays from the oldest surviving horse-drawn tram to Tube simulators and the original London Underground map (p466). Its hands-on, jump-on and full-on exhibits are popular with all ages, there's an interactive trail specifically for the kiddies and there are often imaginative temporary exhibitions. The **Museum Depot** at Acton Town contains the 370,000 items that can't be displayed in the museum proper, and can be visited by **guided tour** (once a month; adult/concession £10/8.50) and on occasional **open weekends** (£6.95/4.95; check website for details of both). You can get your Mind the Gap boxer shorts and knickers at the shop.

ROYAL OPERA HOUSE Map p452

☎ 7304 4000; www.royaloperahouse.org; Bow St WC2; adult/concession £8/7; ⌚ tours 10.30am, 12.30pm & 2.30pm Mon-Sat; ⊖ Covent Garden; ♿

On the northeastern flank of the piazza is the gleaming, redeveloped – and practically new – Royal Opera House. Unique 'behind the scenes' tours take you through the venue, and let you experience the planning, excitement and hissy fits that take place before a performance at one of the world's busiest opera houses. As it's a working theatre, plans can change so you'd best call ahead. Of course, the best way to enjoy it is by seeing a performance (see p324).

PHOTOGRAPHERS' GALLERY

Map p452

☎ 7831 1772; www.photonet.org.uk; 5 & 8 Great Newport St WC2; admission free; ⌚ 11am-6pm Mon-Sat, 12-6pm Sun; ⊖ Leicester Sq/Covent Garden/ Charing Cross; ♿

So small that it uses the walls of its neighbouring café as additional exhibition space, this cutting-edge gallery punches well above its weight in influence. Past winners of its prestigious Photography Prize (held January to March every year) include Richard Billingham, Luc Delahaye, Andreas Gursky, Boris Mikhailov and Juergen Teller. The gallery is always exhibiting something thought-provoking, while the shop is an excellent place to browse for coffee-table books, style magazines and quirky gifts.

LEICESTER SQUARE Map p452

Enormous cinemas, nightclubs and a colossal comedy venue dominate this cheerless, disagreeable square, which is badly in need of a mayor-driven makeover (reported to be on the cards). Although it is central, pedestrianised and stacked with options for entertainment (Britain's glitzy film premieres take place here), it still feels very much like a place to pass through, quickly, rather than a destination.

It's obviously a bit of a comedown since the 19th century, when the square was so fashionable that artists Joshua Reynolds and William

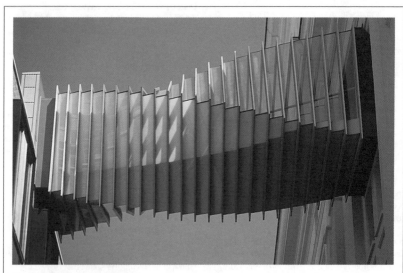

The Royal Opera House (above)

Hogarth chose to hang their hats here. There's a small statue of Charlie Chaplin to one side, and plaques in the ground (not that you'd ever be able to see them for the crowds) list the distances from central London to the capitals of various Commonwealth countries.

CHINATOWN Map p452
Immediately north of Leicester Sq – but a world away in atmosphere – are Lisle and Gerrard Sts, the focal point for London's Chinese community and the nearest thing London has to a 24-hour zone. Although not as big as Chinatowns in many other cities – it's just two streets really – this is a lively quarter with Chinese street signs, red lanterns, dragon-adorned moon gates and more restaurants than you could shake a chopstick at. To see it at its effervescent best, time your visit with Chinese New Year in late January/early February (p10). Do beware that the quality of food here varies enormously – it pays to get recommendations (see p234) as many places are mediocre establishments aimed squarely at the tourist market.

ST GILES-IN-THE-FIELDS Map p452
☎ 7240 2532; 60 St Giles High St; ⏰ 9am-4pm Mon-Fri; ⊖ Tottenham Court Rd
Another church built in what used to be countryside between the City and Westminster, St Giles isn't much to look at but has an interesting history. The current structure is the third to stand on the site of an original chapel built in the 12th century to serve the leprosy hospital. Until 1547, when the hospital closed, prisoners on their way to be executed at Tyburn stopped at the church gate and quaffed from St Giles's Bowl, a large cup of soporific ale and their last refreshment. From 1650 they were also brought back here to be buried in the church grounds. An interesting relic in the church is the pulpit that was used for 40 years by John Wesley, the founder of Methodism.

THEATRE MUSEUM Map p452
☎ 7943 4700; www.theatremuseum.org; Russell St WC2; admission free; ⏰ 10am-6pm Tue-Sun; ⊖ Covent Garden
Conveniently located in the heart of theatreland, this museum is dedicated to British drama from Tudor times to the late 20th century, and also has increasingly impressive exhibitions on opera and ballet. There's a vast collection of costumes, stage sets, painting, posters and assorted memorabilia in the mostly underground space, and the overall effect can be quite disorientating unless you've got a special interest in things thespian. If you don't, focus on a few specific displays – like the Wind in the Willows From Page to Stage exhibition, or profiles of famous actors – and you'll probably get more from your visit. Kids, however, won't have any problems getting into it, as there are lots of activities such as theatre make-up demonstrations and craft workshops.

HOLBORN & THE STRAND
This area – compacted here for convenience's sake – comprises the rough square wedged between the City to the east, Covent Garden to the west, High Holborn to the north and the Thames to the south. Past glory and prominence are its key characteristics: Fleet St was the former home of British journalism while the Strand, connecting Westminster with the City, used to be one of the most important streets in London and was lined with fabulous town houses built by local luminaries and aristocrats. This rich history is only vaguely evident today, but while much of this pocket is soulless and commercial, it is saved by some architectural gems, a few splendid galleries and the calm, green recesses of the charming Inns of Court, the cradle of English law. Behind the Strand run the Victoria Embankment Gardens, a lovely place for a picnic, a stroll and splendid views across the Thames to the recharged South Bank.

Fleet St was named after the River Fleet, which in the 17th and 18th centuries was a virtual sewer filled with entrails and other grisly bits from Smithfield Market (p124) upriver. Holborn was named after one of its tributaries and both were filled in the late 18th century. The area was a notorious slum in Victorian times and although efforts were made to smarten it up in the early 20th century, it was probably no great loss when the Germans flattened much of it during WWII, after which the current business moved in.

SOMERSET HOUSE Map p452
☎ 7845 4600; www.somerset-house.org.uk; ⏰ the House 10am-6pm, Great Court 7.30-11pm; ⊖ Temple/ Covent Garden
Passing beneath the arch towards this splendid Palladian masterpiece, it's hard to believe that the magnificent courtyard in front of you, with its 55 dancing fountains, was a car park for tax collectors up until a spectacular refurbishment in 2000! William Chambers designed the house in 1775 for royal societies and it now contains three fabulous museums. The courtyard is

transformed into a lively ice rink in winter and used for a mixed programme of concerts in summer. Behind the house, there's a lovely sunny terrace and café overlooking the embankment.

Immediately to your right as you enter the grounds of Somerset House from the Strand, you'll find the **Courtauld Institute of Art** (☎ 7848 2526; www.courtauld.ac.uk; adult/concession/UK students £5/4/free, free 10am-2pm Mon; ☉ 10am-6pm), a superb gallery connected to the Courtauld Institute of Arts, Britain's foremost academy of art history. If you can't face the crowds at the National Gallery (and even if you can), treat yourself to an unhampered stroll between the walls of this wonderful place, lined with works from the most important old masters, impressionists and postimpressionists. The collection was recently augmented with a series of long-term loans, and now counts Rubens, Botticelli, Cranach, Cézanne, Degas, Renoir, Manet, Monet, Matisse, Gauguin, van Gogh and Toulouse-Lautrec among its contributors. There are **lunchtime talks** on specific works or themes from the collection at 1.15pm every Tuesday and a delightful little café provides sustenance.

The vaults beneath the South Terrace boast one of the finest Thames views and are home to the **Gilbert Collection of Decorative Arts** (Map pp448–9; ☎ 7420 9400; www.gilbert-collection.org .uk; adult/concession/UK students £5/4/free; ☉ 10am-6pm), including Italian mosaics, European silver, gold snuffboxes and portrait miniatures bequeathed to Britain in 1996 by Anglo-American businessman and 'magpie' extraordinaire Arthur Gilbert. The part-dazzling, part-gaudy display has been described as the most generous gift ever made to the nation. There are one-hour **guided tours** (adult/concession including admission £6.50/6) each Saturday. Visit two collections on the same day and you can save a quid; see all three and save £2.

Finally, it's usually worth visiting the relatively recent addition of the **Hermitage Rooms** (☎ 7845 4630; www.hermitagerooms.com; adult/concession/UK students £5/4/free; ☉ 10am-6pm). This charming gallery is an outpost of the State Hermitage Museum in St Petersburg (which holds some three million pieces that make up one of the finest art collections in the world). Small but fascinating Russian-themed exhibits from the Hermitage collection revolve every six months. Recent successes included Circling the Square, a display of Russian avant-garde porcelain. The galleries are modelled on those in the Imperial Winter Palace, and there's a live feed to St Petersburg and a short video on the State Hermitage Museum itself to get you in the mood.

ROYAL COURTS OF JUSTICE Map pp448-9
☎ 7936 6000; 460 the Strand; admission free; ☉ 9am-4.30pm Mon-Fri; ⊖ Temple

Where the Strand joins Fleet St, you'll see the entrance to this gargantuan melange of Gothic spires, pinnacles and burnished Portland stone, designed by aspiring cathedral builder GE Street in 1874. (It took so much out of the architect that he died of a stroke shortly before its completion.) Inside the Great Hall there's an exhibition of legal costumes, as well as a list of cases to be heard in court that day. If you like to watch, leave your camera behind and expect airport-like security.

THE STRAND Map pp448-9
At the end of the 12th century, nobles built sturdy stone houses with gardens stretching down to the 'beach' (from the German word *strand*) of the Thames, which connected the City and Westminster, the two centres of power. It was one of the most prestigious places in London in which to live; indeed, the 19th-century prime minister Benjamin Disraeli pronounced it 'the finest street in Europe'.

Well it certainly isn't now; these days the Strand is much less than the sum of its parts. Although it contains hallowed hostelries such as the Savoy and Simpson's-in-the-Strand, and the wonderful Somerset House with all its riches, the street still feels like a bleak, cheerless and none-too-salubrious place. But concentrating on the good things, check out **Twinings** at No 216, a teashop opened by Thomas Twining in 1706 and believed to be the oldest company in the capital still trading on the same site and owned by the same family. The **Wig & Pen Club** at No 229–30 – note the symbolic wigs and pens in the plasterwork – is the only original Strand building to survive the Great Fire of 1666. Otherwise it's a fairly bland place, home to numerous high-street stores and fast-food outlets, although it's also the centre of London philatelic life, with stamp- and coin-collector's mecca **Stanley Gibbons** at No 339.

SIR JOHN SOANE'S MUSEUM
Map p452
☎ 7405 2107; www.soane.org; 13 Lincoln's Inn Fields WC2; admission free; ☉ 10am-5pm Tue-Sat, 6-9pm 1st Tue of month; ⊖ Holborn

One of the most atmospheric and fascinating sights in London, Sir John Soane's Museum is partly a beautiful, bewitching house and partly a small museum brimming with surprising effects and curiosities, representing the taste of

Inns of Court

Clustered around Holborn to the south of Fleet St are the Inns of Court, whose alleys, open spaces and atmosphere provide an urban oasis. All London barristers work from within one of the four inns, and a roll call of former members ranges from Oliver Cromwell to Charles Dickens and from Mahatma Gandhi to Margaret Thatcher. It would take a lifetime working here to grasp the intricacies of the protocols of the inns – they're similar to the Freemasons, and both are 13th-century creations – and it's best to just soak in the dreamy atmosphere, relax, and thank goodness you're not one of the bewigged and deadly serious barristers scurrying about you.

Lincoln's Inn (Map pp448-9; ☎ 7405 1393; Lincoln's Inn Fields WC2; ☿ grounds 9am-6pm Mon-Fri, chapel 12.30-2.30pm Mon-Fri; ⊖ Holborn) Lincoln's Inn is the most attractive of the four inns and has a chapel, pleasant square and picturesque gardens that invite a stroll, especially early or late in the day when the legal eagles aren't flapping about. The court itself, although closed to the public, is visible through the gates and is relatively intact, with original 15th-century buildings, including the Tudor Lincoln's Inn Gatehouse on Chancery Lane. Inigo Jones helped plan the chapel, built in 1623 and pretty well preserved.

Gray's Inn (Map pp448-9; ☎ 7458 7800; Gray's Inn Rd WC1; ☿ grounds 10am-4pm Mon-Fri, chapel 10am-6pm Mon-Fri; ⊖ Holborn/Chancery Lane) This inn – destroyed during WWII, rebuilt and expanded – is less interesting than Lincoln's Inn although the peaceful gardens are still something of a treat. The walls of the original hall absorbed the first ever performance of Shakespeare's *Comedy of Errors*.

Inner Temple (Map pp448-9; ☎ 7353 8559; King's Bench Walk EC4; ⊖ Temple/Blackfriars) Duck under the archway next to Prince Henry's Room and you'll find yourself in the Inner Temple, a sprawling complex of some of the finest buildings on the river. The church (see p106) was originally planned and built by the secretive Knights Templar between 1161 and 1185. At the weekend you'll usually have to enter from the Victoria Embankment.

Staple Inn (Map pp448-9; Holborn; ⊖ Chancery Lane) The 16th-century shop front façade is the main interest at Staple Inn (1589), the last of eight Inns of Chancery whose functions were superseded by the Inns of Court in the 18th century. The buildings, mostly postwar reconstructions, are now occupied by the Institute of Actuaries and aren't actually open to the public, although nobody seems to mind a discreet and considerate look around. On the same side of Holborn but closer to Fetter Lane stood Barnard's Inn, redeveloped in 1991. Pip lived here with Herbert Pocket in Dickens' *Great Expectations*.

celebrated architect and hoarder extraordinaire Sir John Soane (1753–1837).

Soane, the son of a country bricklayer, is most famous for designing the Bank of England. In his work and life, he drew on ideas picked up while on an 18th-century grand tour of Italy. He married into money, which he then poured into building this house and the one next door, which at the time of writing had been acquired by the museum and was expected to form an extension for exhibits in 2006.

The heritage-listed house is largely as it was when Sir John was carted out in a box, and is itself a main part of the attraction. It has a glass dome which brings light right down to the basement, a lantern room filled with statuary, rooms within rooms, and a picture gallery where each painting folds away when pressed to reveal another one behind it. It contains Soane's choice paintings, including Canalettos and Turners, drawings by Christopher Wren and Robert Adam, and the original *Rake's Progress*, William Hogarth's set of cartoon caricatures of late-18th-century London lowlife,

for which a specific gallery was built. Among his more unusual acquisitions are an Egyptian hieroglyphic sarcophagus, an imitation monk's parlour, ancient vases and countless *objets d'art*.

Note that groups of seven or more need to book ahead and are not admitted on Saturdays, which is by far the museum's busiest day. Tours depart at 2.30pm Saturdays (tickets cost £3, and are sold from 2pm). Evenings of the first Tuesday of each month are a choice time to visit as the house is lit by candles and the atmosphere is even more magical.

HUNTERIAN MUSEUM Map pp448-9

☎ 78☉ 6560; www.rcseng.ac.uk/services/museum; Royal College of Surgeons, 35-43 Lincoln's Inn Fields WC2; admission free; ☿ 10am-5pm Tue-Sat; ⊖ Holborn

One of the least known yet most fascinating of London's museums, this curious place is inspired by the work of pioneering surgeon John Hunter (1728–93). The collection of Hunter's anatomical specimens ranges from the skeleton of a 7ft 7in (2.3m) giant to half of mathematician Charles Babbage's brain (one can't help wondering where the other half is) via myriad other beings in jars. It's a lot more than pure gore and curiosity though – animal digestive systems are forensically documented in formaldehyde, including such wonders as the 'hearing organ' of a blue whale. The entire museum was refitted in 2005 in a huge overhaul and its upstairs now includes a display on plastic surgery techniques, which will impress and disgust in equal measure.

TEMPLE CHURCH Map pp448-9

☎ 7353 3470; www.templechurch.com; Temple EC4; admission free; ⏰ usually Wed-Sun approx 2-4pm, but call or email ahead to check; ⊖ Temple/Chancery Lane

This magnificent church lies within the walls of the Temple, built by the legendary Knights Templar, an order of crusading monks founded in the 12th century to protect pilgrims travelling to and from Jerusalem. The order moved here around 1160, abandoning its older headquarters in Holborn. Today the sprawling oasis of fine buildings and pleasant traffic-free green space is home to two Inns of Court (housing the chambers of lawyers practising in the city), the Middle and the Lesser Temple.

The Temple Church has a distinctive design: the Round (consecrated in 1185 and designed to recall the Church of the Holy Sepulchre in Jerusalem) adjoins the Chancel (built in 1240), which is the heart of the modern church. Both parts were severely damaged by a bomb in 1941 and have been lovingly reconstructed. Its most obvious points of interest are the life-size stone effigies of nine knights that lie on the floor of the Round. These include the Earl of Pembroke, who acted as the go-between for King John and the rebel barons, eventually leading to the signing of the Magna Carta in 1215.

In recent years the church has become a site of modern pilgrimage of another kind: readers of *The Da Vinci Code* flock here (see p132). During the week, the easiest access to the church is via Inner Temple Lane, off Fleet St. At the weekends, you'll need to enter from the Victoria Embankment.

ST CLEMENT DANES Map pp448-9

☎ 7242 8282; Strand WC2; ⏰ 8.30am-4.30pm Mon-Fri, 9am-3.30pm Sat, 9am-12.30pm Sun; ⊖ Temple

'Oranges and lemons, say the bells of St Clements.' Remember the nursery rhyme that incorporated the names of London churches and ended with the sleep-inducing line, 'Here comes a chopper to chop off your head'? Well this *isn't* the St Clements referred to in the

Top Five Places of Worship

- St Martin-in-the-Fields (p101)
- St Paul's Cathedral (p110)
- Temple Church (left)
- Westminster Abbey (p133)
- Westminster Cathedral (p138)

first line of that 18th-century verse, although historical fact needn't get in the way of a (feel) good story, and the bells of this church chime the old tune every day at 9am, noon and 3pm. Sir Christopher Wren designed the original building in 1682 but only the walls and a steeple added by James Gibbs in 1719 survived the Luftwaffe, and the church was rebuilt after the war as a memorial to allied airmen. Today it is the chapel of the RAF, and there are some 800 slate badges of different squadrons set into the pavement of the nave.

The statue in front of the church quietly and contentiously commemorates the RAF's Sir Arthur 'Bomber' Harris, who led the bombing raids that obliterated Dresden and killed some 10,000 civilians during WWII.

ST ANDREW HOLBORN Map pp448-9

☎ 7353 3544; Holborn Viaduct EC4; ⏰ 9am-4.30pm Mon-Fri; ⊖ Chancery Lane

This church on the southeastern corner of Holborn Circus, first mentioned in the 10th century, was rebuilt by Wren in 1686 and was the largest of his parish churches. Even though the interior was bombed to smithereens during WWII, much of what you see inside today is original 17th century as it was brought from other churches.

BLOOMSBURY & FITZROVIA

Immediately north of Covent Garden, wonderfully English Bloomsbury is the traditional academic and intellectual heart of London, dominated by its university and many faculties, and home to what must be one of the best museums in the world, the fabulous British Museum. To its north run pleasant Georgian and Victorian streets, which meet at beautiful squares once colonised by the group of artists and intellectuals of the so-called Bloomsbury Group, which included Virginia Woolf and EM Forster. They were merely carrying on a tradition, of sorts, begun by the likes of Charles Dickens, Charles Darwin, William Butler Yeats and George Bernard Shaw, who

Neighbourhoods – The West End

all lived here or hereabouts. The many blue plaques dotted around are testament to the area's former prominence.

After the war, Fitzrovia to the west was a forerunner to Soho as a bohemian enclave populated by struggling artists and writers who frequented its many pubs, particularly the Fitzroy Tavern. It's a bit of a tourist blind spot these days, its one main sight, the 1960s BT Tower – once the highest structure in London – having closed years ago as a result of terrorist threats.

Today Bloomsbury continues to teem with students, bookshops and cafés, while remaining relatively uncommercial. At its heart, London's largest green square, Russell Sq, is looking better than ever with an excellent refit and tidy up a few years ago. It remains a wonderful place for lunch and people watching.

BRITISH MUSEUM Map p452

☎ 7323 8000, tours ☎ 7323 8181; www.thebritish museum.ac.uk; Great Russell St WC1; admission free, £3 donation suggested; ⏱ galleries 10am-5.30pm Sat-Wed & 10am-8.30pm Thu & Fri, Great Court 9am-6pm Sun-Wed & 9am-11pm Thu-Sat; ⊖ Tottenham Court Rd/Russell Sq; ♿

One of the world's oldest and finest museums, the British Museum started in 1749 in the form of royal physician Hans Sloane's 'cabinet of curiosities', which he later bequeathed to the country. The collection now comprises some seven million items, augmented over the years through judicious acquisition and the controversial plundering of empire. It is London's most visited attraction, drawing an average of five million punters each year.

The Great Court of the British Museum

Before launching into the collection, bear in mind that the back entrance at Montague Pl is usually quieter than the porticoed main one off Great Russell St, although nothing nearly as grand. The museum's inner courtyard, hidden from the public for almost 150 years, was covered with a spectacular glass-and-steel roof designed by Norman Foster and opened as the **Great Court** in 2000; it is the largest covered public square in Europe. The stunning design opens up the labyrinth that is the British Museum and makes its mind-bogglingly vast collection just a tad more accessible, although it's still pretty daunting. If you have the luxury of time, you'd be well advised to make a few visits. Don't try and see too much or you'll end up savouring nothing. Relax, take a few deep breaths, peruse the written guides available at the information desk, consider the choice of tours (p108) and decide which part of the collection you want to focus on.

It's an exhaustive and exhilarating stampede through world cultures, with galleries devoted to Egypt, Western Asia, Greece, the Orient, Africa, Italy, the Etruscans, the Romans, prehistoric and Roman Britain and medieval antiquities. To help whet your appetite, the following are some highlights that you should definitely try to catch.

The **Rosetta Stone** (Room 4), discovered in 1799, is written in two forms of ancient Egyptian and Greek and was the key to deciphering Egyptian hieroglyphics, which had stymied scholars up to that time. The **Parthenon Marbles** (Room 18), better known – although it's no longer politically correct – as the Elgin Marbles (see p108), once adorned the walls of the Parthenon on the Acropolis in Athens, and are thought to show the great procession in the temple that took place during the Panathenaic Festival, on the birthday of Athena, one of the grandest events in the Greek world. Their presence here remains controversial as the Greek government is trying to have them returned to Athens; the British Museum's side of the story is told in a leaflet entitled 'Why are the Parthenon Sculptures always in the news?'

Tucked away at the foot of the eastern staircase is the Mexican Gallery (room 27), featuring the 15th-century Aztec **Mosaic Mask of Tezcatlipoca (The Skull of the Smoking Mirror)**, with a turquoise mosaic laid over a human skull. Beyond that, in rooms 33 and 34, the Asian collections contain the wonderful **Amaravati Sculptures** (room 33A), Indian goddesses, dancing Shivas and serene cross-legged Buddhas in copper and stone.

The stunning **Oxus Treasure** (Room 52) is a collection of 7th- to 4th-century BC pieces of Persian gold, which originated in the ancient Persian capital of Persepolis and ended up here after it was rescued from bandits in a Rawalpindi bazaar. The **Lindow Man** (Room 50) is a 1st-century unfortunate who appears to have been smacked on the head with an axe and then garrotted. His remains were preserved in a peat bog until 1984 when a peat-cutting machine sliced him in half. The **Sutton Hoo Ship Burial** (Room 41) is an Anglo-Saxon ship burial site dating from 620, which was excavated in Suffolk in 1939.

In the centre of the Great Court – and the heart of the museum – is the world-famous **Reading Room**, which was formerly the British Library and where George Bernard Shaw and Mahatma Gandhi studied, Oscar Wilde and William Butler Yeats mused, and scruffy Karl Marx wrote *The Communist Manifesto*. The northern end of the courtyard's lower level houses the terrific new **Sainsbury African Galleries**, a fascinating romp through the art and cultures of historic and contemporary African societies.

The restored **King's Library**, an 1820 architectural gem that used to contain the library of George III (now relocated to the British Library), is Room 1 and specialises in the evolution of the museums. The **Wellcome Gallery of Ethnography** provides exhibition space for many previously warehoused items.

The museum offers nine free 50-minute **eye-Opener tours** of individual galleries throughout the day, and 20-minute **eyeOpener spotlight talks** daily at 1.15pm focusing on different themes from the collection. Ninety-minute **highlights tours** (adult/concession £8/5) leave at 10.30am,

1pm and 3pm daily. If you want to go it alone there is a series of **audio tours** (£3.50) available at the information desk, including a family-oriented one narrated by comedian, writer and all-round top bloke Stephen Fry. One specific to the Parthenon Marbles is available in that gallery. You could also check out Compass, a multimedia public access system with 50 computer terminals that lets you take a virtual tour of the museum, plan your own circuit or get information on specific exhibits.

DICKENS HOUSE MUSEUM Map pp442-3
☎ 7405 2127; www.dickensmuseum.com; 48 Doughty St WC1; adults/under 16yr/concession £5/3/4; ◉ 10am-5pm Mon-Sat, 11am-5pm Sun; ⊖ Russell Sq
This handsome four-storey house is the sole surviving residence of the many that the great and restless Victorian novelist occupied before moving to Kent (leaving a trail of blue plaques behind him). The two-and-a-half years spent here, from 1837 to 1839, were prolific and Dickens dashed off *The Pickwick Papers*, *Nicholas Nickleby* and *Oliver Twist* between bouts of worry over debts, deaths and his ever-growing family. The house itself was saved from demolition and opened as a museum in 1925, and is one of the most interesting of its kind. The drawing room has been restored to its original condition while the other 10 rooms are stuffed with memorabilia. In the dressing room you can see texts Dickens had prepared for his reading tours, which include notes and instructions to himself like 'slapping the desk'. You can also see the very same slapped desk, a velvet-topped bureau he had made for his public reading events.

Nations Squabble over Marbles

Wonderful as it is, the British Museum can sometimes feel like one vast repository for stolen booty. Much of what's on display wasn't just 'picked up' along the way by Victorian travellers and explorers, but stolen or purchased under dubious circumstances.

Restive foreign governments occasionally pop their heads over the parapet to demand the return of 'their' property. The British Museum says 'no' and the problem goes away until the next time. Not the Greeks, however, who have been kicking up a stink demanding the return of the so-called Elgin Marbles, the ancient marble sculptures that once adorned the Parthenon. The British Museum, and successive British governments, steadfastly refuse to hand over the priceless works that were removed from the Parthenon and shipped to England by the British ambassador to the Ottoman Empire, the Earl of Elgin, in 1806. (When Elgin blew all his dough, he sold the marbles to the government.) All along, the British Museum has sniffed that the marbles were better off under *its* protective care. This arrogance proved tragicomic when it was discovered that earlier in the 20th century the museum had 'cleaned' the marbles using chisels and wire brushes, thereby destroying the finishing applied by the ancient Greeks.

The Greek government has upped the ante in recent years and has almost completed work on an €86 million museum in Athens designed specifically to exhibit the marbles as they were originally displayed in the 5th century BC. Only time will tell where the marbles will end up.

PERCIVAL DAVID FOUNDATION OF CHINESE ART Map pp440-1

☎ 7387 3909; www.pdfmuseum.org.uk; 53 Gordon Sq WC1; admission free; ⏰ 10.30am-5pm Mon-Fri; ⊖ Russell Sq

Although it feels like a fusty old institution, the friendly staff, lack of crowds and quirky collection here make for a rewarding visit. With some 1700 pieces, it's the largest collection of Chinese ceramics from the 10th to 18th centuries outside China. Sir Percival David donated it to the University of London in 1950 on the condition that every single piece be displayed at all times. Consequently, there are a few very ordinary pieces – of great significance, no doubt, just not very interesting to the casual enthusiast – to sift through before you reach the really exquisite stuff, such as wares that used to belong to Chinese emperors. Among the highlights are the David Vases (1351), the earliest dated and inscribed blue-and-white Chinese porcelain, named after Sir Percival himself.

PETRIE MUSEUM OF EGYPTIAN ARCHAEOLOGY Map pp440-1

☎ 7679 2884; www.petrie.ucl.ac.uk; University College London (UCL), Malet Pl WC1; admission free; ⏰ 1-5pm Tue-Fri, 10am-1pm Sat; ⊖ Goodge St

If you've got any interest in things Egyptian, you'll love this quiet and oft-overlooked gem, where some 80,000 objects make up one of the most impressive collections of Egyptian and Sudanese archaeology in the world. Behind glass – and amid an atmosphere of academia – are exhibits ranging from fragments of pottery to the world's oldest dress (2800 BC). The museum is named after Professor William Flinders Petrie (1853–1942), who uncovered many of the exhibits during his excavations and donated the collection to the university in 1933. The entrance to the museum is through the University's Science Library.

POLLOCK'S TOY MUSEUM Map pp448-9

☎ 7639 3452; www.pollockweb.co.uk; 1 Scala St; adult/child £3/1.50; ⏰ 10am-5pm Mon-Sat; ⊖ Goodge St

Possibly a bit creepy for kids but fascinating for adults, this deceptively large museum has what feels like a dusty collection of thousands of old toys, including board games, tin toys, puppets, doll houses, teddy bears, wax dolls, comics and craft toys from around the world. The most impressive collection, however, is of toy theatres, which should be no surprise

as Benjamin Pollock was the leading Victorian manufacturer of these popular toys. This really is a magical little place (not least because you go up three flights of stairs, come down four and leave by the same door!). You follow a higgledy-piggledy trail up creaking stairs and around a warren of rooms, each dedicated to a different toy theme. For anyone over 30, it'll be a poignant prance down memory lane. The shop has a fantastic range of wooden toys you're unlikely to see anywhere else.

THE SQUARES OF BLOOMSBURY
Map pp448-9

At the very heart of Bloomsbury is **Russell Square**, the largest in London. Originally laid out in 1800 by Humphrey Repton, it was recently given a striking facelift and a new 10m-tall fountain.

The centre of literary Bloomsbury was **Gordon Square** where, at various times, Bertrand Russell lived at No 57, Lytton Strachey at No 51 and Vanessa and Clive Bell, Maynard Keynes and the Woolf family at No 46. Strachey, Dora Carrington and Lydia Lopokova (the future wife of Maynard Keynes) all took turns living at No 41. Not all the buildings, many of which now belong to the university, are marked with blue plaques.

Lovely **Bedford Square**, the only completely Georgian square still surviving in Bloomsbury, was home to many London publishing houses until the 1990s, when they were swallowed up by multinational conglomerates and relocated. They included Jonathan Cape, Chatto and the Bodley Head (set up by Woolf and her husband Leonard), and were largely responsible for perpetuating the legend of the Bloomsbury Group by churning out seemingly endless collections of associated letters, memoirs and biographies.

ST GEORGE'S BLOOMSBURY
Map p452

☎ 7405 3044; Bloomsbury Way WC1; ⏰ 9.30am-5.30pm Mon-Fri, 10.30am-12.30pm Sun; ⊖ Holborn/Tottenham Court Rd

Not far from the British Museum, this Nicholas Hawksmoor church (1731) is distinguished by its classical portico of Corinthian capitals and a steeple that was inspired by the Mausoleum of Halicarnassus. It is topped with a statue of George I in Roman dress, and you can imagine how the sight of a bloke in a toga went down in 18th-century London. The church underwent a much-needed restoration in 2005, the results of which are superb.

EAST CENTRAL

Eating p239-44; Drinking p281-4; Shopping p340-1; Sleeping p360-1

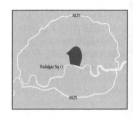

As London's commercial and residential rents rose dramatically in the 1980s and 1990s, a long-forgotten flank of the capital east of Bloomsbury and Islington began to see redevelopment from postindustrial wasteland to thriving modern counterweight to the West End. Ask any vaguely hip Londoner where they go out these days and all will mention at least one bar or club in Shoreditch, Hoxton or Clerkenwell. The area reached its height of cool in the late 1990s when it was defined by the Hoxton fin (an indigenous haircut still sported by the *homo hoxtonis*) and the term Shoreditch Twat became a self-deprecating phrase used by the cognoscenti to describe themselves and their mates who hung out in the run-down backstreets of Old St. Home to *Dazed and Confused*, the *Guardian* and even good old Lonely Planet, this neighbourhood remains the most creative, fast changing and fun in the whole of London. From media-yuppie Clerkenwell to *Blade Runner*–like Barbican and the funky nightlife of Kingsland Rd, no-one should miss out on East Central London.

Top Five – East Central

- 30 St Mary Axe (p113)
- Geffrye Museum (p123)
- Museum of London (p116)
- St Paul's Cathedral (below)
- Tower of London (p118)

THE CITY

It's confusing to arrive in London and discover a City within a city. While 'the city' might refer loosely to the entire metropolis of London, 'the City' (with a capital) definitely refers to the 'Square Mile' on the northern bank of the Thames, effectively the birthplace of London where the Romans built a walled community 2000 years ago. Nowadays it's overrun by stockbrokers and other money people carrying on the proud Roman tradition of empire building (albeit strictly financial these days). Despite being a desert for entertainment (it's a virtual ghost town after 7pm and at weekends), the City has more to offer curious visitors than almost any other corner of London, including the world-famous Tower of London, nearby Tower Bridge and the fabulous dome of St Paul's Cathedral.

ST PAUL'S CATHEDRAL Map pp454-5 & p111
☎ 7236 4128; www.stpauls.co.uk; St Paul's Churchyard; adult/senior & student/6-16yr £8/3.50/7; ⊕ 8.30am-4pm (last entry) Mon-Sat; ⊖ St Paul's; limited ♿
Occupying a superb position atop Ludgate Hill, one of London's most recognisable build-

ings is Sir Christopher Wren's masterwork, completed in 1697 after the previous building was destroyed in the Great Fire of 1666. The proud bearer of the capital's largest church dome, St Paul's Cathedral has seen a lot in its 300-plus years, although Ludgate Hill has been a place of worship for almost 1400 years, the current incarnation being the fifth to stand on this site. St Paul's almost didn't make it off the drawing board, as Wren's initial designs were rejected. However, since its first service in 1697, it's held funerals for Lord Nelson, the Duke of Wellington and Winston Churchill, and has played host to Martin Luther King as well as the ill-fated wedding of Charles and Diana. For Londoners the vast dome, which still manages to loom amid the far higher skyscrapers in the Square Mile, is a symbol of resilience and pride – miraculously surviving the Blitz unscathed.

However, despite all the fascinating history and its impressive interior, people are usually most interested in climbing the dome for one of the best views of London imaginable. It's actually three domes, one inside the other, but it made the cathedral Wren's *tour de force* and only a handful of others throughout the world (mostly in Italy) outdo it in size. Exactly 530 stairs take you to the top, but it's a three-stage journey. The cathedral is built in the shape of a cross, with the dome at its intersection. So first find the circular paved area between the eight massive columns supporting the dome, then head to the door on the western side of the southern transept (ie at about 'five o'clock' as you face the altar). Some 30m and precisely 259 steps above, you reach the interior walkway around the dome's base. This is the **Whispering Gallery**, so called because if you talk close to the wall it really does carry your words around to the opposite side, 32m away.

Climbing even more steps (another 119) you reach the **Stone Gallery**, which is an exterior viewing platform, with 360-degree views of London, all of which are rather obscured by pillars and other suicide-preventing measures.

The further 152 iron steps to the **Golden Gallery** are steeper and narrower than below but are really worth the effort as long as you don't suffer from claustrophobia. From here, 111m above London, the city opens up to you, your view unspoilt by superfluous railings; you'll be hard pushed to see anything better.

Of course, back on the ground floor, St Paul's offers plenty of riches for those who like to keep their feet firmly on its black-and-white tiled floor – and the interior has been stunningly restored in recent years. Just beneath the dome, for starters, is a compass and an epitaph written for Wren by his son: *Lector, si monumentum requiris, circumspice* (Reader, if you seek his monument, look around you).

In the northern aisle you'll find the **All Souls' Chapel** and the **Chapel of St Dunstan**, dedicated to the 10th-century archbishop of Canterbury, and the grandiose **Duke of Wellington Memorial** (1875). In the north transept chapel is Holman Hunt's celebrated painting **The Light of the World**, which depicts Christ knocking at an overgrown door that, symbolically, can only be opened from the inside. Beyond, in the cathedral's heart, are the particularly spectacular **quire** (or chancel) – its ceilings and arches dazzling with green, blue, red and gold mosaics – and the **high altar**. The ornately carved **choir stalls** by Grinling Gibbons on either side of the quire are exquisite, as are the **ornamental wrought-iron gates**, separating the aisles from the altar, by Jean Tijou (both men also worked on Hampton Court Palace). Walk around the altar, with its massive gilded oak canopy, to the **American Memorial Chapel**, a memorial to the 28,000 Americans based in Britain who lost their lives during WWII.

Around the southern side of the ambulatory is the **effigy of John Donne** (1573–1631). The one-time dean of St Paul's, Donne was also a metaphysical poet, most famous for the immortal lines 'No man is an island' and 'Ask not for whom the bell tolls, it tolls for thee' (both in the same poem!).

ST PAUL'S CATHEDRAL

GROUND FLOOR
1 Queen Anne Statue
2 Great West Door
  (Main Entrance)
4 All Souls' Chapel
5 Exterior Entrance to
  Crypt Café & Shop
6 Monument to the
  People of London
7 Chapel of St Dunstan

8 Duke of Wellington
  Memorial
11 Holman Hunt's
  The Light of the World
12 Dome & Wren's Epitaph
15 Quire
16 Choir Stalls
18 High Altar
19 American Memorial
  Chapel

20 Wrought-iron Gates
21 St Paul's in WWII
  Photos
23 John Donne
  Effigy
24 Entrances to Crypt
25 Entrance to Dome &
  Whispering Gallery
27 Chapel of St George
  & St Michael

CRYPT (keyed in italics)
3 Crypt Café
9 Toilets
10 Treasury
13 Nelson's Tomb
14 Wellington's
  Tomb
17 OBE Chapel
22 Wren's Tomb
26 Cathedral Shop

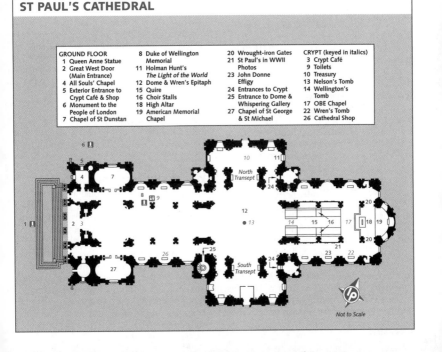

Not to Scale

On the eastern side of both the north and south transepts are stairs leading down to the crypt, treasury and OBE Chapel, where weddings, funerals and other services are held for members of the Order of the British Empire. The **crypt** has memorials to up to 300 military demigods, including the Duke of Wellington, Florence Nightingale, Lord Kitchener and Admiral Nelson, the last of which is directly below the dome in a black sarcophagus. On the surrounding walls are plaques in memory of those from the Commonwealth who died in various conflicts during the 20th century.

Wren's own tomb is in the crypt, while architect Edwin Lutyens and poet William Blake are also remembered here. In a niche, there is also an exhibit of Wren's controversial plans for St Paul's and his actual working model. St Paul's was one of the 50 commissions the great architect was given after the Great Fire of London wiped out most of the city.

The **treasury** displays some of the cathedral's plate, along with some spectacular needlework, including Beryl Dean's jubilee cope (bishop's cloak) of 1977, showing spires of 73 London churches, and its matching mitre. There is a **Crypt Café** (🕙 9am-5pm Mon-Sat, 10.30-5pm Sun) and the restaurant **Refectory** (🕙 9am-5.30pm Mon-Sat, 10.30am-5.30pm Sun), in addition to a **shop** (🕙 9am-5pm Mon-Sat, 10.30am-5pm Sun).

Just outside the north transept (that's to the left as you face the cathedral's entrance stairway), there's a simple **monument to the people of London**, honouring the 32,000 civilians killed (and another 50,000 seriously injured) in the defence of the city and the cathedral during WWII. Also to the left as you face the entrance stairway is **Temple Bar**, one of the original gateways to the city of London. This medieval stone archway once straddled Fleet St, but was removed to Middlesex in 1878. With the redevelopment of Paternoster Sq to its horribly sterile current state came the return of Temple Bar to the centre of London.

Audioguide tours lasting 45 minutes cost £3.50 for adults, or £3 for seniors and students; **guided tours** lasting 1½ to two hours (adult/child aged six to 16 years/senior and student £2.50/1/2) leave the tour desk at 11am, 11.30am, 1.30pm and 2pm. There are free **organ recitals** at St Paul's at 5pm most Sundays, as well as **celebrity recitals** (adult/concession £8/5.50) at 6.30pm on the first Thursday of the month between May and October. Evensong takes place at 5pm most weekdays and at 3.15pm on Sunday.

CENTRAL CRIMINAL COURT (OLD BAILEY) Map pp448-9

☎ 7248 3277; cnr Newgate & Old Bailey Sts; admission free; 🕙 10am-1pm & 2-5pm Mon-Fri; ⊖ St Paul's

Just as fact is often better than fiction, taking in a trial in the Old Bailey leaves watching a TV courtroom drama for dust. Of course, it's too late to see author Jeffrey Archer being found guilty of perjury here, watch the Guildford Four's convictions being quashed after their wrongful imprisonment for IRA terrorist attacks or view the Yorkshire Ripper Peter Sutcliffe being sent down. However, 'the Old Bailey' is a byword for crime and notoriety. So even if you sit in on a fairly run-of-the-mill trial, simply being in the court where such people as the Kray twins and Oscar Wilde (in an earlier building on this site) once appeared is memorable in itself.

Choose from 18 courts, of which the oldest – courts one, two and three – usually have the most interesting cases. As cameras, video equipment, mobile phones, large bags and food or drink are all forbidden inside, and there are no cloakrooms or lockers, it's important not to take these with you. Take a cardigan or something to cushion the hard seats though, and if you're interested in a high-profile trial, get there early.

The Central Criminal Court gets its nickname from the street on which it stands: *baillie* was Norman French for 'fortified church'. The current building opened in 1907 on the combined site of a previous Old Bailey and Newgate Prison. Intriguingly, the figure of justice holding a sword and scales in her hands above the building's copper dome is *not* blindfolded (against undue influence, as is traditionally the case). That's a situation that has sparked many a sarcastic comment from those being charged here.

GREAT FIRE MEMORIAL Map pp448-9

This small statue of a corpulent boy opposite St Bartholomew's Hospital, at the corner of Cock Lane and Giltspur St, has a somewhat odd dedication: 'In memory put up for the fire of London occasioned by the sin of gluttony 1666'. All becomes clear, however, when you realise the Great Fire was started in a busy bakery. On this site, the Fortune of War tavern once stood. This is where 'resurrectionists' (body snatchers) took corpses to be sold to the hospital's surgeons for use when practising surgery (see p83).

DR JOHNSON'S HOUSE Map pp448-9

☎ 7353 3745; www.drjohnsonshouse.org; 17 Gough Sq EC4; adult/child/concession/family £4/1/3/9; ⊙ 11am-5.30pm Mon-Sat May-Sep, 11am-5pm Mon-Sat Oct-Apr; ⊖ Chancery Lane/Blackfriars

The birthplace of the first serious dictionary of English and one-time home to the man who proclaimed 'When a man is tired of London, he is tired of life', this museum doesn't exactly crackle with Samuel Johnson's immortal wit. It's a beautifully preserved Georgian town house, that's for sure, with creaky floorboards and pastel walls, but the numerous paintings of Dr Johnson and his associates, including his black manservant Francis Barber and his clerk and biographer James Boswell, offer little insight into the good doctor's way with words.

There's a rather ponderous video, plus leaflets telling how the lexicographer and six clerks (Boswell wasn't among them, yet) developed the first English dictionary in the house's attic during the period he lived here from 1748 to 1759. Children will love the Georgian dressing-up clothes on the top floor. However, for adults the best part is the bookshop, where you can learn more about Boswell's hero worship of his employer or snap up a £3.50 pamphlet called *Dr Johnson said…* containing wry aphorisms from the 18th-century magazine the *Idler* and other sources.

Across Gough Sq is a statue of Johnson's cat, Hodge, sitting above the full (sexist) quote explaining why when a man is tired of London, he is tired of life: 'For there is in London all that life can afford.'

ST BRIDE'S, FLEET STREET Map pp448-9

☎ 7427 0133; St Bride's Ave EC4; ⊙ 8am-4.45pm Mon-Fri,10am-3pm Sat, services at 11am & 6.30pm Sun; ⊖ St Paul's/rail Blackfriars/City Thameslink

Rupert Murdoch might have frog-marched the newspaper industry out to Wapping in the 1980s, but this small church off Fleet St remains 'the journalists' church'. Candles were kept burning here for reporters John McCarthy and Terry Anderson during their years as hostages in Lebanon during the 1990s, and a memorial plaque was unveiled in October 2003 to 18 who lost their lives in Iraq (including Australian cameraman Paul Moran, ITN's Terry Lloyd, Channel 4 News' Gaby Rado, Reuters' Taras Protsyuk and Mazen Dana, Al-Jazeera's Tareq Ayoub and BBC translator Kamaran Muhamed). Outside there's a memorial tree for, among others, young Reuters photographer Dan Eldon, whose amazing scrapbook travel diaries formed the much-acclaimed cult book *The Journey is the Destination*.

There's a brief, well-presented history of the printing industry in the crypt, dating from 1500 when William Caxton's first printing press was relocated next to the church after Caxton's death. St Bride's is also of architectural interest. Designed by Sir Christopher Wren in 1671, its add-on spire (1703) reputedly inspired the first tiered wedding cake.

HOLBORN VIADUCT Map pp448-9

⊖ St Paul's/Farringdon

This fine iron bridge was built in 1869 in an effort to smarten up the area, as well as to link Holborn and Newgate St above what had been a valley created by the River Fleet. The four bronze statues represent Commerce and Agriculture (on the northern side) and Science and Fine Arts (on the south).

30 ST MARY AXE Map pp454-5

☎ 7071 5023; www.30stmaryaxe.com; St Mary Axe EC3; ⊖ Aldgate/Bank

Known to one and all as 'the Gherkin' for obvious reasons when you see its incredible shape, 30 St Mary Axe – as it is officially and far more prosaically named – remains London's most distinctive skyscraper, dominating the city despite actually being slightly smaller than the neighbouring NatWest Tower. In some ways the phallic Gherkin's futuristic, sci-fi exterior could be said to do for London what the Pudong Tower does for Shanghai.

Built in 2002–03 to a multi-award-winning design from Norman Foster, this is London's first eco-friendly skyscraper: after doing research with the legendary architect Buckminster Fuller, Foster laid out the offices so they spiral around internal 'sky gardens'. The windows (one of which popped out of its frame in 2005) can be opened and the gardens are used to reprocess stale air, so air conditioning is kept to a minimum. Its primary fuel source is gas, low-energy lighting is used throughout the building and the design heightens the amount of natural light let into the building, meaning that less electricity is used.

Its 41 floors mainly house the reinsurance giant Swiss Re's London offices, and tours are possible, but at a price. You need to book in advance to allow time for security clearances to be carried out, and a tour for up to eight people isn't exactly cheap at £250. Sadly the gorgeous top-floor restaurant is open only to staff and guests.

LLOYD'S OF LONDON Map pp454-5
☎ 7623 1000; 1 Lime St EC3; ⊖ Aldgate/Bank

While the world's leading insurance brokers are inside underwriting everything from trains, planes and ships to cosmonauts' lives and film stars' legs, people outside still stop to gawp at the stainless steel external ducting and staircases of the Lloyd's of London building. French free climber, or 'spiderman', Alain Robert even felt moved to scale the exterior with his bare hands in 2003.

Lloyd's is the work of Richard Rogers, one of the architects of the Pompidou Centre in Paris, and although it was a watershed for London when it was built in 1986, it's since been overtaken by plenty of other stunning architecture throughout the capital. However, its brave-new-world postmodernism still strikes a particular contrast with the olde worlde Leadenhall Market next door.

While you can watch people whizzing up and down the outside of the building in its all-glass lifts, sadly you can't experience it yourself. Access to the elevators and the rest of the interior is restricted to employees or professional groups, who must book in advance.

LEADENHALL MARKET Map pp454-5
Whittington Ave EC1; ⏰ 7am-4pm Mon-Fri; ⊖ Bank

Like stepping into a small slice of Victorian London, a visit to this dimly lit, covered mall off Gracechurch St is a minor time-travelling experience. There's been a market on this site since the Roman era, but the architecture that survives is all cobblestones and late-19th-century ironwork; even modern restaurants and chain stores decorate their façades in period style here. The market also appears as Diagon Alley in *Harry Potter and the Philosopher's Stone*. For details of what's on sale, see p351.

BANK OF ENGLAND MUSEUM
Map pp454-5

☎ 7601 5545; www.bankofengland.co.uk; Bartholomew Lane EC2; admission free, audioguides £1; ⏰ 10am-5pm Mon-Fri; ⊖ Bank

When James II declared war against France in the 17th century, he looked over his shoulder and soon realised he didn't have the funds to finance his armed forces. A Scottish merchant by the name of William Paterson came up with the idea of forming a joint-stock bank that could lend the government money and, in 1694, so began the Bank of England and the notion of national debt. The bank rapidly expanded in size and stature and moved to this site in 1734. During a financial crisis at the end of the 18th century, a cartoon appeared depicting the bank as a haggard old woman, and this is probably the origin of its nickname 'the Old Lady of Threadneedle St', which has stuck ever since. The institution is now in charge of maintaining the integrity of the sterling and the British financial system. The gifted Sir John Soane built the original structure, although the governors saw fit to demolish most of his splendid bank in the early 20th century and replace it with a utilitarian, no-frills model that they would soon regret.

The centrepiece of the museum – which explores the evolution of money and the history of this venerable institution, and which is not *nearly* as dull as it sounds – is a post-war reconstruction of Soane's original stock office complete with mannequins in period dress behind original mahogany counters. A series of rooms leading off the office are packed with exhibits ranging from photographs and coins to a gold bar you can lift up (it's amazingly heavy) and the muskets once used to defend the bank.

BANK Map pp454-5

By its very nature, much of the work of the City goes on behind closed doors. However, a short exploration of the streets around Bank

Shopfront at Leadenhall Market (left)

tube station will take you to the door of many financial, as well as political and religious, landmarks. Here, at the tube station's main exit, seven bank-filled streets converge. Take Princes St northwestwards to get to the Guildhall or head northeastwards along Threadneedle St for the Bank of England Museum.

The **Royal Exchange** is the imposing, colonnaded building you see at the juncture of Threadneedle St and Cornhill to the east. It's the third building on a site originally chosen in 1564 by Thomas Gresham and the former home of the London International Financial Futures Exchange. Today, however, it's simply an upmarket office complex and shopping mall, where you can take in the fabulous architecture while buying a Prada bag or Paul Smith shirt. There's also a Conran restaurant, **Grand Café & Bar** (p239), in the central courtyard. Alternatively, you can simply stand on the huge steps, enjoying the view of the Bank of England across Threadneedle St. The Futures Exchange has now moved slightly northeast along Threadneedle St to the Stock Exchange and is hence no longer open to the public.

Turning southeast, you enter Lombard St, which takes its name from the Italian bankers who ran London's money markets between the 13th and 16th centuries after Jewish financiers were expelled. The large signs bearing the banks' founding dates – a grasshopper (1563), a running mare for Lloyd's (1677), a cat and a fiddle – were once banned after they started falling in high winds and killing people. Only during Edward VII's 1901 coronation were they reaffixed (securely).

In the angle between Lombard St and King William St further south you'll see the twin towers of Hawksmoor's **St Mary Woolnoth** (☎ 7626 9701; ◷ 8am-5pm Mon-Fri), built in 1717. The architect's only City church, its interior Corinthian columns are a foretaste of his Christ Church in Spitalfields.

Between King William St and Walbrook stands the grand, porticoed **Mansion House** (☎ 7626 2500; www.cityoflondon.gov.uk), the official residence of the Lord Mayor of London, which was built in the mid-18th century by George Dance the Elder. It's not open to the public, though group tours are sometimes available when booked in advance.

Along Walbrook, past the City of London Magistrates Court, is **St Stephen Walbrook** (☎ 7283 4444; 39 Walbrook EC3; ◷ 10am-4pm Mon-Thu, 10am-3pm Fri), built in 1679. Widely considered to be the finest of Wren's City churches and a forerunner to St Paul's

Cathedral, this light and airy building is indisputably impressive. Some 16 pillars with Corinthian capitals rise up to support its dome and ceiling, while a large cream-coloured boulder lies at the heart of its roomy central space. This is an altar by sculptor Henry Moore, cheekily dubbed 'the Camembert' by critics.

Queen Victoria St runs southwestwards from Bank. A short way along it on the left, in front of Temple Court at No 11, you'll find the remains of the 3rd-century AD **Temple of Mithras**. Truth be told, however, there's little to see here. If you're interested in this Persian God and the religion worshipping him, you're better off checking out the **Museum of London** (p116), where sculptures and silver incense boxes found in the temple are on display.

Due west of Bank is Poultry. The modern building at the corner, with striped layers of blond and rose stone, is by Stirling Wilford (the Wilford in question is also behind the much-acclaimed Lowry centre in Salford Quays near Manchester). Behind this, Poultry runs into Cheapside, site of a great medieval market. On the left you'll see another of Wren's great churches, **St Mary-le-Bow** (☎ 7248 5139; Cheapside EC2; ◷ 6.30am-6pm Mon-Thu, 6.30am-4pm Fri), built in 1673. It's famous as the church whose bells dictate who is – and who isn't – a cockney. Its delicate steeple is one of Wren's finest works and the modern stained glass is striking. There's a good café called the **Place Below** (p244).

MONUMENT Map pp454-5
☎ 7626 2717; Monument St EC3; adult/5-15yr £2/1; ◷ 9.30am-5pm; ⊖ Monument

This is a huge memorial to the Great Fire of London of 1666, which, in terms of the physical devastation and horrifying psychological impact it wreaked on the city, must have been the 9/11 of its day. Fortunately, this event lies further back in history and few people died, so it's possible to simply enjoy Sir Christopher Wren's 1677 tower and its panoramic views of London. Slightly southeast of King William St, near London Bridge, the Monument is exactly 60.6m from the bakery in Pudding Lane where the fire started and exactly 60.6m high. To reach the viewing platform, just below a gilded bronze urn of flames that some call a big gold pincushion, you will need to climb 311 narrow, winding steps. On descent, you're given a certificate to say you did it, and if you did go all the way to the top, you'll feel it's justly deserved.

Neighbourhoods – East Central

MUSEUM OF LONDON Map pp454-5

☎ 0870 444 3852, 7600 0807; www.museumof
london.org.uk; London Wall EC2; admission free;
🕑 10am-5.50pm Mon-Sat, noon-5.50pm Sun;
⊖ Barbican; ♿

Hiding its light under the bushel of the Barbican and surrounding offices is one of London's most engaging museums. It's a relaxed place to while away a few weekend hours, as locals themselves frequently do when the Square Mile is all but deserted. The museum chronicles the city's evolution from the Ice Age to the 20th century, and is the world's largest urban-history museum.

The newest gallery, called London Before London, outlines the development of the Thames Valley from 450 million years ago. Harnessing computer technology to enliven its exhibits and presenting impressive fossils and stone axe heads in shiny new cases, it somehow feels less warm and colourful than the more-established displays. In these you begin with the city's Roman era and move anticlockwise through the Saxon, medieval, Tudor and Stuart periods. Continuing down a ramp and past the ornate Lord Mayor's state coach, this history continues progressively until 1914. Unfortunately this is the museum's cut-off point, despite the fact that the some of the city's darkest hours as well as its finest have occurred since then.

Aside from the magnificently OTT state coach, highlights include the 4th-century lead coffin, skeleton and reconstructed face of a well-to-do young Roman woman whose remains were discovered in Spitalfields in 1999; the Cheapside Hoard, an amazing find of 16th- and 17th-century jewellery; the lo-fi but heartfelt Great Fire of London diorama, narrated from the renowned diary of Samuel Pepys; and a timeline of London's creeping urbanisation during the 18th and 19th centuries. There are two mock-ups of city streets – one represents Roman London, the other is called Victorian Walk and harks back to the 19th century (although **Leadenhall Market**, p114, creates a slightly less authentic, but more lively Victorian feeling).

You can pause for a breather in the pleasant garden in the building's central courtyard or head for the adjoining Museum Café, which serves light meals from 10am to 5.30pm (from 11.30am on Sunday). Alternatively, on a sunny day, pack some sandwiches and lunch in the next-door **Barber Surgeon's Herb Garden**.

When arriving, look for the Barbican's gate seven; before leaving, don't forget to have a browse through the well-stocked bookshop.

BARBICAN Map pp454-5

information ☎ 7638 8891, switchboard ☎ 7638
4141; www.barbican.org.uk; Silk St EC2; 🕑 9am-11pm
Mon-Sat, 10.30am-11pm Sun; ⊖ Barbican/Moorgate

Occasionally long-lost Londoners emerge, blinking, from the labyrinthine Barbican, having done unspeakable things to feed and water themselves for years and still believing Margaret Thatcher is prime minister of Britain. OK, we made that one up, but the maze of elevated walkways that leads to Europe's largest multi-arts venue and home of the London Symphony Orchestra (LSO) does make it easy to become confused.

The problem lies in the centre's history. Begun in the 1970s on a huge bombsite abandoned since WWII, it was originally planned as just a housing scheme – the theatres, concert halls, cinemas and art gallery that attract most visitors were a last-minute addition. Most of the apartments sit in narrow, six- or seven-storey concrete slab blocks on stilts, which are arranged to form the sides of a staggered rectangle (embellished with three towers, a few stray curves and extra paths). And one has to negotiate one's way around, or through, this citadel to find the arts centre, which opened in 1982.

Yet what it lacks it orientation, the Barbican certainly makes up for in culture and these days even retro chic. Besides the world-class London Symphony Orchestra, you'll also find the City of London Symphonia, the English Chamber Orchestra and the BBC Symphony Orchestra performing in the auditoriums. The programme of theatre has been slightly uneven since the Royal Shakespeare Company moved out of the Barbican in 2002; however, dance is a strong part of the Barbican's current repertoire.

The highly regarded **Barbican Gallery** (☎ 7638 8891; Level 3, Barbican Centre, Silk St EC2; adult £8, senior, student & 12-17yr £6; 🕑 11am-8pm, until 6pm Tue & Thu) stages some of the best photographic exhibits in London.

With a recent £7 million refit and a highly regarded brasserie, the Barbican is much better loved than London's other modernist colossus, the South Bank Centre. Trendy urban architects are racing to get hold of the back-in-fashion apartments. The *Daily Telegraph* newspaper is less decided, once describing the complex as a cross between utopia and a public loo.

See the Entertainment chapter for details of the theatres (p330), cinemas (p300) and concert halls (p324).

GUILDHALL Map pp454-5

☎ 7606 3030; www.cityoflondon.gov.uk; Gresham St EC2; admission free; ⏰ 10am-5pm May-Sep, 10am-5pm Mon-Sat Oct-Apr; ⊖ Bank; ♿

Bang in the centre of the Square Mile, the Guildhall has been the City's seat of government for nearly 800 years. The present building dates from the early 15th century, in the sense that the walls survived. Other segments suffered severe damage during both the Great Fire of 1666 and the Blitz of 1940. The oak-panelled roof, for example, was restored in the 1950s by Sir Giles Gilbert Scott, the architect responsible for the Bankside Power Station (now the Tate Modern art gallery).

Most visitors' first port of call is the impressive **Great Hall**, where you can see the banners and shields of London's 12 guilds (principal livery companies), which used to wield absolute power throughout the City. The lord mayor and sheriffs are still elected annually in the vast open hall, with its chunky chandeliers and its church-style monuments. It is often closed for various other formal functions, so it's best to ring ahead. Meetings of the Common Council are held here every third Thursday of each month (except August) at 1pm, and the Guildhall hosts the awards dinner for the Booker Prize, the leading British literary award.

Among the monuments to look out for if the hall is open are statues of Winston Churchill, Admiral Nelson, the Duke of Wellington and the two prime ministers Pitt the Elder and Younger. In the minstrels' gallery at the western end are statues of the legendary giants Gog and Magog; today's figures replaced similar 18th-century statues destroyed in the Blitz. The Guildhall's stained glass was also blown out during the Blitz but a modern window in the southwestern corner depicts the City's history; look out for a picture of London's first lord mayor, Richard 'Dick' Whittington, and his famous cat.

Beneath the Great Hall is London's largest medieval crypt, with 19 stained-glass windows showing the livery companies' coats of arms. The crypt can be seen only as part of a free **guided tour** (☎ 7606 3030 ext 1463).

The buildings to the west house Corporation of London offices and the **Guildhall Library** (☎ 7606 3030; Aldermanbury EC2; ⏰ 9.30am-4.45pm Mon-Sat), founded in about 1420 under the terms of Dick Whittington's will. It is divided into three sections for research: printed books; manuscripts; and prints, maps and drawings. Also here is the **Clockmakers' Company Museum** (☎ 7332 1868; Guildhall Library, Alderman-bury EC2; admission free; ⏰ 9.30am-4.45pm Mon-Fri), which has a collection of more than 700 clocks and watches dating back some 500 years. The clock museum sometimes closes for an hour or two on Monday to wind the clocks.

GUILDHALL ART GALLERY & ROMAN LONDON AMPHITHEATRE Map pp454-5

☎ 7332 3700; www.guildhall-art-gallery.org.uk; Guildhall Yard EC2; adult/senior & student/family £2.80/1/5, all day Fri & daily after 3.30pm free; ⏰ 10am-5pm Mon-Sat, noon-4pm Sun; ⊖ Bank

You'll notice the statue of former prime minister Margaret Thatcher is in a protective glass case here. That's because it was decapitated by an angry punter with a cricket bat (and one of the gallery's own metal stanchions) soon after its installation in 2002. Today, following some tricky neck surgery, the iron lady has finally rejoined the gallery's paintings of London – including some superbly atmospheric portraits of the capital through the centuries.

However, the real highlight of a visit here is deep in the darkened basement, where the archaeological remains of Roman London's amphitheatre, or coliseum, lie. Discovered only in 1988 when work finally began on a new gallery (the original having been badly damaged during the Blitz), they were immediately declared an Ancient Monument, and the new gallery built around them. While only a few remnants of the stone walls lining the eastern entrance still stand, they're imaginatively fleshed out with a black-and-fluorescent-green trompe l'oeil of the missing seating, and computer-meshed outlines of spectators and gladiators. The roar of the crowd goes up as you reach the end of the entrance tunnel and hit the central stage.

ST LAWRENCE JEWRY Map pp454-5

☎ 7600 9478; Gresham St EC2; admission free; ⏰ 7.30am-2.15pm; ⊖ Bank; ♿

To look at the Corporation of London's extremely well-preserved official church, you'd barely realise that it was almost completely destroyed during WWII. Instead, it does Sir Christopher Wren, who built it in 1678, and its subsequent restorers proud, with its immaculate alabaster walls and gilt trimmings. The arms of the City of London adorn the organ above the door at the western end. The Commonwealth Chapel is bedecked with the flags of member nations. Free piano recitals are held each Monday at 1pm; organ recitals at the same time on Tuesday.

As the church name suggests, this was once part of the Jewish quarter – the centre being Old Jewry, the street to the southeast. The district was sadly not without its pogroms. After some 500 Jews were killed in 1262 in mob 'retaliation' against a Jewish moneylender, Edward I expelled the entire community from London to Flanders in 1290. They did not return until the late 17th century.

TOWER OF LONDON Map pp454-5 & p119
☎ 7709 0765; www.hrp.org.uk; Tower Hill EC3; adult/5-15yr/senior & student/family £13.50/9/10.50/37.50; ⏲ 9am-6pm Tue-Sat & 10am-6pm Sun & Mon Mar-Oct, 9am-5pm Tue-Sat & 10am-5pm Sun & Mon Nov-Feb, last admission on all days 1hr before closing time; ⊖ Tower Hill; limited ♿

'Uneasy lies the head that wears the crown' wrote Shakespeare in Henry IV, and the line seems highly appropriate at the Tower of London, where conspiracy and plot have always reigned supreme. Here King Henry VIII's wife Anne Boleyn was beheaded in the 16th century, Sir Walter Raleigh was imprisoned (no less than three times) and the 'princes in the tower' infamously disappeared to ensure they were no threat to their uncle's ambitions.

Easily one of London's top attractions, the tower's vast complex is also home to the stunning British Crown Jewels. It's also the best-preserved medieval castle in London and will fascinate anyone with an interest in history and warfare. Begun during the reign of William the Conqueror (1066–87) and largely unchanged in external appearance for at least 600 years, the Tower of London today combines a large number of curious ceremonial roles with that of a vast tourist attraction.

With over two million visitors per year, the crowds are quite serious in the high season and it's best to buy a ticket in advance as well as to visit later in the day. You can buy Tower tickets at any tube station up to a week beforehand, which can save you a long time when you arrive. Also, after 3pm the groups have usually left and the place is a lot more pleasant to stroll around. During the winter months it's far less crowded, so there's no need to do either of the above.

The Tower is one of London's four World Heritage Sites (the others are Westminster Abbey, Kew Gardens and Maritime Greenwich), and, of course, it's a complex rather than one building. The White Tower at its heart was the original Norman building, around which two walls –an inner wall with 13 towers and an outer wall with

five – were erected between 1190 and 1285 by Kings Henry III and Edward I. A moat that once encircled the outer wall was finally drained of centuries of festering sewage in the late 19th century, necessitated by persistent cholera outbreaks, and a superbly manicured lawn now surrounds the Tower. Other buildings have been built alongside the White Tower in the courtyard, from a Tudor chapel and houses to 19th- and 20th-century museums. In the early Middle Ages, the Tower of London acted as a royal residence (until the early 17th century at least), and also as a treasury, a mint, an arsenal and a prison, meaning you'll find remnants of those various institutions dotted around the grounds. Throughout the ages, murder and political skulduggery have reigned as much as kings and queens, so tales of imprisonment and executions will pepper your trail.

You enter the tower via the West Gate and proceed across the walkway over the dry moat between the **Middle Tower** and **Byward Tower**. Before you stands the **Bell Tower**, housing the tower's curfew bells and one-time home to Thomas More. The politician and author of Utopia was imprisoned here in 1534 before his execution for refusing to recognise King Henry VIII as the new head of the Church of England in place of the Pope. To your left are the **casements of the former Royal Mint**, which was moved from this site to new buildings northeast of the castle in 1812.

Continuing past the Bell Tower along **Water Lane** between the walls you come to the famous **Traitors' Gate**, the gateway through which prisoners being brought by river entered the tower. Above the gate, rooms inside **St Thomas's Tower** show what the hall of Edward I (1272–1307) might once have looked like and also how archaeologists peel back the layers of newer buildings to find what went before. Opposite St Thomas's Tower is **Wakefield Tower**, built by Henry III between 1220 and 1240. Its upper floor is actually entered via St Thomas's Tower and has been even more enticingly furnished with a replica throne and huge candelabra to give an impression of how, as an anteroom in a medieval palace, it might have looked in Edward I's day. During the 15th-century War of the Roses between the Houses of Lancaster and York, Henry VI was almost certainly murdered in this tower.

Below, in the basement of Wakefield Tower, there's a **Torture at the Tower** exhibition. However, torture wasn't practised as much in England as it was on the Continent apparently, and the display is pretty perfunctory, limiting itself to a

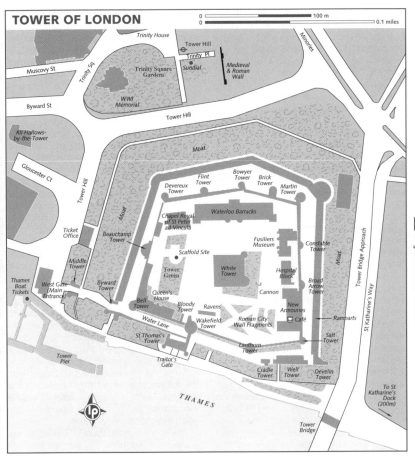

TOWER OF LONDON

0 — 100 m
0 — 0.1 miles

Trinity House

Trinity Pl

Tower Hill

Muscovy St

Trinity St

Trinity Square Gardens

Sundial

Medieval & Roman Wall

Minories

WWI Memorial

Byward St

Tower Hill

All Hallows-by-the-Tower

Gloucester Ct

Moat

Tower Hill

Flint Tower

Bowyer Tower

Brick Tower

Devereux Tower

Martin Tower

Moat

Chapel Royal of St Peter ad Vincula

Waterloo Barracks

Ticket Office

Beauchamp Tower

Fusiliers Museum

Constable Tower

Scaffold Site

Middle Tower

Tower Green

White Tower

Hospital Block

Thames Boat Tickets

West Gate (Main Entrance)

Byward Tower

Queen's House

Cannon

Broad Arrow Tower

Bell Tower

Bloody Tower

Ravens

New Armouries

Water Lane

Wakefield Tower

Roman City Wall Fragments

Café

Ramparts

St Thomas's Tower

Lanthorn Tower

Salt Tower

Tower Pier

Traitor's Gate

Cradle Tower

Well Tower

Develin Tower

To St Katharine's Dock (200m)

THAMES

Tower Bridge

Tower Bridge Approach

St Katharine's Way

Moat

Neighbourhoods – East Central

rack, a pair of manacles and an instrument for keeping prisoners doubled up called a Scavenger's Daughter. Frankly, you'd see scarier gear at any London S&M club. To get to this exhibition and the basement level of Wakefield Tower, you enter the tower courtyard through the arch opposite Traitors' Gate.

As you do so, you'll also see at the centre of the courtyard the Norman **White Tower** with a turret on each of its four corners and a golden weather vane spinning atop each. This tower has a couple of remnants of Norman architecture, including a fireplace and garderobe (lavatory). However, most of its interior is given over to a collection of cannons, guns and suits of armour for men and horses, which come from the Royal Armouries in Leeds. Among the most remarkable exhibits are the 6ft 9in (2m) suit of armour made for John of Gaunt (to

see that coming towards you on a battlefield must have been terrifying) and alongside it a tiny child's suit of armour designed for James I's young son Henry. Another unmissable suit is that of Henry VIII, almost square-shaped to match the monarch's body by his 40s, and featuring what must have been the most impressive posing pouch in the kingdom.

The stretch of green between the Wakefield and White Towers is where the Tower's famous **ravens** are found (see p121). Opposite Wakefield Tower and the White Tower is the **Bloody Tower**, with an exhibition on Elizabethan adventurer Sir Walter Raleigh, who was imprisoned here three times by the capricious Elizabeth I, most significantly from 1605 to 1616.

The Bloody Tower acquired its nickname from the story that the 'princes in the tower', Edward V and his younger brother, were murdered here to annul their claims to the throne. The blame is usually laid at the door of their uncle Richard III, although Henry VII might also have been responsible for the crime.

Beside the Bloody Tower sits a collection of black-and-white half-timbered Tudor houses that are home to Tower of London staff. The **Queen's House**, where Anne Boleyn lived out her final days in 1536, now houses the resident governor and is closed to the public.

North of the Queen's House, across **Tower Green**, is the **scaffold site**, where seven people were executed by beheading in Tudor times: two of Henry VIII's six wives, the alleged adulterers Anne Boleyn and Catherine Howard; the latter's lady-in-waiting, Jane Rochford; Margaret Pole, countess of Salisbury, descended from the House of York; 16-year-old Lady Jane Grey, who fell foul of Henry's daughter Mary I by being her rival for the throne; William, Lord Hastings; and Robert Devereux, earl of Essex, once a favourite of Elizabeth I.

These people were executed within the tower precincts largely to spare the monarch the embarrassment of the usual public execution on Tower Hill, an event that was usually attended by thousands of spectators. In the case of Robert Devereux, the authorities perhaps also feared a popular uprising in his support.

Behind the scaffold site lies the **Chapel Royal of St Peter ad Vincula** (St Peter in Chains), a rare example of ecclesiastical Tudor architecture and the burial place of those beheaded on the scaffold outside or at nearby Tower Hill. Unfortunately, it can only be visited on a group tour or after 4.30pm, so if you aren't already part of a group hang around until one shows up and then tag along. Alternatively, attend a service, which takes place at 9am on Sundays.

To the east of the chapel and north of the White Tower is the building that visitors most want to see: **Waterloo Barracks**, the home of the **Crown Jewels**. You file past footage of Queen Elizabeth II's coronation and videos on some of the more prominent pieces before you reach the vault itself, but once inside you'll be confronted with ornate sceptres, cloaks, plates, orbs and, naturally, crowns. A very slow-moving travelator takes you past the dozen or so crowns that are the centrepiece, including the £27.5 million Imperial State Crown, set with diamonds (2868 of them to be exact), sapphires, emeralds, rubies and pearls, and the platinum crown of the late Queen Mother, Elizabeth, which is famously set with the 105-carat Koh-i-Noor (Mountain of Light) diamond. Surrounded by myth and legend, the 14th-

century diamond has been claimed by both India and Afghanistan. It reputedly confers enormous power on its owner, but male owners are destined to die a tormented death.

The **Fusiliers Museum** to the east of Waterloo Barracks is run by the Royal Regiment of Fusiliers, who charge a separate nominal entrance fee. This museum covers the history of the Royal Fusiliers dating back to 1685, and has models of several battles. A 10-minute video gives details of the modern regiment.

The red-brick **New Armouries** in the southeastern corner of the inner courtyard has an assortment of exhibits. These include pictures of the Royal Menagerie (which was taken from here in 1834 and formed the nucleus of London Zoo) and a list of the Tower's famous prisoners, from Ranulf Flambard, bishop of Durham in 1100, to Hitler's henchman Rudolf Hess in 1941.

There are plenty of other attractions, as well as churches, shops, toilets and a restaurant, within the tower complex, but before you leave you should also walk along the inner ramparts. This **Wall Walk** begins with the 13th-century **Salt Tower**, probably used to store saltpetre for gunpowder, and ends at the **Martin Tower**, which houses an exhibition about the original coronation regalia. Here you can see some of the older crowns, designed so that the jewels in them could be removed. The oldest surviving crown is that of George I, which is topped with the ball and cross from James II's crown. It was from the Martin Tower that Colonel Thomas Blood attempted to steal the Crown Jewels in 1671, disguised as a clergyman.

The hour-long **guided tours** led by the Yeoman Warders are worth sticking with for at least a bit, as they do bring the various nooks and crannies of the tower to life. These tours leave from the Middle Tower every 30 minutes from 9.30am (10am on Sunday) to 3.30pm (2.30pm in winter) daily. The warders also conduct about eight different short talks (35 minutes) and tours (45 minutes) on specific themes. The first is at 9.30am Monday to Saturday (10.15am on Sunday in summer, 11.30am in winter), the last at 5.15pm (3pm in winter). A self-paced audioguide in five languages is available for £3 from the information point on Water Lane. There's an expensive but decent restaurant-café in the new armouries building.

Despite the Tower's World Heritage Site status, the area immediately to the north is fairly disappointing, especially as in recent years much of it has been a construction site. Just outside Tower Hill tube station, a giant bronze **sundial** depicts the history of London from

Raven Mad

For years every English school child – and every visiting tourist – has been pointed to the ravens at the Tower of London and told of a centuries-old superstition that the monarch would fall should the birds ever leave. This superstition is said to date back at least to the time of Charles II, who wished to shoo off a bunch of noisy ravens, but was warned of the ill luck that would ensue. Since then, the story goes, at least six ravens have been kept in residence, with their wings cropped so they may not fly away.

It turns out, however, that this tale is a bigger load of hokum than it first appears. Not only is the superstition itself implausible, it didn't even exist until the 19th century. The whole raven legend was conjured up by the Victorians.

In late 2004 an official Tower historian finally revealed that the first record of ravens being kept here dates back only to 1895. He thought the birds might have been kept as pets by staff who were fans of the hugely popular Edgar Allan Poe poem *The Raven,* or that some of the creatures might even have been a witty gift to the Tower from the highly immodest Earl of Dunraven. Records also show that during WWII the Tower was entirely bereft of ravens, yet none of the dire consequences forecast came to pass.

This news apparently hasn't filtered down to the ravens themselves, whose recent history as a talisman has given them diplomatic immunity to bite visitors who get too close, or to steal visitors' food. With their coats glossy and their wings clipped, they still strut around the place as if they own it – treated like royalty by their 'raven master' and other beefeaters and given their own accommodation budget and love nests (literally). It remains to be seen whether the revelations as to their true history will lead to a drop in their status. But, given that everyone loves a good yarn, it seems unlikely.

AD 43 to 1982. It stands on a platform offering a view of the neighbouring **Trinity Square Gardens**, once the site of the Tower Hill scaffold and now home to Edwin Lutyens' memorial to the marines and merchant sailors who lost their lives during WWI. A grassy area, off the steps leading to a subway under the main road, lets you inspect a stretch of the **medieval wall** built on Roman foundations, with a modern statue of Emperor Trajan (r AD 98–117) standing in front of it. At the other end of the tunnel is a postern (gate) dating from the 13th century.

TOWER BRIDGE Map pp454-5
☻ **Tower Hill**

The sort of iconic symbol of London that school children recognise the world over, Tower Bridge doesn't disappoint up close. There's something about its neo-Gothic towers and blue suspension struts that catch your eye whenever you're in the vicinity. Built in 1894 as a much-needed crossing point in the east, it was equipped with a then revolutionary bascule (seesaw) mechanism that could clear the way for oncoming ships in three minutes. Although London's days as a thriving port are long over, the bridge still does its stuff, lifting some 900 times per year and as many as 10 times per day in summer. (For information on the next lifting ring ☎ 7940 3984 or check the website below.)

The **Tower Bridge Exhibition** (☎ 7940 3985; www .towerbridge.org.uk; adult/under 5yr/senior, student & 5-15yr £5.50/free/4.25, family £10-20; ☽ 10am-6pm Apr-Oct, 10.30am-6pm Nov-Mar) explains the nuts and bolts of it all. If you're not particularly technically minded, however, it's still nice to get inside the bridge and look out its windows along the Thames.

ALL HALLOWS-BY-THE-TOWER
Map pp454-5
☎ **7481 2928; Byward St EC3; admission free;**
☽ **9am-5.45pm Mon-Fri, 10am-5pm Sat & Sun;**
☻ **Tower Hill**

All Hallows is where famous diarist Samuel Pepys recorded his observations of the nearby Great Fire of London in 1666. Above ground it's a pleasant enough church, rebuilt after WWII. There's a copper spire added in 1957 to make the church stand out more, a pulpit from a Wren church in Cannon St destroyed in the war, a beautiful 17th-century font cover by the master woodcarver Grinling Gibbons and some interesting modern banners.

However, a church by the name All Hallows (meaning 'All Saints') has stood on this site since AD 675, and the best bit of the building today is undoubtedly its atmospheric Saxon undercroft, or **crypt** (admission £3; ☽ 10am-4pm Mon-Sat, 1-4pm Sun). There you'll find a pavement of reused Roman tiles and walls of the 7th-century Saxon church, as well as coins and bits of local history.

William Penn, founder of Pennsylvania, was baptised here in 1644 and there's a memorial to him in the undercroft. John Quincy Adams, sixth president of the USA, was also married at All Hallows in 1797.

A 45-minute audioguide tour of the church is available (donation requested). At the **brass-rubbing centre** (☉ 11am-4pm Mon-Sat, 2-4pm Sun) rubbings cost from £2 to £5.

HOXTON, SHOREDITCH & SPITALFIELDS

The phenomenal success of this northeast London enclave of cool continues to astound pretty much everyone, especially given more than five years of self-hating backlash and endless ribbing for its tireless trendiness from the rest of the capital. By the early 1990s, what had been one of London's most uninspiring urban wastelands suddenly became a place where creative types began buying warehouses and converting them into work and living spaces, chased out of the West End by prohibitive rents.

By the late 1990s Old St was seriously cool, having spawned its own indigenous haircut (the Hoxton fin) and even its own self-satirising fanzine (the *Shoreditch Twat*, although it's no longer published). Superslick bars, cutting-edge clubs, galleries and restaurants opened up to cater to the new media-creative-freelance squad and property prices quickly caught up with elsewhere in central London. Yet despite the bursting of the dotcom bubble, and the general expectation that the Shoreditch scene would collapse under the weight of its own trucker hats, the regenerated area is flourishing stronger than ever. On streets where a decade ago there were only newsagents slowly going out of business and the occasional fighting pub, there are now delis, photo labs, busy bars, thriving clothes shops and small independent business start-ups. The entire neighbourhood remains rough enough around the edges to feel a bit of an adventure, although it's already transformed so entirely from its 1990s self as to be almost unrecognisable.

BRICK LANE Map pp454-5

Immortalised in a warm, much-lauded book by Monica Ali, Brick Lane is the centrepiece of a thriving Bengali community in an area nicknamed Banglatown. The lane itself is one long procession of curry and balti houses intermingled with sari and fabric shops, Indian cookery stores and outlets selling ethnic knick-knacks. Sadly, the once high standard of cook-ing in the curry houses is a distant memory, so you're probably better off trying Indian cuisine in Whitechapel (p255) or Tooting (p269). Restaurateurs aside, much of the Bengali community is, like its Huguenot forerunners, involved in the clothes trade.

Just past Hanbury St is the converted **Old Truman's Brewery**. This was once London's largest brewery and the Director's House on the left harks back to 1740, the old Vat House across the road with its hexagonal bell tower is early 19th century, and the Engineer's House next to it dates from 1830. The brewery stopped producing beer in 1989, and in the 1990s became home to a host of independent businesses such as record label Acid Jazz and music mag *Blues & Soul* (and even home to musician Talvin Singh himself). Now you'll find lots of small shops, as well as hip clubs and bars, including **93 Feet East** (p303), the **Vibe Bar** (p283) and **1001** (p281).

DENNIS SEVERS' HOUSE Map pp454-5

☎ 7247 4013; www.dennissevershouse.co.uk; 18 Folgate St E1; Sun/Mon/Mon evening £8/5/12; ☉ noon-2pm 1st & 3rd Sun of the month, noon-2pm Mon following 1st & 3rd Sun of the month, every Mon evening (times vary); ⊖ Liverpool St

This quirky hotchpotch of a cluttered house is named after the late American eccentric who restored it, and long may his name ring. He turned his residence into what he called a 'still-life drama', but could also be described as part opera, part murder mystery. Visitors find they have entered the home of a 'family' of Huguenot silk weavers so common to the Spitalfields area in the 18th century. However, while they see the fabulous restored Georgian interiors with meals and drinks half-abandoned and rumpled sheets, and while they smell cooking and hear creaking floorboards, their 'hosts' always remain tantalisingly just out of reach. It's a unique and intriguing proposition by day, but the 'Silent Night' tours by candlelight every Monday evening are an even more memorable trip (the word is used advisedly). Booking for the 'Silent Night' tours is essential.

Top Five Quirky London

- **Cabinet War Rooms** (p136)
- **Dennis Severs' House** (above)
- **Old Operating Theatre Museum** (p171)
- **Pollock's Toy Museum** (p109)
- **Tyburn Convent** (p146)

Dennis Severs' House (opposite)

under 16yr £2/free). It's the absolute attention to detail that impresses, right down to the vintage newspaper left open on the breakfast table (and apparently that contemporary-looking square glass vase really is period). The setting is so delicate, however, that this small almshouse is only open once a month and numbers are limited, so check the website or call ahead. Meanwhile, special gardening events revolve around the museum's lovely herb garden.

MUSEUM OF IMMIGRATION & DIVERSITY Map pp454-5

☎ 7247 5352; www.19princeletstreet.org.uk; 19 Princelet St E1; admission free, donations requested; ⊖ Liverpool St/Shoreditch

This unique Huguenot town house was built in 1719 and housed a prosperous family of weavers, before subsequently becoming home to waves of immigrants including Polish, Irish and Jewish families, the last of which built a synagogue in the back garden in 1869. In keeping with the house's multicultural past, it now houses a museum of immigration and diversity, whose carefully considered exhibits are aimed at both adults and children. Unfortunately the house is in a terrible state of repair and as such opens only infrequently (sometimes as little as 10 times per year). Check the website for dates, and jump at the chance to see this magnificent place.

SPITALFIELDS Map pp454-5

Dennis Severs' House is not the only fine Georgian house in Folgate St, north of Spitalfields market; the street is lined with them, and they too were once occupied by the Protestant Huguenots who fled religious persecution in France to settle here in the late 17th century. Bringing with them their skills as silk weavers, their presence is still recalled by such street names as Fleur-de-Lis St and Nantes Passage.

Diagonally opposite the market on the corner of Commercial and Fournier Sts is **Christ Church, Spitalfields** (☎ 7247 7202; www.christchurch spitalfields.org; ⊖ 1-4pm Sun, 11am-4pm Tue), where many of the weavers worshipped. The magnificent 'English Baroque' structure, with a tall spire sitting on a portico of four great Tuscan columns, was designed by Nicholas Hawksmoor and completed in 1729. Looking up at its haunting outline at night, you understand a little how Hawksmoor got his diabolical reputation. A comprehensive restoration was completed in 2004.

GEFFRYE MUSEUM Map pp442-3

☎ 7739 9893; www.geffrye-museum.org.uk; 136 Kingsland Rd E2; admission by donation; ⊙ 10am-5pm Tue-Sat, noon-5pm Sun; ⊖ Old St/Liverpool St; ⓖ

Definitely Shoreditch's most accessible sight, this utterly charming museum begins to work its magic on you before you even go inside; on a distinctly run-down part of Kingsland Rd dominated by local-authority blocks, this 18th-century ivy-clad almshouse with an inviting sun-dappled green lawn and herb garden draws you in immediately.

Inside, the Geffrye Museum plots the history of English interior furnishings, beginning with 17th-century oak furniture and panelling and ending up with a remarkably realistic contemporary London loft and its Ikea-strewn interior. It's a fascinating glimpse at the changing styles and fashions and there are temporary exhibits and a reference library for those with a developed interest in domestic design.

The 14 almshouses were originally built to provide homes for the elderly poor, with funds bequeathed by Robert Geffrye, a late-16th-century London mayor. However, it was the preponderance of furniture makers and other interior design trades in the neighbourhood that led to the decision to turn these houses into this sort of museum in 1914.

A recent addition has been the exquisite restoration of a **historic almshouse interior** (adult/

Across from the church is the glorious late-Victorian **Spitalfields Market**. Until 1991 this was the city's fruit and vegetable market. Its proximity to Hoxton and Shoreditch means the Sunday market here is still the market of the moment, but with young clothes designers and producers of trendy furniture and ornaments selling their wares. Organic produce is on sale Friday and Saturday; see p351 for further details.

There are yet more restored Georgian houses along Fournier St, leading to a building that throughout history has demonstrated the sort of religious tolerance that today's world needs. Before the **Great Mosque** here became an Islamic place of worship in 1975, it was a synagogue for Jewish refugees from Russia and central Europe. Before that, it was called the New French Church and echoed with the prayers of Huguenots from 1743 to 1899.

WHITE CUBE GALLERY Map pp442-3

☎ 7930 5373; www.whitecube.com; 48 Hoxton Sq N1; admission free; ◷ 10am-6pm Tue-Sat; ⊖ Old St

Alongside Charles Saatchi, owner of the **Saatchi Gallery** (p150), the White Cube's Jay Jopling was the man responsible for bringing 'Britart' (see p47) to the public's attention during the 1990s. He worked with a young Damien Hirst before Saatchi came on the scene, showcased the works of sculptor Antony Gormley (responsible for Gateshead's huge *Angel of the North* sculpture) and married artist Sam Taylor-Wood. Now firmly part of Britain's 'new establishment', Jopling has refurbished his White Cube gallery (the original White Cube in St James's has been shut) to include two new floors. The White Cube differs from the Saatchi Gallery in that it's a place where collectors actually come to buy works, but shows by Damien Hirst, Tracey Emin and other less well-known artists also mean it's worth coming simply to view.

CLERKENWELL & ISLINGTON

Historic Clerkenwell, on the fringes of the City, lies in the valley of the River Fleet (from where the clerks' well the neighbourhood is named after sprang), although the river itself has long been bricked over. Like Shoreditch, Clerkenwell has profited enormously from redevelopment since the late 1980s, and many once-empty warehouses have been converted into expensive flats and work spaces. More famous for its clubs, pubs and restaurants than its history these days (this was where crusaders would depart for the Holy Land in the 12th century), Clerkenwell is still a great place to see historic landmarks from throughout London's history, including magnificent Smithfield Market, St John's Gate and St Bartholomew's Church.

Islington is perceived as a chichi upper-middle-class neighbourhood synonymous with the centre-left 'New Labour' political project, despite its pockets of very real social deprivation. Since Prime Minister Tony Blair and many liberal-minded professionals bought restored Georgian homes here, 'Islington' has virtually become a term of tabloid newspaper abuse, implying a love of expensive foreign food and bleeding-heart liberalism. It's principally a night-time destination, and Upper St in particular is lined with ethnic eateries and animated bars. By day, it's worth visiting the Estorick Collection or perhaps tracing the area's literary associations. George Orwell was living at 27 Canonbury Sq when he published *Animal Farm* in 1945, and the playwright Joe Orton stayed at 25 Noel Rd for seven years in the 1960s.

SMITHFIELD MARKET Map pp448-9

☎ 7248 3151; West Smithfield EC1; ⊖ Farringdon

Smithfield is central London's last surviving meat market. Built on the site of the notorious St Bartholomew's fair, where witches were traditionally burned at the stake, and described in terms of pure horror by Dickens in *Oliver Twist*, this was once the armpit of London, where animal excrement and entrails created a sea of filth. Today it's an increasingly smart area full of bars and the market itself is a wonderful building, constantly under threat of destruction and redevelopment into office blocks. There's an interesting display of photos on Grand Ave detailing the market's history and its bombing during the Blitz.

ST BARTHOLOMEW-THE-GREAT

Map pp448-9

☎ 7606 5171; www.greatstbarts.com; West Smithfield EC1; ◷ 8.30am-5pm Tue-Fri, 10.30am-1.30pm Sat, 8am-8pm Sun; ⊖ Farringdon/Barbican

This spectacular Norman church dates from 1123, originally a part of the monastery of Augustinian Canons, but becoming the parish church of Smithfield in 1539 when King Henry VIII dissolved the monasteries. The authentic Norman arches, the weathered and blackened stone, the dark wood carvings and the low lighting lend this space an ancient calm – especially as there's sometimes only a handful of visitors.

Crime & Punishment

London's gruesome past is notorious and chances are you'll pass one of the sites connected with the city's harsh administration of justice during your visit. Smithfield, now the site of a huge meat market, was the original site of public executions in the Middle Ages. Traditionally the condemned would be hanged, burned or boiled alive here; thousands of witches met their ends at Smithfield, as well as both Catholic and Protestant martyrs in the 16th century.

However, the gallows were removed to Tyburn (today's Marble Arch) during the reign of Henry IV in the early 15th century. While Smithfield continued to be the place for burning heretics, witches, traitors and the like, condemned common criminals would be transported like cattle from Newgate, stopping in St Giles where they'd be given a last drink of ale, before continuing to Tyburn where they would be hanged in front of a braying, drunken crowd, for whom the public mass hangings were the equivalent of a football match or pop concert. The nooses would be attached to the criminals' necks and then the horse given a lash of the whip, leaving all the condemned dangling as the cart disappeared from beneath their feet. Relatives and friends would pull on the bodies to aid a quick death, and once the corpses were cut down there would be mayhem as people rushed to touch the bodies, believing them to be the source of extreme good luck.

There are historical associations with the painter William Hogarth, who was baptised here, and with politician Benjamin Franklin, who worked on site as an apprentice printer. The church sits on the corner of the grounds of St Bartholomew's Hospital, on the side closest to Smithfield Market. Another selling point for modern audiences is that scenes from the Oscar-winning *Shakespeare in Love* (and parts of *Four Weddings and a Funeral*) were filmed here. The location managers for those movies knew what they were doing: St Bartholomew-the-Great turns out to be one of the capital's most atmospheric places of worship.

KARL MARX MEMORIAL LIBRARY

Map pp442-3

☎ 7253 1485; www.marxlibrary.net; 37a Clerkenwell Green EC1; admission free; ⊙ 1-6pm Mon-Thu, to 8pm Wed, 10am-1pm Sat; ⊖ Farringdon

Clerkenwell has quite a radical history. An area of Victorian-era slums (the so-called Rookery), it was settled by mainly Italian immigrants in the 19th century. Political revolutionary Mazzini joined them and Italy's founding father Garibaldi dropped by in 1836. During his European exile, Lenin edited the Bolshevik newspaper *Iskra* (Spark) from this building in 1902–03. Copies of the newspaper have been preserved in today's library, along with a host of other socialist literature. Nonmembers are free to look around between 1pm and 2pm, but you need to become a member (£11 per year) to use the library or borrow its books.

ST JOHN'S GATE Map pp448-9
⊖ Farringdon

What looks like a toy-town medieval gate cutting across St John's Lane turns out to be the real thing. It dates from the early 16th century

but was heavily restored 300 years later. The Knights of St John of Jerusalem were soldiers who took on a nursing role during the Crusades, establishing a priory in Clerkenwell that originally covered around four hectares. The gate was built in 1504 as a grand entrance to their church, St John's Clerkenwell in St John's Sq. (This had a round nave like the one at Temple Church, and you can still see some of the circular outline picked out in grey tiles on the newly refurbished square outside.)

Although most of the buildings were destroyed when Henry VIII dissolved every priory in the country between 1536 and 1540, the gate lived on. It had a varied afterlife, not least as a Latin-speaking coffee house run, without much success, by William Hogarth's father during Queen Anne's reign. The restoration dates from the period when it housed the Old Jerusalem Tavern in the 19th century.

ORDER OF ST JOHN MUSEUM

Map pp448-9

☎ 7324 4070; www.sja.org.uk/museum; St John's Lane EC1; admission free; ⊙ 10am-5pm Mon-Fri, 10am-4pm Sat; ⊖ Farringdon

Inside St John's Gate is the small Order of St John Museum. It recounts the history of the knights and their properties around the world (gently admitting the immorality of the Crusades when seen through modern eyes), and of their successors, the modern British Order of St John and the St John Ambulance brigade. It also offers a potted history of Clerkenwell in photographs and documents.

Definitely try to arrive at 11am or 2.30pm on Tuesday, Friday or Saturday for a **guided tour** (adult/senior £5/4) of the gate and the restored church remains. This includes the fine Norman crypt with a sturdy alabaster monument commemorating a Castilian knight (1575), a battered monument showing the last prior, William Weston, as a skeleton in a shroud, and stained-glass windows showing the main figures in the story. You'll also be shown the sumptuous Chapter Hall where the Chapter General of the Order meets every three months.

CHARTERHOUSE Map pp448-9

☎ 7251 5002; Charterhouse Sq EC1; admission £10; ⓨ guided tours 2.15pm Wed Apr-Sep; ⊖ Barbican/ Farringdon

You need to book nearly a year in advance to see inside this former Carthusian monastery, whose centrepiece is a Tudor hall with a restored hammer-beam roof. Its incredibly popular summer two-hour guided tours begin at the 14th-century gatehouse on Charterhouse Sq, before going through to the Preachers' Court (with three original monks' cells in the western wall), the Master's Court, the Great Hall, and the Great Chamber, where Queen Elizabeth I stayed on numerous occasions.

Founded in 1371, the monastery was confiscated by Henry VIII in 1537 and bought by philanthropist Thomas Sutton in 1611. Today it's home to three dozen pensioners who lead the tours. For tickets, send a stamped self-addressed envelope, a covering letter giving at least three dates when you would like to attend and a cheque made payable to 'Charterhouse' to Tour Bookings, Charterhouse, Charterhouse Sq, London EC1M 6AN.

ESTORICK COLLECTION OF MODERN ITALIAN ART Map pp442-3

☎ 7704 9522; www.estorickcollection.com; 39a Canonbury Sq N1; adult/concession £3.50/2.50; ⓨ 11am-6pm Wed-Sat, noon-5pm Sun; ⊖ Highbury & Islington

The only museum in Britain devoted to Italian art, and one of the leading collections of futurist painting in the world, the Estorick Collection is housed in a listed Georgian house and stuffed with works by such greats as Giacomo Balla, Umberto Boccioni, Gino Severini and Ardengo Soffici. The collection of paintings, drawings, etchings and sculpture, amassed by American writer and art dealer Eric Estorick and his wife Salome, also includes drawings and a painting by the even more famous Amedeo Modigliani. Well-conceived special exhibitions might concentrate on Italian divisionism or a collection of classic Italian film posters. The museum also encompasses an extensive library, café and shop. Highly recommended.

WEST CENTRAL

Eating p245-50; Drinking p285; Shopping p342-4; Sleeping p362-6

London has many well-heeled neighbourhoods but none is so frightfully Jimmy Choo-ed up as this. A pristine swath of territory primed with blue blood and old money, its swank restaurants and bars are the first port of call for tabloid paparazzi stalking designer-clad trust-fund babes or stick-thin 'It' girls with double-barrelled names.

The wealth and power flow largely unabated from Mayfair – as any Monopoly player knows, the most expensive place in London – to Chelsea, the natural habitat of the 1980s phenomenon known as the Sloane Ranger (a sobriquet that has never quite disappeared). Along the way you'll pass Her Majesty's 'hood of St James's, the Prime Minister's gaff along Whitehall and the mother of all parliaments at Westminster. Only the immediate area around Victoria seems a little more urban and grimy, thanks principally to its large railway station.

With locals having money to burn, it's no wonder that Knightsbridge, in the middle of this district, is synonymous with upmarket shopping. Harrods is far from the only household name; every luxury brand conceivable has an outlet here, and then there's always Harvey Nick's. South Kensington takes a more cultured, highbrow tone with its world-class museums and famous concert hall.

Despite the enormous wealth and ingrained privilege, west central London isn't somewhere anyone need feel intimidated. The posh locals are extremely used to rubbing shoulders with tourists and most take it all with jolly-hockey-sticks good humour and equanimity.

All the same, if the air of supreme confidence that permeates this part of London isn't your thing, Hyde Park – central London's biggest green space – always provides a wonderful breath of fresh air.

MAYFAIR & ST JAMES'S

The neighbourhoods of Mayfair and St James's are where the fabulously wealthy live and play. St James's is a mixture of exclusive gentlemen's clubs (the Army and Navy sort as opposed to lap-dancing), historic shops and elegant buildings. Despite much commercial development, its matter-of-fact elitism remains pretty much intact.

Just south of St James's the real reason this area is so exclusive becomes apparent as you enter the seat of royal London, where the grand, processional Mall sweeps alongside attractive St James's Park, up to Buckingham Palace and the Queen's driveway. The district took shape when Charles II moved his court to St James's Palace in the 17th century, and the toffs followed. The great Georgian squares – Berkeley, Hanover and Grosvenor – were built in the next century, by which time St James's was largely filled. By 1900 it was the most fashionable part of London, teeming with theatres, restaurants and boutiques. Savile Row is still where gentlemen go for tailoring, Bond Sts (old and new) are where ladies go for jewellery, and Cork St is where they go together for expensive art. Some residents couldn't keep up with the Joneses of St James's and moved out – to be replaced by businesses, offices and embassies. Grosvenor Sq is dominated by the US embassy.

Mayfair is also west of Regent St and is where high society gives high-fives to one another; defining features are silver spoons and old-fashioned razzamatazz. But, in its southwestern corner, nudging Hyde Park, Shepherd Market is near the site of a rowdy and debauched fair that gave the area its name. The fair was finally banned in 1730, and today 'the old village centre of Mayfair' is a tiny enclave of pubs and bistros.

BUCKINGHAM PALACE Map pp448-9

☎ 7766 7300, for disabled access ☎ 7766 7324; www.the-royal-collection.com; SW1; adult/child/concession £13.50/7/11.50; 🕑 9.30am-4.30pm early Aug-Sep, timed ticket with admission every 15min; ✈ St James's Park/Victoria/Green Park; book for 🅰

Built in 1705 as Buckingham House for the duke of the same name, this palace has provided the royal family's London lodgings since 1837, when St James's Palace was judged too old-fashioned and insufficiently impressive. It's difficult to miss but if you're having trouble, it stands at the end of the Mall where St James's Park and Green Park converge at a large roundabout dominated by the 25m-high **Queen Victoria Memorial**. Tickets for the palace are on sale from a kiosk in Green Park.

After a series of crises and embarrassing revelations in the early 1990s, the royal spin-doctors cranked up a gear to try and rally public support behind the royals once again, and

Queen Elizabeth II leaving Buckingham Palace

it was decided to swing open the royal doors of Buck House to the public for the first time. Well, to 19 of the 661 rooms, anyway. And only during August and September, when HRH was holidaying in Scotland. And for a veritable king's ransom, but still, we mustn't quibble – no price is too great for an opportunity to see the Windsors' Polaroids plastered all over the fridge door.

The 'working rooms' are stripped down each summer for the arrival of the commoners, and the usual carpet is replaced with industrial-strength rugs, so the rooms don't look all that lavish. The tour starts in the Guard Room, too small for the Ceremonial Guard who are deployed in adjoining quarters; allows a peek inside the State Dining Room (all red damask and Regency furnishings); then moves on to the Blue Drawing Room, with a gorgeous fluted ceiling by John Nash; to the White Drawing Room, where foreign ambassadors are received; and to the Ballroom, where official receptions and state banquets are held. The biggest laugh is the Throne Room, which features kitschy his-and-hers pink chairs initialled 'ER' and 'P', sitting smugly under what looks like a theatre arch. It's good to see that they've still got a sense of humour – don't they?

The most interesting part of the tour, for all but the royal sycophants, is the 76.5m-long Picture Gallery, featuring splendid works from the likes of Van Dyck, Rembrandt, Canaletto, Poussin, Canova and Vermeer, although the likes of these and much more are yours for free at the National Gallery.

CHANGING OF THE GUARD
☎ 7766 7300; Buckingham Palace, SW1; ☽ 11.30am daily Apr-Jul & alternate days, weather permitting, Aug-Mar; ✈ St James's Park/Victoria

This is a London 'must see', although the idea of it is much more fun than the actual experience. The old guard (Foot Guards of the Household Regiment) comes off duty to be replaced by the new guard on the forecourt of Buckingham Palace, and tourists get to gape – sometimes from behind as many as 10

people – at the bright red uniforms and bear-skin hats of shouting and marching soldiers for just over half an hour. The official name for the ceremony is Guard Mounting, which, we dare say, sounds more interesting.

QUEEN'S GALLERY Map pp448-9
☎ 7766 7300; www.the-royal-collection.com; southern wing, Buckingham Palace; adult/child/concession £7.50/4/6; ☽ 10am-5.30pm; ✈ St James's Park/Victoria; ♿

Works encapsulating more than 500 years of royal, er, taste, from paintings and sculpture to ceramics, furniture and jewellery, go on display in regularly changing exhibitions at this splendid gallery, originally designed by Nash as a conservatory. It was converted into a chapel for Victoria in 1843, destroyed in a 1940 air raid and reopened as a gallery in 1962. A £20 million renovation for the Golden Jubilee in 2002 enlarged the entrance and added a Greek Doric portico, a multimedia centre and three times as much display space. Entrance to the gallery is through Buckingham Gate.

ROYAL MEWS Map pp448-9
☎ 7766 7302; www.the-royal-collection.com; Buckingham Palace Rd SW1; adult/child/concession £6/3.50/5; ☽ 11am-4pm Mar-Jul, 10am-5pm Aug & Sep; ✈ Victoria; ♿

South of the palace, the Royal Mews started life as a falconry but is now a working stable looking after the royals' immaculately groomed horses, along with the opulent vehicles the monarchy uses for getting from A to B. Highlights include the stunning gold coach of 1762, which has been used for every coronation since that of George III, and the Glass Coach of 1910, used for royal weddings. The Mews is closed in June during the four-day racing carnival of Royal Ascot, when the royal heads try to win a few bob on the gee-gees.

ST JAMES'S PARK Map pp448-9
☎ 7930 1793; the Mall SW1; ☽ 5am-dusk; ✈ St James's Park

The most pleasant of London's royal parks also has the best vistas, including those of Westminster, St James's Palace, Carlton Terrace and Horse Guards Parade; the view of Buckingham Palace from the footbridge spanning St James's Park Lake is the best you'll find. The large lake with its waterfowl acts as a focal point, while the flowerbeds – some modelled on John Nash's original 'floriferous' beds of mixed shrubs, flowers and trees – are sumptu-

Top Five Old-Fashioned London
- Buckingham Palace (p127)
- Fortnum & Mason (p342)
- Ritz (p363)
- Inns of Court (p105)
- Wallace Collection (p190)

ous and colourful in summer. Of course, at the merest hint of sunshine, it's not just the flowers that come out, but hordes of pallid sunbathers who drape themselves across the grass, the park benches and the rentable deck chairs. The eye-catching café **Inn the Park** (☎ 7451 9999; ⏰ 8am-11pm Sun-Thu, 9am-11pm Fri & Sat) serves tasty cakes, but in summer you'll be lucky to get a seat.

Nearby stands the new **National Police Memorial**, one column of marble and another of glass. Bizarrely conceived by film director Michael (Death Wish) Winner and less bizarrely designed by architect Norman Foster and artist Per Arnoldi, it pays tribute to 1600 'bobbies' who have lost their lives in the line of duty.

ST JAMES'S PALACE Map pp448-9
Cleveland Row SW1; closed to the public; ⊖ Green Park

The striking Tudor gatehouse of St James's Palace, the only surviving part of a building initiated by the palace-mad Henry VIII in 1530, is best approached from St James's St to the north of the park. This was the official residence of the king and queen for more than three centuries and foreign ambassadors are still formally accredited to the Court of St James, although the tea and biscuits are actually served at Buckingham Palace. Princess Diana, who hated this place, lived here up until her divorce from Charles in 1996, when she moved to Kensington Palace. (Ironically, the powers-that-be thought St James's Palace the most suitable place for her body to lie in state after her death in 1997.) Prince Charles and his sons stayed on at St James's until 2004, before decamping next door to Clarence House, leaving St James's Palace to a brace of minor royals and Charles's famously tetchy sister, Princess Anne. Don't get too close in case she sends out a footman to tell you to naff off.

CLARENCE HOUSE Map pp448-9
☎ 7766 7303, for disabled access ☎ 7766 7324; Cleveland Row SW1; guided tour adult/concession £6/3.50; ⏰ 9.30am-5pm Aug-Oct; ⊖ Green Park; book for ♿

After his beloved granny the Queen Mum died in 2002, Prince Charles got the tradesmen into her former home of Clarence House and spent £4.6 million of taxpayers' money reshaping the house to his own design. The 'royal residences are held in trust for future generations', but the current generation has to pay to have a look at five official rooms when the Prince, his sons and Camilla are away on their summer hols. The highlight is the former Queen Mum's small art collection, including one painting by playwright Noël Coward and others by WS Sickert and Sir James Gunn. Admission is by tour only, which must be booked (far in advance). The house was originally designed by John Nash in the early 19th century, but – as Prince Charles wasn't the first royal to call in the redecorators – has been modified much since.

SPENCER HOUSE Map pp448-9
☎ 7499 8620; www.spencerhouse.co.uk; 27 St James's Pl SW1; adult/concession £9/7; ⏰ 10.30am-5.45pm Sun, last entry 4.45pm, closed Jan & Aug; ⊖ Green Park; ♿

Just outside the park, Spencer House was built for the first Earl Spencer, an ancestor of Princess Diana, in the Palladian style between 1756 and 1766. The Spencers moved out in 1927 and their grand family home was used as an office, until Lord Rothschild stepped in and returned it to its former glory in 1987 with an £18 million restoration. Visits to the eight lavishly furnished rooms of the house are by guided tour only.

The gardens, returned to their 18th-century design, are open only between 2pm and 5pm on a couple of Sundays in summer. Tickets cost £3.50 or £11 for combined house/garden entry.

QUEEN'S CHAPEL Map pp448-9
Marlborough Rd SW1; ⏰ only for Sunday services at 8.30am & 11.15am Apr-Jul; ⊖ St James's Park

We're not all that impressed with the royal sights, but this one is quite moving: it's where all the contemporary royals from Princess Diana to the Queen Mother have lain in their coffins in the run-up to their funerals. The church was originally built by Inigo Jones in the Palladian style and was the first post-Reformation church in England built for Roman Catholic worship. It was once part of St James's Palace but was separated after a fire. The simple interior has exquisite 17th-century fittings and is atmospherically illuminated by light streaming in through the large windows above the altar.

ADMIRALTY ARCH Map p452
⊖ Charing Cross

From Trafalgar Sq, the Mall passes under this grand Edwardian monument, a triple-arched stone entrance designed by Aston Webb in honour of Queen Victoria in 1910. The large central gate is opened only for royal processions and state visits.

APSLEY HOUSE
(WELLINGTON MUSEUM) Map pp448-9
☎ 7499 5676; www.vam.ac.uk; 149 Piccadilly W1;
adult/child/concession incl audio tour £4.95/2.50/3.70;
🕑 10am-5pm Tue-Sun, last entry 4pm; ⊖ Hyde
Park Cnr

This stunning house, one of the finest in the
city, used to belong to the first Duke of Wellington and has the distinction of being known
as No 1 London, because it used to be the first
building one saw when entering town from the
west. It was designed by Robert Adam for Baron
Apsley in the late 18th century, but later sold to
Wellington, who lived here for 35 years until his
death in 1852. The duke cut Napoleon down to
size in the Battle of Waterloo and is well known
for lending his name to a sensible, if none too
flattering, style of waterproof boot.

In 1947 the house was given to the nation,
which must have come as a surprise to the
duke's descendants who still live here; 10 of
its rooms are open to the public today as the
Wellington Museum. The house itself is magnificent and retains many of its original furnishings and collections. Wellington memorabilia,
including his medals, some entertaining old
cartoons and his death mask, fill the basement
gallery, while there's an astonishing collection
of china, including some of the Iron Duke's
silverware, on the ground floor. The stairwell
is dominated by Antonio Canova's staggering 3.4m-high statue of a naked Napoleon,
adjudged by the subject as 'rather too athletic'. The 1st-floor rooms are decorated with
paintings by Velàsquez, Rubens, Brueghel and
Murillo, but perhaps the most interesting is
Goya's portrait of the duke, which some years
ago was discovered to have the face of Napoleon's brother, Joseph Bonaparte, beneath the
duke's. Apparently, the artist had taken a punt
on Napoleon winning the Battle of Waterloo
and had to do a quick 'about face' when news
of Wellington's victory arrived.

BURLINGTON ARCADE Map p450
51 Piccadilly W1; ⊖ Green Park
Flanking Burlington House – home of the Royal
Academy of Arts – on its western side is the
curious Burlington Arcade, built in 1819 and
evocative of a bygone era. Today it is a shopping precinct for the very wealthy and is most
famous for the Burlington Berties, uniformed
guards who patrol the area keeping an eye
out for punishable offences such as running,
chewing gum or whatever else might lower
the arcade's tone. The fact that the arcade
once served as a brothel isn't mentioned.

FARADAY MUSEUM Map p450
☎ 7409 2992; www.rigb.org; 21 Albarmarle St W1; admission £1; 🕑 10am-5pm Mon-Fri; ⊖ St James's Park

This museum in the Royal Institution (of Science) is dedicated to the celebrated physicist
and chemist Michael Faraday, who discovered electromagnetic, er, stuff, that led to the
invention of the dynamo. He also gave his
name to the unit of measurement for electricity. This museum – probably only of interest
to people who know what 'stuff' means –
contains a reconstruction of Faraday's labora-
tory, where he made many of his discover-
ies, and which is furnished with many of his
original apparatus.

GREEN PARK Map pp448-9
Piccadilly W1; 🕑 5am-dusk; ⊖ Green Park
Less manicured than the adjoining St James's,
this park has trees and open space, sunshine
and shade. It was once a duelling ground and
served as a vegetable garden during WWII.

GUARDS MUSEUM Map pp448-9
☎ 7414 3271; www.army.mod.uk; Wellington Barracks,
Birdcage Walk SW1; adult/concession £2/1; 🕑 10am-
4pm Feb-Dec, last entry 3.30pm; ⊖ St James's Park; ♿
Showing that the royal guards are not a
namby-pamby troop employed merely for
decoration and to entertain the tourists, this
small museum covers the history of the five
regiments of foot guards and their role in military campaigns from Waterloo on. It was established in the 17th century during the reign
of Charles II and is packed with uniforms, oil
paintings, medals, curios and memorabilia that
belonged to the soldiers. Perhaps the biggest
draw here is the huge collection of toy soldiers
in the shop.

HANDEL HOUSE MUSEUM Map pp448-9
☎ 7495 1685; www.handelhouse.org; 25 Brook St
W1; adult/child/concession £5/2/4.50; 🕑 10am-6pm
Tue-Sat, to 8pm Thu, noon-6pm Sun; ⊖ Bond St; ♿
This 18th-century Mayfair building, where
George Frederick Handel lived for 36 years
until his death in 1759, opened as a museum
in late 2001. It has been restored to how it
would have looked when the great German-
born composer was in residence, complete
with artworks borrowed from several museums. Exhibits include early editions of Handel's
operas and oratorios, although being in the
hallowed space where he composed and first
rehearsed the likes of *Water Music, Messiah,
Zadok the Priest* and *Fireworks Music* is ample

'I'll Have a House for Mayfair, Please'

Thousands of people throughout the world who've never visited know the name Mayfair via the game of Monopoly. And although the most recent Monopoly edition has replaced Mayfair and Park Lane with contemporary hotspots Canary Wharf and the City, for decades there was no higher goal in that board game than landing on and developing Mayfair. Well, it transpires that in real life – no matter the changes to the game itself – this pursuit is just as profitable as imagined in childhood dreams.

The freehold of some 300 acres in Mayfair and Belgravia is owned exclusively by the Duke of Westminster and his family, the Grosvenors. As a result of his company Grosvenor Estates' interests, the current duke has an estimated personal fortune of £5.5 billion, and for many years he topped the *Sunday Times* Rich List as the wealthiest person in Britain (until expat Russian oligarch Roman Abramovich arrived; see p206).

The duke is a controversial figure who sometimes launches unpopular development schemes. He's also a supporter of the Countryside Alliance, which backs fox hunting.

---

attraction for any enthusiast. Entrance to the museum is on Lancashire Ct.

In a funny twist of fate, the house at No 23 (now part of the museum) was home to a musician as different from Handel as could be imagined: American guitarist Jimi Hendrix (1942–69) lived there from 1968 until his death.

INSTITUTE OF CONTEMPORARY ARTS Map pp448–9

ICA; ☎ 7930 3647; www.ica.org.uk; the Mall SW1; day membership adult/concession Mon-Fri £1.50/1, Sat & Sun during exhibitions £2.50/1.50; ☺ noon-10.30pm Mon, noon-1am Tue-Sat, noon-11pm Sun; ⊖ Charing Cross/Piccadilly Circus; ⑤

Renowned for being at the cutting and controversial edge throughout the arts, the Institue of Contemporary Arts is the place to come any day of the week for all manner of experimental/progressive/radical/obscure films, dance, club nights, photography, art, theatre, music, lectures, multimedia works and book readings. Sure, much of it might seem like 'craftless tat' (as described by one resigning chairman a few years back) and the place has been known to award a £26,000 prestigious sculpture prize for what was essentially a wonky shed. However, the fact that Picasso and Henry Moore had their first UK shows here should be sufficient credentials. The complex includes an excellent bookshop, gallery, cinema, bar, theatre, and the licensed ICA Café & Restaurant.

The **Duke of York Column**, up the steps beside the ICA into Waterloo Pl, commemorates a son of George III. It was erected in 1834, but never quite caught the public imagination like Nelson's Column in Trafalgar Sq, although it's only 6m shorter.

ROYAL ACADEMY OF ARTS Map p450

☎ 7300 8000; www.royalacademy.org.uk; Burlington House, Piccadilly W1; admission varies; ☺ 10am-6pm, to 10pm Fri; ⊖ Green Park; ⑤

Britain's first art school had to play second fiddle to the Hayward Gallery for a long time, but leapt back into the limelight in recent years with a series of perfectly pitched shows, ranging from the gigantically successful Art of the Aztecs to Turks to the Academy's famous – and notoriously patchy – Summer Exhibition from early June to mid-August, which for nearly 250 years has showcased art submitted by the general public. The permanent exhibition in this radically altered Palladian mansion focuses on British art from the 18th century, and features major works from the likes of Reynolds, Gainsborough, Turner, Constable and Hockney.

Today the place is swaddled in scaffolding as the Burlington Project, a plan to more than double the Academy's space by 2008, gets underway. The Academy is already enjoying its new Annenberg Courtyard, which, à la Somerset House, features a dashing stone-paved piazza with choreographed lights and fountains flanking a statue of founder Joshua Reynolds. Pity they're prone to dolling it up with dodgy art from time to time – less is more, Academy.

ST JAMES'S PICCADILLY Map p450

☎ 7734 4511; 197 Piccadilly W1; ☺ 8am-7pm; ⊖ Green Park

The only church Christopher Wren built from scratch and on a new site (most of the others were replacements for ones razed in the Great Fire), this simple building is exceedingly easy on the eye and substitutes what some might call the pompous flourishes of his most famous churches with a warm and elegant

Neighbourhoods – West Central

131

user-friendliness. The simple spire, although designed by Wren, was added only in 1968. This is a particularly sociable church: it houses a counselling service, stages lunchtime and evening concerts, provides shelter for an antiques market and an arts and crafts fair (from 10am to 6pm on Tuesday, and from Wednesday to Sunday, respectively) as well as, what was the last thing…oh, yeah, teaching the word of God and all that jazz.

WELLINGTON ARCH Map pp448-9

☎ 7930 2726; www.english-heritage.org.uk; Hyde Park Cnr W2; adult/student or child/senior £3/1.50/2.30; ⊙ 10am-5pm Wed-Sun; ⊖ Hyde Park Cnr

Opposite Apsley House in the little bit of green space being strangled by the Hyde Park Corner roundabout is England's answer to the Arc de Triomphe, except this one commemorates France's *defeat* (specifically, Napoleon's at the hands of Wellington). The neoclassical arch, erected in 1826, used to be topped by a disproportionately large equestrian statue of Wellington, but this was removed in 1882 and replaced some years later with the biggest bronze sculpture in Britain, *Peace Descending on the Quadriga of War*.

For years the monument served as the capital's smallest police station, but it was restored

and opened up to the public as a three-level exhibition space focusing on London's arches. The balcony affords unforgettable views of Hyde Park, Buckingham Palace and the Houses of Parliament.

WESTMINSTER & WHITEHALL

Whereas the City of London has always concerned itself with the business of making money, Westminster's *raison d'être* for almost a millennium has been as the seat of royal and religious authority, and from the 14th century as the fulcrum of parliamentary power. Predictably, then, most of its sights are tied up with the affairs of the nation; its two dominating features are the most important church in England and the most famous parliament in the world. The whole area is a remarkable spectacle of rare architectural cohesion, and an awesome display of power, gravitas and historical import. Westminster is actually the name of the borough that covers much of the West End but in everyday parlance it applies only to the area immediately around Parliament Sq. Whitehall, a name synonymous with government and administration, is generally regarded as the area between

---

Cracking London's Da Vinci Code

Some consider it a load of old tosh, but not the thousands of tourists who have descended on London in pursuit of Dan Brown's best-selling novel *The Da Vinci Code*. Having sold up to 25 million copies, the book has been turned into a film starring Tom Hanks and Audrey Tatou as the heroes Langdon and Neveu, with Ian McKellen as the arch-villain Teabing. During their search for the Holy Grail and Christ's descendants, these three characters are told that 'In London lies a knight a Pope interred'. In the book, the religious department at **King's College London** (Map p452; the Strand) helps them interpret this cryptic message. Since the book was published, the college laments, it's been taking calls for a Research Institute in Systematic Theology that doesn't exist, from people wanting to use a fictional database.

Whether you're a fan of the book, or just like a good (possibly sneering) laugh, other stops on the 'grail trail' include:

Temple Church (p106) Built by the Knights Templar, who in Brown's novel were the keepers of the Holy Grail secret, this is the only surviving round church in London. However, it's more remodelled and slightly less darkly atmospheric than the novel might lead you to expect. Teabing brings Langdon and Neveu here, on a wild goose chase for a clue to the riddle, which he hints lies among the effigies. The tomb without an orb is on the northern side of the nave, but there is no surviving crypt. Talks on the church and debunking the *Da Vinci Code* are usually held every Friday at 1pm.

St James's Park (p128) Langdon and Neveu are being trailed by a rival investigator, 'The Teacher', who plans to steal what they learn. Before he does that, though, he has to deal with one of his co-workers who's slipped up. This unfortunate accomplice is dispatched in St James's Park.

Westminster Abbey (opposite) Langdon and Neveu visit the tomb of Sir Isaac Newton searching for more clues. A shady character sends them a message to meet him in the abbey's Chapter House, where there's a struggle. Teabing is arrested, while Langdon and Neveu come out on top. Of course. According to one Westminster Abbey staff member, the first question people used to ask was 'Where's the toilet?' Now it's 'Where's Sir Isaac Newton's tomb?'

Westminster and Trafalgar Sq. Millbank runs along the river from Westminster to Vauxhall Bridge and is best known as the home of New Labour spin doctors (the party's HQ are here), as well as Tate Britain.

London's geography would have been inestimably different had Edward the Confessor not moved his royal court near here in the 11th century so he could oversee the construction of Westminster Abbey. Because he did, the royal and commercial centres of London were permanently detached.

Of course, after you've seen the sights, there's sod all to do on a Westminster evening once the earnest civil servants have scurried off home to watch *EastEnders* after another tough day in the office of the nation.

WESTMINSTER ABBEY Map pp448-9

☎ 7222 5152; www.westminster-abbey.org; Dean's Yard SW1; adult/child/concession £8/free/6; ⏲ 9.30am-3.45pm Mon-Fri, to 6pm or 7pm Wed, 9.30am-1.45pm Sat, last entry 1hr before closing; ⊖ Westminster; ♿

This is one of the most sacred and symbolic sites in England. With the exception of Edward V and Edward VIII, every sovereign has been crowned here since William the Conqueror in 1066, and most of the monarchs from Henry III (died 1272) to George II (died 1760) were also buried here. In addition to being the well from which the Anglican Church draws its inspiration, the abbey is also where the nation commemorates its political and artistic idols. It's difficult to imagine its equivalent anywhere else in the world.

The abbey is a magnificent, arresting sight. Though a mixture of architectural styles, it is considered the finest example of Early English Gothic (1180–1280) in existence. The original church was built in the 11th century by King (later St) Edward the Confessor, who is buried in the chapel behind the main altar. Henry III (r 1216–72) began work on the new building but didn't complete it; the French Gothic nave was finished in 1388. Henry VII's huge and magnificent chapel was added in 1519. Unlike St Paul's, Westminster Abbey has never been a cathedral – it is what is called a 'royal peculiar' and is administered directly by the Crown.

Without belittling its architectural achievements, the abbey is probably more impressive from outside than within. The interior is chock-a-block with small chapels, elaborate tombs of monarchy and monuments to various luminaries down through the ages. And, as

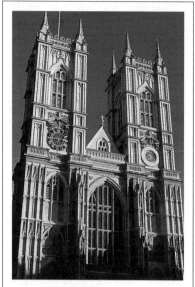

Westminster Abbey

you might expect for one of the most visited churches in Christendom, it can get intolerably busy in here.

Immediately past the barrier through the north door is what's known as **Statesmen's Aisle**, where politicians and eminent public figures are commemorated mostly by staggeringly large marble statues. The Whig and Tory prime ministers who dominated late Victorian politics, Gladstone (who is buried here) and Disraeli (who is not), have their monuments uncomfortably close to one another. Nearby is a monument to Robert Peel, who, as home secretary in 1829, created the Metropolitan Police force. They became known as 'Bobby's boys' and later, simply, 'bobbies'.

At the eastern end of the sanctuary, opposite the entrance to the Henry VII Chapel, is the rather ordinary-looking **Coronation Chair**, upon which almost every monarch since the late 13th century is said to have been crowned. Up the steps in front of you and to your left is the narrow **Queen Elizabeth Chapel**, where Elizabeth I and her half-sister 'Bloody Mary' share an elaborate tomb.

The **Henry VII Chapel**, in the easternmost part of the abbey, has spectacular circular vaulting on the ceiling. Behind the chapel's altar is the elaborate sarcophagus of Henry VII and his queen, Elizabeth of York.

133

Beyond the chapel's altar is the **Royal Air Force (RAF) Chapel**, with a stained-glass window commemorating the force's finest hour, the Battle of Britain. Next to it, a plaque marks the spot where Oliver Cromwell's body lay for two years until the Restoration, when it was disinterred, hanged and beheaded. The bodies believed to be those of the two child princes (allegedly) murdered in the Tower of London in 1483 are buried here. The chapel's southern aisle contains the **tomb of Mary Queen of Scots**, beheaded on the orders of her cousin Elizabeth and with the acquiescence of her son, the future James I.

The **Chapel of St Edward the Confessor**, the most sacred spot in the abbey, lies just east of the sanctuary and behind the high altar; access may be restricted to protect the 13th-century floor. St Edward was the founder of the abbey and the original building was consecrated a few weeks before his death. His tomb was slightly altered after the original was destroyed during the Reformation.

The south transept contains **Poets' Corner**, where many of England's finest writers are buried and/or commemorated; a memorial here is the highest honour the Queen can bestow. Just north is the **Lantern**, the heart of the abbey, where coronations take place. If you face eastwards while standing in the centre, the sanctuary is in front of you. George Gilbert Scott designed the ornate high altar in 1897. Behind you, Edward Blore's chancel, dating from the mid-19th century, is a breathtaking structure of gold, blue and red Victorian Gothic. Where monks once worshipped, boys from the Choir School and lay vicars now sing the daily services.

The entrance to the **Cloister** is 13th century, while the cloister itself dates from the 14th. Eastwards down a passageway off the Cloister are three museums run by English Heritage. The octagonal **Chapter House** (admission with/without abbey ticket £1/2.50; 🕑 9.30am-5pm Apr-Sep, 10am-5pm Oct, 10am-4pm Nov-Mar) has one of Europe's best-preserved medieval tile floors and retains traces of religious murals. It was used as a meeting place by the House of Commons in the second half of the 14th century. The adjacent **Pyx Chamber** (admission with/without abbey ticket £1/2.50; 🕑 10am-4.30pm) is one of the few remaining relics of the original abbey and contains the abbey's treasures and liturgical objects. The **Abbey Museum** (🕑 10.30am-4pm) exhibits the death masks of generations of royalty, wax effigies representing Charles II and William III (who is

on a stool to make him as tall as his wife Mary), as well as armour and stained glass.

To reach the 900-year-old **College Garden** (🕑 10am-6pm Tue-Thu Apr-Sep, 10am-4pm Tue-Thu Oct-Mar), enter Dean's Yard and the Little Cloisters off Great College St.

On the western side of the cloister is **Scientists' Corner**, where you will find **Sir Isaac Newton's tomb**; a nearby section of the northern aisle of the nave is known as **Musicians' Aisle**.

The two towers above the west door are the ones through which you exit. These were designed by Nicholas Hawksmoor and completed in 1745. Just above the door, perched in 15th-century niches, are the latest sacred additions to the abbey: 10 stone statues of international 20th-century martyrs. These were unveiled in 1998 and they include the likes of Martin Luther King and the Polish priest St Maximilian Kolbe, who was murdered by the Nazis at Auschwitz.

To the right as you exit is a memorial to innocent victims of oppression, violence and war around the world. 'All you who pass by, is it nothing to you?' it asks poignantly. Give it some thought.

There are 90-minute **guided tours** (☎ 7222 7110; £3) that leave several times during the day (Monday to Saturday) and limited **audio tours** (£2). One of the best ways to visit the abbey is to attend a service, particularly evensong (5pm weekdays, 3pm at weekends). Sunday Eucharist is at 11am.

There is an extraordinary amount to see here but, unless you enjoy feeling like part of a herd, come very early or very late.

HOUSES OF PARLIAMENT Map pp448-9

☎ 7219 4272; www.parliament.uk; St Stephen's Entrance, St Margaret St SW1; admission free; 🕑 during Parliamentary sessions 2.30-10.30pm Mon, 11.30am-7pm Tue & Wed, 11.30am-6.30pm Thu, 9.30am-3pm Fri; ⊖ Westminster; 🚻

The House of Commons and House of Lords are housed here in the sumptuous Palace of Westminster. Charles Barry, assisted by interior designer Augustus Pugin, built it between 1840 and 1860, when the extravagant neo-Gothic style was all the rage. The most famous feature outside the palace is the Clock Tower, commonly known as **Big Ben**. Ben is the bell hanging inside and is named after Benjamin Hall, the commissioner of works when the tower was completed in 1858. If you're very keen, you can apply in writing for a free tour of the Clock Tower (see the website). Thirteen-ton Ben has rung in the New Year since 1924, and the clock gets its hands and face washed by abseiling cleaners once every five years. The best view of the whole complex is from the eastern side of Lambeth Bridge. At the opposite end of the building is **Victoria Tower**, completed in 1860.

The House of Commons is where Members of Parliament (MPs) meet to propose and discuss new legislation, to grill the prime minister and other ministers, and to get their mugs on TV to show their constituents they are actually working. Watching a debate is not terribly exciting unless it's Prime Minister's Question Time, for which you will have to book advance tickets through your MP or local British embassy.

The layout of the Commons Chamber is based on that of St Stephen's Chapel in the original Palace of Westminster. The current chamber, designed by Giles Gilbert Scott, replaced the earlier one destroyed by a 1941 bomb. Although the Commons is a national assembly of 659 MPs, the chamber has seating for only 437. Government members sit to the right of the Speaker and Opposition members to the left. The Speaker presides over business from a chair given by Australia, while ministers speak from a despatch box donated by New Zealand.

When Parliament is in session, visitors are admitted to the **House of Commons Visitors' Gallery**. Expect to queue for an hour or two if you haven't already organised a ticket. Parliamentary recesses (ie holidays) last for three months over the summer and a couple of weeks over Easter and Christmas, so it's best to ring in advance. To find out what's being debated on a particular day, check the notice board posted beside the entrance, or look in the *Daily Telegraph* or the freebie *Metro* newspaper under 'Today in Parliament'. Bags and cameras must be checked at a cloakroom before you enter the gallery and no large suitcases or backpacks are allowed through the airport-style security gate.

A bulletproof screen sits between members of the public and the debating chamber. After campaign group Fathers 4 Justice managed to lob a condom full of purple powder at the PM in May 2004 and pro-hunt campaigners broke into the Commons that September, security has been further tightened, but not without some difficulties. People kept on souveniring the visitors' badges first introduced, so those had to be abandoned. Unfortunately, the low-cost stickers used to replace them don't stick very well to clothing, but virtually weld themselves to Westminster's ancient flagstones.

Top Five Romantic London

- Kissing in the back of a **black cab** (p403)
- A squeeze on top of the **London Eye** (p149)
- Indulging in a champagne picnic on **Hampstead Heath** (p194) on a summer's evening
- Gazing at the river from the **Millennium Bridge** (p152) or Golden Jubilee Bridge
- Shopping together for lingerie in **Agent Provocateur** (p336)

Another rethink is probably required – but in the meantime try to keep your sticker with you. A new visitors' entrance to the Palace of Westminster is also being considered.

The **House of Lords Visitors' Gallery** (☎ 7219 3107; admission free; ☯ 2.30-10pm Mon-Wed, 11am-1.30pm & 3-7.30pm Thu, 11am-3pm Fri) is also open to outsiders. Against a backdrop of peers' gentle snoring, you can view the intricate Gothic interior that led poor Pugin (1812–52) to an early death from overwork and nervous strain.

As you're waiting for your bags to go through the X-ray machines, look left at the stunning roof of **Westminster Hall**, originally built in 1099 and today the oldest surviving part of the Palace of Westminster, the seat of the English monarchy from the 11th to the early 16th centuries. Added between 1394 and 1401, it is the earliest known example of a hammer-beam roof and has been described as 'the greatest surviving achievement of medieval English carpentry'. Westminster Hall was used for coronation banquets in medieval times, and also served as a courthouse until the 19th century. The trials of William Wallace (1305), Thomas More (1535), Guy Fawkes (1606) and Charles I (1649) all took place here. In the 20th century, monarchs and Winston Churchill lay in state here.

When Parliament is in recess, there are 75-minute **guided summer tours** (☎ 0870 906 3773; St Stephen's Entrance, St Margaret St; adult/ concession £7/5) of both chambers and other historic buildings. Times change, so telephone or check www.parliament.uk for latest details.

TATE BRITAIN Map pp460-1

☎ 7887 8000, 7887 8888; www.tate.org.uk; Millbank SW1; admission free, prices vary for temporary exhibitions; ☯ 10am-5.50pm; ⊖ Pimlico; ♿

You'd think maybe this gallery would be down in the dumps since its sibling, the Tate Modern, stole half its collection and pretty much all of the limelight when it opened in 2000. On the contrary, the venerable Tate, built in 1897, is thriving, too.

First of all, the gallery stretched out splendidly into all its increased space, filling it with its definitive collection of British art from the 16th to the late 20th centuries.

Then in 2005 it rediscovered the blockbuster special exhibition, with its Turner, Whistler and Monet show breaking all attendance records, followed by an attention-grabbing showcase of Joshua Reynolds' work, and another triumvirate in Degas, Sickert and Toulouse-Lautrec.

Away from the headline-grabbing one-offs, the permanent galleries are broadly chronological in order, and you can expect to see some of the most important works by artists such as Constable and Gainsborough – who have entire galleries devoted to them – and Hogarth, Reynolds, Stubbs, Blake, Hockney and Moore, among others. There's a separate room devoted to Lucian Freud and Francis Bacon, and one apiece to contemporary artists Antony Gormley (the sculptor behind the *Angel of the North* statue on the way to Newcastle) and bad-girl Britartist Tracey Emin.

Adjoining the main building is the Clore Gallery, which houses the huge and occasionally superb JMW Turner bequest.

There are several free one-hour **thematic tours** each day, mostly on the hour, along with free 15-minute talks on paintings, painters and styles at 1.15pm Tuesday to Thursday in the Rotunda. **Audio tours** for the collection cost £3/2.50 (adult/concession). A boat connects the two Tates; see p94.

From October to early December every year, Tate Britain hosts the prestigious Turner Prize of contemporary art, temporarily stealing the limelight back from its sister, the Tate Modern.

CHURCHILL MUSEUM & CABINET WAR ROOMS Map pp448-9

☎ 7930 6961; www.iwm.org.uk; Clive Steps, King Charles St SW1; adult/under 16yr/unemployed/senior & student £10/free/5/8; ☽ 9.30am-6pm, last admission 5pm; ✜ Charing Cross/Westminster; ⚹

Down in the bunker where Prime Minister Winston Churchill, his cabinet and generals met during WWII, £6 million has been spent on a huge exhibition devoted to 'the greatest Briton'. This whiz-bang, multimedia Churchill Museum joins the highly evocative Cabinet War Rooms, where chiefs of staff slept, ate and plotted Hitler's downfall, blissfully believing

they were protected from Luftwaffe bombs by the 3m slab of concrete overhead. (Turns out it would have crumpled like paper had the area taken a hit.) Together, these two sections make you forget the Churchill who was a maverick and lousy peace-time politician, and drive home how much the cigar-chewing, war-time PM was a case of right man, right time.

The Churchill Museum contains all sorts of posters, trivia and personal effects, from the man's cigars to a 'British bulldog' vase in his image, and from his formal Privy Council uniform to his shockingly tasteless red velvet 'romper' outfit. So, to be fair, the museum doesn't shy away from its hero's fallibilities. However, it does begin with his strongest suit – his stirring speeches, replayed for each goose-bumped visitor who steps in front of the matching screen. 'I have nothing to offer but blood, toil, tears and sweat', 'We will fight them on the beaches', 'Never in the course of human history has so much been owed by so many to so few'. Elsewhere, silver-tongued Winnie even gets credit for inspiring Orson Welles' famous rant about Switzerland and cuckoo clocks, with a speech he made to Parliament several years before *The Third Man* was filmed.

There's fantastically edited footage of Churchill's 1965 state funeral, making the April 2005 burial of Pope John Paul II look like a low-key family affair, and you can check on what the PM was doing nearly every day beforehand via the huge, table-top interactive lifeline. Touch the screen on a particular year, and it will open up into months and days for you to choose.

In stark contrast, the old Cabinet War Rooms have been left much as they were when the lights were turned off on VJ Day in August 1945 and everyone headed off for a well-earned drink. The room where the Cabinet held more than 100 meetings, the Telegraph Room with a hotline to Roosevelt, the cramped typing pool, the converted broom cupboard that was Churchill's office and scores of bedrooms have all been preserved.

You will pass the broadcast niche where Churchill made four of his rousing speeches to the nation, including one about Germany's fuelling 'a fire in British hearts' by launching the London Blitz. In the Chief of Staff's Conference Room, the walls are covered with huge, original maps that were discovered only in 2002. If you squint two-thirds of the way down the right wall, somebody (possibly even Churchill himself) drew a little doodle depicting a cross-eyed and bandy-legged Hitler knocked on his arse.

The free audioguide is very informative and entertaining and features plenty of anecdotes, including some from people who worked here in the nerve centre of Britain's war effort – and weren't even allowed by their short-tempered boss to relieve the tension by whistling.

WHITEHALL Map pp448-9

Whitehall and its extension, Parliament St, is the wide avenue that links Trafalgar and Parliament Squares, and it is lined with many government buildings, statues, monuments and other historical bits and pieces.

BANQUETING HOUSE Map pp448-9

☎ 7930 4179; Whitehall SW1; adult/concession £4/3; ⏰ 10am-5pm Mon-Sat; ✆ Westminster/Charing Cross; book for ♿

This is the only surviving part of the Tudor Whitehall Palace, which once stretched most of the way down Whitehall and burned down in 1698. It was designed as England's first purely Renaissance building by Inigo Jones after he returned from Italy, and looked like no other structure in the country at the time. Apparently, the English hated it for more than a century.

A bust outside commemorates 30 January 1649 when Charles I, accused of treason by Cromwell after the Civil War, was executed on a scaffold built against a 1st-floor window here. When the royals were reinstated with Charles II, it inevitably became something of a royalist shrine, although its ceremonial functions faded in time and it was used as the Chapel Royal from the 18th century. It is still occasionally used for state banquets and concerts, but fortunately you don't have to be on the royal A-list to visit. In a huge, virtually unfurnished hall on the 1st floor there are nine ceiling panels painted by Rubens in 1635. They were commissioned by Charles I and depict the 'divine right' of kings. Maybe he got what he deserved.

CENOTAPH Map pp448-9

Whitehall SW1; ✆ Westminster/Charing Cross

The Cenotaph (Greek for 'empty tomb') is Britain's main memorial to the Commonwealth citizens who were killed during the two world wars. The Queen and other public figures lay poppies at its base on 11 November.

NO 10 DOWNING STREET Map pp448-9

www.number10.gov.uk; 10 Downing St SW1; ✆ Westminster/Charing Cross

An ambitious real-estate agent might describe this as the British PM's live/work space. It's been the British leader's official office since 1732, when George II presented No 10 to Robert Walpole, and since refurbishment in 1902 it's also been the PM's official London residence. As Margaret Thatcher, a grocer's daughter, put it, the PM 'lives above the shop' here.

For such a famous address, however, No 10 is a small-looking building on a plain-looking street, hardly warranting comparison to the White House, for example. A stoic bobby stands guard outside, but you can't get too close; ever since the IRA fired a rocket at No 10 during John Major's premiership the street has been cordoned off with a rather large iron gate.

Breaking with tradition when he came to power, Tony Blair and his family swapped houses with the then-unmarried Chancellor, who traditionally occupied the rather larger flat at No 11. He also commandeered the offices at No 12, traditional base of the chief whip, claiming the need for more workspace.

HORSE GUARDS PARADE Map pp448-9

☎ 0906 866 3344; ⏰ 11am Mon-Sat & 10am Sun; ✆ Westminster

In a more accessible version of Buckingham Palace's Changing of the Guard, the mounted troopers of the Household Cavalry change guard here daily, at the official entrance to the royal palaces (opposite the Banqueting House). A lite-pomp version takes place at 4pm when the dismounted guards are changed. On the Queen's official birthday in June, the Trooping of the Colour is also staged here.

Fittingly, as the parade ground and its buildings were built in 1745 to house the Queen's so-called 'Life Guards', this is being proposed as the pitch for the beach volleyball during the London 2012 Olympics. When this choice of venue was first announced, it had Tony Blair gloating about what a good view of the bikini-clad players the prime minister would have

Neighbourhoods – West Central

137

from his Downing St back window (and some of the public wondering how long Blair was *really* hoping to stay in power).

JEWEL TOWER Map pp448-9

☎ 7222 2219; Abingdon St SW1; adult/concession £2.60/2; ⏱ 10am-5pm Apr-Sep, 10am-4pm Oct-Mar; ⊖ Westminster

Across the road from the Houses of Parliament, the Jewel Tower was built in 1365 to house the treasury of Edward III and is one of the last vestiges of the medieval Palace of Westminster. The tower has had various functions over the years, although storing the crown jewels was never one of them. Today it houses exhibitions describing the history and procedures of Parliament. There is a 25-minute explanatory video, which occasionally works, and this is a useful first stop if you intend visiting the House of Commons. Otherwise, it's a stocky and handsome building with a few interesting exhibits, such as a 12th-century Saxon sword.

ST JOHN'S SMITH SQUARE Map pp460-1

☎ 7222 1061; www.sjss.org.uk; Smith Sq, Westminster SW1; ⊖ Westminster

In the heart of Westminster, this eye-catching church was built by Thomas Archer in 1728 under the Fifty New Churches Act (1711), which aimed to stem the spread of nonconformism by swamping the market (so *that's* where Starbucks got the idea). With its four corner towers and monumental façades, the church was much maligned for the first century of its existence. Queen Anne is said to have likened it to a footstool, although in the version told by the people who run the church, Queen Anne actually requested a church built in the shape of a footstool. Anyway, it's generally agreed now that the church is a masterpiece of English Baroque, although it's no longer a church. After receiving a direct hit during WWII, it was rebuilt in the 1960s as a classical music venue (p325) and, as such, is renowned for its crisp acoustics. The brick-vaulted restaurant in the crypt is called, as you might guess, the Footstool, and is open for lunch Monday to Friday, as well as for pre- and postconcert dinner.

VICTORIA & PIMLICO

Clinging to Westminster, Victoria has all the pizzazz of its neighbour without any of the attractions, which doesn't add up to very much at all. It's best known for coming and going, via its huge train and coach stations. Despite its function as a transport hub, there's not all that much reason for staying unless you're a backpacker availing of its cheap and predominantly cheerless accommodation. The one attraction worth pausing your journey for is the candy-striped Westminster Cathedral a couple of hundred metres from the tube station.

At least Victoria's unattractiveness gives it a smidgen of character; Pimlico, on the other hand, would probably disappear in an X-ray. Thomas Cubitt built most of it in the 19th century, but the developer had obviously done his dash in the creation of swanky Belgravia nearby and was only creating apathetically plain Pimlico for beer money. Its only redeeming feature is the view it affords across the river to the Battersea Power Station.

WESTMINSTER CATHEDRAL Map pp460-1

☎ 7798 9055; www.westminstercathedral.org.uk; Victoria St SW1; cathedral admission free, tower adult/concession £3/1.50, audioguides £2.50; ⏱ cathedral 7am-7pm, tower 9am-5pm Apr-Nov, 9am-5pm Thu-Sun Dec-Mar; ⊖ Victoria; ♿

In 1895 work began on this cathedral, the headquarters of the Roman Catholic Church in Britain, and although worshippers began flocking here in 1903, the church ran out of money and the project has never been completed. In some ways, it's London's version of Gaudí's La Sagrada Familia in Barcelona – a magnificent work in progress.

John Francis Bentley's design is a superb example of neo-Byzantine architecture: its distinctive candy-striped red-brick and white-stone tower features prominently on the west London skyline. Remarkably few people think to look inside, but the interior is part stunning marble and mosaic and part bare brick, although the stunning bits are slowly climbing up the walls and pillars. The highly regarded stone carvings of the *14 Stations of the Cross* (1918) by Eric Gill and the marvellously sombre atmosphere make this a welcome haven from the traffic outside. The views from the 83m-tall **Campanile Bell Tower** are impressive, as is the fact that there's a lift to save you the climb.

Seven Masses are said daily from Sunday to Friday and five on Saturday. There's a gift shop and a café here, open 10am to 4.30pm daily.

Westminster Cathedral (opposite)

CHELSEA & BELGRAVIA

Chelsea has been one of London's most fashionable precincts ever since chancellor Thomas More moved here in the early 16th century. The 'village of palaces' became one of London's most desirable neighbourhoods, as it was close to the bustle of the City and Westminster yet still concealed behind a big bend in the river. Even when it was consumed by greater London in the 20th century, it retained its aristocratic angle and even managed to mix it with a Bohemian vibe. Its main artery, King's Rd, helped propel London into the swinging '60s and Chelsea even managed to get a big slice of punk cred in the following decade. These days its residents still have among the highest incomes of any London borough (shops and restaurants presume you do too), the community is as cosmopolitan as the local football team and it's still awash with 'trendy' this and that. And that's the big difference: it feels like the folk of Chelsea are trying to be trendy these days, and the area has lost much of its stylish oomph and is now filled with money without much of the magic.

Neighbouring Belgravia, with its white stuccoed squares, has had a reputation for elitism ever since it was laid out by builder Thomas Cubitt in the 19th century. It's a charming, mainly residential enclave with quaint cobbled mews, numerous embassies, a few wonderful old-fashioned pubs and, these days, nowhere near the affectation of its try-hard neighbour.

KING'S ROAD Map pp458-9
⊖ Sloane Sq/South Kensington

In the 17th century, Charles II set up a Chelsea love nest here for him and his mistress, an orange-seller at the Drury Lane Theatre by the name of Nell Gwyn. Heading back to Hampton Court Palace of an evening, Charles would make use of a farmer's track that inevitably came to be known as the King's Rd. The street was at the forefront of London, nay world, fashion during the technicolour '60s and anarchic '70s, and continues to be trendy now, albeit in a more self-conscious way. The street begins at Sloane Sq, to the north of which runs Sloane St, celebrated for its designer boutiques.

CHELSEA OLD CHURCH Map pp458-9
☎ 7795 1019; cnr Cheyne Walk & Old Church St SW3; ⏱ 1.30-5.30pm Tue-Fri & Sun; ⊖ Sloane Sq; &

This church is principally a monument to Thomas More (1477–1535), the former chancellor (and current Roman Catholic saint) who lost his head for refusing to go along with Henry VIII's plan to establish himself as supreme head of the Church of England. Original features include the **More Chapel**, and More's headless body is rumoured to be buried somewhere within the church. (His head, having been hung out on London Bridge according to the practice of the times, is now at rest a long way away in St Dunstan's Church, Canterbury.)

Outside is a gold statue of More, who lived in Chelsea with his family in a property expropriated by Henry VIII after the lord chancellor's execution. Other celebrated former residents of Chelsea, and Cheyne Walk in particular, are *Middlemarch* author George Eliot, who lived and died at No 4, and the painter JMW Turner, who lived at No 119 under the alias 'Booth'.

CHELSEA PHYSIC GARDEN Map pp458-9
☎ 7352 5646; www.chelseaphysicgarden.co.uk; 66 Royal Hospital Rd SW3; adult/concession £5/3; ⏱ noon-5pm Wed & 2-6pm Sun Apr-Oct, noon-5pm daily during the Chelsea Flower Show, 11am-3pm on Snowdrop Days (1st & 2nd Sun in Feb); ⊖ Sloane Sq; &

Established by the Apothecaries' Society in 1673 for students studying medicinal plants and healing, this relatively secret garden – barely known to Londoners – is one of the oldest of its kind in Europe and contains many rare trees, shrubs and plants. Planting beds include a pharmaceutical garden (devoted to plants used in contemporary Western medicine), a garden of world medicine (highlighting plants used by tribal peoples in Australia, China, India, New Zealand and North America) and a garden of perfume and aromatherapy. There are also collections of island plants from Crete, the Canaries and Madeira.

The statue is of Sir Hans Sloane, the philanthropist who saved the garden from going under in the early 18th century. Various beds are devoted to prominent botanists, including Sir Joseph Banks, who was famous for mapping the flora of Australia and Newfoundland.

Opening hours for the garden are limited because the grounds are still used for research and education. Tours – informative and entertaining – can be organised by appointment.

ALBERT & BATTERSEA BRIDGES

Map pp458-9
One of London's most striking bridges, the Albert is a cross between a cantilever and a suspension bridge, buttressed to strengthen it as an alternative to closure in the 1960s. It was designed by Roland Mason Ordish in 1873, but later modified by the engineer Joseph Bazalgette, who then built the companion Battersea Bridge in 1890. Painted white and pink and with fairy lights adorning its cables, it looks stunning during the day and festive by night. The booths at either end survive from the days when tolls applied.

ROYAL HOSPITAL CHELSEA Map pp458-9

☎ 7881 5200; www.chelsea-pensioners.co.uk; Royal Hospital Rd SW3; admission free; ⏰ 10am-noon & 2-4pm Apr-Sep, 10am-noon & 2-4pm Mon-Sat Oct-Mar; ⊖ Sloane Sq; call for ♿
Designed by Christopher Wren, this superb structure was built in 1692 to provide shelter for ex-servicemen. Since the reign of Charles II, it has housed hundreds of war veterans, known as Chelsea Pensioners. They're fondly regarded as national treasures, and cut striking figures in the dark blue greatcoats (in winter) or scarlet frock-coats (in summer) they wear on ceremonial occasions.

At the time of writing, however, the pensioners were in temporary accommodation, awaiting a refurbishment of the residential wing, or 'Long Wards', as well as a new infirmary. Most of the controversy about this – there's a debate over which plans to choose – will

be irrelevant to visitors. It's usually possible to visit the museum (which contains a huge collection of war medals bequeathed by former residents), as well as to look into the hospital's Great Hall, Octagon, Chapel and courtyards. Do note, however, that the hospital is off-limits to visitors when it is hosting events.

The Chelsea Flower Show – definitely open to the public – takes place here in May. For more on that, see www.rhs.org.uk.

NATIONAL ARMY MUSEUM Map pp458-9

☎ 7730 0717; www.national-army-museum.ac.uk; Royal Hospital Rd SW3; admission free but donations requested; ⏰ 10am-5.30pm; ⊖ Sloane Sq; ♿
Next door to the Royal Hospital, appropriately enough, this old-fashioned museum tells the history of the British army from the perspective of the men and women who put their lives on the line for king and country in eras when there was honour in doing such. Refreshingly low-tech, it convey the horrors as well as the glories of war, with exhibits ranging from the skeleton of Napoleon's horse and model trenches, through to the usual arsenal of weapons, artillery and military tactics. Two of the best exhibitions focus on the life and times of the 'Redcoat' (the term for the British soldier from the Battle of Agincourt in 1415 to the American Revolution), and the tactical battle at Waterloo between Napoleon and the Duke of Wellington.

CARLYLE'S HOUSE Map pp458-9

☎ 7352 7087; 24 Cheyne Row SW3; adult/concession £4/2; ⏰ 2-5pm Wed-Fri, 11am-5pm Sat & Sun mid-Mar–Nov; ⊖ Sloane Sq
From 1834 until his death in 1881, the Victorian essayist and historian Thomas Carlyle lived in this three-storey house, writing his famous history of the French Revolution and many other works. Legend has it that when the manuscript was complete, a maid accidentally threw it on the fire, whereupon the diligent Thomas patiently wrote it all again. The small, charming 1798 terraced house is purported to be pretty much as it was when Carlyle and his wife Jane lived here, and the likes of Chopin, Tennyson and Dickens would call around for a natter.

KNIGHTSBRIDGE, SOUTH KENSINGTON & HYDE PARK

Much of west central London is high-class territory and it doesn't get much higher or classier than 'South Ken', which thanks to Prince Albert and the 1851 Great Exhibition is also museum-centric, home to the Natural History, Science and Victoria & Albert Museums all on one road. This is also one of London's most sophisticated stretches, with sizable English, French, Italian and Far Eastern communities all bound together in prosperity. Kensington High St, a lively blend of upmarket boutiques and chain stores, dominates the area of Kensington itself. North of here is Holland Park, a residential district of elegant town houses built around a wooded park. Knightsbridge, once famous for highwaymen and raucous drinking, is now renowned for its swanky shopping and for being a playpen for moneyed and perpetually tanned middle-aged men and ditzy young rich girls, not necessarily playing together. Screening the denizens of these well-to-do neighbourhoods from the decidedly more drab Bayswater and Paddington to the north are the utterly splendid Hyde Park and Kensington Gardens (think of them as one big green entity), around which upmarket hotels and prestigious shops have long since shooed the hoi polloi away.

VICTORIA & ALBERT MUSEUM

Map pp458-9

☎ 7942 2000; www.vam.ac.uk; Cromwell Rd SW7; admission free, prices vary for temporary exhibitions; ☿ 10am-5.45pm, to 10pm Wed & last Fri of month; ➔ South Kensington; ⛨

This vast, rambling museum of decorative art and design is part of Prince Albert's legacy to the nation in the aftermath of the successful Great Exhibition of 1851. It's a bit like the nation's attic, comprising four million objects collected over the years from Britain and around the globe. Some people love the sheer eclecticism of it all; those with shorter attention spans will swiftly be overwhelmed unless they pick their areas of interest carefully.

Spread over nearly 150 galleries, the museum houses the world's greatest collection of decorative arts, including ancient Chinese ceramics, modernist architectural drawings, Korean bronze and Japanese swords, cartoons by Raphael, spellbinding Asian and Islamic art, Rodin sculptures, gowns from the Elizabethan era, dresses straight from this year's Paris fashion shows, ancient jewellery, a 1930s wireless set – you get the picture. But what you see is only the tip of the iceberg, with the vast majority of the rotated collection always in storage. As part of the

museum's FuturePlan lots of renewal work has been taking place recently.

As you enter under the stunning **Dale Chihuly Chandelier** you can pick up a map of the museum at the information and ticket desk. (If the main entrance on Cromwell Rd is too busy, there's another around the corner on Exhibition Rd.) Although it handily points out the museum's highlights, the floor plan is hardly straightforward, and parts of the building frustratingly only connect on certain floors. So if you're prone to getting lost, consider one of the free **introductory guided tours** that leave the main reception area every hour from 10.30am to 4.30pm. There is also family activities information; ask at one of the desks.

Level 1 is mostly devoted to art and design from India, China, Japan and Korea, as well as European art. It's here that you'll find **Room 40** – almost always a highlight of any visit even if you don't generally consider yourself into fashion – and the new **Islamic Galleries**, opened in 2005.

The newly replanted and landscaped **garden** is a lovely, shaded inner courtyard where you can collect your thoughts. Beyond the garden lies a bit of controversy. Two of the three original refreshment rooms dating from the 1860s have been turned back into a café. The problem is that the cheap furniture shoved into the **Gamble and Poynter Rooms** is hardly sympathetic with their ornate Arts and Crafts interiors. Only the **William Morris Room** has been spared the indignity.

The **British Galleries**, featuring every aspect of British design from 1500 to 1900, are found on Levels 2 and 4, while **20th-century design** and **silverware** is on Level 3.

The Three Graces, a famous marble statue by Antonio Canova, is found on Level 4 among the British Galleries. In the 1990s the statue was controversially 'saved' for the nation after the public raised £7.6m to buy it from a private owner and prevent it going to the US. When it was privately owned, the statue of the three sisters used to be revolved so guests could admire their fetching posteriors.

The new **architecture** section is also on Level 4 (although you can't cross from the British Galleries section, but must go back to Level 1 and catch another lift).

The V&A's temporary exhibitions are frequently compelling and it has a brilliant programme of talks, events and even club evenings. For many visitors, these attractions even surpass the permanent collection, so consider yourself warned.

NATURAL HISTORY MUSEUM

Map pp458-9

☎ 7938 9123; www.nhm.ac.uk; Cromwell Rd SW7; admission free, highlights tours (depending on availability) £3, half-hourly tours of 'wet' zoological exhibits in the Darwin Centre free; ⏰ 10am-5.50pm Mon-Sat, 11am-5.50pm Sun; ⊖ South Kensington; ♿

The Natural History Museum is very much a museum of two halves: the **Life Galleries** in the gloriously over-the-top Gothic Revival building (1880) approached from Cromwell Rd, and the slick **Earth Galleries**, whose entrance lies around the corner on Exhibition Rd. The first evokes the fusty, musty moth-eaten era of the Victorian gentleman scientist; the second feels like walking into a swanky Italian nightclub. The only real unifying factor is that both halves are extremely kid-friendly.

The main museum building, designed by Alfred Waterhouse with gleaming blue and sand-coloured brick and terracotta, is largely lined with fossils and glass cases of taxidermied birds. True, its antiquated atmosphere is charming and there are some popular, modern additions, including **animatronic dinosaurs**, a stunning room on **creepy crawlies**, the Ecology Gallery's **Quadrascope** video wall and the vast new **Darwin Centre** of zoological specimens. However, the much-loved **diplodocus dinosaur skeleton** in the entrance hall and the huge, but tired-looking, **blue whale** are undeniably old-school attractions.

The animatronic T-rex dinosaurs and raptors used to be the centre of attention and, although they are often lent out now, one of them will usually be on site. However, the newer Darwin Centre is getting more of the limelight. The first phase, opened in 2002, focuses on taxonomy (the study of the natural world), with some 450,000 jars of pickled specimens shown off during free guided tours every half-hour. The even-more-ambitious phase II of the Darwin Centre will showcase some 22 million zoological, botanical and entomological exhibits in 'a giant cocoon', due to open in 2007.

The Earth Galleries are a more thoroughly modern affair. Displays of crystals, gems and precious rock line the black walls of its entrance hall, while four life-size human statues herald the way to the escalator, which slithers up through a hollowed-out globe into displays about our planet's geological make-up. Volcanoes, earthquakes and storms are all discussed on the upper floor. However, the supposed star attraction, the Kobe earthquake

mock-up – a model of a small Japanese grocery shop that trembles in a manner meant to replicate the 1995 earthquake – is disappointingly lame. Better exhibitions on the lower floors focus on ecology, look at gems and other precious stones and explore how planets are formed. Touch-screen computer displays and gadgetry abound. To avoid crowds during school-term time, it's best to visit early morning or late afternoon, or early on weekend mornings year-round.

SCIENCE MUSEUM Map pp458-9

☎ 0870 870 4868; www.sciencemuseum.org.uk; Exhibition Rd SW7; admission free, adult/concession IMAX Cinema £7.50/6, SimEx Simulator Ride £3.75/2.75, Motionride simulator £2.50/1.50; ⏰ 10am-6pm; ⊖ South Kensington; ♿

This is one of the most progressive and accessible museums of its kind, and does a terrific job of bringing to lustrous life a subject that is often dull, dense and impenetrable for kids and adults alike. With five floors of interactive and educational exhibits, it's informative and entertaining and has something to snag the interest of every age group.

The revamped **Energy Hall**, on the ground floor as you enter, concentrates on 11 machines of the Industrial Revolution, showing how the first steam engines such as Puffing Billy and Stephenson's Rocket helped Britain become 'the workshop of the world' in the early 19th century. Animations show how the machines worked and are accompanied by detailed overall explanations, including a section on the Luddites who opposed the march of technology.

Of course, it's impossible to miss the huge **Energy Ring** that now hangs over the open atrium from the gallery Energy: Fuelling the Future on the 2nd floor. Pop up here to enter your name and answers to several energy questions onto the electronic tickertape messages that run around the inside of the ring. On the same level you will also find a recreation of **Charles Babbage's mechanical calculator** (1832), the famous forerunner to the computer.

The 3rd floor is a favourite place for children, with its gliders, hot air balloon and varied aircraft, including the Gipsy Moth, in which Amy Johnson flew to Australia in 1930. This floor also features an adapted **flight simulator** that's been turned into a 'Motionride'. Level 1 contains displays on food and time, while the 4th and 5th floors contain exhibits on medical and veterinary history.

Crowd outside the Science Museum (opposite)

Nostalgic parents will delight in the old cars and the **Apollo 10 command module**. However, both they and their children will probably most enjoy the hi-tech **Wellcome Wing**, which is spread over several floors at the back of the building. The **SimEx Simulator Ride** and **IMAX Cinema** are found within this wing, with the usual crop of travelogues, space adventures and dinosaur attacks in stunning 3-D. There's a superlative exploration of identity on Level 1 entitled **Who am I?**, plus other hands-on displays for children.

There are no guided tours on offer, but you can pick up trail guides for children (lighter cover for younger kids, darker cover for older ones). The Deep Blue Café on the ground floor of the Wellcome Wing opens from 10.30am to 5.30pm daily. At some point, most parents will find themselves pestered into visiting the huge, revamped ground-floor shop.

MICHELIN HOUSE Map pp458-9
81 Fulham Rd SW3; ⊖ South Kensington
Even if you're not up for dinner at Terence Conran's wonderful restaurant **Bibendum** (p249) in Michelin House, mosey past and have a look at the superb Art Nouveau architecture. It was built for Michelin between 1905 and 1911 by François Espinasse, and completely restored in 1985. The open-fronted ground floor provides space for upmarket fish and flower stalls, the famous roly-poly Michelin Man appears in the modern stained glass, while the lobby is decorated with tiles showing early-20th-century cars. The Conran Shop is also housed here.

KENSINGTON PALACE Map pp444-5
☎ 7937 9561; wwwroyalresidences.com; Kensington Gardens W8; adult/child/concession £11/7.20/8.30, park & gardens free; ☒ 10am-4.30pm; ⊖ Queensway/Notting Hill Gate/High St Kensington
Most readers will probably remember Kensington Palace as the residence of the late Diana, Princess of Wales. And while the carpet of floral bouquets covering the lawn during that September's very un-British period of mourning is but a memory, a collection of the attention-grabbing frocks worn by 'the people's princess' remains. It's still one of this living palace's major draws, forming the highlight of the **Royal Ceremonial Dress Collection**.

Of course, Kensington Palace already had a long history when Diana moved in after her divorce from Prince Charles in 1996. Built in 1605, it became the favourite royal residence under William and Mary of Orange in 1689, and remained so until George III became king and relocated to Buckingham Palace (perhaps spurred by the ignominy of his predecessor's having died of a stroke while squatting on the loo). Even afterwards the royals stayed occasionally, with Queen Victoria being born here in 1819.

London for Kids

Somewhere along the line Londoners, and Britons in general, got the reputation for being excessively strict with their kids. If it used to be the case, it isn't now. Although the old axiom that children should be seen and not heard in public still has a little traction in Britain, London parents are more likely to pamper their princes and princesses these days. That said, you might not always find nappy-changing facilities or high chairs so it sometimes pays to plan and telephone ahead.

The city is jam-packed with things to keep the little ones amused and there are stacks of fun places for all the family. Central London's many parks never disappoint, especially around the new **Princess Diana Memorial Fountain** (opposite), while the **Science Museum** (p142), **Natural History Museum** (p142), **Bethnal Green Museum of Childhood** (p175), **Museum in Docklands** (p178), **Theatre Museum** (p103) and **Ragged School Museum** (p177) are full of engaging gadgets and exhibits. Head to the impressive **Tower of London** (p118). Check out the **London Zoo** (p190), the **Wetland Centre** (p206) and **city farms** (p192), go for a ride on a **canal barge** (p94), hop on a **Duck Tour** (p95), make loud noises at **Firepower** (p185), but don't miss the dizzying heights of the **London Eye** (p149).

In the 17th and 18th centuries, Kensington Palace was variously renovated by Sir Christopher Wren and William Kent. So you'll find yourself taking a self-guided audio tour through the surprisingly small, wood-panelled State Apartments dating from William's time and then the grander apartments by Kent.

Most beautiful of all the quarters is the **Cupola Room**, where the ceremony of initiating men into the exclusive Order of the Garter took place and where Victoria was baptised; you can see the order's crest painted on the trompe l'oeil 'domed' ceiling, which is actually essentially flat.

The **King's Long Gallery** displays some of the royal art collection, including the only known painting of a classical subject by Van Dyck. On the ceiling William Kent painted the story of Odysseus but slipped up by giving the Cyclops two eyes!

The **King's Drawing Room** is dominated by a monumentally ugly painting of **Cupid and Venus** by Giorgio Vasari (1511–74), an Italian mannerist painter who used to brag about the speed at which he worked and was better known for his historical record of the Renaissance. There are splendid views of the park and gardens from here; you can also see the **Round Pond**, once full of turtles for turtle soup but now popular for sailing model boats.

The **King's Staircase** is decorated with striking murals by William Kent, who painted himself in a turban on the fake dome. Also included is a portrait of Peter, the 'wild child' who had been discovered in the woods of Hanover and brought to England to entertain the jaded court.

The **Sunken Garden** near the palace is at its prettiest in summer; the nearby **Orangery**, designed by Vanbrugh and Hawksmoor as a freestanding conservatory in 1704, is a bright, if rather formal, place for tea.

KENSINGTON GARDENS Map pp444–5

🕓 dawn–dusk; ⊖ Queensway/High St Kensington/Lancaster Gate

Immediately west of Hyde Park, across the Serpentine Lake, these gardens are technically part of Kensington Palace, where Princess Diana lived after her divorce from Charles. The Palace and the gardens have become something of a shrine to her memory. If you have kids, visit the **Diana, Princess of Wales Memorial Playground**, in the northwest corner of the gardens.

Art is also characteristic of these gardens – George Frampton's famous **statue of Peter Pan** is close to the lake, beside an attractive area known as Flower Walk. South of the lake, near the main road that runs through the park, are sculptures by Henry Moore and Jacob Epstein.

SERPENTINE GALLERY Map pp444–5

☎ 7402 6075; www.serpentinegallery.org; Kensington Gardens W8; admission free; 🕓 10am–6pm; ⊖ Knightsbridge; ♿

A visit to the Serpentine is one of London's most pleasant gallery outings, being as it's small with usually stunning exhibitions and easily combined with a lazy stroll in the park. This 1930s tea pavilion has huge curtain windows beaming lots of natural light onto its attention-grabbing contemporary art exhibitions. Past shows have included works by Damien Hirst, Andreas Gursky, Louise Bourgeois, Gabriel Orozco and Tomoko Takahashi, while the space readily lends itself to sculpture and interactive displays.

If you visit between May and September, there's the bonus of the temporary summer pavilion, built by leading – sometimes even legendary – architects, such as Alvaro Siza, Oscar Niemeyer, Daniel Libeskind and Zaha Hadid. Reading, talks and open-air screenings take place here.

PRINCESS DIANA MEMORIAL
FOUNTAIN Map pp444-5
Kensington Gardens W8; ⊖ **Knightsbridge/South Kensington**

The drama surrounding this memorial seems a predictably fraught postscript to a life that itself often hovered between Greek tragedy and farce. A 'moat without a castle' draped 'like a necklace' around Hyde Park near the Serpentine Bridge, this circular double stream had to be shut just a fortnight after it opened in 2004. The inclusive design by Kathryn Gustafson initially invited visitors, especially children, to wade in the fountain. But with fans flocking to the site in an unseasonably wet summer, the surrounding grass became muddy and slippery, leaves choked the drains causing an overflow and several people were injured when they slipped on the smooth granite basin.

A year later, the fountain was reopened with a gravel path encircling it to keep the Glastonbury-style mud bath to a minimum, and with park wardens patrolling the area to make sure visitors only delicately dip in their toes. If it's not quite what Gustafson imagined, it is still a marvellous experience, with people mesmerised by the water's flow both left and right from the fountain's highest point, or sunning themselves around it. We've all been here before with the Millennium Bridge. In a recent poll by the Heritage Lottery Foundation, people already rated this as London's second most important contemporary icon after the London Eye – proving, if nothing else, that the English always appreciate a good balls-up.

ALBERT MEMORIAL Map pp444-5
☎ **7495 0916; www.aptg.org.uk; 45min guided tours adult/concession £4.50/4;** ☾ **2pm & 3pm 1st Sun of the month;** ⊖ **Knightsbridge/South Kensington**

On the southern edge of Hyde Park and facing Kensington Gore, this memorial is as over-the-top as the subject, Queen Victoria's German husband Albert (1819–61), was purportedly humble. Albert explicitly said he did not want a monument and 'if (as is very likely) it became an artistic monstrosity like most of our monuments, it would upset my equanimity to be permanently ridiculed and laughed at in effigy'. Ah, he didn't really mean it, they reckoned, and got George Gilbert Scott to build the 52.5m-high, gaudy Gothic monument in 1872, featuring the prince thumbing through a catalogue for his Great Exhibition, and surrounded by 178 figures representing the continents (Asia, Europe, Africa and America), as well as the arts, industry and science. The monument was unveiled again in 1998 after being renovated at huge expense. It's certainly eye-catching when lit up at night.

ROYAL ALBERT HALL Map pp444-5
☎ **7589 3203, tour bookings** ☎ **7838 3105; www .royalalberthall.com; Kensington Gore SW7;** ⊖ **South Kensington;** ♿

This huge, domed, red-brick amphitheatre adorned with a frieze of Minton tiles has turned over a new leaf. The home of the famous Promenade Concerts (or 'Proms'; see p324) every summer, it was ironically never meant to be a concert venue. Instead, this 1871 memorial to Queen Victoria's husband was intended as a hall of arts and sciences, and consequently it spent the first 133 years of its existence tormenting concert performers and audiences with its terrible acoustics. (It was said the only way a British composer could ever hear his work twice was by playing here, so bad was the reverberation around the oval structure.)

In early 2004, however, a massive refurbishment was completed, installing air-conditioning, modernising the backstage areas, moving the entrance to the south of the building and fixing the acoustics. You can now take a 45-minute **guided tour** (adult/under 16yr/senior & student/ family £6/3.50/5/16; ☾ hourly 10am-3pm Fri-Tue) of the Hall.

If the flag-waving patriotism of Rule Britannia and the Proms isn't your thing, you've plenty of other events to choose from, including tennis, circus and book readings. Newsworthy events in the past few years include Brian Wilson's live premiere of his legendary 37-years-in-the-making album *Smile*.

ROYAL GEOGRAPHICAL SOCIETY
Map pp444-5
☎ **7591 3000; www.rgs.org; 1 Kensington Gore SW7; admission free;** ☾ **10am-5pm Mon-Fri;** ⊖ **South Kensington;** ♿

A short distance to the east of the Royal Albert Hall is the headquarters of the Royal Geographical Society, housed in a Queen Anne–style, red-brick edifice (1874) easily identified by the statues of explorers David Livingstone and Ernest Shackleton outside. The society holds a regular talks programme (many after hours) and photography exhibitions, while the **Foyle Reading Room** (☎ 7591 3040; adult/student £10 per day/free) offers access to the society's collection of more than half a million maps, photographs, artefacts, books and manuscripts. The entrance to the society is on Exhibition Rd.

HYDE PARK Map pp444-5

☽ 5.30am-midnight; ⊖ Hyde Park Cnr/Marble Arch/Knightsbridge/Lancaster Gate

London's largest open space weighs in at a whopping 145 hectares, and is an inviting composite of neatly manicured gardens and wild, deserted expanses of overgrown grass. It's a riot of colour in spring and full of milky-white (and soon-to-be-burnt) sunbathers on summer days. It's a magnificent venue for open-air concerts, demonstrations and royal occasions. Gun salutes are fired here and soldiers ride through the park each morning on their way to Horse Guards Parade in Whitehall.

Hyde Park is separated from Kensington Gardens by the squiggly L-shaped Serpentine Lake, which was created when the Westbourne River was dammed in the 1730s; it's a good spot for pleasure boating in summer. Henry VIII expropriated the park from the Church in 1536, after which it became a hunting ground for kings and aristocrats; later it became a popular venue for duels, executions and horse racing. It became the first royal park to open to the public in the early 17th century, and famously hosted the Great Exhibition in 1851. During WWII it became an enormous potato bed.

You'll either love or hate the ornate **Queen Mother's Gates** (designed by Giuseppe Lund and David Wynne) leading on to Park Lane near Hyde Park Corner. The pale-green granite sweep of the new **Australian War Memorial** (Map pp448–9) nearby at Hyde Park Corner is a little more restrained.

SPEAKERS' CORNER Map pp444-5

⊖ Marble Arch

The northeastern corner of Hyde Park is traditionally the spot for oratorical acrobatics and soapbox ranting. It's the only place in Britain where demonstrators can assemble without police permission, a concession granted in 1872 as a response to serious riots when 150,000 people gathered to demonstrate against the Sunday Trading Bill before Parliament. If you've got something on your chest, you can get rid of it here on Sunday, although it'll be largely loonies and religious fanatics you'll have for company. Nobody else will take much notice.

MARBLE ARCH Map pp444-5

⊖ Marble Arch

John Nash designed this huge arch in 1827. It was moved here, to the northeastern corner of Hyde Park, from its original spot in front of Buckingham Palace in 1851, when it was adjudged too small and unimposing to be the entrance to the royal manor. There's a one-room flat inside, London's grandest bedsit. If you're feeling anarchic, walk through the central portal, a privilege reserved for the royal family by law.

TYBURN TREE Map pp444-5

⊖ Marble Arch

A plaque on the traffic island at Marble Arch indicates the spot where the infamous Tyburn Tree, a three-legged gallows, once stood. An estimated 50,000 people were executed here between 1300 and 1783, many having been dragged from the Tower of London.

TYBURN CONVENT Map pp444-5

☎ 7723 7262; www.tyburnconvent.org.uk; 8 Hyde Park Pl; admission free; ☽ tours of the crypt 10.30am, 3.30pm & 5.30pm (call beforehand if you can); ⊖ Marble Arch

One of the buildings of this sorrowful and silent place has the distinction of being the smallest house in London, measuring just over a metre in width. A convent was established here in 1903, close to the site of the Tyburn Tree gallows where many Catholics were executed because of their faith during the 15th century, and which later became a place of Catholic pilgrimage. The crypt contains the relics of some 105 martyrs, along with paintings commemorating their lives and recording their deaths. A closed order of Benedictine sisters lives here, as they have for more than a century.

BROMPTON ORATORY Map pp458-9

☎ 7808 0900; 215 Brompton Rd SW7; ☽ 6.30am-8pm; ⊖ South Kensington

Also known as the London Oratory and the Oratory of St Philip Neri, this Roman Catholic church was built in the Italian Baroque style in 1884. It has marble, candles and statues galore, as well as one very important regular in Prime Minister Tony Blair. There are six daily Masses on weekdays, one at 6pm on

---

Top Five Green Spaces

- Hampstead Heath (p194)
- Hyde Park (above)
- Kew Gardens (p210)
- Regent's Park (p189)
- St James's Park (p128)

Saturday, and nine between 7am and 7pm on Sunday.

COMMONWEALTH INSTITUTE

Map pp444-5

☎ 7603 4535; www.commonwealth.org.uk; Kensington High St W8; ⊖ High St Kensington

On the southern side of Holland Park, just off Kensington High St, an open space with fountains and flagpoles fronts the Commonwealth Institute, designed in 1962 to resemble a large tent and created from materials from all over the British Commonwealth. It looks as horrid as it sounds. The rather pedestrian interior extols the virtues of the 54 Commonwealth countries and houses temporary exhibits.

LINLEY SAMBOURNE HOUSE Map

pp444-5

☎ 7602 3316; www.rbkc.gov.uk/linleysambourne house; 18 Stafford Tce W8; adult/child/concession £6/1/4; ☼ tours Sat & Sun; ⊖ High St Kensington

Tucked away behind Kensington High St, this was the home of *Punch* political cartoonist and amateur photographer Linley Sambourne and his family from 1874 to 1910. It's one of those houses whose owners never redecorated or threw anything away. What you see is pretty much the typical home of a well-to-do Victorian family: dark wood, Turkish carpets and rich stained glass. Visits are by 90-minute guided tour only (with your guide in period costume).

ALONG THE SOUTH BANK

Eating p251-5; Drinking p286; Shopping p345; Sleeping p367

No place in London better represents the city's recent re-invention than the formerly 'wrong' side of the Thames River. In less than a decade it's gone from slightly seedy underbelly to trim, taut and terrific middle. In what the local council likes to call a 'bold vision of urban regeneration', two of 21st-century London's major icons have recently come to be located here. The London Eye has been raised across the water from the neo-Gothic parliament building at Westminster, while the disused Bankside Power Station has morphed into the Tate Modern, opposite St Paul's Cathedral.

Borough Market (p350)

This is where new London faces off with old London, and both come out winners. If you follow the Silver Jubilee Walkway and the Thames Path all the way along the river's southern bank – one of the most pleasant strolls in town – you'll also appreciate just how much its redevelopment has opened up new London vistas. Images of the industrial age have been give a new lease of life, as with the Art Deco Oxo Tower, while the shiny space-age City Hall makes a striking contrast with the medieval Tower of London on the river's northern bank.

It wasn't even a decade ago that film directors were using the South Bank's neglected back streets to express gritty reality, as in Guy (Mr Madonna) Ritchie's *Lock, Stock and Two Smoking Barrels,* while celebrity chef Jamie Oliver's decision to shop at Borough Market was considered avant-garde. Now clusters of new offices, flats, restaurants and bars are springing up all over the place and that same market is one of the most popular in the city. The latest plan is to convert the coach park next to the London Eye into an artificial summertime beach, in the same vein as Paris Plage.

147

LAMBETH NORTH

There's not much to Lambeth North really. The name Lambeth translates into the unappealing 'muddy landing place', conveying the fact that this, like nearby Waterloo, was largely undeveloped swamp until the 18th century. Apparently, the only notables brave enough to live here earlier were the Archbishops of Canterbury, who began coming and going in barges from their waterside Lambeth Palace in the 13th century. It was the arrival of bridges and the railways some 250 years ago that finally connected Lambeth to London. But by the 1930s people were singing the area's praises, in the form of the jiggy song and dance called 'the Lambeth Walk'.

IMPERIAL WAR MUSEUM Map pp460-1

☎ 7416 5320, 0900 160 0140; www.iwm.org.uk; Lambeth Rd SE1; admission free; ✆ 10am-6pm; ✆ Lambeth North/Southwark; limited ♿

Pundits have suggested that if George W Bush had travelled more before becoming US president he would never have invaded Iraq. Perhaps a quick visit to the Imperial War Museum could have done the same trick? Despite the planes, tanks and other military hardware parked in the entrance hall of this huge former psychiatric hospital, this is overall a very sombre, thoughtful museum. Most of its six storeys are given over to exploring the human and social cost of conflict.

Although the museum's focus is officially on military action involving British or Commonwealth troops during the 20th century, it gives 'war' a wide interpretation. So it not only has serious discussion of the two World Wars, Korea and Vietnam, it also covers the Cold War, 'secret' warfare (ie spying) and even the war on apartheid in South Africa.

In the basement there are two wartime recreations. In the Trench Experience you walk through the grim day-to-day reality of life on the Somme front line in WWI, and in the more hair-raising Blitz Experience you cower inside a mock bomb shelter during a WWII air raid and then emerge through ravaged East End streets. On the upper floors you find the two most outstanding, and moving, sections: the extensive Holocaust Exhibition (not recommended for under 16s) and a stark gallery devoted to genocide, featuring a 30-minute film (certificate 12) on crimes against humanity in Cambodia, Yugoslavia and Rwanda.

We can imagine opponents of the Iraq war being pleased to lock Dubya in any of these last four exhibits, or perhaps even to stand him in front of the clock ticking off the number of people killed in war and ask him how many of the 100 million plus deaths he's responsible for. The museum itself hasn't yet included exhibits on 9/11, Afghanistan or Iraq; for historians, these seem too recent.

LAMBETH PALACE Map p460-1

Lambeth Palace Rd SE1; ✆ Lambeth North

The red-brick Tudor gatehouse beside the church of St Mary-at-Lambeth leads to Lambeth Palace, the London residence of the Archbishop of Canterbury. Although the palace is not usually open to the public, the gardens occasionally are; check with a Tourist Information Centre (TIC) for details (p416).

MUSEUM OF GARDEN HISTORY

Map pp460-1

☎ 7401 8865; www.museumgardenhistory.org; St Mary-at-Lambeth, Lambeth Rd SE1; admission free, requested donation £3; ✆ 10.30am-5pm; ✆ Lambeth North

In a city holding out the broad attractions of Kew Gardens, the modest Museum of Garden History is mainly for the seriously greenfingered. Its trump card is the charming knot garden, a replica of a 17th-century formal garden, with topiary hedges clipped into an intricate, twirling design and interspersed with wild daffodils, old roses and herbaceous perennials. Keen gardeners will enjoy the displays on the 17th-century Tradescants, gardeners to Charles I and Charles II and enthusiastic collectors of exotic plants. Nongardeners might like to pay their respects to Captain Bligh (of mutinous Bounty fame), who is buried here.

FLORENCE NIGHTINGALE MUSEUM

Map pp448-9

☎ 7620 0374; www.florence-nightingale.co.uk; St Thomas's Hospital, 2 Lambeth Palace Rd SE1; adult/senior, student & child/family £5.80/4.20/13;

⊙ 10am-5pm Mon-Fri, 10am-4.30pm Sat & Sun, last entry 1hr before closing; ⊖ Westminster/Waterloo; ⅗

If you're wondering where society's obsession with fame and stardom began, here's a good place to start. Yes, with baseball card–style photos sold of the gentle 'Lady of the Lamp' during her lifetime, Florence Nightingale (1820–1910) was one of the world's first modern celebrities. Lauded as the mother of professional nursing, Flo has recently been shown to be more of a canny administrator than a good carer – and a good deal more contrary than her public image as a ministering angel has often admitted. Her fame derives from having persuaded the authorities to let her set up field hospitals in Turkey and Crimea during the 1854–56 Crimean War, and from the fact that the *Times'* first foreign correspondent, William Howard Russell, was there to see it.

Given that, this museum is an important record of a woman who stamped her mark on history, and visitors do seem to enjoy the recent addition of her stuffed pet owl, Athena, as a humanising touch. Still, the exhibition has some catching up to do with more recent interpretations of Nightingale's career.

SOUTH BANK CENTRE & WATERLOO

Six years after the end of WWII the government decided to distract the public from the fact that they were still on restricted rations, by holding a national knees-up called the Festival of Britain. Someone forgot to tidy up properly afterwards, leaving the Royal Festival Hall to shape the face of the South Bank neighbourhood. This would have been all very well, had not some other modernist rubbish also been thrown down here during the 1960s and '70s, resulting in decades of architectural blight.

That cluster of concrete buildings, known as the South Bank Centre, still stands defiant. But today it's undergoing a major makeover to help it keep up with the Joneses – the impressive County Hall and the terrific London Eye.

Waterloo, triumphantly named after the Belgian field where Napoleon met his English nemesis, was nearly all marshland until the 18th century, as the name of the street Lower Marsh still attests. Bridges from the northern bank of the Thames at Westminster and Waterloo changed all that. Waterloo train station was built in 1848. Today it's a gateway to Europe, via the Channel Tunnel.

LONDON EYE Map pp448-9

☎ 0870 500 0600; www.londoneye.com; Jubilee Gardens SE1; adult/5-15yr/senior £12.50/6.50/10; ⊙ 9.30am-8pm, to 9pm May, Jun & Sep, to 10pm Jul & Aug, closed Jan & early Feb; ⊖ Waterloo; ⅗

Given the notoriously lousy British weather, you would have thought that erecting an observation wheel over London was something of a risk. Not so, history has ruled, and it's now hard to remember what the city looked like without its Eye. Since the wheel was cantilevered into place in the millennium year, it's not just fundamentally altered the skyline of the South Bank, but is visible from other surprising parts of the city (such as Borough or St James's). Instantly becoming one of London's top five attractions, the wheel is still found at the end of long queues. In fact, it should have been dismantled by now. However, its phenomenal popularity has meant a change in planning permission, so people will be forming lines here for another 20 years. (That's despite a scare in mid-2005, when the owners of the land on which one of the wheel's struts stands threatened to up the rent massively and it seemed the London Eye would close.)

Not everyone will quite agree with the customers of Pringles crisps who, in a possibly additive-fuelled rush in 2005, voted this the-best-tourist-attraction-in-the-whole-wide-world-ever. However, a ride in one of the wheel's 32 glass-enclosed gondolas is something you really shouldn't miss. It takes a gracefully slow 30 minutes and, weather permitting, you can see 25 miles in every direction from the top of 135m-tall wheel (the world's largest). To the west lies Windsor, while to the east you can gaze out to sea. In between, you have the chance to pick out various landmarks and argue with your friends over which to visit next.

You'll need to book 14 hours in advance if you buy online and arrive 30 minutes before your 'flight' to pick up any advance tickets. If you haven't booked, arrive early to beat the queues.

Top Five London Views

- Buckingham Palace from the footbridge over **St James's Park Lake** (p128)
- From the **London Eye** (above)
- From Waterloo Bridge, preferably at sunset
- From the dome of **St Paul's Cathedral** (p110)
- From the top-floor bar/restaurant of the **Tate Modern** (p152)

COUNTY HALL Map pp448-9

Westminster Bridge Rd SE1; ⊖ Westminster/Waterloo
Directly across Westminster Bridge from the Houses of Parliament, this magnificent building with its curved façade and colonnades was once home to the London County Council and then the renamed (1965) Greater London Council, before it was shut by PM Margaret Thatcher in 1986.

Today the building's reopened, with a vast aquarium in the basement, a museum devoted to the work of the artist Salvador Dalí, the Saatchi Gallery, two hotels and a couple of restaurants.

SAATCHI GALLERY Map pp448-9

advance tickets ☎ 0870 166 0278, recorded information ☎ 7823 2363; www.saatchi-gallery.co.uk; County Hall, Westminster Bridge Rd SE1; adult/senior & student £9/£6.75; ⏰ 10am-6pm, to 10pm Fri & Sat, last entry 45min before closing; ⊖ Westminster/Waterloo
Has it all gone pear-shaped for Charles Saatchi? The advertising supremo might have got hitched to domestic goddess Nigella Lawson, but he seems to have fallen out of love with the YBA (young British art) that was once the mainstay of his collection and reputation. Tragically, some major works went up in smoke in a devastating warehouse fire in 2003, but other disposals have been more deliberate. Damien Hirst – that great pickler of dissected cows and sheep – is rumoured to have bought back 48 pieces, possibly acrimoniously. Reports have

Saatchi Gallery (above)

also had Saatchi trying to sell his entire collection to the Tate, whose director Nicholas Serota allegedly wasn't interested.

We can't vouch for any of this, as the gallery's spokespeople have remained tight-lipped, but we can say that on our most recent visit none of the trademark works that launched the collection was still on display. Instead of the likes of Tracey Emin's *My Bed,* Ron Mueck's *Dead Dad* and Chris Ofili's *The Holy Virgin Mary,* the walls of this venerable building were lined with rather modest Continental European paintings.

The only constant work seems to be Richard Wilson's admittedly fabulous *20:50,* an optically deluding, oil-filled room.

DALÍ UNIVERSE Map pp448-9

☎ 7620 2720; www.daliuniverse.com; County Hall, Westminster Bridge Rd SE1; adult/3-9yr/10-16yr/senior & student/family £8.50/3.50/5.50/7.50/24; ⏰ 10am-5.30pm; Westminster Bridge Rd SE1; ⊖ Westminster/Waterloo
The low-lit black interior of this museum is perfect for showcasing Europe's largest collection of Salvador Dalí's work, as it feels like stepping into the surrealist artist's deliciously twisted subconscious. His regular leitmotifs, including melted watches, fire, crutches and drawers, appear in themed areas: Sensuality & Femininity, Religion & Mythology, and Dreams & Fantasy. And, because he was a master self-publicist who readily admitted, 'modesty is not exactly my speciality', his own impish face crops up regularly. There are more than 500 works displayed, including Dalí's famous Mae West Lips Sofa, the backdrop he painted for Hitchcock's film *Spellbound,* and one of his Lobster Telephones, making this the place for serious fans and the merely curious alike. Temporary exhibitions, which have in the past focused on artists such as Picasso or Warhol, are located in a separate annexe; check for latest details.

LONDON AQUARIUM Map pp448-9

☎ 7967 8000; www.londonaquarium.co.uk; County Hall, Westminster Bridge Rd SE1; adult/3-14yr/senior & student/family £8.75/5.25/6.50/25, Jan, public & school holidays extra £1; ⏰ 10am- 6pm, last entry 5pm; ⊖ Westminster/Waterloo; ♿
It's hard to grasp exactly why one might rush to visit an aquarium in London, a city hardly known for its piscine delights. However, should you so wish, this is Europe's largest. Fish are grouped in tanks according to their geographic origin, from the Pacific to the Atlantic Oceans

and from freshwater to the sea. There's a touch pool with manta rays and an invertebrates zone, where kids can find – and call out – Nemo.

SOUTH BANK CENTRE Map pp448-9

A collection of mostly concrete hulks on the southern London landscape, the South Bank Centre is one of those cultural developments that must have seemed like a good idea at the time. That time was from the late 1950s to the late 1970s, when the architectural world was still in thrall to brutalist modernism. Thankfully, today's different taste is starting to have an impact and much of the centre is, has recently been, or soon will be, under renovation.

The **Royal Festival Hall** (☎ 0870 380 0400; www .rfh.org.uk; Belvedere Rd SE1; ⊖ Waterloo) was the first existing building on the South Bank, having been erected to cheer up a glum postwar populace as part of the 1951 Festival of Britain. Its slightly curved, glass and Portland Stone façade always won it more public approbation than its 1970s neighbours, but all the same it's getting a £60 million refit. This has already seen the opening of new pedestrian walkways, a new outdoor café in Festival Sq behind the building, and new food outlets, bookshops and music stores below it. However, at the time of writing the main Royal Festival Hall building was scheduled to remain closed until early 2007.

In the meantime, concerts and the Meltdown Festival will be transferred to the neighbouring **Queen Elizabeth Hall** and **Purcell Room**. (You'll find there's a real skateboarders' hangout underneath their elevated floor.)

Tucked almost out of sight under the arches of Waterloo Bridge is the **National Film Theatre** (NFT; bookings ☎ 7928 3232, recorded information ☎ 7633 0274; www.bfi.org.uk/nft; South Bank SE1; ⊖ Waterloo), completed in 1958 and now screening some 2000 films a year. Largely a repertory or art-house theatre, it runs regular retrospectives and is also one of the venues for the London Film Festival in November. Most excitingly, it also previews some major releases, usually accompanied by a talk with the director or one of the stars. Popular guests in the past few years have ranged from Clint Eastwood and Cate Blanchett to Jonathan Glazer and Walter Salles. On a more down-to-earth level, there's a buzzing café.

Next door to the NFT, the **Museum of the Moving Image** has been closed and will only be reopened (this time as a space for temporary film exhibitions) after the British Film Institute builds a new film centre. This new centre is only in the initial planning stages.

The **Riverside Walk Market**, with prints and second-hand books, takes place immediately in front of the NFT under the arches of the bridge. See p351 for market details.

The **Hayward Gallery** (information ☎ 7960 5226, bookings ☎ 0870 169 1000; www.hayward .org.uk; Belvedere Rd SW1; adult/student/senior £9/5/6, but can vary, Mon half-price; ⏰ 10am-6pm, to 8pm Tue & Wed, to 9pm Fri; ⊖ Waterloo) has always been generally considered an enormously ugly piece of 'brutalist' architecture, but at least now it has a new foyer and mirrored glass pavilion. If you're not a fan of such buildings, perhaps the best thing to do is to get inside quick, where the fairly bland interior spaces act as an excellent hanging space for modern art and have made it London's leading contemporary art gallery. This is where you'll find major international exhibitions. Admission prices vary according to what's on.

The **National Theatre** (☎ 7452 3000; www.nat ionaltheatre.org.uk; South Bank SE1; ⊖ Waterloo) is the nation's flagship theatre complex, comprising three auditoria: the Cottesloe, Lyttelton and Olivier. Designed in 1976 by the architect Denys Lasdun and modernised to the tune of £42 million in the late 1990s, it's been undergoing an artistic renaissance under the directorship of Nicholas Hytner. Hytner has also been responsible for the extremely popular £10 ticket season, where two-thirds of the seats are offered at this discount price between May and October. **Backstage tours** (adult/concession £5/4; 3 times daily Mon-Sat) are also offered.

A short walk eastwards along the South Bank is **Gabriel's Wharf**, a cluster of twee craft shops, snack bars, cafés and restaurants.

The **Jubilee Gardens**, near the London Eye, are also due to be extended towards the South Bank Centre and Hungerford Bridge, adding to a major revamp of the entire area, which hopefully will see the South Bank Centre's reputation massively improved.

LONDON IMAX CINEMA Map pp448-9

☎ 0870 787 2525; www.bfi.org.uk/imax; 1 Charlie Chaplin Walk SE1; adult/4-14yr/senior & student £7.90/4.95/6.50, plus advance booking fee of £1, additional films £4.20; ⏰ 7 screenings 1-9pm, 2 additional screenings at 10.30am & 11.45am Fri & Sat; ⊖ Waterloo
There's nothing new about the films shown at the London IMAX Cinema; they're the usual mix of 2-D and IMAX 3-D documentaries about travel, space and wildlife, lasting from 40 minutes to 1½ hours. At this BFI venue, size matters: the 458-seat cinema is the largest in Europe, with a screen 10 storeys high and 26m wide.

BANKSIDE

Bankside was once London's very own Sodom and Gomorrah – an Elizabethan pleasure ground of inns, bear-baiting pits and brothels run by the venal Bishops of Winchester, where the audience at Shakespeare's nearby Globe Theatre could have popped out for a quickie during the interval. Fast forward five centuries, and the area's entertainments are altogether more highbrow. Shakespeare has gone all respectable and mainstream, a disused power station has become the world's leading modern art gallery and one of Britain's most acclaimed architects has given us all something to admire in the shape of the magnificent Millennium Bridge.

TATE MODERN Map pp454-5

general enquiries ☎ 7887 8000, tickets ☎ 7887 8888, recorded information ☎ 7887 8008; www .tate.org.uk; Queen's Walk SE1; admission free, special exhibitions £5.50-10, but may vary; ☉ 10am-6pm Sun-Thu, 10am-10pm Fri & Sat; ⊖ St Paul's/ Southwark/London Bridge; &

The public's love affair with this phenomenal modern art gallery shows no sign of cooling. Serious art critics have occasionally swiped at its populism, poked holes in its collection and called it a 'supermarket of art'. However, more than 22 million people visited before its fifth birthday, making it the world's most popular contemporary gallery. Only spoilsports would argue with such success.

The critics are right in one sense, though: this 'Tate Modern effect' is really more about the building and its location than it is about the 20th-century art inside. Leading Swiss architects Herzog & de Meuron won the Pritzker, architecture's most prestigious prize, for their transformation of the empty Bankside Power Station. Leaving the building's central chimney, adding a two-storey glass box to the roof and using the vast Turbine Hall as a dramatic entrance space were three strokes of genius. Then, of course, there are the wonderful views of the Thames and St Paul's the building enjoys, particularly from the coffee bar on the 4th floor or the bar/restaurant on the 7th. There's also a café on the 2nd level, plus places to relax overlooking the Turbine Hall. Herzog & de Meuron are now working on an extension of the entire building.

The collection was originally, and somewhat controversially, arranged according to theme rather than by chronology. Galleries were divided into four topics – Landscape/ Matter/Environment, Still Life/Object/Real Life, History/Memory/Society, and Nude/Action/ Body – which critics said papered over a lack of real masterpieces. From 2006, however, this organisation is to change – although how exactly the gallery wouldn't say until the new look was unveiled.

Some 65,000 works are on constant rotation, and the curators have at their disposal paintings by Georges Braque, Henri Matisse, Piet Mondrian and Andy Warhol, as well as pieces by Joseph Beuys, Marcel Duchamp, Damien Hirst, Rebecca Horn, Claes Oldenburg and Auguste Rodin. Mark Rothko's famous Seagram murals have been given their own space and are on show permanently. Other stalwarts include Roy Lichtenstein's *Whaam!*, Pablo Picasso's *Weeping Woman* and Jackson Pollock's *Summertime*.

Special exhibitions have recently included shows on Frida Kahlo, August Strindberg, and Nazism and 'Degenerate' Art. **Audioguides**, with four different tours, are available for £1.50. Free **guided highlights tours** depart at 11am, noon, 2pm and 3pm daily.

The **Tate-to-Tate** ferry, painted by Damien Hirst, operates between the Bankside Pier at the Tate Modern and the new Millennium Pier at sister museum Tate Britain, stopping en route at the London Eye. Services run 10am to 5.30pm daily, at 40-minute intervals. A three-stop ticket (purchased on board) costs £4 (discounts available).

MILLENNIUM BRIDGE Map pp454-5

Londoners have forgiven, although not completely forgotten, this elegant footbridge's shaky start to life. So while it now provides a smooth crossing between the Tate Modern and St Paul's – and has a firm place in the city's heart – it's still called the wobbly bridge. Opened in June 2000, it had to be closed after just three days because of the alarming way it swayed under the weight of pedestrians. Still, an 18-month refit costing £5 million eventually saw it right, so now it's possible to just admire Sir Norman Foster and Antony Caro's design without worrying about getting seasick. The low-slung frame looks pretty spectacular, particularly lit up at night with fibre-optics, and the view of St Paul's from the Tate Modern end has swiftly become one of London's iconic images. The bridge now carries some 10,000 people per day, and every one of them seems to be on it the same time as you.

SHAKESPEARE'S GLOBE Map pp454-5

☎ 7902 1500; www.shakespeares-globe.org; 21 New Globe Walk SE1; exhibition entrance incl guided tour adult/under 15yr/senior & student/family £9/6/7/25; ⏰ 9am-noon & 12.30-5pm May-Sep, 10am-5pm Oct-Apr, tours every 15-30min; ⊖ London Bridge; ♿

For most of the 20th century, high-school students of English were taught the works of William Shakespeare as high culture, forced to reverentially pore over Macbeth's tragedy or commit to memory Hamlet's soliloquy. However, as has been increasingly recognised in more recent years (Baz Luhrmann's *Romeo + Juliet* and the Reduced Shakespeare Company being just two examples), the Bard was essentially a popular writer. The world's best-known playwright was always willing to play to the gallery, by peppering his scripts with innuendo.

They know this at the rebuilt Globe theatre, where you can see Shakespeare as he was meant to be performed: with cross-dressing actors and heckling condoned. The circular venue itself is only 200m from the original Globe Theatre, which Shakespeare helped found in 1599 and where he worked until 1611. And it's a faithful replica, with a central arena left open to the elements, housing the stage and 500 'groundlings' (standing viewers). That means the actors perform up close and personal with both the standing and seated audience, without stage lighting or sound systems. (There are a few downsides to this set-up, such as the planes flying overhead and the two 'authentic' Corinthian pillars that obstruct much of the view from the seats closest to the stage.) In the cold of winter performances move to the indoor **Inigo Jones Theatre**, a replica of a Jacobean playhouse connected to the Globe. For ticket details see p330.

If you can't make time to catch *Richard III*, *The Taming of the Shrew* or any of the other Elizabethan or contemporary plays on the programme, you can walk the boards and learn about the Globe's history with a daytime guided tour of the theatre and the marvellous exhibition below. The original theatre was closed in 1642 after the English Civil War was won by the Puritans, who regarded theatres as dens of iniquity. Its reconstruction became a decades-long labour of love for American actor (later film director) Sam Wanamaker, who helped raise the necessary money, but sadly died three years before the 1997 opening night. The building has been painstakingly constructed with 600 oak pegs (there's not a nail or a screw in the house), specially fired

Tudor bricks, and thatching reeds from Norfolk; even the plaster contains goat hair, lime and sand, as it did in Shakespeare's time. The **Globe Café** and **Globe Restaurant** are open for lunch and dinner till 10pm or 11pm.

GOLDEN HINDE Map pp454-5

☎ 0870 011 8700; www.goldenhinde.co.uk; St Mary Overie Dock, Cathedral St SE1; adult/child/senior & student/family £3.50/2.50/3/10; ⏰ 9am-5.30pm; ⊖ London Bridge

Okay, it looks like a dinky theme-park ride, and kids do love it, but stepping aboard this replica of Sir Francis Drake's famous Tudor ship will inspire genuine admiration for the admiral and his rather short – generally 5ft 4in (1.6m) – crew. This tiny galleon was home to Drake and company for more than three years, from 1577 to 1580, as they became the first sailors to circumnavigate the globe. Adult visitors wandering stooped around this reconstruction must also marvel at how the taller, modern-day crew managed to spend 20 years at sea on this 37m-long replica, after it was launched in 1973.

Tickets are purchased at the card and souvenir shop just opposite the ship. Theme parties are organised, or you can spend the night aboard for £33 per person, including a supper of stew and bread and a breakfast of bread and cheese.

SOUTHWARK CATHEDRAL Map pp454-5

☎ 7367 6700; www.dswark.org/cathedral; Montague Close SE1; admission free, requested donation £4; ⏰ 8am-6pm; ⊖ London Bridge

The earliest surviving part of this relatively small cathedral is the atmospheric retrochoir, which was part of the 13th century Priory of St Mary Overie (from 'St Mary over the Water'). However, most of the building is Victorian (eg the nave) and the cathedral's ethos is more modern still.

As well as housing in its northern choir aisle a macabre **medieval tomb**, where you can see the ribs of a stone corpse through a shroud, Southwark cathedral also features a **plaque to actor Sam Wanamaker** (1919–93), who was the force behind the rebuilding of the nearby Globe theatre. Near the door, another modern memorial recalls the 1989 **Marchioness disaster**, when a Thames pleasure cruiser hit a dredger and sank with 51 passengers near Southwark Bridge.

Meanwhile in the adjacent visitors' centre you'll find a touch-screen multimedia exhibition of local history called the **Long View of London** (adult/child/senior & student £3/1.50/2.50; with audioguide adult/child/senior & student/family £5/2.50/4/12.50; 🕙 10am-6pm Mon-Sat, 11am-5pm Sun).

Audioguides (adult/child/senior & student £2.50/1.25/2) to the main cathedral, lasting about 40 minutes, are available if you're really keen. Evensong is at 5.30pm weekdays, 4pm Saturday and 3pm Sunday.

A **restaurant** (🕙 10am-5pm) and shop is open to visitors, but the gardens outside are where you'll find neighbourhood workers lunching in summer.

VINOPOLIS Map pp454-5
☎ 0870 241 4040; www.vinopolis.co.uk; 1 Bank End SE1; adult/under 15yr/senior £12.50/free/11.50; 🕙 noon-9pm Mon, Fri & Sat, noon-6pm Tue-Thu & Sun; ⊖ London Bridge; ♿

Half trendy wine bar, half rustic vineyard in appearance, Vinopolis provides a pretty cheesy and essentially soulless tour of the world of wine. It's popular with hen parties; need any more be said? Well, okay, if you really insist, you need to follow the audioguide to make sense of the exhibits, which usually means you'll end up spending more time than you intended. However, those with time and patience – who want to know a little more about wine production and regional varieties from France to South Africa and Chile to Spain – will find it interesting enough. There's the chance to have a little fun sitting on a Vespa for a virtual tour through the Italian hills of Chianti, or 'flying' over Australia's Hunter Valley in the mock-up of an airline cabin.

Serious wine enthusiasts would be better served attending a tasting evening or visiting the gourmet food and wine shop or the nearby branch of the wine retailer Majestic. An onsite restaurant, Cantina Vinopolis, opens for lunch daily and for dinner Monday to Saturday, but during the week it's full of suits.

ROSE THEATRE Map pp454-5
☎ 7902 1500; www.rosetheatre.org.uk; 56 Park St SE1; adult/5-15yr/senior & student £9/6.50/7.50; 🕙 matinee performances May-Oct; ⊖ London Bridge

Now run by the nearby Globe Theatre, the Rose is only open to the public for summer matinee plays. Unlike at the Globe, however, this theatre's original 16th-century foundations have been unearthed. They were discovered in 1989 beneath an office building at Southwark Bridge and given a protective concrete cover. More recent excavations in 2005 revealed just what a raucous party a trip to the theatre was in the 1590s. Cockles, mussels and oysters were consumed in large quantities, beer, ale and wine drunk and tobacco smoked.

CLINK PRISON MUSEUM Map pp454-5
☎ 7378 1558; www.clink.co.uk; 1 Clink St SE1; adult/senior, student & child/family £5/3.50/12; 🕙 10am-6pm, to 9pm Jun-Sep; ⊖ London Bridge

So this is what it feels like to be 'in the clink'? What a letdown. The prison that lent its name to the very experience of being jailed isn't a particularly edifying experience. Once the private jail of the powerful bishops of Winchester who ran the notorious Bankside brothels, it was frequently used to jail prostitutes who displeased their masters, as well as debtors, thieves and even actors. Today, it's just a musty-smelling minor attraction that details what a terrible time such prisoners had, and displays some instruments of torture. Only for those determined to learn more about local history.

WINCHESTER PALACE Map pp454-5
Clink St SE1; ⊖ London Bridge

As if struck down by the hand of a wrathful god, the grand palace of the powerful and corrupt Bishops of Winchester lies in ruins. However, a 14th-century rose window carved in a wall from the Great Hall, high above you, and parts of the flooring, below, are visible from the street. The palace was built in 1109 and remained the bishops' home for more than 500 years, before being converted into a prison for royalists under the puritanical Oliver Cromwell in 1642.

BANKSIDE GALLERY Map pp448-9
☎ 7928 7521; www.banksidegallery.com; 48 Hopton St SE1; admission free; 🕙 10am-5pm Tue-Fri, 11am-5pm Sat & Sun; ⊖ Southwark/St Paul's/London Bridge; ♿

With a fancy new nameplate so people don't confuse it with neighbouring Tate Modern (heaven knows how, but they used to), Bankside Gallery is home to the Royal Watercolour Society and the Royal Society of Painter-Printmakers. It's somewhere to head if you're interested in buying some art, and at its constantly changing exhibitions of watercolours, prints and engravings, prices typically range from £50 to £4,000. Call ahead for the occasional Artists' Perspectives, where artists talk about their work.

(Continued on page 171)

1 *Shopping on Charing Cross Rd (p346)* 2 *Victoria & Albert Museum (p141), South Kensington* 3 *Street performer, Covent Garden (p101)* 4 *Mosaic at Carnaby St, Soho (p96)*

1 Façade of the Royal Albert Hall (p145), home of the Proms 2 The 'Gherkin', 30 St Mary Axe (p113) 3 St Martin-in-the-Fields (p101) hosts classical concerts throughout the year 4 Part of the 25m-high Queen Victoria Memorial, Buckingham Palace (p127)

1 *Apsley House (Wellington Museum, p130)* 2 *The postmodern Lloyd's of London building (p114), designed by Richard Rogers* 3 *Dickens House Museum (p108)* 4 *Christ Church, Spitalfields (p123), designed by Nicholas Hawksmoor*

1 Whitechapel Bell Foundry (p175), the oldest business in London and maker of the clock bells of Big Ben and St Paul's Cathedral *2* The candy-striped red-brick and white-stone tower of Westminster Cathedral (p138) *3* Headstone at Highgate Cemetery (p195) *4* The Great Court of the British Museum (p107), the largest covered public square in Europe

1 Spiral staircase inside City Hall (p171) **2** The neo-Gothic architecture of Tower Bridge (p121) **3** Part of the Queen Victoria Memorial, Buckingham Palace (p127)
4 Statues outside the Natural History Museum (p142), South Kensington

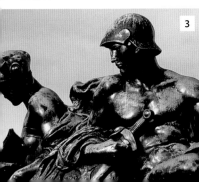

1 *Fountains in the forecourt of the Royal Academy of Arts (p131)*
2 *Apsley House (Wellington Museum, p130)* 3 *Kensington Palace (p143)* 4 *Busker at Covent Garden (p101)*

1 The bank of the River Thames
2 Tourists relax outside Westminster Abbey (p133) *3* A prayer book in the Temple Church (p106), built by the Knights Templar *4* Somerset House (p103), home to three museums

1 Hampstead Heath (p194) *2* Hyde Park (p146) *3* Horse riding in Hyde Park (p146) *4* Kew Gardens (p210)

1 Tourists in Trafalgar Square (p98) 2 Speakers' Corner, Hyde Park (p146) 3 Tulips in St James's Park (p128) 4 Specimen from the Temperate House in Kew Gardens (p210)

1 *Spitalfields Market (p351)*
2 *Shakespeare's Globe (p330), Bankside* **3** *People watching a performance at Victoria Embankment Gardens (p103)* **4** *London Pride parade (p11)*

1 London's famous Harrods department store (p342) 2 Fashion display at children's department store Daisy & Tom (p342) 3 Smiths of Smithfield (p242) sources much of its produce from the eponymous market across the road 4 Comedy Café (p307), Hoxton

1 The Duke of York's Theatre (p331) 2 Waitress at a Notting Hill restaurant (291) 3 Teenagers outside London's Transport Museum (p101), Covent Garden 4 Daddy Kool record store (p349) in Soho, central London's best store for Black music

1 Signs at Portobello Road Market (p350) 2 Movie, rock and entertainment memorabilia (p349) 3 The Jamaica Wine House (p281), actually a historic Victorian pub in the City 4 The London IMAX Cinema (p151), South Bank

FOYLES

Independent Bookshop of the Year   Independent   Bookshop of the Year   Independent Bookshop of the Year

1 Foyle's bookstore (p346) on Charing Cross Rd prides itself on its extensive range *2* Ronnie Scott's jazz club (p323), Soho *3* Punters at a Waterloo bar (p286) *4* Window display in Harvey Nichols (p342), home of local and international high fashion

1 *Window display in Liberty department store (p337) on Regent St* 2 *Street artist* 3 *Restaurant on Gerrard St, Chinatown (p103)* 4 *The Cross, Kings Cross (p303)*

四季火鍋
歡迎預訂

DIM SUM
SERVE DAILY TILL 5 PM

KARAOKE
FULLY AIR CONDITIONED

(Continued from page 154)

BOROUGH & BERMONDSEY

Trendsetters might like to note that this area has been billed as 'the new Hoxton'. Okay, it *might* be in some five to 10 years. Admittedly, all the prerequisites are in place: a nearby trendy market (Borough Market; see p350), a community of creatives living in loft buildings like the former Hartley jam factory, and a growing cluster of gastropubs, restaurants and hip shops in and around popular Bermondsey St. With the area's proximity to the City and a mainline rail station, its already inflated property prices and its pretentious nickname SoBo (South Borough), local real-estate agents like to boast that it's attracted celebrities like Zandra Rhodes, the Chemical Brothers and Marc Almond. One famous rumour (it was just that) even had Robert de Niro buying a penthouse here.

OLD OPERATING THEATRE MUSEUM & HERB GARRET Map pp454-5

☎ 7955 4791; www.thegarret.org.uk; 9a St Thomas St SE1; adult/child/senior & student/family £4.75/2.75/3.75/13; 🕙 10.30am-5pm; ⊖ London Bridge

Tales of delayed hip operations, botched cancer treatments and antibiotic-resistant MRSA bugs have recently made Britain's National Health Service seem a very grim experience. This gory gem provides an antidote; you'll leave praising the heavens for the phenomenon of modern medicine generally.

In this former Victorian surgical theatre you'll see the sharp, vicious-looking instruments 19th-century doctors used, and you'll view the rough-and-ready conditions under which they operated – without antiseptic or anaesthetic on a wooden table in what looks like a modern lecture hall. Placards explain how, without anaesthetic, surgeons had to perform quickly on patients; one minute to complete an amputation was reckoned about right. However, it's even more fascinating, educational and fun to watch bloodless re-enactments of such 'speed surgery', so check the website to see when they're scheduled.

Elsewhere there's information on body-snatching, where the medical profession bought dug-up corpses to practise on, a drawing of famous diarist Samuel Pepys' gallbladder removal (look at the instrument used!) and a life-size anatomical figure from the 18th century, with removable organs. The adjoining herb garret makes a small nod to alternative therapies with bunches of herbs and explanations of their perceived powers; however even this section is dotted with pickled human organs.

This small, quirky but highly recommended museum sits at the top of 32 narrow and rickety stairs, so unfortunately there is no access for visitors with limited mobility.

FASHION & TEXTILE MUSEUM
Map pp454-5

☎ 7403 0222; www.ftmlondon.org; 83 Bermondsey St SE1; adult/student/family £5/3/13; 🕙 11am-5.15pm (last entry) Tue-Sun; ⊖ London Bridge; ♿

We're all dedicated followers of fashion these days, it seems, with the clothing industry long having overtaken ship-building. And London – with its cutting-edge street style and designers including Stella McCartney, Matthew Williamson and Vivienne Westwood – is one of its sizzling hot centres. Therefore, this brainchild of designer Zandra Rhodes is particularly fitting. It's not only fashionistas who come to visit her striking pink, lemon and orange building. Suburban mums and daughters – and even men – come to mooch over the outfits, too.

The plainer concrete interior doesn't detract from the displays and things are arranged over the ground floor and upper mezzanine. There is no permanent collection, simply long temporary exhibitions, which have recently included retrospectives on Rhodes herself and style magazine *i-D*. Check the website for current details.

CITY HALL Map pp454-5

☎ 7983 4100; www.london.gov.uk; Queen's Walk, SE1; admission free; 🕙 8am-8pm Mon-Fri, plus occasional weekends; ⊖ Tower Hill/London Bridge; ♿

Ken Livingstone certainly has enviable luck with his offices. In the early 1980s, as the leader of the Greater London Council, left-wing 'Red Ken' was ensconced in the palatial County Hall (home today to the Saatchi Gallery). Now as London's current mayor, he spends his days in this creation by Norman Foster and Ken Shuttleworth.

Nicknamed 'the egg' – or, more cheekily, 'the testicle' – because of its globular shape, the glass-clad City Hall could also be likened to a spaceman in a helmet. Alternatively, it's the dome of Berlin's Reichstag pushed halfway sideways by a giant hand. The Reichstag was an earlier Foster design and he's used some of the same ideas here. Symbolically transparent,

City Hall also has an interior spiral ramp ascending above the assembly chamber to the building's roof.

There's a visitors centre on the lower ground floor, with a so-called 'London Photomat', an aerial photo of the city stuck to the floor, big enough for you to walk on and pick out individual buildings. There's also an information desk and café (both open 9.30am to 5pm) down here, while an amphitheatre leads off to the outside.

Some other areas, including the ramp, the meeting room on the 6th floor called 'London's Living Room' and outside viewing gallery, open on certain weekends. Check the website for details.

DESIGN MUSEUM Map pp454-5

☎ 7940 8790; www.designmuseum.org; 28 Shad Thames SE1; adult/senior & student/family £6/4/16; ⏰ 10am-5.45pm Sat-Thu, last entry 5.15pm; ⊖ Tower Hill/London Bridge; ♿

There have been some bloody battles inside the white walls of the minimalist Design Museum in recent years. First, chairman James Dyson (the inventor of the suction-free cleaner) resigned, claiming that, under director Alice Rawsthorn, this showcase of contemporary design had developed 'trivialising' policies. Then there was the controversy surrounding the museum's choice for Designer of the Year 2005, who hadn't actually been the architect on the project on which her prize principally rested, but the project manager instead.

For the casual visitor, however, all this is largely ancillary. Rawsthorn has abandoned a permanent collection of 20th- and 21st-century objects to make way for a constant programme of special exhibitions. But although those shows are populist – a display of Manolo Blahnik shoes, a retrospective of designer Saul Bass' movie work in *Psycho, The Man with the Golden Arm* and *Casino* and the evolution of the surfboard, for example – they are also popular. Check the website: you'll know immediately whether the current shows will appeal to you.

As with many museums of its ilk, its shop is an attraction in itself, with lavish coffee-table books on design and architecture, lamps, model chairs and scores of other curios. There are also two places to eat: the infor-

Design Museum (above)

mal **Riverside Café** (🕙 11am-5.30pm Mon-Fri, 10.30am-5.30pm Sat & Sun), and the more formal **Blueprint Café** (p252), which is actually a restaurant.

LONDON DUNGEON Map pp454-5

☎ 7403 7221, recorded information ☎ 0900 160 0066; www.thedungeons.com; 28-34 Tooley St SE1; adult/under 14yr/student & senior £15.50/10.95/12.25; 🕙 10am-5.30pm Apr-Sep, 10am-4.30pm Oct-Mar; ⊖ London Bridge

You have to hand it to the London Dungeon. Despite constant sniping by cynics – including us – the length of the queues to get into the place never seems to diminish.

The reason for the queues, though, lies in the way you have to move through this hammed-up historical house of horrors in a group, and much of your time is spent waiting around for the attendants/actors to finish with an earlier bunch of suckers. It all starts with a stagger through a mirror maze (the Labyrinth of the Lost), followed by a waltz through some plague history, a torture chamber and a Jack the Ripper scene, and a run 'through' the Great Fire of London, where – to give you an idea of the production values – painted, wafting curtains are the 'flames'. The best bits are the vaudeville delights of being sentenced by a crazy judge on trumped-up charges, the fairground-ride boat to Traitor's Gate and the genuinely bitchy undertones when the actors have to deal with a smart-arse visitor.

All in all, though, this camped-up gothic gorefest is rather more underwhelming than even sceptics might suspect. If that doesn't deter you, it would be a good idea to buy tickets online (£2 to £3 surcharge) to avoid the queues.

HMS BELFAST Map pp454-5

☎ 7940 6300; www.hmsbelfast.org.uk; Morgan's Lane, Tooley St SE1; adult/child/senior & student £8/free/5; 🕙 10am-6pm Mar-Oct, 10am-5pm Nov-Feb, last entry 45min before closing; ⊖ London Bridge

Moored in the middle of the Thames, HMS *Belfast* is a big toy that boys of all ages generally love. Of course, for most of its commissioned life this large, light cruiser had a rather more serious purpose than that. Launched in 1938 from the Belfast shipyard Harland & Wolff, it served in WWII, most noticeably in the Normandy landings, and during the Korean War.

Now, as a branch of the Imperial War Museum, it evokes a genuine sense of naval life, laying out everything from its operations room and bridge (where you can sit in the admiral's chair) to its boiler room and living quarters. There's a video of the Battle of the North Cape, off Norway, in which the ship took part, and, on the open deck, there are 16 six-inch guns, whose sights you can peer through.

You need to really concentrate on your Visitors Guide to find your way successfully around the eight zones on nine decks and platforms, although an alternative is to let your nose lead you and see what you find. Either way, you should be prepared for a lot of scrambling up and down steep ladders and steps.

BRAMAH MUSEUM OF TEA & COFFEE

Map pp454-5

☎ 7403 5650; 40 Southwark St SE1; adult/child/senior & student/family £4/3/3.50/10; 🕙 10am-6pm; ⊖ London Bridge; ♿

This is a pleasant, nostalgic place to while away half an hour – provided your visit does not coincide with the arrival of a tour group. Trace the route by which tea conquered the world, making its way to the sitting rooms of Holland and England and further afield from the eastern seaports of China. Alternatively, simply enjoy the chintzy cornucopia of tea- and coffee-drinking equipment, from floral teacups and silverware to Japanese cans of tea.

BRITAIN AT WAR EXPERIENCE

Map pp454-5

☎ 7403 3171; www.britainatwar.co.uk; 64-66 Tooley St SE1; adult/child/concession/family £8.50/4.50/5.50/18; 🕙 10am-5.30pm Apr-Sep, last entry 5pm, 10am-4.30pm Oct-Mar, last entry 4pm; ⊖ London Bridge

If you're not visiting the Churchill Museum or the Imperial War Museum – or you have and you want more – the Britain at War Experience combines elements of the two. There's an 'Anderson' domestic air-raid shelter where you can get an idea of what it must have been like to sit out the Blitz and a BBC Radio Studio allowing you to hear broadcasts by Churchill and Hitler. The other rather musty displays make it feel like you're on a low-budget TV stage-set. The highlight is the colour newsreels of the era.

THE EAST END

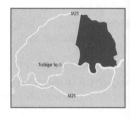

Eating p255-7; Drinking p286-7; Shopping p345

Once the very definition of poverty, during the Victorian era the East End was home to slums, disease, prostitution and utter filth. As the power of the city of London grew exponentially during the 19th century, the East End, which begins at Aldgate on the eastern fringe of the Square Mile, seemed to take on the terrible suffering that was the price of London's global pre-eminence.

A realm of almshouses and the birthplace of both the Salvation Army and the Barnardo's children's charity, the East End was deliberately omitted from most maps of the city, too shocking and miserable to actually believe in for decent folk. Jack the Ripper stalked the streets in the 1880s, when his serial murder of prostitutes had a nation almost paralysed with hysteria, and the East End officially became too horrible to countenance. Even in the early 20th century, American author Jack London found he couldn't get a cab willing to take him to Whitechapel.

Naturally, the East End has changed a lot in the intervening 100 years – it's in the *A-Z* street map, for a start – and as recent gentrification has swept over Hoxton and the neighbouring City, signs of wealth have also started to trickle over into the areas around Whitechapel and Aldgate East. There's even been a growing focus on ramshackle, tube-deprived Hackney and Dalston, while property prices have risen enormously in Mile End, Bethnal Green and Bow.

The waves upon waves of immigrants who came here in search of jobs have given the place a brilliantly multicultural feel. While you can still see the houses of the French Huguenot silk weavers in nearby Spitalfields, from Whitechapel eastwards there are plenty of Bangladeshi restaurants, Italian and Jewish businesses and a vibrant Afro-Caribbean population in Hackney and Dalston.

Docklands is a strange, unnatural enclave in all of this, an earlier, forced attempt at rejuvenation and proof of what happens when you let people who think 'there is no such thing as society, only individuals' meddle in a community. That's what former PM Margaret Thatcher and her cohorts effectively did in the 1980s when they took this dilapidated London docks area and began creating a new financial centre to rival the City. The result is the very essence of anomie: a sci-fi cluster of skyscrapers, much further removed from the rest of London than mere distance could ever indicate.

Top Five – the East End

- **Bethnal Green Museum of Childhood** (opposite)
- **Canary Wharf** (p178)
- **Ragged School Museum** (p177)
- **Museum in Docklands** (p178)
- **Whitechapel Art Gallery** (right)

WHITECHAPEL

Synonymous with poverty and slums during the Victorian era, contemporary Whitechapel is an invigorating experience. The East End's main road, Whitechapel High St, hums with a cacophony of Asian and African languages, its busy shops selling everything from Indian snacks to Nigerian fabrics and Middle Eastern jewellery, as the East End's multitudinous ethnic groupings rub up against each other. It's still a chaotic and poor place, but it's one full of life and aspiration and should not be missed.

WHITECHAPEL ART GALLERY
Map pp454-5
☎ 7522 7888, 7572 7878; www.whitechapel.org; 80-82 Whitechapel Rd; admission free; ⌚ 11am-6pm Tue-Sun, to 9pm Thu; ⊖ Aldgate East; ♿

Among the more interesting of London's contemporary art galleries, the Whitechapel has made its name putting on exhibitions by established and emerging artists including Gary Hume, Robert Crumb and Nan Goldin. It also regularly holds debates or talks by musicians and filmmakers, not to mention its often vastly impressive and ambitiously themed shows that change every couple of months. Check the programme online, but remember there's the very pleasant Whitechapel Art Gallery Café, regardless of what's on. There's an entry fee for one exhibition a year, usually between January and March. This is done to raise cash for the gallery, although entry from 6pm to 9pm on Thursdays remains free during this period.

WHITECHAPEL BELL FOUNDRY

Map pp454-5

☎ 7247 2599; www.whitechapelbellfoundry.co.uk; 32-34 Whitechapel Rd; tours per person £8, children under 14yr not allowed; ⊗ tours 10am & 2pm Sat, shop 9.30am-4.15pm Mon-Fri; ⊖ Aldgate East

The oldest business in London, established nearby in 1570, this place can be said, literally, to resonate with history. It's the birthplace of the Liberty Bell in Philadelphia and the clock bells of Big Ben and St Paul's Cathedral, among others. After 11 September 2001, the foundry also cast a new bell for New York City's Trinity Church. The 1½-hour guided tours on Saturdays offer a revealing insight into a distinguished old trade, but bookings are essential. During office hours you can view a few small exhibits in the foyer or pick up souvenirs from the shop.

WHITECHAPEL ROAD Map pp454-5

Within a few minutes' walk of Whitechapel tube there are a couple of other landmarks that students of modern history might like to see. First find the large East London Mosque; Fieldgate St runs parallel behind it, housing not only the decent restaurant New Tayyab (p257), but also Tower House. Now being redeveloped as luxury apartments, in its previous incarnation as a hostel residents included Stalin, Lenin and author Jack London.

You're now also deep in Jack the Ripper territory. In fact, the serial killer's first victim, Mary Ann Nichols, was hacked to death on 31 August 1888 on what is now Durward St behind Whitechapel tube.

Along Whitechapel Rd itself, the criminal connections continue through the centuries. Just before the intersection with Cambridge Heath Rd sits the Blind Beggar Pub (☎ 7247 6195; 337 Whitechapel Rd), where the notorious gangster Ronnie Kray shot dead George Cornell in 1966, in a turf war over control of the East End's organised crime. A barmaid witnessed the murder, and Kray ended up in the Old Bailey – and jail.

After the intersection with Cambridge Heath Rd, this traditionally poor area's history

takes a more philanthropic turn, with a bust of William Booth, who established the Salvation Army around here in the 1860s, and the Trinity Green Almshouses, poor houses built for injured or retired sailors in 1695. The two rows of almshouses run at right angles away from the street, facing a village-type green; please be considerate when peering through the fence as they are private homes today.

BETHNAL GREEN & HACKNEY

This is the 'proper' East End, as epitomised by the chaos and close-knit community of Bethnal Green and the sprawl of Hackney town, one of the most ethnically diverse areas of the capital. While neither area is on the traditional tourist path, both repay a visit amply – the Bethnal Green Museum of Childhood and Sutton House are both entertaining diversions, and you'll certainly get a flavour of 'real' East End life during your visit.

BETHNAL GREEN MUSEUM OF CHILDHOOD Map pp454-5

☎ 8980 2415; www.museumofchildhood.org.uk; cnr Cambridge Heath & Old Ford Rds E2; admission free; ⊗ 10am-5.50pm Sat-Thu; ⊖ Bethnal Green; ♿

The open hall of this Victorian-era building contains a number of child-friendly, interactive exhibits and resounds with children's laughter and the clomping of tiny feet. Kids can play on oversize dominos boards, dig castles in a sandpit or raid the dressing-up box all for free. Alternatively, they can join nostalgic older visitors admiring vintage dolls and rocking horses. ('You mean there were toys before Xbox, grandma?')

Yes, it's true, and from carved ivory figures to teddy bears, from Meccano to Lego and from peep shows to video games, childhood artefacts from the 17th century to today are on display in this cheery museum. The upstairs gallery, decorated with wrought-iron railings, traces the stages of growing up and showcases toys from Africa, the Caribbean and Eastern Europe, in a reflection of Bethnal Green's multicultural make-up.

It doesn't take very long to get around, but there's a café in the middle of the chequerboard ground floor where tuckered-out little tykes and adults can refuel. At the time of writing, the museum was expected to be closed until October 2006 for a major overhaul.

Museum of Childhood (p175)

HACKNEY MUSEUM Map pp438-9
☎ 8356 3500; www.hackney.gov.uk/museum;
Hackney Learning & Technology Centre, 1 Reading Lane
E8; admission free; ☽ 9.30am-5.30pm Tue-Fri, to 8pm
Thu, 10am-5pm Sat; rail Hackney Central; ☒

Surprisingly appealing, this museum traces
the habitation and reflects the multicultural
make-up of Hackney – one of the most ethnically diverse neighbourhoods in the UK. It
looks like a funky stylist has had a say in the
exhibits, as display boards feature translucent
squares of the same colour and one case puts
single souvenirs and effects from diverse ethnic communities behind square panes of glass
– just as you'd expect to find in *Elle Decor*
magazine. Even the ancient Saxon log boat,
discovered on the marshes, has been placed
in the floor under glass squares, above which
sits a replica, which you can pretend to load.

Yet the design is not so flashy as to interfere
with your enjoyment of what's on show, from
zoetropes and an early-20th-century locality
map to an early pie 'n' mash shop and a hand
with painted fingernails, such as you can have
done in local, Vietnamese-run salons. There's a
copy of the genre-defining London crime novel
Yardie, which was published locally. Meanwhile,
recorded oral histories can be listened to by

picking up phone handsets, and there are several touch-screens where you can learn more.

It's an attraction that's probably not worth
trekking all the way east for, but a must if
you're already in the area. Kids will love it. Alternatively, if you prefer not to mingle with
over-exuberant school groups, try to make it
on a Thursday night or a Saturday.

SUTTON HOUSE Map pp438-9
☎ 8986 2264; www.nationaltrust.org.uk; 2 & 4
Homerton High St E8; adult/child/family £2.50/50p/£5;
☽ 1-5.30pm Fri & Sat, 11.30am-5pm Sun; rail Hackney Central, then bus 106, 253 or D6

It's really quite amazing to think of Tudor nobles living in 'ackney, but as East London's oldest surviving house proves, they did, and in
some style at that. Abandoned and taken over
by squatters in the 1980s (who have left behind
an attic wall of graffiti), 16th-century Sutton
House could have been tragically lost to history, but it's since been put under the care of
the National Trust and magnificently restored.

The first historic room you walk into, the
Linenfold Parlour, is the absolute highlight,
where the Tudor oak panelling on the walls
has been carved to resemble draped cloth.
Unfortunately, after that even the ornate
Tudor and Edwardian chambers, the Victorian
study, the Georgian parlour and the intriguing
mock-up of a Tudor kitchen all seem a trifle
anticlimactic. The only thing that could top
the Linenfold Parlour, we reckon, would be
spotting the alleged resident ghost.

There's a café and shop on site, and on the
last Sunday of each month you can participate
in 'discovery days', when different aspects of
mainly Tudor and occasionally more recent
history are brought back to life.

MILE END & VICTORIA PARK
Mile End is arguably the heart of the modern East End. A busy junction where the
Docklands meet Hackney and the inner
city meets Bow and Stratford Marsh, this

Top Five Multiethnic London
- Dancing at the **Notting Hill Carnival** (p12)
- Having a curry in **Tooting** (p269)
- Hanging in **Brixton** (p201)
- Exploring **Hackney** (p175)
- Walking through **Chinatown** (p103)

is an increasingly popular residential locale with some great bars and restaurants, a unique park that straddles the busy Mile End Rd and a more traditional one in the gorgeous expanse of Victoria Park, the East End's biggest and most attractive green lung. There's nothing to bring the general traveller here, but anyone staying in the area or interested in the East End's history will find their time very profitably spent.

MATT'S GALLERY Map pp438-9
☎ 8983 1771; www.mattsgallery.org; 42-44 Copperfield Rd E3; admission free; ☺ noon-6pm Wed-Sun; ⊖ Mile End

Named after founder Robin Klassnik's dog, this working studio and gallery is one of the East End's more interesting. Here some of London's most respected artists have premiered their works, including Jo Bruton and Mike Nelson. Concentrating mainly on installation and video work, the gallery also regularly shows works in more traditional media too.

MILE END PARK Map pp438-9
⊖ Mile End

The 36-hectare Mile End Park is adjacent to Mile End Rd and the Ragged School Museum. Landscaped to great effect during the millennium year by Tibbalds TM2, it now incorporates a go-kart track, a children's centre for under-10s, areas for public art and an ecology area. The centrepiece, though, is architect Piers Gough's 'green bridge' from the northern edge of the park across Mile End Rd. The bridge itself is actually yellow – confusing until you realise that the 'green' in question refers to the trees that have been planted along its walkway.

RAGGED SCHOOL MUSEUM Map pp438-9
☎ 8980 6405; www.raggedschoolmuseum.org.uk; 46-50 Copperfield Rd E3; admission by donation; ☺ 10am-5pm Wed & Thu, plus 2-5pm 1st Sun of month; ⊖ Mile End

Want to learn a little more about the East End's past? Then pack your books and head to the Ragged School Museum, a combination of mock Victorian schoolroom and social history museum. Both adults and children are inevitably charmed by the hard wooden benches and desks, with slates, chalk, inkwells and abacuses of the re-created classroom on the 1st floor. During term time, the museum runs a schools programme, where pupils are

Worth the Trip
William Morris Gallery (Map p437 ☎ 8527 3782; www.lbwf.gov.uk/wmg; Lloyd Park, Forest Rd E17; admission free; ☺ 10am-1pm & 2-5pm Tue-Sat, plus 1st Sun of month; ⊖ Walthamstow Central) The home where Victorian-era designer and socialist William Morris lived as a teenager is now full of his typically ornate floral wallpaper and chintz. The permanent displays also feature woven rugs and carpets, stained glass, painted tiles and furniture, by either Morris himself or his associates, including Pre-Raphaelite artist Edward Burne-Jones.

Along with Morris' medieval-style helmet and sword, which were made as 'props' for the Pre-Raphaelite murals at the Oxford Union, and the original design for his earliest wallpaper 'Trellis', the downstairs rooms also give an insight into the extremely busy life of a quite fascinating man. The upstairs gallery houses a good selection of Pre-Raphaelite paintings.

From the Underground station, walk northwards along Hoe St for about 15 minutes and turn west (left) on Forest Rd. The gallery is just across the street.

taught reading, writing and arithmetic by a strict schoolma'am in full Victorian regalia; and if you're very good – no talking up the back, there – you can watch and listen to these lessons from the glassed-off gallery. During school holidays, such kinky Victorian role plays are sometimes offered to the general public, so ring ahead.

'Ragged' was a Victorian term used to refer to pupils' usually torn, dirty and dishevelled clothes, and the museum celebrates the legacy of Dr Joseph Barnardo, who founded the first free school for poor East End urchins in this building in the 1860s. So beneath the classroom there's a ground-floor gallery chronicling the area's wider history. The displays manage to touch you with the early poverty of the place and the hardship suffered during and after WWII without ever becoming maudlin – something probably helped by a peppering of colourful anecdotes.

VICTORIA PARK Map pp438-9
⊖ Mile End

If you want a little more green than Mile End Park affords, head north from Mile End tube along Grove Rd, until you reach Victoria Park. This leafy expanse has lakes, fountains, bridges, a bowling green, tennis courts and much more.

DOCKLANDS

You'd never guess it while gazing up at the ultramodern skyscrapers that dominate the Isle of Dogs and Canary Wharf today, but from the 16th century until the mid-20th century this was the industrial heartland of the London docks. Here cargo from global trade was landed, bringing jobs to a tight-knit, working-class community. Even as little as 60 or 70 years ago this community still thrived, but then the docks were badly firebombed during WWII. Never really properly rebuilt, they fell into terminal decline as the British Empire evaporated after the war and container ships were re-routed to deep-water ports further towards the mouth of the Thames River.

The financial metropolis that exists today was begun by the London Docklands Development Corporation (LDDC), a body established by the Thatcher government in the free-wheeling 1980s to take pressure for office space off the City. This rather artificial community had a shaky start. The low-rise toy-town buildings had trouble attracting tenants, the Docklands Light Railway – the main transport link – had obdurate teething troubles and the Canary Wharf Tower itself had to be rescued from bankruptcy twice. Now, however, several newspaper groups and financial behemoths such as Citigroup and HSBC have moved in, and, more than 20 years after it was begun, the area is finally starting to become the mini-Manhattan envisaged – complete with high winds whipping through its streets.

ISLE OF DOGS Map p463

Pundits can't even really agree on whether this is an island, let alone where it got its name. Strictly speaking it's a peninsula of land on the northern shore of the Thames, although without modern road and transport links it would *almost* be separated from the mainland at West India Docks. Similarly, the origin of 'dogs' remains disputed. Some very reputable organisations suggest it's because the royal kennels were located here during Henry VIII's reign. Other equally reputable sources believe it's a corruption of the word *dijks* (dikes), referring to the work of Flemish engineers here in the 19th century.

It can be agreed, however, that the centrepiece of the Isle of Dogs is Canary Wharf. If you want to see how the isle once looked, check out **Mudchute Park & Farm** (☎ 7515 5901; Pier St E14; ⊙ 10am-5pm, from 9am in summer; DLR Mudchute), a short distance to the southeast.

CANARY WHARF Map p463

It's worth visiting Canary Wharf, in the middle of the Isle of Dogs, simply because it's so blimmin' surreal. Cesar Pelli's 244m **Canary Wharf Tower**, built in 1991 at 1 Canada Sq, presides over a toy-town, financial theme park, surrounded by newer towers for HSBC and Citigroup, and offices for Bank of America, Barclays, Lehmann Brothers, Morgan Stanley Dean Witter and more. This thoroughly artificial community is like the set of a sci-fi film. On a good day it's almost utopian, but on a bad day, dark thoughts form about dystopian brainwashing and *Blade Runner*–style replicants.

It took a long time for the place to come this far, even. Canary Wharf Tower, still the tallest building in London and one of the largest property developments in Europe, had to be saved from bankruptcy before it reached today's levels of occupancy. As home to the *Independent* and *Daily Telegraph* newspapers (among other tenants), it's now nicknamed the 'vertical Fleet St'.

Unfortunately, there's no public access to the tower, but on a sunny day you can head for the open air cafés and bars of increasingly trendy West India Quay.

You can arrive here on the DLR. However, the monumental grandeur of Sir Norman Foster's sleek Canary Wharf Underground station, on the Jubilee line, is a better introduction to this otherworldly region.

MUSEUM IN DOCKLANDS Map p463

☎ 0870 444 3857; www.museumindocklands.org.uk; **Warehouse No 1, West India Quay E14; adult/student & under 16yr/senior £5/free/3;** ⊙ **10am-5.30pm (last entry);** ⊖ **Canary Wharf/DLR West India Quay;** ♿

Despite its name, this converted 200-year-old warehouse doesn't confine itself to a simple tale of the docks. Rather, it provides a comprehensive overview of the entire history of the Thames since AD 43, an approach that adults might at times find more taxing than engaging. Ironically, it's at its best when it's dealing with home-turf specifics like the controversial transformation of the decrepit docks into Docklands in the 1980s and the social upheaval and dislocation that accompanied it.

Kids, however, usually adore the place, with its exhibits like 'sailor town' (an excellent re-creation of the cobbled streets, bars and lodging houses of a 19th-century dockside community) and especially the hands-on Mudlarks gallery, where five- to 12-year-olds can explore the history of the Thames, tipping the clipper, trying on old-fashioned diving helmets, learning to use winches and even constructing a simple model of Canary Wharf.

The tour begins on the 3rd floor (take the lift to the top) with the Roman settlement of Londinium and works its way downwards through the ages. Tickets are valid for a year, so if you're in town for a while, or making repeat trips, you can tackle this museum in small bites.

ST KATHARINE'S DOCK Map pp454-5
☻ Tower Hill

Although it's unashamedly touristy, St Katharine's Dock works, albeit in a very limited sense. With its cafés and one great restaurant, **Lightship Ten** (p256), it makes an ideal spot to pause for a brief rest after a morning's sightseeing at Tower Bridge or the Tower of London. There's a row of twee shops and a hokey pub called the **Dickens Inn**, but it's more entertaining just admiring the opulent luxury yachts.

Sadly, the dock's history is rather less appealing than its appearance. More than 1200 houses were razed and 11,000 people made homeless to make way for its creation in 1828. Yet it was never a great success and closed in 1968 – before being resurrected in its current incarnation in the 1980s. Tourists share the space with the financial brokers who work in nearby Commodities Quay.

WAPPING & LIMEHOUSE Map pp454-5

Author John Stow in his 16th-century *A Survey of London* described Wapping High St as a 'filthy strait passage, with alleys of small tenements or cottages'. It's a far cry from that today, but hardly more attractive. It was one of the first failed yuppie projects of the 1980s, where luxury flats were built but remained unsold. Although the converted warehouses and lofts that line the brick road are now mostly occupied, travelling through here is still a fairly unaesthetic experience.

The area was traditionally home to sailors and dockers. One of the historic sites that people like to visit, however, is the **Execution Dock** near the old river police station at Wapping New Stairs. This is where convicted pirates were hanged and their bodies chained to a post at low tide, to be left until three tides had washed over them. A nearby landmark, the **Captain Kidd pub**, recalls one of the more famous people executed in this way in 1701.

Northwards along Wapping Lane and across the Highway, you'll come to **St George-in-the-East**; the shell of the original church you see surrounding the smaller modern building is the remnants of the church erected by Nicholas Hawksmoor in 1726, which was badly damaged by the Blitz in WWII.

Cannon St Rd leads northward to Cable St, where ropes were manufactured in the late 18th century. The length of the street – 180m – was once the standard English measure for cable. Eastwards along Cable St is the former **Town Hall building**, now a library. On a side wall of the building is a large mural commemorates the **Cable Street riots** that took place here in October 1936. The British fascist Oswald Mosley led a bunch of his Blackshirt thugs into the area to intimidate the local Jewish population, but they were resoundingly repelled.

There isn't much to Limehouse, although it became London's first Chinatown in the late 19th century and was also mentioned in Oscar Wilde's *The Picture of Dorian Gray* (1891), when the protagonist passed by this way in search of opium. Today, the most notable attraction is **St Anne's, Limehouse** (cnr Commercial Rd & Three Colt St). This was Nicholas Hawksmoor's earliest church and still boasts the highest church clock in the city. Although building was completed in 1724, it was only consecrated in 1730.

TRINITY BUOY WHARF Map p463
☎ 7515 7153; ☽ 9am-5.30pm 1st Fri of each month; DLR East India

London's only **lighthouse** is located at this brownfield site. The lighthouse was built for Michael Faraday in 1863. Also here is the unusual **Container City**, a community of artists' studios made from shipping containers, stacked side by side and one on top of each other. The web designers, architects and other creative tenants even have their own balconies.

The wharf is open to the public every day (follow the signs to the bird sanctuary) and is much loved for film and modelling shoots. There are great views of the Millennium Dome, too.

SOUTHEAST LONDON

Eating p258; Drinking p287; Shopping p346; Sleeping p368-9

This corner of London feels like a succession of small villages, and that's exactly what many of these suburbs were until as recently as the late 19th century. Although there's evidence of early prehistoric settlements in areas like Forest Hill, Greenwich and Woolwich, for millennia this area was merely on the fringes of the big city.

Greenwich, right on the banks of the Thames, is something of an exception in this. It has powerful royal connections harking back to the Middle Ages, when Humphrey, Duke of Gloucester, the uncle of Henry VI, built a manor house here in 1426–33. King Henry VIII was born here in 1491 in the Tudors' Palace of Placentia (since destroyed) and used this as his main residence, marrying Catherine of Aragon here, signing Anne Boleyn's warrant and awaiting the birth of his first and second daughters, Mary and Elizabeth (later Elizabeth I).

Greenwich has a great seafaring history. Its proximity to the sea made it one of the main points of entry for invading Danes in the 11th century and it was later the site of the Royal Naval College. However, the area's main claim to fame is its special relationship with time. Ever since the Prime Meridian of Longitude was moved here in the 19th century – ironically from London's recent Olympics rival Paris – Greenwich Mean Time has dictated how clocks and watches around the globe are set.

Now a Unesco World Heritage Site, Greenwich's leafy green expanses and white wedding-cake buildings give it an air of semirural gentility. This tranquil aura continues, although to a lesser degree, as you venture further southeast, into a London that few nonlocals see.

GREENWICH

Symmetry's the thing in Greenwich – and great views. Sure, the area does have fascinating connections with royalty, the sea and timekeeping, but repeatedly your eye will be drawn back to its architecture and outlook. Two legendary designers, Inigo Jones and Sir Christopher Wren, are partly responsible for this.

In the early 17th century, Inigo Jones built one of England's first classical Renaissance homes, the Queen's House, which still stands today. Sir Christopher Wren built the Royal Observatory in 1675–76 and, with his acolyte Nicholas Hawksmoor, began work 20 years later on the Royal Hospital for Seamen, which became the Royal Naval College in 1873. Considerately, Wren altered his plans, splitting the college into two perfectly formed halves, to allow uninterrupted views of the Thames from the Queen's House.

The designer of Greenwich Park, Le Nôtre, also left Greenwich a wonderful legacy in the huge expanse of semilandscaped grass that heads uphill.

Back in the centre of 'town', small boho shops give the place an overwhelming village feel.

ROYAL OBSERVATORY Map p463

☎ 8312 6565; www.nmm.ac.uk; Greenwich Park SE19; admission free; ☺ 10am-5pm Oct-May, 10am-6pm Apr-Sep; DLR Cutty Sark

The Royal Observatory allows you to stand with one foot in the world's western hemisphere and the other in the east. It also explains how the prime meridian of time – which you've just persuaded someone to photograph you straddling, right? – came to be located here. The establishment of Greenwich as the point from which all time on the planet is measured harks back to the search for a reliable way to measure longitude in the 17th and 18th centuries (see opposite). Charles II, sick of ships foundering, had the Royal Observatory built on the hill here in 1675, intending that astronomy be used to find an accurate means of navigation at sea. The first astronomer royal, John Flamsteed (1646–1719), set up home here, training his telescope on the skies from the Octagon Room – one of the few surviving interiors designed by Sir Christopher Wren.

In the end, it was a watchmaker who solved the problem of longitude, and John Harrison's original clocks, watches and story are showcased in the second half of the exhibition – although this might be partly closed during ongoing renovations in the next few years, so ring ahead or check the website. Greenwich itself was still named as the prime meridian at an 1884 Washington conference, in recognition of all its work. Every day at midday, or 1pm in the summer, the red time ball at the top of the Royal Observatory drops to mark the accuracy and pre-eminence of Greenwich Mean Time (GMT) as standard time.

The observatory is set to open its state-of-the-art new planetarium and astronomy galleries in spring 2007. In the meantime, a makeshift planetarium has been erected in the **National Maritime Museum** (see below).

NATIONAL MARITIME MUSEUM

Map p463

☎ 8312 6565; www.nmm.ac.uk; Romney Rd SE10; admission free, for special exhibitions charges vary; ☽ 10am-6pm Apr-Sep, 10am-5pm Oct-Mar; DLR Cutty Sark; ♿

Most first-timers think they're coming to Greenwich for the Royal Observatory, but in reality the main National Maritime Museum building is more impressive. From the moment you step through the sound sculpture of gentle washing tides at the entrance to this magnificent neoclassical building you'll be won over. And it just gets better as you progress through the glass-roofed Neptune Court into the rest of this three-storey building.

The exhibits are arranged by theme, focusing on Explorers, Maritime London, Seapower, Trade & Empire and much more. Visual highlights include the golden barge built in 1732 for Frederick, Prince of Wales, and the huge ship's propeller installed on the ground floor. The museum also owns the uniform Britain's greatest sea-faring hero, Horatio Nelson, was wearing when he was fatally shot, plus a replica of the lifeboat *James Caird* used by explorer Ernest Shackleton and a handful of his men on their epic mission for help in Antarctica.

The environmentally minded are catered for with the ever-growing Planet Ocean exhibit, examining the science, history, health and future of the sea. Kids will love steering a Viking long boat or firing a cannon in 'All Hands'. Even fashionistas will be wowed by Rank and Style (Naval uniforms) and the Passengers exhibit (classic travel posters and the mock-up of the cocktail bar of a cruise ship). The temporary exhibitions are usually jaw-droppingly good, too.

The Long Road to Longitude

Rarely has a science story proved so sexy. Dava Sobel's remarkable slim volume on the subject, *Longitude*, became an international bestseller; and the concentrated looks on the faces of Royal Observatory visitors today reveal that 'the true story of a lone genius who solved the greatest scientific problem of his time' (as Sobel's subtitle would have it) still enthrals.

In short, it goes like this. At the start of the 18th century, sailors still had no reliable means to measure a ship's longitude. Calculating how far north or south of the equator they were, or their latitude, was easy; they simply needed to measure with a sextant the height of the sun or the Pole Star on the horizon. But they had only complicated astronomical methods – and some other downright kooky formulas – for measuring how far east or west they were. As a result, they all too regularly miscalculated and catastrophically ran aground.

Already by the 16th century, scientists knew that the answer to measuring one's longitude could lie in comparing local time (measured by the sun) with the reading of a clock set at the time of one's home port. This was based on the knowledge that it takes 24 hours for the earth to complete one revolution of 360°, so a one-hour difference represents 1/24th of a revolution – or 15° longitude.

However, that meant having a clock on board that would accurately continue to record the time back home. Even two hundred years later, at the start of the 18th century, no such technology had been invented; the often violent pitching of a ship at sea and variable temperatures always caused contemporary watches to lose or gain time.

As a leading sea-going nation in an era of discovery, Britain had perhaps the most to lose. So, in 1714, parliament offered an enormous prize of £20,000 to anyone who could discover a method of finding longitude, accurate to within 30 miles.

Some wag suggested a solution involving a wounded dog in London and 'a powder of sympathy' to make a dog on board yelp at certain times, while powerful astronomers, among them Sir Isaac Newton, were convinced the answer lay in the stars. Against a background of intense politicking, humble Yorkshire clockmaker John Harrison persevered with different pendulums, springs and metals until the Royal Observatory authorities were forced to admit that his fourth effort – the watch H4 with its temperature-resistant bimetallic strips – did the trick. The authorities still weren't in a hurry to part with the prize money, though. Harrison was 79 years old by the time he was paid in 1772.

National Maritime Museum (p181)

While the refurbishment of the Royal Observatory is underway (expected to continue until spring 2007), a makeshift **planetarium** (adult/senior, student & child £4/2; ☪ shows 2.30pm Mon-Fri, 1.30pm & 3.30pm Sat, 2pm & 3pm Sun) has been set up here.

OLD ROYAL NAVAL COLLEGE Map p463
☎ 8269 4747, 0800 389 3341; King William Walk SE10; admission free; ☪ 10am-5pm Mon-Sat, 12.30-5pm Sun; DLR Cutty Sark

There are two main rooms open to the public here: the Painted Hall and the chapel. They're in separate buildings, because when Christopher Wren was commissioned in 1692 by King William and Queen Mary to design a hospital and retirement home for wounded naval veterans, he considerately split the building in two, thus giving the existing **Queen's House** (opposite) uninterrupted river views.

Top Five – Southeast London

- **Eltham Palace** (p186)
- **National Maritime Museum** (p181)
- **Painted Hall** (right) of the Old Royal Naval College
- **Royal Observatory** (p180)
- **Thames Flood Barrier** (p185)

Built on the site of the Old Palace of Placentia used by the Tudors, the hospital was initially intended for those wounded in the victory over the French at La Hogue in 1692. In 1869 the building was converted to a Naval College. Now even the navy has left and the premises are home to the University of Greenwich and Trinity College of Music.

The **Painted Hall** is one of Europe's greatest banquet rooms. In the King William Building, it has been covered in decorative 'allegorical Baroque' murals by artist James Thornhill, who also painted the cupola of St Paul's Cathedral. The hall was intended as the naval pensioners' dining room but, rather sadly, was declared too magnificent for that once Thornhill got his hands on it. If you want to see where the poor pensioners were packed off to, visit the Jacobean undercroft of the former palace of Placentia on one of the daily **guided tours** (adult/under 16yr £4/free; ☪ 2pm) leaving from the Painted Hall.

The murals basically pay tribute to the hospital's founders, William and Mary, and took 19 years to complete. But despite the flattery, his bosses only paid Thornhill £1 per square yard for the walls and £3 for the ceilings, so no wonder he drew himself into the picture with an open hand. (He could just be introducing the work, but we doubt it.)

Off the upper hall is the **Nelson Room**, originally designed by Nicholas Hawksmoor, then used as a smoking room and now newly refurbished. For a week over Christmas 1805, this is where the brandy-soaked (for embalming purposes, of course) body of the great naval hero lay, before his state funeral at St Paul's. Today the room boasts a replica of the statue atop Nelson's column in Trafalgar Sq (see p99), plus other memorabilia.

The **chapel** in the Queen Mary Building, opposite, is decorated in a lighter rococo style. It's certainly a beautiful room, but it's more famous for its organ and acoustics. If possible come on the first Sunday of the month, when there's a free organ recital at 3pm, or time your visit for Eucharist, every Sunday at 11am.

QUEEN'S HOUSE Map p463

☎ 8858 4422; Romney Rd SE10; admission free; ☉ 10am-5pm early Sep-May, 10am-6pm Jun-early Sep; DLR Cutty Sark

This building was first called the 'House of Delight' and that's certainly true – it is. The first Palladian building by architect Inigo Jones after he returned from Italy, it's far more enticing than the art collection in it, even though that contains some Hogarths and Gainsboroughs. One of the few examples of Jones' work to survive, it was begun in 1616 for Anne of Denmark, wife of James I. However, it wasn't completed until 1635, when it became the home of Charles I and his queen, Henrietta Maria. The Great Hall is the principal room – a lovely cubical space, with a gallery at 1st-floor level and a helix-shaped Tulip Staircase.

GREENWICH PARK Map p463

☎ 8858 2608; DLR Cutty Sark/rail Maze Hill

This is one of London's largest and loveliest parks, with a grand avenue, wide-open spaces, a rose garden and rambling, picturesque walks. It's partly the work of Le Nôtre, who landscaped the palace gardens of Versailles for Louis XIV. It contains several historic sights, a café and a deer park called the Wilderness.

If you continue south of the park you come to **Blackheath** (p184).

CUTTY SARK Map p463

☎ 8858 3445; Cutty Sark Gardens SE10; adult/5-16yr/family £3.95/2.95/9.80; ☉ 10am-5pm; DLR Cutty Sark

Rust and rot have been eating away at the last of the great tea clippers to sail between China and England in the 19th century and she's due to go in for repairs towards the end of 2006. Before then, however, you're still welcome on board to see the world's largest collection of colourful ship's figureheads (great for kids), or to learn how the superspeedy *Cutty Sark* – the fastest ship of her day – furthered the cause of globalisation by bringing Britons home a fresh load of tea.

From 2007 parts of the ship will be closed, but visitors will be able to take hard-hat tours focusing on preservation techniques.

The *Cutty Sark* takes its name from a Robert Burns' poem where it means 'short shirt'. The ship used to be accompanied by a smaller craft, the *Gipsy Moth IV* (www.gipsymoth.org), in which Francis Chichester sailed around the world in 1967. However, this is now based on the Isle of Wight.

Tunnel Visions

One moment the Greenwich foot tunnel beneath the Thames is the most claustrophobic place in London, with a spine-chilling aura of fear and mystery. (Will the river burst through before I reach the other side? What's that clunking echo behind?) The next it's just a mundane pedestrian underpass between Greenwich and Island Gardens, which has safely withstood the water pressure from above for more than 100 years.

The crime novelist PD James succumbed to the first interpretation with a terrified character in *Original Sin*, and certainly the way the tunnel gradually slopes down towards the middle does initially lend an air of nightmarish infinity. People coming towards you appear first as just feet, before gradually their legs, body and face are revealed.

But then you pass the halfway mark, the exit comes into view and you know you're home and dry, literally. That's the time to reflect on the tunnel's usefulness. Built in 1902 so that workers in Greenwich could reach the docks without having to catch a ferry, it's open 24 hours for those prepared to traverse the 88 or 100 steps at either end. (There's CCTV for security.) Otherwise, the lifts in both dome-shaped entrances will take you up and down from 7am to 7pm Monday to Saturday and 10am to 5.30pm on Sunday.

On a more fanciful note, the tunnel can be seen as an analogy for London's continuing north-south divide. Crossing to the other side is a slightly uncomfortable, but somehow thrilling, rite of passage for the many Londoners – from both north and south – who treat the Thames as if it were the River Styx. Artists haven't missed this mythic potential, either; one art installation here once used red strip-lighting and sound to make it feel like you were pulsing along an artery.

FAN MUSEUM Map p463

☎ 8305 1441; www.fan-museum.org; 12 Croom's Hill SE10; adult/concession £3.50/2.50; ⊙ 11am-5pm Tue-Sat, noon-5pm Sun; DLR Cutty Sark; ⟨⟩

Proving that fans aren't just something for delicate ladies prone to fainting and swooning, but artworks in their own right, this collection contains ivory, tortoiseshell, peacock feather and folded-fabric examples alongside kitsch battery-powered versions and huge, ornamental Welsh fans. The Georgian town house in which the collection resides also has a Japanese-style garden with an orangery serving **afternoon teas** (full/half-tea £4.50/3.50; ⊙ 3-5pm Tue & Sun).

RANGER'S HOUSE Map p463

☎ 8853 0035; www.english-heritage.org.uk; Greenwich Park SE10; adult/under 5yr/5-15yr/senior & student £5/free/2.50/3.50; ⊙ 10am-5pm Wed-Sun Apr-Sep; DLR Cutty Sark

The potpourri of jewellery, paintings, porcelain, silverware and tapestries here belonged to Julius Wernher, a German-born diamond- and gold-miner who made his riches in South Africa in the 19th century. Any park ranger who owned this many treasures would clearly have been on the take.

ST ALFEGE CHURCH Map p463

☎ 8858 6828; Church St SE10; admission free; ⊙ 10am-4pm Mon-Sat, 1-4pm Sun; DLR Cutty Sark

Designed by Nicholas Hawksmoor in 1714 to replace a 12th-century building, this parish church features a restored mural by James Thornhill (the artist behind the Painted Hall at the Royal Naval College). St Alfege was the archbishop of Canterbury, killed on this site by Vikings in 1012.

BLACKHEATH Map p437
rail Blackheath

Looking at a map, you could easily mistake Blackheath for a southern extension of Greenwich Park, but the common and surrounding 'village' have a character very much their own. Known by some as the 'Hampstead of the south', the 110-hectare expanse of open common has played a greater role in the history of London than its much bigger sister to the north. The Danes camped here in the early 11th century after having captured Alfege, the archbishop of Canterbury, as did Wat Tyler before marching on London with tens of thousands of Essex and Kentish men during the Peasants' Revolt in 1381. Henry VII fought off Cornish rebels here in

1497, and the heath was where Henry VIII met his fourth wife, Anne of Cleves, in 1540 (he had agreed to marry her based on a portrait by Holbein, but disliked her immediately in the flesh). Later Blackheath became a highwaymen's haunt, and it was not until the area's development in the late 18th century, when the lovely **Paragon**, a crescent of Georgian mansions on the southeastern edge of the heath, was built to entice 'the right sort of people' to move to the area, that Blackheath was considered safe. The name of the heath dates from the 12th century, so is thought to derive from the colour of the soil, not from its alleged role as a burial ground during the Black Death, the bubonic plague of the 14th century.

Today the windswept heath is the starting point for the London Marathon in April, a pleasant place for a stroll or somewhere to go fly a kite. It's not uncommon to see artists dabbing away at their easels; apparently these Turner wannabes find the light has a special quality on the heath. There are a couple of historic pubs within reach: the Hare and Billet and the Princess of Wales.

Along with the Paragon, other notable buildings include the fieldstone **All Saints' church** (1858), with its needle-sharp spire to the south, and **Morden College**, the Ritz of almshouses, built in 1695 to house 'decayed Turkey Merchants' who had fallen on hard times. The building, now a nursing home and closed to the public, is believed to be a Christopher Wren design.

To reach Blackheath from Greenwich Park, walk southwards along Chesterfield Walk and past the Ranger's House (or southwards along Blackheath Ave and through Blackheath Gate) and then cross Shooters Hill Rd.

CHARLTON & WOOLWICH

From early Iron Age hillforts to one mammoth Millennium Dome, humankind has been determined to leave a mark on these areas over the centuries. One of the most enduring landmarks has been the Royal Arsenal, which followed Henry VIII's royal dockyards out here in the 16th and 17th centuries. When it was finally closed in 1994, it made way for a museum.

MILLENNIUM DOME Map p463
⊖ **North Greenwich**

Since it closed at the end of 2000, having failed miserably in its bid to attract 12 million visitors, the huge circus tent–shaped Millennium Dome hasn't really done much except star in a

James Bond movie and sit glumly on the horizon waiting for Londoners to curse at it. Many are annoyed at the way this 380m-wide white elephant on Greenwich Peninsula has snuffled up more than £1 billion in public funds. Now, however, it's finally about to be transformed into something useful.

Work is underway on turning it into a 26,000-seat sports and entertainment venue, which is also planned to be used during the 2012 Olympics. An expansive plaza, Millennium Sq, is planned between the tube station at North Greenwich and the entrance to the dome.

Meanwhile, in a later stage of the development, offices, shopping centres, a school, a hotel and 10,000 homes (4100 of them low-cost homes) will be built on the surrounding 76 hectares.

There's still not much to see yet, however, and the area around the dome is still pretty derelict. If you want to get a good view, you can see it from Docklands or by taking a Thames River cruise (see right). **Trinity Buoy Wharf** (see p179) is also an excellent vantage point.

THAMES FLOOD BARRIER Map p437

⊖ North Greenwich/rail Charlton, then bus 161, 177, 180 or 472/bus 177 or 180

The sci-fi looking Thames Flood Barrier has saved London from flooding nearly 70 times. And with global warming increasing the city's vulnerability to rising sea levels and surge tides, the barrier is likely to be of growing importance in coming years. Completed in 1982, it has 10 movable gates anchored to nine concrete piers, each as tall as a five-storey building. The silver roofs on the piers house the operating machinery to raise and lower the gates against excess water and they're vaguely reminiscent in shape of the Sydney Opera House, or Glasgow's Armadillo building.

The barrier was built in response to a disaster in 1953, when 300 people drowned after the Thames burst its banks (it took so long to green-light the project because of shipping issues). Today environmentalists are already talking about a bigger, wider damming mechanism further towards the mouth of the river, before the current barrier comes to the expected end of its design life in 2030.

The barrier looks best when it's raised, and the only guaranteed time this happens is once a month, when the mechanisms are checked. For exact dates and times, ring the **Thames Barrier Visitors Centre** (☎ 8305 4188; www.environment-agency.gov.uk; 1 Unity Way SE18; admission to barrier free, admission to downstairs information centre adult/child/senior £1.50/75p/£1; ✆ 11am-3.30pm Oct-Mar, 10.30am-4.30pm Apr-Sep). This tiny centre will also fill you in on the science of daily tides, spring tides and surge tides that threaten the city.

To get to the visitors centre, you need to go by tube, rail or bus. If you're coming from central London, take a train to Charlton from Charing Cross or London Bridge. Then walk, or take bus 161, 177, 180 or 472 to the Thames Barrier stop. If you're coming from Greenwich, you can pick up bus 177 or 180 along Romney Rd and get off at the Thames Barrier stop (near the Victoria Pub, 757 Woolwich Rd). From there Westmoor St leads northwards to the visitors centre.

Boats also travel to and from the barrier, although they don't land. From Westminster it's a three-hour round trip; from Greenwich it takes one hour. From late March to October direct services run by **Thames River Services** (☎ 7930 4097; www.westminsterpier.co.uk; adult/child/senior/family one way £6.80/3.40/5.60/18.70, return £8.60/4.30/7.10/23.60) leave Westminster Pier on the hour from 10am to 3pm (leaving Greenwich from 11am to 4pm), passing the Dome along the way. From November to March there's a reduced service from Westminster between 10.40am and 3.20pm. See the website for exact times.

CHARLTON HOUSE Map p437

☎ 8856 3951; Charlton Rd SE7; admission free; ✆ 9am-11pm Mon-Fri, 9am-5.30pm Sat; rail Charlton/bus 53, 54, 380 or 442

Lucky Charlton to have this red-brick Jacobean house as a community centre. Fortunately, because community groups use the building day and night during the week, you can also pop in to look at the oak staircase, ornate ceilings and marble fireplaces. On Saturdays the place is very popular for weddings.

The formal gardens, part of which are thought to have been designed by leading 17th-century architect Inigo Jones, have been replanted and landscaped in recent years. There are now separate herb and shrub gardens. Elsewhere in the grounds there's a mulberry tree dating from 1608.

FIREPOWER Map p437

☎ 8855 7755; www.firepower.org.uk; Royal Arsenal, Woolwich SE18; adult/5-15yr/senior & student/family £5/2.50/4.50/12; ✆ 10.30am-5pm Wed-Sun Apr-Oct, 10.30am-5pm Fri-Sun Nov-Mar; rail Woolwich Arsenal

Not a place for pacifists or those of a nervous disposition, Firepower is a shoot-'em-up display of how artillery has developed throughout the ages. This history proceeds from catapults to nuclear warheads, while the multimedia extravaganza Field of Fire tries to convey the experience of artillery gunners from WWI to Bosnia. There's a gunnery hall and a medals gallery, and a Real Weapons gallery where you can even try your hand at shooting a tank or a rifle on a simulator. It's loud and it flashes, but the kids just can't get enough of the place.

ELTHAM

Eltham was the favoured home of the Plantagenet kings who came before the Tudors, as a handy stopover on the trip back from France. However, after the royal favours were switched to Greenwich, Eltham Palace lay neglected for more than five hundred years. Only when the wealthy Courtauld family arrived in the 1930s to build their fabulous home were the remains of the original palace restored.

ELTHAM PALACE Map p437

☎ 8294 2548; www.english-heritage.org.uk; Court Rd SE9; adult/under 5yr/5-15yr/concession £7.30/ free/3.50/5.50; ⏲ 10am-4pm Sun-Wed Nov-Mar, 10am-5pm Sun-Wed Apr-Oct; rail Eltham; ♿

No self-respecting fan of Art Deco should miss a trip to Eltham Palace, not for the scarce remnants of the palace building itself – although that has its own attractions – but for the fabulous Courtauld House in the grounds. If you like 1930s style, you'll be fantasising about moving in.

The house was built during that decade by the well-to-do textile merchant Stephen Courtauld and his wife Virginia; and from the impressive entrance hall with its dome and huge circular geometrically patterned carpet to the marbled bathrooms and advanced electrical fittings it appears the couple had taste as well as money. They also, rather fashionably for the times, had a pet lemur, and the heated cage for the spoiled (and vicious) 'Mah-jongg' is also on view.

Little remains of the 14th- to 16th-century palace where Edward IV entertained and Henry VIII spent his childhood before decamping for Greenwich, apart from the restored Great Medieval Hall. Its hammer-beam roof is generally rated the third best in the country, behind those at Westminster Hall and Hampton Court Palace.

DULWICH & FOREST HILL

As its name suggests, Dulwich is not exactly London's most exciting quarter. Instead it's a comfortable middle-class enclave, helped along by one powerful freeholder, Dulwich Estate, which has kept out the riff-raff. Somehow, though, both Margaret Thatcher and Hammer Horror bloodsucker Peter Cushing are on the roll as former residents – now there's a meeting we would like to have seen. Explorer Ernest Shackleton also went to school here.

The name Forest Hill was devised by an unimaginative property developer in the late 18th century to describe this, er, leafy, hilly district. Its most famous former

Worth the Trip

Danson House (Off Map p437; ☎ 8303 6699; http://dansonhouse.com; Danson Park, Bexleyheath DA6; adult/ concession £5/4.50; ⏲ 11am-5pm, last entry 4.15pm, Wed, Thu & Sun Mar-Oct; rail Bexleyheath) This restored Palladian villa is testament not only to one man's love for his new wife, but to the luxury in which wealthy East India Company executives lived at the height of Britain's trading power in the late 18th century. The numerous dining-room friezes celebrating love and romance have been cleaned, while the octagonal salon in which John Boyd would have sat with his second wife, Catherine Capone, is returned to its original splendour.

Red House (Map p437; ☎ 0149 475 5588; www.nationaltrust.org.uk; 13 Red House Lane, Bexleyheath DA6; adult/ child £6/3; ⏲ 11am-3.30pm Oct-Feb, 11am-4.15pm Mar-Sep; rail Bexleyheath, plus 15min walk) From the outside, this one-time home of Victorian designer William Morris might remind you of an exquisite gingerbread house. It's a red-brick construction with a pointy red-tiled roof that somehow contrives to look both gothic and homy. Inside elements of the 'Arts and Crafts' style to which Morris adhered are slowly being revealed during ongoing restoration. Furniture by Morris and the house's designer Philip Webb are in evidence, as are paintings and stained glass by Edward Burne-Jones. Entry is by guided tour only, which must be prebooked.

resident was the Victoria tea merchant Frederick John Horniman, whose eclectic collection forms the basis of a notable museum.

DULWICH PICTURE GALLERY Map p437

☎ 8693 5254; www.dulwichpicturegallery.org.uk; Gallery Rd SE21; adult/student & child/senior £4/free/3, admission free Fri; ⊙ 10am-5pm Tue-Fri, 11am-5pm Sat & Sun; rail West Dulwich

The Dulwich Picture Gallery is the UK's oldest public art gallery. It was designed by Sir John Soane between 1811 and 1814 to house the Dulwich College's collection of paintings by Raphael, Rembrandt, Rubens, Reynolds, Gainsborough, Poussin, Lely, Van Dyck and others. Unusually, the collectors, Noel Desenfans and painter Francis Bourgeois, chose to have their mausoleums placed among the pictures.

A new annexe built for the millennium contains space for temporary exhibitions, and there's also now an open-air café. The museum is a 10-minute walk northwards along Gallery Rd, which starts almost opposite West Dulwich station.

HORNIMAN MUSEUM Map p437

☎ 8699 1872, 8699 2339; www.horniman.ac.uk; 100 London Rd SE23; admission free; ⊙ 10.30am-5.30pm Mon-Sat, 2-5.30pm Sun; rail Forest Hill

An Art Nouveau building with a clock tower houses this eclectic little museum. Based on the collection of Victorian tea merchant Frederick John Horniman, it encompasses everything from Africa's largest mask to Emperor angelfish to a wonderful collection of concertinas.

In the ethnographic section you'll find 'African Worlds', the first permanent gallery of African and Afro-Caribbean art and culture in the UK. The revamped natural history area features a large walrus, animal skeletons and pickled specimens. The Music Room has instruments from 3500-year-old Egyptian clappers to early English keyboards, with touch-screens so you can hear what they sound like. (If that's not sufficient there's a small 'hands-on' section where you can bash away to your heart's content – don't go here with a hangover!) On top of all this, there's an aquarium, beehive, conservatory and café.

To get here from Forest Hill station, turn left out of the station along Devonshire Rd and then right along London Rd. The Horniman is on the right.

NORTH CENTRAL

Eating p259-62; Drinking p288-9; Shopping p347; Sleeping p369-72

Including some of the most desirable residential neighbourhoods of the capital, North Central has the sophistication and fast pace of the West End without its crowds, dirt and general chaos. Crammed full of superb sights and interesting museums, not to mention Regent's Park, one of London's finest, this is an area you won't want to miss out on.

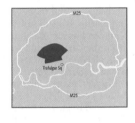

Marylebone, the plush residential neighbourhood north of Mayfair, is one of the most exciting culinary destinations in the capital, with Marylebone High St now a veritable foodies' mecca. Until the 18th century, Marylebone was a mostly rural community known after its parish church, which sat on a bank of the River Tyburn: somehow 'St Mary's by the Bourne' morphed into the incomprehensible Marylebone (marlee-bone). Not only has it been home to supersleuth Sherlock Holmes (of Baker St), the world's best and most expensive medical practitioners (on Harley St), the venerable BBC (on Regent St), and the spirit of cricket (through the Marylebone Cricket Club, the guardians of the game), it also presents London's greatest conundrum: how come Madame Tussaud's is the city's most popular paying attraction when the wonderful and free Wallace Collection is virtually overlooked? Not even Arthur Conan Doyle's debonair detective could solve that one.

North of restful Regent's Park is the amiable and affluent Primrose Hill, all the more amiable since its residents made a stand against the scourge of Starbucks, and booted globalisation out of Regent's Park Rd. Famously home to London's most glamorous models, actors and pop stars, it remains surprisingly laid-back with some charming drinking and eating options. The hill, itself a park, provides wonderful vistas over the centre of London. Further north again is the leafy residential enclave of Belsize Park, where it always feels like Sunday afternoon.

North of Hyde Park, Paddington is best known for its train station (with its splendid mid-19th-century iron girder roof) and as the place where a very cute bear arrived after his trip from darkest Peru. It's never had much of a reputation, not least because of its proximity to the notorious gallows at Tyburn. These days, it can be described as scruffy at best and sordid at worst; there's nothing to bring you here although you might pass through on the Heathrow Express. Similarly, Bayswater – named after Bayard's Spring, which supplied the city's drinking water in the Middle Ages – holds little of interest. It's a uniformly bland residential area, bisected by the predominantly naff Queensway. However, given the central location of these areas, their fashionable neighbours, the demand for space and London's fondness for reinventing itself, it can only be a matter of time before Paddington and Bayswater are 'the next big things', even though they are arguably too expensive already to attract people creative and young enough to ensure reinvention.

Despite ongoing efforts to transform the district – including the opening of the fabulous British Library and the ongoing building of the Eurostar high-speed rail link (due to open in 2007) – King's Cross and Euston are still notoriously dodgy and forbidding. Two ugly train stations and an absolutely magnificent one dominate the area, while the streets are choked with traffic, lined with ugly grey buildings and paved with general cheerlessness. Street prostitution, crime, drug abuse and drunkenness all feature, and while transformation efforts continue, the noise and closed-off roads are just adding to the general unpleasantness for now.

Few parts of London can match the breakneck pace with which Camden has been made over and under in the last 50 years. Traditionally home to huge numbers of poor Irish and Greek immigrants, it was run-down and neglected until the early 1970s, when all of a sudden it gained the brio of bohemia, and became the place where struggling actors like those of *Withnail & I* fame hung out and drank hard. When the world-famous market started, Camden became a weekend destination for many Londoners and up sprang many artists' studios and music venues that were the incubators for some of London's finest. It peaked in the early '90s when the market was the home of all things hip and Camden was the epicentre of Britpop. Inevitably, its cool credentials attracted middle-class homebuyers and moneyed wannabes, and the area gradually fell on the sword of its own popularity. It's still savvy and spirited – with the best small music venues in town – but Camden has lost much of the edge that used to set it apart. The drunks – who swigged from their bottles and watched bemused as their locale morphed from one unrecognisable place into another – have partly reclaimed the litter-strewn Camden High St and are raving once again.

Upper-class St John's Wood, a leafy suburb of genteel houses and overdressed residents, is due west of Regent's Park. Local attractions are limited to two prominent addresses and a painted road. The Beatles recorded most of their albums at 3 Abbey Rd, including *Abbey Road* (1969) itself, with the famous shot for the album cover taken on the zebra crossing outside. The other important address is that of world cricket, at Lord's Cricket Ground.

Slightly southwest are Maida Vale and the unexpectedly pretty corner of London known as Little Venice, with its tree-lined streets, handsome locks and colourful boats on Regent's Canal, one of London's most expensive neighbourhoods.

MARYLEBONE & REGENT'S PARK

One of London's smartest neighbourhoods, Marylebone is packed full of things to see and do, including the inevitable Madame Tussaud's waxworks. Bustling Marylebone High St is one of London's choicest shopping streets and a huge draw for the capital's foodies with its excellent delis and restaurants. Regent's Park, with its staggering mansions, is also a must-see and one of London's loveliest open spaces.

MADAME TUSSAUD'S Map pp444–5
☎ 0870 400 3000; www.madame-tussauds.com; Marylebone Rd NW1; adult/under 16yr £20/16 (incl London Planetarium); �9.30am-5.30pm Mon-Fri, 9am-6pm Sat & Sun; ↔ Baker St; &

Almost three million people visit London's famous waxworks each year, so if you want to avoid the queues (particularly in summer) arrive early in the morning or late in the afternoon, or buy your tickets in advance from a ticket agency, online or over the phone and get a timed entry slot. For our money, this is one of London's most overrated experiences, and few

Top Five – North Central

- **British Library** (p191)
- **Camden Market** (p193)
- **Regent's Park** (right)
- **St Pancras Chambers** (p192)
- **Wallace Collection** (p190)

could convincingly argue that it's anything more than a staggeringly overpriced tourist trap.

Madame Tussaud's dates back more than two centuries when the eponymous Swiss model-maker started making death masks of the people killed during the French Revolution. She came to London in 1803 and exhibited around 30 wax models in Baker St, on a site not far from this building, which has housed the waxworks since 1885.

The waxworks were an enormous hit in Victorian times, when the models provided the only opportunity for visitors to glimpse the famous and infamous before photography was widespread and long before the advent of TV. Just why so many people pay so much money to see the models today is beyond us, though. We're not total killjoys; if the queues weren't so long and the prices so steep, it could be a laugh but unfortunately this isn't the case.

Much of the modern waxworks is made up of the **Garden Party** exhibition at the beginning, featuring the celebrities *du jour*, and the **Grand Hall** where world leaders line up. The famous **Chamber of Horrors** details the horrors of Jack the Ripper, all kinds of torture devices and some notorious Victorian murderers, and is usually a huge hit with children. The **Chamber Live** seeks to terrify people unaffected by the Chamber of Horrors, and does seem to do the trick (you need to pay extra for this treat, and it's off limits to under 12s).

Finally you can take a ride in the **Spirit of London 'time taxi'**, where you sit in a mock-up of a London black cab and are whipped through a five-minute historical summary of London, a mercifully short time to endure the god-awful scripts and hackneyed commentary.

In case you were wondering what happens to the models of those people whose 15 minutes have passed, their heads are removed and stored in a cupboard just in case they should ever revisit the fickle world of fame, while their less fortunate bodies are melted down to become a bit of the latest boy band or J-Lo's most recent husband.

LONDON PLANETARIUM Map pp444-5

☎ 0870 400 3000; www.london-planetarium.com; Marylebone Rd NW1; entry included in ticket for Madame Tussaud's, no separate tickets available; ⏱ 12.30-5.30pm Mon-Fri, 10.30am-6pm Sat & Sun; ⊖ Baker St; ♿

Shame, shame and more shame! Until recently you were able to buy (very reasonably priced) tickets for this excellent establishment, which projects a 20-minute star show onto the dome ceiling, zooming through the cosmos in an attempt to explain the origins of the universe and the solar system. However, now you can only visit by buying an overpriced ticket to Madame Tussaud's next door, which includes the planetarium as an afterthought. A really nasty bit of corporate greed, it would appear.

REGENT'S PARK Map pp440-1

☎ 7486 7905; ⏱ 5am-dusk; ⊖ Baker St/ Regent's Park

The most elaborate and ordered of London's many parks, Regent's was created around 1820 by John Nash, who planned to use it as an estate upon which he could build palaces for the aristocracy. Although the plan never quite came off – like so many at the time – you can get some idea of what Nash might have achieved from the buildings along the Outer Circle, and in particular from the stuccoed Palladian mansions he built on Cumberland Tce.

Like many of the city's parks, this one was used as a royal hunting ground, and then as farmland, before it was used as a place for fun and leisure during the 18th century. These days it's a well-organised but relaxed, lively but serene, local but cosmopolitan haven in the heart of the city. Among its many attractions are the London Zoo, the Grand Union Canal along its northern side, an ornamental lake, an open-air theatre in Queen Mary's Gardens where Shakespeare is performed during the summer months, ponds and colourful flowerbeds, rose gardens that look spectacular in June, football pitches and summer games of softball.

On the western side of the park is the impressive **London Central Islamic Centre & Mosque** (☎ 7724 3363; www.iccuk.org; 146 Park Rd NW8; ⊖ Marylebone), a huge white edifice with a glistening dome. Provided you take your shoes off and dress modestly you're welcome to go inside, although the interior is fairly stark.

LONDON ZOO Map pp440-1

☎ 7722 3333; www.zsl.org/london-zoo; Regent's Park NW1; adult/child/concession £14/10.75/12; ⏱ 10am-5.30pm mid-Mar–Oct, 10am-4pm Nov-Jan, 10am-4.30pm Feb–mid-Mar; ✈ Baker St/Camden Town

Established in 1828, these zoological gardens are among the oldest in the world and it was actually from here that the word 'zoo' originated. After receiving a lot of flak in recent years, London Zoo has become one of the most progressive in the world. It's in the middle of a long-term modernisation plan and the emphasis is now firmly placed on conservation, education and breeding, with fewer species and more spacious conditions.

A great way to visit the zoo is by canal boat from Little Venice or Camden, but you can also reach it by walking along the canal towpath. There's a delightful **children's zoo**, which is built almost entirely from sustainable materials, and busy programmes of events and attractions (like elephant bathing and penguin feeding) throughout the year.

The **Web of Life**, a glass pavilion containing some 60 live animal exhibits (from termites and jellyfish to the birds and the bees), has interactive displays and, yes, on-show breeding groups to see, making a visit to the zoo worthwhile by itself. Elsewhere don't miss the enclosures housing the big cats, the elephants and rhinos, the small mammals and the birds, or the new **walk-through monkey house**. The elegant and cheerful **Penguin Pool**, designed by Berthold Lubetkin in 1934, is one of London's foremost modernist structures, although the penguins don't seem to be particularly interested in this fact.

WALLACE COLLECTION Map pp448-9

☎ 7563 9500; www.wallacecollection.org; Hertford House, Manchester Sq W1; admission free; ⏱ 10am-5pm; ✈ Bond St; ♿

Arguably London's finest small gallery (relatively unknown even to Londoners), the Wallace Collection is an enthralling glimpse into 18th-century aristocratic life. The sumptuously restored Italianate mansion houses a treasure trove of 17th- and 18th-century paintings, porcelain, artefacts and furniture collected by generations of the same family and bequeathed to the nation by the widow of Sir Richard Wallace (1818–90) on condition it should always be on display in the centre of London.

Among the many highlights here – besides the warm and friendly staff – are paintings by the likes of Rembrandt, Hals, Delacroix, Titian, Rubens, Poussin, Van Dyck, Velàzquez, Reynolds and Gainsborough in the stunning and aptly named **Great Gallery**. There's a spectacular array of medieval and Renaissance armour (including some to try on), a Minton-tiled smoking room, stunning chandeliers and a sweeping staircase that is reckoned to be one of the best examples of French interior architecture in existence. There are also temporary exhibitions (admission payable) and very popular 'day in the 18th century' events (£1 suggested donation), bringing alive a day in the life of your average 18th-century French aristocrat, complete with ballroom dancing in full costume. Throw in the excellent glass-roofed restaurant, Café Bagatelle, which occupies the central courtyard, and you've got one of the most outstanding attractions in the whole of London.

SHERLOCK HOLMES MUSEUM
Map pp448-9

☎ 7935 8866; www.sherlock-holmes.co.uk; 221b Baker St; adult/child £6/4; ⏱ 9.30am-6pm; ✈ Baker St

This museum gives its address as 221b Baker St, but the house in which Sherlock Holmes

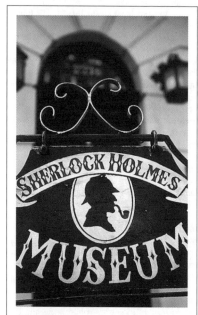

Sherlock Holmes Museum (above)

fictionally resided is actually the Abbey National building a bit further south. Fans of the books will enjoy examining the three floors of reconstructed Victoriana, deerstalkers, burning candles, flickering grates, and maybe even the dodgy waxworks of Professor Moriarty and 'the Man with the Twisted Lip', but might wonder why there isn't more on Arthur Conan Doyle.

BROADCASTING HOUSE Map pp448-9

☎ 0870 603 0304; www.bbc.co.uk; Portland Pl; ✆ shop 9.30am-6pm Mon-Sat, 10am-5.30pm Sun; ⊖ Oxford Circus

Broadcasting House is the iconic building from which the BBC began radio broadcasting in 1932, and where much of the BBC's radio output still comes from. There's a shop stocking any number of products relating to BBC programmes, even though the majority of the Beeb's output is produced in the corporation's glassy complex in Shepherd's Bush (hop on the website if you want to get tickets to a recording). Broadcasting House is currently having a vast extension built onto it, to where the World Service will relocate when its lease on its current premises, Bush House on the Strand, expires in 2008.

ALL SOULS CHURCH Map pp448-9

☎ 7580 3522; www.allsouls.org; Langham Pl W1; ✆ 9am-6pm, closed Sat; ⊖ Oxford Circus

A Nash solution for the curving, northern sweep of Regent St was this delightful church, which features a circular columned porch and distinctive needle-like spire, reminiscent of an ancient Greek temple. Built from Bath stone, the church was very unpopular when completed in 1824; a contemporary cartoon by George Cruikshank shows Nash rather painfully impaled on the spire through the bottom with the words 'Nashional Taste!!!' below it. It was bombed during the Blitz and renovated in 1951, and it's now one of the most distinctive churches in central London.

KING'S CROSS & EUSTON

Never an area that is going to charm, the traffic-choked Euston Rd runs east–west past two of London's major stations, King's Cross and Euston, and in the best tradition of large railway stations, the area has been a haven for shady characters of every description for decades. King's Cross in particular, despite being the centre of a huge ongoing redevelopment and regeneration campaign, is one of the few places in London where you should proceed with caution when walking alone at night-time. Policing has been improved in recent years, but be aware that some side streets around the station are really not safe for wandering around after dark.

BRITISH LIBRARY Map pp440-1

switchboard ☎ 7412 7000, visitor services ☎ 7412 7332; www.bl.uk; 96 Euston Rd NW1; admission free; ✆ 10am-6pm Mon, 9.30am-6pm Tue-Thu, 9.30am-6.30pm Fri & Sat; ⊖ King's Cross; ♿

The British Library moved to these spanking new premises between King's Cross and Euston Stations in 1998, and at a cost of £500 million it was Britain's most expensive building, and not one that is universally loved; Colin St John Wilson's exterior of straight lines of red brick, which Prince Charles reckoned was akin to a 'secret-police building', is certainly not to all tastes. But even people who don't like the building from the outside can't fault the spectacularly cool and spacious interior.

It is the nation's principal copyright library and stocks one copy of every British publication as well as historical manuscripts, books and maps from the British Museum. The library counts some 186 miles (300km) of shelving on four basement levels and will have some 12 million volumes when it reaches the limit of its storage capacity.

At the centre of the building is the wonderful **King's Library**, the 65,000-volume collection of the insane George III, which was given to the nation by his son, George IV, in 1823 and now housed in a six-storey, 17m-high glass-walled tower. To the left as you enter are the library's excellent bookshop and exhibition galleries.

Most of the complex is devoted to storage and scholarly research, but there are also several public displays including the **John Ritblat Gallery: Treasures of the British Library**, which spans almost three millennia and every continent. Among the most important documents here are the Magna Carta (1215); the Codex Sinaiticus, the first complete text of the New Testament, written in Greek in the 4th century; a Gutenberg Bible (1455), the first Western book printed using movable type; Shakespeare's First Folio (1623); manuscripts by some of Britain's best-known authors (eg Lewis Carroll, Jane Austen, George Eliot and

Thomas Hardy); and even some of the Beatles' earliest hand-written lyrics.

You can hear historic recordings, such as the first one ever, made by Thomas Edison in 1877, James Joyce reading from *Ulysses* and Nelson Mandela's famous speech at the Rivonia trial in 1964, at the **National Sound Archive Jukeboxes**, where the selections are changed regularly. The **Turning the Pages** exhibit allows you a 'virtual browse' through several important texts including the *Sforza Book of Hours*, the *Diamond Sutra* and a Leonardo da Vinci notebook.

The **Philatelic Exhibition**, next to the John Ritblat Gallery, is based on collections established in 1891 with the bequest of the Tapling Collection, and now consists of over 80,000 items including postage and revenue stamps, postal stationery and first-day covers from almost every country and from all periods.

The **Workshop of Words, Sounds and Images** documents the development of writing and communicating through the written word by carefully examining the work of early scribes, printers and bookbinders. The sound section compares recordings on different media, from early-20th-century wax cylinders to modern CDs. The **Pearson Gallery** hosts some sensational special exhibitions, ranging from 'Oscar Wilde: A Life in Six Acts' to 'Chinese Printing Today'.

Access to the reading rooms is by reader's pass only. See the website for details of how to apply for one and the conditions that need to be met.

There are **guided tours** (adult/child £6/4.50) at 3pm Monday, Wednesday and Friday and at 10.30am and 3pm Saturday of the library's public areas and another that includes a visit to one of the **reading rooms** (adult/concession £7/5.50) at 11.30am and 3pm Sunday. Call the main number to make a booking.

ST PANCRAS CHAMBERS Map pp442-3
☎ 7713 6514; www.lcrproperties.com; Euston Rd NW1; tours £5 (no booking); ⏰ tours 11am & 1.30pm Sat & Sun; ⬤ King's Cross St Pancras

If you use the tube for any length of time, chances are you'll pass through King's Cross St Pancras station, in which case you should rise to the surface and check out this fabulously imposing Victorian Gothic masterpiece, which was built as a hotel by the renowned architect George Gilbert Scott in 1876. At the back is a dramatic glass-and-iron train shed, engineered by the great Brunel. There are plans to convert the chambers back into a

---

Barnyard Blitz

So young Londoners don't grow up thinking cows' udders are shaped like milk bottles, a number of farms have been set up across the city where real live farm animals moo, bleat, oink, eat, roll around in shit and do whatever else it is that comes naturally to barnyard beings. If you and your kin need a break from urban London, head to one of these:

Coram's Fields (Map pp442–3; ☎ 7837 6138; 93 Guildford St WC1; ⏰ 9am-7pm Jun-Sep, 9am-6pm Oct-May; ⬤ Russell Sq)

Hackney City Farm (Map pp438–9; ☎ 7729 6381; 1a Goldsmith's Row E2; ⏰ 10am-4.30pm Tue-Sun; ⬤ Bethnal Green/rail Cambridge Heath)

Kentish Town City Farm (Map p465; ☎ 7916 5420; 1 Cressfield Close NW5; ⏰ 9.30am-5.30pm; ⬤ Kentish Town)

Spitalfields Farm (Map pp454–5; ☎ 7247 8762; Weaver St E1; ⏰ 10.30am-5.30pm Tue-Sun; ⬤ Shoreditch/Liverpool St)

---

hotel, but do call in advance to see if the tours are still running. Bear in mind that there are no lifts or disabled access and to follow the tour you'll have to climb several flights of stairs.

ST PANCRAS NEW CHURCH Map pp440-1
☎ 7388 1461; www.stpancraschurch.org; cnr Euston Rd & Upper Woburn Pl WC1; ⏰ 9am-5pm Tue-Fri, 9.15-11am Sat, 7.45am-noon & 5.30-7.15pm Sun; ⬤ Euston

The striking Greek Revival St Pancras New Church has a tower designed to imitate the Temple of the Winds in Athens, a portico with six Ionic columns mirroring the Erechtheion on the Acropolis and a wing decorated with caryatids, again like the Erechtheion. When it was completed in 1822 this was the most expensive new church to have been built in London since St Paul's Cathedral. Within the porch you can see a large tablet in memory of the 31 people who lost their lives in the King's Cross tube station fire of November 1987.

LONDON CANAL MUSEUM Map pp442-3
☎ 7713 0836; www.canalmuseum.org.uk; New Wharf Rd N1; adult/child/student 3/1.50/2; ⏰ 10am-4.30pm Tue-Sun & Bank Holidays; ⬤ King's Cross

This quirky and old-fashioned museum is housed in an old ice warehouse (with a deep well where the frozen commodity was stored) and traces the history of Regent's Canal, the ice business and the development of ice cream through models, photographs, exhibits and archive documentaries. The ice trade was huge in late Victorian London, and 35,000 tonnes of it were imported from Norway in 1899.

CAMDEN

Few people can put their finger on the protean beast that is Camden Town. Conjuring up images of Goths, drug addicts and tourist tat to many, the rather unpleasant stretch that runs from Camden Town tube station to Camden Lock is actually just one part of this exciting place. Explore on your own and you'll find lovely quiet pubs, cool clubs and a smattering of excellent restaurants.

Once home to Britpop, and slowly becoming fashionable again after being deserted in favour of Shoreditch by many artists and musicians in the late 1990s, Camden will rarely inspire indifference.

CAMDEN MARKET Map pp440-1
cnr Camden High & Buck Sts NW1; 9am-5.30pm Thu-Sun; Camden Town/Chalk Farm

Although – or perhaps because – it stopped being cutting-edge several thousand cheap leather jackets ago, Camden market gets a whopping 10 million visitors each year and is London's most popular 'unticketed' tourist attraction. What started out as a collection of attractive craft stalls by Camden Lock on the Grand Union Canal now extends most of the way from Camden Town tube station to Chalk Farm tube station to the north. You'll find a bit of everything but in particular a lot of tourist-oriented tack (see p350 for more information). It's completely mobbed at the weekend, and something preferably to avoid on those days.

JEWISH MUSEUM Map pp440-1
7284 1997; www.jewishmuseum.org.uk; Raymond Burton House, 129-31 Albert St NW1; adult/child/senior/family £3.50/1.50/2.50/8; 10am-4pm Mon-Thu, 10am-5pm Sun; Camden Town;

This branch of the Jewish Museum examines Judaism and Judaic religious practices in the prestigious **Ceremonial Art Gallery**, and the story of the Jewish community in Britain from the time of the Normans to the present day

through paintings, photographs and artefacts in the **History Gallery**. There's also a gallery for temporary exhibitions.

The **Jewish Museum, Finchley** (Map p437; 8349 1143; Sternberg Centre, 80 East End Rd N3; adult/child/concession £2/free/1; 10.30am-5pm Mon-Thu, 10.30am-4.30pm Sun; Finchley Central) houses the museum's social-history collections, including the oral history and photographic archives, and hosts changing exhibitions. Its permanent collection includes reconstructions of the tailoring and cabinet-making workshops from the East End, as well as a Holocaust exhibition focusing on the experience of one Jewish Briton who survived Auschwitz.

ST JOHN'S WOOD & MAIDA VALE

SJW is synonymous with cricket and the Beatles, and two very different kinds of obsessives usually find themselves making the pilgrimage here for Lord's and Abbey Rd respectively. Next door Maida Vale is stuffed full of very smart houses and mansion blocks, some good eating and drinking, but precious little to see or do beyond that.

LORD'S CRICKET GROUND Map pp440-1
tours office 7616 8595, switchboard 7616 8500; www.lords.org; St John's Wood Rd NW8; tours adult/child/concession/family £7/4.50/5.50/20; tours 10am, noon & 2pm Apr-Sep, noon & 2pm Oct-Mar when there's no play; St John's Wood; limited

The next best thing to watching a Test at Lord's is the absorbing and anecdotal 90-minute tour of the ground and facilities, which takes in the famous Long Room, where members watch the games surrounded by portraits of cricket's great and good, and a museum featuring evocative memorabilia that will appeal to fans old and new. Australian fans will be keen to pose next to the famous little urn containing the Ashes, which remain in English hands no matter how many times the Aussies beat them.

The ground itself is dominated by a striking media centre that looks like a clock radio, but you should also look out for the famous weather vane in the shape of Father Time and the remarkable tentlike modern Mound Stand.

NORTH LONDON

Eating p263-4; Drinking p289-90; Shopping p348; Sleeping p372

Fashionable north London is made up of villages that inter-
connect in the hills of the Thames Valley and retain atmos-
pheres unique to their history despite the encroachment of
modern London. In descending order of social status, they
begin at Hampstead with its vast, wild and rambling heath,
which has been a popular area with writers, artists and the
moneyed since the early 19th century, when Romantic poet
John Keats spent two of his few years knocking about here. The refined and picturesque
village of Highgate, perched on top of its own hill, has superb views of London in case the
privileged locals get bored with the pleasant parks and verdant woods surrounding them.
Muswell Hill and Crouch End, further north and east respectively, also feel like small towns
just outside London because the tube reaches neither and they are both self-contained oases
of life you'd expect to see more in the home counties than in zone 2. Edwardian Muswell
Hill has a string of exceptional shops, a convivial vibe and the inimitable Alexandra Palace
but, curiously, not one good pub. Crouch Enders have it all, just with more celebrities and
kids. Stoke Newington isn't part of the chain of hills that make up the centre of north London, though it may as well be as it can be reached only by bus and is cheerfully detached
from the megalopolis. It's dominated by hippy-chic Church St, lined with good shops, pubs,
restaurants and one of London's best places to be dead, the lovely Abney Park Cemetery.

Top Five – North London

- **Hampstead Heath** (below)
- **Highgate Cemetery** (opposite)
- **Highgate Wood** (opposite)
- **Keats House** (opposite)
- **Kenwood House** (opposite)

HAMPSTEAD & HIGHGATE

Two of London's most charming villages,
Hampstead and Highgate wash over you
and enamour you with their respective
wonders. The famous heath is one of the
few places you can feel lost in nature within
the M25, and the outrageously lovely cottages and cobbled streets of Hampstead
village will inspire real-estate envy in even
the least materialistic. Highgate's gorgeous
cemetery is a must, as is the wood, one of
the loveliest places to take a stroll in the
capital.

HAMPSTEAD HEATH Map p465

☎ 7485 4491; ⊖ Hampstead/rail Gospel Oak/
Hampstead Heath/bus 214 or C2 to Parliament Hill Fields
Sprawling Hampstead Heath, with its rolling
woodlands and meadows, is a million miles
away – well, approximately four – from the
city of London. It covers 320 hectares, most of
it woods, hills and meadows, and is home to
about 100 bird species. It's a wonderful place

for a ramble, especially to the top of Parliament
Hill, which offers expansive views across the
city and is one of the most popular places in
London to fly a kite. Alternatively head up the
hill in North Wood.

If walking is too pedestrian for you, another
major attraction is the bathing ponds (separate
ones for women and men and a mixed pond),
which have recently – and thankfully – been
saved from closure. There is now a charge to use
the ponds (which until recently were free), although locals are refusing to pay. Sections of the
heath area are also laid out for football, cricket
and tennis. Those of a more artistic bent should
make a beeline to **Kenwood House** (opposite) but
stop to admire the sculptures by Henry Moore
and Barbara Hepworth on the way.

If you work up a thirst, there's no better
place to quench it than at the atmospheric
– and possibly haunted – **Spaniard's Inn** (p289),
which has a fascinating history and a terrific
beer garden.

By night the West Heath is a gay cruising
ground that is so well established that the police pitch up to protect the men who spend
their nights here. On South Green, opposite
Hampstead Heath station, is one of Britain's
oldest lavatories, which was built in 1897 and
restored in 2000. This was gay playwright Joe
Orton's lavatory of choice for 'cottaging' (cruising for gay sex). George Orwell worked in a
bookshop opposite the toilets and doubtless
used them now and then for their originally
intended purpose.

HIGHGATE CEMETERY Map p465

☎ 8340 1834; www.highgate-cemetery.org; Swain's Lane N6; admission £2 (plus £1 per camera); ☉ 10am-5pm Mon-Fri & 11am-5pm Sat & Sun Apr-Oct, 10am-4pm Mon-Fri & 11am-4pm Sat & Sun Nov-Mar; ⊖ Highgate

Most famous as the final resting place of Karl Marx and other notable mortals, Highgate Cemetery is set in 20 wonderfully wild and atmospheric hectares with dramatic and overdecorated Victorian graves and sombre tombs. It's divided into two parts. On the eastern side you can visit the grave of Marx who, coincidentally, is buried opposite the free-market economist Herbert Spencer – Marx and Spencer, does it ring a bell? This slightly overgrown and wild part of the cemetery is a very pleasant walk but it's merely the overflow area. It's the wonderfully atmospheric western section of this Victorian Valhalla that is the main draw. To visit it, you'll have to take a tour and deal directly with the brigade of stroppy silver-haired ladies who run the cemetery and act like they are the home guard defending it from the Germans (eyes straight, shoulders back, chest out, march!). It is a maze of winding paths leading to the Circle of Lebanon, rings of tombs flanking a circular path and topped with a majestic, centuries-old cedar tree. The guides are engaging and gladly point out the various symbols of the age and the eminent dead occupying the tombs, including the scientist Michael Faraday and the dog-show founder Charles Cruft. 'Dissenters' (non–Church of Englanders) were buried way off in the woods. Tours (£3, plus £1 per camera) depart 2pm Monday to Friday (book ahead by phone) and every hour 11am to 4pm Saturday and Sunday (no bookings).

The cemetery still works – the best plots still go to those with the most money – and closes during burials, so you might want to call ahead just to be sure it will be open.

HIGHGATE WOOD Map p465

☉ dawn-dusk; ⊖ Highgate

With more than 28 hectares of ancient woodland, this park is a wonderful spot for a walk any time of the year. It's also teeming with life, and some 70 different bird species have been recorded here, along with five types of bat, 12 of butterfly and 80 different kinds of spider. It also has a huge clearing in the centre for sports, a popular playground and nature trail for kids and a range of activities – from falconry to bat-watching – throughout the year.

KEATS HOUSE Map p465

☎ 7435 2062; www.keatshouse.org.uk; Wentworth Pl, Keats Grove NW3; adult/under 16yr/concession £3.50/free/1.75; ☉ 1-5pm Tue-Sun; ⊖ Hampstead/rail Hampstead Heath

A stone's throw from the lower reaches of the heath, this elegant Regency house was home to the golden boy of the Romantic poets from 1818 to 1820. Never short of generous mates, Keats was persuaded to take refuge here by Charles Armitage Brown, and it was here that he met his fiancée Fanny Brawne, who was literally the girl next door. Keats wrote his most celebrated poem, *Ode to a Nightingale,* while sitting under a plum tree in the garden (now replaced) in 1819. Unfortunately, the most valuable mementos – including original manuscripts and love letters – are in need of careful conservation and are no longer on display. That said, there is still plenty to see and the house is dripping with atmosphere, thanks in part to the collection of Regency furniture amassed here in recent years. Rather than supplying pamphlets or audioguides, the staff here tell stories about Keats and the house as you wander around, perhaps examining the ring he gave Fanny (which she wore for the rest of her life) or the bust of Keats, which is set at the poet's exact height: barely 5ft 1in (1.5m)!

American visitors might like to know that the house was saved and opened to the public largely due to the donations of Keats' fans in the US. Staff are playing a kind of US state bingo and need visitors from only two more states to have the full set (so be sure to let them know where you're from). If you're coming to Hampstead specifically to visit the house at any time, you should probably call ahead just to make sure it's open, as ongoing repairs are required.

KENWOOD HOUSE Map p465

☎ 8348 1286; www.english-heritage.org.uk; Hampstead Lane NW3; admission free; ☉ house 11am-5pm Apr-Oct, 11am-4pm Nov-Mar, the Suffolk Collection (upstairs) 11am-4.30pm Thu-Sun; ⊖ Archway/Golders Green, then bus 210; ♿

At the northern end of the heath, this magnificent neoclassical mansion stands in a glorious sweep of landscaped gardens leading down to the picturesque lake, around which classical concerts take place in summer (see p324). The house was remodelled by Robert Adam in the 18th century, and rescued from the clutches of developers by Lord Iveagh Guinness who donated it and the wonderful collection of art it contains to the nation in 1927. The Iveagh Bequest contains paintings by the likes of Gainsborough, Reynolds, Turner, Hals, Vermeer and Van Dyck and is one of the finest small collections in Britain.

Robert Adam's Great Stairs and the library, one of 14 rooms open to the public, are especially fine. The Suffolk Collection has limited opening hours and occupies the 1st floor. It includes Jacobean portraits by William Larkin and royal Stuart portraits by Van Dyck and Lely. The subjects were, pardon the pun, no oil paintings.

The **Brew House Café** has excellent grub, from light snacks to full meals, and plenty of room on the lovely garden terrace.

NO 2 WILLOW ROAD Map p465
☎ 7435 6166, 0149 475 5570; www.nationaltrust .org.uk; 2 Willow Rd NW3; adult/concession £4.60/2.30; ☾ noon-5pm Thu-Sat Apr-Oct, noon-5pm Mar & Nov, guided tours at noon, 1pm & 2pm; ⊖ Hampstead/rail Hampstead Heath

Fans of modern architecture may want to swing past this property, the central house in a block of three, designed by the 'structural rationalist' Ernö Goldfinger in 1939 as his family home. Although the architect was following Georgian principles in creating it, many people think it looks uncannily like the sort of mundane 1950s architecture you see everywhere. They may look similar now, but 2 Willow Rd was in fact a forerunner; the others were mostly bad imitations. The interior, with its cleverly designed storage space and collection of artworks by Henry Moore, Max Ernst and Bridget Riley, is certainly interesting and accessible to all.

BURGH HOUSE Map p465
☎ 7431 0144; www.burghhouse.org.uk; New End Sq NW3; admission free; ☾ noon-5pm Wed-Sun & 2-5pm Bank Holidays; ⊖ Hampstead

If you happen to be in the neighbourhood, this late-17th-century Queen Anne mansion houses the **Hampstead Museum** of local history, a small art gallery and the delightful Buttery tearoom, where you can get a decent and reasonably priced lunch from Wednesday to Saturday.

FENTON HOUSE Map p465
☎ 7435 3471; www.nationaltrust.org.uk; Windmill Hill, Hampstead Grove NW3; adult/child £4.80/2.40; ☾ 2-5pm Wed-Fri & 11am-5pm Sat & Sun Apr-Oct, 2-5pm Sat & Sun Mar; ⊖ Hampstead

One of the oldest houses in Hampstead, this late-17th-century merchant's residence has a charming walled garden with roses and an orchard, fine collections of porcelain and keyboard instruments – including a 1612 harpsichord played by Handel – as well as 17th-century needlework pictures and original Georgian furniture.

Underground (tube) sign

Worth the Trip

Freud Museum (Map pp440-1; ☎ 7435 2002; www
.freud.org.uk; 20 Maresfield Gardens NW3; adult/
under 12yr/concession £5/free/2; ☒ noon-5pm
Wed-Sun; ⊖ Finchley Rd) After fleeing from Nazi-
occupied Vienna in 1938, Sigmund Freud came to
London and to this house where he lived the last 18
months of his life. His daughter – a renowned child
psychologist – lived here until she died in 1986, after
which, and according to her wishes, it became the
Freud Museum. Along with Freud's original couch,
the house is crammed with his extensive collection
of books and artefacts, while commentary is provided through extracts from his writings. A poignant
photograph shows how meticulously Freud tried to
re-create his Viennese home in the unfamiliar surroundings of quiet and leafy residential London.

Royal Air Force Museum (Map p437; ☎ 8205 2266;
www.rafmuseum.org.uk; Grahame Park Way, Hendon
NW9; admission free; ☒ 10am-6pm; ⊖ Colindale,
plus easy 10min walk) For all things aeronautical,
plane spotters should hurry out to Henley and the
'birthplace of British Aviation'. You can trace the history of human flight with the help of more than 70
aircraft, photo exhibitions, flight simulators and a
spectacular sound-and-light show called 'Our Finest
Hour', which focuses on the Battle of Britain.

MUSWELL HILL & CROUCH END

Muswell Hill is another comfortable north
London village, a charming Edwardian suburb of the capital, from which it can feel
entirely removed. Its only claim to fame
is being the home of Alexandra Palace,
which has some lovely parkland to wander
in. Nearby Crouch End is a more upmarket
version, often pronounced by other north
Londoners in a silly French accent ('croosh-
on'), playing on its extremely upper-middle-
class image and residents.

ALEXANDRA PARK & PALACE Map p437
☎ 8365 2121; www.alexandrapalace.com; Alexandra
Palace Way N22; rail Alexandra Palace

Built in 1873 as north London's answer to
Crystal Palace, Alexandra Palace suffered the
ignoble fate of burning to the ground only
16 days after opening. Encouraged by attendance figures, investors decided to rebuild and
it reopened just two years later. Although it
boasted a theatre, museum, lecture hall, library
and Great Hall with one of the world's larg-

est organs, it was no match for Crystal Palace.
It housed German POWs during WWI and in
1936 the world's first TV transmission – a variety show called *Here's Looking at You* – took
place here. The palace burned down again in
1980 but was rebuilt for the third time and
opened in 1988. Today 'Ally Pally' (as it is af-
fectionately known, even though locals are
paying increased council rates since it was rebuilt) is largely a multipurpose conference and
exhibition centre with a number of additional
facilities, including an indoor ice-skating rink,
the panoramic Phoenix Bar & Beer Garden and
funfairs in summer.

The park in which it stands sprawls over
some 196 hectares consisting of public gardens,
a nature conservation area, a deer park and various sporting facilities including a boating lake,
pitch-and-putt golf course and skate park, making it a great place for a family outing.

STOKE NEWINGTON

Stoke Newington is a medieval village that,
while now swallowed up by the British capital, has never truly become a part of it. In
the heart of the much-maligned borough
of Hackney, Stokey, as most locals know it,
is scruffy but charming and has provided a
refuge for Londoners from London since
the 17th century. One of the most culturally
diverse parts of London, Stoke Newington
is today a great place to eat, drink and shop
as well as being an excellent detour from
the beaten tourist track.

ABNEY PARK CEMETERY Map p437
☎ 7275 7557; Stoke Newington Church St N16; admission free; ☒ 8am-dusk; rail Stoke Newington/bus 73,
106 or 243

Unfairly dubbed 'the poor man's Highgate'
by some, this magical place was bought up
and developed by a private firm from 1840 to
provide burial grounds for central London's
overflow. It was the first cemetery for dissenters and many of the most influential London
Presbyterians, Quakers and Baptists are buried
here, including the founder of the Salvation
Army, William Booth, whose grand tombstone
greets you as you enter from Church St. Since
the 1950s the cemetery has been left to fend
for itself and, these days, is as much a bird and
plant sanctuary as a delightfully overgrown
ruin. The derelict chapel at the heart of the
park could be straight out of a horror film, and
the atmosphere of the whole place is nothing
short of magical.

WEST LONDON

Eating p264-7; Drinking p291-2; Shopping p348-9; Sleeping p372-4;

The sprawl west of Hyde Park in all directions is one of the most vibrant areas of London and few parts of the capital can boast the area's sheer variety – its rampant multiculturalism (the Caribbean community in Notting Hill, the Poles in Hammersmith and the Australian home-from-home in Earl's Court), its exciting bars (check out Portobello Rd or Westbourne Grove) and its grand parks and mansions (wander the back streets of Holland Park to see how the rich and famous *really* live).

The status of the famous Notting Hill Carnival reflects the multicultural appeal of this part of west London, into which West Indian immigrants moved in the 1950s. After decades of exploitation, strife and the occasional race riot, the community took off in the 1980s and this is now a thriving, vibrant corner of the city and an emblem for multicultural London.

Despite the unsightliness of Shepherd's Bush Green and the general chaos that rules here, the curiously named west London hub is in the process of a very real renaissance and is a great place to hang out and eat. The strange name reputedly comes from the fact that shepherds would graze their flocks on the common here, en route for Smithfield Market in east London, back when Shepherd's Bush was another rural village outside the city. Synonymous for many with the sprawling BBC Television Centre in nearby White City that opened in 1960, the area had actually become famous 50 years earlier as the site of the 1908 London Olympics, as well as the Great Exhibition of the same year. The Olympics were held here again in 1948, but the stadium was torn down in 1984, so nothing remains from London's Olympic past today. During the '60s, Shepherd's Bush was used as the setting for the Who's film *Quadrophenia,* so mods on pilgrimage are not an uncommon sight.

NOTTING HILL & WESTBOURNE GROVE

Although there's not a lot to see in Notting Hill – and it's nothing like its portrayal in the eponymous, saccharine Richard Curtis film – there's plenty to do, with lots of highly individual shops, restaurants and pubs. Narrow Portobello Rd is its heart and soul (as opposed to traffic-choked Notting Hill Gate) and most well known these days for hosting London's best market (p350). The neighbourhood also gives its name to the Notting Hill Carnival, a highlight of most Londoners' summer (see p12). Unfailingly fashionable Westbourne Grove, roughly in the northeastern corner, is lined with distinctive shops, pubs, artists' galleries and studios.

KENSAL GREEN CEMETERY Map pp438-9
Harrow Rd, Kensal Green W10; tours £5; ⊙ tours 2pm Sun; ⊖ Kensal Green
Thackeray and Trollope are among the eminent dead folk at this huge and handsome Victorian cemetery, which made a name for itself in the 19th century as the place where the celebrities preferred to RIP. Supposedly based on the Cimetière du Père-Lachaise in Paris, the cemetery is distinguished by its Greek Revival architecture, arched entrances and the outrageously ornate tombs that bear testimony to 19th-century delusions of grandeur. Ambitious two-hour tours start from the Anglican chapel in the centre of the cemetery.

LEIGHTON HOUSE Map pp458-9
☎ 7602 3316; www.rbkc.gov.uk; 12 Holland Park Rd W14; admission by donation; ⊙ 11am-5.30pm Wed-Mon; ⊖ High St Kensington
Near Holland Park and Kensington – but frequently overlooked – is Leighton House, a gem of a house designed in 1866 by George Aitchison. It was once the home of Lord Leighton (1830–96), who was a painter belonging to the Olympian movement; he decorated parts of the house in Middle Eastern style. The finest of all the rooms is the exquisite Arab Hall, added in 1879 and densely covered with blue and green tiles from Rhodes, Cairo, Damascus and Iznik (Turkey) and with a fountain tinkling away in the centre. Even the wooden lattice work of the windows and gallery was brought from Damascus. The house contains notable Pre-Raphaelite paintings by Burne-Jones, Watts, Millais and Lord Leighton himself. Restoration of the back garden has returned it to its Victorian splendour – as has work on the stairwell and upstairs rooms.

EARL'S COURT & WEST BROMPTON

As west London fades from the old money of Kensington into the urban sprawl of Hammersmith, the two meet seamlessly in Earl's Court, a hard-to-define no-man's-land. Its '80s nickname 'Kangaroo Valley' attests to the area's popularity with backpackers from Down Under, which is still the case today. In the 1980s Earl's Court was the original gay village, later overtaken by Soho, but still not forgotten today. Freddie Mercury lived and died at 1 Garden Pl and remains the neighbourhood's most famous resident.

West Brompton is even quieter and less remarkable, but is home to one of London's most magnificent cemeteries and is pleasant for a stroll.

BROMPTON CEMETERY Map pp458-9
☎ 7351 9936; www.royalparks.gov.uk; Old Brompton Rd SW5; tours £3; ☼ 8am-dusk, tours Sun; ⊖ West Brompton

One of the seven London cemeteries opened in the early 19th century as London's vast population exploded, Brompton Cemetery is a long expanse running between Fulham Rd and Old Brompton Rd with a chapel and colonnades, modelled after St Peter's in Rome, at one end.

Tours depart 2pm Sundays from the South Lodge, near the Fulham Rd entrance. While the most famous resident is Emmeline Pankhurst, the pioneer of women's suffrage in Britain, the cemetery is most interesting as the inspiration for many of Beatrix Potter's characters. A local resident in her youth before she moved to the North, Potter seems to have taken many names from the deceased of Brompton Cemetery and immortalised them in her world-famous books. Names to be found include Mr Nutkin, Mr McGregor, Jeremiah Fisher, Tommy Brock – and even a Peter Rabbett.

SHEPHERD'S BUSH & HAMMERSMITH

Today Shepherd's Bush is a multiethnic place full of quirky cafés, bars and character. It won't disappoint those looking for good venues to eat and drink in, especially since a slew of gastropubs have opened in recent years. The world-famous Shepherd's Bush Empire, on the Green, is also one of London's best concert venues, and regularly hosts world-class music acts.

Hammersmith is a different story, a very urban neighbourhood dominated by a huge flyover and roundabout, with little to entice the visitor save some decent restaurants and

---

Worth the Trip

Shri Swaminarayan Mandir (Map p437; ☎ 8965 2651; www.madir.org; 105-119 Brentfield Rd, Neasden NW10; admission to Mandir free, to exhibition adult/student £2/1.50; ☼ 9am-6pm; ⊖ Neasden) The Mandir, London's huge Hindu Temple, was consecrated in 1995, having been constructed by a Hindu sect modelling the design on the Akshardam in Gujarat, India. It's an amazingly impressive and slightly surreal place rising above the drab reality of suburban Neasden and is built from over 5000 tonnes of marble and limestone. While it's a working temple, visitors are welcome, but should dress conservatively (no shorts or skirts shorter than knee-length) and leave their shoes at the entrance.

Osterley Park & House (Map p437; ☎ 8232 5050; www.nationaltrust.org.uk; Osterley Park; house adult/5-15yr/family £4.50/2.25/11.20, park free; ☼ house 1-4.30pm Wed-Sun Apr-Oct, 1-4.30pm Sat & Sun Nov-Mar, park 9am-dusk year-round; ⊖ Osterley) Set in 300 acres of landscaped park and farmland, Osterley House started life in 1575 as the country retreat of Thomas Gresham, the man responsible for the Royal Exchange, but was extensively remodelled in the mid-18th century by Robert Adam. There are wonderful paintings, plasterwork and furniture, but many people rate the downstairs kitchen and the Tudor Grand Stables as even more interesting. The charming park is a great place to walk.

To get there from Osterley tube, walk eastward along the Great West Rd and turn left into Thornbury Rd, bringing you to Jersey Rd and the park entrance. The house is 500m to the north.

Pitshanger Manor (Map p437; ☎ 8567 1227; www.ealing.gov.uk/pitshanger; Walpole Park, Mattock Lane W5; admission free; ☼ 1-5pm Tue-Fri, 11am-5pm Sat; ⊖/rail Ealing Broadway) This manor was bought by the architect John Soane in 1800 and rebuilt in the Regency style. Parts of the manor now house a collection of pottery, designed by the Martin Brothers of Southall in the late 19th century. Not everyone will care for their grotesque designs, although the owl jars with swivel heads are undoubtedly good fun. There is also an adjacent art gallery that houses temporary exhibits.

the famously arty **Riverside Studios** (p301). With time to spare there's a good set of riverfront pubs on the Chiswick side of Hammersmith Bridge plus a pleasant 2-mile (3km) walk along the Thames from the shopping centre beside the bridge to Chiswick itself.

BBC TELEVISION CENTRE Map pp438-9
☎ 0870 603 0304; Wood Lane W12; adult/student & child over 10yr £7.95/5.95 (no children under 10yr);
✈ White City; book for ♿

The chance to visit the vast complex of studios and offices that bring the BBC's TV programmes to the world will appeal to anyone interested in TV production. Two-hour-long guided tours

(bookings essential), which change route and itinerary in accordance with broadcasting schedules, take in the BBC News and Weather Centres as well as studios where shows are being made, and it's a fascinating glimpse into the Corporation at shop-floor level. TVC, as it's known to BBC staff, opened in 1960 and is where TV favourites from *Little Britain* to *Top Gear* are still filmed each week. Keep your eyes peeled, as part of the fun is the endless TV-star-spotting between locations. Alternatively, if you book in advance online, it is possible to go and watch the recording of certain shows for free at one of the BBC's many London studios. Log on to www.bbc.co.uk/whatson/tickets to see what's available during your stay.

SOUTH LONDON

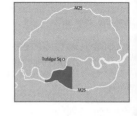

Eating p268-70; Drinking p293-4; Shopping p352

'Sarf' (South) London gets a bad rap. The idea that it's bleaker and offers less to do has been successfully propagated by – guess who? – north Londoners. It is true to say that public transport is worse, because only a small percentage of the Underground network ventures here. However, it really ain't so grim down south. In recent years even former north Londoners have discovered there's something rather pleasant about the more affordable property prices and relaxed lifestyle of the river's former B-list side (referring here, of course, to all the place names beginning with that letter, from Battersea to Brixton).

Clapham has long been the flag-bearer for south London style, with plenty of upmarket restaurants and bars lining its high street since the late 1980s. However, in the mid-1990s, anarchic and artistic Brixton started to become gentrified, too.

Attention has started to focus even more recently on Battersea, with the construction of a landmark luxury flats complex, Montevetro, by leading architect Richard Rogers. The architectural conversion of the monolithic Battersea Power Station is finally underway, too.

Kennington has some lovely streets lined with neo-Georgian terraced houses, so it can only be a matter of time before the gentrification of 'Little Portugal' – Stockwell – begins.

Battersea Power Station (p202)

Ghetto Fabulous

The West End, west London and Primrose Hill in north London might provide the capital's best star-spotting opportunities, but those born, raised or living in the historically poorer suburbs of Brixton and Stockwell have also made a notable contribution to public life. So here's an antidote to all those sarky north London jibes: a list of just a few local alumni you will certainly have heard of, or are worth getting to know.

- Floella Benjamin – celebrated *Play School* presenter and writer of children's books, BAFTA executive and Brixton resident
- David Bowie – once outrageous, gender-bending rock star (now all grown up); born David Jones at 40 Stansfield Rd
- Harold Macmillan – Conservative British prime minister; born in Brixton
- Linton Kwesi Johnson -'dub poet' and icon for black British artists; has lived in Brixton for more than 40 years
- John Major – often pilloried former British prime minister; born to a circus family and raised here, married in St Matthew's Church
- Magnus Mills – bus driver on the 159 route; became a bestselling novelist with *The Restraint of Beasts*
- Roger Moore – formerly the Saint and James Bond 007; born in Stockwell, where his father was a local policeman
- Chris Morris – bad-boy comedian, resident of Brixton; caused public worry about the new drug 'cake' and announced the 'death' of very healthy Tory MP Michael Heseltine
- Will Self – provocative novelist, perhaps most famous for *My Idea of Fun* (very twisted) and *Great Apes;* Stockwell resident
- Paul Simenon – bass player of rock band the Clash was born and raised here (later moved to west London); wrote song 'Guns of Brixton'

BRIXTON

'We gonna rock down to Electric Avenue,' sang Eddy Grant optimistically in 1983, about Brixton's first shopping street blessed with electric lights (just to the left of the Underground station exit). But the Clash's 'Guns of Brixton' took a much darker tone when talking about the riots of the 1980s and community discontent with the police that provoked the street disturbances. Historically, those are just two sides to this edgy, vibrant, multicultural potpourri of a neighbourhood.

There was a settlement here as early as a year after the Norman invasion in 1066. However, Brixton remained an isolated, far-flung village until the 19th century, when the new Vauxhall Bridge (1816) and the railways (1860) linked it with central London.

The years that most shaped contemporary Brixton, however, were the postwar 'Windrush' years, when immigrants arrived from the West Indies in reply to the British government's call for help in solving the labour shortage of the time. (*Windrush* was the name of one of the leading ships that brought these immigrants to the UK.) A generation later the honeymoon period was over, as economic decline and hostility between the police and particularly the black community (who accounted for only 29% of the population of Brixton at the time) led to the riots in 1981, 1985 and 1995. These centred on Railton Rd and Coldharbour Lane.

Some of the problems still remain. However, the overall mood has been decidedly more upbeat in the last few years. Soaring property prices have sent house-hunters foraging in these parts, and pockets of gentrification sit alongside the more run-down streets. Whatever edge is left from the dark days of the 1980s has only added to the excitement of the area's restaurants (p268) and clubs. Hip-hop and reggae still blares from car radios.

Besides coming here to go eating, clubbing, to a gig at the **Brixton Academy** (p313) or to a film at the historic **Ritzy** (p301), probably the best way to experience the area's Caribbean flavour is to visit **Brixton Market** (p350). Here, you can drink in the heady mix of incense and the smells of the exotic fruits, vegetables and meat on sale. It's a good place to get red snapper or pigs' trotters for your shopping basket, or to splash out on African clothes and trinkets.

Near Brixton, in Brockwell Park, you'll also find London's best lido, or outdoor swimming pool, **Brockwell Park Lido** (p311).

BATTERSEA & WANDSWORTH

Against the proud silhouette of the Battersea Power Station, this area is in bloom. Southwest along the Thames from Lambeth, it was a site of industry until the 1970s. Now its abandoned factories and warehouses are fast being replaced by luxury flats. Even residents from well-heeled Chelsea are defecting across the Thames.

Wandsworth, slightly downriver again, has become similarly yuppified. You'll hear the area repeatedly referred to as 'nappy valley' and probably think that's an overstatement. It's not! Just visit the main thoroughfare of Northcote Rd.

BATTERSEA DOGS HOME Map pp460-1

☎ 7622 3626; www.dogshome.org; 4 Battersea Park Rd; ☼ 10.30am-4.15pm Mon-Wed & Fri, 10.30am-3.15pm Sat & Sun; rail Battersea Park

If you're a reader putting down roots in London, you can pick yourself up a new best friend at this famous shelter for stray dogs. Singer Geri Halliwell even collected a handbag-sized puppy a few years back here to help get her through life's tough times, and to act as a fashion accessory. Before joining her as a proud pooch owner, though, remember the RSPCA's motto that a dog is for life, not just for Christmas.

BATTERSEA PARK Map pp458-9

☎ 8871 7530; www.batterseapark.org; ☼ dawn-dusk; rail Battersea Park

These 50 hectares of greenery stretch between Albert and Chelsea Bridges. With its Henry Moore sculptures and a **Peace Pagoda**, erected in 1985 by a group of Japanese Buddhists to commemorate Hiroshima Day, its tranquil appearance belies a bloody past. It was once the site of an assassination attempt on King Charles II in 1671 and of a duel in 1829 between the Duke of Wellington and an opponent who accused him of treason.

The park has had a recent £7.5 million refurbishment, so there's never been a better time to visit. The 19th-century landscaping has been reinstated, and the grand riverside promenade spruced up. At the same time, the Festival of Britain pleasure gardens, including the spectacular Vista Fountains, have been restored. There are lakes, plenty of sporting facilities, an art gallery, the **Pump House** (Map pp460–1; ☎ 7350 0523; Battersea Park SW11; ☼ 11am-5pm Wed, Thu & Sun, to 4pm Fri & Sat) and a small **Children's Zoo** (☎ 7924 5826; Battersea Park SW11; adult/child/family £4.95/3.75/15.50; ☼ 10am-5pm Apr-Oct).

BATTERSEA POWER STATION Map pp460-1

www.thepowerstation.co.uk; rail Battersea Park

This abandoned monolith has never attracted *quite* the same unquestioning affection as architect Giles Gilbert Scott's other industrial creation, Bankside Power Station (now the Tate Modern). Curiously, as an icon it's almost been as much loathed as it's been loved. But the fact that readers of stuffy *Country Life* magazine recently voted it one of the four British structures they'd most like to knock down ought to be grounds enough to rescue it, and now it seems it has been. The 38-acre building – the largest brick building in Europe – is planned to open in 2008 as, gulp, a '24-hour destination', with two hotels, a 2,000-seat theatre, a 16-screen cinema and 750 new flats. The scheme involves crystal palaces, hanging gardens, a vast greenhouse growing vegetables, a ballroom big enough to hold two jumbo jets and even a helipad. The four smokestacks that make it resemble an upside-down table will remain. However, one will house a thrill ride and all will be joined by a glass-covered atrium. The £1 billion redevelopment by Parkview International has its critics and sceptics, but it is intended to upgrade Battersea Park train station, too.

Opened in two stages, in 1933 and 1953, the original plant stopped generating electricity in 1983 and fell into disrepair, despite its Grade II heritage listing. In 1995 it was a location in a film version of *Richard III* starring Ian McKellen. It's also appeared on several album covers, including the Orb's 1991 *Adventures beyond the Ultraworld* and Pink Floyd's 1977 *Animals*. (Hilariously, when a huge 40ft pig-shaped balloon was being photographed flying over the power station for the latter cover, it broke free from its moorings and caused a massive civil aviation alert over London, before coming down on a farm in Kent. Proof not only that pigs might fly, but also that sometimes they do!)

WANDSWORTH COMMON Map pp438-9

rail Wandsworth Common/Clapham Junction

Wilder and more overgrown than the nearby common in Clapham, Wandsworth Common is full of couples pushing prams on a sunny day. On the common's eastern side is a pleasant collection of streets known as the **toast rack**, because of their alignment. Baskerville, Dorlcote, Henderson, Nicosia, Patten and Routh Rds are lined with Georgian houses. There's a blue plaque at 3 Routh Rd, home to the former British prime minister David Lloyd George.

In the northeast corner of the common, off Trinity Rd, is the **Royal Victoria Patriotic Building**. This listed Gothic colossus has towering steeples and cobblestone courtyards, and was built for orphans of servicemen who had served in the Crimean War of the early 19th century. Today the building houses a drama school, apartments and a main hall that's very popular as a wedding venue. There's also an atmospheric restaurant.

YOUNG'S RAM BREWERY Map pp438-9

☎ 8875 7000; 68 High St SW18; brewery tour adult/14-17yr/senior & student £5.50/3/4.50; ⏰ visitors centre 10am-6pm Mon-Sat; rail Wandsworth Town

Beer ('bitter', not lager) has been brewed here since the late 16th century; 1½-hour tours of the brewery leave at noon and 2pm Monday to Thursday and Saturday – call in advance to book. Under-18s must be accompanied by an adult.

To get here from Wandsworth Town station (trains from Waterloo station), walk west on Old York Rd, cross over to Armoury Way and then go south along Ram St to the visitors centre on High St.

CLAPHAM

The so-called 'man on the Clapham omnibus' – English law's sexist definition of the ordinary person – has largely left this neighbourhood. Instead, Clapham is now the spiritual home of well-off young professionals in their 20s and 30s, who eat in the area's many restaurants, drink in its many bars and generally drive up property prices. It was the railways that originally conferred on Clapham its status as a home for everyday commuters from the late 19th century. Clapham Junction is still the largest UK rail interchange, and in 1988 the tragic site of one of Britain's worst privatised rail disasters.

Reaching further back in history, the area was first settled after the Great Fire of Lon-don in 1666, when the well-off, including noted diarist Samuel Pepys and explorer Captain James Cook, escaped the desecration of the City to build homes here. Its name dates back much further still, believed to derive from the Anglo-Saxon for 'Clappa's farm'.

CLAPHAM COMMON Map p462

⊖ Clapham Common

This large expanse of green is the heart of the Clapham neighbourhood. Mentioned by Graham Greene in his novel *The End of the Affair*, it's also now a venue for many outdoor summer events (see http://clapham highstreet.co.uk). The main thoroughfare, Clapham High St, starts at the western edge, and is lined with many of the bars, restaurants and shops that people principally come to Clapham for. However, for a simple stroll it's much more pleasant to explore the more upmarket streets of **Clapham Common North Side** and **Clapham Old Town**, both to the northwest of the tube station.

On the corner of Clapham Park Rd and Clapham Common South Side you'll find the **Holy Trinity Church**. This was home to the 19th-century Clapham Sect, a group of wealthy Christians that included William Wilberforce, a leading antislavery campaigner. The sect also campaigned against child labour and for prison reform.

KENNINGTON, OVAL & STOCKWELL

Only cricket lovers and those who set up home here will really venture into this neck of the woods. It centres on Kennington Park, which isn't that much to look at, but which has an interesting history. Off Kennington Lane, just west of its intersection with Kennington Rd, lies a lovely enclave of leafy streets – Cardigan St, Courtney St and Courtney Sq – with neo-Georgian houses. They're not really worth travelling to see, but make a nice diversion should rain interrupt play at the Oval.

KENNINGTON PARK Map pp460-1

⊖ Oval

This unprepossessing space of green has a great rabble-rousing tradition. Originally a common, where all were permitted entry, it acted as a south London speakers' corner.

Preachers of the 18th and 19th century used to deliver hellfire-and-brimstone speeches to large audiences here; John Wesley, Methodist Church founder and antislavery advocate, is said to have attracted some 30,000 believers. After the great Chartist rally on 10 April 1848 (where millions of working-class people turned out to demand the same voting rights as the middle classes), the royal family promptly fenced off and patrolled the park. Today, some locals are again objecting to its renewed political use. During the 18th century, Jacobite rebels seeking Scottish independence were also hanged, drawn and quartered in the park.

OVAL Map pp460-1

☎ 7582 7764; www.surreyccc.co.uk; Kennington Oval SE11; test matches £45, last day £10, county fixtures £5-10; ☎ booking office 9am-12.30am & 1-4pm Mon-Fri Apr-Sep; ⊖ Oval

Home to the Surrey County Cricket Club, the Oval is London's second cricketing venue after Lord's. As well as Surrey matches, it also regularly hosts international Test matches – where the English team have staged a renaissance in recent years. The season runs from April to September.

Worth the Trip

Peckham Library (☎ 7525 0200; Peckham Sq SE15; admission free; 🕙 9am-8pm Mon-Fri, from 10am Wed, 9am-5pm Sat, noon-4pm Sun; rail Peckham Rye/Queen's Road/Peckham; ♿) In a relatively deprived area, this award-winning building stands out like a beacon. It looks like a capital letter F, with its 12m-high upper storey cantilevering out well beyond the five-floor vertical block below. Plus it's fun and colourful with green patinated copper cladding and a prominent red 'tongue' and the word 'Library' above the roof.

Architect Will Alsop, who won 2000's prestigious Stirling Prize for this design, also had a serious intent. The upper storey overlooks not only nearby Peckham Sq but also the lights of the City and the West End, connecting Peckham to the bright lights of London. Visitors are free to enter the library, although large groups should book and photography is not allowed.

AROUND STOCKWELL Map pp460-1
⊖ Stockwell

Another London neighbourhood that only longer-term visitors would get to see, Stockwell does harbour **Vincent van Gogh's home** from 1873 to 1874. The troubled Dutch genius lived at 87 Hackford Rd.

Peckham Library (above)

SOUTHWEST LONDON

Eating p271-2; Drinking p294-5; Shopping p352; Sleeping p375

It's the common pursuit of a large proportion of the London populace to find bits of London that aren't like London at all, and much of Southwest London represents such a beacon of bucolic relief. It's here that you escape to the country without leaving the city at all. The best time to visit is on a warm sunny day, when the hours seem to stretch on forever. The area loses some of its shine under grey skies so is best saved for the summer if you have the choice.

During the day Southwest London is a fairly quiet residential area; you'll see lots of young mothers out pushing prams and doing their shopping. This is the best time to enjoy the area's many green spaces – walk along the Thames Path from Putney Bridge to Barnes, lounge by the river in Bishop's Park, play tennis in South Park, sup on a pint by Parson's Green or picnic on Barnes Common.

It's at night that the area comes alive and the resident Antipodean and ex–public school populations make themselves known. Fulham is a very popular place to go out in town with a plethora of good pubs, bars and restaurants. Putney and Barnes like to think that they're a little more refined, though a trip to any of the pubs on the High St on a Saturday night will put paid to that opinion.

Although southwest London is a little far out if you're only in London for a long weekend, it's the perfect place to base yourself for a longer stay, which is probably why there are so many Aussies and Kiwis living and working here.

FULHAM & PARSON'S GREEN

Fulham and Parson's Green merge neatly into one neighbourhood that sits comfortably in a curve of the Thames between Chelsea and Hammersmith. While the attractive Victorian terraces and riverside location have drawn a very well-to-do crowd, Fulham's blue-collar roots are still evident in the strong tradition of support for Fulham Football Club. After a couple of seasons away, Fulham are back at their home ground at Craven Cottage, on Stevenage Rd down by the river.

FULHAM PALACE Map pp438-9

☎ 7736 3233; Bishop's Ave SW6; ☉ 2-5pm Wed-Sun Mar-Oct, 1-4pm Thu-Sun Nov-Feb; admission free, children under 16 must be accompanied; ⊖ Putney Bridge; ☊

Summer home of the bishops of London from 704 to 1973, Grade One–listed Fulham Palace is an interesting mix of architectural styles set in beautiful gardens and once enclosed by the longest moat in England. You can enjoy the small botanic gardens as Catherine of Aragon and Elizabeth I, who both stayed here, once did and learn about the history of the palace and its inhabitants in the museum. Although most of the palace is not open to the public, guided tours can be booked in advance through the museum and cost £4.

The surrounding land, once totalling 36 acres but now reduced to just 13, forms Bishop's Park, and consists of a shady promenade along the river, a bowling green, tennis courts, a rose garden, a café and even a paddling pond with fountain for cooling off in on a hot day.

CHELSEA VILLAGE Map pp458-9

☎ 0870 603 0005; Fulham Rd SW6; www.chelsea village.com; ⊖ Fulham Broadway

To his credit, Roman Abramovich, the new billionaire owner of champion Chelsea Football Club (see p206), is said not to like this commercialised development surrounding the team's Stamford Bridge stadium. On top of two interlinked hotels (see p375) there are also restaurants, a nightclub and a luxury health club.

The club's newly won trophies, such as the Carling Cup (2004–05) and FA Premiership (2004–05), are on display in the **Megastore**

Top Five – Southwest London

- **Barnes Common** (p206)
- **Chelsea Village** (above)
- **Fulham Palace** (left)
- **Thames Path** (p207)
- **Wetland Centre London** (p206)

The Chelski Revolution

Money might not buy you happiness, but as expatriate Russian billionaire Roman Abramovich has proved, it sure doesn't hurt when you're constructing a champion English football team. Chelsea weren't exactly languishing when Abramovich snapped them up for £140 million in summer 2003, but as fourth in the league the Blues did fall into the 'could do better' category. Less than two seasons and £213 million in transfer fees later, they'd done better, coming top of the FA Premiership for the first time in 50 years.

The Russian oligarch's purchases included Didier Drogba for £24 million, Damien Duff for £17 million, Claude Makelele for £16.6 million, Adrian Mutu for £15.8 million and brilliant goalkeeper Petr Cech for £7 million. However, his most astute signing was undoubtedly the Portuguese coach Jose Mourinho, who took the helm in summer 2004 after predecessor Claudio Ranieri was unable to immediately satisfy his new Russian owner's desire for absolute supremacy. (Chelsea only came – horrors! – second in 2003–04.)

Mourinho has since created controversy off the field in the way he's courted other teams' players, insulted a referee and freely admitted his own arrogance. However, he's widely recognised as instilling discipline and genuine camaraderie in his team – although Chelsea still has improvements to make in FA Cup and European Championships performances.

The owner of Russian oil giant Sibneft, Abramovich has an estimated personal fortune of £7.5 billion. Several journalists have journeyed to Siberia to ask hard questions about how he became so rich so quickly. But if you raise the matter with most Chelsea fans, who've rarely seen the depths of poverty in Russia, they're just not that interested.

(🕙 10am-6pm Mon-Sat, 11am-4pm Sun) or you can take a **tour** (adult/child £10/6; 🕙 11am, 1pm & 3pm Mon-Fri, noon & 2pm Sat & Sun) of the ground.

Getting to see the team play is much, much trickier, especially as they are now the darlings of the league. However, you could try on ☎ 7915 2951.

PUTNEY & BARNES

Putney is most famed as the starting point of the Oxford and Cambridge Boat Race (opposite), which is beamed live to millions of people across the globe each spring. There are references to the race in the pubs and restaurants in the area and along the Thames Path.

Barnes is less well known and more villagey in feel. Its former residents include author Henry Fielding.

The best way to approach Putney is to follow the signposts from Putney Bridge tube station for the footbridge (which runs parallel to the rail track), admiring the gorgeous riverside houses, with their gardens fronting the murky waters of the Thames, and thereby avoiding the tatty High St until the last possible minute. If you have the time, walking the Thames Path from Putney or meandering across the Common from Putney train station are good ways to reach Barnes. Otherwise, catch the overland train from Vauxhall or Waterloo.

WETLAND CENTRE LONDON
Map pp438-9

☎ 8409 4400; www.wwt.org.uk; Queen Elizabeth's Walk SW13; adult/child/concession £6.75/4/5.50; 🕙 9.30am-5pm winter, 9.30am-6pm summer, last entry 1hr before closing; ⊖ Hammersmith, then bus 283 ('the duck bus'), 33, 72 or 72/rail Barnes

Europe's largest inland wetland project, the 105-acre Wetland Centre was superbly transformed from four Victorian reservoirs in 2000 and attracts some 140 species of birds and 300 types of moths and butterflies – not to mention 100,000 visitors. From the shop and entrance hall, the outdoor paths divide into two walks around the grounds, both of which take in the habitats of its many residents. While the information cards allude to some of the more exotic wetland creatures, the animals you can realistically expect to see are ducks, swans, geese and coots. The odd heron and rarer variation, such as the mandarin duck, can also be found. When the ducklings are young (in spring and summer) this is a wonderful place to watch the tame birds swim and play – they have no fear of humans, so you can come very close. An excellent place to bring the kids.

BARNES COMMON & GREEN

Barnes Common consists of rambling, open parkland, scythed by roads but large enough that it's easy to escape the traffic – and to get very lost. This is a great place for an aimless ramble or a picnic (stock up at the delis on Church Rd or Barnes High St). Glam fans may like to hunt out the tree, festooned with tributes, that brought Marc Bolan's life to a premature end in 1977.

The Green, at the western edge of the Common, is in some way responsible for the village feel of Barnes itself and is the highlight for local children, who come armed with bread with which to feed the many ducks bobbing on top of its pond. The village stocks used to stand by the water – parents may like to point this out to any misbehaving children.

THAMES PATH
www.thames-path.co.uk
The section of the Thames Path that runs between Putney and Barnes is a great spot to take in a small part of the 210-mile riverside walk. The initial stretch along the Embankment is always a merry hive of activity, with rowers setting off and returning to their boat clubs and punters from nearby pubs lazing by the water. The majority of the walk, though, is intensely rural – at times the only accompaniment is the call of songbirds and the gentle swish of old Father Thames (yes, we *are* still in London).

BEVERLEY BROOK WALK
www.londonwalking.com, www.tfl.gov.uk/streets/walking/home.shtml
The gentle 7-mile walk from Putney to New Malden station follows a tributary of the Thames and takes in the splendours of Putney Lower Common, Barnes Common, Richmond Park and Wimbledon Common. Much of the walk is rural in nature and offers an ideal opportunity to tramp across parkland and woodland. There are many pubs and cafés on the way for those in need of victual encouragement.

The Boat Race
Even those with absolutely no interest in rowing or in Oxbridge find themselves drawn to the Varsity Boat Race, which takes place along the 4-mile stretch of water between Putney and Mortlake at the end of March or beginning of April each year. Maybe it's the tradition, maybe it's the romance of 18 men in the prime of youth pitting their strength and wits against one another, or maybe it's the prospect of the boats sinking and their hoity-toity young contents spilling into the river. If you're heading down to watch (get here early to bag a spot on the bank), here are some facts with which to stun and amaze the 250,000 people with the same idea:

- The 2003 Boat Race was the closest ever – the margin between ecstasy (Oxford) and agony (Cambridge) was just 1ft; the biggest margin of victory saw Cambridge win by 20 lengths in 1900.
- The boats have sunk six times, most recently in 1978.
- The 1877 race ended in a dead heat.
- The fastest time of 16 minutes and 19 seconds was achieved by Cambridge in 1998.
- Both teams pull an average of 600 strokes to complete the course.
- The heaviest oarsmen tipped the scales at 17 stone and 5lbs; the lightest oarsmen came in at 9 stone and 6.5lbs.
- Cambridge notched up a record 13 successive victories between 1924 and 1936.

For more details, dip into the official website at www.theboatrace.org.

UP RIVER
Eating p272-4; Drinking p295-6; Shopping p352; Sleeping p375-6

The well-to-do have been retreating from the city to the palaces and villas of the riverside boroughs of southwest London for over 500 years, and its appeal to those wishing to escape the more frenetic pace of life in zones 1 and 2 is still very much apparent. Richmond, Chiswick and Kew in particular offer an expensive slice of village life far removed from the crowds of central London.

Anyone wanting to get out of London for the day without too much trouble or expense should take a trip here, and for people who aren't big-city fans but need to be in London, it's a great place to stay.

CHISWICK

Mention Chiswick to most Londoners and they will groan at the sheer bourgeois, golf-playing dullness of the place. Ask how many have actually visited, and perhaps you'll be surprised – Chiswick to many represents an idea rather than a reality, and this quiet west London enclave does not deserve the flak it gets for its well-heeled residents and unfeasibly grand mansions.

Chiswick High Rd itself is an upmarket yet uninspiring main drag, full of pubs and twee shops with the odd decent restaurant – there will be little to waylay you, so best to head straight down to Hogarth Lane, Church St and the riverfront.

CHISWICK HOUSE Map p437

☎ 8995 0508; www.english-heritage.org.uk; Chiswick Park W4; adult/child/senior & student £4/2/3; ⊗ 10am-5pm Wed-Sun Apr-Oct, prebooked appointments only Nov-Mar; rail Chiswick/ ⊖ Turnham Green

This is a fine Palladian pavilion with an octagonal dome and colonnaded portico. It was designed by the third Earl of Burlington (1694–1753) when he returned from his grand tour of Italy, fired up with enthusiasm for all things Roman. Lord Burlington used it to entertain friends and to house his library and art collection.

Inside, certain rooms have been completely restored to a grandeur some will find overpowering. The dome of the main salon has been left ungilded and the walls are decorated with eight enormous paintings. In the Blue Velvet Room look for the portrait of Inigo Jones, the architect much admired by Lord Burlington, over one of the doors. The ceiling paintings are by William Kent, who also decorated the Kensington Palace State Apartments.

Lord Burlington also planned the house's original gardens, now Chiswick Park, but they have been much altered since his time. The restored Cascade waterfall is bubbling again after being out of action for years. The house, which is about 1 mile southwest of the tube station, is opposite the start of Burlington Lane.

CHISWICK VILLAGE

Walking around the Hogarth Roundabout (use the subways), take the exit onto Church St where the charming remains of Chiswick village are incongruously situated not 30 seconds from the monstrous A4 road out of London and some shockingly uninspired modern development. Walking down here you can get a good feel of how Chiswick looked in the 19th century and before – some of the buildings date from the 16th century. If you turn right by the church, you will get to **Chiswick Old Cemetery** (⊗ 9am-dusk), where among the many graves you can see Hogarth's and Whistler's. Continuing down Church St you reach **Chiswick Mall**, one of London's most exclusive addresses, where vast mansions front the Thames. The walk up the mall along the Thames Walk towards Hammersmith is delightful on a good day, and there are plenty of riverside pubs at which to stop for a drink or some lunch. The **Old Ship** (p296) is our top pick.

FULLER'S GRIFFIN BREWERY

☎ 8996 2063; Chiswick Lane South W4; adult/14-18yr £5/3.50; ⊗ tours 11am, noon, 1pm & 2pm Mon & Wed-Fri; ⊖ Turnham Green/rail Chiswick

Of interest to anyone who enjoys bitter and wants to see it being made (or to those who want to avail themselves of the opportunity to enjoy a comprehensive tasting session), Fuller's Brewery is one of two remaining breweries in London (the other being Young's, just up the road in Wandsworth). The brewery is accessible by 1½-hour tour only, which must be booked in advance by phone.

HOGARTH'S HOUSE Map p437

☎ 8994 6757; Hogarth Lane, Great West Rd W4; admission free; ⊗ 1-5pm Tue-Fri, 1-6pm Sat & Sun Apr-Oct, 1-4pm Tue-Fri, 1-5pm Sat & Sun Nov, Dec, Feb & Mar; ⊖ Turnham Green

Home between 1749 and 1764 to artistic and social commentator William Hogarth, this now showcases his caricatures and engravings, including famous works such as the haunting *Gin Lane, Marriage à la mode* and a copy of *Rake's Progress*. More obscurely, there are the private engravings *Before* and *After* (1730), commissioned by the Duke of Montagu and bearing the immortal inscription 'every creature is sad after intercourse'. Although the house is pretty, no furniture remains, so this is really a destination for locals or ardent Hogarth fans. Other examples of his work, including the original *Rake's Progress*, can be seen in **Sir John Soane's Museum** (p104).

SYON HOUSE Map p437

☎ 8560 0883; www.syonpark.co.uk; Syon Park, Brentford TW7; adult/concession/family £7.50/6.50/17, gardens only £3.75/2.50/9; ☽ 11am-5pm Wed, Thu & Sun mid-Mar–Nov, gardens 10.30am-dusk; ⊖ /rail Gunnersbury, then bus 237 or 267

Appearing in the Robert Altman film *Gosford Park*, this converted Tudor mansion is an abject lesson in the *dreadful* things even the richest English aristocrats apparently have to do to pay the upkeep on their stately homes these days. An aquatic park with crocodiles and piranhas, a snakes-and-ladders indoor playground and a trout fishery have all been established in the grounds to give the Duke of Northumberland's manor extra family appeal, while a neighbouring hotel is due to be built to help to pay the bills. There goes the neighbourhood.

There was a bitter row in 2002 when the Duke announced he wish to sell the Raphael masterpiece *The Madonna of the Pinks* – then on loan to the National Gallery – to the Getty Museum in Los Angeles to support Syon House and Alnwick Castle in Northumberland (incidentally a *Harry Potter* film location). All was smoothed over, however, when the Heritage Lottery Fund and public donations raised £21 million to keep it permanently for the gallery and the nation.

Syon House started life as a medieval abbey named after Mt Zion, but in 1542 Henry VIII dissolved the order of Bridgettine nuns who were peacefully established there and had the abbey rebuilt into a handsome residence. (In 1547, they say, God got his revenge when Henry's coffin was brought to Syon en route to Windsor for burial and burst open during the night, leaving the king's body to be set upon by the estate's hungry dogs.)

The understated exterior gives way to a neoclassical interior built by Robert Adam and decorated with a slew of old masters. There are beautiful views towards Kew Gardens. The house's own 40-acre gardens were modelled by the ubiquitous 'Capability' Brown and feature a truly magnificent conservatory.

RICHMOND

'If I have to choose between Richmond and death, I choose death!' exclaims Nicole Kidman as Virginia Woolf in *The Hours*. The sentiment may seem a bit extreme, but Richmond today remains anathema to zone 1 snobs, although it's loved by almost everyone else for its incredible park and lovely walks. Centuries of royal history, some stunning Georgian architecture and the graceful curve of the Thames has made this one of London's swankiest locales, home to ageing rock stars and city high-fliers alike.

Richmond was historically named Sheen, but Henry VII, having fallen in love with the place, renamed the village after his Yorkshire Earldom. This started centuries of royal association with the area; the most famous local, Henry VIII, acquired nearby Hampton Court Palace from Cardinal Wolsey after the latter's fall from grace in 1529, while his daughter Elizabeth I died here in 1603.

RICHMOND GREEN Map p464

On exiting Richmond station, you'll find the town itself does not look much different from any other English high street. However, a short walk beyond the Quadrant will reveal the enormous open space of Richmond Green with its mansions and delightful pubs, and you'll realise that this is quite a special place. Crossing the green diagonally will take you to what remains of **Richmond Palace**, just the main entrance and gatehouse, built in 1501. You can see Henry VII's arms above the main gate: he built the Tudor additions to the edifice, although the palace had been in use as a royal residence since 1125. The green itself was used to feed the village's sheep herds, and hosted jousting matches for the king's pleasure.

RICHMOND PARK Map p437

☎ 8948 3209; www.royalparks.gov.uk/richmond_park; admission free; ☽ 7am-dusk (from 7.30am winter); ⊖ /rail Richmond/bus 371

The largest urban parkland in Europe, Richmond Park is quite something, offering everything from formal gardens and ancient woodland of oak and chestnut to unsurpassed views of the city 12 miles away. Established by Edward II in the 13th century, the royal park has changed little since that time – though perhaps there wouldn't have been quite so many 4WDs trundling through in his day. It's easy enough to escape the several roads that cut up the rambling wilderness, making the park an excellent spot for a quiet walk or picnic, even in summer when Richmond's riverside can be heaving. Such is the magic of the place, it somehow comes as no surprise to happen upon herds of remarkably docile red and fallow deer basking under the trees.

Coming from Richmond, it's easiest to enter via Richmond Gate or from Petersham Rd. Take a map with you and wander around the grounds – flower lovers should make a special trip to **Isabella Plantation** in late spring, when the rhododendrons and azaleas are ablaze and the gardens at their most impressive.

Pembroke Lodge, the childhood home of Bertrand Russell, is now a cafeteria set in beautiful gardens and affording great views towards central London.

Particularly attractive are the two large lakes at **Pen Ponds**, in the very centre of the park. There is a **deer pen** next to **White Lodge** for those who want to see the red deer up close (they breed so successfully here that there are two annual culls to control their numbers). However, it's far more exciting to see the deer wild in the park, although this involves a degree of luck. It is possible to go horse riding in the park – there are four stables in the immediate vicinity. Call the main park number for more information.

ST PETER'S CHURCH Off Map p464
Church Lane, Petersham TW10; admission free;
♥ 3-5pm Sun; ⊖ /rail Richmond/bus 65

St Peter's is a pleasing Norman church that has been a place of worship for 1300 years – parts of the present structure date from 1266. It's a fascinating place, not least for its curious Georgian box pews, which local landowners would rent while the serving staff and labourers sat in the open seats in the south transept. Against the north wall of the chancel is the **Cole Monument**, which depicts barrister George Cole, his wife and child, all reclining in Elizabethan dress – an unusual design for an English church. The family vault lies under the chancel.

Of interest to any Canadian, St Peter's is also the burial place of Captain George Vancouver, who was laid to rest here in 1798, having contributed a vast amount to the charting of the earth, including, of course, the discovery of Vancouver Island. His unshowy tomb is on the boundary wall of the cemetery. Pastry fans of a peculiar bent may also like to seek out the tomb of Mary Burdekin, who is thought to have originated the Maids of Honour pastries (see p274).

THE THAMES
The stretch of the river bank from Twickenham Bridge down towards Petersham and Ham is one of the prettiest in London. The action is concentrated around **Richmond Bridge**, an original structure from 1777 and London's oldest surviving crossing, only widened for traffic in 1937. The lovely walk upriver to Petersham is often overcrowded in nice weather – best to cut across **Petersham Meadows** and continue on to Richmond Park if it's peace and quiet you seek. There are several companies near Richmond Bridge offering skiff hire (adult/child £12/4) and, for the less energetic, boat tours up to Hampton and back into the city (from £4.50).

KEW
The town of Kew is world-famous for its World Heritage–listed Botanic Gardens, and rightly so – a day at Kew Gardens can be fascinating and appealing even to someone with no knowledge of plants and flowers. This smart west London suburb is also a pleasant place for an idle wander – watch out for cricket matches played on central Kew Green in summer.

KEW GARDENS Map p437
☎ 8332 5000, 8940 1171; www.rbgkew.org.uk; Kew Rd TW9; adult/under 16yr/senior, student & 16-18yr £10/free/7; ♥ gardens 9.30am-6.30pm Mon-Fri, 9.30am-7.30pm Sat & Sun late-Mar–Aug, 9.30am-6pm Sep-Oct, 9.30am-4.15pm Nov-Feb, glasshouses 9.30am-5.30pm late-Mar–Oct, 9.30am-3.45pm Nov-Feb; ⊖ /rail Kew Gardens; ⑤

The Royal Botanic Gardens at Kew give a whole new meaning to the term 'the greenhouse effect': their famous metal-and-glass **Palm House** (1848) and other hothouses lure one million visitors each year. Kew's 120-hectare expanse of lawns, formal gardens and parkland are especially popular during spring and summer, but it's these climate-controlled conservatories that make a visit worthwhile in any season.

As well as being a public garden, Kew is an important research centre, and it maintains its reputation as the most exhaustive botanical collection in the world. One of its most important new acquisitions is a 200-million-year-old Wollemi Pine, discovered in Australia after being thought long extinct. The gardens will breed saplings to sell to the public and help the conservation effort in Australia.

The Palm House, near the main Victoria Gate, is home to exotic – if perhaps not quite so exotic as the Wollemi – tropical greenery. There's a tiny **Water Lily House** (♥ Mar-Dec) to the northwest, and further north lies the **Princess of Wales Conservatory** (1985), with plants in 10 different computer-controlled climate zones –

Kew Garden's Palm House (opposite)

everything from a desert to a cloud forest. It's here you find the most famous of Kew's 38,000 plant species, the 2m-tall **Titan Arum**, or 'corpse flower', which is overpoweringly obnoxious-smelling when it blooms. The garden staff have been successful beyond their wildest dreams in getting this plant to flower, and it now blooms nearly every year.

Beyond that is the **Kew Gardens Gallery** bordering Kew Green, which houses exhibitions of paintings and photos, mostly with a horticultural theme.

Heading westwards from the gallery you will arrive at the red-brick **Kew Palace**, a former royal residence once known as Dutch House, dating from 1631. It was very popular with George III and his family (his wife Charlotte died here in 1818). The gardens surrounding the palace are especially pretty. At the time of writing, the palace was expected to reopen in 2006, after extensive renovations.

Other highlights include the **Temperate House** and **Queen Charlotte's Cottage** – the latter also popular with 'mad' George III and his wife. Don't forget to see the **Japanese Gateway** and the celebrated **Great Pagoda** (1761), designed by William Chambers. The **Marianne North Gallery** features paintings on a botanical theme, while **Museum No 1** demonstrates how plant materials have been fashioned into clothes, medicines and implements. The **Orangery** near Kew Palace contains a restaurant, café and shop.

If this Unesco World Heritage Site seems too vast, the **Kew Explorer minitrain** (adult/child £3.50/1.50) will whizz you around in 40 minutes.

You can get to Kew Gardens by tube or train. Come out of the station and walk straight (west) along Station Rd, cross Kew Gardens Rd and then continue straight along Lichfield Rd. This will bring you to Victoria Gate. Alternatively, from March to September (with reduced services in October), boats run by the **Westminster Passenger Services Association** (☎ 7930 2062; www.wpsa.co.uk) sail from Westminster Pier to Kew Gardens up to four times a day (see p94).

TWICKENHAM

As Wimbledon is to tennis, so Twickenham is to rugby, and you'll find one of the few museums in the world devoted to the sport here. Otherwise there's not much to detain you in this quiet and pretty Middlesex suburb aside from the delights of the fine Marble Hill House overlooking the Thames.

MARBLE HILL HOUSE Map p437

☎ 8892 5115; www.english-heritage.org.uk; Richmond Rd; adult/under 15yr/senior & student £4/2/3; ⏰ 10am-2pm Sat & Sun Apr-Oct, open for prebooked tours only Nov-Mar; rail St Margaret's

This is an 18th-century Palladian love nest, built originally for George II's mistress Henrietta Howard and later occupied by Mrs Fitzherbert, the secret wife of George IV. The poet Alexander Pope had a hand in designing the park, which stretches down to the Thames. Inside you'll find an exhibition about the life and times of Henrietta, and a collection of early-Georgian furniture.

To get there from St Margaret's station, turn right along St Margaret's Rd. Then take the right fork along Crown Rd and turn left along Richmond Rd. Turn right along Beaufort Rd and walk across Marble Hill Park to the house.

MUSEUM OF RUGBY Map p437

☎ 8892 8877; www.rfu.com; Gate K, Twickenham Stadium, Rugby Rd; stadium guided tour & museum adult/child/family £9/6/30, entry to museum only (on match days, for match ticket holders only) £3; ⏰ 10am-5pm Tue-Sat, 11am-5pm Sun; rail Twickenham

A state-of-the-art museum that will appeal to all rugby lovers, the Museum of Rugby is tucked behind the eastern stand of the stadium. Relive highlights of old matches in the video theatre and then take a tour of the grounds. Tours depart at 10.30am, noon and 1.30pm (with an additional tour at 3pm on Sunday) but there are no tours on match days.

WIMBLEDON

For a few weeks each summer the sporting world fixes its glare on the quiet southern suburb of Wimbledon, as it has since 1877 (see p23); and then the circus leaves town and Wimbledon returns to unremarkable normality. That said, it's a pleasant little place, and the Wimbledon Lawn Tennis Museum will excite any tennis fan, even in darkest December.

WIMBLEDON LAWN TENNIS MUSEUM

☎ 8946 6131; www.wimbledon.org; Gate 4, Church Rd SW19; adult/concession £6/5; ⏰ 10.30am-5pm, spectators only during championships; ✪ Southfields/ Wimbledon Park

This museum is of specialist interest, dwelling as it does on the minutiae of the history of tennis playing, traced back here to the invention of the all-important lawnmower in 1830 and of the India-rubber ball in the 1850s. It's a state-of-the-art presentation, with plenty of video clips to let fans of the game relive their favourite moments. The museum houses a tearoom and a shop selling all kinds of tennis memorabilia.

WIMBLEDON COMMON

Running on into Putney Heath, Wimbledon Common covers 440 hectares of south London, and is a wonderful expanse of open space for walking, nature trailing and picnicking. There are a few specific sights on Wimbeldon Common, most unexpectedly **Wimbledon Windmill** (☎ 8947 2825; Windmill Rd SW19; adult/child £1/50p; ⏰ 2-5pm Sat, 11am-5pm Sun & public holidays Apr-Oct; ✪ Wimbledon), a fine smock mill dating from 1817. It was during a stay in the mill in 1908 that Robert Baden-Powell was inspired to write parts of his wonderfully named *Scouting for Boys*.

On the southern side of the common, the misnamed **Caesar's Camp** is a prehistoric earthwork that proves that Wimbledon was settled before Roman times.

BUDDHAPADIPA TEMPLE

☎ 8946 1357; 14 Calonne Rd SW19; admission free; ⏰ grounds 8am-9.30pm summer, 8am-6pm winter, temple 9am-5pm Sat & Sun; ✪ Wimbledon, then bus 93

Another unexpected sight, this time found in a residential neighbourhood half a mile from Wimbledon Village, is as authentic a Thai temple as ever graced this side of Bangkok. The Buddhapadipa Temple was built by an association of young Buddhists in Britain and opened in 1982. The *wat* (temple compound) boasts a *bot* (consecrated chapel) decorated with traditional scenes by two leading Thai artists. Remember to take your shoes off before entering the *bot*.

To get to the temple take the tube or train to Wimbledon and then bus 93 up to Wimbledon Parkside. Calonne Rd leads off it on the right.

HAMPTON

Out in London's southwestern outskirts, the wonderful Hampton Court Palace is pressed up against 400-hectare Bushy Park, a semiwild expanse with herds of red and fallow deer.

HAMPTON COURT PALACE

☎ 8781 9500; www.fhrp.org.uk; East Molesey; all-inclusive ticket adult/5-15yr/senior & student/family £12/7.80/9/35; ⏰ 10am-6pm Apr-Oct, 10am-4pm Nov-Mar; rail Hampton Court

London's most spectacular Tudor palace is the 16th-century Hampton Court Palace, located in the city's suburbs and easily reached by train from Waterloo Station. Here history is palpable – from the kitchens where you can see food being prepared and the grand living quarters of Henry VIII to the spectacular gardens complete with 300-year-old maze. This is one of the best days out the city has to offer and should not be missed by anyone with any interest in British history. Set aside plenty of time to do it justice, bearing in mind that if you come by boat from central London the trip will have already eaten up half the day.

Hampton Court Palace, like so many royal residences, was not built for the monarchy at all. In 1514 Cardinal Thomas Wolsey, Lord Chancellor of England, decided to build himself a palace in keeping with his lofty sense of self-importance. Unfortunately, even Wolsey couldn't persuade the pope to grant Henry VIII a divorce from Catherine of Aragon and relations between king and chancellor soured rapidly. Against that background, Wolsey felt obliged to present Hampton Court Palace to the wrathful Henry some 15 years later. The hapless cardinal was charged with high treason but died before his trial in 1530.

As soon as he acquired the palace, Henry set to work expanding it, adding the **Great Hall**, the exquisite **Chapel Royal** and the sprawling kitchens. By 1540 this was one of the grandest and most sophisticated palaces in Europe. In the late 17th century, King William and Queen Mary employed Sir Christopher Wren to build extensions. The result is a beautiful blend of Tudor and 'restrained Baroque' architecture.

At the ticket office by the main **Trophy Gate** be sure to pick up a leaflet listing the daily programme, which will help you plan your visit; this is important as some of the free guided tours require advance booking.

The **Clock Court** is your starting point, from which you can visit the six sets of rooms in the complex, which can be visited in any order.

The stairs inside Anne Boleyn's Gateway lead up to **Henry VIII's State Apartments**, including the Great Hall, the largest single room in the palace, decorated with tapestries and what is considered the country's best hammer-beam roof. The Horn Room, hung with impressive antlers, leads to the Great Watching Chamber

where guards controlled access to the king. Leading off from the chamber is the smaller Pages' Chamber and the Haunted Gallery. Arrested for adultery and detained in the palace in 1542, Henry's fifth wife Catherine Howard managed to evade her guards and ran screaming down the corridor in search of the king. Her woeful ghost is said to do the same thing to this day.

Further along the corridor you'll come to the beautiful Chapel Royal, built in just nine months. The blue-and-gold vaulted ceiling was originally intended for Christ Church, Oxford, but was installed here instead, while the 18th-century reredos was carved by Grinling Gibbons.

Also dating from Henry's day are the Tudor kitchens, again accessible from Anne Boleyn's Gateway and originally able to rustle up meals for a royal household of some 1200 people. The kitchens have been fitted out to look as they might have done in Tudor days and palace 'servants' turn the spits and stuff the bustards. Don't miss the Great Wine Cellar, which handled the 300 barrels each of ale and wine consumed here annually in the mid-16th century.

Returning again to the Clock Court and passing under the colonnade to the right you reach the **King's Apartments**, built by Wren for William III towards the end of the 17th century. Highlights here include the King's Presence Chamber, which is dominated by a throne backed with scarlet hangings. The King's Great Bedchamber, with a bed topped with ostrich plumes and the King's Closet (where His Majesty's toilet has a velvet seat) should also not be missed.

William's wife, Mary II, had her own separate **Queen's Apartments**, which are accessible up the Queen's Staircase, decorated by William Kent. When Mary died in 1694 work on these rooms was incomplete; they were finished under George II's reign. The rooms are shown as they might have been when Queen Caroline used them for entertaining between 1716 and 1737. In comparison with the King's Apartments, those for the queen seem rather austere, although the Queen's Audience Chamber has a throne as imposing as that of the king's.

Also worth seeing are the **Georgian Rooms** used by George II and Queen Caroline on the court's last visit to the palace in 1737. The first rooms you come to were designed to accommodate George's second son, the Duke of Cumberland, whose bed is woefully tiny for its grand surroundings. In the **Cartoon Gallery**, the real Raphael

Cartoons (now in the **Victoria & Albert Museum**; p141) used to hang; nowadays you have to make do with late-17th-century copies.

Beyond the Cartoon Gallery are the Queen's Private Rooms: her drawing room and bedchamber, where she and the king would sleep if they wanted to be alone. Particularly interesting are the Queen's Bathroom, with its tub set on a floor cloth to soak up any spillage, and the Oratory, an attractive room which was looking rather bare at the time of writing as roof leaks had led to the removal of its exquisite 16th-century Persian carpet.

Once you're finished with the palace interior there are still the wonderful gardens to appreciate. Carriage rides for up to five people around the gardens are available; they cost £10 and last 20 minutes. Look out for the **Real Tennis Court**, dating from the 1620s and designed for real tennis, a rather different version of the game from that played today. In the restored 24-hectare Riverside Gardens, you'll find the **Great Vine**. Planted in 1768, it's still producing around 300kg of grapes per year; it's an old vine, no doubt about it, but not the world's oldest, as they say it is here. The **Lower Orangery** in the gardens houses Andrea Mantegna's nine *Triumphs of Caesar* paintings, bought by Charles I in 1629; the Banqueting House was designed for William III and painted by Antonio Verrio. Look out, too, for the iron screens designed by Jean Tijou.

No-one should leave Hampton Court without losing themselves in the famous 800m-long **maze**, which is made up of hornbeam and yew planted in 1690. The average visitor takes 20 minutes to reach the centre. Jerome K Jerome set a famous scene of his novel *Three Men In a Boat* here, where the protagonists get thoroughly lost despite dismissing it as incredibly simple and 'absurd to call it a maze'. The maze is included in entry, although those not visiting the palace can enter the maze for £3.50 (or £2.50 for children). Last admission is at 5.15pm in summer and 3.45pm in winter.

There are trains every half-hour from Waterloo direct to Hampton Court station (30 minutes), from where it's a three-minute walk to the palace entrance. The palace can also be reached from Westminster Pier in central London on one of three riverboats operated by **Westminster Passenger Services Association** (☎ 7930 2062; www.wpsa.co.uk) from April to September, with reduced sailings in October. This is a great trip if the weather is good, but be aware that it takes three hours. For details see p94.

Walking Tours

Walking Tours

London might well seem totally unsuited to walking at first glance. The city's vast traffic-choked thoroughfares and overcrowded shopping streets are something to endure rather than savour, and even the best-intentioned Londoner can get pretty pushy steaming impatiently through a crowd of gaping tourists. But the truth is that there's no better way to experience London life than on foot, and at weekends you'll be joining hundreds of Londoners who love nothing better than a stroll through the deserted City, along the artistic South Bank or around one of the massive manicured parks that the capital has in such abundance.

More and more pedestrian areas are being opened all the time, from Trafalgar Sq to the excellent towpaths of the Thames, making for no shortage of carefree areas in which to amble. In London, museums are largely free, so you can just pop your head in for a noncommittal glance if you don't feel like trawling through an entire collection. On foot, you'll be able to see the city up close and personal, and, most importantly, enjoy its many pubs with a well-earned drink at the end of each tour.

THE SOUTH BANK WALK

A stroll along the South Bank of the Thames is one of the most awe-inspiring in London. You'll not only pass many of the city's newer major attractions, including the London Eye and Tate Modern, but, gazing across the river to the northern bank's magnificent skyline, you'll also gain a real appreciation of how great this city really is.

Starting from the hyper-modern **Westminster tube station** 1, cross Westminster Bridge, which gives you spectacular views of the Houses of Parliament and Big Ben. **County Hall** 2 (p150) –

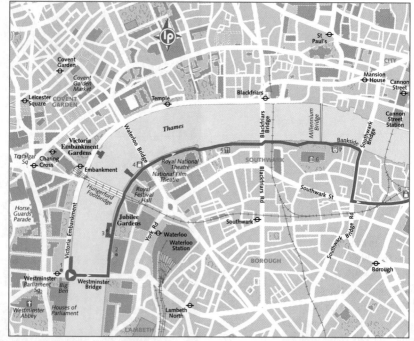

once the power base of the so-called 'loony left' Greater London Council (GLC) under the leadership of 'Red' Ken Livingstone – is the imposing 1922 building at the end of the bridge, now containing a hotel, the Saatchi Gallery (p150), London Aquarium (p150) and a small Salvador Dalí museum, Dalí Universe (p150). The GLC was finally dissolved by Margaret Thatcher after it dared disagree with her one too many times. However, while Lady Thatcher is rarely heard from these days, Ken Livingstone has gone on to take the ultimate prize, becoming mayor of London,

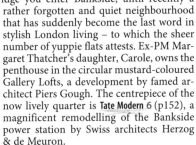

Walk Facts

Best time Any time
Start Westminster tube station
End Tower of London/St Katharine's Dock
Food en route Borough Market for a gourmet picnic
End-of-walk drink Tower Thistle Hotel
Distance 2 miles (3.2km)
Time Two hours

and you'll come across his new office later in this walk. The stretch of the embankment from Westminster Bridge to the **London Eye** 3 (p149) is always busy. If you plan to go up the Eye to enjoy the unbeatable view it offers, it's best to book. There are plans to build an artificial beach in the park next to the Eye in summertime, although this might not come off.

The Thames curves gracefully towards Waterloo here, and you'll walk past the newly refurbished Golden Jubilee Bridge (formerly the Hungerford Bridge), which is stunning at night when floodlit. Follow the Thames' path, and you'll see the **South Bank Centre** (p151) on your right, a large part of which will be under wraps until early 2007. The Royal Festival Hall will be closed during this period, although new shops have opened at its base. Further on, the complex houses the National Film Theatre (NFT; p301) and the National Theatre (p330), which has been a hot ticket lately. At weekends the Riverside **second-hand book market** 4 (p351) under Waterloo Bridge offers excellent bargains.

Continuing along the Thames you'll pass the redeveloped **Oxo Tower** 5 (p251). This handsome building hosts plenty of shops and art galleries, as well as the eponymous restaurant on the 8th floor. Past Blackfriars Bridge you enter Bankside, until recently a rather forgotten and quiet neighbourhood that has suddenly become the last word in stylish London living – to which the sheer number of yuppie flats attests. Ex-PM Margaret Thatcher's daughter, Carole, owns the penthouse in the circular mustard-coloured Gallery Lofts, a development by famed architect Piers Gough. The centrepiece of the now lively quarter is **Tate Modern** 6 (p152), a magnificent remodelling of the Bankside power station by Swiss architects Herzog & de Meuron.

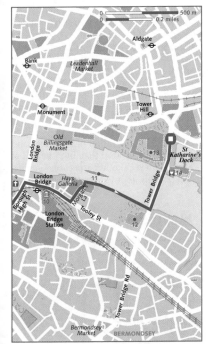

Take advantage of the free admission and wander through this incredible space – even if just to look into the enormous turbine hall. There are also a couple of places where you can enjoy breathtaking views over the river (an example is the coffee bar on the fourth floor).

In front of Tate Modern, the Millennium Bridge (p152), a fabulous Norman Foster creation, spans the Thames and affords magnificent views of St Paul's Cathedral on the other side of the river. However, stay on the south bank and continue east to **Shakespeare's Globe** 7 (p153), a replica of the London theatre that William Shakespeare co-owned. The original burned down during a performance of *Henry V* in 1613; the replica is definitely worth a visit. You can

:r through the fascinating exhibition that charts the history of the theatre, take a ed tour and – even better – watch a matinee performance.

From the theatre walk down Bankside to Southwark Bridge. Take Southwark Bridge Rd south to Southwark St and turn left towards the heart of Borough. This wonderful area has a village feel and a sense of community that are rare finds in London. Its centrepiece is the fantastic **Borough Market 8** (p350), where food has been sold since the 13th century. On Friday and Saturday the market is abuzz with shoppers checking out a fantastic range of gourmet stalls. This is a great place to pick up a picnic lunch, which you can enjoy in the lovely grounds of the **Southwark Cathedral 9** (p153) – walk up Borough High St towards the Thames and you'll see the cathedral to your left.

From London Bridge, briefly take Tooley St towards Bermondsey. However, just after you pass the **London Dungeon 10** (p173) head through Hay's Galleria back to the riverbank, where you will see the sky-scraping 30 St Mary Axe, or the Gherkin, across the river. You'll pass **HMS Belfast 11** (p173) and **City Hall 12** (p171), before coming to Tower Bridge (p121). You can even take a lift into the 'roof' of the bridge, for great views. Once north of the river, the truly hardy could tackle the **Tower of London 13** (p118), while most will prefer to have a drink at the **Tower Thistle Hotel 14**, or one of the other bars in nearby St Katharine's Dock.

THE SOHO WALK

Soho, the 'village' at the heart of London, appears seedy, grubby and chaotic at first glance. However, taking this walk provides an insight into the usually overlooked history that echoes down its crowded, littered pavements.

Starting at the transport and advertising hub of Piccadilly Circus (p97), walk up Sherwood St and look into the **Devonshire Arms 1** pub on the left; this unassuming place was a haunt of Soho's gangland leaders throughout the '50s and '60s. They would frequently meet in the upstairs room, where you can now enjoy a good pub lunch.

Turn right onto Brewer St and follow it towards Great Windmill St, passing lap-dancing clubs and 'bookshops'. Juxtaposed with them are nevertheless some great shops. **Arigato 2**, the unmarked Japanese supermarket (No 48–50), is a great place to pick up some interesting Japanese delicacies, while **Anything Left Handed 3** (No 57) and the **Vintage Magazine Store 4** (No 39–43) both sell a great range of potential presents.

Turn left up Lexington St and you'll arrive at the **John Snow 5** pub, named after the local doctor who isolated the water pump on Broadwick St as the source of the Soho cholera outbreak in 1854. There's a replica water pump on the site of the original at the intersection of Poland and Broadwick Sts, to commemorate the 5000 people who died before Snow made the vital connection. Turn right from Broadwick St into Berwick St, with its lively **market 6** (p351) and sense of real community (between the prostitutes and the drug addicts, some might cynically say).

Keep walking down Berwick St, where aside from the market stalls there are some excellent record shops. As you approach the end of Berwick St, the concentration of sex shops and sleaze suddenly reaches its peak in the appropriately named **Walker's Court** that links the end of Berwick St to Brewer St. Walk through Walker's Ct to absorb yet another aspect of Soho life, then make a quick right turn back onto Brewer St and possibly grab a snack from the superb Italian deli **Lina 7** (No 18). Walk back past Walker's Ct to the fabled nightspot **Madame Jo Jo's 8** (p305). This is one Soho institution that shows no sign of flagging – it's seamy, glamorous, fun and camp all at once, with cabaret and dancing every night.

At the end of Brewer St turn left up Wardour St, one of Soho's busiest arteries. You'll pass the famous rocker/punk/goth hang-out that is the Intrepid Fox. Turn right into Meard St, a gorgeous side street with original Huguenot town houses perfectly preserved and still inhabited today.

Walk Facts

Best time Weekend mornings, when Soho is at its most village-like
Start Piccadilly Circus tube station
End Cambridge Circus
Food en route Italian deli Lina
Drink en route Coach & Horses pub
Distance 1 mile (1.6km)
Time About one hour

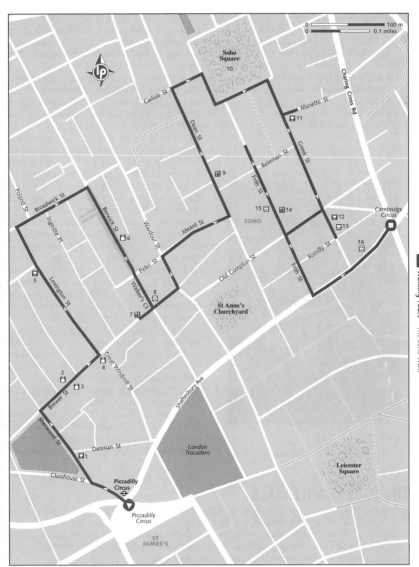

Walking Tours – The Soho Walk

At the end of Meard St turn left onto Dean St, former home of Karl Marx, who moved to No 28 in 1851. Marx lived above what is now the beautiful restaurant **Quo Vadis 9** (p233), and his name appears at the site in large letters on the wall. The interior has obviously improved since Marx's day. A Prussian agent visited the thinker, only to report back that 'Everything is broken, tattered and torn, finger-thick dust everywhere, and everything in the greatest disorder…it is dangerous to sit down.'

Follow Dean St as far as Carlisle St – turn right here and you'll walk into **Soho Square 10**, the graceful and charming green lung of Soho. On a summer's day, office workers in their hundreds crowd every available centimetre of the lawns to enjoy lunch, but the rest of the year it's usually far quieter and is a lovely place to sit and people watch.

Having walked through the gardens and seen the curious mock-Tudor 'house' at the centre (now the gardener's shed), walk out of the square down Greek St. This happening strip of bars and restaurants was once home to Casanova, and you can take a diversion through the archway on your left onto Manette St, where Francis Bacon's haunt, the **Pillars of Hercules** 11, on the corner of Manette, still packs them in.

Crossing over Old Compton St, the epicentre of London's sprawling gay scene, Greek St continues. **Maison Bertaux** 12 (p234) is a favourite among Soho bohos who love to drink tea all day long in this little cake house. Next door, the **Coach & Horses** 13 (p277) pub is where legendary *Spectator* columnist Jeffrey Barnard used to retire on his way to becoming 'unwell' (leading to the famous by-line and the play *Jeffrey Barnard Is Unwell*).

Double back and turn left into chilled-out Old Compton St, and try to guess which bars are gay. Even the straight bars in Soho are gay-friendly, so it's often a bit hard to tell. Turn right onto Frith St and you'll find post-clubbing institution **Bar Italia** 14 (p234), immortalised by Jarvis Cocker in the eponymous Pulp song and a place in which revellers have been enjoying cappuccinos for decades. Above Bar Italia, John Logie Baird changed the world as we know it by giving the first-ever demonstration of TV in 1926 in front of an audience of 50 scientists. Mozart lived next door (No 20), opposite the world-famous **Ronnie Scott's** 15 (No 47; p323). Every jazz great has performed here at some time since it was founded in 1959 by the unfortunately named Ronald Schatt, who came up with a suitable tweak to his name to make it sound just right. The essayist William Hazlitt lived and died at No 6 Frith St and is buried in St Anne's Churchyard on lower Wardour St, where a monument to him was restored in 2003.

To end the walk, stroll back down Frith St all the way to Shaftesbury Ave. Turn left up the avenue, past the wonderful cinema **Curzon Soho** 16 (p300) to Cambridge Circus.

Bar Italia (p234)

THE SQUARE MILE WALK

Whereas Soho is seedy and throbbing with life at the weekend, the financial district of the City is eerily quiet outside the hours of 9am to 5pm Monday to Friday. Yet, as the site of Londinium, the ancient Roman city, no part of the capital has such a long and continuous history as the so-called Square Mile. Weekends are the best time to appreciate its wild juxtaposition of sci-fi skyscrapers and medieval churches.

Starting from St Paul's tube station, you'll find one of the city's most recognisable landmarks, Sir Christopher Wren's **St Paul's Cathedral** 1 (p110). From the cathedral entrance, follow St Paul's Churchyard onto Cannon St. On arrival at Mansion House tube station, take Queen Victoria St until you reach the **Temple of Mithras** 2 on your right. These remains of an ancient Roman temple, dating from AD 240 and devoted to the Persian god Mithras, look almost comical, situated on this busy street in front of a Japanese banking corporation's anonymous-looking headquarters. Yet this is the very essence of the City in all its glorious incongruity.

Continuing up Queen Victoria St you reach the heart (if not the soul) of the Square Mile – the imposing buildings of the **Bank of England** 3, Royal Exchange and Mansion House. Stop here and admire the last, the official residence of the Lord Mayor of London, which distinguishes itself as the only private residence in the country to have its own law courts

Walk Facts

Best time Any time at the weekend
Start St Paul's tube station
End Whitechapel tube station
Food en route Snacks at one of the Spitalfields Market stalls
End-of-walk drink Blind Beggar Pub
Distance 3 miles (4.8km)
Time Two hours

and prison cells. It is also the scene of the Chancellor of the Exchequer's annual address to the great and the good of the City. The Bank of England has a fascinating museum (p114), while there's the **Grand Café & Bar 4** (p239) within the Royal Exchange.

Leaving Bank, as this traffic-packed confluence of streets has been dubbed due to the tube station it masks below ground, walk down genteel King William St until you reach Monument tube station. Cross over to the other side of the road and walk down until you reach the **Monument 5** (p115). Christopher Wren and Robert Hooke erected this commemorative Doric column between 1671 and 1677 to mark the 1666 Great Fire. Although it dominated the skyline of the city in the late 17th century, at 66m it's now dwarfed by surrounding buildings.

As you walk north from the Monument up Gracechurch St, a small detour down Leadenhall St will allow you to wander the fascinating **Leadenhall Market 6** (p114), built in the 14th century and now covered by a beautifully painted arcade. This was Diagon Alley in the film *Harry Potter and the Philosopher's Stone*, and has clothes stores and curio shops, a fishmonger, a butcher and a cheesemonger. Further along you can ogle the striking **Lloyd's of London 7** (p114) building on Lime St, designed by Richard Rogers.

Double back along Leadenhall St and turn right into Bishopsgate, the old Roman road that leads all the way to York. Pass the city's transport hub, Liverpool St station, and then turn right into Folgate St, which is lined with fine Georgian houses. It was in this area that Huguenots settled in the late 17th century, bringing with them their skills as silk weavers. Street names such as Fleur-de-Lis St and Nantes Passage recall their presence.

At 18 Folgate St is **Dennis Severs' House 8** (p122), named after the late American eccentric who restored it to its 18th-century splendour.

Turn right (south) along Commercial St and you'll see hip **Spitalfields Market 9** (p351) on the right, part of which has been snatched from the hands of redevelopers. On Sundays, one of London's more interesting markets takes place in the area.

On Commercial St, virtually opposite the market, you can't miss the arresting façade of **Christ Church, Spitalfields 10** (p123). A magnificent English-Baroque structure, it was designed by Sir Christopher Wren's acolyte Nicholas Hawksmoor and completed in 1714 for the Huguenot weavers who lived in the area. The fact that it is sited over a former Roman

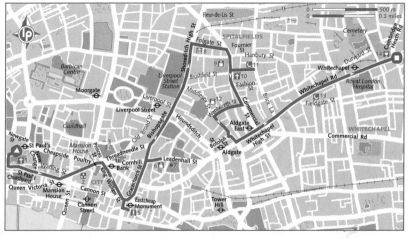

cemetery, the alleged sexual symbolism of its windows (they're long and narrow, and point into small holes), and general devil-worship rumours about Hawksmoor and several of his other churches have all led to Christ Church enjoying something of a Satanic reputation. The fact that it was hit by lightning in 1841 was only grist to the mill.

Anyhow, leaving interesting but ultimately kooky theories behind, turn down Fournier St, to the left of Christ Church, and check out the beautifully restored Georgian houses with their wooden shutters. Most were built between 1718 and 1728 for wealthy London merchants, and were later taken over by the silk weavers and their families.

At the Brick Lane end of Fournier St is the **Great Mosque** 11 of the Bengali community. Before it became a mosque in 1975 it was a synagogue for Jewish refugees from Russia and central Europe. Before 1899, when it became a synagogue, it was the New French Church, built for the Huguenots in 1743.

Retrace your steps back to Commercial St and possibly pause for a drink in the Ten Bells, a lovely old pub with a hip clientele and a 'no Jack the Ripper tours' policy. After this, wander past Christ Church down the ramshackle rows of clothing bulk-buy outlets and fabric shops to Wentworth St. This will take you to Middlesex St, where **Petticoat Lane Market** 12 (p351) operates on Friday and Sunday. Unlike the swish organic food stalls of Spitalfields Market, Petticoat Lane is a true East End tradition of cheap knock-off fashions, beauty products and leather goods.

The back of the market leads you into Aldgate, the site of the old eastern gate to London. Walk down Aldgate to Whitechapel High St – you have now entered Jack the Ripper territory. The 19th-century serial killer's identity remains a mystery and is still the subject of speculation; what is certain is that in 1888 he butchered five prostitutes in the wretched backstreets of the Victorian East End: Mary Anne Nichols died in Bucks Row (now Durward St), north of Whitechapel tube station; Annie Chapman in Hanbury St, near the Ten Bells (hence the pub's policy), Spitalfields; Elizabeth Stride in Berner St (now Henriques St), west of Commercial Rd; Catherine Eddowes in Mitre Sq, near Aldgate; and Mary Kelly in Miller's Ct (now a car park). For information about organised tours of the murder sites, see p95.

Travel along Whitechapel High St, which becomes Whitechapel Rd, and turn right onto Fieldgate St, where you'll find some good Pakistani restaurants and the Fieldgate Great Synagogue, now part of the modern **Whitechapel Mosque** 13. Alternatively, continue east on Whitechapel Rd to the junction with Cambridge Heath Rd and you'll see the **Blind Beggar Pub** 14 (p175) at No 337, notorious as the place where Ronnie Kray shot George Cornell in 1966 in a gang war over control of the East End's organised crime. Whitechapel tube is a short distance west of the pub.

THE HIGHGATE & HAMPSTEAD WALK

One of the loveliest areas of London, the hilly, leafy villages of Highgate and Hampstead (p194) have long enchanted visitors, as well as being home to the city's moneyed intellectuals. This walking tour begins in Highgate, with a visit to the world-famous cemetery, and takes you across glorious Hampstead Heath to old Hampstead village.

Starting from Archway tube station, walk northwest up Highgate Hill. This was the spot where, according to legend, Dick Whittington heard Bow Bells (the church bells of St Mary-le-Bow, in the East End) ringing out 'turn again, Whittington, Lord Mayor of London', and dutifully he did, going on to fulfil his destiny as Lord Mayor four times. While obviously untrue – being able to hear Bow Bells on Highgate Hill would have been some achievement, not to mention rendering the posh residents cockneys – it's a nice story, and there's the **Whittington Stone** 1 to mark the 'event'.

Continuing up Highgate Hill, turn left into Dartmouth Park immediately after you pass the distinctive **St Joseph's Church** 2

Walk Facts

Best time Any day during the summer months
Start Archway tube station
End Hampstead tube station
Food en route A posh café or restaurant on Hampstead High St
End-of-walk drink The Hollybush pub
Distance 3 miles (4.8km)
Time Three hours

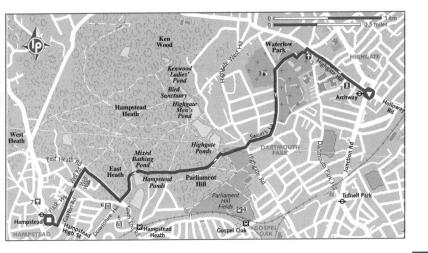

on your left. The entrance to the lovely Waterlow Park is then a little way down the road on the right. Waterlow Park is a beautiful, uncrowded spot to wander, with lovely ponds and hills. It was donated to London at the end of the 19th century by Sir Sydney Waterlow and takes you out onto bucolic Swain's Lane. It's hard to believe you are still in London here, and that was obviously the intention behind the building of Holly Village, a private residential enclave erected in 1865. It's off Swain's Lane to your left after Highgate Cemetery.

Walk left down Swain's Lane and you will come to Highgate's most famous spot, its **cemetery 3** (p195). The western section can be visited only on a guided tour (such are its complexities); however, you are free to stroll at leisure in the eastern section. Most famous of all the greats buried here is Karl Marx, and the cemetery was something of a pilgrimage spot for communists during the 20th century. Nowadays, diplomats from the few surviving communist governments in the world are the only people who seem to bring flowers. If you have time to join the tour of the western cemetery, it's definitely the more interesting of the two, being far more atmospheric and magical with its catacombs and maze-like pathways adorned with elaborate family crypts.

Follow the pretty curve of Swain's Lane down to the right, and it will lead you straight to Hampstead Heath (p194) and onto Parliament Hill, with its glorious views over the centre of London. Hampstead Heath offers almost endless leisure activities – you can swim at numerous refreshing ponds or the always chilly **Parliament Hill Lido 4** (p311), play football or tennis, ride bikes, rollerblade or just drink in the scenery.

But as you're already doing plenty of exercise on this walk, you might want to just head to **Keats House 5** (p195). Make your way across Parliament Hill and down towards Hampstead Ponds, then leave the heath at South End Rd and walk down to Keats Grove to see the house – this is where the poet lived for two years until 1820. From Keats House, take South End Rd back towards the heath and wander up East Heath Rd.

Lovers of modernism may be interested in the unique building at **No 2 Willow Road 6** (p196), which is on the left as you walk up, just off Downshire Hill. The international modernist building style was pioneered by Ernö Goldfinger, and this fascinating example is now maintained by the National Trust.

Carrying on up East Heath Rd, wander the incredibly village-like side streets of Well Rd and Well Walk, where beautiful little ivy-clad cottages vie with one another to be the most attractive. Walking down Well Walk will take you through Gayton Rd to Hampstead High St. This is the centre of Hampstead village and a great place to stop for a spot of lunch and a well-earned drink. You'll do well to try one of Hampstead's best-loved taverns, the **Hollybush 7** (p289) on Holly Mount.

223

THE WORLD IN LONDON WALK

If you want to get under the skin of multicultural London, into an area less visited by mainstream visitors, this walk will take you from the Bengali community in Shoreditch to the West African hub of Dalston to the Turkish diaspora in Stoke Newington. It's a fairly long hike, but a good stretch of it can be done by bus if you get tired.

Starting at Aldgate East tube station, make your way left onto Osborn St from Whitechapel High St and follow the road up as it becomes Brick Lane. In 1550 this was just a country road leading to brickyards, and by the 18th century it had been paved and lined with houses and cottages inhabited by the Spitalfields weavers. Today this vibrant street is taken up almost entirely by touristy curry houses, with greeters trying to lure you in. (Standards are no longer high, and you really need to know where to go.) During festivals the street is beautifully lit and festooned with decorations. There are plenty of shops along the way, selling a huge range of fabrics and clothing, as well as knick-knacks and other Bengali exotica. All the street names are in Bengali as well as English (along with Chinatown and Southall, this is one of the few truly bilingual areas of London).

Halfway up you'll pass the **Vibe Bar** 1 (p283) and the **Truman Brewery** 2. The Truman was the biggest brewery in London by the mid-18th century, and the Director's House standing to the left dates from 1740. The old **Vat House** 3, which dates from the turn of the 19th century and has a hexagonal bell tower, is across the road. Next to it stands the 1830 Engineer's House and a row of former stables. The brewery shut down in 1989, and the Truman today is an arts centre that showcases the work of up-and-coming young artists from all media.

If you detour left near the brewery along Dray Walk, you'll find some interesting shops, and along Brick Lane you'll pass more. Also look right at Cheshire St. There's a **flea market** 4 (p351) on Sunday at Brick Lane around Shoreditch tube station, where some good bargains can be had, particularly for furniture.

At the far end of Brick Lane, some of the original Jewish families who settled the neighbourhood continue to dwell, and there are a couple of excellent bagel outlets, including **Brick Lane Beigel Bake** 5 (p244), which operates 24 hours a day and is usually busy with Shoreditch clubbers throughout the night.

From Brick Lane, if it's a Sunday, cross Bethnal Green Rd and go up Swanfield St until you get to Columbia Rd, scene of London's most colourful **market** 6 (p351). Here,

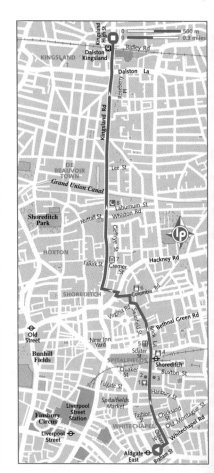

Brick Lane (p122)

every Sunday from dawn, market stalls selling freshly cut flowers, plants and orchids feed flora-starved Londoners who come in droves. Arrive early to see the market in all its glory, and, if you aren't too hung over from Saturday night, make a beeline for the food stalls behind the main flower sellers. Here you can enjoy fried king prawns and sweet chilli sauce as an exotic London breakfast.

Make your way east down Columbia Rd until you reach Hackney Rd; cross over and follow your way to Kingsland Rd. This now achingly cool strip boasts a big range of bars, clubs and cafés. The planned new Hoxton tube station and endless series of warehouse conversions make it pretty certain that property prices here will continue to soar.

The **Geffrye Museum** 7 (p123), on the right as you walk up the road, is an imposing inlet of Victorian almshouses, which now hosts a fascinating museum devoted to English furniture through the ages.

After the Geffrye Museum you can either walk the stretch of road up to Dalston or take the bus (all buses on the side of the road opposite the museum stop in Dalston). The walk to Dalston takes about 15 minutes and includes the impressive **Sulemaniye Mosque** 8 at 212–216 Kingsland Rd and the Grand Union Canal that flows under the road as you head north.

Dalston, hardly an impressive sight at first, starts with a slew of fried-chicken takeaways. However, as you approach Dalston Junction you suddenly begin to wonder what country you are in. The chaos, brilliant colour and animation of the African community here are all-encompassing. The traffic is always chaos, Ridley Rd Market (p351) is always chaos, Dalston is always chaos – it's unlike any other part of London. Kingsland Rd sweeps on up to Stoke Newington, where the African community is replaced gradually by the enormous Turkish diaspora that has established itself across northeast London from Haringey to Islington.

We recommend you stop here, but should you still have some life in your legs, carry on to atmospheric, rambling Abney Park Cemetery (p197), whose residents don't have any life left at all. Reward yourself with a well-deserved pint at the Birdcage (p290) in Stamford Hill.

THE RIVERSIDE & RICHMOND WALK

Looking to get out of the city, but don't want to go too far? This walk is a quick introduction to the leafy delights of Richmond. It's best started at Richmond tube station, but if you've got plenty of time you could reach Richmond by taking the river taxi from Waterloo, which will give you the chance to see some of the most picturesque parts of Old Father Thames. However you arrive, first make your way to the green. From the tube, take the Quadrant left from the station exit and follow it until the junction with Eton St, where you turn right towards the green.

Walking across the diagonal of **Richmond Green** 1 with its lovely houses and crowds of families playing ball games, it's surprisingly easy to imagine it as the site of jousting contests throughout the Middle Ages, watched by the king and the royal family. The path across the green takes you to the site of **Richmond Palace** 2, a royal residence since the 12th century and where Queen Elizabeth I spent her last years. Little of the palace remains today, save its fine Tudor gates, bearing the arms of Henry VII, who built the Tudor extensions to the old Norman Palace. You can look through the gates, but don't try to enter, as the site is now a very private housing development.

Taking Old Palace Lane, the sleepy side street that links the green to the Thames towpath, you can see some fine mansions on the site of Richmond Palace. The **White Swan pub** 3 (p296) makes for a great pit stop in hot weather and serves good food. The path ends at the Thames – and the riverfront is always bustling with couples, boat touts and bemused local dog-walkers. This is one of the loveliest stretches of the Thames, with the pretty greenery of **Corporation Island** 4 and the bizarre colonisation of the trees by colourful parakeets.

Ahead, **Richmond Bridge 5** is London's oldest river crossing still in use, dating from 1777, and gracefully curves over the Thames towards Twickenham and St Margaret's. The Richmond ice rink was demolished on the Twickenham side of the river a few years ago, and now it plays host to an enormous property development for yet more of Richmond's wealthy. It's rather an eyesore on an otherwise lovely patch of river.

Walk on down the lovely towpath, past the various pubs, restaurants and hotels that line the river on the way to Petersham

Walk Facts

Best time Any time
Start Richmond tube station
End Richmond town centre
Food en route Traditional pub lunch at the Dysart
End-of-walk drink Old Ship pub
Distance 4 miles (6.4km)
Time About three hours

and Ham. As the path swings right, take the dark redwood gate that takes you off the main strolling route, and down across **Petersham Meadow 6**. This lovely path leads through a cow field and on down a narrow pathway towards Richmond Park. Stop on your left before the end of the road to admire the unique **St Peter's Church 7**, a Saxon place of worship since the 8th century, which nowadays features an unusually laid out Georgian interior, complete with

boxed pews. (Unfortunately, the church is only open to visitors on Sunday afternoons, but even if its main door is shut, you can still stroll in the fascinating graveyard, which includes the tombstone of Captain George Vancouver.)

Church Lane, as the footpath has become, takes you out onto Petersham Rd, where the **Dysart pub** 8 (p296) to your left makes an agreeable refreshment point or pub-lunch place. Slightly up the road from the Dysart is the Petersham entrance to Richmond Park, and it's a great place to begin a walk through this most sumptuous of London's green spaces. Walk up the steep hill for a great view to the west, and then continue to the enclosure around **Pembroke Lodge** 9. The gardens here are lovely to walk through, and there are amazing, unbroken views to the centre of London to be had.

Carry on out of Pembroke Lodge and its vast gardens, and you'll find yourself out in the wilds of Richmond Park, completely surrounded by a sea of unbroken green. There is no set route you should follow, as exploration is part of the joy here, but those who want to see the herds of wild red deer that breed so successfully here should head to the long grass and keep back from the roads that unfortunately dissect the parkland.

Another highlight is the Isabella Plantation. There are sporadic signposts to help you get there, but it's best just to rely on a map and general sense of direction. The plantation is a haven of formalised gardening in the otherwise completely wild park, and its fine layout includes duck ponds and enormous forests of azaleas and rhododendrons.

Coming out the other side of the plantation, try to follow your way round to the left and you'll find some heavily wooded areas – Prince Charles' Spinney and Spanker's Wood – that lead up to **Pen Ponds** 10, the lovely showpiece of the park at its geographical centre. You can wander through Duchess' Wood to the **Deer Pen** 11 to see red deer in captivity, if you haven't seen them in the wild, before continuing northwest up to Richmond Gate.

This lovely walk through the highlights of Richmond Park brings you out at the top of marvellous **Richmond Hill** 12. Local residents crowd the pubs and small park areas that give views over the curve of the Thames, Hampton Court Palace and Ham in the valley below. Richmond Hill's charming antiques shops, traditional pubs and fashionable clothes shops will ease you back into London after a good stroll through the 'countryside', and once you reach the bottom you'll have the choice of Richmond's many pubs and cafés to tempt you. We recommend the **Old Ship** 13 (p296) on King St.

THE HYDE PARK WALK

Escape from the urban jungle and meander through this renowned Royal Park – one of the so-called lungs of the city. With plenty of opportunities to stop to smell the roses or to take a nap under a tree, this relaxing walk is ideal for less athletic readers of all ages. However, it's particularly suitable if you have primary school–aged children in tow. If they get tired, there are several junctures where you could break off proceedings midway.

Start at **Wellington Arch** 1 (p132), perhaps paying to ascend to the balcony and enjoy great views. In the same small square of green, you will also find the rather tasteful **Australian War Memorial** 2, a wall of eucalypt-green granite, inaugurated in 2003.

From here, cross to Hyde Park through the Ionic columns of the **Decimus Burton Screen** 3, the original grand entrance to the park, and head to the nearest information board. To your right you'll spy the ornate – some say too ornate – **Queen Elizabeth Gate** 4, commissioned from sculptors Giuseppe Lund and David Wynne to honour the late Queen Mother in 1993. To your left lies the wonderfully named Rotten Row, built in 1690 to link the palaces of Westminster and Kensington and the first lamp-lit road in the UK.

Start walking along Rotten Row, but veer right, or north, soon afterwards, heading through the relaxing **Rose Garden** 5. Just on

Walk Facts

Best time A summer weekday, when most people are at work
Start Hyde Park Cnr tube
End Lancaster Gate tube
Food en route Coffee and cake at the Lido café
End-of-walk drink The Swan or the Island Restaurant & Bar
Distance 2.5 miles (4km)
Time About 1½ hours

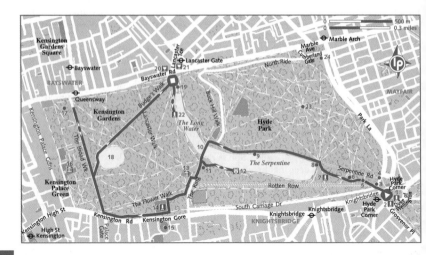

the other side of the garden is a remarkable **tree** 6 whose branches have grown outwards and downwards, forming a natural tent of foliage. Kids love the hide-and-seek atmosphere of stepping inside, but you're not supposed to climb on any of the trees in Hyde Park.

Passing the **Holocaust Memorial** 7, keep going to the **Dell Restaurant** 8, not for refreshment but to take in the view along the Serpentine Lake from the restaurant's deck. Bear right, following the lake's northern bank, just in case you should want to interrupt your walk by renting a paddle boat from the **Serpentine Boathouse** (9; 10am-4pm Feb & Mar, 10am-6pm Apr-Jun, 10am-7pm Jul & Aug, 10am-5pm Sep & Oct, 10am-5pm Sat & Sun Nov) and taking a quick spin on the water. Take care to avoid the swans; they're the property of the Queen!

Otherwise, keep going until you reach the **Serpent Bridge** 10 and cross over onto the south bank to the **Princess Diana Memorial Fountain** 11 (p145). Despite early teething problems, this concrete 'ring' of water sitting on perfectly manicured lawn is a popular chill-out spot today. Water flows from the highest point in both directions, into a small pool at the bottom. Bathing is forbidden, although you are allowed to dip your feet.

Just east of the fountain lies the **Lido Café** (12; 9am-7.30pm Apr-Oct, 9am-4pm Nov-Mar). Near here every Christmas Day, members of the Serpentine Swimming Club jump into the freezing water (sometimes having to break the ice beforehand to do so) in the annual 'Peter Pan Christmas Day Race'. The race has been held since 1864, with author JM Barrie, creator of Peter Pan, donating the first trophy some years later.

Now head back towards the bridge and cross the road to the **Serpentine Gallery** 13 (p144). This former teahouse is now one of the city's best contemporary art galleries, and the space is small enough to get around before any kids accompanying you get bored.

The opulent **Albert Memorial** 14 (p145) is southwest of the gallery, across grass and through trees. The circular building you can see across the road from here is the **Royal Albert Hall** 15 (p145), another memorial to Queen Victoria's beloved husband.

Strictly speaking, you've already crossed the boundary from Hyde Park into Kensington Gardens, and if you continue westwards to the Broad Walk, and turn north, you'll soon see **Kensington Palace** 16 (p143) to your left.

If you do have young children with you, you won't want to skip a trip further north to the **Diana, Princess of Wales Memorial Playground** 17. If you're all adults, head northeast from the **Round Pond** 18 to the **Italian Garden and Fountains** 19.

There's plenty more to see in the park, if you have time, stamina and the strength of will to resist merely having a snooze on the grass or stopping in at the **Swan** (20; 7262 5204; 66 Bayswater Rd W2; 10am-11pm) or the **Island Restaurant & Bar** (21; 7551 6070; Lancaster Tce W2; noon-11pm). Other well-known features include the **Peter Pan Statue** 22, the **Reformer's Tree** 23 and, of course, **Speaker's Corner** 24.

Eating

Eating

'The best place in the world to eat right now' – that was the verdict of respected US *Gourmet* magazine on London in 2005. However, bear in mind that its journalists were eating on expense accounts. Just two months later one of the city's most respected food critics, the *Evening Standard*'s Fay Maschler, was decrying how overhyped and overpriced some of London's top restaurants had become.

Without doubt the leading chefs in London have broken through some earthly flavour barrier, conjuring up heavenly tastes that explode on your tongue and leave your tastebuds tingling. With the likes of Gordon Ramsay, Alan Yau, David Thompson and Tom Aikens overseeing the kitchens, this city really is *the* place to treat yourself to an unforgettable meal.

However, while all British food has improved immeasurably over the past decade (see p16), everyday dining is still – if we're perfectly honest – a trifle patchy. Eating out at random without a guidebook or reading reviews could result in a few expensive disappointments – especially with minor-league chefs sometimes getting out of their depth with experimentation. As Maschler so scathingly put it in her article, serving something as 'inventive' as Big Mac ice cream does not make you Heston Blumenthal (for more on Blumenthal, see p17).

With that in mind, this chapter steers you towards the best restaurants and cafés, distinguished by their location, unique features, original settings, value for money and, of course, outstanding grub.

Tipping

Most restaurants now automatically tack a 'recommended' 12.5% service charge onto the bill. If they *still* cheekily leave space for a tip on the credit-card slip, remember you're perfectly free to ignore that. If you want know whether the servers are benefiting from this charge, just ask. It's perfectly possible to scratch the charge from the bill and tip the server directly.

Hours & Meal Times

Londoners follow fairly loose fuelling schedules, although, in contrast to people in Continental Europe, they like to eat their evening meal early, generally between 7pm and 9.30pm. Most places serve lunch between noon and 2.30pm (or 3pm in more informal restaurants), and dinner from 7pm to 10pm, although many midrange restaurants stay open throughout the day. Hours can change from place to place – for example, many restaurants in Soho close on Sunday, and those in the City close for the whole weekend – and we've noted with each venue where places stray from the standard. However, if you're going out of your way, it's always safest to call first and check.

Booking Tables

Making reservations has become just about compulsory for all central restaurants in London from Thursday to Saturday, and for the hippest places at any time. A good Internet booking service is www.toptable.co.uk, which is reliable and often offers substantial discounts. Many of the high-end restaurants – the ones that cost the most and where you'd most like to linger – run the exceedingly annoying system of multiple sittings, where you have the option of an early or late slot, for example 7pm to 9pm or 9pm to 11pm. It's probably best to go for the later window and not be rushed.

Top Five Food Markets

Details of these markets can be found on p350-1.
- Berwick Street
- Borough
- Brixton
- Ridley Road
- Smithfield

Farmers Markets

For fresh fruit, vegetables, dairy, meat, bread and other foodstuffs that taste the way they did when you were a kid (ie with flavour), head to one of the growing number of weekend farmers markets that have been springing up around London. Here producers sell their own wares, the atmosphere is sociable and the plumpest, crispiest produce is guaranteed. You can check out all the markets online at www.lfm.org.uk; these are some of the best and most central.

Blackheath (station car park; ☉ 10am-2pm Sun; rail Blackheath)

Islington (Map pp442–3; Essex Rd, opposite Islington Green; ☉ 10am-2pm Sun; ⊖ Angel) The original market, Islington sells organic produce.

Marylebone (Map pp448–9; Cramer St car park; ☉ 10am-2pm Sun; ⊖ Baker St/Bond St)

Notting Hill (Map pp444–5; Kensington Pl, car park behind Waterstone's; ☉ 9am-1pm Sat; ⊖ Notting Hill Gate)

Palmer's Green (station car park; ☉ 10am-2pm Sun; rail Palmer's Green)

Peckham (Peckham Sq, Peckham High St; ☉ 9.30am-1.30pm Sun; rail Peckham Rye)

Pimlico Road (Map pp460–1; Orange Sq, cnr Pimlico Rd & Ebury St; ☉ 9am-1pm Sat; ⊖ Sloane Sq)

Swiss Cottage (Map pp438–9; next to Camden Library; ☉ 10am-4pm Wed; ⊖ Finchley Rd)

Wimbledon (Havana Rd; ☉ 9am-1pm Sat; ⊖ Wimbledon Park)

Smoking

Most restaurants – at least midrange and upwards – provide no-smoking areas, but you won't always have that luxury, and smokers at the next table won't hesitate in sparking up even if you're halfway through your main. More and more venues are turning smoke-free, especially since mooted legislation is likely to force the issue over the next few years. If you're a heavy nonsmoker, make sure to say so when you book.

How Much?

Perhaps the most compelling reason for scouring this chapter and choosing your restaurant carefully is that dining out here is outlandishly expensive compared with the US, Australia and most of Europe. And if you don't earn sterling, chances are that you'll rarely get what you consider value for money. Go to a top restaurant, have a martini at the bar, order three courses à la carte and wash it down with a decent European red, and two of you will be lucky to get change out of £250. Then again, you can have an excellent meal for half that if you arrive at times when you can opt for a set meal, or avoid the restaurants *du jour*. If you choose carefully it is possible to have a meal that you both remember fondly for £40 (without drinks). The West End and west-central London are the most expensive places to eat.

Self-Catering

Along with Londoners' new-found passion for dining out comes a greater appreciation for food in general, and if you're keen to self-cater you'll find lots of great little farmers markets (see above), continental delis, and ethnic and organic stores dotted all over town.

Vegetarian Dining ✳

London has long been one of the best places for vegetarians to dine. That's firstly due to its many Indian restaurants, which always cater for people who don't eat meat for religious reasons. Several health scares over British beef, and many celebrity vegetarians, have also increased Britons' propensity to shun meat. For dedicated vegetarian joints, try **Food for Thought** (p237), the **Gate** (p267), **Manna** (p261), **Mildred's** (p233), the **Place Below** (p244), **Rasa** (p264), **Red Veg** (p238) and **Woodlands** (p260).

THE WEST END

Many of London's most eclectic, fashionable and, quite simply, best restaurants are dotted around the thrilling West End. As with most things in London, it pays to be in the know: while there's a huge concentration of mediocre places to eat along the main tourist drags, the best eating experiences are frequently tucked away on back streets and not at all obvious. New restaurants open here weekly, but if they're good you'll rarely be able to walk in off the street without a booking, so plan ahead whenever possible. You'll find everything here, from Hungarian to Jamaican and from sandwich counter to *haute cuisine*. Chinatown, as you might guess, is a great spot for inexpensive Chinese food, although some restaurants can be little more than tourist traps – choose with care.

SOHO

ANDREW EDMUNDS

Map p450   Modern European
☎ 7437 5708; 46 Lexington St W1; mains £7.95-15;
⊖ Oxford Circus/Piccadilly
This tiny place is exactly the sort of restaurant you should be able to find in Soho with no trouble, but unfortunately the real deal is extremely thin on the ground. Two floors of cramped, wood-panelled bohemia with a mouth-watering menu of French and European country cooking, it's a real favourite of those in the Soho know. Reservations are usually essential.

BACK TO BASICS Map pp448-9   Fish
☎ 7436 2181; www.backtobasics.uk.com; 2a Foley St W1; mains £12.95-14.95; ⊗ closed Sun; ⊖ Oxford Circus
There are other options on the menu, but fish is the focus at this superb corner restaurant, which you'll find cosy or cramped, loud or just lively depending on your mood. A dozen varieties of exceedingly fresh fish, and a dozen original, mouth-watering ways to cook them, are chalked up on a blackboard daily, meaning that unfortunately you won't always get our favourite of monkfish with spicy, garlicky prawn couscous.

CRITERION Map p450   French
☎ 7930 0488; 224 Piccadilly W1; mains £11-17;
⊗ closed Sun; ⊖ Piccadilly Circus
This beautiful Marco Pierre White restaurant is all chandeliers, mirrors, marble and sparkling mosaics – one breathless wag has compared it to the inside of a Fabergé egg – but its most spectacular feature is the modern French food, which ranges from the delicate mussel and saffron soup to a hefty and heavenly steak tartare. Unfortunately, it's one of those places where dinner is in shifts; arrive for the second sitting so you won't be so rushed. Vegetarians shouldn't arrive at all.

GAY HUSSAR Map p450   Hungarian
☎ 7437 0973; www.gayhussar.co.uk; 2 Greek St W1; mains £12-18; ⊖ Tottenham Court Rd
Elegant without being stuffy, the Gay Hussar takes you back to the Soho of the 1950s via Budapest, where dinner is served in a wood-panelled dining room with brocade and sepia prints on the walls, and a conspiratorial ambience. The menu is rich, authentic and meaty, and the portions are colossal. The 'Gypsy quick dish' of pork medallions, onions and green peppers is a standout.

LA TROUVAILLE Map p450   French
☎ 7287 8488; www.latrouvaille.co.uk; 12a Newburgh St W1; set dinner £24.50; ⊗ closed Sun; ⊖ Oxford Circus
Nowhere is quite as perfect for a romantic dinner as this Soho treat. Here you'll find a gorgeous, warm space perfect for candlelit canoodling, and an excellent menu of rich traditional French cuisine on this charming cobbled backstreet.

LINDSAY HOUSE Map p450   Irish
☎ 7439 0450; www.lindsayhouse.co.uk; 21 Romilly St W1; set lunch/dinner £25/48; ⊖ Leicester Sq
Richard Corrigan is the Irish chef and character behind this superb restaurant, where you'll be won over to 'new Irish cuisine' – no sniggering, it's something to behold. Dishes are simple and hearty but exquisitely executed (like poached ballotine of sea bass with pickled cabbage and oysters). The restaurant still has the atmosphere of the 18th-century residence

Top Five – the West End

- **Ivy** (p235)
- **J Sheekey** (p235)
- **Red Fort** (opposite)
- **Sketch** (p246)
- **Hakkasan** (p237)

Sketch restaurant (p246)

Eating – The West End

it occupies; you have to ring the bell to get in, and the décor comprises all natural materials and tones. Service is warm and sincere.

MASALA ZONE Map p450 *Indian*
☎ 7287 9966; 9 Marshall St W1; mains £6-11;
⊖ Oxford Circus

This spacious and tranquil light space in Soho gets mobbed for lunch but remains one of the best budget Indian choices in London. Thoroughly modern in design, the meals it serves up (centred on its famous thalis) remain authentic and give a taste of India from regional dishes to national staples. Service can shake when it's busy, and there can even be people queuing for a table, but these are minor gripes in an otherwise excellent establishment.

MILDRED'S Map p450 *Vegetarian*
☎ 7494 1634; www.mildreds.co.uk; 45 Lexington St W1; mains £6-8; ⊖ Tottenham Court Rd

This is central London's best veggie restaurant and is a treat for carnivores and herbivores alike. Although Mildred's moved to bigger premises a few years ago, lunchtimes are still heaving. Don't be shy about sharing tables or you'll miss out on excellent, inexpensive and hugely portioned wholesome veggie fare from salads and stir-fries to bean burgers and a memorable ale pie. Drinks include juices, coffees, beers and organic wines, and the staff are friendly and unruffled.

QUO VADIS Map p450 *Italian*
☎ 7437 9585; 26-29 Dean St W1; mains £14-32;
☾ closed Sun; ⊖ Tottenham Court Rd

Quo Vadis used to be a cosy arrangement between superchef Marco Pierre White and Britartist Damien Hirst. After a very public spat in 1999, Marco ridded the walls of Damien's art and replaced it with his own parodies. It has settled back into a very snazzy groove these days, exuding elegance and intimacy in its light and airy interior. Marco is only executive chef now, so he can't take all the credit for the excellent food (try the mushroom risotto or skate with capers). Service is warm and extremely well organised – an all-round winner.

RED FORT Map p450 *Indian*
☎ 7437 2525; www.redfort.co.uk; 77 Dean St; mains £12-20; ⊖ Tottenham Court Rd

The Red Fort has always been a trailblazing place, and back in the dark days of London cuisine in the 1980s this was one of the few places offering real Indian cooking in London. Today it's largely retained its reputation and remains an upmarket and glamorous Soho Indian restaurant, serving up delicious dishes including *Nizami kaliya* (kingfish in a spicy sauce with curry leaves) and *mahi tikka* (smoked dorado with fresh mint, garlic and green chilli).

Top Five Soho Cafés

Soho presents the nearest thing London has to a sophisticated café culture to match that of its Continental neighbours. The area has been synonymous with sipping, smoking and schmoozing since the Victorians established the first coffee houses here. Its café heyday came with the mod hang-outs of the '60s, but whatever your inclination or mood there are still plenty of places from which to choose. These five will get you started.

- **Bar Italia** (Map p450; ☎ 7437 4520; 22 Frith St W1; sandwiches £3.50-5; ⏰ 24hr; ❸ Leicester Sq/Tottenham Court Rd) Pop into this Soho favourite at any time of day or night – or in any state – and you'll see slumming celebrities lapping up reviving juices and hunky paninis amid cool 1950s décor. It's always packed and buzzing, but you can normally get a seat after 1am.
- **Maison Bertaux** (Map p450; ☎ 7437 6007; 28 Greek St W1; cakes about £3; ❸ Tottenham Court Rd) Bertaux has exquisite confections, unhurried service, a French bohemian vibe and 130 years of history on this spot.
- **Monmouth Coffee Company** (Map p452; ☎ 7836 5272; 27 Monmouth St WC2; ❸ Tottenham Court Rd/ Leicester Sq) Essentially a shop selling beans from just about every coffee-growing country in the world, characterful Monmouth also has a few wooden alcoves at the back where you can squeeze in, sit and savour the blends from Nicaragua and Guatemala to Kenya and Ethiopia (although you'd probably catapult through the window after all that). This place is the antithesis of the café chains in every way.
- **Pâtisserie Valerie** (Map p450; ☎ 7437 3466; 44 Old Compton St W1; sandwiches £3.50-5.95; ❸ Tottenham Court Rd/Leicester Sq)This sweet Soho institution was established in 1926, and has delicious, delicate pastries, stylish sandwiches, filled croissants and a strict no-mobile-phones policy. There are four more branches around town, and you'll be lucky to get a seat at any of them.
- **Star Café** (Map p450; ☎ 7437 8778; 22 Great Chapel St W1; mains £5-8; ❸ Tottenham Court Rd) So Soho, this wonderfully atmospheric café has vintage advertising and continental décor that makes it feel like not much has changed since it opened in the 1930s. It's best known for brekky, particularly the curiously named Tim Mellor Special of smoked salmon and scrambled eggs. Cold roast lamb and new potatoes makes a terrific lunch as well, and the service is bright and friendly whatever the time of day.

VEERASWAMY Map p450   *Indian*

☎ 7734 1401; www.veeraswamy.com; 99 Regent St (entrance on Swallow St) W1; mains £8-20; ❸ Piccadilly Circus

This institution claims to be the UK's oldest Indian restaurant, having opened in 1927. It's under newish management now, but the standards are as high as ever and the kitchen knocks out some real winners, such as firm customer favourite mussels in ginger sauce and an excellent Malabar lobster curry with unripe mango.

YAUATCHA Map p450   *Dim Sum*

☎ 7494 8888; www.yauatcha.com; 15 Broadwick St W1; mains £3-15; ❸ Oxford Circus

Alan Yau, the restaurateur famous for Busaba Eathai, Wagamama and Hakkasan, has poured a staggering £4 million into creating this most glamorous of dim-sum restaurants and teahouses. It's not hard to see where the money has gone, though – the upstairs tea room offers an exquisite blue-bathed oasis of calm from the chaos of Berwick St Market (and the cakes on display are hypnotisingly beautiful), while the convivial dining space downstairs has a smarter, more atmospheric feel with

constellations of light-bulb stars in the ceiling and an exquisite and original dim-sum menu. Reservations are usually essential.

COVENT GARDEN & LEICESTER SQUARE

CALABASH Map p452   *African*

☎ 7836 1973; Africa Centre, 38 King St WC2; mains £5-8; ❸ Covent Garden

This easy and relaxed eatery in the Africa Centre pulls in flavours from all over the continent and has a descriptive menu to guide the uninitiated on a gastronomic tour from *egusi* (Nigerian meat stew) to *yassa* (Senegalese chicken).

CHINESE EXPERIENCE Map p450   *Chinese*

☎ 7437 0377; www.chineseexperience.com; 118 Shaftesbury Ave W1; mains £6-10; ❸ Leicester Sq

One of the new wave of Chinatown restaurants, this simple yet smart place presents a full range of Chinese cooking, from Cantonese to Peking to Sichuan. The staff are impeccably polite, and the prices are good value for the high standards. Definitely one of Chinatown's best.

CHRISTOPHER'S Map p452 *American*

☎ 7240 4222; www.christophersgrill.com; 18 Wellington St WC2; mains £12.50-25; ⊖ Covent Garden

Popular with the political classes when they aren't ensconced in Westminster, this sleek American restaurant is housed in a vast Georgian mansion. Its interior is suitably grand, with a busy downstairs bar and a stylish upstairs dining room, where classic but clever dishes such as blackened salmon with potato and cherry tomato salad and Maytag blue-cheese dressing are served up next to a wonderful range of lobster and steaks.

CHUEN CHENG KU Map p450 *Chinese*

☎ 7437 1398; 17 Wardour St W1; dim sum £2, mains £6-12; ⊖ Leicester Sq

This Chinatown champ is ideal for the uninitiated, as all the dishes – dumplings, noodles, paper-wrapped prawns – are trundled, sometimes raced, around on trolleys so you can just point out what you want (and then cross your fingers). The dim-sum starters are mostly moist and perky, while the main courses burst with flavour. There are lots of vegetarian options, even if 'crabmeat and tofu' doesn't quite fit the bill.

IVY Map p452 *Modern British*

☎ 7836 4751; 1 West St WC2; mains £10-25; ⊖ Leicester Sq

That the Ivy is famously the preferred restaurant of the great and the good seems incidental compared to its magnificent menu and wonderful buzzing atmosphere, at once intimate and exciting, at the heart of London's theatreland. Liveried doormen and a gaggle of paparazzi outside may intimidate you on the way in, but once you're inside you are treated to excellent service no matter who you are, and you may well find yourself sitting next to George Michael or Christian Slater. The fare consists of glorious versions of British staples such as shepherd's pie (doubtless the best in town, so probably the best in the world), steak tartare and kedgeree, and the desserts are superb (frozen berries with ice cream get our vote). Unfortunately, you do need to book months and months in advance.

J SHEEKEY Map p452 *Fish*

☎ 7240 2565; 28-32 St Martin's Ct WC2; mains £11-25; ⊖ Leicester Sq

A jewel of the local scene, this incredibly smart restaurant has four elegant, discreet and spacious wood-panelled rooms in which to savour the riches of the sea, cooked simply and exquisitely. The fish pie is justifiably legendary; fortuitously, it's the cheapest thing on a menu that can work out quite reasonably if you're restrained about side dishes, wine and extras but escalates alarmingly the moment you start to get carried away.

JOE ALLEN Map p452 *American*

☎ 7836 0651; www.joeallenrestaurant.com; 13 Exeter St WC2; mains £9-15.50; ⊖ Covent Garden

This late-night theatreland restaurant is packed every night of the week with West End actors and crew members for whom this cosy subterranean restaurant is a home from home. Its burgers (not on the menu) are famous and delicious, even though they look distinctly ungourmet. The menu is not cheap, but you are paying for atmosphere, the late opening hours and some great star-spotting opportunities.

MELA Map p452 *Indian*

☎ 7836 8635; www.melarestaurant.co.uk; 152-156 Shaftesbury Ave; mains £5-19; ⊖ Leicester Sq

No tourist trap despite its location, this bustling Shaftesbury Ave eatery remains one of our favourite West End spots for dinner. While it doesn't look particularly special from the outside, its warm and friendly atmosphere and fantastic Ayurvedic regional Indian menu (which offers a magnificent choice for vegetarians) makes it a real winner.

ORSO Map p452 *Italian*

☎ 7240 5269; www.orsorestaurant.com; 27 Wellington St WC2; mains £13-16; ⊖ Covent Garden

This refined, subterranean Italian eatery is especially popular with journalists by day (perhaps drawn by the free Bloody Mary with the set lunch) and tourists on their way to the theatre in the evening. The fare is typically excellent, and there's a superb wine list.

PORTRAIT Map p452 *British*

☎ 7312 2490; www.npg.org.uk; St Martin's Pl WC2; mains £11-19; ☺ restaurant 11.45am-2.45pm Sat-Wed, 11.45am-2.45pm & 5.30-8.30pm Thu & Fri, lounge & bar 10am-5pm Sat-Wed, 10am-10pm (last orders food 8pm) Thu & Fri ⊖ Charing Cross

This stunningly located restaurant above the excellent National Portrait Gallery is where Clive Owen made a thoroughly indecent proposal to Julia Roberts in *Closer*. It's better employed as a place for a decent meal after the gallery, though, or for a buzzing evening dinner (for which you should book). The views over Trafalgar Sq and Westminster are, unsurprisingly, wonderful. Unfortunately, Portrait is restricted in its opening times by the gallery, so it only serves dinner on Thursday and Friday.

RULES Map p452 *Traditional British*
☎ 7836 5314; 35 Maiden Lane WC2; mains £18-24; ⊖ Covent Garden

Established in 1798, this very posh and very British establishment is London's oldest restaurant and specialises in classic game cookery, serving up some 18,000 birds a year. Despite the history, it's not a museum piece and its sustained vitality attracts locals as well as the tourist masses.

HOLBORN & THE STRAND

HOMAGE Map p452 *Modern European*
☎ 7759 4080; www.homagegrandsalon.co.uk; Waldorf Hilton, Aldwych WC2; mains £8-19; ⊖ Holborn/Temple

After an impressive refit the Waldorf reopened in 2005 to some acclaim, featuring Homage as its main restaurant, so named in a nod to the great café societies of Paris and Vienna. Quite something to look at, housed in the former Waldorf Grill Room, Homage is a sumptuous neoclassical feast of a place, modernised by a black marble bar and some purposefully incongruous modern additions to the pillars. The food is of a very good standard, with well-sourced fresh ingredients oozing flavour and a varied and interesting modern European menu.

MATSURI Map p452 *Japanese*
☎ 7430 1970; www.matsuri-restaurant.com; Mid City Place, 71 High Holborn; set menus £22-45; ⊖ Holborn

The second venue for this high-quality, authentic Japanese restaurant on the fringe of the City can sometimes feel a little sterile, although the quality of the food is extremely high. With a sushi bar, upstairs dining room and large *teppanyaki* basement where the meals are prepared in all seriousness (no food throwing here) by Japanese chefs, there's plenty of choice.

SHANGHAI BLUES Map p452 *Chinese*
☎ 7404 1668; www.shanghaiblues.co.uk; 193-197 High Holborn WC1; mains £10-40; ⊖ Holborn

The former St Giles Library now houses its own slice of China in David Yiu's newest and most impressive venture to date. The dark and atmospheric interior recalls imperial Shanghai with modern twists, and the

menu is just as disarming, particularly its large and adventurous range of seafood dishes, its delightful desserts (try Red Bean and Quan Fa tea flavoured pudding…) and its vast tea selection.

SIMPSON'S-IN-THE-STRAND
Map p452 *Traditional British*
☎ 7836 9112; 100 Strand WC2; mains £15; ⊖ Covent Garden

If you have a craving for traditional English roasts and joints off the trolley (we're still talking about meat), head to this rather stuffy old stalwart, which has been dishing up fleshy fare in a fine panelled dining room since 1848. It's a gorgeous place, although something of a museum piece these days.

BLOOMSBURY & FITZROVIA

ABENO Map p452 *Japanese*
☎ 7405 3211; 47 Museum St WC1; mains £5-25; ⊖ Tottenham Court Rd

This understated little restaurant specialises in *okonomiyaki*, a kind of Japanese savoury pancake that is combined with the ingredients of your choice (there are over 20 varieties including anything from sliced meats and vegetables to egg, noodles and cheese) and cooked in front of you on the hotplate that makes up most of your table. It can get a little warm, and the staff can go a bit overboard with the sauces, but the food is tasty, making this an interesting and novel gastronomic diversion.

BAM-BOU Map p450 *Vietnamese*
☎ 7323 9130; www.bam-bou.co.uk; 1 Percy St W1; mains £10-16; ⊖ Goodge St/Tottenham Court Rd

This listed Georgian house attracts the media darlings from all over Fitzrovia with its winning colonial French–Vietnamese cuisine. It can feel a little cliquish, and some of the staff are less than welcoming, but the mostly modern Vietnamese fare (sesame prawns, pan-fried duck) is a winner.

Top Five Designer Eats

- Amaya (p247)
- Hakkasan (opposite)
- Les Trois Garçons (p241)
- Sketch (p246)
- Yauatcha (p234)

BUSABA EATHAI Map p450   *Thai*
☎ 7299 7900; 22 Store St WC1; mains £5-8;
🚇 Goodge St

We prefer the slightly less hectic Store St premises of this West End favourite, but there's also a **Wardour Street branch** (Map p450; 106-110 Wardour St; 🚇 Tottenham Court Rd). Here the sumptuous Thai menu greets you in an informal communal dining situation. This isn't the place to come for a long and intimate dinner, but it's a superb option for an excellent, speedy meal, although at peak times it can be a little mad. There's a private dining room downstairs for a more leisurely experience.

FINO Map p450   *Spanish*
☎ 7813 8010; www.finorestaurant.com; 33 Charlotte St (entrance on Rathbone St); tapas £3-18.50;
🚇 Tottenham Court Rd

Critically acclaimed (and it's easy to see why), Fino represents the resurgence of Spanish cuisine in a London all too dominated by dreary and uninventive tapas bars. Set in a glamorous basement on one of the city's premier eating strips, Fino is nevertheless relentlessly about the food. Try the superb baby leeks or the Jerusalem artichoke cooked with mint for a feast of innovative and delightful Spanish cooking.

HAKKASAN Map p450   *Chinese*
☎ 7907 1888; 8 Hanway Pl W1; mains £6-30; 🚇 Tottenham Court Rd

This basement restaurant – hidden down a lane like all the most fashionable haunts should be – combines celebrity status, stunning design, persuasive cocktails and surprisingly sophisticated Chinese food. Presentation and taste are both remarkable, and this was the first Chinese restaurant to get a Michelin star. The low, nightclub-style lighting makes it a good spot for dating (as Hugh Grant and Rachel Weisz did in *About A Boy*), while the long, glinty bar is a great cocktail space. As the main restaurant can take itself a bit too seriously, however, and the service can be somewhat snooty at dinner, the trick is to come for lunch in the more informal Ling Ling lounge.

HAN KANG Map p450   *Korean*
☎ 7637 1985; 16 Hanway St W1; mains average £12;
🚇 Tottenham Court Rd

You wouldn't expect to find a culinary gem on dodgy Hanway St, which wears its seediness on its sleeve, but Han Kang is the very thing. It's not much to look at – and nonsmokers might not be able to cope with the uninterrupted cloud left by Korean students – but the food here is a revelation, from *kimchi* (pickled, spicy cabbage) to *bulgogi* (literally 'fire meat', marinated slices of beef).

NORTH SEA FISH RESTAURANT
Map pp442-3   *Fish*
☎ 7387 5892; 7-8 Leigh St WC1; mains £8-17;
🚇 Russell Sq

This restaurant cooks fresh fish and potatoes, a simple ambition that it realises with aplomb. Look forward to jumbo-sized plaice or halibut steaks, deep-fried or grilled, and a huge serving of chips. The setting is characterless, but the charisma of the staff more than makes up for it.

RASA SAMUDRA Map p450   *Indian*
☎ 7637 0222; 5 Charlotte St W1; mains £8-13;
🚇 Goodge St

Behind Rasa Samudra's loud interior, this under-appreciated restaurant showcases the tantalising seafood cuisine of Kerala (in the southern tip of India), supported by a host of more familiar vegetarian staples. The fish soups are outstanding, the breads superb and the various curries heavily and heavenly spiced. The staff are cheeky and charming.

CHEAP EATS
FOOD FOR THOUGHT
Map p452   *Vegetarian*
☎ 7836 0239; 31 Neal St WC2; mains £3-6.50;
🚇 Covent Garden

This valued vegetarian joint is big on sociability and flavour, and small on price and space. Food ranges from soups and salads to stir-fries and stews. It's earthy, unpretentious and deservedly packed.

HAMBURGER UNION Map p452   *Fast Food*
☎ 7379 0412; www.hamburgerunion.com; 4/6 Garrick St; meals £4-8; 🚇 Leicester Sq

Highly recommended, Hamburger Union delivers gourmet, calorific fast-food favourites to you in two smart and perennially packed central London locations – there's a second branch at 25 Dean St (Map p450). Pay at the counter, and your food will be brought to your table where you can enjoy the sophisticated and fun atmosphere. All meat is additive free and free range, while vegetarians are guaranteed a minimum choice of two main meals each day.

IKKYU Map p452 — *Japanese*

☎ 7439 3554; 7-9 Newport Pl WC2; sushi £1.50-2.50, noodle dishes £5-8; ⊖ Leicester Sq

This Chinese-owned restaurant with Japanese cooks has à la carte sushi, sashimi and noodle dishes, but the great draws for budget travellers are the four different set lunches and the all-you-can-eat Japanese buffet from 5pm.

KULU KULU Map p450 — *Japanese*

☎ 7734 7316; 76 Brewer St W1; sushi £1.20-3; ⊖ Piccadilly Circus

Bare and bustling, this is the best inexpensive conveyor-belt sushi place in the city. There are no menus, and you just grab colour-coded plates of whatever takes your fancy before it rushes past on the carousel. Portions are petite, so it can quickly cease to be a cheap eat if you lose the run of yourself, but the spinach dish (which comes around way too rarely) and the aubergine are stunners.

LEON Map p450 — *Modern European Fast Food*

☎ 7437 5280; www.leonrestaurants.co.uk; 35 Great Marlborough St W1; mains £3-6; ⊖ Oxford Circus

A definite standout of Soho's cheap eats, Leon is delightful – cheap, friendly, delicious and perfectly located. Serving such treats as chicken with winter *salsa verde*, Moroccan meatballs and garlic mushrooms, Leon has about as much in common with fast food as McDonald's apple pie does with, erm, apple pie. Busy for lunch, it's a real find in the evening, when you're always guaranteed a seat. Final props: it's fully licensed and serves vodka smoothies.

MR JERK Map p450 — *Jamaican*

☎ 7287 2878; 189 Wardour St; mains £5-8; ⊖ Tottenham Court Rd

Favoured by many Soho office workers, this cramped but immensely characterful Wardour St canteen serves up delicious Jamaican dishes – focused on jerk chicken, as its name suggests. You'll fill up nicely and quickly here.

Oxo Tower Restaurant & Brasserie (251)

RED VEG Map p450 — *Vegetarian Fast Food*

☎ 7437 3109; 95 Dean St W1; mains £3-5; ⊖ Tottenham Court Rd

A brilliant concept that will hopefully spread across the city sometime soon (there's already a second branch in Brighton), Red Veg offers delicious veggie and vegan fast food – burgers, falafels, wraps, fries and organic soft drinks – from its tiny Soho premises. A winner, despite the tiny eating area.

TAI Map p450 — *Vegan/Chinese*

☎ 7287 3730; 10 Greek St W1; lunch/dinner buffet £5/6; ⊖ Tottenham Court Rd

This lifeline for vegans in Soho is also a great option for anyone who wants an interesting, healthy and exceptionally good value meal. From its little outlet just off Soho Sq, Tai has a huge all-you-can-eat buffet featuring noodles, fried tofu and a delicious selection of vegetable dishes that you can gorge yourself on throughout the day.

TOKYO DINER Map p452 — *Japanese*

☎ 7287 8777; 2 Newport Pl WC2; set menus £5.90-8.50; ⊖ Leicester Sq

Everyday Japanese food at everyday prices is what Tokyo Diner's all about, and you can't ask for fairer than that. The Japanese waiters are discreet and graceful in their service, and knowledgeable about the food. The miso is ordinary, but the Japanese-style curry is tops. All round this is a terrific place to pop in for a quick bowl of noodles or a plate of sushi.

Top Five Tables with a View

- Blueprint Café (p252)
- Oxo Tower Restaurant & Brasserie (p251)
- Portrait (p235)
- Ubon (p257)
- Vertigo 42 (p240)

EAST CENTRAL

The total explosion of east-central London as a fashionable counterweight to the West End has meant that it now plays host to some of the city's most exciting restaurants. Less than a decade ago culinary boundaries between the City, with its expense-account diners, and the hip Hoxton scene were clearly drawn. Now, the lines between 'establishment' and 'stylish' have started to blur, with Spitalfields and Shoreditch accommodating plenty of cool places where even stockbrokers want to be seen. Less scruffy Clerkenwell is another place where City prices are married with Shoreditch levels of cool. By comparison, Islington, once the capital's foodie hub, has definitely lost its '90s cachet as a home of innovation. That said, it's still got more than its fair share of great restaurants, and a walk down Upper St will rarely disappoint.

THE CITY

CAFÉ SPICE NAMASTE Map pp454-5 *Indian*
☎ 7488 9242; 16 Prescot St E1; mains £9.50-15; 🕑 closed lunch Sat & Sun; ⊖ Tower Hill

This restaurant is too good, really, for its predominantly City-worker customers to have to themselves. Admittedly, it's a bit off the beaten track, but it is only a 10-minute walk from Tower Hill. Parsee chef Cyrus Todiwala has taken an old magistrates' court and spiced it up in bright-patterned Oriental colours. The Parsee/Goan menu is famous for its superlative *dhansaak* (traditionally lamb, but now also vegetable, stew with rice and lentils). However, there are plenty of other pleasant surprises, such as the *papeta na pattice* – mashed potato cakes filled with green peas, grated coconut, chopped nuts and spices.

CHANCERY Map pp448-9 *French*
☎ 7831 4000; www.thechancery.co.uk; 9 Cursitor St EC4; 3-course set menu £32; ⊖ Chancery Lane

Sadly located slap-bang in the legal heart of the capital, the Chancery is unsurprisingly patronised by a crowd of barristers and can feel a bit stuffy as a result. It's a shame, as the charming staff and superb food deserve to be shared by the general public. Delicate and precise mains such as grilled calves liver, artichoke purée and caramelised onions make this worth the effort to find.

GRAND CAFÉ & BAR
Map pp454-5 *Modern European*
☎ 7618 2480; www.conran.com; Royal Exchange, Threadneedle St EC2; dishes £5.50-£14.50; 🕑 breakfast, lunch & dinner Mon-Fri; ⊖ Bank

This newish Conran venue is really just a very swish pavement café, but its excellent location in the middle of the beautiful Royal Exchange building makes it a great place for an informal business meeting. The food ranges from sandwiches (crab, honey-roasted ham, lobster) to dishes such as leek-and-fontina tart and langoustines with mayonnaise.

Top Five – East Central
- **Bistrotheque** (p240)
- **Coach & Horses** (p241)
- **Flâneur** (p242)
- **Ottolenghi** (p243)
- **Refettorio** (below)

PATERNOSTER CHOPHOUSE
Map pp454-5 *British*
☎ 7029 9400; www.conran.com; Warwick Court, Paternoster Sq EC4; mains £14.50-25; 🕑 lunch & dinner Mon-Fri, dinner Sat & Sun; ⊖ St Paul's

Conran's latest City project is this magnificently located chophouse right next to St Paul's Cathedral. While you'll need a shoehorn to get through the door at lunchtime, it's far quieter in the evenings. Delightfully British fare is on offer, ranging from the 'beast of the day' to a huge shellfish and grill selection and other traditional favourites such as bubble and squeak, and haggis. City prices certainly, but few people who dine here seem to be paying for themselves.

REFETTORIO Map pp448-9 *Italian*
☎ 7438 8052; www.tableinthecity.com; Crown Plaza London, 19 New Bridge St EC4; mains £16-21.50; ⊖ Blackfriars

Though it's a much needed addition to the city's eating scene, Refettorio's detractors say that it's not as convivial or warm as its West End equivalents, but on our last visit this proved to be anything but the case. The vast dark-wood refectory table was humming with chatter and laughter, and the food (overseen by Giorgio Locatelli, one of London's hottest chefs) was excellent. Cured meats and regional cheeses are the specialities here, and the various platters will not disappoint, while the meaty mains and the vegetarian-friendly antipasti are divine.

SWEETING'S Map pp454-5 — *Seafood*
☎ 7248 3062; 39 Queen Victoria St EC4; mains £10-£22; ⊗ lunch Mon-Fri; ⊖ Bank/rail Cannon St
Old-fashioned Sweeting's is a City institution, having been around for more than 50 years. It still carries a sense of history with its small sit-down restaurant area, mosaic floor and narrow counters, behind which stand waiters in white aprons. Dishes include wild smoked salmon, oysters (in season from September to April) and even eels.

VERTIGO 42 Map pp454-5 — *Seafood*
☎ 7877 7842; www.vertigo42.co.uk; Tower 42, 25 Old Broad St EC2; snacks & light meals £3.80-£12.50; ⊗ noon-3pm & 5-10pm Mon-Fri; ⊖ Bank
Not so much a bar/restaurant with a view but a view with attached bar/restaurant, Vertigo 42 offers the best panorama of the city aside from the London Eye. Chairs and benches for eating are arranged around the glass outer walls of this circular space, 42 floors and 590ft up. Evenings are the better time to visit, when you can watch the lights come on across London. However, for security and space reasons, you must book at least 24 hours in advance and accept a certain time slot. And, with 30 varieties of champagne on offer, under-18s are not allowed. The modern international food, with a strong seafood bent, is frankly secondary.

HOXTON, SHOREDITCH & SPITALFIELDS

ARKANSAS CAFÉ
Map pp454-5 — *North American*
☎ 7377 6999; Unit 12, Spitalfields Market, 107b Commercial St E1; mains £4-12.50; ⊗ lunch Sun-Fri; ⊖ Liverpool St/Aldgate East
Good ole down-home country cookin' is served up in this unprepossessing unit on the edges of Spitalfields market (it's reached via the inside of the market). Whether you're tucking into ribs, corn-fed chicken or steak, you can rest assured they'll be of truly excellent quality, with lots of potatoes, coleslaw and stuff on the side. It's the kind of place to give vegetarians a real fright, but meat-loving City workers flock here.

BISTROTHEQUE — *French*
☎ 8983 7900; www.bistrotheque.com; 23-27 Wadeson St E2; mains £9-15; ⊖ Bethnal Green/rail Cambridge Heath
It's a sign of the times when the hippest restaurant in London has an 0208 phone number. Shoreditch's colonisation by the great and gorgeous has even made neighbouring Haggerston glamorous, and no more so than at this stunning and unusually located place. Bistrotheque has a cocktail bar downstairs where drinks are prepared with a semi-religious rigour, while upstairs the spacious, minimalist restaurant knocks out some absolutely top-notch food. On our most recent visit two excellent starters of foie gras and oysters were followed by the rarest, tenderest steak we've ever eaten and a sole meunière that actually *was* a religious experience. Reservations recommended.

EYRE BROTHERS
Map pp442-3 — *Spanish/African*
☎ 7613 5346; 70 Leonard St EC2; mains £16-25, set-menu starters £5.50, mains £13.50; ⊗ closed lunch Sat & Sun; ⊖ Old St
Geographically located in Shoreditch, but stylistically with one foot in the City, this dark panelled, low-ceilinged den excels with an interesting range of fare inspired by the food of Spain, Portugal and Mozambique. Slightly older diners tuck into a largely vegetarian-unfriendly menu, including clams with *jamón Serrano*, grilled Mozambique prawns with *piri-piri* sauce and lamb marinated with anchovies, garlic and rosemary. The Eyre brothers were behind London's first gastropub, the Eagle. They still know what they're doing.

FIFTEEN Map pp442-3 — *Italian*
☎ 0871 330 1515; www.fifteenrestaurant.com; 15 Westland Pl; mains £25-29; ⊗ lunch & dinner Mon-Sat, brunch Sun; ⊖ Old St
If you're interested enough to be reading this because you plan on visiting, you'll know the deal, and the idea of paying £7 for fancy beans on toast won't deter you. This is Jamie Oliver's gaff, where he trains and employs 15 young chefs and the profits go to charity. It's difficult to get a reservation, but two-thirds of the seating in the downstairs trattoria is kept for walk-ins. While Oliver is undoubtedly overexposed, we have a renewed respect for the man, not just for his crusade for healthier school dinners but also because he refused to shake Bill Clinton's hand because most of the ex-prez's party were on the silly South Beach diet.

Eating – East Central

LES TROIS GARÇONS Map pp442-3   French

☎ 7613 1924; www.lestroisgarcons.com; 1 Club Row E1; mains £15-26; ☽ dinner Mon-Sat; ⊖ Liverpool St

One of Hoxton's most outstanding restaurants, you won't quickly forget a trip to the viscerally hip three boys of the restaurant's name. The animal trophies – antelopes, a tiger and even a giraffe – wearing diamanté tiaras and necklaces join forces with the long, square chandeliers, the crowned alligator carrying a sceptre and a centrepiece of hanging handbags to make this converted pub as camp as Christmas. The French food with a modern twist is very good, although the service can sometimes be so attentive as to be almost overbearing.

REAL GREEK Map pp442-3   Greek

☎ 7739 8212; www.therealgreek.co.uk; 15 Hoxton Market N1; mains £14-18; ☽ closed Sun; ⊖ Old St

The newfangled menu certainly doesn't seem to be what most of us understand as authentic Greek food (usually Greek Cypriot), but when it comes to sheer deliciousness this is the real deal. Mains might include *giouvarlakia* (meat dumplings) or pot-roasted pork with pickled flat cabbage, served with Greek pasta and Cretan goat's cheese. The less expensive and more relaxed Souvlaki Bars in Farringdon (Map pp442–3) and Bankside (Map pp454–5) are better for a light lunch/snack and a drink (*metaxa*, ouzo and vodka cocktails or surprisingly good Greek wine), rather than a full-on meal.

ST JOHN BREAD & WINE

Map pp454-5   British

☎ 7247 8724; www.stjohnbreadandwine.com; 94-96 Commercial St; mains £5-14; ☽ closed dinner Sun; ⊖ Liverpool St

The newer St John outlet is cheaper and more relaxed than its Clerkenwell cousin, St John, but offers similar 'nose to tail' eating (duck legs and carrots, or duck hearts on toast, for example) in an airy, inviting space popular with Spitalfields creative types. There's also a takeaway service for the breads, excellent puddings and wine.

CLERKENWELL

CICADA Map pp442-3   Modern Asian

☎ 7608 1550; 132-136 St John St EC1; mains £8-11; ☽ closed lunch Sat & Sun; ⊖ Farringdon

A hip-looking open-plan bar/restaurant with plenty of outside seating, Cicada serves a pan-Asian menu, from Japanese tempuras to Thai salads. It can be pretty hectic in this restaurant, sister to Notting Hill's **E&O** (p264), so book early to grab one of the brown leather booths.

CLERKENWELL

Map pp448-9   Modern International

☎ 7253 9000; www.theclerkenwell.com; 67-73 St John St EC1; mains £13-17; ☽ closed lunch Sat & dinner Sun; ⊖ Farringdon

A discreet but sleek Clerkenwell eatery that embraces the more staid residents of the neighbourhood, the Clerkenwell's head chef, Andrew Thompson, once worked at the famous L'Escargot, where his cooking won him a Michelin star. His à la carte dishes here manage to be both imaginative and traditional: seared skate wing and crab risotto sits next to pot-roasted partridge with *dauphinoise* potatoes on the regularly changing menu.

CLUB GASCON Map pp448-9   French

☎ 7796 0600; 57 West Smithfield EC1; tapas £5-25; ☽ closed lunch Sat & Sun; ⊖ Farringdon/Barbican

One of Clerkenwell's leading restaurants since it was awarded a Michelin star in 2002, Club Gascon takes a different approach to fine dining, with a selection of tapas-style portions (that would, naturally, leave an ordinary tapas restaurant for dust). There's duck, squid, cassoulet and an entire menu section devoted to foie gras. A set menu is £35, but if you go off piste you're looking at more like £50 and up per head.

COACH & HORSES Map pp448-9   Gastropub

☎ 7278 8990; www.thecoachandhorses.com; 26-28 Ray St EC1; mains £10-14; ⊖ Farringdon

Just around the corner from London's original gastropub, the Eagle, the Coach & Horses has zipped past the competition to become one of London's most talked about dining destinations. Despite this, it's spookily easy to get a seat within its traditional walls and absorb the menu, which has never been anything short of dazzling.

EAGLE Map pp442-3   Mediterranean

☎ 7837 1353; 159 Farringdon Rd EC1; mains £4.50-14; ☽ closed dinner Sun; ⊖ Farringdon

London's first gastropub is still going strong. Even though the original owners and many chefs have left, the customers still come, at lunch or after work, for its Mediterranean-influenced food. As it's no longer part of the 'scene' per se, the atmosphere is nicely relaxed.

FLÂNEUR

Map pp448-9   *French/Mediterranean*
☎ 7404 4422; www.flaneur.com; 41 Farringdon Rd
EC1; mains £10-16; ✪ Farringdon

Dining while shoppers browse around you may not sound particularly appealing, but it's just part of the charm of this Farringdon gourmet deli and unsurprisingly excellent restaurant. Beautifully attired in woods with unfeasibly high shelves stocked with all manner of rare and wonderful delicacies, tables are scattered around, and diners keep the place busy for both lunch and dinner. The menu is a rich and clever combination of French and Mediterranean cuisine, and the accompanying wine list is breathtakingly comprehensive.

LE CAFÉ DU MARCHÉ Map pp448-9 *French*
☎ 7608 1609; 22 Charterhouse Sq, Charterhouse
Mews EC1; 3-course set menu £26; ✆ closed lunch
Sat & Sun; ✪ Farringdon/Barbican

This quaint, authentic French bistro might become less of a state secret with the new hotel Malmaison (p360) next door in Charterhouse Sq. Then again, tradition is a watchword in this exposed-brick warehouse, from the hearty steaks with garlic and rosemary flavours to the piano playing and jazz upstairs, so hopefully it won't change. Meals are set-menu only.

MEDCALF BAR Map pp442-3 *British*
☎ 7833 3533; 40 Exmouth Market EC1; mains £8.50-
13.50; ✆ kitchen noon-3pm & 6-10pm Mon-Thu,
noon-3pm Fri, noon-4pm & 6-10pm Sat, noon-4pm Sun;
✪ Farringdon

Despite its erratic kitchen hours (the bar itself is open all day), Medcalf is one of the best-value hang-outs on Exmouth Market. A beautifully converted butcher shop, the innovative yet very British feel to the menu delivers some superb and relatively affordable food. Highlights on our visit were an excellent beetroot and walnut salad, delicious smoked salmon and anchovy terrine and a Cippolini onion risotto that was richly textured and had just the right amount of bite.

MORO Map pp442-3 *North African/Spanish*
☎ 7833 8336; www.moro.co.uk; 34-36 Exmouth
Market N1; mains £11-15.50; ✪ Farringdon

The exulted Moro's reputation precedes it, especially since it released a book of its North African, Spanish and Portuguese fusion cuisine. And the weight of expectation is probably why opinions are so mixed. Some diners love it, while others complain about odd season-ings and small portions. The constantly changing menu might include dishes such as crab *brik*, a crispy deep-fried packet served with piquant harissa sauce, wood-roasted red mullet with sharp Seville orange, and char-grilled lamb with artichokes.

QUALITY CHOP HOUSE

Map pp442-3   *British*
☎ 7837 5093; 92-94 Farringdon Rd EC1; mains £6.75-
24; ✆ closed lunch Sat; ✪ Farringdon

Hmmm. The self-description as 'a progressive working-class caterer' is a bit pretentious, but the food is good and we see what they mean. This former workmen's caf with a white-and-black tiled floor and wooden benches (or are they church pews?) now serves old-fashioned British staples to a middle-class media crowd. Starters include eels, while Toulouse sausages and mash, lots of red meat and the widely recommended salmon fish cakes are among the mains.

ST JOHN Map pp448-9 *British*
☎ 7251 0848; www.stjohnrestaurant.co.uk; 26 St
John St EC1; mains £15-18; ✆ closed lunch Sat & Sun;
✪ Farringdon

Clerkenwell's most famous restaurant has spawned its own book (*Nose to Tail Eating*, by chef Fergus Henderson), and indeed this much-acclaimed, enduringly hip place really is for adventurous carnivores who want to sample Ye Olde English cuisine. The signature dish is bone-marrow salad, and the changing daily menu includes such specialities as veal heart and chicken neck. There are more familiar choices such as duck, fish and even lentils (one of a few token veggie dishes). However, St John, with its minimalist white dining room and patient staff, is overwhelmingly a Rabelaisian experience.

SMITHS OF SMITHFIELD

Map pp448-9   *Modern British*
☎ 7236 6666; 67-77 Charterhouse St EC1; mains
£3.50-29; ✆ breakfast, lunch & dinner Mon-Fri, dinner
Sat; ✪ Farringdon

After the hubbub of the cavernous bar and café on the ground floor, where you can grab breakfast and lunch (all-day breakfast £3.50 to £6.50), there are two quieter places to dine: the brasserie on the 2nd floor (mains all £10.50) and the rooftop dining room (mains £19 to £29), which has great views of St Paul's. The linking factor is a focus on top-quality British meat and organic produce, much of which comes from the eponymous market across the road.

ZETTER Map pp448-9 *Italian*

☎ 7324 4444; www.zetter.com; 86-88 Clerkenwell Rd EC1; mains £10-17; ⊖ Farringdon

Not simply the restaurant for Clerkenwell's long-overdue boutique hotel, also called **Zetter** (p361), this place is destination dining in its own right. The space is magnificently light, with huge bay windows on three sides and staff who make its crisp white tablecloths and chic modern Italian cooking seem totally informal. The menu changes monthly and is always a treat, featuring seasonal specialities with clever twists and full flavours. The suits who populate it during the week disappear come Friday, and Clerkenwell's media classes make up the bulk of the clientele, giving it a far less stuffy feel.

ISLINGTON

ALMEIDA Map pp442-3 *French*

☎ 7354 4777; www.almeida-restaurants.co.uk; 30 Almeida St N1; mains £14.50-19; ⊖ Angel/Highbury & Islington

A treat for after-theatre dining opposite the Islington playhouse of the same name, the Almeida is a big success story for the Conran empire. The staff hit the right balance between Gallic perfectionism and chatty friendliness, while the classic French menu is excellent, albeit entirely in French. Steak tartare was a standout success on our last visit, while the main course of Chateaubriand *à la moëlle* with Béarnaise sauce (£38 for two people) was also faultless.

DUKE OF CAMBRIDGE

Map pp442-3 *Gastropub*

☎ 7359 9450; 30 St Peter's St N1; mains £6.50-15; ☾ closed lunch Mon; ⊖ Angel

It has a typical London gastropub feel, with bare wooden boards, tables and sofas, but there's something different about the Duke of Cambridge. Everything here, even the lager, is organic, making it the first of its kind in the UK. The Italian/French/Spanish-influenced menu can be a little inconsistent in quality, but generally it's worth coming here for more than just the novelty.

FREDERICK'S

Map pp442-3 *Modern International*

☎ 7359 2888; Camden Passage; mains £13-18.50, 2-/3-course lunch & early-evening dinner set menus £12.50/£15.50; ☾ closed lunch Sat & Sun; ⊖ Angel

Probably Islington's premier upmarket eatery, and popular with the expense-account brigade, Frederick's is more establishment than

Top Five Veggie

- **Eat & Two Veg** (p259)
- **Food For Thought** (p237)
- **Gate** (p267)
- **Manna** (p261)
- **Mildred's** (p233)

cutting edge. The main dining room is under a glass-vaulted roof and overlooks a garden, much like a conservatory. Within the eclectic menu the pepper-roasted duck is widely recommended, although you'll also find lots of fish, beef and lamb.

HOUSE Map pp442-3 *Gastropub*

☎ 7704 7410; 63-69 Canonbury Rd N1; mains £9.50-17; ☾ closed Sun & lunch Mon; ⊖ Highbury & Islington/ rail Essex Rd

House combines a funky bar with an informal dining room. The menu is strong on seafood dishes like risotto of calamari with mascarpone and salt cod *marinière*, as well as an excellent range of starter salads.

METROGUSTO Map pp442-3 *Italian*

☎ 7226 9400; www.metrogusto.co.uk; 11-13 Theberton St N1; mains £15.50-17.50; ☾ dinner Mon-Sat, lunch Fri-Sun; ⊖ Angel

This laid-back restaurant serves progressive, modern Italian cuisine, where you can rely on tasty pizzas, as well as mains including *carne del giorno* and *pesce di mercato* (meat and fish of the day). There's a good mix of happy diners.

OTTOLENGHI Map pp442-3 *Italian*

☎ 7288 1454; 287 Upper St N1; set menus £9.50-11.50; ⊖ Highbury & Islington/Angel

The second Ottolenghi – the original is in Notting Hill (Map pp444–5) – is the new Upper St branch, a superb addition to the Islington dining scene. Sleek minimalist white, the bakery-cum-restaurant looks as good as its food tastes, and that's saying something. The set menu is great value for food of this quality, although the desserts are the real highlight. (Before you ask, the electricity cables and plugs hanging over the table are for toasters at breakfast.)

PASHA Map pp442-3 *Turkish*

☎ 7226 1454; 301 Upper St N1; mains £6.95-14; ⊖ Highbury & Islington/Angel

The Ottoman wall paintings, the fountain and the decadent, cushion-filled alcoves convey that this is an upmarket kind of Turkish restaurant, and it doesn't disappoint. The meze, while small-ish, is great. Mains run the gamut of seafood *tagine*, lamb couscous and aubergine *pilaf*.

SOCIAL Map pp442-3 *Gastropub*
☎ 7354 5809; Arlington Sq N1; mains £9-13;
🕑 lunch & dinner Sat & Sun, dinner Mon-Fri;
⊖ Angel/rail Essex Rd

This venue for 20- and 30-somethings – plus the odd B- or C-list celeb – serves excellent gastropub fare. If you come on a Friday, Satur-day (usually) or Sunday (always) evening, you can enjoy your crisp roast belly of pork, char-grilled rib-eye steak, roast salmon in polenta crumb or risotto cake with butternut squash while a DJ spins funky laid-back tunes in the corner. The name over the door says Hanbury Arms, which can't be changed as it's listed.

CHEAP EATS

AFGHAN KITCHEN Map pp442-3 *Afghani*
☎ 7359 8019; 35 Islington Green N1; mains £ 4.50-6;
🕑 lunch & dinner Tue-Sat; ⊖ Angel

This tiny gem serves up some of Islington's best-value food, not to mention some of its most interesting: traditional Afghan dishes such as *dogh*, a yogurt and mint concoction, and lamb cooked with spinach alongside a large vegetarian selection including *borani kado* (pumpkin with yogurt) and lentil dhal. All this, a delightful location and friendly staff make this a super place.

BRICK LANE BEIGEL BAKE
Map pp442-3 *Bakery*
☎ 7729 0616; 159 Brick Lane E2; bagels 15p-£1.80;
🕑 24hr; ⊖ Liverpool St/Aldgate East

This renowned round-the-clock bakery turns out some of London's springiest, chewiest ba-gels, and attracts daytime and after-club crowds. It's a slice of real London, but not kosher (in the Jewish sense). You can take away plain bagels or get them filled – the salt beef is excellent. The staff have a real East End charm.

FRYER'S DELIGHT Map pp448-9 *Fish & Chips*
☎ 7405 4114; 19 Theobald's Rd EC1; mains £1.50-5;
⊖ Holborn

A Clerkenwell classic that seems to always be busy, the Fryer's Delight has real retro charm with its 1960s interior and comfy booths, where (rarely for a chip shop) you can sit in and enjoy your fried fish.

GALLIPOLI Map pp442-3 *Turkish*
☎ 7359 0630; 102 Upper St N1; mains £5-7;
⊖ Angel/Highbury & Islington

A crammed, popular, cheek-by-jowl restaurant with funky Turkish decorations and not bad food, from the meze to the spicy vegetarian moussaka. There's an overspill restaurant, **Gal-lipoli Again** (Map pp442–3; 120 Upper St).

LE MERCURY Map pp442-3 *French*
☎ 7354 4088; 140a Upper St N1; mains £5.95;
⊖ Angel/Highbury & Islington

Given the low prices here and the more-than-reasonable food, it's all the more surprising that this budget French eatery favours silver-ware and white linen over the usual rustic décor. There are occasional specials, and the food is of very good quality for the price.

PLACE BELOW Map pp454-5 *Vegetarian*
☎ 7329 0789; St Mary-le-Bow Church, Cheapside EC2;
🕑 lunch Mon-Fri; ⊖ Bank/Mansion House

In a church crypt, this pleasant veggie restau-rant is of the old school. Think spinach and mushroom quiche, celeriac and blue cheese gratin and (steady on, getting a bit modern here) sun-dried tomatoes and rice salad.

PREEM Map pp454-5 *Indian*
☎ 7247 0397; 120 Brick Lane E1; mains £6.50-8.50;
🕑 noon-2am; ⊖ Liverpool St/Aldgate East

The cuisine is generally less oily than most, and tastier, making this one of the best curry houses on Brick Lane. Filling set menus are £10.

SÔNG QUÊ Map pp442-3 *Vietnamese*
☎ 7613 3222; 134 Kingsland Rd E2; mains £3.50-8.50
⊖ Old St, then bus 55 or 243

The critics are right, this is London's best Viet-namese restaurant. However, the much-lauded competition is in fact terribly poor – Chinese really – so connoisseurs beware that this ac-colade doesn't say as much as it could.

ZIGNI HOUSE Map pp438-9 *Eritrean*
☎ 7226 7418; 330 Essex Rd N1; mains £6-8; 🕑 6-11pm; ⊖ Angel/Highbury & Islington

It's a surprise to see such a treat at the shabby end of Essex Rd. A recent addition, Zigni House is packed most nights with groups enjoying huge platters of delicious Eritrean cooking on beds of *injera* (pancake flatbread), brought to you here by Tsige Haile, East Africa's answer to Delia Smith. The *zigni*s of the name refer to the spicy Eritrean stews, which are a speciality. Serv-ice can be slow, but the food's worth the wait.

WEST CENTRAL

Naturally, quality gravitates to where the money is, and you'll find some of London's finest establishments in the swanky hotels and ritzy mews of these areas, particularly Mayfair and Chelsea. The king of them all, Gordon Ramsay, has three Michelin stars in its crown and resides in Chelsea. Many of London's most dazzling new restaurants have sprung up around Mayfair, while chic and cosmopolitan South Kensington has always been reliable for pan-European options.

Top Five – West Central

- **Amaya** (p247)
- **Daquise** (p250)
- **Gordon Ramsay** (p248)
- **Nahm** (p249)
- **Wolseley** (p246)

MAYFAIR & ST JAMES'S

EMBASSY Map p450 *French*

☎ 7851 0956; www.embassylondon.com; 29 Old Burlington St W1; mains £15-25, 2-/3-course set lunch £17/20; ⏰ lunch Mon-Fri, dinner Mon-Sat; ⊖ Green Park/Piccadilly Circus

You wouldn't necessarily realise from Embassy's fairly corporate décor (white leather chairs and a fair bit of gold) that it attracts such a rock-and-roll clientele, but the downstairs members' club has been known to pull in everyone from Nicole Appleton to Pharrell Williams of a weekend (and coming to dine at the restaurant means automatic admission to the club, too). Chef Gary Hollihead is renowned for the consistency and excellence of his cooking and, even if the portions are famously small, £20 for three courses at this level is a steal.

GORDON RAMSAY AT CLARIDGE'S

Map pp448-9 *Modern British*

☎ 7499 0099; www.gordonramsay.com; 53 Brook St W1; set lunch £30, set dinner £55-65; Bond St

The coming together of London's most celebrated chef and its grandest hotel was probably a match made in heaven and sent down as His way to apologise for the historic awfulness of British food. All is forgiven. A meal in this gorgeous Art Deco dining room is a special occasion indeed; the Ramsay flavours will have you reeling, from the mosaique of foie gras and duck confit with a salad of green beans and shallot salad à la grecque all the way to the cheese trolley, whether you choose the one with French, British or Irish number plates.

MAZE Map pp448-9 *Modern International*

☎ 7107 0000; 10-13 Grosvenor Sq W1; dishes £3.50-8.50; ⏰ noon-3pm & 6-11pm; ⊖ Bond St

Talented chef Jason Atherton is the man slaving in the kitchen at Gordon Ramsay's latest 'egalitarian' enterprise. The idea is to serve exquisite food in a relaxed informal environment and the focus is very much on the tapas-style 'grazing' menu. Portions of grilled spring lamb with cinnamon sweetbreads, cos lettuce with bacon, onions and Moroccan spices, tempura of monkfish with mango and chilli dressing or pressed foie gras and smoked eel with pickled ginger and rhubarb are all just too good – and frankly just too small – to share with your fellow diners. The room is minimalistically decorated in earthy tones, although the tables are very close together.

Gordon Ramsey restaurant (248)

MOMO Map p450   *North African*
☎ 7434 4040; www.momoresto.com; 25 Heddon St W1; mains £14.50-19.50, 2-/3-course set lunch £17/20; ⊖ Piccadilly Circus

The souk comes to the West End at this wonderfully atmospheric and maximalist North African restaurant, which is stuffed with cushions and lamps, and manned by all-dancing, tambourine-playing waiters. It's a funny old place that manages to be all things to all diners, who range from romantic couples to raucous office-party ravers. Service is very friendly and the dishes are as exciting as you dare to be, so eschew the traditional and ordinary *tagine* and tuck into the splendid Moroccan speciality of nutmeg and pigeon pie.

NOBU Map pp448-9   *Japanese*
☎ 7447 4747; www.noburestaurants.com; Metropolitan Hotel, 19 Old Park Lane W1; mains £5-28, set lunch from £25, set dinner from £70; ⊖ Hyde Park Cnr

Not so much a Japanese restaurant as a London designer's *idea* of a Japanese restaurant, this is nonetheless a strong contender for the best Asian food in town. It's comfortably minimalist in décor, anonymously efficient in service, and out of this fricken world when it comes to exquisitely prepared and presented sushi and sashimi. The black cod is worth sneaking past customs. Amorous couples thinking about sharing the chocolate *bento* box (a cake shell packed with gooey chocolate) might want to order a cab first and have it waiting.

SKETCH Map p450   *Modern European*
☎ 0870 777 4488; www.sketch.uk.com; 9 Conduit St W1; gallery mains £15-45, Lecture Room mains £45-60; ⓨ closed Sun; ⊖ Oxford Circus

The collection of bars and restaurants at the former Christian Dior headquarters in Mayfair remains a huge draw for fashion world parties, the great, the gorgeous and the downright loaded. The gallery restaurant downstairs buzzes informally in shimmering white and features video art projections. There two excellent bars adjacent serve food from a small but brilliant menu and become a nightclub from 10pm. There's a stunning patisserie at the building's entrance, which is great for tea and cakes, while the ultimate attraction is the more formal Lecture Room upstairs, where the high prices and *haute cuisine* in sumptuous surroundings from three-starred Michelin chef Pierre Gagnaire attracts an unsurprisingly exclusive crowd. Booking is essential – go to the gallery for cool; go upstairs to impress.

SQUARE Map pp448-9   *Modern International*
☎ 7495 7100; www.squarerestaurant.com; 6-10 Bruton St W1; 2-/3-course set lunch £25/30, 3-course dinner £60, tasting menu £75; ⓨ lunch Mon-Fri, dinner Mon-Sat; ⊖ Piccadilly Circus/Green Park

Many people sum up chef Phillip Howard's two-Michelin starred restaurant by saying you pay for what you get. But when what you get is consistently exquisite cuisine, an extensive wine list and impeccable service, just as many people (albeit mainly businessmen) seem happy to drop £85 to £100 per head. Despite the lack of atmosphere, this is still an excellent place to head on an expense account.

TAMAN GANG
Map pp444-5   *Indonesian Fusion*
☎ 7518 3160; www.tamangang.com; 141 Park Lane W1; mains £15-45; ⓨ dinner Tue-Sat; ⊖ Marble Arch

Just metres from the traffic chaos of Marble Arch, the staircase down to this basement restaurant transports you to a world of magnificent tranquillity, suffused with incense and humming with a smart yet surprisingly informal Park Lane crowd. The interesting menu fuses Indonesian with Chinese and Japanese classics. On our last visit, tuna tartare with wasabi was superb, while fried veal and cashews in a tart plum sauce was of a similarly high standard but an alarmingly small serving for a main course. The desserts sealed the deal, however, and were perhaps the highlight of the entire meal.

TAMARIND Map pp448-9   *Indian*
☎ 7629 3561; www.tamarindrestaurant.com; 20 Queen St W1; mains £14-25, 2-/3-course set lunch £14.50/16.50; ⓨ closed lunch Sat; ⊖ Green Park

This is one of those places where you're passed along a chain of assorted staff before you actually get to park your bum (beneath huge inverted tea-lights) – not quite Bobby de Niro in *GoodFellas*, but you get the picture. The slightly older crowd is froufrou, in keeping with the beautiful restaurant and neighbourhood, while the food – a cavalcade of Indian classics – is out of this world.

WOLSELEY Map p450   *Modern European*
☎ 7499 6996; www.thewolseley.com; 160 Piccadilly W1; mains £8.75-26; ⓨ 7am-midnight Mon-Fri, 9am-midnight Sat, 9am-11pm Sun; ⊖ Green Park

The former owners of the Ivy and J Sheekey have transformed this former Bentley car showroom into an opulent Viennese-style brasserie and somewhere it would be silly to miss during any London visit. The golden chandeliers and black-and-white tiled floors look fantastic, the silver-service morning and afternoon tea beats the more expensive Ritz, and it's a great place for celeb-spotting. That said, the Wolseley tends to work better for breakfast, brunch or tea, rather than lunch or dinner, when the meals (apart from the salads) are slightly stodgy and the black-attired staff cagey about giving away tables at such a premium.

WESTMINSTER & WHITEHALL

CINNAMON CLUB Map pp448-9 *Indian*

☎ 7222 2555; www.cinnamonclub.com; Old Westminster Library, 30 Great Smith St W1; mains £11-26; 🕒 lunch Mon-Fri, dinner Mon-Sat; ⊖ St James's Park

Domed skylights, high ceilings, parquet flooring and a book-lined mezzanine evoke an atmosphere reminiscent of when this place was the Westminster Library. Hushed, eager-to-please waiters hover like anxious footmen, although they really have no need to be concerned, because the Indian food here is consistently of the highest quality and fit for a rajah.

VICTORIA & PIMLICO

KEN LO'S MEMORIES OF CHINA

Map pp460-1 *Chinese*

☎ 7773 7734; 67-69 Ebury St SW1; mains £5-29; 🕒 lunch & dinner Mon-Sat; ⊖ Victoria

This is where fine Chinese food arrived in London, with the late Ken Lo many moons ago, and if food is more important than buzz this is still the best Chinese restaurant in the city. The interior is elegant, oriental minimalism and the noise levels are agreeably low because this place isn't filled with highly strung first dates like London's more fashionable restaurants. There are several set menus – including a veggie one and an unforgettable 'Gastronomic Tour of China' – and all the well-proportioned dishes feature a splendidly light touch and wonderful contrasts of flavours and textures.

OLIVO Map pp460-1 *Italian*

☎ 7730 2505; 21 Eccleston St SW1; mains £13.50-15; 🕒 lunch & dinner Mon-Sat; ⊖ Victoria/Sloane Sq

This colourful restaurant specialises in the food and wine of Sardinia and Sicily, and has a dedicated clientele of sophisticates who, quite frankly, would rather keep it to themselves. Not surprising, really, because it's a little gem. As a general rule, drink Sicilian and eat Sardinian, particularly the famous spaghetti bottarga (which is a delicacy with mullet roe served simply with oil, garlic, parsley and flakes of red pepper).

VINCENT ROOMS

Map pp460-1 *International*

☎ 7802 8391; www.westking.ac.uk; Westminster Kingsway College, Vincent Sq SW1; mains £6.50-8.50, 3-course set menu £20; 🕒 lunch noon-3pm Mon-Fri, last orders 1.15pm, dinner 6-9pm Tue & Thu, last orders 7.30pm term time only; ⊖ Victoria

Oh, the indignity! Not only are you essentially offering yourself up as a guinea pig for the student chefs at Westminster Kingsway College here, you have to book to do it. You might even find yourself grovelling, in the hope of discovering the next Jamie Oliver, as the Naked Chef also trained here. You usually won't (find him or her), of course, but as this *is* fine dining at very decent prices you won't regret the experience. Service is nervously eager to please, the atmosphere smarter than expected and the food (including veggie options) ranges from well-executed to occasionally exquisite.

CHELSEA & BELGRAVIA

AMAYA Map pp444-5 *Indian*

☎ 7823 1166; www.realindianfood.com; Halkin Arcade, 19 Motcomb St SW1; mains £8-17.50, express lunch £16.50; ⊖ Knightsbridge

Hidden down a little arcade behind Starbucks lies a swish, stylish restaurant that was crowned London's best in 2005. The low-lit interior looks suitably regal, with Indian statues, colourful jewelled inlays in the wood, hanging crystal strings and chandeliers. The thing that will hold your attention, though, is the chefs at work in the open kitchen, as they slave over an iron skillet, charcoal grill or clay oven to bring you such exquisite dishes as lamb osso bucco, fragrant lime curry or mussels *piri-piri*. Varied set menus put the emphasis on sharing dishes with fellow diners, and there's a special £26 menu for vegetarians.

BLUEBIRD DINING ROOMS & BLUE-BIRD CAFÉ Map pp458-9   Modern European

☎ 7352 4441; www.conran-restaurants.co.uk; 350 King's Rd SW3; mains £13-25, café dishes £5-12.50; ⊖ Sloane Sq, then bus 11,19, 22, 49 or 319

There are two eateries here; do not confuse them. The dining rooms (upstairs) are decent enough, if arguably overpriced, working out at about £50 a head. A former private members' club thrown open to the public by Terence Conran's son and heir-apparent, Tom, this attracts lots of see-and-be-seen types with its capable British food and revamped 1930s surrounds. If you think you might get a taste of the same in the café, forget it. Having paid £6.75 for a meagre handful of lettuce, four (maybe five) croutons and one anchovy masquerading as a Caesar salad, we reckon it's only worth coming to the bar here for a drink.

CHEYNE WALK BRASSERIE & SALON

Map pp458-9   French

☎ 7376 8787; www.cheynewalkbrasserie.com; 50 Cheyne Walk SW3; mains £9-30; 2-/3-course set lunch £16.95/19.95; ⊙ lunch & dinner Mon-Sat, brunch Sun; ⊖ Sloane Sq

This brasserie's *belle époque* decoration is appealingly kitsch, with turquoise banquettes, red leather chairs, chandeliers and crystal lamps topped with pink shades. With a reputation for especially tender steaks, the focus of the food preparation is the large open grill in the centre of the ground-floor dining room. However, you might prefer sardine *pissaladière*, onion soup or lobster and avocado salad with raspberry dressing. In the star-dotted upstairs cocktail salon are great views of the Thames near the Albert Bridge.

GORDON RAMSAY

Map pp458-9   Modern European

☎ 7352 4441; www.gordonramsay.com; 68-69 Royal Hospital Rd SW3; set lunch/dinner/degustation £35/65/80; ⊙ lunch & dinner Mon-Fri; ⊖ Sloane Sq

One of Britain's finest restaurants, and the only one in the capital with three Michelin stars, this is hallowed turf and obviously the creation of Mr Ramsay himself. This is as close to perfect as we may ever experience, a blissful treat right through from the taster to the truffles. The only quibble is that you don't get time to savour it. Bookings are made in specific eat-it-and-beat-it slots and, if you've seen the chef on TV, you won't argue for fear he might come rushing out of the kitchen with a meat cleaver.

GORING Map pp460-1   British

☎ 7396 9000; www.goringhotel.co.uk; Goring Hotel, 15 Beeston Pl SW1; set lunch/dinner from £26.50/35; ⊙ lunch & dinner Mon-Fri, dinner Sat & Sun; ⊖ Sloane Sq

Whether you call it stately or starchy, this is the real trad-English deal, with chandeliers, brocade curtains, penguin waiters and silver settings. There's an emphasis on seasonal and regional English ingredients, as the chefs' light touch with dishes such as grouse, guinea fowl and lamb won the place an award for best hotel restaurant in 2005. If you can't get into Ramsay's, the three-course Sunday lunch for £25 is a brilliant deal.

LA POULE AU POT Map pp460-1   French

☎ 7730 7763; 231 Ebury St SW1; mains £26.50-19.50, 2-/3-course set lunch £15.50/17.50; ⊖ Sloane Sq

Some Londoners claim the 'Chicken in the Pot' is the best country-style French restaurant in town, and we've yet to prove them wrong (although we could name five places that offer better value). What you're paying for here is the romantic, candlelit ambience – which makes it virtually impossible to read the menu – although it might all backfire if your accent isn't as sexy as zee waiter's.

PAINTED HERON Map pp458-9   Indian

☎ 7351 5232; www.thepaintedheron.com; 112 Cheyne Walk SW10; mains £12-14; ⊙ lunch Mon-Fri, dinner Mon-Sat; bus 11, 19, 22 or 319

There are several decent posh Indian restaurants in Chelsea and Knightsbridge, and this riverside venue is the starchiest of the lot, with white tablecloths, expensive silverware and a neutrally decorated main dining room. All the imagination of the place has been directed towards the frequently changing menu, where you'll find an east-west mix summed up by rabbit leg tikka, guinea fowl in green herb chutney sauce and so on. Watch out for special dishes during the Chelsea Flower Show, such as edible petals and spiced potato cake, strawberries in hot curry and elderflower sorbet.

TUGGA Map pp458-9   Portuguese

☎ 7351 0101; www.tugga.com; 312-314 King's Rd SW3; mains £13.50-22, tapas £1.50-12; ⊖ Sloane Sq, then bus 11, 19, 22, 49 or 319

A Portuguese restaurant in Chelsea seems incredibly timely and, indeed, Chelsea FC's famous coach, José Mourinho, was one of the first through the door of this vibrantly coloured room. The psychedelically floral wallpaper and cerise and purple cushions make it a favourite with the Chelsea set, who come to enjoy the Portuguese cuisine (which is sold as modern but is actually more classic).

KNIGHTSBRIDGE, SOUTH KENSINGTON & HYDE PARK

BIBENDUM Map pp458-9 *Modern European*
☎ 7581 5817; www.bibendum.co.uk; 81 Fulham Rd SW3; mains £19-42; ✪ South Kensington
This restaurant occupies the striking Art Nouveau Michelin House (1911), one of the finest settings in London. Upstairs dining is in a spacious and light room with stained-glass windows, where you can savour fabulous and creative food, and tolerate very ordinary service. Downstairs in the Bibendum Oyster Bar you can really feel at the heart of the architectural finery while lapping up terrific native and rock oysters.

BOXWOOD CAFÉ

Map pp444-5 *Modern European*
☎ 7235 1010; www.gordonramsay.com; Berkeley Hotel, Wilton Pl SW1; most mains £15-25; ✪ Knightsbridge
This New York–style café is Gordon Ramsay's mostly successful attempt to kick back with the young folk and make fine dining in London 'a little bit more relaxed'. It's the kind of place you can come for a single course or a glass of wine, and while the layout is a little flat – even dreary down in the depths of the main restaurant – the food is generally first rate. Simple starters like fried oysters, fennel and lemon are generally tastier than the fussier mains. While here, pop through the swing doors upstairs to the Berkeley's fabulous Blue Bar.

NAHM Map pp448-9 *Thai*
☎ 7333 1234; www.halkin.co.uk; Halkin Hotel, Halkin St SW1; mains £19.50-21.50, set lunch/dinner £18/26; ✪ lunch Mon-Fri, dinner Mon-Sat; ✪ Hyde Park Cnr
Aussie chef David Thompson is a world authority on Thai food and responsible for the scandalously good tucker at this hotel restaurant, the only Thai eatery outside the kingdom to have a Michelin star. Eating here is like taking a pulse-pounding gastronomic tour of Thailand, which more than atones for the sterile setting. On offer are Thai classics like jungle curry of monkfish as well as more exotic fare like crab and pomelo with roasted coconut and caramel dressing.

RACINE Map pp458-9 *French*
☎ 7584 4477; 239 Brompton Rd SW3; mains £11-19.50, 2-/3-course lunch & early-evening dinner set menus £15.50/17.50; ✪ Knightsbridge
The key to the success of this splendid creation is that it limits its ambitions and then achieves them with panache. Regional French cooking is the vehicle and all-round, dedicated service to the customer the destination. Expect the likes of scallops with slow-roasted tomatoes, Morecambe Bay shrimps and smoked duck. Being French, dishes might feel heavy to some, but the sauces, the very foundation of 'la cuisine grandmère', and the desserts are all spot on.

SHIKARA Map pp458-9 *Indian*
☎ 7581 6555; 87 Sloane Ave SW3; set menus £13.95-16.95; ✪ South Kensington
This calm and sophisticated Indian restaurant – think white walls, wood floor and black leather

Bibendum Oyster Bar (left)

banquettes – puts some modern flair into its mainly, although not exclusively, north Indian cuisine. (Try the Malabar curry.) There's a nod to healthy eating, too, with customers able to choose whether to have their food cooked in ghee or oil, for example. Most of all, given its chic appearance, it's remarkably good value.

TOM AIKENS

Map pp458-9   *Modern European*
☎ 7584 2003; 43 Elystan St SW3; 3-course set lunch/dinner £29/£55; ☽ lunch & dinner Mon-Fri; ⊖ South Kensington

A notorious firebrand in the kitchen, the Tom of the title made his name by picking up two Michelin stars at Pied à Terre by the time he was only 26. He disappeared for a few years but returned with an enormous splash in mid-2003 with this handsome and understated restaurant. The food is fab, and the pork belly and truffle entrée is just about the best darn starter we've ever had. Mains hop along the lines of rabbit confit, and frogs' legs are equally good.

ZAFFERANO Map pp460-1   *Italian*
☎ 7235 5800; 15-16 Lowndes St SW1; 3-course set lunch/dinner £29/42; ☽ closed dinner Sun; ⊖ Knightsbridge

This glamorous place, sparkling with diamonds and wall-to-wall with perma-tans, serves excellent seasonal and inspired Italian dishes. That said, the service is sometimes snooty, and they might try to fob you off with an inferior table.

ZUMA Map pp444-5   *Japanese*
☎ 7584 1010; www.zumarestaurant.com; 5 Raphael St SW7; mains £3.50-28.50; ☽ closed Sun; ⊖ Knightsbridge

The 'opulently minimalist' décor at this jolly Japanese place features glass, steel, teak and swaths of granite, and it's a favourite setting for celebrities out for a quick bite and a slow cocktail. The exceptionally long menu is outstanding from top to tail; all the dishes are bursting with flavour, especially anything that's just come from under the robata grill (chicken wings, pork skewers, tiger prawns etc). You can dine at the counter with the plebs or at the chef's table, but the most delicious display of eye candy can be found around the rectangular bar. Unfortunately, that bar is understaffed and the staff aren't overfriendly.

CHEAP EATS

CHELSEA KITCHEN Map pp458-9   *European*
☎ 7589 1330; 98 King's Rd SW3; mains £3.50-6.50; ⊖ Sloane Sq

This spartan place – part of the Stockpot empire – has some of the cheapest food in London and is *almost* like eating out at a restaurant. Sturdy staples include the likes of French onion soup, spaghetti bolognese, lasagne and steak.

DAQUISE Map pp458-9   *Polish*
☎ 7589 6117; 20 Thurloe St SW7; most mains £5.50-9.80; ⊖ South Kensington

A wonderful anachronism, this attractively dowdy Polish diner is as authentic and charming as you're likely to find in the centre of London these days. Staff are welcoming and friendly, and the menu consists of lots of vegetarian as well as meat options.

JAKOB'S Map pp458-9   *Armenian*
☎ 7581 9292; 20 Gloucester Rd SW7; mains £6.50-11; ⊖ Gloucester Rd

If you want to spend your money on shopping rather than restaurant frills like décor and menus, this charismatic Armenian restaurant is a revelation. It serves delicious and wholesome salads, vegetarian lasagne, filo pie, falafel and kebabs that are a treat for your palate as well as a relief for your purse. Desserts are also good.

JENNY LO'S TEA HOUSE

Map pp460-1   *Chinese*
☎ 7259 0399; 14 Eccleston St SW1; mains £5.50-7.50; ⊖ Victoria

This simple place in Westminster was established by the daughter of the late Chinese food supremo Ken Lo, and is particularly good value for the neighbourhood. It serves soups and rice dishes, but noodles are this place's speciality.

PIZZA ORGANIC Map pp458-9   *Pizza*
☎ 7589 9613; 20 Old Brompton Rd SW7; pizzas £6.50-9; ⊖ South Kensington

At this family-friendly place on a busy corner of South Kensington, a squadron of black-clad waiters are primed to spring into action. The actual pizzas occupy a delicious middle ground between Roman-style pizzas, with thin crusts, and Neapolitan, with thick and moist crusts.

ALONG THE SOUTH BANK

Interesting eateries just keep on springing up on the South Bank, after the Oxo Tower and Tate Modern started bringing people here in the late 1990s and early noughties. There are clusters of interesting venues near Waterloo and the theatres in the Cut, around the foodies' mecca of Borough Market, and along up-and-coming Bermondsey St.

SOUTH BANK CENTRE & WATERLOO

ANCHOR & HOPE Map pp448-9 *Gastropub*
☎ 7928 9898; the Cut SE1; mains £11-14; ⓨ lunch Tue-Sat, dinner Mon-Sat; ⊖ Southwark/Waterloo

The hope is that you'll get a table without waiting hours, because you can't book and you're liable to have your chair 'borrowed' by a fellow customer in the uncomfortable bar area. The anchor of the enterprise, meanwhile, is the gutsy, unashamedly carnivorous food. The critics love this place, but with dishes including snails, pink lamb's neck, pig's heart or pigeon, veggies may blanche just reading the menu.

BALTIC Map pp448-9 *Polish/Eastern European*
☎ 7928 1111; www.balticrestaurant.co.uk; 74 Blackfriars Rd SE1; mains £9.50-14; ⓨ closed lunch Sun; ⊖ Southwark

There's no point in coming to Baltic half-heartedly. Go straight to the main restaurant. Do not stop at the shiny bar, where you'd need all those vodkas to survive the naff after-work environment. Do not settle for the bar menu. Head straight for the airy, high-ceilinged dining room, where you can eat in proper style and comfort under its inverted V-shaped beams. The food, including *pierogi* and caviar, black pudding and smoked eel, is 90% Polish, despite being usually billed as Eastern European.

LAUGHING GRAVY
Map pp448-9 *Modern International*
☎ 7721 7055; 154 Blackfriars Rd; mains £12.50-15.50; ⓨ lunch & dinner Mon-Fri, dinner Sat; ⊖ Southwark

Just far enough away from the crowded Cut to usually guarantee a table, this casual pub has a delightfully shambolic atmosphere. With its large sauce-bottle collection, vintage ad posters, paintings, potted plants and piano, it resembles a bohemian late-1940s living room. The food includes some adventurous offerings like springbok and wild boar, and only rarely disappoints. The small bar area, which fills up more quickly, is well stocked with whisky or 'laughing gravy' (also the name of silent comedians Laurel and Hardy's dog).

Top Five – Along the South Bank
- Anchor & Hope (left)
- Baltic (left)
- Garrison (p253)
- Oxo Tower (below)
- Tas (p254)

MESÓN DON FELIPE Map pp448-9 *Spanish*
☎ 7928 3237; 53 the Cut SE1; tapas £3.95-4.95; ⓨ closed Sun; ⊖ Southwark/Waterloo

A veritable institution on the local scene, predating most of its neighbours, this tapas bar is still a perpetual scrum of customers crowding around the central bar and making enough noise to drown out the struggling guitarist. The only answer is to perch yourself on a stool and hunch protectively over your *patatas bravas* (incidentally, some of the best in town).

OXO TOWER RESTAURANT & BRASSERIE
Map pp448-9 *Modern International*
☎ 7803 3888; www.harveynichols.com; 8th fl, Barge House St SE1; brasserie mains £11-17, restaurant mains £17.50-26; ⊖ Waterloo

The Oxo Tower is about event dining, with the emphasis more on the event than the food. You have a front-row seat to probably the best view in London here, and you're paying for this, not the fusion food. True, the cuisine's much improved, but it's still not particularly memorable (seafood is best), and the place is disconcertingly noisy. A cocktail in the crowded bar *seems* like the next best option, but then you find all these chatty diners are blocking your view.

OZU Map pp448-9 *Japanese*
☎ 7928 7766; County Hall, Westminster Bridge Rd SE1; most mains £4.50-15, set menus £23.50 & £35.50; ⓨ closed Sun; ⊖ Waterloo

For those whose idea of Japanese food extends beyond plates of sushi whizzing round on a conveyor belt – you can get that across the road at Yo! Sushi – this bamboo-bedecked brasserie-style restaurant at the back of County Hall is a real treat. The chef's 'introduction to new flavours and ingredient to try' (as charmingly described on the menu) include *aonori* seasoned tempura fish cakes, *natto* (fermented soy bean) and *nametake* mushrooms served with grated *daikon*. There are also *kamado* rice pots (cooked in stock and served with different toppings), traditional Japanese starters, as well as the usual soup, sashimi and sushi.

BANKSIDE
MENIER CHOCOLATE FACTORY
Map pp454-5   *French*
☎ 7378 1712; www.menierchocolatefactory.com; 51/53 Southwark St SE1; mains £8-16.50, set pre-theatre menu including theatre ticket £20; ✆ lunch & dinner Mon-Fri, dinner Sat; ✆ London Bridge

Many theatre restaurants are disappointing afterthoughts; not so at this converted Bankside factory, which houses one of London's most exciting fringe venues (see p332) and a superlative French restaurant to boot. The menu heaves with rich and politically incorrect delicacies – swordfish steak, foie gras and veal to name but a few – and the warm atmosphere and high standard of cooking make this a destination in itself, whether or not you're seeing a performance.

BOROUGH & BERMONDSEY
BERMONDSEY KITCHEN
Map pp454-5   *International*
☎ 7407 5719; 194 Bermondsey St SE1; mains £9-13; ✆ lunch & dinner Mon-Sat, brunch Sun; ✆ London Bridge

As it's a great place to curl up on the sofas with the Sunday newspapers, or to escape the heaving crowds at the nearby Garrison on a weeknight, it's hardly surprising that many

locals seem to have made this their second living room. The Mediterranean food that comes from the open grill is as homy and unpretentious as the rough-hewn tables. And, just to complete the package, it comes in refreshingly filling portions.

BLUEPRINT CAFÉ
Map pp454-5   *International*
☎ 7378 7031; www.conran-restaurants.co.uk; Design Museum, Butler's Wharf SE1; mains £12.50-22; ✆ closed dinner Sun; ✆ Tower Hill

Behind glass at the Design Museum, and aided by opera glasses at each table, customers of this 1st-floor restaurant have stunning views of Tower Bridge and the 'Gherkin' at 30 St Mary Axe, which makes it easier to overlook the slightly uneven service. Food is simple but tasty, with the most straightforward dishes usually working best – such as nettle soup, beetroot salad and roast duck on our last group visit.

BUTLER'S WHARF CHOP HOUSE
Map pp454-5   *Modern British*
☎ 7403 3403; www.conran-restaurants.co.uk; Butler's Wharf Bldg, 36e Shad Thames SE1; mains £13.50-17; ✆ closed dinner Sun; ✆ Tower Hill

A poster child for 1990s modern British cuisine, Terence Conran's Chop House is still turning out upmarket variants on bangers and mash, burgers and steaks. It has, however, recently added the ancient dish of rook pie to the menu, should you be feeling more adventurous. A great view is thrown into the deal if you can get an outdoor table along this touristy strip.

CHAMPOR-CHAMPOR Map pp454-5 *Asian*
☎ 7403 4600; www.champor-champor.com; 62-64 Weston St SE1; 2/3 courses £19/26; ✆ lunch Mon-Sat; ✆ London Bridge

You won't find Malaysian food like this anywhere else, not even in Malaysia, because *champor-champor* means mix and match. Its unusual east-west cuisine includes innovations such as braised ostrich fillet in sweet soy sauce, peppercorn-crusted lamb cutlets with caramel and tamarind sauce, and several vegetarian options that the waiter will probably have to explain. When the dishes work – usually every two out of three courses – they're truly divine, but they sometimes misfire, and while the eclectic Oriental décor is a delight, both the music and the 15% service charge are cheesy. So, mix and match is more of a mixed bag – but worthwhile for gourmands looking for something unique.

DELFINA Map pp454-5 *International*
☎ 7357 0244; www.delfina.org.uk; 50 Bermondsey St SE1; mains £9.95-14; ⏰ lunch & morning & afternoon tea Mon-Fri; ⊖ London Bridge

It's a crying shame that this upmarket artists' canteen only serves meals at weekday lunch-times, because this means besuited office workers from surrounding financial institutions are the ones who most often get to sample its superior modern international cuisine. The room is light-filled and spacious; the menu changes fortnightly. If you can't make lunch, coffee and cakes are served 10am to noon and 3pm to 5pm Monday to Friday.

GARRISON Map pp454-5 *Gastropub*
☎ 7089 9355; www.thegarrison.co.uk; 99 Bermond-sey St SE1; mains £7-14; ⏰ breakfast, lunch & dinner daily, brunch Sat & Sun; ⊖ London Bridge

There's always a sign outside the Garrison advising 'Advance Booking Here', which tells you all you need to know about its popularity. With good reason, too. The traditional green-tiled exterior and minimalist beach-shack interior are both appealing, it has a cinema in its basement, and the actual food at this gastropub is the best casual bite along this strip. If don't fancy nearly bashing your neighbour's elbow every time you fork a mouthful of risotto, though, come for a weekend brunch or breakfast any day of the week.

Le Pont de la Tour (right)

Top Five Outdoor Tables
- **Butler's Wharf Chop House** (opposite)
- **Engineer** (p261)
- **Jason's** (p262)
- **Lauderdale House** (p263)
- **Terrace café** at **Somerset House** (p103)

HARTLEY Map pp454-5 *Gastropub*
☎ 7394 7023; www.thehartley.com; 64 Tower Bridge Rd SE1; lunch mains £3.50-9.50, dinner mains £9.50-12.50; ⏰ lunch & dinner Mon-Sat, lunch Sun; ⊖ London Bridge

Despite this neighbourhood's aspirations to be known as 'SoBo' (South Borough), the large, high-ceilinged Hartley is still a pioneer here, and its menu is careful not to scare off the area's traditional residents…except perhaps when it comes to lime-mousse *brûlée*. Lunch even includes a fish-finger sandwich, fer chrissakes, although you might prefer the more sophisti-cated salmon or smoked-salmon fishcakes, or the pork. The staff are charm itself, making you feel a valued regular even on the first occasion you show your face.

KWAN THAI Map pp454-5 *Thai*
☎ 7403 7373; www.kwanthairestaurant.co.uk; the Riverfront, Hay's Galleria SE1, entrance on Queen's Walk; mains £9-14; ⏰ lunch & dinner Mon-Fri, dinner Sat; ⊖ London Bridge

In an unlikely and pretty sterile setting, this restaurant attracts a mostly corporate clien-tele, although passers-by who wander in will be pleasantly taken with the food. There's the usual range of green, red and jungle curries, but seafood, grills, stir-fries and salads are the specialities. Particularly recommended are the stir-fried roasted duck with chilli, aubergine and lime leaves, or the salmon mixed with curry paste, coconut cream and herbs, then wrapped in banana leaves.

LE PONT DE LA TOUR Map pp454-5 *French*
☎ 7403 8403; www.conran-restaurants.co.uk; Butler's Wharf Bldg, 36d Shad Thames SE1; bar & grill mains £12.50-19.50, 2-/3-course set lunch £13.95/16.95, restaurant mains £12.50-35, 3-course set lunch £29.50; ⏰ noon-3pm & 6-11pm; ⊖ Tower Hill

Too famous and obviously located to ignore, the main room of Le Pont is the starchiest Conran restaurant in the neighbourhood. All in all, it's probably better to go to the **Blueprint Café** (op-posite) for its superior outlook, but if you can't

Eating – Along the South Bank

get a table there, or are really fussy about good service, settle in here for some elegant modern European/French dishes. For something a little more relaxed, head to the bar-and-grill side.

ROAST Map pp454-5 *British*
1st fl, Borough Market SE1; ⊖ London Bridge
Iqbal Wahhab, of revered Cinnamon Club fame, has situated his new restaurant directly over Borough Market, so he won't have to go far should he need to pop out for a cup of sugar

or any other ingredient. The centrepiece is the open spit, where the ribs of beef, suckling pigs, birds or game will be roasted. With an emphasis on seasonal ingredients, there are also lighter dishes from salads through to grilled seafood.

WOOLPACK Map pp454-5 *Gastropub*
☎ 7357 9269; 98 Bermondsey St; mains £6.60-10;
🕒 food served noon-9pm; ⊖ London Bridge
There's still something of a smoky old pub about this place, despite the now shiny brown

---

The London Chain Gang

While, of course, the usual bleak offerings of chain restaurants are to be found all over the capital, London also boasts some excellent chains of inventive and interesting restaurants, commanding massive loyalty from locals. Here are some of our favourites below – check their websites for a full list of outlets.

Carluccio's

Inventive and authentic, these Italian restaurants have a great ambience, helped along by the open space created by the deli-counter each outlet has. Not too pricey given the excellent food. (www.carluccios.com)

Giraffe

There's a kind of sunny Californian feel to family-friendly Giraffe, where the likes of coarse-cut chips, burritos, veggie salad wraps and burgers are on the menu, and friendly service is a given. (www.giraffe.net)

Gourmet Burger Kitchen

The burgers here are the real deal, made from prime Scottish beef and lovingly enlivened by specially created sauces and superb chips (veggie versions available). The Bayswater branch on Westbourne Grove (Map pp444–5) is probably the most useful. (www.gbkinfo.co.uk)

Royal China

The city's number one dim-sum chain also does a selection of Cantonese specialities. The **Westferry branch** (Map p463; ☎ 7719 0888; 30 Westferry Circus) has impressive Thames views and is quieter on weekends than the most famous branch, on Queensway (Map pp444–5). (www.royalchinagroup.co.uk)

Tas

Excellent Turkish restaurants with a roll call of Anatolian stews and grills that never disappoint. There are branches near **Waterloo** (Map pp448–9; ☎ 7928 2111; 33 the Cut SE1) and **Borough Market** (Map pp454–5; ☎ 7403 7200; 72 Borough High St SE1), plus a touristy branch near the **Globe theatre** (Map pp454–5; ☎ 7633 9777; 20-22 New Globe Walk SE1) selling pide (Turkish pizzas) and kitted out in ethnic décor. (www.tasrestaurant.com)

Wagamama

There's nothing new or exciting about this chain of noodle bars, but the food's reliable and the bench seating excellent for solo travellers. (www.wagamama.com)

Yo! Sushi

It's time to resurrect London's original Sushi chain, which brought dining on an conveyer belt to the Brits in the late 1990s. Smart makeovers and modernisations in the past year or so have made this a great place to come once again. The original outlet on **Poland Street** (Map p450; ☎ 7287 0443) and branches at Harvey Nichols and Selfridges are among the 14 outlets across London. (www.yosushi.com/consumer)

tiling on the walls, the stripped-back wooden floors, the 1970s retro touches and the hip, relaxed clientele. (Perhaps it's the boozy, smoky environment and weekend football fans that convey that impression?) The menu screams 'pub grub' with all its burgers, chips and steaks, but the tortillas are a cut above.

CHEAP EATS

DEGUSTIBUS Map pp454-5 *English*
☎ 7407 5048; www.degustibus.co.uk; 4 Southwark St SE1; mains £2-5; ☼ lunch Thu-Sat; ⊖ London Bridge
Salads, wraps, big fat sandwiches and plump muffins are the stock in trade of this cheerful sandwich bar/deli next to Borough Market. The *pièce de résistance* is the tortino, a huge thick triangle of pastry and Mediterranean vegetables that's halfway between a slice of pizza and a calzone.

EL VERGEL Map pp454-5 *Latin American*
☎ 7357 0057; www.elvergel.co.uk; 8 Lant St SE1; mains £4.50-6.50; ☼ 8.30am-3pm Mon-Fri; ⊖ Borough
This small café is most notable for its breakfasts of fried Chilean bread and bacon, but also has specialities like *empanadas*, tacos and Peruvian flat bread sandwiches, all to the tune of a funky beat.

MASTERS SUPER FISH
Map pp448-9 *Seafood*
☎ 7928 6924; 191 Waterloo Rd SE1; most mains £6.50-10.50; ☼ dinner Mon, lunch & dinner Tue-Sat; ⊖ Southwark/Waterloo
No lie, we've once been eating Masters' delicious-looking and -smelling fish and chips at the nearest bus stop when a passing car pulled over and the passenger asked to try a bite! We're not sure we'd go to *quite* such lengths ourselves but, given it resembles a typical greasy spoon, Masters' seafood is excellent – fresh daily from Billingsgate market and grilled rather than fried if desired. Other humble dishes, including vegetarian lasagne, are also on the menu and can all be eaten in (not just at the bus stop).

TAS CAFÉ Map pp454-5 *Turkish*
7403 8557; www.tasrestaurant.com; 72 Borough High St; snacks £1.75-4.50; ☼ breakfast, lunch & dinner; ⊖ London Bridge
Several of the excellent Tas restaurants are located on the South Bank, but this café is even less formal, offering toasted Turkish sandwiches (with cheese or *suchuk* sausage), mezes, wraps, salads and extremely syrupy baklava and other sweets, all to have in or take away.

THE EAST END

While Brick Lane is now a landscape of restaurant 'greeters' trying to entice you inside, and lads out on the piss trying to outdo each other in competitions as to who can eat the hottest vindaloo, real curry fans have moved on to Whitechapel (and Tooting, see Worth the Trip, p269). The East End's famous multiculturalism means its ethnic cuisine doesn't stop there, either. You'll find pretty well anything – from Turkish to Latin American and even Georgian.

BETHNAL GREEN & HACKNEY

ARMADILLO Map pp438-9 *Latin American*
☎ 7249 3633; www.armadillorestaurant.co.uk; 41 Broadway Market E8; mains £10-14; ☼ dinner; rail London Fields/bus 106, 253, 26, 48 or 55
Armadillo is the jewel in the crown of Broadway Market's increasingly funky scene, a simple neighbourhood restaurant that people travel across London to visit. There's a constantly changing mix of excellent Argentine, Brazilian and Peruvian food, a friendly vibe and sparse decoration with Latino-kitsch touches (beaded curtains with pictures of Jesus and Frida Kahlo, lizard-shaped toilet-roll holders). Typical dishes might include roast suckling pig, criolla cabbage and chestnuts, Peruvian duck *seco* and fried cassava or pancakes with *dulce de leche* (a sweeter, thicker condensed milk).

CILICIA Map pp438-9 *Mediterranean*
☎ 7249 8799; www.cilicia.co.uk; 1 Broadway Market E8; mains £10-14; ☼ 9am-11pm; rail London Fields/bus 106, 253, 26, 48 or 55
Just by the canal, this is the newer and larger of two Cilicia outlets – the original is on Stoke Newington Church St – and a welcome addition to the eating strip on Broadway Market. The welcoming staff serves up a great range of Turkish-, Greek- and Italian-accented cooking using the freshest ingredients in a convivial and laid-back atmosphere.

Eating – The East End

CROWN ORGANIC Map pp438-9 *Gastropub*
☎ 8981 9998; 223 Grove Rd E3; mains £7.50-15;
⊖ Mile End/bus 8 or 277

The cooking is a little more variable at this off-shoot of Islington's Duke of Cambridge, but with its elegant upstairs dining room and its pleasant balcony, it's a bit of a boon in this area.

LITTLE GEORGIA Map pp438-9 *Georgian*
☎ 7249 9070; 2 Broadway Market E8; mains £10-14;
🕒 dinner Tue-Sat; rail London Fields/bus 106, 253, 26, 48 or 55

This charming slice of the Caucasus in East London is an excellent place to try out one of the best but least-known cuisines in Europe. Here the menu includes dishes such as *nigziani* (red pepper or aubergine stuffed with walnuts, herbs and roast vegetables), chicken *satsivi* in walnut sauce and the Georgian classic staple *khachapuri* (cheese bread). Service can be a little unpredictable, but Little Georgia comfortably gets away with that.

DOCKLANDS

LIGHTSHIP TEN Map pp454-5 *Danish*
☎ 7481 3123; www.lightshipx.com; 5a St Katharine's Way, St Katharine Docks E1; lunch mains £5.50-14, dinner mains £11-18.50; 🕒 lunch Tue-Fri, dinner Tue-Sat; ⊖ Tower Hill

This is a memorable restaurant aboard the world's oldest lightship, serving, wait for it, nouveau Danish cuisine. In recent years a certain French tone has crept into the menu, with foie gras this and *dauphinoise* that, Béarnaise sauce, tarte tartin and filet mignon. However, this colonisation only adds to the appeal for those who haven't acquired a taste for open-faced sandwiches, meatballs, gravadlax, pork or herrings and aquavit. The lacquer-red dining room remains a wonderfully romantic space.

PLATEAU Map p463 *Japanese*
☎ 7715 7100; www.conran-restaurants.co.uk; Canada Place, Canada Sq E14; bar & grill mains £9.50-18.50, 2-/3-course set menus £16.50/20, restaurant mains £14.50-27, 3-/4-course set menus £24.75/29.75; 🕒 bar & grill noon-11pm Mon-Sat, noon-3pm Sun, restaurant noon-3pm & 6-10.30pm Mon-Fri, 6-10.30pm Sat; ⊖ Canary Wharf

At last the financial worker bees at Canary Wharf have somewhere to go that's not All Bar One. For while their bosses are exercising the company plastic in the formal restaurant, the bar and grill offers fresh dishes like swordfish steak, Guinness-batter halibut and duck leg with caramelised plum at affordable prices. The rooms are light and airy with Eero Saarinen Finnish Tulip chairs and Castiglioni Arco floor lamps, but most notably they overlook Canada Sq. Its E14 postcode means this is unlikely to become a destination restaurant, but when that square is looking all sci-fi lit up at night, perhaps it should.

UBON Map p463 *Japanese*

☎ 7719 7800; 34 Westferry Circus E14; mains £5-30; ⌚ lunch Mon-Fri, dinner Mon-Sat; ⊖ Canary Wharf/DLR Westferry

Roman Abramovich reportedly once sent a private jet from Russia to pick up takeaway from this Canary Wharf restaurant, but that's kind of missing the point. Ubon is certainly no disgrace to its big sister, **Nobu** (p246), in the food stakes. While customers argue over whether you really get value for money here, the selling point has to be the breathtaking Thames views.

WAPPING FOOD

Map pp454-5 *Mediterranean*

☎ 7680 2080; Wapping Wall E1; mains £11-19, brunch £4-9; ⌚ lunch & dinner Mon-Sat, lunch Sun, brunch Sat & Sun; ⊖ Wapping

Unusually for the many converted factories that populate the post-industrial world, this Mediterranean restaurant has chosen to leave all the hydraulic equipment *in situ*, giving you the chance to admire the turbines and sniff the engine grease (it's not at all unpleasant, really!) while enjoying your Mediterranean food. The staff are very pleasant, the wine list all-Australian and the ingredients fresh. A good choice.

CHEAP EATS
FRIZZANTE@CITY FARM

Map pp438-9 *Italian*

☎ 7739 2266; www.frizzanteltd.co.uk; Hackney City Farm, 1a Goldsmith's Row E2; mains £3-7; ⊖ Bethnal Green/rail Cambridge Heath

The ramshackle Frizzante, located at Hackney City Farm, was voted *Time Out's* family restaurant of the year in 2005, and it's easy to see why. The plentiful servings of good Italian food are great value, and the next-door city farm makes it a great place to bring children, who can be kept entertained watching sheep, pigs, cattle and hens being looked after before, erm, eating them.

Top Five – the East End

- **Armadillo** (p255)
- **LMNT** (right)
- **Mangal** (right)
- **New Tayyab** (right)
- **Wapping Food** (above)

LAHORE KEBAB HOUSE

Map pp454-5 *Indian*

☎ 7488 2551; 2 Umberston St E1; mains £5-6.50; ⊖ Whitechapel/Aldgate East

This smoky glass-walled restaurant is not an aesthetic experience, and ever since City workers discovered this local the standard of cooking seems to have slipped a little bit. Still, it's okay for a fast and functional fill-up of curry or lamb kebabs.

LAHORE ONE Map pp454-5 *Indian*

☎ 7791 0112; 218 Commercial Rd E1; mains £3.75-5.50; ⌚ to 2am; ⊖ Whitechapel

You'll be lucky to bag a table at this tiny outlet, but it also does takeaway. The proprietors boast that the food is made to order, with no artificial or packet sauces, in charcoal-fired ovens, and they're certainly doing something right. Spicy lamb kebabs (70p each) are a popular starter, while mains are mostly meat and veggie biryanis or *karahai* (their spelling) wok dishes.

LMNT Map pp438-9 *International*

☎ 7249 6727; 316 Queensbridge Rd E8; mains before/after 7pm £5.45/7.95; rail London Fields

The ornate Egyptian interior, with seating in elevated alcoves in the corners, over the bar and inside a huge gilt jar, comes as a shock as you enter from the nondescript street. The food is also good and plentiful at this less-wealthy person's Les Trois Garçons.

MANGAL Map pp438-9 *Turkish*

☎ 7275 8981; 10 Arcola St E8; mains £6.50-8.50; rail Dalston Kingsland

Mangal serves some of the best Turkish meze, grilled lamb chops, pigeon and salads in north London. Gilbert & George, *enfants terribles* of the British art scene, are regulars.

NEW TAYYAB Map pp454-5 *Indian*

☎ 7247 9543; 83 Fieldgate St E1; mains £3-10; ⌚ dinner; ⊖ Whitechapel

From the enticing aroma on entering, it's clear this buzzing Punjabi restaurant is in another leage than its Brick Lane equivalents. *Seekh* kebabs, *masala* fish and other starters served on sizzling hot plates are delicious, as are accompaniments like nan, raita and mango lassi. But meat mains are definitely the strong point here. The vegetarian *karahi* wok dish, while tasty, is atypically oily. New Tayyab has been so popular that a new extension has been built, making it less of a crush at weekends. BYO alcohol.

SOUTHEAST LONDON

It's not that we've been lazy in compiling the following brief section, it's just that southeast London's culinary reputation is only starting to emerge, if at all. Even locals despair about where to eat in Greenwich; you'll pass plenty of eateries along the main street, but few places are really decent. Dulwich is starting to support a gastropub culture, but nothing that's really noteworthy has arrived yet. Come back in a few years.

GREENWICH

INSIDE Map p463 *Modern European*
☎ 8265 5060; www.insiderestaurant.co.uk; 19 Greenwich South St SE10; mains £12-17, 2-/3-course lunch & early dinner set menus £15/18; ☺ lunch Wed-Sun, dinner Mon-Sat, brunch Sat & Sun; DLR Greenwich/Cutty Sark

With white and aubergine walls, modern art and linen table cloths, Inside looks quite formal, but they won't bat an eyelid if you turn up in jeans. The crisp food typically includes fresh-tasting pea soup or truffle-and-mixed-mushroom risotto, and desserts such as dark-chocolate tart with white-chocolate ice cream. This is Greenwich's best restaurant.

SE10 RESTAURANT & BAR

Map p463 *Modern European*
☎ 8858 9764; www.se10restaurant.co.uk; 62 Thames St SE10; mains £11.75-17.75; ☺ lunch Mon-Sat, dinner Tue-Sat, brunch Sun; DLR Cutty Sark

Don't be deterred by the scruffy exterior and location, and study the map carefully before setting out, because this is a deceptively worthwhile detour. Inside the place is light and airy, and surprisingly posh. For a restaurant so near the river, there's a good concentration of fish dishes, plus traditional British dishes (sadly only a few veggie options). The desserts are pure comfort food, especially the sticky-toffee pudding.

TRAFALGAR TAVERN

Map p463 *British/Mediterranean*
☎ 8858 2437; Park Row SE10; mains £8.30-13; DLR Cutty Sark

It's lovely here being able to enjoy a magnificent river view, while tucking into fish, British staples or the celebrated whitebait (for which Parliament used to come to a halt when it first came into season). However, you won't be the only one to have the idea; this place is pretty touristy.

CHEAP EATS

ROYAL TEAS Map p463 *Vegetarian*
☎ 8691 7240; 76 Royal Hill SE10; meals £2.50-5.50; ☺ 10am-6pm; DLR Cutty Sark/Greenwich

Planning issues have put the existence of this delightful – and tiny – café under the spotlight, but it seems like, fingers crossed, it's here to stay. It's not quite vegetarian, in that you can get smoked salmon at breakfast, but there are also baguettes, soups and stews. We come for the ginger cake (and the American breakfast, and…).

Goddards Pie House (opposite)

NORTH CENTRAL

Marylebone High St is now one of the most talked about restaurant strips in London, consistently churning out new and dazzling eating that has Londoners making regular pilgrimages. Like mini-Marylebones, Primrose Hill and Maida Vale both offer a couple of knock-out local restaurants still largely unknown to the wider city population, which makes them well worth a trip, while Camden, a food hub for years, has well and truly rested on its laurels with little of excitement to show for the last few years. However, there's still a great deal there thanks to the frantic pace of change in the 1990s.

MARYLEBONE & REGENT'S PARK

EAT & TWO VEG Map pp448-9 *Vegetarian*
☎ 7258 8595; www.eatandtwoveg.com; 50 Marylebone High St W1; mains £6-10; ⊖ Baker St

One of the best vegetarian experiences in London, Eat & Two Veg is a huge success despite its rather awful name. Bright and breezy with charming, friendly staff and a smart 21st-century American diner look, the ambience is great (with none of the more sanctimonious elements of some veggie places). The menu is international – the satay chicken wings tasted like the real McCoy and were delicious, while the burgers and fries made us double-check the place really was vegetarian. Plenty on offer for vegans too, and desserts (particularly the bread and butter pudding) are flawless.

Pie 'n' Mash

Among all London's trendy modern eateries, maybe you should try how the English used to eat, and sample a pie made from minced beef and gravy, and 'mash' (fake mashed potatoes made from powder). Eels, mushy peas and 'liquor' (a parsley sauce) are optional extras. It's something of an acquired taste, although veggie pies are frequently available. The **Square Pie Company** (Map pp454–5; ☎ 7377 1114; Spitalfields Market E1), with what tastes like real mashed potatoes, is most likely to appeal to modern tastes. Other options:

Castle's (Map pp440-1; ☎ 7485 2196; 229 Royal College St NW1; ⊖ Camden Town/rail Camden Rd)

F Cooke (☎ 7729 7718; 150 Hoxton St N1; ⊖ Old St/Liverpool St)

Goddards Pie House (Map p463; ☎ 8293 9313; 45 Greenwich Church St SE10; DLR Cutty Sark)

Manze's (Map pp454-5; ☎ 7407 2985; 87 Tower Bridge Rd SE1; ⊖ London Bridge)

GOLDEN HIND map pp448-9 *Fish & Chips*
☎ 7486 3644; 73 Marylebone Lane W1; mains £4-10; ⊖ Bond St

This 90-year-old chippie has a classic interior, chunky wooden tables and contractors sitting alongside pinstriped business types. From the vintage fryer comes quite possibly the best cod and chips in London. Attentive service and fresh fish cooked well – could you ask for anything more? BYO alcohol.

LE PAIN QUOTIDIEN Map pp448-9 *French*
☎ 7486 6154; www.lepainquotidien.com; 72-75 Marylebone High St W1; mains £4.75-10; ⊖ Baker St

The attractively simple, stripped-down wooden interior of the dining room here makes for a lovely spot for lunch or dinner – 'Daily Bread' has a bakery section selling, among other things, jams too. This new place on foodie central Marylebone High St has been a real hit, although service can be atrocious – a pity, as the food is delicious, based on a selection of *tartines* complemented by salads and soups.

LOCANDA LOCATELLI Map pp444-5 *Italian*
☎ 7935 9088; www.locandalocatelli.com; 8 Seymour St W1; mains £19-29; ⊖ Marble Arch

This place has become something of a cult eatery in London, and its co-founder, celebrity chef Giorgio Locatelli, has brought some of the best Italian cooking to England in the past decade. While it's still hard to get a table here without booking months in advance, it's worth the effort of so doing despite some recurring gripes about the slow service, as this is sublime Italian cooking at its best.

ORRERY Map pp448-9 *Modern European*
☎ 7616 8000; www.conran.com; 55 Marylebone High St W1; mains £22-29; ⊖ Baker St

From the moment you walk into this surprisingly unshowy restaurant bathed in natural light you'll be made to feel totally welcome by the generous and attentive staff. Worth every point of its Michelin star, this Conran gem has perhaps the best service of any of

London's fine-dining establishments. The French-leaning food is also outstanding, with dishes like roast Icelandic cod fillet or sea bass semolina gnocchi a thorough treat. But Orrery's star attraction is its selection of some 40 cheeses that you'll remember long after your meal here is over. Stunning.

OZER Map pp448-9 — *Turkish*

☎ 7323 0505; 5 Langham Pl W1; mains £7.50-13; closed Sun; ✪ Oxford Circus

The 'Ottoman cuisine' here is lighter and more refined than the Turkish norm, as local workers and shoppers fully appreciate. This restaurant's Ankara sibling is supposed to be one of the best in Turkey. Portions are 'elegant' (okay, that means small), but mains like roasted shoulder of lamb with kumquat marmalade are powerful. It's a classy joint, but if you don't agree complain to Ozer, whose mobile number is on the table!

PROVIDORES & TAPA ROOM

Map pp448-9 — *Spanish Fusion*

☎ 7935 6175; www.theprovidores.co.uk; 109 Marylebone High St W1; tapas £2-13, mains £16-23; ✪ Baker St/Bond St

Kiwis Peter Gordon and Anna Hansen are the kitchen alchemists behind this sassy, sociable and sexy place, which gives fusion back its good name. The restaurant is split over two levels, with tempting tapas grazers on the ground floor and full meals along the same innovative lines – Spanish and just about everything else – in the elegant and understated dining room above.

QUIET REVOLUTION Map pp448-9 — *Café*

☎ 7487 5683; 28 Marylebone High St W1; mains £5-9; closes 6pm; ✪ Baker St/Bond St

Just walking into this wholly organic place (located behind Aveda) is enough to lift flagging spirits and put the spring back in your step. It's a terrific place to unwind and fill up during the day on the vigorous juice combos, creative but simple brekkies like herb omelettes, and zingy salads and mouth-watering quiches for lunch. Bills come with a free promotional beauty product from Aveda.

WOODLANDS

Map pp448-9 — *Vegetarian/Indian*

☎ 7486 3862; 77 Marylebone Lane W1; mains £5-15; ✪ Bond St

In India the 'Voodies' chain is pretty decent, but here it's wow. Superb thalis (all-you-can-eat mixed plates) and *dosas* are highlights, but there are no real duds on the South Indian menu. Their rallying call is 'let vegetation feed the nation' and they put up a persuasive argument.

PADDINGTON & BAYSWATER

COUSCOUS CAFÉ Map pp444-5 — *Moroccan*

☎ 7727 6597; 7 Porchester Gardens W2; mains £10-16; ✪ Bayswater

If Moroccan is your cup of mint tea then get yourself down to this vividly decorated place, which does a faultless line in familiar favourites from all over North Africa but really excels with tangy *tagines*, sweet pastries and slightly exaggerated service.

LEVANTINE Map pp444-5 — *Lebanese*

☎ 7262 1111; www.levant.co.uk; 26 London St W2; mains £9.50-19; ✪ Paddington

Paddington's most interesting restaurant (although this is hardly a huge feat), Levantine is cosy, atmospheric and yet thoroughly contemporary. The set menus are the best value (make a point of asking to see the set-menu list), and the fare is delicious, including wonderful renditions of Lebanese staples such as tahini, hummus and *muhammara* as well as more complex grills. Don't miss the *Thousand and One Nights*–style fantasy toilets, and beware of the inevitable belly dancer.

MANDARIN KITCHEN

Map pp444-5 — *Chinese*

☎ 7727 9468; 14-16 Queensway W2; mains £5.95-25; ✪ Bayswater/Queensway

This perennially popular Cantonese restaurant specialises in seafood and keeping customers waiting ages for their table. With that gripe out of the way – oh, and the décor's not up to much – we can focus on the fare, which is most likely the best Chinese seafood in London. Specialities include stuffed whole chicken with shark fin (£70) – a treat for an entire family.

CAMDEN

BAR GANSA Map pp440-1 *Spanish*
☎ 7267 8909; 2 Inverness St NW1; tapas £2.60-4.50, mains £12; ⏲ closed Sun; ⊖ Camden Town

This place bears more than a passing resemblance to a traditional Spanish tapas joint – it's smoky, loud and cramped, and the staff often seem to speak a different language. The menu ranges from tasty titbits to manly mains. This is a focal point of the Camden scene, has a late licence and is howlingly popular. It's good, but we could cope with a little less attitude.

CAFÉ CORFU Map pp440-1 *Greek*
☎ 7269 8088; 7-9 Pratt St NW1; mains £8-12; ⊖ Camden Town

Corfu is among the best of a host of Greek restaurants around here. Décor is sleek and simple, the delicious food feels light but fills, and there's more than retsina to slake your thirst. A belly dancer helps with digestion at the weekend, but be warned: on her second spin the buxom beauty takes partners.

CAFÉ DELANCEY Map pp440-1 *French*
☎ 7387 1985; 3 Delancey St NW1; mains £9-15.50; ⊖ Camden Town

The granddaddy of French-style brasseries in London, Delancey offers the chance to get a decent cup of coffee with a snack or a full meal in relaxed European-style surroundings complete with newspapers. The cramped toilets, bickering staff and Charles Aznavour crooning in the background seem suitably Parisian.

COTTONS RHUM SHOP, BAR & RESTAURANT Map pp440-1 *Caribbean*
☎ 7482 1096; 55 Chalk Farm Rd NW1; mains £10-15; ⊖ Chalk Farm

Easily more enticing than it sounds, Cottons is one of the most authentic Caribbean eateries in town, and offers island specials like jerk chicken and curried goat, head-banging rum-based cocktails, and a friendly atmosphere in cheerful surroundings.

EL PARADOR Map pp440-1 *Spanish*
☎ 7387 2789; 245 Eversholt St NW1; tapas £3-6; ⊖ Mornington Cres

This laid-back Spanish place has a huge selection of tapas – including mucho vegetarian titbits – from all over Spain. There's a walled garden for when the sun's out and you're feeling moderately Mediterranean (the rea-

sonably priced rioja might help). The only thing we don't like about this place is the odd booking protocol: fewer than three can forget it.

ENGINEER Map pp440-1 *Gastropub*
☎ 7722 0950; 65 Gloucester Ave NW1; mains £10-15; ⊖ Chalk Farm

One of London's original and best gastropubs, the Engineer serves up consistently good international cuisine – from tempura prawns to racks of lamb – and is hugely popular with impeccably hip north Londoners. The pub itself is quite decadent, with red-velvet curtains and gold candelabras hanging from the high ceilings upstairs, although the splendid walled garden is the highlight.

JAMÓN JAMÓN Map pp440-1 *Spanish*
☎ 7284 0606; 38 Parkway N1; tapas £2-7; ⏲ noon-midnight; ⊖ Camden Town

Authentically Spanish, Jamón Jamón features, as you would expect, an extensive menu of pork-based dishes, bursting with flavour and served up in large, cosy premises a short walk from the chaos of Camden High St.

MANGO ROOM Map pp440-1 *Caribbean*
☎ 7482 5065; www.mangoroom.co.uk; 10 Kentish Town Rd NW1; mains £9.50-13; ⊖ Camden Town

Among the litter and lowlife of this part of Camden, Mango Room is a relaxed Caribbean experience popular with everyone from pre-clubbers to the occasional brigade of silver-haired ladies out for a special occasion. It's kind of decaf Caribbean, although there's no holding back with the food, especially things fishy or with mango – grilled goat's cheese with mango and pesto, and grilled barracuda with courgettes and coconut sauce were highlights, as was the banana and mango *crème brûlée*. The early-ska/Jamaican-jazz soundtrack is wicked.

MANNA Map pp440-1 *Vegetarian*
☎ 7722 8082; www.manna-veg.com; 4 Erskine Rd NW1; mains £9.50-13; ⊖ Chalk Farm

Tucked away on a side street in London's most glamorous inner-city village, this gorgeous little place does a brisk trade in inventive vegetarian cooking. The menu features mouth-watering dishes such as couscous-crusted aubergine-and-celeriac cakes with blue cheese. Prices are, naturally, not low – this is Primrose Hill after all – but Manna is often heavenly.

Top Five Celebrity Spotting

- **Ivy** (p235)
- **Gordon Ramsay** (p248)
- **Nobu** (p246)
- **Sketch** (p246)
- **Wolseley** (p246)

TROJKA Map pp440-1   *Eastern European*
☎ 7483 3765; 101 Regent's Park Rd NW1; mains £6-9;
❸ Chalk Farm
This Primrose Village place serves good-value Eastern European/Russian dishes, such as herrings with dill sauce and Russian salad, Polish *bigosz* (a cabbage 'stew' with mixed meats) and salt beef, in an attractive skylit restaurant frequented by local bohos. Avoid the house wine by bringing your own.

ST JOHN'S WOOD & MAIDA VALE

GREEN OLIVE Map pp444-5   *Italian*
☎ 7289 2469; 5 Warwick Pl W9; 3-course set lunch/dinner £15/45; ❸ Warwick Ave
The Maida Vale cognoscenti hold this neighbourhood Italian place in high esteem. Dishes, although creative and very tasty, are rather daintily portioned, so you don't want to arrive with a mean appetite. The plain brickwork and bubbly staff give it an upmarket rustic kinda vibe.

JASON'S Map pp444-5   *Fish*
☎ 7286 6752; wwww.jasons.co.uk; Jason's Wharf, opposite 60 Blomfield Rd W9; mains £12-20; ❂ lunch Wed-Sun, dinner Tue-Sat; ❸ Warwick Ave
One to remember when the sun's out, canalside Jason's has cosy outside tables, and a main dining room in a high wooden-ceilinged boathouse that is basic but feels almost alfresco. Happily, the exotic fare is more reliable than the weather; you can expect superb fish and seafood dishes with French, Mauritian and Creole influences and overtones.

CHEAP EATS

ADDIS Map pp442-3   *Ethiopian*
☎ 7278 0679; 42 Caledonian Rd N1; mains £4.50-8.50; ❸ King's Cross St Pancras
It always feels like summer in Addis, with its golden sunset hues, cheery staff and very laidback vibe. It's normally full of Ethiopian and

Sudanese punters, which is a good sign, and serves up a lip-smacking parade of exotic fare like *ful masakh* (a salad with feta and spicy falafel), the best sign of all.

ASAKUSA Map pp440-1   *Japanese*
☎ 7388 8533; 265 Eversholt St NW1; mains £5-10; ❸ Mornington Cres
This scruffy but clean place has cheap sushi for £1 to £2 per piece, along with more elaborate, reasonably priced set menus.

DIWANA BHEL POORI HOUSE
Map pp440-1   *Indian*
☎ 7387 5556; 121 Drummond St; mains £3-6.50; ❸ Euston/Euston Sq
The first of its kind – and still the best on this busy street, according to many – Diwana specialises in Bombay-style *bhel poori* (a sweet and sour, soft and crunchy 'party mix' snack) and *dosa*s (filled pancakes). There's an all-you-can-eat lunchtime buffet for £6.

KONSTAM Map pp442-3   *Café*
☎ 7833 5040; 109 King's Cross Rd WC1; mains £4-8; ❂ 7.30am-4pm Mon-Fri; ❸ King's Cross St Pancras
Despite its uninspiring environs – or perhaps because of them – Konstam is a real gem, serving tasty, healthy, good-value sandwiches and specials in a charming, friendly atmosphere.

MANDALAY Map pp444-5   *Burmese*
☎ 7258 3696; 444 Edgware Rd W2; mains £5-8; ❂ closed Sun; ❸ Edgware Rd
Despite looking not unlike a greasy spoon and being located on this particularly grim part of Edgware Rd, Mandalay is actually one of the capital's most wonderful secrets, not to mention its only Burmese restaurant. The delicious fritters and the spicy *mokhingar* soup with noodles make great starters, while king prawns in noodles with tamarind and ginger sauce is simply the best we've ever had.

TERRA BRASIL Map pp440-1   *Brazilian*
☎ 7388 6554; 36-38 Chalton St NW1; set buffet £5; ❸ Euston
Don't think less of Terra because of the bracket it's in; this is the best eatery in the whole of Euston (although we concede that that's a bit like saying the best slalom skier in the desert). It's a particularly warm and cosy place, where the *caipirinha* cocktails are mighty and the plates are laden with tasty Brazilian fare like *feijoada* (an assorted platter of thinly sliced meats with black beans, rice and citrus slices).

NORTH LONDON

None of these restaurants are destinations in themselves, but a visit to any one of them will certainly improve your outing. A couple are in parks, while most of the others are on the high streets of each of the different neighbourhoods; Stoke Newington Church St, Crouch End Broadway and Muswell Hill Broadway are particularly good strips.

HAMPSTEAD & HIGHGATE

JIN KICHI Map p465 — *Japanese*
☎ 7794 6158; 73 Heath St NW3; mains £5.50-13;
Ⓥ lunch & dinner Sat & Sun, dinner Mon-Fri;
Ⓔ Hampstead

A disproportionate number of London's Japanese live in Hampstead, and a disproportionate number of them eat at this slightly shabby and cramped little place, regarded as one of the best Japanese restaurants in north London. It's a particularly good bet for grilled meats and other nonstandard Japanese flavours, none of which you'll be able to enjoy unless you book.

LAUDERDALE HOUSE Map p465 — *Café*
☎ 8348 8716; Waterlow Park, Highgate Hill N6;
mains £6; Ⓔ Archway

The best place to eat in Highgate during the day – and only a short walk from fascinating **Highgate Cemetery** (see p195) – Lauderdale House is a lovely 16th-century residence that doubles as a community arts centre. The outdoor tables in the big garden that leads out into the park are much coveted on sunny weekend afternoons by families and hungover funsters. Standard dishes include reasonable fish cakes, chips, salads and lasagnes, although the creative specials like stuffed avocado are often your best bet. The coffee is very good.

WELLS TAVERN Map p465 — *Gastropub*
☎ 7794 3785; www.thewellshampstead.co.uk;
30 Well Walk NW3; 2-/3-course lunch Mon-Sat £12.95/14.95, 2-/3-course dinner & Sun lunch £21/26;
Ⓔ Hampstead

The Wells was once a raucous venue for 'clandestine or unpremeditated marriages'. Now it's a 'very naice' gastropub, with mulberry-coloured pillows plumped up on black leather and brown corduroy couches, dark walls and big flower arrangements. The modern European food is well above average and, particularly at lunch, offers pretty good value – for Hampstead. However, it's the style and indisputably gorgeous location that attract the well-heeled, frequently older crowd.

MUSWELL HILL, CROUCH END & STOKE NEWINGTON

BANNERS — *Modern European*
☎ 8348 2930; 21 Park Rd N8; mains £8-11; Ⓔ Finsbury Park, then bus W7

They say some people move to Crouch End to be closer to this café, although we suspect that 'they' might be the owners. It's always buzzing – too much so when the babies and infants start acting up – and it's got an inexplicable magnetic power. The food can be hit and miss (veggie sausages and mash hit, cooked brekkies generally miss), the smoothies are invigorating, and the staff are friendly to locals and polite to strangers.

BLUE LEGUME — *Vegetarian*
☎ 7923 1303; 101 Stoke Newington Church St N16; mains £5-8; rail Stoke Newington, then bus 73

Buzzing with familiarity, this lively and laid-back local has mosaic tables and slightly kooky décor (such as a big plaster sun hanging from the ceiling), although there's nothing odd about the big, late breakfasts or the selection of satisfying smoothies. Throughout the day there are light veggie snacks such as ciabatta and crostini, hot specials like courgette burgers, and trays of delicate, delicious pastries.

CAFÉ ON THE HILL — *Modern European*
☎ 8444 4957; www.cafeonthehill.com; 46 Fortis Green Rd N10; mains £8-14; Ⓔ Highgate, then bus 134

Largely organic and very veggie, this place has been a real hit with locals, who come here in droves. It's all you could hope for in a local café – seasonal menus, all-day brekkies, good

> ### Top Five – North London
> - Wells Tavern (left)
> - **Rasa** (p264)
> - **Özlem** (p264)
> - **Café on the Hill** (above)
> - **Toff's** (p264)

coffee, light lunches, afternoon tea, substantial and relatively adventurous evening meals, newspapers, and a welcoming atmosphere.

TOFF'S
Fish & Chips

☎ 8883 8656; 38 Muswell Hill Broadway N10; mains £9-17; ⊙ closes at 10pm; ⊖ Highgate, then bus 134

This former British chipper of the year has a rather smelly takeaway counter at the front and a more salubrious dining room out the back. The staff are very friendly, and Toff's is renowned for providing large quantities of fresh fish, beautifully battered and flawlessly fried.

CHEAP EATS

ÖZLEM
Map pp438-9 *Turkish*

☎ 7275 9974; 2 Prince George Rd N16; mains £3-6; rail Dalston Kingsland

The staff here barely speak any English – the clientele are 99% from the local Turkish diaspora in Stoke Newington – but they seem genuinely delighted that any non-Turks should visit their canteen. It's not going to win any prizes for design with its bright strip light-

Top Five Gastropubs

- **Anchor & Hope** (p251)
- **Coach & Horses** (p241)
- **Cow** (left)
- **Duke of Cambridge** (p243)
- **Lots Road Pub & Dining Room** (p271)

ing and nonexistent décor, but the delicious authentic food more than compensates, and prices are ludicrously low.

RASA
Map p437 *Indian/Vegetarian*

☎ 7249 0344; 55 Stoke Newington Church St N16; mains £4-6; rail Stoke Newington, then bus 73

This superb South Indian vegetarian restaurant can't be missed (not with that shocking-pink façade anyway). Friendly service, a calm atmosphere, jovial prices and outstanding food from the Indian state of Kerala are its distinctive features. Don't bother with the menu, just bring on the three-course feast. Rasa Travancore, across the road, is more of the same, but with fish and meat.

WEST LONDON

The sheer variety on offer in multicultural west London means rich pickings for those seeking truly excellent restaurants. Notting Hill is the epicentre of this zone and offers a superb range of eateries whatever the size of your belly or purse, from venerated chippers to fashionable fusion. Shepherd's Bush is constantly abuzz with new openings and revamps of old favourites, while Earl's Court offers a good range of cheaper options and some great people-watching. Hammersmith makes up for its lack of sights with some unique eateries, which are well worth travelling for.

Top Five – West London

- **Chez Kristof** (p266)
- **E&O** (right)
- **Harlem** (opposite)
- **Patio** (p267)
- **River Café** (p267)

NOTTING HILL & WESTBOURNE GROVE

COW
Map pp444-5 *Gastropub*

☎ 7221 5400; 89 Westbourne Park Rd W2; mains £8-16; ⊖ Westbourne Park/Royal Oak

Owned by Tom Conran, the son of renowned restaurateur Sir Terence, this superb pub was

transformed from a dilapidated old side-street boozer into a unique and thrilling gastropub with outstanding food and a jovial pub-is-a-pub atmosphere. Seafood is a highlight (predictably, the fresh oysters with Guinness are a speciality; a pint of prawns and mayonnaise is a delight) and, despite its fair share of trust-funded west Londoners, it's still a great hang-out.

E&O
Map pp444-5 *Asian Fusion*

☎ 7229 5454; 14 Blenheim Cres W11; mains £6-20; ⊖ Notting Hill Gate/Ladbroke Grove

This Notting Hill hot spot is about the best – certainly the trendiest – in a notable neighbourhood. The Eastern & Oriental presents fusion fare, which usually starts with an Asian base and then pirouettes into something resembling Pacific Rim, eg red pumpkin, aubergine and litchi curry. The décor is stark and minimalist, but you'd better appreciate it at lunch because the evenings are mental. You can dim sum at the bar if a table is unavailable.

ELECTRIC BRASSERIE

Map pp444-5   *American*
☎ 7908 9696; www.electricbrasserie.com; 191 Portobello Rd W11; mains £10-22; ⊖ Ladbroke Grove
The name comes from the adjoining cinema, but it's possible to believe that it's a comment on the atmosphere here too, as this place never seems to stop buzzing. Whether it's for brunch over the weekend, a hearty lunch or a full dinner, the Electric certainly draws a trendy and wealthy Notting Hill crowd with its British-European menu, which includes treats such as Dover sole and wild-mushroom potpie.

GEALES Map pp444-5   *Fish & Chips*
☎ 7727 7528; 2 Farmer St W8; fish & chips £10;
⊖ Notting Hill Gate
Gregarious Geales was established in 1939 and has become a popular faux-seaside fixture with locals and tourists alike. It prices everything according to weight and season, and while it's more expensive than your everyday chipper, it's a lot better and worth every penny.

HARLEM Map pp444-5   *American*
☎ 7985 0900; 78 Westbourne Grove W2; mains £8.75-22; ⊖ Bayswater/Royal Oak
The funky feel, chunky chandeliers and smiling staff are just the first things that might impress you about this excellent new addition to the west London dining scene. The menu is just as noteworthy, though, expanding on the usual array of burgers and steaks to accommodate more off-piste dishes such as buttermilk fried chicken and char-grilled tuna steak. A great place for a meal, and with breakfast served until 6pm everyday, you know you're onto a winner.

MANDOLA Map pp444-5   *African*
☎ 7229 4734; 139-141 Westbourne Grove W2; mains £5-7; ⊖ Bayswater/Notting Hill Gate
This bright and breezy Sudanese joint offers staples such as *tamia* (a kind of falafel), *fifilia* (a vegetable curry) and meat dishes such as the unusual *shorba fule* (a meat and peanut soup). The owners are so relaxed that they sometimes can't be bothered opening.

MARKET THAI Map pp444-5   *Thai*
☎ 7460 8320; Market Bar, 240 Portobello Rd; mains £5-8; ⊖ Ladbroke Grove
Drippy white candles, carved arches and wrought-iron chairs mark out the interior of this delightful restaurant, which occupies the

Eating – West London

Geales (above)

first floor of the Market Bar but feels way, way, way beyond the market crowds. Hospitable staff and fresh, delicately spiced Thai cuisine make this place a little money very well spent.

TAWANA Map pp444-5   *Thai*
☎ 7229 3785; 3 Westbourne Grove W2; mains £5.50-8; ⊖ Bayswater/Royal Oak

Try the delicious chicken satay and succulent king-prawn dishes at this diminutive Thai place, which is decorated with potted plants and rattan chairs. The exceedingly friendly waiters will help you make some sense of the huge menu – including a large veggie section – should you need help. Or you could just take our advice.

EARL'S COURT & WEST BROMPTON

LOU PESCADOU Map pp458-9   *Fish*
☎ 7370 1057; 241 Old Brompton Rd SW5; mains £14-16; ☽ dinner; ⊖ Earl's Court/West Brompton

Simplicity and elegance meet at this wonderful seafood restaurant, which stands out among the many neighbouring eateries on Old Brompton Rd. Should you have trouble understanding the all-French menu, the staff are surprisingly democratic about assisting you, and the results are usually very rewarding.

MR WING Map pp458-9   *Chinese*
☎ 7370 4450; 242-244 Old Brompton Rd SW5; mains £7-12; ⊖ Earl's Court/West Brompton

The oddly named Mr Wing is a very smart Asian-fusion place offering Chinese cuisine with elements of Thai and Mongolian cooking. To recommend it are a plush, dark interior, helpful staff and a basement where live jazz is played. This is one of London's more interesting Chinese restaurants, yet Mr Wing is surprisingly well priced.

SHEPHERD'S BUSH & HAMMERSMITH

BUSH BAR Map pp438-9   *Modern European*
☎ 8746 2111; www.bushbar.co.uk; 45a Goldhawk Rd W12; mains £9.50-17; ☽ lunch & dinner, closed dinner Sun; ⊖ Goldhawk Rd

You have to search for this trendy media hang-out, housed in a converted warehouse and with its entrance down an alleyway off

Goldhawk Rd. It's light and breezy, and the decent restaurant attracts a BBC crowd after work with its great cocktails as much as its food. The menu is inventive and particularly strong on fresh fish and salads.

CHEZ KRISTOF Map pp438-9   *French*
☎ 8741 1177; www.chezkristof.co.uk; 111 Hammersmith Grove W6; mains £11.50-16; ⊖ Goldhawk Rd/Hammersmith

On a very unlikely stretch of road between Hammersmith and Shepherd's Bush, Chez Kristof entices you in with its fairy lights and genial, intimate atmosphere. On offer here is a sumptuous menu of regional French cooking – braised rabbit with asparagus and chanterelles, baked whole red mullet with red-pepper sauce, and traditional *coq au vin* are all exceptional quality, given the perfectly reasonable prices. The adjacent **deli** (☽ 8am-8pm) offers a great range.

ESARN KHEAW Map pp438-9   *Thai*
☎ 8743 8930; 314 Uxbridge Rd W12; mains £5-8.50; ☽ lunch & dinner Mon-Fri, dinner Sat & Sun; ⊖ Shepherd's Bush

Welcoming you back into the '70s is the green and kitsch interior of this superb Thai restaurant, which has won awards consistently throughout the last seven years. The fish-cake starters are sublime and the staff extremely friendly. The biographical detail on the menu that traces the owner's journey from Thailand to owning his own restaurant via Trusthouse Forte is a gem.

Lou Pescadou (left)

GATE Map pp438-9 *Vegetarian*

☎ 8748 6932; www.thegate.tv; 51 Queen Caroline Rd W6; mains £8.50-12.50; ✆ lunch & dinner Mon-Fri, dinner Sat; ⊖ Hammersmith

Widely considered the best vegetarian restaurant in town, Gate has an unlikely location, rented from the next-door church. The staff are exceptionally friendly and welcoming, and the relaxed atmosphere, despite the restaurant's being full most nights of the week, contributes to the uniqueness of this place. Surprisingly enough, it's the cheesecake that gets recurring rave reviews, as does the stuffed aubergine, the simple but inspired starters and the fine wine list. It's a good opportunity to convert meat-eaters. Bookings are advisable.

PATIO Map pp438-9 *Polish*

☎ 8743 5194; 5 Goldhawk Rd W12; mains £7-10; ✆ lunch & dinner Mon-Fri, dinner Sat & Sun; ⊖ Shepherd's Bush/Goldhawk Rd

Welcome to a Warsaw sitting room, c 1972. Here, amid the clutter and bizarre antiques, you'll be made truly welcome by the kindly matriarch who presides over this slice of Poland in Shepherd's Bush. Very decent set menus are great value and include traditional favourites such as blini with smoked salmon and duck *à la polonaise*, not to mention the complementary vodka. This place is brilliant.

RIVER CAFÉ Map pp438-9 *Italian*

☎ 7386 4200; www.rivercafe.co.uk; Thames Wharf, Rainville Rd W6; mains £26-30; ✆ lunch & dinner Mon-Sat, lunch Sun; ⊖ Hammersmith

The restaurant that spawned the world-famous cookbooks, the River Café is a serious treat off Fulham Palace Rd, overlooking Barnes across the river. The simple, precise cooking showcases seasonal ingredients sourced with fanatical expertise. Booking is essential, as it's still a hot favourite of the Fulham set, not to mention the New Labour elite, as the wine list and prices will confirm.

CHEAP EATS

BLAH BLAH BLAH Map pp438-9 *Vegetarian*

☎ 8746 1337; 78 Goldhawk Rd W12; mains £8-10; ✆ lunch & dinner Mon-Sat, dinner Sun; ⊖ Goldhawk Rd

This vegetarian institution has been packing them in for years with imaginative, well-realised food and a great, informal atmosphere. You can bring your own bottle, which makes an already medium-priced night out very good value indeed. Crayons are supplied for doodling on your table while you wait for your order.

CHURRERÍA ESPAÑOLA

Map pp444-5 *Spanish/British*

☎ 7727 3444; 177 Queensway W2; mains £4-8; ⊖ Bayswater

This unlikely café serves a variety of cheap dishes, from English breakfasts to a range of Spanish staples, including paella and several veggie specials. There are a few outdoor tables during the summer, and staff are delightful year round.

COSTA'S FISH RESTAURANT

Map pp444-5 *Fish & Chips*

☎ 7229 3794; 12-14 Hillgate St W8; mains £4-7; ⊖ Notting Hill Gate

This fondly regarded local puts a Cypriot spin on the traditional chippy and has a huge array of fresher-than-fresh fish dishes at market prices, which many prefer to the more up-market Geales nearby.

KRUNGTAP Map pp458-9 *Thai*

☎ 7259 2314; 227 Old Brompton Rd SW10; mains £4-6; ⊖ Earl's Court/West Brompton

Krungtap is the Thai name for Bangkok, and this eponymous restaurant is a busy, friendly café-style undertaking serving very good-value Thai food. There is also karaoke from 7pm to midnight Friday to Sunday, so be warned.

MANZARA Map pp444-5 *Turkish*

☎ 7727 3062; 24 Pembridge Rd W11; mains £5-8; ⊖ Notting Hill Gate

There's cheap, fresh and well-prepared Turkish food, with great *pides*, kebabs, pseudo-pizzas and lots of vegetarian options, at this simple place. The organic burger is superb.

TROUBADOUR Map pp458-9 *Home Cooking*

☎ 7370 1434; 265 Old Brompton Rd SW5; mains £6-7; ✆ breakfast, lunch & dinner; ⊖ Earl's Court/West Brompton

Bob Dylan and John Lennon have performed here, and the Troubadour remains a wonderfully relaxed bohemian hang-out decades later – great for coffee or a reasonably priced, home-cooked meal. There's still live music most nights and a large, pleasant garden for summer. Come for the atmosphere and the friendly service, and to make new friends with other boho inhabitants of west London.

Eating – West London

SOUTH LONDON

South London's best retort to all those sniffy jokes by north Londoners is its wonderful restaurant scene. You'd actually travel here just to visit some of the restaurants in Clapham and Wandsworth, while Brixton lays out a reasonably priced multicultural spread.

Eating – South London

BRIXTON

BRIXTONIAN HAVANA CLUB

Map p462   *Caribbean*

☎ 7924 9262; 11 Beehive Pl SW9; mains £15;
🕑 dinner; ⊖ Brixton

There are them folk that come to this club late for its *caipirinhas*, rum punches and dancing, and them that head upstairs earlier for the food. If you're a connoisseur of Caribbean nosh, it's certainly worth trying dishes like roast pepper and ginger soup and baked ham with sweet sorrel sauce. Each month the kitchen highlights the cuisine of a different island in the Caribbean. Whether dinner is being served depends on demand, so you must book ahead.

BUG Map p462   *Modern International*

☎ 7738 3366; St Matthew's Church Brixton Hill SW2; mains £7.50-10.50; 🕑 lunch & dinner Sun, dinner Mon-Sat; ⊖ Brixton

Once famed for its faux-ecclesiastical theme – it is a former church, after all – Bug finally went secular with a minimalist makeover in 2005. The healthy cuisine is the same, all either organic, vegetarian or free range, with Cantonese mock duck, nut Wellington, swordfish, chicken satay and Sunday roasts.

FUJIYAMA Map p462   *Japanese*

☎ 7737 2369; 5-7 Vining St SW9; mains £5-10; ⊖ Brixton

For that healthy rush that Japanese food can sometimes give you, come to this womblike restaurant, with its dark-red interior and communal benches. Apart from a large choice of *bento* boxes, noodles, tempuras, *gyoza* dumplings, miso soup and fantastic juices are also on the menu.

NEON Map p462   *Pizza*

☎ 7738 6576; www.neonbrixton.co.uk; 71 Atlantic Rd SW9; mains 7-15; 🕑 dinner Tue-Sat, all day Sun; ⊖ Brixton

With its vibrant red façade standing out like a beacon on Atlantic Rd you can't miss Brixton's favourite pizzeria. The interior design is a bit more sedate, with long, communal, backless benches. The food can be variable, but the cocktails are good.

BATTERSEA & WANDSWORTH

CHEZ BRUCE Map p437   *French*

☎ 8672 0114; www.chezbruce.co.uk; 2 Bellevue Rd SW17; 3-course set weekday lunch/weekend lunch/dinner £23.50/25/32.50; rail Wandsworth Common

The Bruce in question is chef Bruce Poole, and people still, rightly, trek right across London to visit his Michelin-starred abode. Then, funnily enough, on arriving they find it actually feels like a real local. The restaurant's rustic façade, beside Wandsworth Common, belies a modern interior. The fixed-price-only setup means that there's fortunately no need to scrimp on desserts, but selecting a fine French wine on top of your food can easily double the bill.

GREYHOUND Map pp438-9   *Gastropub*

☎ 7978 7021; 136 Battersea High St SW11; 2-/3-course lunch £10/13.50, dinner £23/28.50; 🕑 noon-11pm Tue-Sat, noon-4pm Sun; rail Battersea Park/Clapham Junction

This superlative Australian-run enterprise is too good to be called a gastropub really. Chef Tom Martinovic's CV even includes a stint with Heston Blumenthal of Fat Duck fame. The menu is lean and disciplined, with only three choices per course at dinner and two at lunch. (If you're a fussy eater, call to check beforehand; if you're a veggie, call a day ahead.) Service is not always as speedy as the signature creature, so get hold of one of the many bottles of excellent wine early on, and then relax.

RANSOME'S DOCK

Map pp458-9   *Modern European*

☎ 7223 1611; www.ransomesdock.co.uk/restaurant; 35-37 Parkgate Rd SW11; mains £10.50-20; 🕑 closed Sun; ⊖ Sloane Sq, then bus 19, 49, 239, 319 or 345

Diners flock here not because of its location on a narrow inlet of the Thames, but for the superbly prepared modern British food: smoked Norfolk eel with buckwheat pancakes and crème fraîche, noisettes of English lamb, and calf's liver with Italian bacon and field mushrooms.

Worth the Trip

Although the street is still awash with the aromas of turmeric, cumin and garam masala, it's no longer considered as cool as it once was to head to Brick Lane for a curry, and in truth the standard of cooking has deteriorated over the years. But never mind, for Tooting is the new Brick Lane.

If you have time for the journey to surburban SW17, head to Tooting Broadway or Tooting Bec tube stations; you'll be rewarded by a similar promenade through neighbouring curry houses. Even better, as opposed to Brick Lane, where the restaurants are mainly Bengali, in Tooting there's an array of subcontinental cuisine, from north to south, from Bangladeshi to Sri Lankan. You want more? This great cuisine is generally pretty cheap. Some of the best places to try:

Jaffna House (☎ 8672 7786; 90 Tooting High St SW17) The food here is fiery as hell but nevertheless great for veggies.

Kastoori (☎ 8767 7027; 188 Upper Tooting Rd SW17) Excellent Gujerati cuisine, by way of Africa, which is obviously lovingly homemade rather than churned out on an assembly line. Like no other Indian food you'll ever eat.

Lahore Karahi (☎ 8767 2477; 1 Tooting High St SW17) Cheap-as-poppadums Pakistani café.

Masaledar (☎ 8767 7676; 121 Upper Tooting Rd SW17) Tandoori house with East African specialities.

Radha Krishna Bhavan (☎ 8767 3462; 86 Tooting High St SW17) Serving superlative Keralan cuisine.

CLAPHAM

ABBEVILLE Map p462   *Gastropub*
☎ 8765 2201; www.theabbeville.co.uk; 64 Abbeville Rd SW4; mains £8.50-14.50; ⏲ lunch & dinner Mon-Fri, brunch & dinner Sat & Sun; ⊖ Clapham South
Well removed from Clapham High St, this country-style gastropub is worth the detour. There are several interconnecting rooms, including the traditional dark wooden bar where middle-class locals hang out, and comfy lounge chairs near the fire. Cuisine ranges from Mediterranean and seafood to a traditional English Sunday roast.

CINNAMON CAY
Map pp438-9   *Modern International*
☎ 7801 0932; 87 Lavender Hill SW11; mains £9.50-14.50, 2-course set lunch Mon & Tue £12; ⏲ lunch & dinner Mon-Sat; rail Clapham Junction, then bus 77A or 137
Everyone's noisily enjoying their South East Asian–influenced fusion food here, to the tune of pulsating music, extractor fans and the occasional wok fire in the open kitchen. The spicy food is delicious and offers great value; the green-lipped mussels and Sichuan pepper fillet are regular recommendations, although we also like the pepper swordfish with pea pancakes. Veggies are well catered for. Throw in friendly service and you have a little gem.

VERSO Map p462   *Italian*
☎ 7720 1515; 84 Clapham Park Rd SW4; mains £6.50-12.50, 2 courses before 6.30pm £10; ⏲ 6-11.30pm Mon-Fri, noon-11.30pm Sat, 4-11.30pm Sun; ⊖ Clapham Common
Eco (162 Clapham High St) is the name in Clapham pizzas, but this unpretentious neighbourhood restaurant proves consistently superior. It has the natural confidence to serve such slightly unfamiliar specials as rocket, grilled prawn and courgette pizza *bianca* (without tomato paste), alongside seafood and terrific homemade desserts. Well away from the high street, this seems to be *terra incognita* to Clapham's gangs of loud 20-somethings. However, if you don't share the Italian love of children, order your pizza to go.

WHITE HOUSE
Map p462   *Modern International*
☎ 7498 3388; www.thewhitehouselondon.co.uk; 65 Clapham Park Rd SW4; mains £7.50-14.50; ⏲ dinner Mon-Sat; ⊖ Clapham Common
Attracting Clapham's beautiful people with its stylish low-lit interior – all tan sofas, small square tables, expansive bar and polished wooden floors – this chic cocktail bar also boasts a more than decent restaurant out the back and a fantastic roof terrace in summer. The changing menu presents a global assortment ranging from soy-glazed blue-fin tuna and crespelle filled with ricotta and spinach to Scottish rib-eye steak.

KENNINGTON, OVAL & STOCKWELL

REBATO'S Map pp460-1   *Spanish*
☎ 7735 6388; www.rebatos.com; 169 South Lambeth Rd SW8; tapas £2.95-5.50, mains £11.95; ⏲ lunch & dinner Mon-Fri, dinner Sat; ⊖ Stockwell
The cluttered Mediterranean décor (patterned tiles, hanging plants, stucco façade) of this

Top Five – South London

- Abbeville (p269)
- Brixtonian Havana Club (p268)
- Chez Bruce (p268)
- Cinnamon Cay (p269)
- Greyhound (p268)

old-fashioned neighbourhood restaurant definitely wouldn't win any design awards, but that's not the point here. The point is the deliciously authentic tapas – which lean heavily towards seafood and meat, with whitebait, sardines, sherried kidneys and chicken livers – and a warm, frequently Spanish-speaking atmosphere.

CHEAP EATS

ASMARA Map p462   *Eritrean*
☎ 7737 4144; 386 Coldharbour Lane SW9; mains £4-7.50; ☽ dinner; ⊖ Brixton

A rare Eritrean restaurant, Asmara serves spicy meat and vegetable dishes that you scoop up using a piece of *injera* (sourdough pancake). Staff provide a flash of colour in their traditional costumes, while there's a nod to the former colonial power, Italy, with a smattering of pasta on the menu.

BAMBOULA Map p462   *Caribbean*
☎ 7274 8600; 12 Acre Lane SW9; mains £7-8.50; ⊖ Brixton

Patriotically decorated in the yellow and green of the Jamaican flag, this takeaway/restaurant is cheap and cheerful, serving jerk chicken, oxtail, curried goat, ackee and saltfish, rice and peas, plantain, and other 'eeyrie' classics. Bread pudding laced with rum does the trick, too.

BRIXTON BAR & GRILL
Map p462   *Modern International*
☎ 7737 6777; 15 Atlantic Rd SW9; tapas £2-6.75; ☽ dinner; ⊖ Brixton

The Brixton Bar & Grill is a cave-like bar under the railway arches. It's principally for drinking, but does have a very interesting tapas menu, ranging from grilled sardines with couscous, walnut and red-pepper sauce to *kumera* (sweet potato) chips and Mediterranean wontons with avocado and goat's cheese fondue.

BRUNO Map p462   *Vegetarian/Vegan*
☎ 7738 6161; 42 Coldharbour Lane SW9; mains £3.50-6; ⊖ Brixton

Paninis, salads, risotto, faux bangers and mash, crispy polenta, and lots of mix 'n' match pastas in different sauces are served in this refreshing café.

PEPPER TREE Map p462   *Asian*
☎ 7622 1758; 19 Clapham Common South Side SW4; mains £4-6; ⊖ Clapham Common

This noodle bar–style canteen in Clapham has communal benches and is great for a functional fill-up. The adequate Thai food includes curries listed according to colour (red, yellow, green) and variety (including beef, chicken and vegetable).

Giraffe restaurant (p254)

SOUTHWEST LONDON

Although not universally known for its cuisine, this area of London can lay claim to a number of decent gastronomic outposts, some of which are well worth crossing town for. If you're in Fulham, wander down Fulham Rd, up New King's Rd and along Wandsworth Bridge Rd for a good choice. In Putney, head down the high street or the roads heading off it.

Top Five For Kids

- **Banners** (p263)
- **Blue Kangaroo** (right)
- **Frizzante@CityFarm** (p257)
- **Giraffe** (see The London Chain Gang, p254)
- **Pizza Organic** (p250)

FULHAM & PARSON'S GREEN

1492 Map pp458-9   *Latin American*
☎ 7381 3810; www.1492restaurant.com; 404 North End Rd SW6; mains £8.50-17; ⊗ dinner Mon-Fri, lunch & dinner Sat & Sun; ⊖ Fulham Broadway
This relaxed, not-too-themed restaurant distinguishes itself by delving into corners untouched by most Latin American restaurants in London, such as Venezuelan, Cuban and Brazilian cuisine. There's an Argentinian *parilla* grill and sticky-sweet *dulce de leche* desserts. And if you have a taste for Mexican chicken *molé* (in chocolate and chilli sauce) or Peruvian *yuquitas* (cheese and cassava fritters) you should bring it here.

ATLAS Map pp458-9   *Mediterranean*
☎ 7385 9129; www.theatlaspub.co.uk; 16 Seagrave Rd SW6; mains £8-12; ⊖ Fulham Broadway/West Brompton
This Victorian gastropub is a small, perfectly formed gem with a cosy, relaxed feel contributed to by a clientele of well-behaved locals in their late 20s and 30s, out for a quiet meal with friends. The food is delicious, although you might find the menu descriptions slightly over the top, and there's a lovely little courtyard. Unpretentious and delightful.

BLUE ELEPHANT Map pp458-9   *Thai*
☎ 7385 6595; www.blueelephant.com; 4-6 Fulham Broadway SW6; mains £11-28; ⊗ lunch & dinner Sun-Fri, dinner Sat; ⊖ Fulham Broadway
The sumptuous surroundings, attentive staff and excellent food make dining at the Blue Elephant a memorable experience. The atmosphere is romantic, with candlelit tables, fountains and lush foliage. It's wise to book for dinner.

BLUE KANGAROO Map pp458-9   *Brasserie*
☎ 7371 7622; www.thebluekangaroo.co.uk; 555 King's Rd SW6; mains adult £8.50-16, child £4.95; ⊗ 9.30am-7pm Mon-Fri, 9.30am-8pm Sat & Sun; ⊖ Fulham Broadway
In all senses a different beast to the previous listing, this family-oriented restaurant lets you enjoy a meal while watching, via CCTV, your under-eights run wild in the downstairs playroom (£3). Adult nerves are soothed with butternut risotto, Thai king prawns and organic omelettes. Although the children's 'yummy' menu has burgers and nuggets, they're all homemade and 100% meat, of which even health-conscious chef Jamie *(School Dinners)* Oliver might approve. Turkey Twizzlers would be scared to appear here – as would nonparents.

FARM Map pp458-9   *Gastropub*
☎ 7381 3331; www.thefarmfulham.co.uk; 18 Farm Lane SW6; mains lunch £4-10, dinner £9-17; ⊖ Fulham Broadway
A bit too upmarket for somewhere so close to Chelsea FC's Stamford Bridge stadium, Farm has a credit-card-only policy. This is presumably to discourage the football fans, but it also slows down service. The interior, even behind the bar, is very stylish, however, and well suited to a fine-dining experience.

LOTS ROAD PUB & DINING ROOM
Map pp458-9   *Gastropub*
☎ 7352 6645; 114 Lots Rd SW10; mains £8.50-12.50; ⊖ Fulham Broadway
Great vibe, great food, great room – what's not to like about this tucked-away gastropub, aside from the minor affectation of prices being listed in hundreds of pence? Light floods through the windows into the high-ceilinged, wood-lined

Top Five – Southwest London

- **Atlas** (left)
- **Chosan** (p272)
- **Enoteca Turi** (p272)
- **Lots Road Pub & Dining Room** (above)
- **Ma Goa** (p272)

dining area and onto the grey, black and chrome bar, where choice wines are sold by the glass. The regularly changing menu reads as pretty standard fare – burgers, steak, lamb, salmon etc – but if our delicious fishcakes were anything to go by the meals arrive with interesting spicing and sauces. The sticky-toffee pudding should not be missed, but share it between two.

WIZZY Map pp458-9   Korean
☎ 7736 9171; 616 Fulham Rd SW6; mains £7.50-15; ⊖ Parsons Green

Chef Hwi Shim (Wizzy) is making a bold attempt to bring Korean food to a wider audience, with a few contemporary twists. Having done stints at Hakkasan and Nobu, she reinvents some dishes, such as *kaysan* (marinated crab) and gives them a *nouvelle cuisine* presentation. Other classics are left untouched. The menu translations are rather odd, however.

PUTNEY & BARNES

CHOSAN Map pp438-9   Japanese
☎ 87880 9626; 292 Upper Richmond Rd SW15; mains £3.30-19; ⊖ Putney Bridge

One of those rare restaurants you can recommend without reservation, Chosan doesn't look much from the outside – or the inside for that matter – but it does turn out excellent food. The *bento* boxes are a favourite, although the range of fish is also inviting and sometimes unusual.

ENOTECA TURI Map pp438-9   Italian
☎ 8785 4449; 28 Putney High St SW15; ☽ lunch & dinner Mon-Sat; mains £14-17, set lunch £12.50; ⊖ Putney Bridge

And, relax…you've arrived at a little oasis of calm on the high street. The atmosphere is serene, the service is charming and the interior is all understated elegance (linen tablecloths, don't you know). Enoteca Turi devotes equal attention to the grape as to the food, which means that each dish, be it a shellfish *tagliolini* or calf's liver, comes recommended with a particular glass of wine (or you can pick from the 300-strong wine menu if you think you know best).

LA MANCHA Map pp438-9   Spanish
☎ 8780 1022; www.lamancha.co.uk; 32 Putney High St SW15; tapas £3.95-6.95, mains £8.85-12.95; ⊖ Putney Bridge

La Mancha is the place to visit for some good, wholesome fun, and at weekends it's packed with young Putneyites having exactly that. It serves a vast variety of tapas from all over Spain, from old favourites to dishes you're less likely to see on the Costa del Sol.

MVH Map p437   International
☎ 8392 1111; 5 White Hart Lane SW13; 2-/3-course set menus £26/29; ☽ dinner; rail Barnes Bridge

Notable for its quirky décor and its excellent food, MVH is an experience you won't forget. The theme here seems to be heaven (the white dining room, with occasional nude sculpture) and hell (blood-red walls). In between unusual dishes such as green seafood curry with lime *risottini* and scallops with bright-green caviar, you'll be served a succession of complimentary *amuse-bouche*.

CHEAP EATS

MA GOA Map pp438-9   Indian
☎ 8780 1767; 242-244 Upper Richmond Rd 15; mains £6.50-9.50; ☽ dinner Tue-Sun; ⊖ Putney Bridge

The speciality is the Portuguese-influenced cuisine of Goa, served up in terracotta bowls by cheery staff. Sausages may not be the first dish that springs to mind when you think of the subcontinent, but the cinnamon-infused pork snags are worth the booking alone.

MOOMBA WORLD CAFÉ
Map pp438-9   Global
☎ 8785 9151; 5 Lacy Rd SW15; mains £6.25-8.95; ☽ brunch, lunch & dinner; rail Putney/ ⊖ Putney Bridge

Taking its name from the Aboriginal word meaning 'to get together and have a good time', Moomba is a convivial place to spend a few weekend hours. Locals loll about, occasionally breaking from conversations to pick up crayons and puzzles (provided by Moomba) for their offspring. Of an evening, however, it can get a bit hot, sticky and smoky.

UP RIVER

In keeping with its high standard of living along the gentrified banks of the river, restaurants in this part of London are usually exquisitely presented, featuring superlative food and wine lists. Don't miss out on the full French experience at La Trompette and the above-average dining scene in Twickenham, and be sure to visit one of the area's riverside restaurants on a summer's day.

CHISWICK

FISH HOEK Map p437   *Fish & Seafood*
☎ 8742 0766; 6-8 Elliott Rd W4; mains £10-25, 2-/3-course set lunch & early dinner £12/14.50; ⊕ lunch & dinner Tue-Sun; ⊖ Turnham Green

Fish Hoek's small, neat dining room acts as a restrained backdrop to its extraordinary menu. The focus is on fresh South African 'and other exotic' fish and seafood, with dishes ranging from the sublime (grilled Indian Ocean swordfish with sweet-potato mash) to the adventurous (you'd like the oven-baked stumpnose and char-grilled Mauritian Mahi Mahi fillet, yes?). More locally gathered *pesces* ensure that supporters of the British fishing industry are kept well satisfied. The menu changes frequently, providing ample reason to return.

LA TROMPETTE Map p437   *French*
☎ 8747 1836; www.latrompette.co.uk; 5-7 Devonshire Rd W4; set menus £27.50-£32.50; ⊖ Turnham Green

Worth crossing London for, this elegantly understated French restaurant frequently tops polls as the capital's best neighbourhood restaurant. The sleek interior and terrace, together with the stunning *carte* and impressive wine list, draw both locals and visitors again and again. The menu offers traditional French cuisine with an imaginative twist – from oysters with champagne *mousseline* to roast loin of pork. Each sitting boasts a capacity crowd, so booking is advisable.

RICHMOND

BURNT CHAIR

Map p464   *Modern International*
☎ 8940 9488; www.burntchair.com; 5 Duke St; mains £12-18, pre-theatre menus before 7pm £15.00, 2-/3-course set dinner £18/20; ⊕ dinner Tue-Sat; ⊖ /rail Richmond

All is well with the world when you step into the Burnt Chair's pleasant candlelit dining room, full of dark furniture and dazzling white tablecloths. Things only get better after a peruse of the menu, which combines flavours and textures without getting itself in knots of fussiness or overambition. Whether you choose mullet with chorizo and courgette risotto or duck with pumpkin, chestnuts and blackcurrants, you'll find that all the dishes are accomplished, particularly when accompanied by a tipple from the expertly selected wine list.

CANYON Map p464   *American*
☎ 8948 2944; www.jamiesbars.co.uk; the Tow Path, Riverside TW10; mains £10-16, 2-/3-course set lunch £12.50/15; ⊖ /rail Richmond

Canyon's superb location on the Thames is just one reason to visit – the food is excellent without being showy, the American menu borrowing enough from modern European cuisine to make it inventive yet familiar. The theme is Arizona, with the garden crafted to look like the American West (as much as the Thames embankment can). Service can be slow and occasionally erratic, but this shouldn't detract from the generally relaxed dining experience on offer.

CHEZ LINDSAY Map p464   *French*
☎ 8948 7473; www.chezlindsay.co.uk; 11 Hill Rise TW10; mains £11.25-15.75, galettes £2.90-8.75; ⊕ restaurant lunch & dinner Mon-Sat, all day Sun, creperie all day Mon-Sun; ⊖ /rail Richmond

Offering a slice of Brittany at the bottom of Richmond Hill, Chez Lindsay's simply furnished dining rooms draws visitors with its wholesome Breton cuisine and comfortable ambience. The house specialities include seafood (from whelks with aioli to puff pastry with scallops and leek) and galettes with a myriad of tasty fillings, washed down with a variety of hearty Breton ciders. So relaxing is the experience of eating here that it's a considerable struggle dragging yourself away.

PETERSHAM CAFÉ

Off Map p464   *Modern European*
☎ 8940 5230; www.petershamnurseries.com; Petersham Nurseries, off Petersham Rd TW10; mains £11.95-22; ⊕ lunch Fri-Sun; ⊖ /rail Richmond, then bus 65

At the back of the gorgeously situated Petersham Nurseries is this café straight out of the pages of *The Secret Garden* – huge mismatched tables sit amongst statutory, upturned flower pots and improbably billowing plants. Well-to-do locals tuck into confidently executed food that often began life in the nursery gardens – organic vegetable dishes, such as baked aubergine with tarragon and cream, feature alongside seasonal plates of, say, crumbed chicken with coleslaw or veal chops with courgettes and spinach. It's heaven, whether you're into your horticulture or not.

RESTAURANT AT THE PETERSHAM

Off Map p464   *British*
☎ 8939 1084; www.petershamhotel.co.uk; Nightingale Lane TW10; 2-course set lunch Mon-Sat £16.50, 3-course set lunch Sun £28, à la carte dinner £29; ♥ lunch & dinner Mon-Sat, lunch Sun; ⊖ /rail Richmond

Neatly perched on the slope down Richmond Hill leading across Petersham Meadows towards the Thames, the Petersham Hotel offers stunning, Arcadian views at every turn. Its restaurant, with its large windows gazing down to the river, has the very best of these. The menu is as pleasing to the tastebuds as the view is to the eye – you might choose duck lacquered with seven spices, or steamed fillet of sole, and be disappointed with neither. It's quite a polite experience all round, so best saved for a formal occasion.

KEW

GLASSHOUSE Map p437   *Modern European*
☎ 8940 6777; www.glasshouserestaurant.co.uk; 14 Station Pde W9; set menu £35; ⊖ /rail Kew Gardens

A meal at this splendid restaurant a stone's throw from Kew Gardens tube station is a great way to cap off a day spent at the botanical gardens. Its (wait for it) glass-fronted exterior reveals a delicately lit, low-key interior, whose unassuming décor ensures that the focus remains on the divinely cooked food. Punters choose from a set menu that combines traditional English mainstays with modern European innovation. The Glasshouse is sister restaurant to **La Trompette** (p273) and **Chez Bruce** (p268).

TWICKENHAM

BRULA   *Modern European*
☎ 8892 0602; 43 Crown Rd, Middlesex; mains £10-15; ♥ lunch & dinner Mon-Sat, lunch dinner Sun; rail St Margaret's

This attractive and upmarket restaurant near Marble Hill House seems to get it just right. The service and elegant décor complement the fantastically fresh and clever menu of modern French cooking, and the stained-glass windows give the place a unique feel that keeps the locals coming in droves.

MA CUISINE   *French*
☎ 8607 9849; 6 Whitton Rd, Middlesex; 3-course set lunch/dinner £19/29; rail Twickenham

Sister restaurant to **McClements** (below) next door, Ma Cuisine looks not unlike a French take on a greasy spoon, with its linoleum tablecloths. However, nothing could be further from the truth, as the complex and mouthwatering French menu quickly demonstrates. Excellent value given the standard of the cooking, this is another Twickenham highlight.

MCCLEMENTS   *Modern European*
☎ 8744 9610; www.mcclementsrestaurant.com; 2 Whitton Rd, Middlesex TW1; 3-course set lunch/dinner £25/48; ♥ closed Sun & Mon; rail Twickenham

This elaborate Michelin-starred restaurant is one for an occasion, serving a heady mix of traditionally prepared European dishes, such as Gressingham duck with a raviolo of its own leg. The two menus, *traditionnel* and *gourmand*, allow you the choice between four and eight courses – and four is quite enough for anyone.

CHEAP EATS

See also **Chez Lindsay** (p273), whose delicious Breton galettes make for a very reasonable meal.

DON FERNANDO'S Map p464   *Spanish*
☎ 8948 6447; 27f the Quadrant, Richmond; tapas £3-6, mains £8-10; ♥ lunch & dinner Mon & Tue, all day Wed-Sun; ⊖ /rail Richmond

Richmond station seems an unlikely place for one of the best tapas bars in London, but the Izquierdo family have been serving superb cuisine from their native Andalucia for 15 years now, and their enthusiasm shows no signs of waning. With an exhaustive list of Spanish beers, wines and culinary specialities, and cheerful, animated service, this makes a great place for a good lunch or a slow supper.

NEWENS MAIDS OF HONOUR
                          Traditional English
☎ 8940 2752; 288 Kew Rd, Kew W9; set tea £5; ♥ 9.30am-5.30pm Tue-Sun; ⊖ Kew Gardens

The name of this quirky Kew tearoom comes from its famed dessert, supposedly created by Anne Boleyn, Henry VIII's ill-fated second wife. It is made of puff pastry, lemon, almonds and curd cheese, and anyone visiting should try it. The incongruous establishment looks far more like it belongs in a Cotswolds village but is in fact just a short distance from the main entrance to Kew Gardens at Victoria Gate.

Drinking

Drinking

The pub is the heart of London's social existence; it's the great leveller where status and rank are made redundant, generation gaps are bridged, inhibitions are lowered and tongues are loosened. Virtually every Londoner has a 'local', and some go by the quality of the nearest pubs when deciding on whereabouts in this massive city to pitch themselves. Sampling a range of boozers is, for our money, one of the highlights of any visit to the capital. From ancient and atmospheric taverns to slick DJ bars, London has much to offer the discerning tippler, no matter how hard the themed and chain bars try to take over.

Britain is the very cradle of pub culture, and you'll find some of the world's greatest drinking dens here, carrying on their business the way they have for centuries. Their histories are often written all over their walls and etched in the occasionally bloated and bloodshot faces of the regulars who prop up their bars.

As with just about every other facet of London life, the drinking culture has been undergoing something of a transformation in recent decades, and these days there's a huge choice of sensational venues, whether you're swilling beers, sipping cocktails or quaffing wine. DJ bars, in particular, have been springing up all over the shop, and many are now destinations in their own right (as opposed to being simply pre-club warm-ups).

But while *every* change in the restaurant scene has been an improvement, the dictates of fashion have not been universally kind to the drinking culture. Some atmospheric and traditional old boozers have sadly been converted into alcoholic theme parks, cocktail lounges, bland gastropubs and whatever else has been the flavour of recent days. Then there are the myriad chain pubs that have taken over high streets all over the city. These are, quite clearly, the deeds of the devil. Learn to walk past establishments that look vaguely like pubs and feature the words 'slug', 'lettuce', 'all', 'bar', 'one', 'firkin', 'parrot', 'O'Neills', 'Weatherspoons', 'hog's' and 'head' in their names, and your visit will be immeasurably improved.

While here we can't even begin to include *all* the great pubs and bars in a city of London's size, we heartily recommend that you check out a few drinking strips for yourself. Try Islington's Upper St or Essex Rd; Hoxton's Old St or Shoreditch High St; Soho's Dean St or Greek St; West London's Portobello Rd; the Cut on the Southbank; Clapham High St and Borough High St in south London; or Parkway and Camden High St in Camden Town for a guaranteed surfeit of choice.

We reckon it's the traditional pubs that make drinking in London so special, although throughout these pages we've tried to provide an even spread of the timeless and the hip. We've provided info on many of *our* favourite drinking dens here, although there's no substitute for individual research – your liver's the only limit.

Opening Hours

At the time of going to press, Britain was in the midst of the biggest shake-up to its arcane drinking laws for almost a century. Beginning in November 2005, new licences granted at the discretion of local authorities came into effect, which allowed pubs and bars to stay open after 11pm. Quite how the changes will affect the drinking culture in London is extremely hard to predict. However, it should now be a lot easier for revellers to drink into the early hours as a result.

That the English, with their long tradition both of libertarianism and fondness for drink, should *ever* have put up with the ridiculous restrictions that are only now being lifted is fascinating in itself. In fact, the 11pm closing laws were a hangover from WWI – we kid you not – when the government ordered pubs to close in good time to alleviate the problem of drunk munitions workers. The new laws, which we warmly welcome as long overdue, having ourselves had many a great evening out cut short in the past, will mean that cut-off times will vary from pub to pub – but in central areas you should always be able to get a drink without having to pay a cover charge or end up in an illegal dive bar, as was once invariably the case on a Friday or Saturday night.

Under the new laws, any establishment can apply for later opening times – up to 24 hours a day – although the likelihood is that the vast majority will retain an 11pm closing time during the week, and extend by an hour or two only at the weekend. While we've noted places that open late at the time of writing in the reviews following, be aware that 2006 will inevitably be a period of huge change for London's bars and pubs, and so while none of the following will close before 11pm (or 10.30pm on Sunday), you should call ahead and check out the latest details if you want to carry on into the early hours. Unless otherwise stated, all pubs and bars reviewed here close at 11pm from Monday to Saturday and at 10.30pm on Sunday.

THE WEST END

Going out in the West End is a trick few Londoners can confidently say that they have mastered. It's ridiculously crowded at the weekend, so you need to know where to go and do some serious strategic planning if you want anything coming close to a seat. However, it's easy to see why the crowds come – nothing can beat the excitement in the air on a Friday night in Soho, bar hopping with friends before heading off clubbing or rounding the evening off in a late-night semi-legal drinking den. Come here for the cool and cutting-edge, but be discerning – there are an awful lot of wannabes out there.

SOHO

AKA Map p452
☎ 7836 0110; www.akalondon.com; 18 West Central St W1; ☽ to 3am Tue-Fri, to 7am Sat, to 4am Sun; ⊖ Holborn

In one of the West End's deadest parts, you'll find one of its liveliest DJ bars, which, despite being almost a decade old, is still managing to cling to its cred by filling its cavernous interior with a chunky sound system and a young, good-looking clientele propelled by precision-made cocktails.

BARCODE Map p450
☎ 7734 3342; www.bar-code.co.uk; 3-4 Archer St W1; ☽ to 1am Mon-Sat; ⊖ Piccadilly Circus

Tucked away down a side street is this fun gay bar, full of a diverse range of people enjoying a pint or two and some evening cruising. There are frequent club nights in the downstairs area, including a very popular gay comedy night every Tuesday.

CANDY BAR Map p450
☎ 7494 4041; www.thecandybar.co.uk; 4 Carlisle St W1; ☽ to 2am Fri & Sat, to 11.30pm Sun-Thu; ⊖ Tottenham Court Rd

This is the hottest lesbian bar in town, a great, friendly place, with a long bar on the ground floor and a mini-club in the basement where DJs play most nights. Look out for karaoke every Tuesday, which is a blast. Men are admitted as guests to women (one man per one woman).

COACH & HORSES Map p450
☎ 7437 5920; 29 Greek St W1; ⊖ Leicester Sq

Famous as the place where *Spectator* columnist Jeffrey Bernard drank himself to death, this small, busy and thankfully unreconstructed boozer retains an old Soho bohemian atmosphere with a regular clientele of soaks, writers, hacks, tourists and those too pissed to lift their heads off the counter. Pretension will be prosecuted.

EDGE Map p450
☎ 7439 1313; www.edge.uk.com; 11 Soho Sq W1; ☽ to 1am Mon-Sat; ⊖ Tottenham Court Rd

No, it's not a U2 theme bar. Overlooking Soho Sq in all its four-storey glory, the Edge is London's largest gay bar and heaves from the early evening until the early hours with pre-clubbing revellers fuelling up for the night ahead. Great in summer, when the crowd pours out into Soho Sq, it's a good place to start the night any time of the year.

FRENCH HOUSE Map p450
☎ 7437 2799; 49 Dean St W1; ⊖ Leicester Sq

This decadent and charming bar (it doesn't serve pints so doesn't deserve to call itself a pub) was the meeting place of the Free French Forces during WWII, and De Gaulle is said to have drunk here often. More importantly, renowned drinkers such as Dylan Thomas, Brendan Behan and Peter O'Toole frequently ended up on its wood floors. There's red wine and a regular clientele of curiosities.

FRIENDLY SOCIETY Map p450
☎ 7434 3805; 79 Wardour St W1; ⊖ Piccadilly Circus
Definitely one of Soho's hippest gay bars, and thankfully one of the few fashionable queer drinking establishments that hasn't initiated a dubious door policy or membership scheme to ensure that only the rich and beautiful arrive. A fun and up-for-it crowd assemble in the early evening, and drink beer under S&M Barbie and Ken and chill out to live DJs all evening.

GARLIC & SHOTS Map p450
☎ 7734 9505; 14 Frith St W1; ☾ to midnight Mon-Wed, to 1am Thu-Sat, to 11.30pm Sun; ⊖ Tottenham Court Rd
This vampire-themed boozer is popular with Londoners and Scandinavian Goths alike. With garlic-stuffed food upstairs, a great garden out the back warmed by Brazilian heaters in the winter and an ever-so-slightly scary downstairs bar where you'll feel out of place without violent make up and Robert Smith's wig on, this place is a winner and never gets too crowded.

PLAYER Map p450
☎ 7494 9125; www.thplyr.com; 8 Broadwick St W1; ☾ to midnight Mon-Wed, to 1am Thu-Sat, closed Sun; ⊖ Oxford Circus
This basement cocktail bar in Soho was a key, erm, player, in the late-'90s London cocktail revolution. The '70s-style lounge down a dark Soho staircase is surprisingly large, and while it's got a rather suity after-work feel early on in the evening, a far cooler Soho crowd heads down here later on. The cocktail list is superb, but unfortunately only members are admitted after 11pm.

SAK Map p450
☎ 7439 4159; 49 Greek St W1; ☾ to 1am Mon & Tue, to 3am Wed-Sat, closed Sun; ⊖ Tottenham Court Rd
This place should be rammed. It's a sleek, unpretentious Soho bar with free entry, a late licence and a religiously professional approach to cocktail making. But it's usually perfectly easy to get a seat and enjoy a stonking cocktail in an oasis of calm in the middle of Soho. Weekends are much busier, and the velvet rope and suited ape make an inevitable appearance, but this is still a rare Soho delight.

SHAMPERS Map p450
☎ 7437 1692; 4 Kingly St W1; ⊖ Oxford Circus/Piccadilly Circus
It's standing room only in this traditional wine bar at the back of a more contemporary dining room, and it's packed most nights with punters jostling between dark-green walls lined with bottles and sampling the terrific and educational changing wine menu.

SUN AND 13 CANTONS Map p450
☎ 7734 0934; 21 Great Pulteney St W1; ⊖ Oxford Circus/Piccadilly Circus
Certainly Soho's oddest-named pub, the Sun is a music-industry mainstay and a great place for young hopefuls to network. Everyone from the Chemical Brothers (first London gig) to Underworld (global smash hit written here) has links to this place, and there are still regular DJ nights downstairs. A far better reason to visit is the historic décor and relaxed drinking vibe upstairs.

TRASH PALACE Map p450
☎ 7734 0522; www.trashpalace.co.uk; 11 Wardour St W1; ☾ to midnight Sun-Thu, to 3am Fri & Sat; ⊖ Piccadilly Circus
This cool two-floor space from the people who revolutionised London's gay scene with indie club Popstarz has great staff and an alternative yet unpretentious feel. The lines outside can be big at the weekends, so get here early – as with most cool places in London, demand way outstrips supply. There's a small dance floor downstairs with a more relaxed lounge upstairs.

TWO FLOORS Map p450
☎ 7439 1007; 3 Kingly St W1; ☾ closed Sun; ⊖ Oxford Circus/Piccadilly Circus
Unrecognisable from the outside – as cool bars need to be – Two Floors attracts an unfailingly cool mix of bohemian and trendy types, and always seems to be playing the music that you've just got into. The bar staff are friendly and sassy, the décor loungey and scruffy, but drinks are sadly restricted to bottled beers and cocktails.

COVENT GARDEN & LEICESTER SQUARE
CORK & BOTTLE WINE BAR Map p452
☎ 7734 7807; 44-46 Cranbourn St WC2; ⊖ Leicester Sq
Londoners have taken to wine in a big way over recent years, although most of them don't know much about it, which is why Kiwi Chairman Don does so well with this downstairs stone-floored cellar, where you can sip or swig from hundreds of his personal favourites

and nibble on a buffet of cheeses and cured meats amid bustling conviviality.

FREEDOM BREWING CO Map p452
☎ 7240 0606; 41 Earlham St WC2; ⊖ Covent Garden
Even though it was fairly recently refitted and the beer is brewed elsewhere these days, the attractions of London's most popular micro-brewery haven't changed: tasty beers (particularly the pale ales), a cosy semi-chic interior, considerate lighting and staff who, oddly for a London bar, seem intent on serving customers the best way they can.

FREUD Map p452
☎ 7240 9933; 198 Shaftesbury Ave WC2; ⊖ Covent Garden
Make this the first stop on your crawl because there's no way you'll make it down the stairs (not much more than a ladder) after a few bevies. It's a small basement bar/café/gallery with the sort of beige walls that could look just plain dirty, but there are purposefully arty pictures to head off scrutiny. The décor is suitably scruffy and arty, and the cocktails are fat and fancy, but beer is sadly only by the bottle.

SALISBURY Map p452
☎ 7836 5863; 90 St Martin's Lane WC2; ⊖ Leicester Sq
Facing off the super-chic St Martin's Lane Hotel, the Salisbury offers everything its opposite number doesn't: warmth, centuries of history, and a glorious, traditionally British pub interior. The Salisbury is packed in the evenings by pre- and post-theatre drinkers, and while it can be a little touristy, it's still a true London gem.

HOLBORN & THE STRAND
GORDON'S WINE BAR Map p452
☎ 7930 1408; www.gordonswinebar.com; 47 Villiers St WC2; ⊖ Embankment/Charing Cross
We shouldn't really include Gordon's here, as this place is already too crowded as soon as the offices on the Strand empty out of an evening, but there's a good reason for this – it's simply one of London's most brilliant wine bars. Every evening a friendly crowd quaffs reasonably priced French and New World wines, and munches on bread and cheese in the quaint and charming bar. The low ceiling and gothic atmosphere in the main hall are wonderful, although you'll have to fight for a seat.

LAMB Map pp448-9
☎ 7405 0713; 94 Lamb's Conduit St WC1; ⊙ closed Sun; ⊖ Russell Sq
The venerable and atmospheric Lamb has a central mahogany bar with beautiful Victorian dividers and terrific tucker. It's wildly popular, though, so come early to bag a booth. There's a decent selection of Young's bitters and a genial atmosphere perfect for unwinding

NA ZDOROWIE Map p452
☎ 7831 9679; 11 Little Turnstile WC1; ⊖ Holborn
You have to know about this total gem of a Polish vodka bar, as you're certainly unlikely to be passing by it, tucked away as it is on the tiniest imaginable alleyway behind Holborn tube station. Eschewing the smarter Eastern European bar style, Na Zdorowie ('cheers') is thankfully unpretentious and fun, with a huge Polish vodka range and great food available as well.

Members Only...
Typically, Londoners despise snotty door policies and anything that smacks of exclusivity – until they're suddenly let in, and then it's a rather different story. Until recently the antediluvian English drinking laws meant that private members' clubs were an essential extension of any serious drinker's social make-up. Soho abounds with the most famous – the media and celeb-heavy Groucho Club remains the spot to party in style with the well connected, while Soho House, a vast, sprawling complex on Greek St, is usually packed with actors and PR people. Blacks is for the more staid literary crowd, while relative newcomer Century has the cream of West End theatreland drinking there thanks to its policy of giving free membership to actors starring in nearby hits. Home House on Portland Sq is for the seriously loaded; set in an old aristocratic town house, it features gorgeous gardens, a hotel and some exquisitely opulent bars. Despite more relaxed drinking laws, London's private members' clubs are more popular than ever, and getting a peep inside one is a conduit to the city's secretly status-obsessed soul. Most clubs are very tricky to get into unless you know a member. Some will let you drink in the bar if you are eating dinner there or staying in the club (many double as small hotels).

PERSEVERANCE Map pp448-9
☎ 7405 8278; 63 Lamb's Conduit St WC1;
⊖ Holborn/Russell Sq

Playing second fiddle no more to the Lamb, which has always been Lamb's Conduit St's most popular boozer; the newly revamped Perseverance is a charming Victorian boozer downstairs with a very pleasant upstairs dining room. It's always busy with office workers during the week, but it also does a brisk trade with locals over the weekend, when you can be guaranteed a seat.

PRINCESS LOUISE Map p452
☎ 7405 8816; 208 High Holborn WC1; ⊖ Holborn

We might have used the word gem before, but we take all of the other instances back. This late-19th-century Victorian pub is spectacularly decorated with a riot of fine tiles, etched mirrors, plasterwork and a stunning central horseshoe bar. There are invariably more bums than seats until the after-workers split.

SEVEN STARS Map pp448-9
☎ 7242 8521; 53-54 Carey St WC2; ⊖ Holborn/Temple

On a tiny street behind the Royal Courts of Justice, this delightful and minute pub has more character in its 30 sq metres than most other pubs could ever dream of. Originally aimed at sailors, over the centuries the Seven Stars has been repopulated by the local legal community. The great selection of ales and the ever-friendly Tom Paine, cat in residence, make this a superb Holborn hideaway.

BLOOMSBURY & FITZROVIA

BRADLEY'S SPANISH BAR Map p450
☎ 7636 0359; 42-44 Hanway St W1; ⊖ Tottenham Court Rd

Low ceilings, cramped quarters, vaguely Spanish décor, a vintage vinyl jukebox and a convivial atmosphere are the features of this charming hostelry, which is one of the most ordinary boozers in the West End and therefore among the best. Although it's tucked away behind Oxford St, enough punters know about it and they regularly spill out onto the street. Treat yourself to the Cruzcampo.

KING'S BAR Map pp442-3
☎ 7837 6470; Hotel Russell, Russell Sq WC1; ⊖ Russell Sq

Nestled behind the awesome Victorian Gothic façade of the Hotel Russell, the King's Bar is a well-kept secret in a neighbourhood sorely lacking in decent bars. The grand Edwardian décor, huge leather armchairs and table service make the prices worthwhile. There's a great selection of cocktails and wines, and you're always guaranteed a seat.

LORD JOHN RUSSELL Map pp442-3
☎ 7388 0500; 91 Marchmont St WC1; ⊖ Russell Sq

Having a pint here will instantly transport you to studentdom in the most pleasant way. Here under- and post-grads alike escape the local halls of residence for good company and a pint in this traditional one-room bar that sums up conviviality in one simple image.

MUSEUM TAVERN Map p452
☎ 7242 8987; 49 Great Russell St WC1; ⊖ Tottenham Court Rd

This is where Karl Marx used to retire for a sup after a hard day inventing communism in the British Museum Reading Room. An atmospheric traditional pub set around a long bar, it has friendly staff and is popular with academics and students alike.

QUEEN'S LARDER Map pp448-9
☎ 7837 5627; 1 Queen Sq WC1; ⊖ Russell Sq

In a lovely square southeast of Russell Sq, this pub is so called because Queen Charlotte, wife of 'Mad' King George III, rented part of the pub's cellar to store special foods for him while he was getting treatment nearby. There are benches outside for fair-weather fans and a good dining room upstairs.

The Princess Louise (left)

EAST CENTRAL

While the West End is the standard first port of call for visiting revellers, you'll set yourself apart straight away by heading instead to the far hipper offerings of Shoreditch and Clerkenwell. Walking up Old St on a weekend night you'll see a parade of life, and many of the freaks that were once West End features before high prices drove them into the run-down arms of Hoxton. Bars here range from the chic and stylish to the rough and ready, but this is still the part of London where you'll find the liveliest parties and the hippest new openings. Islington is less trendy, but still full of great drinking places, attracting a middle-class north London crew of revellers. However, while the City is great for traditional pubs, it's one to avoid at weekends, when it's dead – it's strictly a Monday to Friday after-work deal here.

THE CITY

JAMAICA WINE HOUSE Map pp454-5
☎ 7626 9496; 12 St Michael's Alley EC3; 🕓 closed Sat & Sun; ⊖ Bank

Not a wine bar at all but a historic Victorian pub, the 'Jam Pot' stands on the site of what was the first coffee house in London (1652), and consequently is more a place to enjoy beer rather than wine.

VERTIGO 42 Map pp454-5
☎ 7877 7842; 25 Old Broad St EC2; 🕓 closed Sat & Sun; ⊖ Bank

The stratospheric views from this 42nd-storey bar are matched by the stratospheric prices, and for security reasons you *must* book. Seats are arranged around the glass-walled circular space, where you quaff champagne while taking in an unforgettable view. The crowd, as you might expect, is made up of city plutocrats and is the least inspiring thing about the place.

YE OLDE CHESHIRE CHEESE Map pp448-9
☎ 7353 6170; Wine Office Ct, 145 Fleet St EC4; ⊖ Blackfriars

The entrance to this historic pub is via a picturesque alley. Cross the threshold and you'll find yourself in a wood-panelled interior (the oldest bit dates from the mid-17th century) with sawdust on the floor and divided up into various bars and eating areas.

HOXTON, SHOREDITCH & SPITALFIELDS

1001 Map pp442-3
☎ 7247 9679; 1 Dray Walk E1; 🕓 to midnight Fri & Sat; ⊖ Aldgate East/Shoreditch

A laid-back food and coffee place during the day, in the evenings 1001 offers a rich programme of DJs who spin while the Spitalfields crowd knock back beers and cocktails in the dark upstairs lounge, where seated areas are padded by enormous cushions and the atmosphere enhanced with candles and comfy booths.

BAR KICK Map pp442-3
☎ 7739 8700; 127 Shoreditch High St E1; ⊖ Old St

A much larger sister venue to Clerkenwell's **Café Kick** (Map pp442–3), this place has a slightly edgier Shoreditch vibe. This time, too, there's some floor space left over after four footy tables were installed, so there are leather sofas and simple tables and chairs.

BLUU Map pp442-3
☎ 7613 2793; www.bluu.co.uk; 1 Hoxton Sq N1; 🕓 to 11.30pm Mon-Thu, to midnight Fri & Sat; ⊖ Old St

When you first walk in, Bluu might feel cold and unwelcoming; that's the effect of all that exposed concrete. Sink into one of the comfy seats and knock back a few cocktails, though, and you'll see why locals regard it fondly as a comfy old favourite.

BRICKLAYERS ARMS Map pp442-3
☎ 7739 5245; 63 Charlotte Rd EC2; ⊖ Old St

A determinedly down-to-earth stalwart of the Hoxton scene, the Bricklayers Arms attracts an unpretentious but cool-looking, generally mid-to-late-20s crowd. This essentially old-style pub is often seen as a solid place to start the evening, before heading off elsewhere.

CANTALOUPE Map pp442-3
☎ 7613 4411; www.cantaloupe.co.uk; 35-43 Charlotte Rd EC2; 🕓 to midnight Mon-Fri, to 11pm Sun; ⊖ Old St/Liverpool St

One of the first of the new generation of Hoxton bars and *the* bar that focused the media's eyes on it in the late 1990s, the Cantaloupe was a bit hectic during the dot-com boom. Now it's far less crowded, but it's still a great place to come and spread out with friends around the large tables. There's a decent restaurant at the back, too.

CARGO Map pp442-3

☎ 7749 7840; www.cargo-london.com; 83 Rivington St EC2; ☾ to 1am Mon-Thu, to 3am Fri & Sat, to midnight Sun; ⊖ Old St/Liverpool St

Housed beneath three railway arches, the excellent Cargo advertises itself as a combined MDF (music, drinks, food) experience. During the week you can park yourself on a dishevelled sofa bench to enjoy a quiet drink – or head to the courtyard with its hammock – but at weekends the clubroom takes precedence, with live bands and some of the best Hoxton DJs.

DRAGON BAR Map pp442-3

☎ 7490 7110; 5 Leonard St N1; ☾ to 11pm Sun & Mon, to midnight Tue & Wed, to 1am Thu, to 2am Fri & Sat; ⊖ Old St

Dragon's super cool, in that louche, moody (as opposed to overtly posey) Hoxton way. It's easy to miss it, as the name is only embossed on the entrance stairs, but once inside it's all exposed brick, Chinese lanterns, velvet curtains and – a suitably ironic touch here – one of those illuminated waterfall pictures you buy on Brick Lane. A place where you feel comfortable in the latest street style but definitely not in a suit.

DREAMBAGSJAGUARSHOES
Map pp442-3

☎ 7729 5830; 34-36 Kingsland Rd E2; ☾ to midnight; ⊖ Old St

Despite the unusual moniker (the original names of the two shop spaces the bar occupies), this is a typical example of Shoreditch shabby chic: wooden floors, exposed brick/concrete walls, leather and canvas sofas rescued from somewhere like a skip, with lads wearing that mussed-up 'just got out of bed' hair look and sleeker-looking gals. Check out the graffiti wall downstairs.

FOUNDRY Map pp442-3

☎ 7739 6900; www.foundry.tv; 84-86 Great Eastern St EC2; ⊖ Old St

The eccentric Foundry so genuinely doesn't give a hoot about being hip that it manages to be impossibly hip and welcoming to all simultaneously. The ramshackle furniture, makeshift bar and piano renditions of, oh, say, vintage David Bowie, are reminiscent of an illegal squat bar somewhere in Eastern Europe. Brilliant.

GEORGE & DRAGON Map pp442-3

☎ 7012 1100; 2 Hackney Rd E2; ⊖ Old St

Despite a notorious write-up in the *Observer* describing it as the trendiest bar in the UK,

the George (as ye shall dub it if you value your Shoreditch High Street cred) remains the epicentre of the Hoxton scene. It's a truly fun place unless it's busy, in which case it's pure (yet cutting-edge) misery. Some of the best DJ nights in London are on offer here, with a brilliant atmosphere of total fun and mindless hedonism generally ruling. Not a place for a quiet pint.

GOLDEN HART Map pp454-5

☎ 7247 2158; 110 Commercial St E1; ⊖ Liverpool St

It's an unsurprisingly trendy Hoxton crowd that mixes in the surprisingly untrendy interior of this brilliant Spitalfields boozer. As it's famously a hang-out for the YBAs (Young British Artists), you may well catch Tracey Emin giving it some to her interlocutor over a pint and chips, although most agree that the person to come and see here is the charming (and, yes, possibly bonkers) landlady, Sandra, who ensures that the bullshit never outstrips the fun. Smashing.

JOINERS ARMS Map pp442-3

☎ 7739 9854; 116 Hackney Rd E2; ☾ to 2am Fri & Sat; ⊖ Shoreditch/Old St

Determinedly run-down and cheesy, the Joiners is Hoxton's only totally gay pub/club (perhaps reflecting the degree to which such distinctions are blurred around E2). It's a crowded, funky, smoky old boozer where hip gay boys hang out at the bar, dance and watch people play pool all night. The toilets are miserable, though, with ridiculous queues – why not install a urinal in a bar populated 90% by men?

LOUNGELOVER Map pp442-3

☎ 7012 1234; 1 Whitby St E1; ☾ to midnight Mon-Thu, to 1am Fri & Sat, closed Sun; ⊖ /rail Liverpool St

Evincing the same junk-shop-rearranged-by-gay-stylist look of its sister establishment, Les Trois Garçons, trendy Loungelover is totally over the top and addictive. It's like stepping into another world, where chandeliers, antiques, street lanterns and comfy lounge chairs materialise just seconds away from the run-down streets outside. Coming here once is never enough, even though the drink prices are pretty high.

MEDICINE BAR Map pp442-3

☎ 7704 9536; 89 Great Eastern St EC2; ☾ to 2am Wed-Sat, to midnight Sun; ⊖ Old St

This larger offshoot of the Islington bar (p284) has been welcomed in Hoxton. Its upstairs room is pleasant enough and attracts a cool crowd, but it's the downstairs DJ bar that's the main draw. Those to have played here include Norman Cook (Fatboy Slim), Norman Jay, Jon Carter (Radio 1 DJ Sara Cox's main squeeze), Sancho Panza and Ashley Beedle. There's a cover charge of £6 after 9pm on Friday and Saturday.

MOTHER BAR Map pp442-3
☎ 7739 5949; www.333mother.com; 333 Old St;
🕑 to midnight Sun-Thu, to 2am Fri & Sat; ⊖ Old St
Still one of the best in town, Mother is the bar above Shoreditch's original hipster club, 333. Mobbed at weekends, it's still a great place to come, with a lounge, a dance floor and a fun, up-for-it crowd. It's open until late.

OLD BLUE LAST Map pp442-3
☎ 7739 5793; 39 Great Eastern Rd, EC2; ⊖ Old St/Liverpool St
The latest of the Shoreditch pubs to be flooded by the Hoxton Fin Society, in 2004 the Old Blue Last was bought by *Vice* magazine, the hipster bible that has become a global conglomerate. It hosts some of the best Shoreditch parties, has a rocking juke box and does a mean square pie to boot, all in the guise of a sawdust-and-spit kind of fighting pub.

SMERSH Map pp442-3
☎ 7739 0092; 5 Ravey St EC2; ⊖ Old St
How can anyone not love this studenty Shoreditch dive bar? The manager/barman/DJ is of the old-fashioned type (people pour their hearts out to him over whisky), while the décor is unique – Soviet memorabilia and hilarious articles from East German propaganda magazines.

T BAR Map pp442-3
☎ 7729 2973; www.tbarlondon.com; 56 Shoreditch High St E1; 🕑 to midnight Thu-Sat; ⊖ Liverpool St/Shoreditch
Housed on the ground floor of the Tea Building, a creative hub for various hip companies cashing in on Shoreditch's aching coolness, the T Bar is a truly vast expanse of, well, very little actually. Such a huge space can be overwhelming, although when there's an event on (frequently) such as Satanica Pandamonia's gay bingo, the place seems to attract every single person in Shoreditch and can be great fun. There's decent bar food available too.

VIBE BAR Map pp454-5
☎ 7377 2899; Truman Brewery, 91-95 Brick Lane E1;
⊖ Old St/Aldgate East
Once the epicentre of the Hoxton scene, the Vibe is part bar, part club and still attracts a regular crowd, although it's safe to say that its time has long passed. On quieter nights drinkers can still enjoy themselves in the spacious bar, which has scuffed leather sofas, arcade games and computer terminals.

CLERKENWELL

CHARTERHOUSE BAR Map pp448-9
☎ 7608 0858; www.charterhousebar.co.uk; 38 Charterhouse St EC1; 🕑 to midnight Wed & Sun, to 1am Thu, to 2am Fri & Sat; ⊖ Barbican/Farringdon
Charterhouse Bar is a convivial wedge-shaped bar (a traditional Clerkenwell warehouse design) boasting DJs every evening and free entry at all times. The music can get a little loud in here at weekends, when you'll find yourself shouting 'What?' repeatedly. The bar food is great though, so head here for brunch if you don't enjoy bleeding ears.

FLUID Map pp448-9
☎ 7253 3444; 27 Charterhouse St EC1; 🕑 to midnight Mon-Wed, to 2am Thu-Sat, closed Sun;
⊖ Barbican/Farringdon
Behind its vibrant neon sign, this Japanese-themed bar oozes laid-back, unpretentious cool. In the dim light, punters sit sipping raspberry-flavoured Tokyo martinis, losing the freestyle sushi off their chopsticks or necking Asahi beer, while others play the '70s video arcade games or investigate the mothballed beer-dispensing machine. Downstairs there's a DJ space with a Tokyo photomontage on the wall. On Saturdays there's a cover charge (£5).

JERUSALEM TAVERN Map pp448-9
☎ 7490 4281; 55 Britton St EC1; ⊖ Farringdon
It's hard to know what to rave about most at the small Jerusalem Tavern – the 18th-century

Drinking – East Central

283

décor where plaster walls are adorned with occasional tile mosaics, or the range of drinks, which includes organic bitters, cream stouts, wheat and, mmm, fruit beers. This was actually one of the first London coffee houses (founded in 1703), but its recent incarnation has sought to pass it off as a ye olde London drinking den, and despite this faux-tradition it's still a charming place.

THREE KINGS OF CLERKENWELL
Map pp448-9

☎ 7253 0483; 7 Clerkenwell Close EC1; ⊖ Farringdon
A friendly pub near Clerkenwell Green, the Three Kings of Clerkenwell is festooned with papier-mâché models, including a giant rhino head situated above the fireplace. This is an unpretentious boozer in one of the most nouveau-trendy areas of London, and locals mix very happily with media darlings throughout the night. There's food and extra seating upstairs.

YE OLDE MITRE Map pp448-9
☎ 7405 4751; 1 Ely Ct EC1; ⊖ Chancery Lane/Farringdon
A delightfully cosy historic pub, tucked away in a back street off Hatton Garden, Ye Olde Mitre was built for the servants of Ely Palace. There's still a memento of Queen Elizabeth, in the shape of the stump of a cherry tree around which she once danced. There's no music, so the snug rooms only echo to the sound of amiable chitchat.

ISLINGTON

ALBION Map pp442-3
☎ 7607 7450; 10 Thornhill Rd N1; ⊖ Angel/Highbury & Islington
Renowned for its wisteria-covered beer garden out the back, which makes it seem like a true country pub, the Albion's best suited for a drink on a sunny weekend afternoon. It's a magnet then for young families and children.

ELBOW ROOM Map pp442-3
☎ 7278 3244; 89-91 Chapel Market N1; ⊖ Angel
Don't be fooled by the row upon row of pool tables, this place is packed on the weekends with punters just as interested in the cocktails, beer, bar food and DJs. It's relaxed, unposey and reckoned by many men to be a top place to meet members of the opposite sex. Entry on Saturday costs about £5.

ELK IN THE WOODS Map pp442-3
☎ 7226 3535; 39 Camden Passage N1; ⊖ Angel
Part Laura Ashley, part East London hip, this is by far the coolest bar in Islington and equally notable for its food, although we tend to use it as a watering hole. With its old mirrors, stuffed deer head and gloriously friendly staff, this is a spot to savour, especially as you can usually get a seat.

EMBASSY Map pp442-3
☎ 7359 7882; 119 Essex Rd N1; ☾ to1am Fri & Sat; ⊖ Angel
Behind those black walls and smoky windows, cool muso and media types quaff beer in the comfy sofas or enjoy the DJs in the street-level bar and more recent basement bar. The buzz about Embassy's street-cred has grown, so it's now one of Islington's premier venues; there's a cover charge (£3) on weekends. Get there early.

KINKY MAMBO Map pp442-3
☎ 7704 6868; www.kinkymambo.co.uk; 144-145 Upper St; ☾ to 2am; ⊖ Angel/Highbury & Islington
This recent addition to the already impressive collection of cool bars on Upper St is a very sleek cocktail and dancing venue set over two floors. DJs spin every night, and its late license is a godsend – there's no charge for entering after 11pm either.

LUSH BAR Map pp442-3
☎ 7704 0977; www.lushlondon.com; 235 Upper St; ☾ to 2am Fri & Sat; ⊖ Highbury & Islington
This newcomer to the Islington scene is a welcome change of pace – relaxed and friendly, what it lacks in hip it makes up for with its easy going attitude. With good cocktails and DJs who spin on Friday and Saturday, this is a great local hang-out.

MEDICINE BAR Map pp442-3
☎ 7704 9536; 181 Upper St N1; ☾ to midnight Sun-Thu, to 2am Fri & Sat; ⊖ Highbury & Islington
Still one of the coolest bars along Upper St, the Medicine Bar attracts 30-something clubbers and drinkers, as well as a younger crowd. One reason you'd come to this converted dark-red pub, with low sofas and dim lighting, is its music, ranging from jazzy funk to hip-hop; another attraction is minor celebrity spotting – you might catch sight of your fave DJ, model or TV star (if you can see through the crowds, that is).

WEST CENTRAL

Although a few slick new bars costing serious money, and with an incredible per-square-metre ratio of beautiful people, have opened up around here in recent years, the traditional pubs are so beautiful and atmospheric that they can't be toppled from our best-of list. It's safe to say that there's nothing particularly hip here, but if the timeless and high fashion is for you, this is the place to join old-money London for a £12 cocktail.

MAYFAIR & ST JAMES'S

CALMIA LOUNGE Map pp448-9

☎ 7747 9380; 23 St James's St W1; ☺ to 1am Mon-Sat, closed Sun; ➍ Green Park

Although the upstairs restaurant had closed at the time of writing, the exclusive cognoscenti bars downstairs remained very much a place to be seen drinking for the Mayfair set. Famous for being owned by Roger Moore's son Geoffrey, the bar keeps the local fashionistas and aristocrats happy with what is reputedly the best bellini in St James's. Effortlessly cool, this is definite model-spotting territory.

GUINEA Map pp448-9

☎ 7409 1728; 30 Bruton Pl W1; ➍ Green Park/Bond St

Top-quality Young's beers, famous autographs on the toilet walls and the whiff of money define this quiet and out-of-the-way pub in London's most exclusive neighbourhood of Mayfair. There are very few places to sit, though, and it sometimes feels little more than a waiting room for the rear restaurant (renowned for its pies).

SALT WHISKY BAR Map pp444-5

☎ 7402 1155; www.saltbar.com; 82 Seymour St W1; ➍ Marble Arch

A fantastic, sophisticated addition to this neighbourhood, perched on the corner of Edgware Rd, Salt exudes cool self-confidence with its sleek, dark wood interior. There's a vast array of whiskies and whisky cocktails to be had at the friendly bar or in the comfortable lounge. Staff are knowledgeable and keen to share their tips with customers.

KNIGHTSBRIDGE, SOUTH KENSINGTON & HYDE PARK

COOPERS ARMS Map pp458-9

☎ 7376 3120; 87 Flood St SW3; ➍ Sloane Sq/South Kensington

This classic Chelsea pub just off King's Rd, decorated with stuffed critters and vintage rail-way advertising, has a bright and sunny bar, a mixed clientele and bonhomie by the barrel.

CUBA Map pp444-5

☎ 7938 4137; www.cubalondon.co.uk; 11-13 Kensington High St W8; ☺ to 2am Mon-Sat, to midnight Sun; ➍ High St Kensington

If you're really into traditional English pubs but have somehow strayed onto these pages, you might enjoy a romp through this Latin-themed bar that positively fizzes with a combination of lethal rum-based cocktails, sexy samba dancers and leery Latino lads. Dress to sweat.

NAG'S HEAD Map pp444-5

☎ 7235 1135; 53 Kinnerton St SW1; ➍ Hyde Park Cnr

Located in a serene mews not far from bustling Knightsbridge, this gorgeously genteel early-19th-century drinking den has eccentric décor, a sunken bar and no mobile phones. A dreamy delight; don't bother if you're not pure of pub heart.

STAR TAVERN Map pp444-5

☎ 7235 3019; 6 Belgrave Mews West SW1; ➍ Knightsbridge/Sloane Sq

This cheery place is best known for West End glamour and East End skulduggery; it's where Christine Keeler and John Profumo rendezvoused for the scandalous Profumo affair and where the Great Train Robbers are said to have planned their audacious crime. These days it's just a lovely boozer with reliable Fuller's beers.

WINDOWS Map pp448-9

☎ 7493 8000; Hilton Hotel, 28th fl, Park Lane W1; ☺ to 2am Mon-Thu, to 3am Fri & Sat; ➍ Hyde Park Cnr

If you make one observation in London, it should probably be from this 28th-floor bar of the Hilton Hotel. The views of the city are breathtaking, particularly at dusk, and there are drinks from beer to cocktails and cognac to slake your thirst. Although it's open fabulously late, be aware that nonguests arriving after 11pm will have to pay a £7.50 cover charge.

ALONG THE SOUTH BANK

Most of the drinking establishments in this area are good, down-to-earth boozers, which just happen to have been here for hundreds of years. Despite a smattering of trendier new places, the traditional English pub with a good set of ales is what keeps people heading down here.

SOUTHBANK CENTRE & WATERLOO

KING'S ARMS Map pp448-9
☎ 7207 0784; 25 Roupell St SE1; ⊖ Waterloo/Southwark

A really well-kept secret (yeah, sorry about that) in a terraced Waterloo back street, the King's Arms is a delightful winter-warmer boozer. Full of character, the large traditional bar area serving up a good selection of ales and bitters gives way to a fantastically odd conservatory bedecked with junk store eclectica. It's a relaxed and friendly place; you'll find few better in London.

BOROUGH & BERMONDSEY

ANCHOR BANKSIDE Map pp454-5
☎ 7407 1577; 34 Park St SE1; ⊖ London Bridge

Come rain or shine, this 18th-century pub is the business. If the weather's poor you can shelter in its warren of historic rooms, including one where Samuel Johnson (1709–84) wrote part of his famous dictionary. When it's sunny, the riverside terrace is justly popular.

GEORGE INN Map pp454-5
☎ 7407 2056; Talbot Yard, 77 Borough High St SE1; ⊖ Borough/London Bridge

It doesn't even fully explain the 'wow' factor of the George to say it's London's last surviving galleried coaching inn and a National Trust pub; you have to see its low-ceilinged, dark-panelled rooms for yourself. Dating from 1676, it's mentioned in Charles Dickens' *Little Dorrit*.

MARKET PORTER Map pp454-5
☎ 7407 2495; 9 Stoney St SE1; ☽ 6.30-8.30am Mon-Fri; ⊖ London Bridge

This pub opens early on weekdays for the traders at Borough's wholesale market. It's good during normal opening hours, too, for its convivial atmosphere and large selection of real ales and bitters. This is the stuff of great pubs, and it's well worth making a detour for.

ROYAL OAK Map pp454-5
☎ 7357 7173; 44 Tabard St SE1; ⊖ Borough

Tucked away down a side street behind a huge apartment development that might yet make this part of Borough trendy, this is a pub for serious lovers of beer. Regulars look mildly surprised to see new faces, but after a pint of the tasty Harveys you'll be feeling more comfy.

WINE WHARF Map pp454-5
☎ 7940 8335; www.winewharf.co.uk; Stoney St SE1; ⊖ London Bridge

Located in a smart warehouse space conveniently close to the culinary joys of Borough Market, the Wine Wharf's range of wines will delight oenophiles and people just coming along for a drink alike. The range is truly enormous, and the staff are more than happy to advise, offering you the chance to taste before buying. It's packed after work, and you'll do much better here at the weekends.

THE EAST END

Once famous for gangster assassinations and Saturday night fights at kicking out time, the pubs of the East End have improved hugely in the past few years. There are still some fairly unpleasant dives and pubs where only locals will feel comfortable, but those listed below are treats.

WHITECHAPEL

GEORGE TAVERN Map pp454-5
☎ 7790 1763; 373 Commercial Rd; ⊖ Shadwell

Some will object to the virtual desecration of this once good-looking East End pub, but it's undeniably East London's best-kept hipster secret, with its '70s Stepney's disco out the back and its oh-so-cool front bar full of beautiful young pop stars in waiting. Regular gigs by local legends such as Babyshambles and the Paddingtons have confirmed the pub's cult status.

George Tavern (opposite)

rambling series of rooms is good at any time for its wide range of Belgian beer, but there's something about its dim back room, with its ethnic boho chic, that makes this pub a great place to hunker down against the chill.

DOCKLANDS

GRAPES Map p463
☎ 7987 4396; 76 Narrow St E14; DLR Westferry
One of Limehouse's renowned historic pubs – just follow the street signs from the DLR – the Grapes is cosy and snug. Actually, it's absolutely tiny, especially the riverside terrace, which can only really comfortably fit four to six people. However, it radiates olde-worlde charm.

MAYFLOWER Map pp454-5
☎ 7237 4088; 117 Rotherhithe St SE16; ⊖ Rotherhithe
This 15th-century pub is named after the ship that took the pilgrims to America in 1620. The ship set sail from Rotherhithe, and the captain supposedly charted out its course here while supping schooners. There's now a long jetty, from which you can view the river.

PROSPECT OF WHITBY Map pp454-5
☎ 7481 1095; 57 Wapping Wall E1; ⊖ Wapping
Although undeniably touristy, the 16th-century Whitby is still a lovely atmospheric old pub, with dim lighting, flagstone floor and pewter bar. You need to be pretty lucky to grab one of the tables by the windows overlooking the Thames, but there's a river terrace, which is great in summer. One of London's oldest surviving drinking houses, the pub also features an upstairs restaurant and open fires in winter.

BETHNAL GREEN & HACKNEY

CAT & MUTTON Map pp438-9
☎ 7254 5599; www.catandmutton.co.uk; 76 Broadway Market E8; rail London Fields/bus 106, 253, 26, 48 or 55
As if to seal the deal on East London's most up-and-coming eating and drinking strip, the once terrifying fighting pub on the corner of London Fields has been reborn as an airy, friendly and well-run gastropub. Serving great ales and offering a full wine list and modern European menu, this family-friendly place is a welcome addition to London's drinking scene.

DOVE FREEHOUSE & KITCHEN
Map pp438-9
☎ 7275 7617; 24 Broadway Market; rail London Fields/bus 106, 253, 26, 48 or 55
On a Sunday winter's evening it's lovely to come here for a comforting roast. Okay, this

SOUTHEAST LONDON
If you're looking for pubs straight out of Dickens, this area can oblige – and throw in some wonderful views to boot. We'd steer clear of the new bars in the area looking to accommodate recent arrivals – stick to traditional boozers and you won't go wrong.

GREENWICH

NORTH POLE Map p463
☎ 8853 3020; 131 Greenwich High Rd SE10; DLR/rail Greenwich
This funky Greenwich bar attracts a fairly trendy crowd. It's over two levels. Upstairs is all animal-print sofas and a warm red glow. Downstairs, at the South Pole, there's an air-craft theme. There's a mix of R & B and ga-rage on the DJs' decks. The food gets good reports too.

TRAFALGAR TAVERN Map p463
☎ 8858 2437; Park Row SE10; DLR Cutty Sark, rail Maze Hill
Charles Dickens once drank at this historic pub and mentions it in *Our Mutual Friend*. Prime ministers Gladstone and Disraeli used to dine on the celebrated whitebait. Today it still has a historic feel, with dark-wood panelling and curved windows overlooking the Millennium Dome. However, the nearby University of Greenwich has brought in a large student clientele during term time. In summer, tourists take over.

NORTH CENTRAL

Marylebone and Camden Town are the two busiest neighbourhoods for drinking options here, both offering a mix of hip and traditional, with some crossover. Maida Vale and St John's Wood have some London classics too – you won't be wasting an evening spent anywhere around here.

MARYLEBONE & REGENT'S PARK

DUSK Map pp448-9
☎ 7486 5746; 79 Marylebone High St W1; ✪ Baker St
Everyone looks more attractive at dusk, and we're not just talking about that moment when demanding day slides into sensual night. This recently made over bar feels designer on both sides of the counter, and has boutique beers and choice cocktails.

LOW LIFE Map pp448-9
☎ 7935 1272; 34A Paddington St W1; ✪ Baker St
In contrast to many of the smarter venues around Marylebone village, Low Life caters, while not exactly to the people advertised in its name, to a nevertheless young and cheerful crowd of early-20s party boys and girls in its trendy basement area. The cocktails aren't anything special, but some of the party nights here enliven an otherwise very staid area.

O'CONNOR DAN Map pp448-9
☎ 7935 9311; 88 Marylebone Lane W1; ✪ Bond St
A great Irish pub free of bullshit and blarney, O'Connor Dan is big, dark and handsome, with table service, scuffed wooden surfaces and bar and restaurant food that is several cuts above the pub norm.

KING'S CROSS

RUBY LOUNGE Map pp442-3
☎ 7837 9558; 33 Caledonian Rd N1; ✪ King's Cross St Pancras
How you come up with such a friendly and unintimidating King's Cross bar is anyone's guess. You'll have to push your way past an assortment of junkies and prostitutes to get to it, but it's worth it, for a fun, warm interior with great DJs and an up-for-it pre-clubbing crowd, in this, what must be London's armpit.

CAMDEN

BAR VINYL Map pp440-1
☎ 7681 7898; 6 Inverness St NW1; ✪ Camden Town
Although deeply chilled and effortlessly cool, this archetypal DJ bar has a very welcoming vibe, and propping up on a bar stool or plopping into comfy retro chairs here is a genuine treat midweek, accompanied by unfailingly groovy sounds. It's equally good at the weekend, just without the chance of a seat.

BARTOK Map pp440-1
☎ 7916 0595; 78-79 Chalk Farm Rd NW1; ☾ to 1am Mon-Thu, to 2am Fri & Sat, to midnight Sun; ✪ Chalk Farm/Camden Town
We love the fact that in Camden, the cradle of Britpop, you can head to this bar and savour a pint with a little classical concerto for audible company. Named after the Hungarian composer and pianist, Bartok has low comfy sofas, intimate lighting and huge drapes as the setting for some brilliant DJ sets blending jazz, classical and world music.

CROWN & GOOSE Map pp440-1
☎ 7485 8008; 100 Arlington Rd NW1; ✪ Camden Town
One of our favourite London pubs, this square room has a central wooden bar between British-racing-green walls studded with gilt-framed mirrors and illuminated by big, shuttered windows. More importantly, it combines a good-looking crowd, easy conviviality, top tucker and good, inexpensive beer.

EDINBORO CASTLE Map pp440-1
☎ 7255 9651; 57 Mornington Tce NW1; ✪ Camden Town
This beautifully attired, relaxed and welcoming pub has more of a Primrose Hill atmosphere than that of a Camden boozer. It boasts a full menu, gorgeous furniture designed for slumping, and a huge outdoor seating area that is perfect for summer evenings.

QUEEN'S Map pp440-1
☎ 7586 0408; 49 Regent's Park Rd NW1; ✪ Camden Town/Chalk Farm
While the ghost of actress, royal 'friend' and former next-door neighbour Lillie Langtry is said to reside in the cellar of this spirited joint, the pub proper is haunted by contemporary beauties such as Jude Law and the other fashionistas of Primrose Hill. The food and drinks won't disappoint, and there's plenty to look at among the clientele, but if you hanker after

something more, head across the road to the hill and splendid views of London.

WORLD'S END Map pp440-1
☎ 7482 1932; 174 Camden High St NW1; ☉ Camden Town

'Meetcha at the World's End, the one beside Camden tube station,' are the famous last words uttered by tourists every day before they find themselves (and nobody else) in this huge, boisterous and manically popular pub that claims to sell a million pints of beer a day. Hell knows what the décor looks like, but it sure feels lively.

ST JOHN'S WOOD & MAIDA VALE

PRINCE ALFRED Map pp444-5
☎ 7286 3287; 5a Formosa St W9; ☉ Warwick Ave

Pubs don't really come much better than this charming place. Despite being renovated and adding a locally celebrated restaurant in 2002, the PA's original interior has been retained, with gorgeous carved-wood dividers radiating from the bar, creating a series of intimate booths. It's a great place to gather and chew the fat with friends.

Top Five Hotel Bars

- **American Bar**, the Savoy (p357)
- **Blue Bar**, Berkeley Hotel (see Boxwood Café, p249)
- **Refuel**, Soho Hotel (p356)
- **Light Bar**, St Martin's Lane (p357)
- **Claridge's Bar**, Claridge's (p362)

WARRINGTON HOTEL Map pp440-1
☎ 7266 3134; 93 Warrington Cres W9; ☉ Warwick Ave/Maida Vale

This former hotel and brothel is now an ornate Art Nouveau pub with heaps of character and an atmosphere that's so laid-back it's virtually horizontal. The huge saloon bar, dominated by a marble-topped hemispherical counter with a carved mahogany base, is a fabulous place to sample a range of real ales. There's outdoor seating and a good Thai restaurant upstairs.

WARWICK CASTLE Map pp444-5
☎ 7432 1331; 6 Warwick Pl W9; ☉ Warwick Ave

The attraction of this place is that it doesn't try too hard and it's a lovely, low-key local on a quiet street near the canal. It's one of a dying breed of London pubs actually owned by a landlord rather than a brewery or corporation.

NORTH LONDON

Head to the hills if you want to savour pubs that haven't changed in centuries, incoherent celebrities and north Londoners at play. The villages boast some knockout pubs, some of which make you pinch yourself to believe they are real, while there are also plenty of new bars – Stoke Newington and Dalston are ever-growing weekend meccas due to their young and lively residents.

HAMPSTEAD & HIGHGATE

BOOGALOO Map p465
☎ 8340 2928; www.theboogaloo.org; 312 Archway Rd N6; ☽ to midnight Thu, to 1.30am Fri & Sat; ☉ Highgate

Unquestionably the oddest location we'll send you to, this is not somewhere that gets a lot of passing tourist trade. This old pub was converted recently from a very cool local frequented by some of London's best musicians and comedians to a more self-consciously cool place, albeit with great music. The jukebox is regularly reprogrammed by celebrity musicians.

HOLLYBUSH Map p465
☎ 7435 2892; 22 Holly Mount NW3; ☉ Hampstead

A beautiful pub that makes you envy the privileged residents of Hampstead, Hollybush

has an antique Victorian interior, a lovely secluded hilltop location, open fires in winter and a knack for making you stay longer than you had intended at any time of the year. Set above Heath St, it's reached via the Holly Bush Steps.

SPANIARD'S INN Map p465
☎ 8731 6571; Spaniards Rd NW3; ☉ Hampstead, then bus 21

This marvellous tavern dates from 1585 and has more character than a West End musical. Dick Turpin, the dandy highwayman (or was that Adam Ant?) was born here and used it as a hang-out, while more savoury sorts such as Dickens, Shelley, Keats and Byron also availed themselves of its charms. There's a big, blissful garden, and the food ain't half bad (English for good).

289

WRESTLERS Map p465
☎ 8340 4397; 98 North Rd N6; ✆ Highgate

Another great, great local where the ambience, beer, food and décor just combine to make you happy to be alive, although when the very friendly Irish governor gets chatting you can begin to have second thoughts.

STOKE NEWINGTON
AULD SHILLELAGH
☎ 7249 5951; 105 Stoke Newington Church St N16; bus 73

Light relief for heavy drinkers, the Auld Shillelagh is one of the best Irish pubs in London. Typically, it's many things to many people: a theatre and a cosy room, centre stage and a sanctuary, a debating chamber and a place for silent contemplation. What's more, the staff are sharp, the Guinness is good, and the live entertainment is frequent and varied.

BIRDCAGE
☎ 7249 5951; 58 Stamford Hill N16; rail Stoke Newington

Once one of Stoke Newington's roughest and least inviting pubs (and that's quite an accolade), the Birdcage has been refitted in a manner more suitable for N16's increasingly young and hip population. It's now a trendy

gastropub-cum-DJ-bar, although it's most profitably employed as a boozer. There are DJs most nights (and even during Sunday lunch, when the new local arrivals lounge around reading the *Observer* and complaining about property prices).

FOX REFORMED
☎ 7254 5975; 176 Stoke Newington Church St N16; rail Stoke Newington/bus 73

Stoke Newington's indomitable wine bar has been packing them in for over two decades now, and it's not at all hard to see why. With its comfortable, quiet atmosphere, stripped wooden interior and lovely garden filled with people playing backgammon in the summer months, you'll probably be tempted to join them.

JAZZ BAR DALSTON
☎ 7254 9728; 4 Bradbury St N16; ☽ to 1am Mon-Thu, to 2am Fri & Sat, to midnight Sun; rail Dalston Kingsland

Dalston's most excellent bar, the Jazz Bar really is an unexpected find just off the chaos of Dalston Junction. Housed within glass walls, it's not really a jazz bar but a cocktail place where the neighbourhood's hip and friendly inhabitants congregate at the weekends to party on to hip hop, R&B and reggae.

Hollybush pub (p289)

WEST LONDON

One of London's busiest and most reliable drinking strips is fabulous Portobello Rd, which in the inimitable London way takes in everything from illegal drinking dens to super-exclusive cocktail bars populated by the local beautiful crowd. There are even more set back in the side streets waiting to be discovered. Away from the 'trustafarian' hang-outs of Notting Hill and Fulham, the bars and pubs of the more down-to-earth areas of west London are a refreshing departure. Shepherd's Bush is particularly lively, although Earl's Court attracts young travellers, particularly from Australia and South Africa.

Top Five Historic Pubs

- **Ye Olde Mitre** (p284)
- **Ye Olde Cheshire Cheese** (p281)
- **George Inn** (p286)
- **Salisbury** (p279)
- **Jerusalem Tavern** (p283)

NOTTING HILL & WESTBOURNE GROVE

CASTLE Map pp444-5

☎ 7221 7103; 225 Portobello Rd W11; ⊖ Ladbroke Grove

An industrial theme meets Moorish charm and comfortable furniture at this marketside pub that has recently enjoyed a much-needed face-lift. The bar serves Leffe and even strawberry beer to a crowd of local characters who keep the place buzzing all day long. There's a full menu and live jazz on Saturday and Sunday evenings.

EARL OF LONSDALE Map pp444-5

☎ 7727 6335; 277-281 Portobello Rd W11; ⊖ Notting Hill Gate/Westbourne Park

This incongruously refined and traditional gin palace on Portobello Rd is a real change of pace for an area full of ultra-cool cocktail lounges and bustling boozers. The huge bar is split up into booths where you can enjoy intimate conversation, the bar serves Samuel Smith ales, and there's a fantastic smoke-free back saloon (which looks more like a private members' club), complete with huge leather armchairs to sink into.

LONSDALE Map pp444-5

☎ 7727 4080; www.thelonsdale.co.uk; 48 Lonsdale Rd W11; ⏲ to midnight Mon-Sat, to 11.30pm Sun; ⊖ Notting Hill Gate/Westbourne Park

The super-slick Lonsdale looks like Buck Rogers' pad with its bumpy space-age walls suffused in purple light and given a traditional touch

with tiny red candles beneath a stunning oval skylight. The exceptional cocktails are what people come for, although there are also beers and wines. The punters are extremely well groomed, and the staff, even the door-man, are friendly.

MARKET BAR Map pp444-5

☎ 7229 6472; 240a Portobello Rd W11; ⊖ Ladbroke Grove

The unofficial base for carnival- and market-goers, this deconstructed boho bar chills out on other days with a steady stream of locals and tourists supping stout and coffee respectively, and gets mobbed in the evenings, when the music's cranked up (by DJs Friday and Saturday, and a jazz band late on Sunday afternoon). There's a more than decent Thai restaurant upstairs (see p265).

TRAILER HAPPINESS Map pp444-5

☎ 7727 2700; www.trailerhappiness.com; 177 Portobello Rd W11; ⏲ closed Sun & Mon; ⊖ Notting Hill Gate/Ladbroke Grove

This intimate Tiki cocktail bar is ultralounge in both décor and atmosphere. Kitted out in 1950s Americana/Hawaiian kitsch – low-slung tables, a bead curtain, beanbags and a couple of Tretchikoff prints – it's pretty laid-back and fun considering that a fair number of fashionistas, minor stars and general Portobello poseurs drop in. In fact, with friendly staff who know their drinks, and interesting enough food, the only discouraging thing about it is sometimes trying to get in. Early in the week there's less need to book.

TWELFTH HOUSE Map pp444-5

☎ 7727 9629; www.twelfth-house.co.uk; 35 Pembridge Rd W11; ⊖ Notting Hill Gate

This is a great place for a quiet drink in busy Notting Hill, an upmarket coffee house and bar dominated by an amazing astrological clock. As the place is run by astrologer Priscilla (we're not making this up), you'll be asked your star sign the moment you arrive and brought a card detailing your foibles; you can even get a full astrological chart made up while you drink wine, and that's got to be worth something.

WESTBOURNE Map pp444-5
☎ 7221 1332; 101 Westbourne Park Villas W2; ⊖ Royal Oak/Westbourne Park

This is another great pub. The Westbourne is virtually opposite the **Cow** (p264), and the summer crowds spilling out from both boozers sometimes get within touching distance. The Westbourne has the larger outdoor area, although inside it's more cramped and there is a little more attitude. As you'd expect, the crowd is beautiful and trust-fund fuelled.

WINDSOR CASTLE Map pp444-5
☎ 7243 9551; 114 Campden Hill Rd W8; ⊖ Notting Hill Gate

One of London's most delightful hang-outs, this relatively out-of-the-way tavern between Notting Hill and Kensington High St oozes history, warmth and charm. With its fireplace, great beer garden, historic interior and friendly regulars, this down-to-earth place in one of London's most exclusive residential areas is a real find.

EARL'S COURT

PRINCE OF TECK Map pp458-9
☎ 7373 3107; 161 Earl's Court Rd SW5; ⊖ Earl's Court

This Earl's Court mainstay is nearly always packed with travellers and is festooned with Australiana (well, stuffed kangaroos, anyway). It's large and comfortable, and has big screens

---

Campaigning for Real Ales

Although young Londoners like to think of themselves as discerning beer drinkers, many if not all seem content to guzzle flat and lifeless lagers delivered to them over the year by massive ad campaigns and monopolising breweries. And these drinks, while rubbish to begin with, are often made worse by a total lack of consideration and care on the part of the publicans and bar staff. Thankfully, a trend that has existed elsewhere in Britain for years has begun to take hold in the capital. Although it's not exactly hip, more and more drinkers are turning to real ales, ie naturally effervescent cask-conditioned ales, which are made to distinctive recipes and – hang on, what's this? – have flavour. For the best real ales in London, look for signs denoting the regional breweries of Young's and Fuller's (in that order).

---

on both floors. This is the default pub for young Aussies and Kiwis in the neighbourhood.

SHEPHERD'S BUSH & HAMMERSMITH

ALBERTINE Map pp438-9
☎ 8743 9593; 1 Wood Lane W12; ⊖ Shepherd's Bush

This pleasant wine bar just off Shepherd's Bush Green has a great wine list, and is a laid-back place for a drink and possibly a meal (mains £6 to £9) amid the humming conversation of after-work drinkers. The room upstairs is quieter and often available for those in a decent-sized group. The menu is largely French but also incorporates other European cuisines.

DOVE Map pp438-9
☎ 8748 5405; 19 Upper Mall W6; ⊖ Hammersmith/Ravenscourt Park

The perfect place to stop off for a drink on a walk down the river, this 17th-century pub is also famed for having the smallest bar in England. Legend has it that *Land of Hope and Glory* was written between these walls, although most visitors will be more impressed that this was Graham Greene's local. The dark-wood interiors are charming, but if the sun is shining fight for a place on the terrace and enjoy traditional ales overlooking the Thames.

GINGLIK Map pp438-9
☎ 8749 2310; www.ginglik.co.uk; 1 Shepherd's Bush Green W12; ☺ to 1am Thu-Sat, to 11.30pm Sun; ⊖ Shepherd's Bush

In a converted Victorian public convenience under Shepherd's Bush Green lurks the local smart set's drinking tavern. This private members' bar is populated by the arty and the gorgeous: you'll have to be taken by a well-connected friend or else apply in advance for temporary membership through the website. Either way, Ginglik makes for a fun and offbeat night out – the bar plays host to various underground DJs and has regular showings of cult films.

OLD SHIP Map p437
☎ 8748 2593; 25 Upper Mall W6; ⊖ Hammersmith

This funky towpath pub is packed at weekends with families and couples getting some liquid refreshment during their walks down the Thames. Its position is its greatest selling point, looking south across the lazy bend of the river towards Putney. It's popular during the rest of the week too, with its outdoor dining area, terrace and 1st-floor balcony.

SOUTH LONDON

Brixton pub regulars turn up their noses at all the pretentious posing that goes on in many of London's neighbourhoods du jour, but nearby Battersea and Clapham have a stylish bar or two. Brixton remains one of the most vibrant and exciting places to go out drinking in London.

BRIXTON
BRIXTONIAN HAVANA CLUB Map p462
☎ 7924 9262; 11 Beehive Pl SW9; ⊖ Brixton
While it is a restaurant (see p268), and sort of a club too (with DJs), most punters here seem to come for the cocktails, which oil the wheels of a super-friendly atmosphere. Take your pick from *mojitos*, *caipirinhas* and rum punches or even just stick to beer.

BUG BAR Map p462
☎ 7738 3366; St Matthew's Church, Brixton Hill; SW2; ⊖ Brixton
This sumptuously Gothic bar in a church crypt is a good place to shelter with friends and a glass of wine – possibly even switching over to the restaurant at some point for a meal (see p268).

DOGSTAR Map p462
☎ 7733 7515; 389 Coldharbour Lane SW9; ⊖ Brixton
Downstairs this long-running local institution has a cavernous bar, always mobbed with a young, casual and trendy South London crowd loudly milling among the tables around the floor. Upstairs there's a house-music club, open to 3am; after 9pm on Friday and Saturday a cover charge applies. And there are queues.

PLAN B Map p462
☎ 7733 0926; 418 Brixton Rd SW9; ⊖ Brixton
It doesn't have to be plan B – it could be an evening's plan A, if you're looking for a friendly, low-key DJ bar any night from Thursday to Sunday. Even on Tuesday and Wednesday nights the decent cocktails are enough to woo you to this large room, decorated in an urban minimalist style – all concrete, exposed brick and benches with frosted-glass side panels.

WHITE HORSE Map p462
☎ 8678 6666; 94 Brixton Hill SW2; ☽ to midnight Sun-Thu, to 3am Fri & Sat; ⊖ Brixton
Does this place *ever* shut? Often a destination for those who've been ejected from other

Brixton institutions such as the Dogstar, the White Horse appears to house some people for the duration of the entire weekend. It consists of just one big room decorated with modern art against one long bar, but it's lots of fun.

BATTERSEA & WANDSWORTH
DUSK Map pp460-1
☎ 7662 2112; www.duskbar.co.uk; 339 Battersea Park Rd SW11; rail Battersea Park
If there is such a thing as destination drinking, this place has to be it, as this rather remote stretch of Battersea Park Rd seems a truly unusual location for this glamorous, dark-wood-clad bar. Staff make killer cocktails despite being a little pleased with themselves and their award-winning bar design. This aspirational, smart place is a hit with the crowd who call Battersea 'South Chelsea' – and it plays to all their deepest, chicest desires with aplomb.

SHIP Map pp438-9
☎ 8870 9667; 41 Jew's Row SW18; rail Wandsworth Town
Though the Ship is right by the Thames, the views aren't spectacular (unless you're partial to retail parks and workaday bridges). Still, the outside area is large, the summer barbecues a treat and the conservatory bar fun in any weather.

CLAPHAM
GROVE Off Map p462
☎ 8673 6531; 39 Oldridge Rd SW12; ⊖ Balham
The Grove is reason enough to make the long trip to Balham. It's vast yet intimate, with a mixed crowd of locals and people who've made the effort to visit for a modern yet delightful pub experience. The food is superb value for money, and not your usual gastropub fare either – come to eat and stay to drink.

PRINCE OF WALES Map p462
☎ 7622 3530; 38 Old Town SW4; ⊖ Clapham Common

While pubs that hang crap from their ceilings in a bid to seem quirky and offbeat are always rather tedious, the Prince of Wales is still a very pleasant Clapham hang out, and its décor, unlike that of most pubs of the genre, is genuinely collected rather than supplied en masse. This is a quiet and unpretentious place for a drink and a plate of delicious hot nuts (the speciality snack).

SAND Map p462
☎ 7622 3022; 156 Clapham Park Rd SW4; ⊖ Clapham North/Clapham Common

Sand sure is sleek and good looking, with sand-textured walls, Islamic-style room dividers, leather pouffes, low-slung tables and lots of interesting features such as wall alcoves, candles, breeze blocks and a huge sand timer. The mood is cosy and relaxed on weekdays, and mobbed at weekends, when there are DJs (entry £5 after 9pm).

SO.UK Map p462
☎ 7622 4004; 165 Clapham High St SW4; ⊖ Clapham Common

Owned by two celebs (including Leslie Ash of *Men Behaving Badly* fame), So.uk is a stylish Moroccan-themed bar that's light and airy and serves unusual cocktails, such as Harissatinis. It's extremely popular, with the chance to spot a few well-known faces. Otherwise, you couldn't put it any better than the *Independent*, which called this a pulling place for Clapham professionals.

TIM BOBBIN Map p462
☎ 7738 8953; 1-3 Lillieshall Rd SW4; ⊖ Clapham Common

It's well worth searching out this charming little pub, set back a short walk from the Common. As one local put it, 'it's not nearly as bad as most of the pubs in Clapham'; that's to say you can get a seat here most nights of the week, chat to the friendly staff and play darts without fear of being cornered by city boys on the piss – something that gives drinking in Clapham a bad name.

SOUTHWEST LONDON

Going out in Fulham is mainly about cheesy nights with lots of drinking, dancing on tables and generally behaving badly. Don't head to this part of town if you want a classy evening. Putney and Barnes offer an altogether more sedate experience – there are few more enjoyable ways to spend a sunny afternoon in London than whiling away the hours in a pub on the river.

FULHAM & PARSONS GREEN
ECLIPSE
☎ 7731 2142; 108-110 New King's Rd SW6; ☽ noon-late; ⊖ Parsons Green

This cool but comfortable cocktail bar looks pretty swanky, but the Fulhamites always manage to drag the party down to their level. You won't find any uptight Sloanes giving you the cold shoulder in here, just sociable locals having a fun night out.

FIESTA HAVANA Map pp458-9
☎ 7381 5005; 490 Fulham Rd SW6; ☽ 5pm-2am Mon-Sat, 5pm-midnight Sun; ⊖ Fulham Broadway

The epitome of a cheesy night out, you'll have to be up for it to enjoy yourself at Fiesta Havana. If you're looking to pull, success is almost guaranteed; Havana has a reputation as a meat market, so be prepared to fight off unwanted attention if snogging a stranger wasn't what you had in mind. The music's great, though (groovy Latin beats), and there

are free dance classes at the beginning of the evening.

MITRE Map pp458-9
☎ 7386 8877; 81 Dawes Rd; ⊖ Fulham Broadway

A decent pub with a large semicircular bar and walled courtyard at the back, the Mitre gets very crowded in the evenings and at the weekends, mainly with toffs, but don't let that put you off – they're generally pretty friendly.

WHITE HORSE Map pp458-9
☎ 7736 2115; 1-3 Parson's Green; ⊖ Parsons Green

Right on the green, the White Horse is an inviting pub with a diverse clientele. Come here for the good hearty fare, barbecues during summer, the warm and friendly atmosphere, and the extensive range of beers (Belgian Trappist beers feature heavily, along with a selection of draught ales). Every year in November the White Horse is host to the Old Ales Festival, during which you can sample traditional ales.

PUTNEY & BARNES

COAT & BADGE Map pp438-9
☎ 8788 4900; 8 Lacy Rd SW15; ⊖ Putney Bridge
The Coat & Badge has gone for a tried and tested lounge-room approach (large sofas, second-hand books on shelves, sport on the telly, impartial décor), which seems to please the local Aussies. It has a short but excellent menu (the Sunday roasts are particularly good) and a fantastic large terrace out the front.

GREEN MAN
☎ 8788 8096; Putney Heath; ⊖ Putney Bridge/rail Putney, then bus 14 or 85
This tiny little pub on the heath is your real local's local, with old men perched on bar stools, chewing the fat with anyone who happens to be in vocal range. The Green Man is decidedly battered inside but has a certain rough charm. The pub's walled garden is *vast* and gorgeous, and hosts barbecues in the summer.

JOLLY GARDENERS Map pp438-9
☎ 8780 8921; 61-63 Lacy Rd SW15; ⊖ Putney Bridge/rail Putney
The antithesis to formulaic decorating and a tribute to all things chilled, this is our favourite pub in Putney. And it's not even on the river. It's been lovingly and eclectically kitted out (you'd never guess that Victorian oak cabinets went quite so well with Art Deco lamps or that thick drapes looked good next to bare bricks and wood-panelled walls). Jolly Gardeners plays host to amiable 30-somethings, and boasts a cheeky little wine menu and innovative food. Its large terrace fronting a quiet road compensates for the lack of riverside location.

The mosaic shingle advertising the Fiesta Havana bar (opposite)

YE WHITE HART
☎ 8876 5177; the Terrace SW13; rail Barnes
Of the three Young's pubs in Barnes, this is the nicest. It has a lovely terrace on the river, somewhat marred by the busy road outside and the view of the mother ship upstream – the source of the pint in your hand perhaps. If you have been to a Young's pub before, you will know exactly what the interior looks like: just think swirly carpets, fruit machines, old man at bar smoking B&Hs…

UP RIVER

Quieter and more traditional, the pubs up river are often real neighbourhood hubs, unlike the more anonymous pubs in central London, where the transience of both staff and punters is a major theme. Often centuries old, many of the best pubs overlook the river and make a great place to stop for a drink at any time of day.

CHISWICK

BOLLO PUB & DINING ROOM
☎ 8994 6037; 13 Bollo Lane W4; ⊖ Chiswick Park
Out of the way even by Chiswick's high standards, this inevitably elevated gastropub has been a huge success, run by local restaurateurs who redeveloped it from a simple local. The Bollo Pub & Dining Room is not the place to catch up with disaffected youth (they're probably all at boarding school anyway) but a great place for an older, wealthier crowd looking for a pub and dining room rolled into one.

295

RICHMOND

DYSART Off Map p464
☎ 8940 8005; 135 Petersham Rd, Richmond; ⊖ /rail Richmond

Formerly the Dysart Arms Hotel, the newly re-fitted Dysart is a great family pub facing Rich-mond Park's Petersham entrance. Apart from the mock-Gothic interior, which is a serious breach of good taste, the Dysart succeeds on all fronts: families are made to feel welcome, although children are not allowed to run riot, the food is good, and the large terrace is packed on a warm afternoon.

OLD SHIP Map p464
☎ 8940 3461; 3 King St, Richmond; ⊖ /rail Richmond

This charming old pub in the centre of Rich-mond attracts a down-to-earth crowd who seem largely oblivious to the toffs and suits of Richmond. There's a firm emphasis on sport, with several large screens, but also the nice traditional elements of the old English pub. It's packed on match days, but you can usually get a seat the rest of the week.

WHITE SWAN Map p464
☎ 8940 0959; Old Palace Lane, Richmond; ⊖ /rail Richmond

Facing the site of Richmond Palace, this great little pub nestles between the Thames tow-path and Richmond Green. Its historic façade gives way to a modern, airy interior, but it's friendly and comfortable, with good Thai food and a pleasant garden.

TWICKENHAM

BARMY ARMS
☎ 8892 0863; the Embankment, Twickenham; rail Twickenham

This is a popular local pub that gets packed to capacity on international match days. It's just by Eel Pie Island, a once-funky hippy hangout that still attracts the alternative crowd, despite its heyday being long gone. There's also de-cent pub food and a charming beer garden to recommend it.

WHITE SWAN
☎ 8892 2166; Riverside, Twickenham; rail Twickenham

This traditional pub is a London classic on what must be one of the most English-looking streets in London. It boasts a fan-tastic riverside location, a great selection of beer and a loyal crowd of locals. If you are in Twickenham the White Swan is a nearby treat, and if you're not too far away, this is one pub worth a detour.

WIMBLEDON

BAR SIA
☎ 8540 8339; www.barsia.com; 105-109 the Broad-way SW19; ⊖ Wimbledon

Hands down the best-designed bar in Wim-bledon (an area hardly noted for its banging nightlife, it must be owned), Bar Sia is located in a Turkish bath that used to serve the actors of the next-door Wimbledon Theatre. With two bars and a dance floor, this unique place features leather sofas and sleek green décor with white tiling, and is quite unlike most places you'll drink in. It's popular with a local crowd on the pull.

FOX AND GRAPES
☎ 8946 5599; 9 Camp Rd SW19; ⊖ Wimbledon

This traditional Wimbledon inn started serving pints in 1787 and is one of the most popular locals. The low-ceilinged bar is nonsmoking, while the bigger bar (converted from the sta-bles) is beautiful (with high beams) and brim-ming with traditional atmosphere. The Pacific Rim bar menu is also worth a look.

Entertainment

Entertainment

London is synonymous with all possible forms of entertainment. When Dr Johnson castigated those who were tired of London as being 'tired of life', he undoubtedly had a valid point, and when he added that there's 'all in London that life can afford' he could have been talking about today's endless choice and downright hedonism as well as the curious spectacles on offer in his own time. London teems with cutting-edge clubs, film festivals, innovative theatre productions, unique gigs, great comedy and world-class sporting events – and whatever complaints you may have about your trip here, being bored is definitely the least likely.

Of course the one snag is that you'll pay for your fun – even kicking back and relaxing in London is overpriced – but swallow that and you'll have a choice on offer that even a New Yorker or Parisian will be impressed by. Whether it's witnessing the latest scandal-clad indie superstars performing in a sweaty shoebox club in East London or seeing the cream of the British theatrical establishment treading the boards in the West End, you'll never be short of something to do on a night out in this most entertaining of cities.

For those looking for edifying and thrilling artistic pursuits, the capital is steeped in culture. Not only is there a good chance of watching a major Hollywood star such as Gwyneth Paltrow or Kevin Spacey strut their stuff on a stage in the West End, but there's also a wealth of homegrown talent. British actors who've gained international movie stardom, such as Dame Judi Dench, Sir Ian McKellen, Ralph Fiennes and Rhys Ifans, still tread the boards here, and it can be pure magic to witness. What's even more impressive is that they're backed by well-trained supporting casts and visionary directors who arguably make London theatre the best on the planet.

The Royal Shakespeare Company, the Royal Opera, the Royal Ballet and four major orchestras all cater to discerning highbrow tastes, while popular musicals such as *Chicago, Bollywood Dreams, Mary Poppins* and *Mamma Mia* woo the crowds. However, London also excels at producing the adventurous, the experimental and the unexpected genius. In recent years, for example, it's been the crucible for the world-famous all-male ballet *Swan Lake* and it's thrown up an entirely new genre by adapting the confessional TV show into *Jerry Springer – the Opera*.

The city harbours the unique experience of seeing Shakespeare staged in a bawdy Elizabethan manner, in an authentic reconstruction of the theatre where the Bard worked. It also has plenty of fun with the English language's most revered playwright: the Reduced Shakespeare Company has managed to compress his works into a mere 90-minute performance, while others have turned his works into hip-hop comedies.

There are plenty of stylish bars, clubs and gig venues stretching from Soho to Shoreditch and beyond. Alternatively, if you simply want a cheesy good time, London lets you relive your hormonally charged teenage years at School Disco or take you back to the '70s with Carwash. Soho, Brixton and Notting Hill also act as fantastic nightlife hubs, taking in everything from arts clubs to head-banging metal nights.

When it comes to cinema, American visitors might at first throw down the London film listings in disgust, thinking they've seen all the movies months before. But read on beyond the Hollywood blockbusters and you'll find an amazing diversity. French art house, Asian martial arts, African dramas, Eastern European black comedies and Latin American love stories all get the screen time here usually denied them by your average multiplex.

Finally, there's London's live rock and pop music scene, which simply can't be beaten. Creatively, the city has been recovering from a millennial lull with a new burst of guitar-based and electronic talent, but anyhow, anyone who's anyone plays the English capital at some time. Among the hundreds of venues there's bound to be a performance to grab your attention nearly every night. New York might boast that it's the city that never sleeps but London brushes off its archaic licensing laws and somnolent public transport to party just as hard.

WHAT'S ON

Competition for tickets to the best theatre, dance, opera, gigs and exclusive club events can be stiff, so make the most of online booking forums before you come to London if there's something specific you want to see. If you can, it's best to buy direct from the venue to save yourself commission charges. Most theatre box offices are open around 10am to 8pm from Monday to Saturday, but almost never on Sunday. However, events in London sell out astonishingly quickly, and agencies tend to have tickets after the venue has sold out. **Ticketmaster** (☎ 0870 534 444; www.ticketmaster.co.uk), **Stargreen** (☎ 7734 8932; www.stargreen .co.uk), **Ticketweb** (☎ 7771 2000; www.ticketweb.co.uk) and **Keith Prowse Ticketing** (☎ 0870 906 3838, www.keithprowse.com) all have 24-hour telephone and online booking.

For theatre productions you may be able to buy a returned ticket on the day of the performance, although for something really popular you might need to start queuing before the returns actually go on sale. On the day of performance only you can buy discounted tickets, sometimes up to 50% off, for West End productions from the **Tkts Booth** (Map p452; ☯ 10am-7pm Mon-Sat, noon-3pm Sun; ⊖ Leicester Sq) in the clock tower on the south side of Leicester Sq. It's run by the nonprofit **Society of London Theatre** (SOLT; ☎ 7836 0971) and wholly legitimate, although it levies a £2.50 service charge per ticket and has a limit of four tickets per customer. Payment is by cash or credit/debit card (Visa, MasterCard, American Express, Switch). Note that commercial ticket agencies nearby, particularly those along Cranbourn St, advertise half-price tickets without mentioning the large commission added to the price. Student stand-by tickets are sometimes available on production of identity cards one hour before the performance starts.

For all gigs, be wary of ticket touts outside the venue on the night. Of course, many of these are perfectly genuine tickets, so if you're happy with a mark-up then it's usually fine. Be sure to check with the holder of a genuine ticket before buying, though, to avoid the possibility of buying a forgery.

CINEMA

The UK film industry may be in a rather woeful state (despite its enormous visibility on the world stage, mainly through US-funded movies being filmed in Britain), but London is a city of cineastes and it's just not done to schlep down to the local multiplex and see the new J Lo vehicle on a Saturday night – at least not when there's a choice of several top-notch film festivals, retrospectives, seasons, new foreign films and cult classics available every night of the week.

Of course, if you want nothing more challenging than the latest Hollywood blockbusters, there are plenty of those, too. Check newspaper or magazine listings for the Warner Villages, Odeons or UGCs – and be prepared to pay up to an astonishing £12 for a first-run film. Many major premieres are held in Leicester Sq, so check when you're in town if you want a chance to see some of the world's major film stars doing public walkabouts.

If your tastes are a little more eclectic, try one of the cinemas below. They're not necessarily cheaper than the multiplex chains, but they certainly offer greater choice.

Typically, in either art-house or mainstream cinemas there are price discounts on Monday and for most weekday-afternoon screenings.

If you're in town in October or November, do keep an eye out for the **Times London Film Festival** (www.rlff.com), Europe's largest of its kind, with plenty of previews, debates and talks.

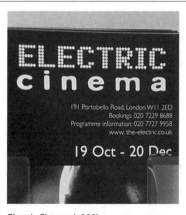

Electric Cinema (p300)

BARBICAN Map pp454-5

info ☎ 7382 7000, bookings ☎ 7638 8891; www
.barbican.org.uk; Silk St EC2; ⊖ Moorgate/Barbican

You don't get any walk-in trade here at London's self-contained arts village, but the several screens at the Barbican still manage to
pull in the crowds with innovative and unusual programming, regular film festivals, and
talks by directors and stars. The main screen
was voted the most comfortable in London
recently – it's a dream to watch a film here,
with no worries about your view being obscured even if you sit behind Marge Simpson and legroom that first-class transatlantic
flights would be proud of.

CINÉ LUMIÈRE Map pp458-9

☎ 7073 1350; 17 Queensberry Pl SW7; ⊖ South
Kensington

The large and well-appointed Ciné Lumière
is attached to South Kensington's excellent
French Institute. It shows mainly French films
subtitled in English but also has a very wide
remit to promote French coproductions from
all over the world as well as festivals and
retrospectives.

CLAPHAM PICTURE HOUSE Map p462

info ☎ 7498 2242, bookings ☎ 7498 3323; www
.picturehouse-cinemas.co.uk; 76 Venn St SW4;
⊖ Clapham Common

One of the capital's best local cinemas, the
Picture House has four screens and the kind
of café/bar where locals arrive well before the
film starts just so they can hang out for a bit.
The programme runs the gamut from first-run
blockbusters to Chinese art-house cinema.

CURZON MAYFAIR Map pp448-9

info ☎ 7495 0501, bookings ☎ 7495 0500; www
.curzoncinemas.com; 38 Curzon St W1; ⊖ Hyde Park
Cnr/Green Park

One of the few avant-garde outposts in London's wealthiest area, the Curzon Mayfair is
posher and not quite so relaxed as its Soho
sister (see below). The original Curzon nevertheless shows an interesting range of mostly
new independent and foreign films.

CURZON SOHO Map p452

info ☎ 7439 4805, bookings ☎ 7734 2255; www
.curzoncinemas.com; 93-107 Shaftesbury Ave W1;
⊖ Leicester Sq/Piccadilly Circus

The Curzon beats other West End cinemas
hands down, and that's not even because of

its good taste and art-house leanings in the
programming department. Upstairs it has a
great coffee counter, also serving healthy tea
and cakes, while downstairs you'll find the
coolest movie-house bar in the centre of
town. The programme contains left-field current releases, an excellent repertory selection,
and frequent retrospectives and minifestivals.

ELECTRIC CINEMA Map pp444-5

☎ 7908 9696, 7229 8688; www.electriccinema.co.uk;
191 Portobello Rd W1; ⊖ Ladbroke Grove/Notting
Hill Gate

A night out at this Rolls Royce of cinemas is
no ordinary evening at the pics. The Edwardian building, the UK's oldest purpose-built
cinema, has been luxuriously fitted out with
leather armchairs, footstools, tables for food
and drink in the auditorium, and an upmarket
brasserie. Of course, such pampering comes
at a slightly higher cost; on full-price nights
the seats are £12.50, or £30 for a two-seater
sofa. However, there's a great programme of
films as well as regular events and premieres.
This is probably the hippest venue in town.

EVERYMAN HAMPSTEAD Map p465

☎ 0870 066 4777; 5 Holly Bush Vale NW3;
⊖ Hampstead

This cosy art-house cinema has two screens.
The newer, smaller auditorium downstairs can
seat 90 people in comfy armchairs and will
screen slightly older foreign or left-of-centre
films, while the main feature is shown in the
original hall upstairs.

GATE Map pp444-5

☎ 7727 4043; 87 Notting Hill Gate W1; ⊖ Notting
Hill Gate

The Gate's single screen has one of London's
most charming Art Deco cinema interiors –
although the bar area is a little squished. It's
the programming it prides itself on, however,
introducing new art-house and independent
films.

INSTITUTE OF CONTEMPORARY
ARTS Map pp448-9

☎ 7930 3647; www.ica.org.uk; Nash House, the Mall
SW1; ⊖ Charing Cross/Piccadilly Circus

The Institute of Contemporary Arts (ICA) has
two screens: one of them extremely small, the
other more capacious and with a bit more legroom. Both show rarer, arty flicks and foreign
films that otherwise barely get cinematic re-

lease in the UK, making it the boho/art-house cinema to hang out in (just check out the poseurs at the lovely bar afterwards if you need any confirmation).

NATIONAL FILM THEATRE Map pp448-9
☎ 7928 3232; www.bfi.org.uk; South Bank SE1;
⊖ Waterloo/Embankment

The large auditorium at Britain's national repository of film is often used by directors and actors – occasionally including major Hollywood stars – to present and talk about their films, both new releases and golden oldies dusted off for retrospectives. There are two other, smaller screens, a good bookshop and a pleasant café/bar. Overall, the National Film Theatre arguably offers the most exciting and balanced mix of new and repertory film in the capital.

NOTTING HILL CORONET Map pp444-5
☎ 7727 6705; 103 Notting Hill Gate W8; ⊖ Notting Hill Gate

This *fin-de-siècle* stunner is one of London's most atmospheric places to watch a film. Indeed, a lovesick Hugh Grant munches popcorn here while watching Julia Roberts on the big screen in *Notting Hill*. The wonderful Edwardian interior, including a gorgeous balcony and even boxes, recalls the glory days of cinema, when filling a 400-seat house for every showing was easy. The Coronet faced closure recently, however, as economic reality caught up with it, but it was saved by a local church group in 2004.

PRINCE CHARLES Map p450
info ☎ 0901 272 7007 (25p per min), bookings
☎ 7494 3654; Leicester Pl WC2; ⊖ Leicester Sq

Central London's cheapest cinema (tickets generally cost from £1 to £4, with the best deals on Monday Madness night) is not for highbrow cinema buffs but for self-proclaimed movie geeks. Famously, the cinema also transformed *The Sound of Music* into a phenomenal – and very camp – sing-a-long hit. The audience members, straight and gay, still dress up as nuns or schoolgirls in plaits, mimicking Maria and booing Baron von Trapp (admission £10).

RENOIR Map pp442-3
☎ 7837 8402; Brunswick Centre, Brunswick Sq WC1;
⊖ Russell Sq

A basement-level oasis of mainly French chic in the drab, concrete Brunswick Centre, the Renoir has a good range of art-house DVDs on sale in the lower foyer, and serves warming coffee and cake. Along with a healthy dose of French film, you'll also be able to catch all sorts of international cinema, from Iranian morality tales to Taiwanese love stories. This cinema is a real Bloomsbury gem, close to the hearts of generations of London students.

RIO Map pp438-9
☎ 7241 9410; www.riocinema.ndirect.co.uk; 107 Kingsland High St E8; rail Dalston Kingsland

Showing a range of new releases, art-house pics and classic cinema, Dalston's Rio was thoroughly modernised in the late '90s, but you can still see traces of the lovely Art Deco theatre it was in its single-screen auditorium. It's where you'll find the Kurdish Film Festival and the Turkish Film Festival (in autumn and December respectively), and it's a venue for the Spanish Film Festival and the Gay & Lesbian Film Festival (held in April and March respectively).

RITZY Map p462
☎ 7733 2229; www.picturehouses.co.uk; Brixton Oval, Coldharbour Lane SW2; ⊖ Brixton

A renovation in the mid-'90s saw a move towards the multiplex model, with four new screens added to this 1911 building, but Brixton's local cinema still has plenty of style. The large original auditorium, with its proscenium arch, survived the conversion (making for five screens in all) and there is a funky bar and café.

RIVERSIDE STUDIOS Map pp438-9
☎ 8237 1111; Crisp Rd W6; ⊖ Hammersmith

Once a film and TV studio itself, where classics such as *Dr Who* and *Hancock's Half-Hour* were shot, the cinema at the Riverside now shows classic art-house flicks and those you might have missed a few months back. Unusual events, such as a programme of international ads, are also sometimes held here.

SCREEN ON THE GREEN Map pp442-3
☎ 7226 3520; 83 Upper St N1; ⊖ Angel

At a bustling junction of Islington's busy nightlife, this film house has a single auditorium with one large screen, attracting a trendy, upmarket crowd with a taste for edgy independent cinema (and good ice cream). Pity about the seats, though – bring a cushion and don't be over 6ft.

CLUBBING

London's hedonistic edge over its European counterparts is nowhere more apparent than in its absolutely thriving clubbing scene, the variety and energy of which leaves most other cities around the world eating the British capital's dust.

It's an expensive pastime, to be sure, although not exclusively. Midweek prices are reasonable, and there are plenty of student nights or those oriented to a less wealthy crowd if you search through the listing magazines during your visit. Saturday is the really big night, when you can expect to pay up to £20 for the pleasure of entering one of London's hipper 'superclubs' such as world-famous Fabric, relentless Turnmills or superglam Pacha. Thursday, Friday and Sunday are the other big party nights in town, when you can absolutely assured of a huge range of superlative clubbing options.

Exclusivity is not such an issue as is it is in, say, New York or Moscow – very few people are turned away from London clubs, but queuing in the cold while the gorgeous and connected jump out of cabs and straight into the warmth of the club can be a humiliating experience. As ever, get there early and try to get advance (or 'queue-jump') tickets for bigger events if you can't bear being left in door-whore limbo.

Dress codes vary widely. The reviews following should give you some idea, but ring ahead if you're unsure. Unlike in many provincial British cities, trainers/sneakers are *the* thing to wear in most clubs, and save in the smartest (usually West London) venues, wearing 'shoes' (ie anything chic in Italian black leather) will set you apart as an out-of-towner.

Many of the specific club nights mentioned have already moved venue several times, so it's always a good idea to check up-to-date listings in *Time Out* or the *Evening Standard*.

Unsurprisingly, the heart of London's nightlife is the West End, which includes some of the capital's longest-established and best nightclubs, although there are some real tourist traps around Leicester Sq to avoid. As Soho is the epicentre of London's gay and lesbian scene, the West End has a higher-than-average proportion of the city's leading gay clubs.

93 FEET EAST Map pp454-5

☎ 7247 3293; www.93feeteast.co.uk; 150 Brick Lane E2; ⏱ 5-11pm Mon-Thu, 5pm-1am Fri, noon-1am Sat, noon-10.30pm Sun; ⊖ Liverpool St/Aldgate East

Probably the most popular club in Shoreditch, 93 Feet East runs some top music nights, including the monthly Chibuku Shake Shake, giving Liverpool's best promoters the chance to wow London with hip-hop, soul and house. The venue itself is appealing, too: there's a courtyard, three good-sized rooms packed with a typically cool East London crowd and an outdoor terrace. However, all those doormen milling around menacingly are a little bit of overkill.

333 Map pp442-3

☎ 7739 5949; 333 Old St EC1; ⏱ 10pm-5am Fri, 10pm-4am Sat & Sun; ⊖ Old St

A real Hoxton old-timer, 333 remains determinedly down to earth in the face of all that is pretentious and silly in Shoreditch. Just off Hoxton Sq, it's simultaneously scruffy and innovative, featuring nights as diverse as Friday's supercool Radio Clash and Sunday's gay alternative Monster.

AQUARIUM Map pp442-3

☎ 7251 6136, 0870 246 1966; 256-260 Old St EC1; ⏱ 10pm-3am Sat, 10pm-4am Sun; ⊖ Old St

The Saturday night hitch-up between '70s disco evening Carwash and this converted gym seems like an excellent match: clubbers dressed in sexy, retro gear – compulsory, but disco wigs not allowed – now mingle around the huge pool or in the trendy bar. The following evening the Aquarium is host to Absolutely Sunday, with a focus on old-school house, garage and R&B. There's also a Russian night on Thursday which is very popular with a glamorous and extremely wealthy Eastern European set. Trainers are not welcome here.

ASTORIA Map p450

☎ 7434 9592, 7434 6963; 157 Charing Cross Rd WC2; ⏱ 10.30pm-4am Mon & Thu, 11pm-4am Fri, 10.30pm-5am Sat; ⊖ Tottenham Court Rd

This dark, sweaty and atmospheric venue hosts London's largest gay club, G-A-Y. Saturday is the big night, with commercial beats and frequent big-name PAs from the likes of Kylie and the latest boy bands. There's a 'Pink Pounder' cheap night on Monday, Thursday night is Music Factory and Friday night is Camp Attack.

BAR RUMBA Map p450

☎ 7287 2715; 36 Shaftesbury Ave W1; ⏱ 10.30pm-3am Mon & Wed, 8.30pm-3am Tue, Thu & Fri, 9pm-5am Sat, 8pm-1.30am Sun; ⊖ Piccadilly Circus

A small club in the heart of Soho with a loyal following, Bar Rumba is best known for Monday's THIS! (That's How It Is), where resident DJ Raw Deal pushes the envelope with an eclectic mix of drum 'n' bass, jazz, hip-hop and global beats.

CARGO Map pp442-3

☎ 7739 3440; www.cargo-london.com; 83 Rivington St EC2; ⏱ noon-1am Mon-Thu, noon-3am Fri, 6pm-3am Sat, noon-midnight Sun; ⊖ Old St/Liverpool St

One of the area's best clubs, Cargo has three different spaces under brick railway arches. The music policy is pretty innovative, with a rolling programme of Latin house, nu-jazz, funk, groove and soul, DJs, global (particularly Latin) bands, up-and-coming bands, demos and rare grooves. The Scratch Perverts' Friday night outing, The Remix Night and Saturday's hip-hop extravaganza Friends & Family win regular plaudits from discerning clubbers. There's also an excellent bar on the premises (see p282).

CHERRY JAM Map pp444-5

☎ 7727 9950; 58 Porchester Rd W2; ⏱ 6pm-late Mon-Sat, 4-11pm Sun; ⊖ Royal Oak

Whether you want to call it a DJ bar or a club, there are three things certain about Cherry Jam: it's small, usually crowded and super fine. Part-owner Ben Watt (of the Notting Hill Arts Club and formerly of Everything But the Girl) is one of the DJs on Saturday. Other club nights are from Wednesday to Sunday, and include Thursday's famous Yo-Yo. Bands play Tuesday, while Monday there are readings and other arty events.

CRASH Map pp460-1

☎ 7820 1500; 66 Goding St SE11; ⏱ 10.30pm-6am Sat; ⊖ Vauxhall

If Vauxhall in general is one of London's newest gay hang-outs, then Crash, in particular, is its Muscle Mary heaven. There are two dance floors churning out hard beats, four bars and even a few go-go dancers.

CROSS Map pp442-3

☎ 7837 0828; Goods Way Depot, York Way N1; ⏱ 10.30pm-5am Fri & Sat, 10.30pm-4am Sun; ⊖ King's Cross St Pancras

This is one of London's best venues, comprising several low brick rooms built under railway arches hidden in the wasteland off York Way. Friday has mixed/gay Fiction, with soulful funk and garage. Sunday is run by Vertigo, a Continental-style clubbing operation, who bring over lots of Italian guest DJs. There's a great outdoor terrace for the summer months, too.

DOGSTAR Map p462
☎ 7733 7515; 389 Coldharbour Lane SW9; 9pm-3am Fri & Sat; ⊖ Brixton

You'll have to push your way through the huge downstairs bar (see p293) of this converted pub to get to the house-music club upstairs, but that's what a hell of a lot of southside clubbers do.

EGG Map pp442-3
☎ 7428 7574; 5-13 Vale Royal N1; ◷ 10pm-4am Fri, 10pm-5am Sat; ⊖ King's Cross St Pancras

One of London's newer, hotter venues, omnisexual Egg has been likened to a club in New York's meat-packing district because of its bare walls and exposed concrete. Located off York Way, the club has three floors, two roof terraces and an outside courtyard. Friday is gay/mixed, with Zerox (electro-punk, funk with classic electronic). At weekends after 11pm, a free shuttle bus runs from King's Cross to the venue every 30 minutes.

END Map p452
☎ 7419 9199; 18 West Central St WC1; ◷ 10pm-3am Mon & Wed, 10pm-4am Thu, 10pm-5am Fri, 9.30pm-6am Sat; ⊖ Holborn

The End is a glam club – with minimalist industrial décor – situated in a West End back street. Friday and Saturday are devoted to guest DJs, including big names such as Darren Emerson and LTJ Bukem. Wednesday's Swerve with Fabio is mega-popular, and the rest of the week includes Sunday's hard-house Riot and one of London's coolest club nights, Monday's disco/glam/punk/'80s electronica Trash.

FABRIC Map pp448-9
☎ 7336 8898, 7490 0444; www.fabriclondon.com; 77a Charterhouse St EC1; ◷ 9.30pm-5am Fri & Sun, 10pm-7am Sat; ⊖ Farringdon

This most impressive of superclubs (one of a millennial rash that has not only survived but actually flourished) is still the first stop on the London club scene for many international clubbers, as the lengthy queues attest (worst from about 9pm to 11pm). A smoky warren of three floors, three bars, many walkways and unisex toilets, it has a kidney-shaking 'sonic boom' dance floor where you can feel the music, literally. The crowd is hip and well dressed without overkill, and the music – mainly electro, house, drum 'n' bass and breakbeat – is as superb as you'd expect from London's top-rated. Celebrated Friday-nighter Fabric Live sees resident DJs James Lavelle, Joe Ransom and Ali B regularly joined by big names ranging from the Scratch Perverts to Andrew Weatherall and beyond, while Sunday's DTPM is one of the longest-running and most hedonistic gay nights in town.

FIRE Map p460-1
☎ 0790 503 5682; South Lambeth Rd SW8; 10pm-4am; ⊖ Vauxhall

Sealing Vauxhall's reputation as the new gay nightlife centre of London, Fire is another expansive, smart space under the railway arches. Currently hosting the infamous Rude Boyz on Thursday night – the first London club especially for gay chavs and their admirers.

FRIDGE Map p462
☎ 7326 5100; 1 Town Hall Pde SW2; ◷ 9pm-2.30am Mon-Thu & Sun, 10pm-6am Fri & Sat; ⊖ Brixton

This is one of London's longest-running venues and it is still extremely popular. The Fridge is an excellent bar and club venue that is not too big and not too small. It runs a wide variety of club nights and live music ranging from African gospel and Cuban salsa to reggae and punk. On weekends, though, the music's generally a mix of trance and hard house.

GHETTO Map p450
☎ 7287 3726; 5-6 Falconberg Ct W1; ◷ 10pm-3am Mon-Thu, from 10.30pm Wed, 10.30pm-4.30am Fri & Sat; ⊖ Tottenham Court Rd

In a sweaty basement, this leading gay club has nevertheless established itself as the hippest Soho has to offer, with its 1950s American milk bar–style white seats and red walls. The most talked about night is Nag Nag Nag, where both Boy George and Yoko Ono have appeared, followed by Friday's in-yer-face Cock. There's also Thursday's indie-music Misshapes and Saturday's trashy Wig Out.

HAMMERSMITH PALAIS Map pp438-9
☎ 8600 2300; 242 Shepherd's Bush Rd W6; ◷ 10pm-3am Sat; ⊖ Hammersmith

Formerly Po Na Na Hammersmith, the Palais is now the notorious home for supremely successful School Disco, held every Friday night and attracting uniform fetishists, cheeky schoolboys and girls, and the odd teacher. A uniform is compulsory or you'll be expelled – check the website for details (www.schooldisco.com).

HEAVEN Map p452

☎ 7930 2020; www.heaven-london.com; Villiers St WC2; ☾ 10.30pm-3am Mon & Wed, 10pm-3am Fri, 10pm-5am Sat; ⊖ Embankment/Charing Cross

This long-standing and perennially popular gay club, under the Arches Shopping Arcade, has always had some mixed nights, but its big draws are its three long-established nights: Saturday is still the flagship night for gay clubbers who like very commercial house music, while Monday is the cheap and cheerful student-oriented Popcorn, possibly gay London's best-value night out. Wednesday is cheeky midweeker Fruit Machine.

HERBAL Map pp442-3

☎ 7613 4462; 10-14 Kingsland Rd E2; ☾ 9pm-2am Wed, Thu & Sun, 9pm-3am Fri, 10pm-3am Sat; ⊖ Old St

You'll recognise Herbal by all the plastic grass stapled to its front wall. Inside is a two-level bar/small club. The laid-back, grown-up loft upstairs has a small dance floor, seating and a window overlooking Shoreditch. Downstairs is more minimalist and can get very sweaty. There's a mix of drum 'n' bass, house, funk-house and hip-hop, interspersed with live shows.

KOKO Map pp440-1

☎ 0870 432 5527; www.koko.uk.com; 1a Camden High St NW1; ☾ 10pm-2.30am Tue, 10pm-6am Fri & Sat; ⊖ Mornington Cres

It was a sad day for scruffy Camden youth past and present when the legendary Camden Palace was closed, refitted and reopened as Koko in 2004. Charlie Chaplin, The Goon Show, The Sex Pistols and Madonna are just a few greats to have performed on the stage, but there's no doubt that the Palace was in desperate need of renovation. In fact, the former theatre with its fantastic main dance floor and balconies is still a great venue, although the mainstay is nowadays club nights for a cashed up and not-so-Camden crowd. Koko Saturday is your best bet for good house and techno.

MADAME JO JO'S Map p450

☎ 7734 2473; 8 Brewer St W1; ☾ 10.30pm-3am Wed-Fri, from 9.30pm Thu, cabaret 7-10pm & club 10pm-3am Sat; ⊖ Leicester Sq/Piccadilly Circus

The renowned subterranean cabaret bar and all its sleazy, fun kitsch gives way to a deep-house/nu-jazz club night on Saturday. But Keb Darge's Deep Funk night on Friday is equally legendary, attracting a cool crew of breakers, jazz dancers and people just out to have a good time.

MASS Map p462

☎ 7737 1016; St Matthew's Church SW2; ☾ 10pm-6am Fri & Sat; ⊖ Brixton

Mass is an appropriately named venue, situated in St Matthew's Church, with its vaulted ceilings, pews and frescoes. Friday night is Fetish Night, while Saturday rolls around for Dekefex, an award-winning mix of drum 'n' bass and hip-hop.

MEAN FIDDLER Map p450

☎ 7434 0403; 165 Charing Cross Rd W1; ☾ 10.30pm-4am Wed-Sat; ⊖ Tottenham Court Rd

The little sister to the Astoria, the Mean Fiddler (still known to many as the LA2) is a great venue over two floors, one overlooking the other through thick glass. Downstairs there's a stage for live acts and dark nooks for all kind of rock-and-roll goings-on. Saturday's alternative night Frog is an unpretentious, madly popular event, while traditional rock is played on Friday at the night suitably called Rock.

Top Five Club Nights

- **Trash** (End, opposite; www.trashclub.co.uk; ☾ Mon) One of the coolest parties in town, Trash attracts the truly indulgent Monday night hedonists with its excellent live bands and dressed-up punk-funk-guitar-fuelled fun.

- **Fabric Live** (Fabric, opposite; www.fabriclondon .com; ☾ Fri) Proving itself to be the only one of several so-called 'superclubs' to live up to its name, Fabric Live continues to impress with cutting-edge line-ups and a cool party crowd. You won't hear music like this anywhere else – look no further for the cool London clubbing experience.

- **Koko Saturday** (Koko, left; www.koko.uk.com; ☾ Sat) The newest addition to London's great Saturday nighters is at the revamped Camden Palace, featuring local stars 2ManyDJs, Tiga and Manhead belting out some of the coolest sounds in the capital in the main room.

- **Scratch** (Forum, p314; www.meanfiddler.com; ☾ Sat) Continuing to win plaudits from across the board, Scratch is the hottest hip-hop party in town, hosted at this cult north London venue and boasting some of the best names in British urban music as regular guests.

- **Nag Nag Nag** (Ghetto, opposite; www.nagnag nag.info; ☾ Wed) The cream of London's club world comes to this superb weekly event, where electro meets punk and models meet pop stars. Come early and expect to queue if you have the audacity not to be on the guest list.

Entertainment – Clubbing

MINISTRY OF SOUND Map pp454-5

☎ 7378 6528; www.minstryofsound.com; 103 Gaunt St SE1; ☿ 10.30pm-6am Fri, midnight-9am Sat; ⊖ Elephant & Castle

No longer a mere club but an enormous global brand, the Ministry of Sound naturally doesn't have the edge it once did. However, it has been trying to grab back some of that revolutionary feel since a major refurbishment in late 2003, which included a total overhaul of its main room, new bars, luxurious loos and a green glass box apparently floating in mid-air. Join the queue.

NEIGHBOURHOOD Map pp444-5

☎ 7524 7979; 2 Acklam Rd W10; ☿ 6pm-late Thu-Sun; ⊖ Ladbroke Grove

On the site of the long-running Subterania, Cherry Jam and Notting Hill Arts Club supremo Ben Watt has launched another excellent venue, with a capacity of 500 and a mixed programme from author readings to house nights.

NOTTING HILL ARTS CLUB Map pp444-5

☎ 7460 4459; 21 Notting Hill Gate W11; ☿ 6pm-1am Tue-Sat, 6pm-2am Fri & Sat, 4-11pm Sun; ⊖ Notting Hill Gate

This laid-back, funky basement club attracts an eclectic crowd. Anyone from dreadlocked students to the occasional celebrity can be found between its white walls. Sunday's legendary Lazy Dog has been replaced with house night Underdog, with the result that the media have now focused on Wednesday's Death Disco – a rock-and-roll, indie and punk evening from Creation Records founder Alan McGee, which has attracted celebs like Courtney Love.

PACHA Map pp460-1

☎ 7833 3139; www.pacha.com; Terminus Pl SW1; ☿ 10pm-6am Fri & Sat; ⊖ /rail Victoria

The London outpost of the seminal 'Ibeefa' club is one of London's most sumptuous venues, eschewing the 'industrial' look that dominates London clubland for the oak-wood panelling, upholstered booths and stunning stained-glass ceiling of a 1920s gentleman's club. Changing Saturday nights include the very popular bi-monthly Kinky Malinki.

PLASTIC PEOPLE Map pp442-3

☎ 7739 6471; 147-149 Curtain Rd EC2; ☿ 10pm-2am Thu, 10pm-3am Fri & Sat; ⊖ Old St

Afrobeat, jazz dance, future dance, broken beats and garage are all on the playlist in this small downstairs club with Balance on Saturday nights. On Friday it's an even more eclectic

Entertainment – Clubbing

Top Five Gay Club Nights

- **Rude Boyz** (Fire, p304; ☿ Thu) At this immensely popular club for scallies and their admirers, dress council (think white trainers, shell suits and Burberry caps). There's lots of risqué fun for an amused and amusing young crowd.
- **DTPM** (Fabric, p304; ☿ Sun) The name apparently stands for Drugs Taken Per Minute, and that has some resonance when you see the glam crowd that rolls up here – none of them appear to have slept since Thursday. However, the atmosphere is incredible, with superb music in a superb venue.
- **Monster** (333, p303; ☿ Sun) This is one of the clubbing week's highlights, attracting a cool EC2 crowd as well as some out-of-area muscle boys in a mixed environment of great music and end-of-weekend hedonism.
- **Fiction** (Cross, p303; ☿ Fri) Some of the best music on the gay scene for a cool, carefree crowd of serious clubbers. Come early, as the queues can be huge. Enjoy the excellent range of music, spread over three small dance floors, in this beautifully converted space in the King's Cross wasteland.
- **Duckie** (Vauxhall Tavern, Map p460–1; ☿ Sat) Get here by 10.30pm to avoid a massive queue because Duckie, hosted by the marvellous Amy Lamé, is the perfect antidote to pretension on the gay scene. Great indie tunes and some of the most unusual cabaret in London await you here.

---

mix of punk, funk, acid disco, sleazy electro and left field for the superb night And Did We Mention Our Disco? Highly recommended.

SCALA Map pp442-3

☎ 7833 2022; 275 Pentonville Rd N1; ☿ 10pm-5am Fri & Sat; ⊖ King's Cross

On Friday this multilevel former cinema hosts Popstarz, a laid-back gay/mixed potpourri of indie, alternative and kitsch. On Saturday it's UK garage night Cookies and Cream. The venue is expansive but excellent, with a glass bar at its centre overlooking the stage but insulated from the noise.

TURNMILLS Map pp448-9

☎ 7250 3409; 63 Clerkenwell Rd EC1; ☿ 6pm-midnight Tue, 10.30pm-7.30am Fri, 9pm-5am Sat; ⊖ Farringdon

This cavernous long-running institution still manages to pull in big-name DJs, including the likes of Judge Jules, Sister Bliss and Roger Sanchez, with its kickin' beats. Any weekend Clerkenwell Rd is heaving with clubbers and long lines around the block to get in.

COMEDY

Comedy in London is bigger than in just about any other city we've ever visited, and there are more than 20 major clubs hosting regular gigs and big names from the circuit, along with countless other venues – including pubs that try to get in on the act at least one night a week. Some of the world's most famous comedians hail from, or made their names in, London.

To whet your appetite a quick roll call from recent decades might include Peter Sellers, Peter Cook, Spike Milligan, Dudley Moore, Tommy Cooper, Dawn French, Jennifer Saunders, Ruby Wax, Lenny Henry, Ben Elton, Alexei Sayle, Harry Enfield, Victoria Wood, Julian Clary, Rowan Atkinson, Reeves & Mortimer, Eddie Izzard, Jo Brand, Ali G, Ricky Gervais, Matt Lucas and David Walliams.

On the club circuit, look out for London-based American comedian Rich Hall, who, for our money, is the greatest stand-up of his time. Ross Noble is a uniquely gifted, sonic-waffling Geordie whose stream of consciousness shtick should come with a health warning, while musician, poet and Luton-towner John Hegley is the uncrowned king of rhythm on the London circuit. Other names that will guarantee memorable moments are Mark Thomas, Alan Carr, Arthur Smith, Richard Herring, Bill Bailey, Daniel Kitson and Simon Munnery.

AMUSED MOOSE SOHO Map p450

☎ 7383 7283; Moonlighting, 17 Greek St W1;
⊖ Tottenham Court Rd

One of the city's best clubs, Soho's Amused Moose is popular with audiences and co-medians alike, perhaps helped along by the fact that heckling is 'unacceptable' and all of the acts are 'first date–friendly' in that they're unlikely to humiliate the front row. At Camden's **Enterprise pub** (p326) there's also Amused Moose Camden, with a similar crowd and policy.

BOUND & GAGGED

☎ 8450 4100; Fox, 413 Green Lanes N13; admission £8;
⊙ Fri & Sat; rail Palmers Green

This 200-seater has long been one of the best rooms in London comedy and was only improved by a 2003 refurbishment. Expect to see some of the best of the moment.

CHUCKLE CLUB Map pp448-9

☎ 7476 1672; Three Tuns Bar, London School of Economics, Houghton St; admission around £10; ⊙ Sat;
⊖ Holborn/Temple

The comedian's favourite, this club has a great atmosphere thanks to comedy stalwart, resident host and all-round lovely bloke Eugene Cheese, who begins every night with the Chuckle Club warm-up song.

COMEDY CAFÉ Map pp442-3

☎ 7739 5706; 66-68 Rivington St EC2; admission Wed free, Sat up to £14; ⊙ Wed-Sat; ⊖ Old St

We really don't like the whole meal-and-show vibe, and this purpose-built comedy club in Hoxton is a little too try-hard and wacky for our tastes, but it has some good comedians and the Wednesday night try-out spots are excruciatingly entertaining.

COMEDY CAMP Map p450

☎ 7483 2960; 3-4 Archer St W1; admission £9;
⊙ 8.30pm Tue; ⊖ Piccadilly Circus

This is an interesting new idea, a gay (but straight-friendly) comedy club in the basement area of one of Soho's more enjoyable gay bars, **Barcode** (p277). Comedy Camp features both up-and-coming queer comedy acts as well as more established gay and lesbian comics.

COMEDY STORE Map p450

☎ 7344 4444; Haymarket House, 1a Oxendon St SW1; admission £13; ⊙ Tue-Sun; ⊖ Piccadilly Circus

This was one of the first (and is still one of the best) comedy clubs in London. It was established down the road in Soho in 1979, the year Margaret Thatcher came to power, which we're sure was no coincidence. Although it's a bit like conveyor-belt comedy, it gets some of the biggest names, plus the Comedy Store Players, the most famous improv outfit in town, on Wednesday and Sunday, featuring the superb Paul Merton – a definite reason to go.

DOWNSTAIRS AT THE KING'S HEAD

☎ 8340 1028; 2 Crouch End Hill N8; admission £7;
⊙ Sat & Sun; ⊖ Finsbury Park, then bus W7

Another club that has thrived thanks to the efforts of its dedicated manager, Downstairs is a busy, smoky and intimate room with a giving atmosphere and top acts.

HEADLINERS

☎ 8566 4067; George IV, 185 Chiswick High Rd W4; admission £10; ⏱ Fri & Sat; ↔ Turnham Green

The first purpose-built venue in west London, Headliners is comfortable and has a traditional shape in that the compere introduces the act and scarpers, try-outs open the night, and the best is saved until last.

JONGLEURS Map pp440-1

☎ 0870 787 0707; Dingwalls, 11 East Yard, Camden Lock NW1; admission from £15; ⏱ Fri & Sat; ↔ Camden Town

The McDonald's of the comedy world, this international chain combines eating, drinking and laughing and is so popular you'll probably have to book for Friday and Saturday nights. The bill normally features one terrific big-name comic and a couple of guys on unicycles (or there-

abouts). There are other venues in Battersea (Map pp438–9) and Bow (Map pp438–9).

LEE HURST'S BACKYARD COMEDY
CLUB Map pp438-9

☎ 7739 3122; 231-237 Cambridge Heath Rd E2; admission £10-13; ⏱ Fri & Sat; ↔ Bethnal Green

Established and maintained by the likeable comic and dedicated promoter of the venue's name, this place benefits by being one of those that the comics most like to play.

UP THE CREEK Map p463

☎ 8858 4581; 302 Creek Rd SE10; admission £10-14; ⏱ Fri & Sat; rail Greenwich/DLR Cutty Sark

Without meaning to encourage them, sometimes the hecklers are funnier than the acts at this great club, run and occasionally still compered by the legendary Malcolm Hardee, the patron sinner of British comedy, who stole Freddie Mercury's 40th birthday cake and donated it to his local old folks home.

Jongleurs (above)

DANCE

London is home to five major dance companies and a host of small, experimental ones. The Royal Ballet, the best classical-ballet company in the land, is based at the Covent Garden Royal Opera House (p324); the Coliseum (Map p452) is another venue for ballet at Christmas and in summer.

The annual contemporary dance event in London is Dance Umbrella (p12). For more information about dance in the capital, visit the London Dance Network's website at www .londondance.com.

Other occasional dance venues include Riverside Studios (p301), the ICA (p300), and the home of the English National Opera, the London Coliseum. For more information about dance in London, see p54. For information about dance schools and classes, see p55.

BARBICAN Map pp454-5

☎ 7638 8891; www.barbican.org.uk; Silk St EC2; admission £6.50 30, student & over 60yr on day of performance £6.50-9; ⊖ Moorgate/Barbican

Increasingly, the Barbican Centre is staging dance performances, particularly through its multidisciplinary BITE (Barbican International Theatre Events) festival, which runs year round.

LABAN Map p463

☎ 8691 8600; www.laban.org; Creekside SE8; admission £1-15; ⊖ Deptford Bridge/DLR Greenwich

This is an independent dance training school, but it also presents student performances, graduation shows and regular pieces by its resident troupe, Transitions, as well as other assorted dance, music and physical performances. Its £22-million home was designed by Tate Modern's architects Herzog & de Meuron.

PEACOCK THEATRE Map p452

☎ 7863 8222; www.sadlers-wells.com; Portugal St WC2; admission £10-37; ⊖ Holborn

This small venue in the West End is part of the **Sadler's Wells complex** (see right). It hosts parodies of modern dance and performances from the less established companies.

PLACE Map pp440-1

☎ 7387 0031; www.theplace.org.uk; 17 Duke's Rd WC1; admission £5-15; ⊖ Euston

The birthplace of modern British dance (a Martha Graham–style school was established here in 1969), the Place concentrates on challenging, contemporary and experimental choreography, with a regular dash of Asian influences and dance theatre. Behind the late-Victorian façade you'll find a recently refurbished 300-seat theatre, an arty, creative café atmosphere and six training studios.

ROYAL BALLET Map p452

☎ 7304 4000; www.royalballet.co.uk; Royal Opera House, Bow St WC2; admission £4-80; ⊖ Covent Garden

Although the Royal Ballet has modernised its programme around the edges, classical ballet is still, as one newspaper critic has put it, 'the mother lode of the Royal Ballet's identity'. So this is where to head if you want to see traditional performances such as *Giselle* or *Romeo & Juliet*, performed by stars such as Sylvie Guillem, Irek Mukhamedov and Tamara Rojo. Standing tickets cost £4 to £5. There are same-day tickets, one per customer, from 10am for £8 to £40, and half-price stand-by tickets.

SADLER'S WELLS Map pp442-3

☎ 7863 8000; www.sadlers-wells.com; Rosebery Ave EC1; admission £10-40; ⊖ Angel

Sadler's Wells has a long and distinguished history. The theatre site dates from 1683, but more recently it's been credited with bringing modern dance into the mainstream by staging Matthew Bourne's revolutionary all-male *Swan Lake*. (Bourne's New Adventures troupe usually still does the Christmas show here.) Made over in 1998, the glittering main theatre attracts renowned international dancers and performances. The smaller Lilian Baylis Theatre stages more left-of-centre studio productions.

SOUTH BANK CENTRE Map pp448-9

☎ 7960 4242; www.rfh.org.uk; Belvedere Rd SE1; admission £6-60; ⊖ Waterloo

Every August the spotlight is put on dance for the Summer on the South Bank community dance festival. The Royal Festival Hall, Queen Elizabeth Hall and Purcell Room are also regular venues for the Dance Umbrella citywide festival.

HEALTH & FITNESS

In a city famed for its drinking and nightlife, it's reasonable to expect Londoners to eschew such puritan pastimes as going to the gym in favour of shameless hedonism. In fact, many people indulge in both, and you will never be far from some sporting facility or swimming pool. In fact, gym attendance in London has never been higher, with up-market chains being the order of the day, often staying open until late at night for the convenience of office workers. Like most other things in London, keeping fit in the capital can be expensive and riddled with snobbery – the gym you're a member of says a lot about you.

Gyms are either local authority–run at the bottom end of the market or private enterprises at the top, with the latter often coming in large chains. A swimming pool can send a gym's membership rates soaring in the increasingly space-conscious city, although not in all cases.

Opening hours vary hugely even within certain leisure centres, where some facilities open or close before others. As a rule, most gyms are open until at least 9pm. However, it's best to call ahead.

GYM CHAINS

CANNONS
☎ 0870 758 2333; www.cannonsclubs.co.uk
Cannons has some 14 clubs in central London and its pricier suburbs, and with no minimum contract of a year to sign it offers some of the best deals. Most of its London outlets are smart and well maintained, and some include a pool.

FITNESS FIRST
☎ 01202-845000; www.fitnessfirst.co.uk
The largest health club in the UK as well as the whole of Europe, this pan-London organisation has a reputation as a good middle-range gym chain. Handily, you can use any Fitness First club, no matter where you joined up. With branches all over the city, this chain is the most popular with short-term visitors to London. You can get a free gym pass to test out any location in the capital.

HOLMES PLACE
☎ 7795 4100; www.holmesplace.co.uk
This yuppie behemoth spans the classier areas of London, and offers top-notch facilities for people with more money than time. Locations include several in the city, Docklands, Notting Hill, Putney and throughout suburban London. Tariffs vary from club to club, but it's not cheap – it costs £80 per month just for the honour of using another branch of the pan-London network. However, there are generous student discounts and off-peak membership schemes.

LA FITNESS
☎ 7366 8080; www.lafitness.co.uk
With over 20 gyms in all areas of London, from Victoria to the City, LA Fitness is another big player on the scene. Its gyms are modern and well equipped, and the membership packages are extremely flexible.

INDIVIDUAL GYMS

CENTRAL YMCA Map p450
☎ 7343 1700; www.centralymca.org.uk; 112 Great Russell St WC1; per day/week £15/42.50;
⊖ Tottenham Court Rd
The gym at London's YMCA remains a very popular place and is always busy. Membership also gives you the chance to use the pool. The YMCA compares favourably with many of the more expensive and elitist London gyms, and of course it's very friendly. It is not, however, a youth hostel!

EQVVS PERSONAL TRAINING
Map pp458-9
☎ 7838 1138; www.eqvvs.com; 43a Cheval Pl SW7;
⊖ Knightsbridge
This personal training centre offers top-of-the-range facilities and orientates itself squarely toward models, actors and other unworldly beings that are able to pay for the personal services of Marco Bellagamba. The centre offers more alternative therapies as well, from yoga to reflexology. Prices are high and vary according to the services required.

QUEEN MOTHER SPORTS CENTRE
Map pp460-1
☎ 7630 5522; 223 Vauxhall Bridge Rd SW1; per day £7.10; ⊖ Victoria
This place is another reliable, central London gym, named after the dear Queen's late mum. It features three pools and comprehensive sporting facilities.

SEYMOUR LEISURE CENTRE
Map p444-5

☎ 7723 8019; Seymour Pl W1; per day gym £7.60, pool £3.05; ⊖ Marble Arch/Edgware Rd

The Seymour is a long-standing London leisure centre and, despite being a little shabby, it's a perfectly functional place that is well equipped and friendly. Its main advantage is its central London location and its reasonable prices, which means it always tends to be quite busy.

THIRD SPACE Map p450

☎ 7439 6333; www.thethirdspace.com; 13 Sherwood St W1; per month £111; ⊖ Piccadilly Circus

The Groucho Club of gyms, this pretentiously named Piccadilly Circus establishment is the last word in gym chic, make no mistake. The sumptuous facilities provide everything necessary for your busy Soho media exec to relax in or work up a sweat on. All at a hefty price, naturally, and the minimum time period for membership is one month.

SWIMMING

London has some lovely 1930s Art Deco 'lidos' – what much of the rest of the world just calls swimming pools. The separate term historically denotes an open-air establishment in this traditionally chilly climate. But while the lidos are obviously best in the summer, most are open all year round for the hardy. Often, you have to be a member of the local swimming club in order to use the pool.

BROCKWELL PARK LIDO Map p462

☎ 7274 3088; www.thelido.co.uk; Dulwich Rd SE24; ☾ 6.45am-7pm mid-Jun–Aug, weather dependent rest of year; admission £2-5; ⊖ Brixton/rail Herne Hill

A beautifully designed 1930s lido, Brockwell is hugely popular in summer and was recently fully restored. It's one of London's best, as witnessed by the multitudes that descend in the summer months.

HAMPSTEAD HEATH PONDS Map p465

Hampstead Heath, Gordon House Rd NW5; adult/concession £2/1; rail Gospel Oak/Hampstead Heath/bus 214, C2 or 24

If you prefer things a little more *au naturel*, Hampstead Heath ponds offer a slightly chilly dip and have recently been saved from closure over a row about lifeguards. The men's

pond is a bit of a gay cruising ground; the secluded women's pond is markedly less so. The mixed pond can sometimes get rather crowded and isn't so scenically located, so many real devotees head to one of the other two.

IRONMONGER BATHS Map pp442-3

☎ 7253 4011; www.aquaterra.com; Ironmonger Row EC1; per swim £3.20; ⊖ Old St

The Ironmonger Baths is a local authority–run gym and pool complex which is popular but not too crowded, and has a great pool and friendly atmosphere. There's a popular sauna and steam bath here too.

OASIS Map p452

☎ 7831 1804; 32 Endell St WC2; adult/concession £3/1.10; ⊖ Tottenham Court Rd/Covent Garden

This bizarre pool has the advantage of being right in the heart of London. It's often very crowded, although the experience of swimming outdoors on the roof should not be missed. There's an indoor pool for fresher London days.

PARLIAMENT HILL LIDO Map p465

☎ 7485 3873; Hampstead Heath, Gordon House Rd NW5; admission adult/concession 7-9am £2/1, 10-6pm £4/2; rail Gospel Oak/bus 214, C2

This classic lido on Hampstead Heath is a wonderful place to come for a bracing morning swim during the summer months. It attracts a friendly but dedicated bunch of locals and boasts a children's paddling pool and sunbathing area.

PORCHESTER BATHS Map pp444-5

☎ 7792 2919; Porchester Centre, Queensway W2; admission £3.20; ⊖ Bayswater/Royal Oak

The lovely Porchester Baths' pool and gym are enduringly popular with west Londoners. The place has seen better days, as is visible from the swimming pool's ceiling, but it's often next to empty, which makes swimming a joy.

SERPENTINE LIDO Map pp444-5

☎ 7298 2100; Hyde Park W2; ⊖ Hyde Park Cnr/Knightsbridge

Perhaps the ultimate London pool, the fabulous Serpentine Lido is usually open in July and August. Admission prices and opening times are always subject to change, so it's essential to call ahead.

TOOTING BEC LIDO

☎ 8871 7198; Tooting Bec Rd SW17; ⊙ May-Sep; adult/concession/under 5yr £3.65/£2.50/free; ⊖ Tooting Bec

The first-ever public lido in London, Tooting Bec was built in 1906 and remains one of the largest in Europe at 90m by 36m. It was refurbished in 2002 and now includes Jacuzzis and saunas.

SPAS

ELEMIS DAY SPA Map pp448-9

☎ 8909 5060; www.elemis.com/dayspa.html; 2-3 Lancashire Ct; ⊖ Bond St

This incredible Mayfair spa recently won European day spa of the year, and it's easy to see why. The place is almost ridiculously elaborate and features themed suites – Balinese, Moroccan, the purple room and the emerald room, for example. Upmarket and offering a huge range of services, this is one hell of a place to treat yourself. Book ahead.

K SPA

☎ 0870 027 4343; www.k-west.co.uk; Richmond Way W12; day membership basic/luxury £25/£35; ⊖ Shepherd's Bush

The K Spa is an important part of the **K West hotel** (p374), and has a good range of facilities – a Jacuzzi, eucalyptus steam room, sauna and two gyms. Alternatively, you can choose from a range of exotic treatments such as the Espa hot-stone treatment, as well as a full range of massages and body and facial treatments. It's one of the best complexes in West London.

PORCHESTER BATHS SPA Map pp444-5

☎ 7792 2919; Porchester Centre, Queensway W2; day membership £19.98; ⊖ Bayswater ⊙ Mon, Wed & Sat

The Porchester Centre contains a spa, which is not connected to the swimming pool and gym next door. It's one of the cheaper places to go and spend the day pampering yourself, although it only operates three days a week.

MUSIC
POPULAR

London was famously the centre of the world music scene in the mid-'90s, when Britpop ruled the radio waves and Blur, Oasis, Suede, Pulp, Garbage, Elastica and Radiohead proffered the most cutting-edge sounds from the British capital. By 2000, though, the scene was washed up and London was suddenly not so hip any more. Things have swung back in the capital's favour recently, however, and a bumper crop of recent London bands (Coldplay, the Libertines, the Scissor Sisters, Babyshambles, Bloc Party) as well as much of the rock and pop royalty choosing to make London their home (from Madonna and Bono to Franz Ferdinand) have ensured that London is still one of the best places to see live performances anywhere in the world.

Other major groups continue to consider London an essential place to tour. As well, there's always a core of up-and-coming local bands, and some superstars of the 1980s and 1990s (from Dave Gahan to Steve Strange) have even reappeared. Together, these artists and bands keep London's wide range of rock and pop venues – from the aircraft hangar–sized Earl's Court Exhibition Centre (p314) or Wembley Arena (p314) to the tiny Borderline (opposite) or Barfly (below) – humming and full. For a more in-depth round-up of London music, see p44.

ASTORIA Map p450

☎ 7434 9592; www.meanfiddler.com; 157 Charing Cross Rd WC2; ⊖ Tottenham Court Rd

An extremely popular though not particularly salubrious venue, the Astoria is busy most nights of the week with indie, pop and rock acts before becoming a club later on in the evening. The adjacent **Mean Fiddler** (p305), at No 165, is far more intimate but doesn't get used as much.

BARFLY@THE MONARCH Map pp440-1

☎ 7691 4244, 7691 4245; www.barflyclub.com; Monarch, 49 Chalk Farm Rd NW1; ⊖ Chalk Farm/ Camden Town

Barfly, Charles Bukowski, lounge lizards – you get the picture. This typically grungy, although not unpleasant, Camden venue is full of small-time artists looking for their big break. Alternative-music radio station Xfm and music weekly NME host regular nights.

BORDERLINE Map p450

☎ 7734 2095; www.borderline.co.uk; Orange Yard W1;
⊖ Tottenham Court Rd

Through the Tex-Mex entrance off Orange Yard and down into the basement, you'll find a packed, 275-capacity venue that really punches above its weight. Read the writing on the walls (literally, there's a gig list): Crowded House, REM, Blur, Counting Crows, PJ Harvey, Lenny Kravitz, Debbie Harry, plus many anonymous indie outfits, have all played here. The crowd's equally diverse but full of music journos and talent-spotting record-company A&Rs.

BRIXTON ACADEMY Map p462

☎ 7771 2000; www.brixton-academy.co.uk; 211 Stockwell Rd SW9; ⊖ Brixton

It's hard to have a bad night at the Brixton Academy, even if you leave with your soles sticky with beer, as this cavernous former theatre (holding 4000) always thrums with bonhomie. There's a properly sloping floor for good views, as well as plenty of bars. You can catch international acts of the ilk of Madonna (once), but more likely bands are Beck, Queens of the Stone Age or the Dandy Warhols.

BULL & GATE Map p465

☎ 7485 5358; www.bullandgate.co.uk; 389 Kentish Town Rd NW5; ⊖ Kentish Town

An old-skool, smoky music venue, despite recent renovations, the legendary Bull & Gate still pulls in the punters with lots of guitar bands hoping to be the next big thing.

CARGO Map pp442-3

☎ 7739 3440; www.cargo-london.com; 83 Rivington St EC2; ⊖ Old St

Multi-talented Cargo spices up its club nights (p303) with performances from up-and-coming bands or visiting cult bands from overseas.

CARLING ISLINGTON ACADEMY
Map pp442-3

☎ 7288 4400; www.islington-academy.co.uk; N1 Centre, 16 Parkfield St N1; ⊖ Angel

Formerly the Marquee, this totally rebuilt space is modern and has great acoustics. It attracts left-of-centre pop and indie acts, and what it might lack in atmosphere it makes up for with an up-for-it Islington crowd of serious musos. The upstairs room hosts up-and-coming groups and can be a great place to see new talent.

Earl's Court Exhibition Centre (p314)

DINGWALLS Map pp440-1
☎ 7267 1577; 11 East Yard, Camden Lock NW1;
✈ Camden Town
More a comedy venue (see p308) and better suited to that really, Dingwalls does however host indie acts on the less busy days from Sunday to Thursday.

DUBLIN CASTLE Map pp440-1
☎ 7485 1773; 94 Parkway NW1; ✈ Camden Town
This famous pub has a back room for gigs and is where many successful bands cut their indie teeth. Madness launched their careers here, and the likes of Blur have passed through.

EARL'S COURT EXHIBITION CENTRE
Map pp458-9
☎ 7385 1200, 0870 903 9033; Warwick Rd SW5;
✈ Earl's Court
The kind of large, soulless venue that gave stadium rock its bad name, Earl's Court has nevertheless scored a coup in recent years by playing host to the annual Brit music awards – where Justin Timberlake was famously photographed pawing Kylie Minogue's bum. You'll see huge internationally famous artists such as Madonna and U2 here.

FORUM Map p465
☎ 0870 534 4444; www.meanfiddler.com; 9-17 Highgate Rd NW5; ✈ Kentish Town
Once the famous Town & Country Club, this medium-sized hall, with stalls and a mezzanine, remains one of the better places in town to see the newly famous, and keeps the ticket touts swarming around Kentish Town tube.

GARAGE Map pp442-3
☎ 7607 1818; www.meanfiddler.com; 20-22 Highbury Cnr N5; ✈ Highbury & Islington
Ever since the likes of the Strokes and the Vines announced the return of guitar-based rock, this indie-kid venue has been enjoying a minor renaissance – although in truth it never went away. The smaller upstairs room is slightly less heaving and sweaty than the main floor. This was where Pete Doherty was photographed performing on heroin in pictures that launched a media frenzy around the young singer in 2005.

HALF MOON Map pp438-9
☎ 8780 9383; www.halfmoon.co.uk; 93 Lower Richmond Rd SW15; ✈ Putney Bridge
It's an unlikely location for a legendary London venue, but the Half Moon has seen the likes of the Stones, U2 and Elvis Costello on its stage. It's more likely to book tribute bands these days, but check the website for listings (the Hamsters remain regulars today).

RHYTHM FACTORY Map pp454-5
☎ 7247 9386; www.rhythmfactory.co.uk; 16-18 Whitechapel Rd E1; ☽ to 3am Sun-Thu, to 5am Fri & Sat; ✈ Aldgate East
One of the best small venues in London is the consistently hip Rhythm Factory. During the day it's a relaxed and friendly coffee shop, but come the evening it opens up the large back room, and bands from the Libertines to the Paddingtons and DJs of all genres keep the up-for-it crowd happy until late.

SHEPHERD'S BUSH EMPIRE Map pp438-9
☎ 7771 2000; www.shepherds-bush-empire.co.uk; Shepherd's Bush Green W12; ✈ Shepherd's Bush
The midsized Empire is one of the cleanest and most civilised music venues in town. It's the sort of place you'll find a slightly older, chilled out but still hip crowd watching the likes of Interpol and the Handsome Family or comeback artists such as Evan Dando and Dave Gahan. One gripe: the floor doesn't slope, so if you're under 6ft tall, it's a little difficult to see from up the back in the stalls – it's worth paying for the balcony.

SPITZ Map pp454-5
☎ 7392 9032; www.spitz.co.uk; 109 Commercial St E1; ✈ Aldgate East/Liverpool St
In the row of buildings lining Spitalfields market, Spitz is a restaurant and café/music venue. It's pretty relaxed in both demeanour and music policy, with the latter including anything from beats-driven jazz fusion to experimental Icelandic singing and everything in between.

UNDERWORLD Map pp440-1
☎ 7482 1932; www.theunderworldcamden.co.uk; 174 Camden High St NW1; ✈ Camden Town
An underground warren beneath the **World's End pub** (p289), only midsized but with plenty of nooks and crannies, Underworld has indie, punk, rock and metal bands performing and fills in the blanks with similarly tuned club nights.

WEMBLEY ARENA Map p437
☎ 8902 0902; Empire Way, Wembley; ✈ Wembley Park
A huge, unappealing barn that's a fair hike – you'd really only bother going to this 10,000-capacity venue if your favourite band was on.

(Continued on page 323)

1 Caribbean restaurant Mango Room (p261) in Camden **2** Trojka (p262) serves Eastern European and Russian dishes **3** Peppers at Brixton Market (p350) **4** Bakery at Borough Market (p350)

de gustibus
borough market
bakers

1 *Coffee and cake* 2 *Roast beef and Yorkshire pudding* 3 *Moro (p242) in Clerkenwell, specialising in North African and Spanish cuisine* 4 *Sliced bread with fillings at Borough Market (p350), London's top food market*

1 Turkish restaurant Gallipoli (p244) *2* Les Trois Garçons (p241), an outstanding French restaurant in Hoxton *3* Fish and chips (p252) *4* The Engineer (p261), one of London's best gastropubs

1 Vibe Bar (p283) in Hoxton
2 Pint of beer in the Windsor Castle (p292), a down-to-earth Notting Hill pub 3 Cool Japanese-themed bar Fluid (p283)
4 Victorian pub Princess Louise (p280) in Holborn 5 Band at the Underworld (p314)

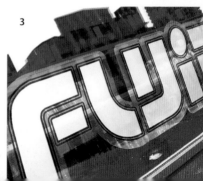

1 Nightclubbers at The Cross, Kings Cross (p303) *2* French House (p277), Soho *3* Market Porter (p286), Borough *4* The National Film Theatre (p301), South Bank

1 Portobello Road Market (p350)
2 Shop on Oxford St (p335)
3 English teddy bears at Hamleys (p336), reportedly the largest toystore in the world 4 A clothes stall at Camden Market (p350)

1 Camden High St (p347) is lined with clothes boutiques **2** Shopfront at Leadenhall Market (p351) **3** Riverside Walk book market (p351), held weekends outside the National Film Theatre **4** Camden Lock Market (p350)

1 Threadneedles hotel (p360), the City **2** Great Eastern Hotel (p360), Hoxton **3** The Ritz (p363), 100 years old in 2006 **4** Claridge's (p362) in Mayfair

JAZZ

London has always had a thriving jazz scene, and – with its recent resurgence thanks to acid jazz, hip-hop, funk and swing – it's stronger than ever.

100 CLUB Map p450

☎ 7636 0933; www.the100club.co.uk; 100 Oxford St W1; ⊖ Tottenham Court Rd/Oxford Circus

This legendary London venue concentrates on jazz, but it once showcased the Stones and was at the centre of the punk revolution as well as the '90s indie scene. There are still free lunchtime jazz sessions from noon to 3pm on Friday.

606 CLUB

☎ 7352 5953; 90 Lots Rd SW10; ⊖ Fulham Broadway/Earl's Court

This out-of-the-way basement jazz club and restaurant showcases contemporary British jazz bands. There's also a jam with famous tenor player Tim Whitehead on the third Thursday of every month. The club frequently opens until 2am, although you have to dine at weekends to gain admission (booking is advised).

BULL'S HEAD

☎ 8876 5241; www.thebullshead.com; 373 Lonsdale Rd SW13; rail Barnes Bridge

This traditional pub dates from Tudor times and has hosted modern jazz concerts in its Jazz Room since 1959. It continues to offer some of the best British jazz nightly and at Sunday lunchtime.

JAZZ CAFÉ Map pp440-1

☎ 7916 6060; www.meanfidler.com; 5 Parkway NW1; ⊖ Camden Town

The jazz club that's really made the most of jazz's crossover to the mainstream, this trendy industrial-style restaurant mixes its jazz with Afro, funk, hip-hop, R&B and soul styles with big-name acts and a faithful bohemian Camden crowd.

PIZZA EXPRESS JAZZ CLUB Map p450

☎ 7439 8722; www.pizzaexpress.co.uk/jazz.htm; 10 Dean St W1; ⊖ Tottenham Court Rd

Believe it or not, this is one of the most consistently popular and excellent jazz venues in London. It's a bit of a strange arrangement, having a small basement venue beneath the main chain restaurant, but it seems to work well. Patrons listen attentively to modern jazz, and lots of big names perform here.

RONNIE SCOTT'S Map p450

☎ 7439 0747; www.ronniescotts.co.uk; 47 Frith St W1; ⊖ Leicester Sq

A quintessential Soho experience, Ronnie's (as it's known to one and all) has survived the death of its namesake owner in 1996 and continued to build upon its formidable reputation as London's best jazz club. Everyone from Bill Evans to Nina Simone has played here, while today you'll find a huge range of knowns and unknowns playing in this most atmospheric of places. Door staff are terribly rude, however, which is our only real gripe. In general, headline acts are American, with British support. Gigs usually last until 2am daily.

Jazz Jams *Gabriel Gatehouse*

London probably has the most vibrant jazz scene anywhere in the world outside the United States, and if you want to hear it at its rawest and most spontaneous, head for one of the capital's many jam sessions, where up-and-coming young players cut their teeth and vie with the more established musicians. Obviously the quality of the playing varies from session to session, but while you may have to sit through a few dud numbers, you will almost certainly stumble across an unexpected gem or two and get a taste of where the new generation is heading. In addition, it's usually free.

Jams are where musicians go to show their peers what they can do, and the atmosphere, while friendly, can get quite competitive. If you're a rhythm-section player and want to sit in, you can usually turn up empty handed. If you're a horn player travelling without your instrument, your best bet is to bring your own mouthpiece, scan the crowd for a friendly face, and ask nicely.

Sunday is the most popular day for jams, but you can find somewhere to play any night of the week – if you know where to look; check the weekly *Time Out* listings. A good place to start is the **Effra Hall Tavern** (Map p462; ☎ 7274 4180; 38 Kellett Rd SW2; ⊖ Brixton) on Sunday night. Lauren Dalrymple, who runs the show, also sings the best version of 'Mercy' you'll hear for free in London. For a funkier vibe, Camden's **Jazz Café** (above) holds a session on Sunday afternoon. Rising stars of the jazz scene go to saxophonist Tim Whitehead's jam at the **606 Club** (above) on the third Thursday of every month – worth a visit even if you don't feel like sitting in.

FOLK & WORLD MUSIC

London's music scene is not limited to guitar-based rock and jazz – the more esoteric types from English traditional to African can also be found.

AFRICA CENTRE Map p452

☎ 7836 1973; www.africacentre.org.uk; 38 King St WC2; ⊖ Covent Garden

The centre offers African-music concerts most Friday nights and one-offs on other nights.

CECIL SHARP HOUSE Map pp440-1

☎ 7485 2206; www.efdss.org; 2 Regent's Park Rd NW1; ⊖ Camden Town

The headquarters of the English Folk Dance & Song Society, this is *the* venue for English folk music (an acquired taste, it must be said). Get in touch if you want to take part in Morris dancing or a clog class, or see a fiddle recital.

CLASSICAL MUSIC

London is a major classical-music capital, with four world-class symphony orchestras, two opera companies, various smaller ensembles, brilliant venues, reasonable prices and high standards of performance. There's so much on that you may have trouble deciding what to pick. On any night of the year, the choice will range from traditional crowd-pleasers to new music and 'difficult' composers. Opera is naturally more costly. Despite recent hiccups at the English National Opera, the overall standard is high.

BARBICAN Map pp454-5

☎ 7638 8891; www.barbican.org.uk; Silk St EC2; admission £6.50-30, student & over 60yr on day of performance £6.50-9; ⊖ Moorgate/Barbican

The Barbican has plenty to offer the classical-music buff: it's the home of the wonderful London Symphony Orchestra, but scores of leading international musicians also perform here every year. The lesser known BBC Symphony Orchestra, City of London Symphonia and English Chamber Orchestra are also regulars. The halls' acoustic qualities were greatly improved by renovations a few years back.

KENWOOD HOUSE Map p465

☎ 0870 154 4040; www.ticketmaster.co.uk; Hampstead Lane NW3; admission £16.50-24.50; ⊖ Archway/Golders Green, then bus 210

A highlight of any sunny summer is to attend an outdoor concert in the grounds of Hampstead's Kenwood House for Proms on the Heath. People sit on the grass or on deck chairs, eat strawberries, drink chilled white wine, and listen to classical music and opera (staying for the fireworks) on selected weekend evenings in July and August.

ROYAL ALBERT HALL Map pp444-5

☎ 7589 8212; www.royalalberthall.com; Kensington Gore SW7; admission £5-150, Proms admission £4-75; ⊖ South Kensington

This splendid, and recently refurbished, Victorian concert hall hosts many classical-music, rock and other performances, but is most famous as the venue for the (BBC) Proms – one of the world's biggest classical- music festivals, still with a touch of flag-waving 'Rule Britannia' patriotism on the last night. Booking is possible, but from mid-July to mid-September Proms punters also queue for £4 standing (or 'promenading') tickets that go on sale one hour before curtain up. Otherwise, the box office and prepaid ticket collection counter are both through door No 12 on the south side of the hall.

SOUTH BANK CENTRE Map pp448-9

☎ 7960 4242; www.rfh.org.uk; Belvedere Rd SE1; admission £6-60; ⊖ Waterloo

The Royal Festival Hall, usually London's premier concert venue, is closed for refurbishment until early 2007, during which time performances will be transferred to the smaller Queen Elizabeth Hall and Purcell Room. Stand-by tickets (from £6 to £10) are available for some performances.

WIGMORE HALL Map pp448-9

☎ 7935 2141; www.wigmore-hall.org.uk; 36 Wigmore St W1; admission £6-35; ⊖ Bond St

This Art Nouveau hall has arguably the best acoustics in town, and its traditional atmosphere and exquisite Art Deco detailing make it one of the best concert venues in London. There's a great variety of concerts and recitals. The recitals at 11.30am on Sunday (£10) are particularly good. There are lunchtime concerts at 1pm on Monday (adult/senior £8/6).

OPERA

ROYAL OPERA HOUSE Map p452

☎ 7304 4000; www.royaloperahouse.org; Royal Opera House, Bow St WC2; admission £6-150, midweek matinees £6.50-50; ⊖ Covent Garden

The once starchy Royal Opera House has been attracting a younger, wealthy audience since its £210 million redevelopment at the turn

Church Venues

Many churches host evening concerts or lunch-time recitals year round or during the summer months. Sometimes they are free (with a suggested donation requested); at other times there is a charge. A few of the city's redundant churches now serve as concert halls.

St James's Piccadilly (Map p450; ☎ 7734 4511; 197 Piccadilly W1; £7.50-17; ✪ Piccadilly Circus) Concerts at 1.10pm on Monday, Wednesday and Friday; donation requested. Evening concerts at 7.30pm (days vary).

St John's Smith Square (Map pp460–1; ☎ 7222 1061; Smith Sq SW1; admission £6; ✪ Westminster/St James's Park) Concerts at 1pm on Monday.

St Martin-in-the-Fields (Map p452; ☎ 7839 8362; Trafalgar Sq WC2; lunchtime donation requested £3.50, evening tickets £6-18; ✪ Charing Cross) Concerts at 1.05pm on Monday, Tuesday and Friday. Evening concerts by candlelight from Thursday to Saturday at 7.30pm.

St Paul's Cathedral (Map pp454–5; ☎ 7236 4128; New Change EC4; organ recitals £6; ✪ St Paul's) Organ recitals at 5pm on Sunday. Evensong at 5pm Monday to Saturday and at 3.15pm Sunday, special events permitting.

Southwark Cathedral (Map pp454–5; ☎ 7367 6700; Montague Close SE1; ✪ London Bridge) Organ recitals at 1.10pm on Monday; other concerts at 1.10pm on Tuesday. Evensong at 5.30pm on Tuesday, Thursday and Friday, at 4pm on Saturday and at 3pm on Sunday.

Westminster Abbey (Map pp448–9; ☎ 7222 5152; www.westminster-abbey.org; Dean's Yard SW1; tickets usually £5-18; ✪ Westminster) Free organ recitals at 5.45pm every Sunday. Evensong on weekdays at 5pm (excluding Wednesday) and at 3pm on Saturday and Sunday. Ring or check the website for details of the spring/summer organ festival sometime between May and August.

---

of the century, with more adventurous programming, including operas like *Woyczek*. The renovated Floral Hall is now open to the public during the day, with free lunchtime concerts at 1pm on Monday, exhibitions and daily tours. The Travelex £10 season has become a favourite with Londoners – you enter an online raffle

Wigmore Hall (opposite)

for some of the best seats in the house for just a tenner – a bargain indeed.

ENGLISH NATIONAL OPERA Map p452
☎ 7632 8300; www.eno.org; Coliseum, St Martin's Lane WC1; admission £3-65; ✪ Leicester Sq/Charing Cross
Generally renowned for making opera modern and relevant, the ENO is currently clawing itself back from a miserable few years of bad reviews, financial difficulties and media flak. Having renovated to great acclaim and moved back to the Coliseum, a more democratic pricing system has been introduced, and 500 £10-and-under tickets are now available for all weekday performances. All opera at the ENO is sung in English.

OPERA HOLLAND PARK Map pp444-5
☎ 0845 230 9769; www.operahollandpark.com; Holland Park W8; admission £25-40; ✪ High St Kensington
An 800-seat canopy is temporarily erected every summer for a nine-week season in the middle of Holland Park, just off Kensington High St. It's an excellent place to see opera in the suitably grand surroundings of one of London's wealthiest areas. The atmosphere's relaxed, you're in a beautiful setting and you can enjoy a picnic beforehand. The programme mixes crowd pleasers such as *Tosca* and *Fidelio* with rare works such as *L'Arlesiana* and attracts a wide range of guests.

SPOKEN WORD

As one of the epicentres of the English language, Londoners treat their literati like glitterati, and London is an extremely good place to see writers read their own work. It's not just home-grown UK talent like Monica Ali, Louis de Bernieres, Patrick Neate, Zadie Smith, Tony Parsons, Will Self or even occasionally JK Rowling you might find here, but international writers like Bill Bryson, Douglas Coupland and Andrey Kurkov on promotional tours.

As they tend to rely on the author's availability, many of these readings are organised on an ad-hoc basis, so if you're interested it's best to keep an eye on the listings in *Time Out* or the *Evening Standard's Metro Life* supplement on Thursday. Chain bookstores, particularly Waterstone's and Books Etc, often have readings, and some major authors now appear at the **South Bank Centre** (p151). Meanwhile, clubs such as **Cargo** (last Sunday of the month, p303), **Cherry Jam** (one Monday a month, p303) and **Vibe Bar** (p283) have spoken-word performances, open-mic sessions, poetry slams and similar events.

Otherwise, the following venues most regularly appear in spoken-word listings pages.

ENTERPRISE Map pp440-1
☎ 7485 2659; www.expressexcess.co.uk; 2 Haverstock Hill NW3; ⊖ Chalk Farm

A weekly writers' session is held every Wednesday at this pub. From small beginnings in 1996, the Express Excess evening has since managed to attract top names in British writing. John Cooper Clarke, John Hegley, Will Self and Murray Lachlan Young have all appeared in the cosy room at the top of this typically grungy Camden pub.

INSTITUTE OF CONTEMPORARY ARTS Map pp448-9
☎ 7930 3647; www.ica.org.uk; Nash House, the Mall SW1; ⊖ Charing Cross/Piccadilly Circus

Writers in all media, from books to film and beyond, give readings here. A roster of well-known writers, from the hip to the seriously academic, often appear at the Institute for Contemporary Arts to read from and discuss their work. The best events are those in the wonderful, high-ceilinged Nash Room upstairs.

POETRY CAFÉ Map p452
☎ 7420 9888; 22 Betterton St WC2; ⊖ Covent Garden

With performances by established poets and a regular poetry and jazz evening every Saturday, it's little wonder this is a favourite destination for lovers of the spoken word. You can also polish your own prose at writing workshops or show what you've learnt on Tuesday's Poetry Unplugged open-mic evening.

SPORT

As capital of a sports-mad nation, you can expect London to be brimming over with sporting spectacles throughout the year. The entertainment weekly *Time Out* is the best source of information on fixtures, times, venues and ticket prices. For information on gyms, swimming pools and spas, see p310.

FOOTBALL

Wembley Stadium, in northwest London, has been the premier national stadium since it was built in 1923. It's where England traditionally plays its international matches and where the FA Cup final is contested in mid-May. Its greatest moment came when the victorious England captain, Bobby Moore, held the World Cup trophy aloft in 1966. Controversially, the great stadium and its two landmark towers were demolished in 2001; at the time of writing, a new 80,000-capacity, state-of-the-art Norman Foster–designed complex was due for completion in 2006.

There are a dozen league teams in London, and usually around five or six play in the Premier League, meaning that on any weekend of the season – from August to mid-May – top-quality football is just a tube or train ride away (if you can manage to get hold of a ticket). If you really want to see a match, you might consider dropping a division and going to see one of the first-division teams, for which you can normally just rock up on the day.

CRICKET

If you're hot and bothered from seeing the sights, you could do a lot worse than packing up a picnic and spending a day enjoying the thwack of leather on willow and savouring the atmosphere of this most English of sports. Although the game was invented here, the England team has struggled on the international stage in recent years, although of late there have been promising signs and the game of gentlemen continues to flourish.

The **English Cricket Board** (☎ 0870 533 8833; www.ecb.co.uk) has full details of match schedules and tickets, which cost between £20 and £50 and can be difficult to get. Test matches are regularly played at the venerable Lord's and Oval grounds (the latter is known for its distinctive gasholders). Tickets (between £5 and £10) are a lot easier to come by for county games; county teams compete in four-day, one-day and 20-over matches between April and September.

LORD'S Map pp440-1

tours ☎ 7616 8585, switchboard ☎ 7616 8500; www.lords.org; St John's Wood Rd NW8; ⊖ St John's Wood

The 'home of cricket,' a trip to Lord's is often as much a pilgrimage as anything else. As well as being home to Middlesex County Cricket Club, the ground hosts test matches, one-day internationals and domestic finals.

OVAL Map pp460-1

☎ 7582 7764; www.surreycricket.com; Kennington Oval SE11; ⊖ Oval

County side Surrey plays at the Oval.

RUGBY UNION & RUGBY LEAGUE

Between January and March, England competes against Scotland, Wales, Ireland, France and Italy in the Six Nations Championship, and there are always three games at Twickenham Stadium.

Clubs in the Capital

Football is at the very heart of English culture, and attending a game is one of the highlights of any visit to London. Whether you're after the glamour of a premiership tie or the old-fashioned atmosphere of the lower divisions, there's ample opportunity to adopt a team and join the cheering throngs. At the time of writing, Arsenal, Charlton, Chelsea, Crystal Palace, Fulham, Tottenham Hotspur and West Ham were all in the Premiership, with four others aspiring to the same heights. For more on football in London, see p20.

Arsenal (Map p437; ☎ 7704 4040; www.arsenal.com; Avenell Rd N5; admission £25-45; ⊖ Arsenal)

Charlton Athletic (Map p437; ☎ 8333 4010; www.cafc.co.uk; the Valley, Floyd Rd SE7; admission £15-40; rail Charlton)

Chelsea (Map pp458–9; ☎ 0870 300 1212, ☎ 7915 2222, tickets 7915 2951; www.chelseafc.com; Stamford Bridge Stadium, Fulham Rd SW6; admission £11-40; ⊖ Fulham Broadway)

Crystal Palace (Off Map p437; ☎ 0871 200 0071; www.cpfc.co.uk; Selhurst Park, Whitehorse Lane SE25; admission £20-26; rail Selhurst)

Fulham (Map pp438–9; ☎ 0870 442 1234; www.fulhamfc.com; Craven Cottage, Stevenage Rd SW6; admission £25-40; ⊖ Putney Bridge)

Leyton Orient (Map p437; ☎ 8926 1111; www.leytonorient.com; Matchroom Stadium, Brisbane Rd E10; admission £12-16; ⊖ Leyton)

Millwall (Map pp438–9; ☎ 7232 1222; www.millwallfc.co.uk; the Den, Zampa Rd SE16; admission £16-25; rail South Bermondsey)

Queens Park Rangers (Map pp438–9; ☎ 0870 112 1967; www.qpr.co.uk; Loftus Rd W12; admission £14-20; ⊖ White City)

Tottenham Hotspur (Map p437; ☎ 0870 420 5000; www.spurs.co.uk; White Hart Lane N17; admission £12-55; rail White Hart Lane)

West Ham United (Map p437; ☎ 0870 112 2700; www.westhamunited.co.uk; Boleyn Ground, Green St E13; admission £22-39; ⊖ Upton Park)

Union fans should head to southwest London, where mighty teams like the **Harlequins** (☎ 8410 6000; www.quins.co.uk; Stoop Memorial Ground, Langhorn Dr, Twickenham; admission £12-25; rail Twickenham)and **Wasps** (☎ 8993 8298; www.wasps.co.uk; Adams Park, High Wycombe; admission £7-18; Rail High Wycombe) play from August to May. **London Irish** (☎ 01932-783034; www.london-irish.com; Bennet Rd, Reading; admission £7-16; rail Reading) and **Saracens** (☎ 01923-475222; www.saracens.com; Vicarage Rd, Watford; admission £12-35; rail Watford High St) are also in the Premiership. Most matches are played on Saturday and Sunday afternoons.

LONDON BRONCOS Map p437
☎ 8853 8001; www.londonbroncos.co.uk; the Valley, Floyd Rd SE7; rail Charlton
The only place in southern England to see rugby league.

TWICKENHAM RUGBY STADIUM
Map p437
☎ 8892 2000; www.rfu.com; Rugby Rd, Twickenham; ⊖ Hounslow East, then bus 281/rail Twickenham
The home of English rugby union. For information about guided tours, see p212.

TENNIS
Tennis and Wimbledon, in southeast London, are almost synonymous, and SW19 suddenly becomes the centre of the sporting universe for a fortnight in June/July when the world-famous tennis tournament is fought.

WIMBLEDON Off Map p437
☎ 8944 1066, 8946 2244; www.wimbledon.org; Church Rd SW19; ⊖ Southfields/Wimbledon Park
The All England Lawn Tennis Championships have been taking place here in late June/early July since 1877. Most tickets for the Centre and Number One courts are distributed by ballot, applications for which must be made the preceding year. Try your luck by sending a stamped self-addressed envelope to the **All England Lawn Tennis Club** (PO Box 98, Church Rd, Wimbledon SW19 5AE). Limited tickets go on sale on the day of play, though queues are painfully long. The nearer to the finals, the higher the prices; a Centre Court ticket that costs £25 a week before the final will cost twice that on the day. Prices for outside courts are under £10, reduced after 5pm. You might be better off going to the men's warm-up tournament at **Queen's Club** (☎ 7385 3421; www.queensclub.co.uk; Palliser Rd, Hammersmith W14; admission per day £12; ⊖ Barons Ct), which takes place a couple of weeks before Wimbledon.

ATHLETICS
England – and London in particular – has a rich history in athletics and continues to produce world champions. There are major international meets each summer at the grand old venue of Crystal Palace in southeast London, which has been the site of many magical moments in recent years and where every international athlete worth his or her salt has competed.

CRYSTAL PALACE NATIONAL SPORTS CENTRE Off Map p437
☎ 8778 0131; www.crystalpalace.co.uk; Ledrington Rd SE19; rail Crystal Palace
Athletics and swimming meetings attracting major international and domestic stars take place here regularly throughout the summer.

BASKETBALL
'B ball' is becoming more popular in the capital and there are two local teams, **London Leopards** (☎ 01277-230231; Brentwood Leisure Centre, Doddinghurst Rd, Essex; rail Brentwood) and **Kinder London Towers** (☎ 8776 7755; www.london-towers.co.uk; Crystal

<hr>

Greyhound Racing
If you're looking for a cheap and cheesy night out, consider going to the dogs. Greyhound racing, in which six to eight skinny mutts chase a mechanical rabbit around an oval track, costs as little as £1.50 to £5 for a 12-race meeting and is Britain's second most popular sport after football. A flutter or two will guarantee excitement, and you'll rub shoulders with a London subculture both welcoming and slightly shady.

Catford Stadium (Map p437; ☎ 8690 8000; Adenmore Rd SE6; rail Catford Bridge)

Walthamstow Stadium (Map p437; ☎ 8531 4255; Chingford Rd E4; rail Highams Park)

Wimbledon Stadium (Off Map p437; ☎ 8946 8000; Plough Lane SW17; ⊖ Wimbledon Park)

Walthamstow Greyhound Stadium (opposite)

Palace National Sports Centre, Ledrington Rd SE19; rail Crystal Palace) in the British Basketball League. Tickets are about £8.

HORSE RACING

There are several racecourses within striking distance of London for those wanting to have a flutter. The flat racing runs from April to September, while you can see the gee-gees scaling fences from October to April.

ASCOT
☎ 01344-622211; www.ascot.co.uk; Berkshire; admission from £6; rail Ascot

Best known for the fashion circus of Royal Ascot in June.

EPSOM
☎ 01372-470047; www.epsomderby.co.uk; Epsom, Surrey; admission from £5; rail Epsom Downs

With much more racing credibility than Ascot, this famous racetrack's star turn is Derby Day in June, but it meets all year.

KEMPTON PARK
☎ 01932-782292; www.kemptonpark.co.uk; Staines Rd East, Sunbury-on-Thames, Middlesex; admission from £6; rail Kempton Park

Of its all-year meetings, summer-evening events are best.

ROYAL WINDSOR RACECOURSE
☎ 01753-865234; www.windsor-racecourse.co.uk; Maidenhead Rd, Windsor, Berkshire; admission from £6; rail Windsor

An idyllic spot beside the castle.

SANDOWN PARK
☎ 01372-463072; www.sandown.co.uk; Portsmouth Rd, Esher, Surrey; admission from £12; rail Esher

Generally considered the southeast's finest racecourse.

THEATRE

London remains an essential and dynamic centre for theatrical innovation and it continues to bask in the glory of being the world's greatest city for drama. No visit is complete without a West End show, a night at the National or the Old Vic, or just a good old-fashioned pub-theatre performance.

Christian Slater, Kevin Spacey and Kim Cattrall are the most recent A-list stars to have swapped the easy life of Hollywood for theatrical roles in London's West End, continuing a tradition of earning Equity minimum in return for some artistic credibility started by Nicole Kidman (successful in her bid) and Madonna (not) a few years previously.

In recent years the risk-taking and innovation normally seen in fringe theatre has infused and enthused the West End, often leaving audiences on the edge of their seats. At the same, if you just want good-time entertainment, musicals like *Chicago*, *Mary Poppins* and *Mamma Mia!* carry on.

For a comprehensive look at what's being staged, pick up the free *Official London Theatre Guide* or visit www.officiallondontheatre.co.uk. For information on booking agencies and discount tickets, see What's On, p299.

BARBICAN Map pp454-5

☎ 7638 8891; www.barbican.org.uk; Silk St EC2; admission to theatre £5-30, to Pit £15; ⊖ Moorgate/Barbican

After the Royal Shakespeare Company abandoned the Barbican as its London home in 2002 – disastrously for both organisations – this theatre has worked hard to fill its two auditoria, the Barbican Theatre and the smaller Pit. It's not done too badly either, especially with its BITE programme and the runaway success of William Burroughs and Tom Waits' *The Dark Rider* and the surprise hit *Duckie Cabaret* in 2004. Besides music and dance shows, overseas drama companies and local fringe-theatre troupes also perform. Stand-by tickets are available on the day of the performance to students, seniors and the unemployed for about £12.

ROYAL COURT Map pp458-9

☎ 7565 5000; www.royalcourttheatre.com; Jerwood Theatre, Sloane Sq SW1; admission Tue-Sun 10p-£26, Mon £7.50; ⊖ Sloane Sq

Forever associated with John Osborne's *Look Back In Anger* and similar revolutionary post-war pieces, the Royal Court continues to concentrate exclusively on fresh, surprising new writing and is an essential part of London's theatre fabric.

The company's own theatre, the Jerwood, was refurbished during the latter half of the 1990s and now has two comfy modern auditoria, upstairs and downstairs. All tickets on Monday are £7.50; there's a general price for students, under 21s, seniors and the unemployed of £9.50; and 10p standing tickets for eight people are sold just before the performance in the Jerwood theatre. Stand-by tickets are sold an hour before the performance, but at full price.

NATIONAL THEATRE Map pp448-9

☎ 7452 3000; www.nationaltheatre.org.uk; South Bank SE1; admission Olivier & Lyttleton £10-34, Cottesloe £10-25; ⊖ Waterloo

England's flagship theatre showcases a mix of classic and contemporary plays performed by excellent casts. New artistic director Nicholas Hytner is not only using exciting stagings and plays (including transferring *Jerry Springer – the Opera* and commissioning a play from Mike Leigh) to attract new audiences but has also slashed ticket prices. In the revolutionary Travelex season, tickets have been sold at £10 for the peak period of the last few years, and this is set to continue. Otherwise, stand-by tickets (usually £17) are sometimes available two hours before the performance. Students or the unemployed must wait until just 45 minutes before

the curtain goes up to purchase stand-by tickets at a concession price of around £9. Registered disabled visitors are eligible for discounts.

SHAKESPEARE'S GLOBE Map pp454-5

☎ 7401 9919; www.shakespeares-globe.org; admission seated £13-29, standing £5; 21 New Globe Walk SE1; ⊖ London Bridge

The Globe is the home of authentic Shakespearean theatre. It's a near-perfect replica of the building William himself worked in from 1598 to 1611, and also largely follows Elizabethan staging practices. (Some modern variations such as all-female casting have not been well received, not because of the principle but because the individual plays came off badly.)

The building is a wooden O with no proper roof over the central stage area. Although there are covered wooden bench seats in tiers around the stage, many people elect to emulate the 17th-century 'groundlings' who stood in front of the stage, shouting and cajoling as they wished.

Because the building is quite open to the elements, you may have to wrap up. No umbrellas are allowed, but cheap macs are on sale. The theatre season runs from May to September and includes works by Shakespeare, his contemporaries such as Christopher Marlowe, and at least one new work every year.

A warning: two pillars holding up the stage canopy (the 'Heavens') obscure much of the view in section D; you'd almost do better to stand. In winter plays are staged in the new indoor Inigo Jones Theatre (Map pp454–5), a replica Jacobean playhouse at the Globe.

OFF WEST END & FRINGE

London's most challenging and headline-creating theatre is often found in its many off-West-End and fringe-theatre productions. Offering a selection of the amazing, the life-enhancing and the downright ridiculous, some of the better venues are listed here.

ALMEIDA THEATRE Map pp442-3

☎ 7359 4404; www.almeida.co.uk; Almeida St N1; ⊖ Angel

It's got refurbished seats and a new artistic director in Michael Attenborough, but the tiny Almeida hasn't lost its edge. Recent highlights have included the acclaimed Rufus Norris production of Gael Garcia Bernal performing in Lorca's Blood Wedding. Overall the Almeida can be relied on to provide the city with an essential programme of imaginative theatre.

West End Theatres

Every summer the West End theatres stage a new crop of plays and musicals, but some performances really do run and run. Addresses and box-office phone numbers of individual theatres are given below. Consult weekly London bible *Time Out* to see what's on.

Adelphi (Map p452; ☎ 7344 0055; Strand WC2; ⊖ Charing Cross)

Albery (Map p452; ☎ 7369 1740; 85 St Martin's Lane WC2; ⊖ Leicester Sq)

Aldwych (Map p452; ☎ 0870 400 0805; 49 Aldwych WC2; ⊖ Holborn/Covent Garden)

Apollo (Map p450; ☎ 7494 5070; 39 Shaftesbury Ave W1; ⊖ Piccadilly Circus)

Cambridge (Map p452; ☎ 7494 5080; Earlham St WC2; ⊖ Covent Garden)

Comedy (Map p450; ☎ 7369 1731; Panton St SW1; ⊖ Piccadilly Circus)

Criterion (Map p450; ☎ 7413 1437; Piccadilly Circus W1; ⊖ Piccadilly Circus)

Dominion (Map p450; ☎ 0870 607 7400; 268-269 Tottenham Court Rd W1; ⊖ Tottenham Court Rd)

Duke of York's Theatre (Map p452; ☎ 7836 4615; St Martin's Lane WC2; ⊖ Leicester Sq)

Fortune (Map p452; ☎ 7836 2238; Russell St WC2; ⊖ Covent Garden)

Garrick (Map p452; ☎ 7494 5085; 2 Charing Cross Rd WC2; ⊖ Charing Cross)

Gielgud (Map p450; ☎ 7494 5065; 33 Shaftesbury Ave W1; ⊖ Piccadilly Circus)

Her Majesty's Theatre (Map p450; ☎ 7494 5400; Haymarket SW1; ⊖ Piccadilly Circus)

London Palladium (Map p450; ☎ 7494 5020; 8 Argyll St W1; ⊖ Oxford Circus)

Lyceum (Map p452; ☎ 7420 8100; 21 Wellington St WC2; ⊖ Covent Garden)

Lyric (Map p450; ☎ 7494 5045; Shaftesbury Ave W1; ⊖ Piccadilly Circus)

New Ambassadors (Map p452; ☎ 7369 1761; West St WC2; ⊖ Leicester Sq/Covent Garden)

New London (Map p452; ☎ 7405 0072; Drury Lane WC2; ⊖ Holborn/Covent Garden)

Palace (Map p452; ☎ 7434 0909; Shaftesbury Ave W1; ⊖ Leicester Sq)

Phoenix (Map p452; ☎ 7369 1733; 110 Charing Cross Rd WC2; ⊖ Tottenham Court Rd)

Piccadilly (Map p450; ☎ 7478 8800; Denman St W1; ⊖ Piccadilly Circus)

Prince Edward (Map p450; ☎ 7447 5400; 30 Old Compton St W1; ⊖ Leicester Sq)

Prince of Wales (Map p450; ☎ 7839 5987; 31 Coventry St W1; ⊖ Piccadilly Circus)

Queen's Theatre (Map p450; ☎ 7494 5040; Shaftesbury Ave W1; ⊖ Piccadilly Circus)

St Martin's (Map p452; ☎ 7836 1443; West St WC2; ⊖ Leicester Sq)

Savoy Theatre (Map p452; ☎ 7836 8888; Savoy Ct, Strand WC2; ⊖ Charing Cross)

Shaftesbury (Map p452; ☎ 7379 5399; 210 Shaftesbury Ave WC2; ⊖ Tottenham Court Rd/Holborn)

Strand (Map p452; ☎ 7836 4144; Aldwych WC2; ⊖ Covent Garden)

Theatre Royal Drury Lane (Map p452; ☎ 7494 5060; Catherine St WC2; ⊖ Covent Garden)

Theatre Royal Haymarket (Map p450; ☎ 0870 901 3356; Haymarket SW1; ⊖ Piccadilly Circus)

Whitehall Theatre (Map p452; ☎ 7321 5400; 14 Whitehall SW1; ⊖ Charing Cross)

Wyndham's (Map p452; ☎ 7369 1736; Charing Cross Rd WC2; ⊖ Leicester Sq)

BATTERSEA ARTS CENTRE Map pp438-9
☎ 7223 2223; www.bac.org.uk; Lavender Hill SW11; ⊖ Clapham Common/rail Clapham Junction/bus 77, 77A or 345

This is a friendly, down-to-earth community theatre where staff chat to you and the actors mingle in the bar with the audience postshow. Playwrights see it as a valuable nurturer and crucible of new plays and talent. Its big-gest crossover hit has been *Jerry Springer – the Opera*, which went from here to the National, to the West End, to BBC TV.

BUSH THEATRE Map pp438-9
☎ 7610 4224; www.bushtheatre.co.uk; Shepherd's Bush Green W12; ⊖ Shepherd's Bush

For what is essentially a pub theatre, the Bush is exceptionally good. Its success is down to strong writing from the likes of Tina Brown, Jonathan Harvey, Conor McPherson and Stephen Poliakoff. It also attracts top actors. The seating has been renovated, so you no longer have to clamber over other people to reach yours.

DONMAR WAREHOUSE Map p452

☎ 7369 1732; www.donmar-warehouse.com; 41 Earlham St WC2; ✆ Covent Garden

The small Donmar Warehouse is doomed – if that's the right word – to be known as the theatre in which Nicole Kidman administered 'theatrical Viagra' nightly by peeling off her clothes in Sam Mendes' production of *The Blue Room*. Although new director Michael Grandage has done a sterling job in introducing a European flavour to the capital's theatre, there's been nothing quite as headline-grabbing since.

HAMPSTEAD THEATRE Map pp440-1

☎ 7722 9301; www.hampsteadtheatre.com; 98 Avenue Rd NW3; ✆ Swiss Cottage

Actor Ewan McGregor calls this his favourite London theatre. Known for producing the works of new and emerging writers – including some new plays by Harold Pinter way back in the 1960s – it now has a funky new modern building, with two auditoria. One seats 80, the other 325.

LYRIC HAMMERSMITH Map pp438-9

☎ 0870 050 0511; www.lyric.co.uk; King St W6; ✆ Hammersmith

A modern glass entrance leads to a historic plush, red auditorium seating 550, and a smaller 180-seat studio. Expect innovative versions of classic European plays such as *Pericles*, and mixed-media performances with film projection, dance and music. The studio is aimed at audiences under 20.

MENIER CHOCOLATE FACTORY
Map pp454-5

☎ 7909 7060; www.menierchocolatefactory.com; 51-53 Southwark St SE1; ✆ London Bridge

One of London's newest theatres, this gorgeous conversion of a 19th-century chocolate factory is one of the coolest venues in town. There's a superb restaurant on the premises, too, which makes for great combination deals (£20 per person for a two-course dinner and a ticket). The recent production of Philip Ridley's *Mercury Fur* outraged and impressed in equal measure.

OLD VIC Map pp448-9

☎ 0870 060 6628; www.oldvictheatre.com; Waterloo Rd SE1; ✆ Waterloo

There was much excited murmuring in the stalls when Hollywood A-lister Kevin Spacey took over as artistic director at the Old Vic, but his efforts have not met with glowing reviews. Indeed Susannah Clapp of the *Observer* sneered after his *Philadelphia Story* in 2005 that 'Kevin Spacey's Old Vic is becoming a byword for the undistinguished'. One of his few successes was a post-modernist Christmas pantomime featuring Sir Ian McKellen in drag.

SOHO THEATRE Map p450

☎ 0870 429 6883; www.sohotheatre.com; 21 Dean St W1; admission £3-15; ✆ Tottenham Court Rd

It's hard not to blindly praise the Soho Theatre Company, which has operated from its smart Dean St premises since 2000. In that short time it's put on almost 80 new plays and supported a whole new generation of budding playwrights. Full of innovative programmes to support new writing, showcase comedy and even get kids penning drama, the theatre is a great place to see which direction London drama is heading.

SOUTHWARK PLAYHOUSE Map pp454-5

☎ 7620 3494; www.southwarkplayhouse.co.uk; 62 Southwark Bridge Rd SE1; ✆ Borough

The Southwark Playhouse, a relatively new 70-seat theatre, has been getting rave reviews for its challenging work under young artistic director Thea Sharrock. One of the biggest hits to date has been *Through the Leaves* starring Simon Callow, which later transferred to the West End.

TRICYCLE THEATRE Map pp438-9

☎ 7328 1000; www.tricycle.co.uk; 269 Kilburn High Rd NW6; ✆ Kilburn

A venue that knows its local audience well, the Tricycle stages top-class productions with an Irish or black theme, and mostly with a strong political angle. There's a nice cinema and bar on site, too.

YOUNG VIC Map pp448-9

☎ 7928 6363; www.youngvic.org; 66 the Cut SE1; ✆ Waterloo

One of the capital's funkiest and most respected theatre troupes – bold, brave and talented – at the time of writing the Young Vic was still on 'walkabout', and expected to return to a refurbished theatre in 2006. Ring or check the website for the latest details on performances and venues.

Entertainment – Theatre

Shopping

Shopping

From the clever high-street fashion of Topshop to the luxurious delights of Harrods, and from the cutting-edge clothes from young designers at Spitalfields Market to the antiques of Portobello, retail London is all things to all people. Whether you're looking for a snazzy top to impress the folks back home or merely want to take them a simple present of English-breakfast tea (we recommend you skip the 'My brother/sister/mother/daughter/boyfriend etc went to London' souvenir T-shirt), this city's 30,000 shops warmly welcome you.

Of course, there are the big-name emporiums, like Selfridges, Harvey Nichols, Hamleys, Fortnum & Mason and Liberty, which are true Aladdin's caves of consumer goods and frequently sightseeing attractions in their own right. But while chains increasingly take over the high street, one of the capital's true delights remains its side-street boutiques. For every classic Savile Row tailor, a dozen funky street-wear outlets exist in Hoxton, Brick Lane and Spitalfields. Or if you're in the market for something a little more exclusive and expensive, a whole host of hot young British designers, like Stella McCartney and Matthew Williamson, maintain lavish outlets where admiring the setting is an integral part of the experience.

Several classic British brands, particularly Burberry, Mulberry and Pringle, have managed to worm their way into the pages of glossy magazines, and stay there, via radical reinvention. But while fashion is London's prime obsession, the English capital also lays out just about every other ware on the planet. As a quick flick through a comprehensive retail catalogue like the annual *Time Out Shopping Guide* (£9.99) demonstrates, homewares stores sit cheek by jowl with computer stores, bookstores play neighbour to music shops, and markets offer fresh, exotic produce.

The strong pound and the high cost of living might keep London from ever being a bargain, but its sheer array is irresistible. In short, no trip to the English capital would be complete with a shopping interlude. Bring your credit card.

OPENING HOURS

The good news is that you can go shopping every day of the week. The slightly bad news is that this is not universally true throughout the city.

Generally, shops open from 9am or 10am to about 6pm or 6.30pm Monday to Saturday, at least. Shops in the West End (Oxford St, Soho and Covent Garden) open late (normally to 8pm) on Thursday; those in Chelsea, Knightsbridge and Kensington open late on Wednesday.

In the West End and in Chelsea, Knightsbridge and Kensington, many shops are now also open on Sunday, typically from noon to 6pm but sometimes 10am to 4pm. Sunday trading is also common in Greenwich and Hampstead and along Edgware and Tottenham Court Rds.

Conversely, some shops in the Square Mile, or the City of London, only open Monday to Friday. Additionally, smaller designer stores tend to keep hours to suit their owners, opening later of a morning and often closing on a Monday or Tuesday to stay open on weekends. It's a good idea to ring ahead with these places, too, as they often have last-minute changes.

If there's a major market on a certain day – say, Columbia Road Flower Market on a Sunday morning – it's a good bet that neighbouring stores will fling open their doors.

Best Areas to Shop

Mired in bendy-bus gridlock, with two streams of card-wielding humanity flowing down either side, London's famous Oxford St can be a slightly disappointing experience, simultaneously overwhelming (in terms of its crowds) and underwhelming (regarding its offerings). Similarly litter-strewn and mobbed, Camden Market at weekends is just as likely to induce a nervous breakdown as it is to deliver retail therapy. Therefore, better central areas to head to are listed below. (Apart from the chains listed under High St Kensington, where no address details are given for a particular store it is reviewed more fully in the relevant section of this chapter.)

Covent Garden (see below) Away from the touristy old market hall you'll find a whole host of cool fashion, including Ted Baker and Paul Smith, Koh Samui and Poste Mistress and hip menswear shop Duffer of St George. The Thomas Neal Centre on Earlham St is packed with urban/skate/surf fashions from the likes of High Jinks, while Long Acre is lined with affordable high-street chains.

High Street Kensington (see p342) The less crowded, more salubrious alternative to Oxford St, this has all the high-street chains from BHS, Boots, French Connection, H&M and Jigsaw to Kookai, Marks & Spencer, Warehouse and Zara. Trendy stores, including **Diesel** (No 38a) and **Urban Outfitters** (No 36), can also be found here, while towards Church St there's even the chance of snapping up some antiques.

Hoxton, Shoreditch and Spitalfields (see p340) Home on Sunday to Spitalfields Market, this area has become increasingly important as a London shopping 'hood. Up-and-coming designers tout clothes, cutting-edge jewellery and household objects, especially along the main arteries of Brick Lane, Dray Walk and Cheshire St. This is an area for adventurous shoppers who don't mind searching out small boutiques for something cool and unique.

King's Road (see p342) A far cry from its 1960s mod heyday, well-heeled King's Rd is now strong on household goods, with the **Designer's Guild** (No 269), **Habitat** (No 206) and **Heal's** (No 234). Children are well catered for, too; Daisy & Tom and **Trotters** (No 34) provide distractions such as a carousel (D&T) and express train (Trotters), while offering designer children's clothes, toys and haircuts.

Knightsbridge (see p342) Harrods is a national institution, and even sceptics should see its food halls and Egyptian Hall of gifts once. Harvey Nichols is within easy reach, and there are many nearby stores for cashed-up fashionistas. **Mulberry** (171-175 Brompton Rd) and the Queen's lingerie supplier **Rigby & Peller** (3 Hans Rd) are home-grown concerns, while Italian design gets an airing at **Emporio Armani** (191 Brompton Rd).

Marylebone High Street (see p347) In the past few years this has morphed into a mellow, grown-up shopper's dream. Homewares stores such as Cath Kidston, **Conran Shop** (No 55) and **Skandium** (No 86) are joined by cosmetic stores like **Space NK** (No 83a) and **Fresh** (No 92), designer shops such as **Sixty 6** (No 66) and **Madeleine Press** (No 90), and quirky yoga outlet **calmia** (No 52). But food is the neighbourhood speciality. There's bakery Le Pain Quotidien and a branch of **Rococo** (No 45), while just around the corner you'll find cheesemonger **La Fromagerie** (2-4 Moxon St) and pork-obsessed butcher **Ginger Pig** (8-10 Moxon St).

DUTY FREE

In certain circumstances visitors from non-EU countries are entitled to claim back the 17.5% value-added tax (VAT) they have paid on purchased goods. The rebate only applies to items purchased in stores displaying a 'tax free' sign (there are plenty of these along Bond St). To claim it, visitors must be staying in the UK for less than six months.

The procedure to follow is relatively simple: don't forget to pick up the relevant form in the shop at the time of sale, and then hand it in at the airport when you leave.

THE WEST END

This is the heart of London shopping where, even in times of reduced consumer confidence, the tills still turn over the GDP of a small country. Oxford St is *the* quintessential high street and, frankly, unless you're coming to shop, there's little reason to be here. For less hectic retail therapy, you might prefer the side streets of Covent Garden. (Skip the stores inside the old market building at Covent Garden, though, as they tend to be pricey and touristy.) Newburgh and Carnaby Sts are worth checking out for fashion, and Charing Cross Rd is where to head for books. Meanwhile, on a more prosaic level, electronics and computer shops are found all along Tottenham Court Rd.

AGENT PROVOCATEUR Map p450 *Lingerie*

☎ 7439 0229; www.agentprovocateur.com; 6 Broadwick St W1; 🕒 11am-7pm Mon-Sat, to 8pm Thu, noon-5pm Sun; ⊖ Oxford Circus

For women's knickers to die for, die over and die in, pull up to Joseph (son of Vivienne Westwood) Corre's wonderful Agent Provacateur. Its sexy and saucy corsets, bras and nighties for all shapes and sizes exude confident and positive sexuality.

ALGERIAN COFFEE STORES

Map p450 *Food & Drink*

☎ 7437 2480; www.algocoffee.co.uk; 52 Old Compton St W1; 🕒 9am-7pm Mon-Sat; ⊖ Leicester Sq

A delectable aroma of fresh-ground coffee beans greets you, as everything from vanilla to varieties – and even teas – is readied for customers.

ANN SUMMERS Map p450 *Lingerie*

☎ 7434 2475; www.annsummers.co.uk; 79 Wardour St W1; 🕒 10am-6pm Mon-Sat, to 8pm Thu, noon-6pm Sun; ⊖ Piccadilly Circus

You don't need attend one of Ann Summers' saucy Tupperware-style sales parties to get your hands on her lacy, racy lingerie. Just roll up here for that, plus fluffy handcuffs, breast enhancers, G-strings, leather whips, nurse uniforms and other playful accessories.

APPLE Map p450 *Computers*

☎ 7153 9000; www.apple.com/uk/retail/regentstreet; 235 Regent St W1; 🕒 10am-9pm Mon-Sat, noon-6pm Sun; ⊖ Oxford Circus

Stocking every iPod accessory conceivable and offering hands-on technical assistance of all varieties, this white, airy two-storey emporium is Mac-geek heaven. Lesser devotees, meanwhile, use the banks of Internet-enabled iMacs as an impromptu cybercafé (a practice that actually has the blessing of the powers that be).

AQUASCUTUM Map p450 *Fashion & Designer*

☎ 7675 8200; www.aquascutum.co.uk; 100 Regent St W1; 🕒 10am-6.30pm Mon-Sat, to 7pm Thu, 11am-5pm Sun; ⊖ Piccadilly Circus

The store has had a recent facelift, but Aquascutum's mackintoshes, scarves, bags and hats remain traditional. For men, this means classic gabardine; for women, the look is pale and interesting in an Audrey Hepburn kind of way.

BENJAMIN POLLOCK'S TOYSHOP

Map p452 *Toys*

☎ 7379 7866; www.pollocks-coventgarden.co.uk; 1st fl, 44 Covent Garden Market WC2; 🕒 10am-6.30pm Mon-Sat, 11am-4pm Sun; ⊖ Covent Garden

The emphasis at this toyshop is on the traditional and the theatrical, with Victorian paper theatres, wooden marionettes and finger puppets. Some antique teddy bears are also in attendance.

DUFFER OF ST GEORGE

Map p452 *Fashion & Designer*

☎ 7836 3722; www.thedufferofstgeorge.com; 29 Shorts Gardens WC2; 🕒 10.30am-7pm Mon-Fri, to 6.30pm Sat, 1-5pm Sun; ⊖ Covent Garden

The first to bring Evisu jeans to London and a good place for Oeuf T-shirts, Duffer remains the *meister* of London menswear despite growing competition. 'Shield' formal wear like shirts and classic Italian handmade suits, as well as more urban sweats, bags and accessories are all on sale.

EAT MY HANDBAG BITCH

Map p452 *Household*

☎ 7836 0830; www.eatmyhandbagbitch.co.uk; 37 Drury Lane W1; 🕒 10am-6pm Mon-Sat; ⊖ Covent Garden

After it emigrated from Brick Lane to the West End, one might have thought that the retro furniture store with the attention-grabbing name would go mainstream. Not a bit. The same range of 20th-century design classics is on offer. The stylish replica '70s ceramics are the most affordable and transportable.

HABITAT Map pp448-9 *Household*

☎ 7631 3880; www.habitat.net; 196 Tottenham Court Rd W1; 🕒 10am-6.30pm Mon-Sat, to 8pm Thu, noon-6pm Sun; ⊖ Goodge St

Don't be fooled by the young urban dwellers who unfairly nickname this 'Shabby tat'; they're the first to snaffle its reasonably priced but fashionable homewares. Bringing design to ordinary homes since it was founded by Terence Conran in the 1950s, the chain is found across London.

HAMLEYS Map p450 *Toys*

☎ 0870 333 2455, 7494 2000; www.hamleys.com; 188-196 Regent St W1; 🕒 10am-8pm Mon-Sat, noon-6pm Sun; ⊖ Oxford Circus

Reportedly the largest toy store in the world and certainly the most famous, Hamleys is like a layer cake of playthings. Computer games are in the basement, with the latest playground trends at ground level. Science kits are on the 1st floor, preschool toys on the 2nd, girls' playthings on the 3rd, car models on the 4th, while the whole confection is topped off with Lego world and its café on the 5th floor.

HEAL'S Map pp448-9 _Household_
☎ 7636 1666; www.heals.co.uk; 196 Tottenham Court Rd W1; ☯ 10am-6pm Mon-Wed, 10am-8pm Thu, 10am-6.30pm Fri & Sat, noon-6pm Sun; ⊖ Goodge St
This long-established furniture and homewares store is like Habitat's more responsible older brother, with more practical and conservatively classy designs, along with a great kitchenware section.

HIGH JINKS Map p452 _Fashion & Designer_
☎ 7240 5580; Units 24 & 25, Thomas Neal Centre, Earlham St WC2; ☯ 10am-6.30pm Mon-Sat, to 7pm Thu, noon-5pm Sun; ⊖ Covent Garden
There's a real cluster of skate-punk and streetwear shops in the Thomas Neal Cen-

tre, including Mooks, Quiksilver and Skate of Mind. But with no allegiance to any particular brand, and quite a large selection from young designers, this offers arguably the broadest range.

JAMES SMITH & SONS
Map p452 _Accessories_
☎ 7836 4731; www.james-smith.co.uk; 53 New Oxford St WC1; ☯ 9.30am-5.30pm Mon-Fri, 10am-5.30pm Sat; ⊖ Tottenham Court Rd
Nobody makes and stocks umbrellas, canes and walking sticks as elegant as those behind this beautiful shop exterior.

JESS JAMES Map p450 _Jewellery_
☎ 7437 0199; www.jessjames.com; 3 Newburgh St; ☯ 11am-6.30pm Mon-Fri, to 7pm Thu, 11am-6pm Sat; ⊖ Oxford Circus
Special-occasion jewellery, from Jess James and other designers, is artistically arranged around an aquarium at this shop. Customers worried about the provenance of their diamonds can opt for the ethically sourced range.

KOH SAMUI Map p452 _Fashion & Designer_
☎ 7240 4280; www.kohsamui.co.uk; 65-67 Monmouth St WC2; ☯ 10.30am-6.30pm Mon-Sat, to 7pm Thu, 11.30am-6pm Sun; ⊖ Covent Garden
Glamorous floaty pieces from the likes of Brit designers Antonio Berardi, Clements Ribeiro and Julien MacDonald are found in this up-market boutique – and hard to imagine on any Thai island.

LIBERTY Map p450 _Department Store_
☎ 7734 1234; www.liberty.co.uk; 210-220 Regent St W1; ☯ 10am-7pm Mon-Sat, to 8pm Thu, noon-6pm Sun; ⊖ Oxford Circus
An irresistible blend of contemporary styles in an old-fashioned mock-Tudor atmosphere, Liberty has a huge and recently refurbished cosmetics department and an accessories floor, along with a new lingerie section on the 1st floor. A classic London souvenir is a Liberty (fabric) print.

MAPPIN & WEBB Map p450 _Jewellery_
☎ 7734 3801; www.mappin-and-webb.co.uk; 170 Regent St W1; ☯ 10am-6pm Mon-Sat, to 7pm Thu; ⊖ Oxford Circus/Piccadilly Circus
This business has long been a favourite for corporate gifts, designer watches and other off-the-shelf trinkets.

Clothing Sizes
Measurements approximate only, try before you buy

Women's Clothing

Aus/UK	8	10	12	14	16	18
Europe	36	38	40	42	44	46
Japan	5	7	9	11	13	15
USA	6	8	10	12	14	16

Women's Shoes

Aus/USA	5	6	7	8	9	10
Europe	35	36	37	38	39	40
France only	35	36	38	39	40	42
Japan	22	23	24	25	26	27
UK	3½	4½	5½	6½	7½	8½

Men's Clothing

Aus	92	96	100	104	108	112
Europe	46	48	50	52	54	56
Japan	S		M	M		L
UK/USA	35	36	37	38	39	40

Men's Shirts (Collar Sizes)

Aus/Japan	38	39	40	41	42	43
Europe	38	39	40	41	42	43
UK/USA	15	15½	16	16½	17	17½

Men's Shoes

Aus/UK	7	8	9	10	11	12
Europe	41	42	43	44½	46	47
Japan	26	27	27½	28	29	30
USA	7½	8½	9½	10½	11½	12½

Shopping – The West End

Mappin & Webb (p337)

suits and tailored shirts are all laid out on open shelves in this walk-in closet of a shop. Smith also does womenswear. There's also a **sale shop** (Map pp448–9; ☎ 7493 1287; 23 Avery Row W1; ⟨⟩ 10am-6pm Mon-Sat, to 7pm Thu, 1-5pm Sun).

POSTE MISTRESS

Map p452 *Fashion & Designer*
☎ 7379 4040; 61-63 Monmouth St WC2; ⟨⟩ 10am-7pm Mon-Sat, noon-6pm Sun; ⊖ Leicester Sq

It's worth shopping at this boudoir-like store just to get your mitts on one of its delicately floral pale-pink bags. But, stuffed with women's shoes from Emma Hope, Vivienne Westwood or Miu Miu, or the latest strappy wedges from Terry de Havilland, that bag feels even more like Christmas.

PURVES & PURVES

Map pp448-9 *Household*
☎ 7580 8223; www.purves.co.uk; 222 Tottenham Court Rd W1; ⟨⟩ 10am-6pm Mon-Fri, to 7.30pm Thu, 9.30am-6pm Sat, 11.30am-5.30pm Sun; ⊖ Goodge St

The same quality furnishings, lighting, kitchenware and accessories you'd get at Heal's but in more colourful, avant-garde designs – think Alessi kettles and Ritzenhoff mugs. It's also great for quirky gifts.

MOLTON BROWN

Map p452 *Cosmetics & Skin Care*
☎ 7240 8383; www.moltonbrown.co.uk; 18 Russell St WC2; ⟨⟩ 10am-7pm Mon-Fri, 10am-6pm Sat, noon-6pm Sun; ⊖ Covent Garden

Much loved by (and much nicked from the bathrooms of) stylish boutique hotels, this British brand of natural beauty and skin-care products offers plenty of pampering for men and women. In this store you can also have a facial, and buy make-up or even home accessories. There are branches across the city.

NEAL'S YARD DAIRY Map p452 *Food*

☎ 7240 5700; 17 Shorts Gardens WC2; ⟨⟩ 9am-7pm Mon-Sat; ⊖ Covent Garden

Proof that the English can hold their own (nose) when it comes to ripe, smelly cheeses, this stocks more than 70 varieties, including independent farmhouse brands. Condiments, pickles, jams and chutneys are also available.

PAUL SMITH Map p452 *Fashion & Designer*

☎ 7379 7133; www.paulsmith.co.uk; 40-44 Floral St WC2; ⟨⟩ 10am-6.30pm Mon-Sat, to 7pm Thu, noon-5pm Sun; ⊖ Covent Garden

Paul Smith represents the best of British classic with innovative twists. Preppy menswear,

RIGBY & PELLER Map pp448-9 *Lingerie*

☎ 7491 2200; 22a Conduit St W1; ⟨⟩ 9.30am-6pm Mon-Sat, to 7pm Thu; ⊖ Oxford Circus

This old-fashioned place makes the Queen's bras, but Rigby & Peller's fitting and alteration service – open to us plebs – is equally legendary, and many a customer has been surprised to discover they've been wearing the wrong size for years. Off-the-peg underwear and swimwear is also available. There's also a **Knightsbridge branch** (Map pp458–9; 3 Hans Rd).

SPACE NK Map p452 *Cosmetics*

☎ 7379 7030; www.spacenk.co.uk; Thomas Neal Centre, 37 Earlham St WC2; ⟨⟩ 10am-7pm Mon-Sat, to 7.30pm Thu, noon-5pm Sun; ⊖ Covent Garden

The first, and hopefully last, stop before the cosmetic surgeon's office, the UK's leading cult cosmetics store not only stocks hair, skin and make-up products from Dr Hauschka, Eve Lom, Skinethics, Kiehl's and Phyto but also anti-ageing ranges like 24/7 and Dr Sebagh. There are Space NK branches across the city.

TED BAKER Map p452 *Fashion & Designer*

☎ 7836 7808; www.tedbaker.co.uk; 9-10 Floral St;
🕑 10am-7pm Mon-Sat, to 8pm Thu, noon-6pm Sun;
⊖ Covent Garden

Trend-conscious women and men prepared to pay a little extra to lessen the risk of running into people wearing 'their' clothes should pop along to Ted Baker for his stylish, delicate takes on the latest fashions.

TOPSHOP & TOPMAN

Map p450 *Fashion & Designer*

☎ 7636 7700; www.topshop.co.uk; 36-38 Great Castle St W1; 🕑 9am-8pm Mon-Sat, to 9pm Thu, noon-6pm Sun; ⊖ Oxford Circus

The flagships of these two allied national chains deserve a special mention, because they encapsulate London's supreme skill at bringing catwalk fashion to the youth market affordably and quickly. It was a surprise to some Londoners to learn Topshop had become such an international cult, now it's working with up-and-coming design talent and even celebrities openly 'fess up to shopping here.

URBAN OUTFITTERS

Map p452 *Fashion & Designer*

☎ 7759 6390; www.urbanoutfitters.com; Seven Dials House, 42-56 Earlham St WC2; 🕑 10am-7pm Mon-Sat, to 8pm Thu, noon-6pm Sun; ⊖ Covent Garden

This American chain has made a big splash in London with its cool street-wear labels for gals and guys, saucy women's underwear, funky homewares and quirky gadgets. There's also a **Kensington branch** (Map pp444–5; 36-38 High St).

VINTAGE HOUSE Map p450 *Food & Drink*

☎ 7437 2592; 42 Old Compton St W1; 🕑 9am-11pm Mon-Fri, 9.30am-11pm Sat, noon-10pm Sun; ⊖ Leicester Sq

A whisky connoisseur's paradise, this shop stocks more than 1000 single-malt Scotches, from smooth Macallan to peaty Lagavulin.

On the High Street

Overseas retailers, such as Diesel, Gap, H&M, Mambo, Mango, Morgan, Muji and Zara, abound. The UK also has many home-grown clothing and shoe chains, some of which are listed below.

French Connection UK (Map pp448–9; ☎ 7629 7766; 396 Oxford St W1; ⊖ Bond St) This chain's clothes are more sober than the FCUK sobriquet suggests, and sales have been noticeably down in recent years.

Jigsaw (Map pp448–9; ☎ 7491 4484; 126-127 New Bond St W1; ⊖ Bond St) Classic women's clothes grouped by colour.

Joseph (Map pp458–9; ☎ 7823 9500; 77 Fulham Rd SW3; ⊖ South Kensington) Show them who wears the trousers, with classically smart pants and pants suits, plus a whole range of other fashion.

Karen Millen (Map p452; ☎ 7836 5355; 32-33 James St WC2; ⊖ Covent Garden) A tasteful take on womenswear, with figure-hugging, glittery evening frocks and glam trouser suits.

Marks & Spencer (Map pp448–9; ☎ 7935 7954; www.marksandspencer.co.uk; 458 Oxford St W1; ⊖ Bond St) Despite continuing forays into 'fashion', this chain seems doomed to remain best known for its knickers.

Miss Selfridge (Map pp448–9; ☎ 7927 0188; 325 Oxford St W1; ⊖ Oxford Circus/Bond St) Fun, throwaway fashion for female teens.

Oasis (Map p452; ☎ 7240 7445; 13 James St WC2; ⊖ Covent Garden) A more mature version of Topshop.

Office (Map p452; ☎ 7379 1896; 57 Neal St WC2; ⊖ Covent Garden) Shoes that go the distance from work to after-hours drinks.

Question Air (Map pp444–5; ☎ 7221 8163; www.question-air.com; 229 Westbourne Grove W11; ⊖ Notting Hill Gate) Small but growing fast, this chain stocks interesting designs from Juicy Couture, Maharishi, Vivienne Westwood and many more.

Reiss (Map p450; ☎ 7637 9111; www.reiss.co.uk; 14-17 Market Pl W1; ⊖ Oxford Circus) Able to almost pass as a designer boutique, Reiss takes men's and women's street fashion and gives it a mature edge with quality materials and precise tailoring.

Shellys (Map p450; ☎ 7287 0939; 266-270 Regent St W1; ⊖ Oxford Circus) For funky-looking, colourful footwear.

Warehouse (Map p452; ☎ 7240 8242; 24 Long Acre WC2; ⊖ Covent Garden/Leicester Sq) Somewhere between Topshop and Oasis in the fashion stakes.

EAST CENTRAL

The hub of London's street-fashion industry lies east, in the boutiques around Hoxton or Brick Lane and especially among the stalls of Spitalfields Market (p351) every Sunday, where up-and-coming designers lay out their wares. Don't forget to check out the burgeoning Cheshire St as well.

Each June and November there's a major showcase of the latest products, clothes, jewellery and art at the Atlantis Gallery of the Truman Brewery; see www.eastlondondesignshow.co.uk.

Nearby Clerkenwell is mostly known for its jewellery. For classic settings and unmounted stones, visit **Hatton Garden** (Map pp448–9; ⊖ Chancery Lane). The area's funky modern jewellers tend to be, literally, on the other side of the railway tracks. The **Clerkenwell Green Association** (Map pp442–3; www.cga.org.uk; cnr Clerkenwell Green & Clerkenwell Rd) provides an excellent starting point.

ANTONI & ALISON

Map pp442-3   *Fashion & Designer*

☎ 7833 2002; www.antoniandalison.co.uk; 34 Rosebery Ave EC1; ⏱ 10.30am-6.30pm Mon-Fri, noon-4pm Sat; ⊖ Farringdon

Having seen their trademark T-shirts on the telly in the wild east of Ukraine of all places, we reckon Antoni & Alison must be more famous than even they know. Their £40 to £50 men's and women's Tees (pick a transfer and match it with a size, shape and colour) are now joined by a burgeoning range of skirts and women's jackets.

ARIA Map pp442-3   *Household*

☎ 7704 1999; 295-296 Upper St N1; ⏱ 10am-7pm Mon-Fri, 10am-6.30pm Sat, noon-5pm Sun; ⊖ Angel/Highbury & Islington

The crowded window displays will draw you in for a browse through this large household store. It's packed with loads of covetable mugs, toasters, kitchen equipment and furniture.

DIVERSE Map pp442-3   *Fashion & Designer*

☎ 7359 8877; 294 Upper St N1; ⏱ 10am-6pm Mon-Sat; ⊖ Angel

One of London's coolest street-wear boutiques for men has jeans, trainers, shirts and tees from Italy and New York arranged around a fairly minimalist interior. Jeans labels include Blue Blood, Indigo Form, Rogan and Paper Denim.

EC ONE Map pp442-3   *Jewellery*

☎ 7713 6185; www.econe.co.uk; 41 Exmouth Market St EC1; ⏱ 10am-6pm Mon-Fri, 10.30am-6pm Sat; ⊖ Angel/Farringdon

It's obvious from the women's-magazine pages artfully dotted around this store that EC One's modern style is a favourite with the country's fashion stylists. There's an eye-catching use of stones, and some particularly fine bracelets.

HOXTON BOUTIQUE

Map pp442-3   *Fashion & Designer*

☎ 7684 2083; www.hoxtonboutique.co.uk; 2 Hoxton St; ⏱ 10am-6pm Mon-Fri, 11am-5pm Sat, noon-5pm Sun; ⊖ Old St

So hip it hurts, this place has a kind of take-no-prisoners, dedicated attitude to stocking the absolute latest in women's street wear. The white, mirrored interior looks like a gallery space made to resemble a disco (at least, according to the owners).

JUNKY STYLING

Map pp454-5   *Fashion & Designer*

☎ 7247 1883; www.junkystyling.co.uk; 12 Dray Walk, Old Truman Brewery, 91 Brick Lane E1; ⏱ 11am-5.30pm Mon-Fri, 10.30am-6pm Sat & Sun; ⊖ Liverpool St/Aldgate East

On retail-friendly Dray Walk, Junky 'recycles' traditional suits into sleek, eye-catching fashion pieces. A man's jacket might become a woman's halterneck top, for example, or tiny shorts with heart-shaped hot-water bottles for back pockets. Menswear includes short-sleeved half-shirt/half-t-shirts, and jackets with sweat suit–material sleeves and suit-material hoods. Bring your own clothes to be transformed.

LADEN SHOWROOMS

Map pp454-5   *Fashion & Designer*

☎ 7247 2431; www.laden.co.uk; 103 Brick Lane E1; ⏱ noon-6pm Mon-Sat, 10.30am-6pm Sun; ⊖ Liverpool St/Aldgate East

The unofficial flagship for the latest Hoxton street wear, Laden was 'London's best-kept secret'…probably until the thrifty Victoria Beckham declared it as such. Unlike many spartan *über*-cool boutiques, it's stuffed to the gills with a wide variety and large quantity of women's and men's clobber, making it a perfect one-stop shop.

Shopping – East Central

LESLEY CRAZE GALLERY

Map pp442-3 *Jewellery*

☎ 7608 0393; www.lesleycrazegallery.co.uk; 33-35a Clerkenwell Green EC1; ☽ 10am-5.30pm Mon-Sat; ⊖ Farringdon

Considered one of Europe's leading centres for arty, contemporary jewellery, this has exquisitely understated, and sometimes pricey, metal designs. There's also a smaller selection of mixed-media bangles, brooches, rings and the like (to the right of the main door), where prices start from about £20.

MATHMOS Map pp442-3 *Household*

☎ 7549 2700; www.mathmos.co.uk; 22-24 Old St EC1; ☽ 9.30am-6pm Mon-Fri; ⊖ Old St

Purveyors of the original lava lamp since the 1960s, Mathmos has experienced a recent revival. This huge, white showroom offers a range of sizes and designs, from original and rocket-shaped lava lamps to glowing outdoor 'aduki' shapes. The cursed things are all so mesmerising, however, making it difficult to choose.

NO-ONE Map pp442-3 *Fashion & Designer*

☎ 7613 5314; 1 Kingsland Rd E2; ☽ 11am-8pm Mon-Sat, noon-6pm Sun; ⊖ Old St/Liverpool St

A small range of hip women's and men's designs is complemented by fashion magazines, novelty beauty accessories and shoes. But the real bit of genius is the dimly lit, lo-fi café, where you can rest after some retail therapy.

PAST CARING Map pp442-3 *Household*

76 Essex Rd N1; ☽ noon-6pm Mon-Sat; ⊖ Angel

Stuffed full of second-hand retro bric-a-brac from ashtrays to curtain material, this shop is so removed from the modern world that it doesn't even have a phone number.

START Map pp442-3 *Fashion & Designer*

☎ 7739 3636; 42-44 Rivington St; ☽ 10.30am-6.30pm Mon-Fri, 11am-6pm Sat, 1-5pm Sun; ⊖ Liverpool St/ Old St

Punk rock meets designer in a boutique accurately reflecting the character of Brix Smith, former guitarist with the Fall, one-time paramour of spiky-haired violinist Nigel Kennedy and now part of Start's husband-and-wife management. In fact, the designer side has the upper hand, with labels like Cacharel and Issa keeping things fairly pricey. However, Smith prides herself on offering flattering jeans, and these are here in abundance, too. A menswear store (Map pp442-3; 59 Rivington St) is over the road.

Preloved Labels

Ever since Julia Roberts wore a vintage dress to the Oscars, yesteryear's *haute couture* has enjoyed a certain cachet, where finding yourself a classy classic is almost like collecting art. So to join the ranks of collectors try one of these.

Absolute Vintage (Map pp454–5; 7247 3883; 15 Hanbury St E1; ⊖ Liverpool St) This huge barn full of women's frocks and men's suits is handily close to Spitalfields Market.

Exclusivo (Map p465; ☎ 7431 8618; 24 Hampstead High St; ⊖ Hampstead) Men's and women's designer clothing and shoes.

Oxfam Originals (Map p452; ☎ 7836 9666; 22 Earlham St WC2; ⊖ Covent Garden) The best pieces given to the national charity Oxfam end up here.

Rellick (Map pp444–5; ☎ 8962 0089; 8 Golborne Rd W10; ⊖ Westbourne Park) The fashionista's favourite London retro store specialises in the likes of Ossie Clark, Zandra Rhodes and Vivienne Westwood, with prices from £30 to well over £300.

Retro Woman (Map pp444–5; 7221 2055; 20 Pembridge Rd W11; ⊖ Notting Hill Gate) Contains an excellent collection of second-hand designer shoes. More stock is in the unmarked sister store at No 16, while Retro Man is at No 34.

TATTY DEVINE

Map pp442-3 *Fashion & Designer*

☎ 7739 9009; www.tattydevine.com; 236 Brick Lane E1; ☽ 10am-6pm Mon-Fri, 11am-5pm Sat & Sun; ⊖ Liverpool St

Much of Tatty Devine's witty jewellery is the sort of thing you fantasise about making yourself, if only you had the time and, ahem, inspiration. Peas replace pearls in a necklace, price stickers are converted into cuff-links and guitar straps are converted into men's belts. Perspex name necklaces (£25) are also a treat.

VERDE'S Map pp454-5 *Food & Drink*

www.jeanettewinterson.com; 40 Brushfield St, Old Spitalfields Market E1; ☽ 8am-8pm; ⊖ Liverpool St

The headline writers had a field day with 'Oranges are not the only fruit' when novelist Jeanette Winterson decided to open this olde-worlde deli on the ground floor of her listed London home. It's true, though, as Winterson – a genuine foodie – has hit back at supermarket ready meals and air-lifted veggies with local produce and a nostalgic atmosphere. Don't expect to find her serving behind the counter, though.

WEST CENTRAL

Money talks in this fabulously well-heeled section of London, from Savile Row with its world-renowned bespoke tailoring to Chelsea's famously chic King's Rd. International luxury brands line New Bond St, while Knightsbridge draws the hordes with typically English department stores and chichi boutiques. You'll find venerable and atmospheric stores dotted around that have spent centuries catering to the whims and vanities of the refined folk who live here. Meanwhile, High St Kensington has a nice mix of chains and boutiques.

BURBERRY Map pp448-9 *Fashion & Designer*
☎ 7839 5222; www.burberry.com; 21-23 New Bond St SW1; ☿ 10am-7pm Mon-Sat, noon-6pm Sun; ⊖ Bond St

The first traditional British brand to go trendy, Burberry proved a little too successful for its own good, with its signature yellow tartan now seen as a mark of yob or 'chav' fashion (see p18), making it little better than cheap trainers, thick gold chains, baseball caps and hoods. The label's since pulled its head in with the offending pattern and branched out into bright block colours, florals and stripes.

BUTLER & WILSON
Map pp448-9 *Accessories*
☎ 7409 2955; www.butlerandwilson.co.uk; 20 South Molton St SW1; ☿ 10am-6pm Mon-Sat, to 7pm Thu, noon-6pm Sun; ⊖ Bond St

There's a sybaritic 1920s Shanghai vibe to Butler & Wilson's central branch, where costume jewellery, handbags, T-shirts and knick-knacks are sold beneath red Chinese lanterns, watched by Chinese shop dummies. The **Chelsea store** (Map pp458-9; ☎ 7352 3045; 189 Fulham Rd SW3) has a large collection of retro dresses, too.

DAISY & TOM
Map pp458-9 *Children's Department Store*
☎ 7352 5000; www.daisyandtom.com; 181 King's Rd SW3; ☿ 9.30am-6pm Mon-Sat, to 7pm Thu & Sat, 11am-5pm Sun; ⊖ Sloane Sq

This superb children's department store has a marionette show, carousel rides, rocking horses, play areas, traditional and modern toys, and a big book room where kids can loll about while flicking through the latest Harry Potter. Upstairs there are fashion labels fit for (your) little princes and princesses.

DR HARRIS Map pp448-9 *Perfumer/Herbalist*
☎ 7930 3915; www.drharris.co.uk; 29 St James's St SW1; ☿ 8.30am-6pm Mon-Fri, 9.30am-5pm Sat; ⊖ Green Park

Operating as chemist and perfumer since 1790, this shop stocks such esoteric goods as moustache wax, tiny beard-combs and DR Harris

Crystal Eye Drops to combat the visual effects of late nights, early starts and jetlag. Best of all, it has its own hangover cure: a bitter herbal concoction called DR Harris Pick-Me-Up.

FORTNUM & MASON
Map p450 *Department Store*
☎ 7734 8040; www.fortnumandmason.co.uk; 181 Piccadilly W1; ☿ 10am-6.30pm Mon-Sat, noon-6pm Sun; ⊖ Piccadilly Circus

You don't have to be Scott heading to the Antarctic to indulge yourself in the famous food hampers, cut marmalade or unusual foodstuffs from the olde-worlde food hall, although this is where the explorer came for supplies. Clothes occupy the other six floors.

GARRARD Map pp448-9 *Jewellery*
☎ 7758 8520; www.garrard.com; 24 Albemarle St W1; ☿ 10am-5.30pm Mon-Sat; ⊖ Bond St/Green Park

Creative director Jade Jagger (daughter of Mick) helped turn Britain's old-fashioned crown jeweller into somewhere funky enough for Missy Elliot to advertise its bling. Jewel-encrusted clothing and gifts are sold upstairs.

HARRODS Map pp444-5 *Department Store*
☎ 7730 1234; www.harrods.com; 87 Brompton Rd SW1; ☿ 10am-7pm Mon-Sat; ⊖ Knightsbridge

This unique store is like a theme park for fans of the British establishment. It is always crowded with slow tourists and there are more rules than at an army boot camp, but even the toilets will make you swoon and the food hall will make you drool. In such an over-the-top environment it seems odd to single out one feature as especially kitsch, but the memorial fountain to Princess Diana and Dodi Al Fayed (son of Harrods owner Mohamed) probably fits that bill.

HARVEY NICHOLS
Map pp444-5 *Department Store*
☎ 7235 5000; www.harveynichols.com; 109-125 Knightsbridge SW1; ☿ 10am-8pm Mon-Fri, 10am-7pm Sat, noon-6pm Sun; ⊖ Knightsbridge

This is London's temple of high fashion, where you'll find all the names that matter in local and international high fashion. There's a great food hall and café on the 5th floor, a softly lit lingerie department, an extravagant perfume department and exquisite jewellery.

JOHN LEWIS Map pp448-9 *Department Store*
☎ 7629 7711; www.johnlewis.co.uk; 278-306 Oxford St W1; ◷ 9.30am-7pm Mon-Sat, to 8pm Thu; ⊖ Oxford Circus

'Never knowingly undersold' is the motto of this store, whose range of household goods, fashion and luggage is better described as reliable rather than cutting-edge. Strong points include its fabrics department.

KURT GEIGER
Map pp448-9 *Fashion & Designer*
☎ 7758 8020; www.kurtgeiger.com; 65 South Molton St W1; ◷ 10am-7pm Mon-Sat, to 8pm Thu, noon-6pm Sun; ⊖ Bond St

Fashion, quality and affordability all come together at this superlative men's and women's shoe store, where footwear from the likes of Birkenstock, Chloe, Hugo Boss, Marc Jacobs, Paul Smith and United Nude adorns the shelves.

LULU GUINNESS
Map pp460-1 *Fashion & Designer*
☎ 7823 4828; www.luluguiness.com; 3 Ellis St SW1; ◷ 10am-6pm Mon-Fri, 11am-6pm Sat; ⊖ Sloane Sq

It's literally handbags at dawn at Lulu Guiness, where some of her products are even inscribed with that motto. Female silhouettes, dice, board games and various other playful insignia grace her range of coin purses, cosmetic bags, handbags and totes, while some of her collectable evening bags come in striking shapes, such as fans.

MATTHEW WILLIAMSON
Map pp448-9 *Fashion & Designer*
☎ 7629 6200; www.matthewwilliamson.com; 28 Bruton St W1; ◷ 10am-6pm Mon-Sat; ⊖ Bond St/Green Park

Couturier to the stars – Sienna Miller, Keira Knightley, Kate Hudson and Joely Richardson among them – Williamson peddles what the fashion writers often term 'boho-deluxe' style. A little bit hippy and a lot glam, the chiffon dresses at this emporium might set you back £800. For something less pricey, try his Butterfly range at **Debenham's** (Map pp448–9; ☎ 7580 3000; www.debenhams.com; 334-348 Oxford St W1; ⊖ Bond St).

MULBERRY Map pp448-9 *Fashion & Designer*
☎ 7491 3900; www.mulberry.com; 41-42 New Bond St W1; ◷ 10am-6pm Mon-Sat, to 7pm Thu; ⊖ Bond St

After Burberry and Pringle reinvented themselves as hip brands, it seemed inevitable that fellow establishment label Mulberry would do the same. But the unisex clothes here are fairly restrained and only slightly edgy. The leather bags have proved the greatest hit.

PETER JONES
Map pp458-9 *Department Store*
☎ 7730 3434; www.peterjones.co.uk; Sloane Sq SW1; ◷ 9.30am-7pm Mon-Sat; ⊖ Sloane Sq

The slightly more upmarket brother of John Lewis, Peter Jones has been given a makeover in recent years, bringing it more in line with Selfridges and Harvey Nicks. Although upmarket china, furnishings and gifts sections remain on the ground and basement floors, there's a new focus on accessories and cosmetics, plus a new top-floor café.

POSTE Map pp448-9 *Fashion & Designer*
☎ 7499 8002; 10 South Molton St; ◷ 10am-7pm Mon-Sat, noon-6pm Sun; ⊖ Bond St

On one of London's most fashionable streets, this very cool shop is aimed at boys who like good shoes, and stocks everything from vintage street labels to razor-sharp Italian imports.

PRINGLE Map pp448-9 *Fashion & Designer*
☎ 0800 360 200, 7297 4580; www.pringleofscotland .com; 112 New Bond St W1; ◷ 10am-6.30pm Mon-Sat, to 7.30pm Thu; ⊖ Bond St

Having somehow convinced us that golfers jumpers were hip, this trad-Brit brand then found its cardigans perfectly placed to exploit fashion's current penchant for demurer women's fashions. Whatever the appearance, you can't argue with the lovely soft feel of these quality women's and men's knits (roughly £110 to £175).

ROCOCO Map pp458-9 *Chocolates*
☎ 7352 5857; www.rococochocolates.com; 321 King's Rd SW3; ◷ 9am-7pm Mon-Sat, noon-6pm Sun; ⊖ Sloane Sq

This sells proper chocolate, in an entirely different league to most English 'cocoa products' (as the EU would call them). And it comes in glorious moulds and flavours. There are truffles, Swiss chocolates, organic bars, surprising vegan varieties and bags of assorted 'broken chocolate' so you can taste different varieties.

Shopping – West Central

SELFRIDGES Map pp448-9 _Department Store_

☎ 7629 1234; www.selfridges.com; 400 Oxford St W1;
🕐 10am-8pm Mon-Fri, 9.30am-8pm Sat, noon-6pm Sun;
⊖ Bond St

Behind the inventive window displays and impressive Art Deco façade lies the funkiest and most vital of London's one-stop shops. Fashion runs the gamut from street to formal, including local designer labels Boudicca, Luella Bartley, Emma Cook, FrostFrench and TataNaka. The food hall is unparalleled, and the ground-floor cosmetics hall is the largest in Europe.

STELLA MCCARTNEY

Map pp448-9 _Fashion & Designer_
☎ 7518 3100; www.stellamccartney.co.uk; 30 Bruton St W1; 🕐 10am-6pm Mon-Sat, to 7pm Thu; ⊖ Bond St/Green Park

Impeccably tailored trouser suits that flatter and floaty women's tops prone to fall off their hangers are showcased in this three-storey terraced Victorian home. Despite ritzy touches like a glasshouse garden and an olde-worlde 'apothecary' selling perfume, the domestic layout is still evident – which will either put you right at ease or have you feeling like an intruder. Sunglasses, vegetarian shoes and a bespoke tailoring service complete the package.

Suits You, Sir

Looking for the suit of a lifetime? Here are three favourite tailors, on and off Savile Row:

Kilgour (Map p450; ☎ 7734 6905; 8 Savile Row W1; ⊖ Piccadilly Circus) Conventional with a modern twist, Kilgour sells a ready-to-wear range, as well as tailor-made suits from £1400.

Ozwald Boateng (Map p450; ☎ 7437 0620; www.ozwaldboateng.com; 12a Savile Row W1; ⊖ Piccadilly Circus) His flamboyance makes Boateng more a couturier than a tailor, with striking colours and fabrics in his £3000 bespoke suits.

Timothy Everest (Map pp454-5; ☎ 7377 5770; 32 Elder St E1; ⊖ Liverpool St) David Beckham and Tom Cruise are clients here, where bespoke suits cost at least £1500 but off-the-peg shirts start at £150.

TAYLOR OF OLD BOND STREET

Map p450 _Men's Grooming_
☎ 7930 5321; www.tayloroldbondst.co.uk; 74 Jermyn St SW1; 🕐 9am-6pm Mon-Fri, 8.30am-6pm Sat; ⊖ Green Park

This shop has been plying its trade since the mid-19th century and has contributed as much as any other to the expression 'well-groomed gentlemen'. It stocks every sort of razor, shaving brush and flavour of shaving soap imaginable.

VIVIENNE WESTWOOD

Fashion & Designer
☎ 7439 1109; www.viviennewestwood.com; 44 Conduit St W1; 🕐 10am-6pm Mon-Sat, to 7pm Thu; ⊖ Bond St/Oxford Circus

The woman who dressed the punk generation is still designing clothes as bold, innovative and provocative as ever. Nineteenth-century-inspired bustiers, frills and flounces, wedge shoes, and loads of tartan make regular appearances in her couture and diffusion lines.

WRIGHT & TEAGUE Map pp448-9 _Jewellery_

☎ 7629 2777; www.wrightandteague.com; 1a Grafton St W1; 🕐 10am-6pm Mon-Fri, to 7pm Thu, 10am-5pm Sat; ⊖ Green Park

This couple met while studying at St Martins School of Art more than 20 years ago and have been together ever since. Their highly original, elegant and affordable pieces are mainly in silver and gold.

ALONG THE SOUTH BANK

As if it weren't enough to boast the Tate Modern art gallery, the Millennium Bridge, the Globe Theatre, the London Eye and the Saatchi Gallery, the revitalised South Bank is also home to Borough Market (see p350), London's foodie shopping destination *du jour*. Meanwhile, the Oxo Tower houses a range of fashion and household designers, with products to suit every taste. Curious fashionistas might appreciate a quick scout in and around Bermondsey St.

BLACK + BLUM Map pp448-9   *Household*

☎ 7633 0022; www.black-blum.com; Unit 2.07, 2nd fl, Oxo Tower Wharf, Barge House St SE1; ⏱ 9am-5pm Mon-Fri, 11am-4pm Sat & Sun; ⊖ Southwark

This Anglo-Swiss partnership's popular 'James the doorman' (a human-shaped doorstop) and 'Mr and Mrs Hang-up' (anthropomorphic coat hangers that can indicate your mood) are now sold in numerous museum and/or design shops. But here you can pick up other products, including 'reading light' (a bulb with wire arms and legs perusing its newspaper-shaped shade) and 'loo read' (a combined toilet-roll holder and magazine rack).

CANDY ANTHONY

Map pp448-9   *Fashion & Designer*

☎ 7803 0898; www.candyanthony.com; Unit 1.12, 1st fl, Oxo Tower Wharf, Barge House St SE1; ⏱ noon-7pm Mon-Fri, 11am-6pm Sat; ⊖ Southwark/London Bridge

Should you, like millions of the BBC's *Strictly Come Dancing* viewers, have been taken with ballroom glamour, pop in here for girlie evening wear sweet enough to seduce even a grown feminist. Pink satin dresses with black ribbons, or tartan and denim full-circle skirts with lace petticoats just beg for a special occasion to be worn to. It's also a wonderful shop just to browse.

COCKFIGHTER OF BERMONDSEY

Map pp454-5   *Fashion & Designer*

☎ 7357 6482; www.cockfighter.co.uk; 96 Bermondsey St SE1; ⏱ 11am-7pm Tue-Fri, noon-6pm Sat; ⊖ London Bridge

T-shirts with attitude, and other clothing and accessories, are found in this small boutique and worn across the pages of celebrity magazines by DJs and popstars.

ELEY KISHIMOTO

Map pp454-5   *Fashion & Designer*

☎ 7357 0037; 40 Snowsfields SE1; ⏱ 10.30am-6.30pm Thu-Sat; ⊖ London Bridge

Bright, colourful prints are the signature of this husband-and-wife team's womenswear. In recent years there's been a focus on African patterns and themes.

KONDITOR & COOK

Map pp454-5   *Food & Drink*

☎ 7407 5100; 10 Stoney St SE1; ⏱ 7.30am-6pm Mon-Fri, 8am-2.30pm Sat; ⊖ London Bridge

This excellent, and pricey, bakery produces wholesome bread and some of the best cake this side of Vienna. There's also gingerbread, treacle pie and chocolate to satisfy the sweetest tooth.

THE EAST END

Just a few years ago there was very little to lure outside shoppers to this district, with all its low-price household-goods stores and cheap off-the-peg fashions. Today the Burberry connection ensures a steady flow, while **Broadway Market** (www.broadwaymarket.co.uk) in Hackney is one of London's up-and-coming retail scenes.

BURBERRY FACTORY SHOP

Map pp438-9   *Fashion & Designer*

☎ 8985 3344, 8328 4320; 29-53 Chatham Pl E9; ⏱ 11am-6pm Mon-Fri, 10am-5pm Sat, 11am-5pm Sun; ⊖ Bethnal Green, then bus 106 or 256 to Hackney Town Hall/rail Hackney Central

This warehouse stocks seconds and samples from reborn-as-trendy Brit brand's current collection or stuff from last season. Prices can be up to 50% to 70% lower than those in the West End, with the best deals on accessories.

FABRICATIONS Map pp438-9   *Household*

☎ 7275 8043; 7 Broadway Market E8; ⏱ noon-5pm Tue-Sat; rail London Fields/bus 106, 253, 26, 48 or 55

Fabrications is the best-known and most eye-catching store along Broadway Market. The shop's owner, Barley Massey, does a lot for the recycling cause, making clothes and soft furnishings from unexpected material, including everything from rubber inner tubes to used ribbon, and also undertakes commissions.

Books

Anyone who saw the film *84 Charing Cross Road* will know which street to head for first when looking for books. It's much more overrun with chain bookstores today – and No 84 is, disappointingly, a soulless chain pub. While good bookstores are scattered across town, Charing Cross Rd is still the premier bibliophile's strip.

BBC World Service Shop (Map p452; ☎ 7557 2576; www.bbcshop.com; Bush House, Strand WC2; ⊖ Holborn/ Temple) Where to buy that missed episode of *The Office* or catch up on Michael Palin's latest exploits.

Blackwell's (Map p452; ☎ 7292 5100; www.bookshop.blackwell.co.uk; 100 Charing Cross Rd WC2; ⊖ Tottenham Court Rd) Once a specialist in academic titles, this has now branched out into travel and other general-interest books.

Books for Cooks (Map pp444-5; ☎ 7221 1992; www.booksforcooks.com; 4 Blenheim Cres W11; ⊖ Ladbroke Grove) All the recipe books from celeb and non-celeb chefs. The café has a test kitchen where you can sample recipes.

Borders (Map p450; ☎ 7292 1600; www.borders.co.uk; 203 Oxford St; ⊖ Oxford Circus) Five floors of books, magazines and newspapers from around the world, plus CDs, tapes and DVDs.

Daunt Books (Map pp448-9; ☎ 7224 2295; 83-84 Marylebone High St W1; ⊖ Baker St) A beautiful old skylit shop with a wide selection.

Forbidden Planet Megastore (Map p452; ☎ 7836 4179; www.forbiddenplanet.com; 179 Shaftesbury Ave WC1; ⊖ Leicester Sq/Tottenham Court Rd) A massive trove of comics, sci-fi, horror and fantasy literature.

Foyle's (Map p452; ☎ 7437 5660; www.foyles.co.uk; 113-119 Charing Cross Rd WC2; ⊖ Tottenham Court Rd) Thankfully, it no longer arranges books by publisher, but this independent bookstore still prides itself on the breadth of its range. Women's book specialist Silver Moon, music store Ray's Jazz, and a café are found under its roof.

Garden Books (Map pp444-5; ☎ 7792 0777; 11 Blenheim Cres W11; ⊖ Ladbroke Grove) Great place for green-thumbing your way through books on growing plants.

Gay's the Word (Map pp442-3; ☎ 7278 7654; www.gaystheword.co.uk; 66 Marchmont St WC1; ⊖ Russell Sq) For more than 25 years Gay has been the word in everything from advice books on coming out to queer or lesbian literature.

Gosh! (Map p452; ☎ 7636 1011; 39 Great Russell St WC1; ⊖ Tottenham Court Rd) Draw up here for graphic novels, manga, newspaper-strip collections and children's books like Tin Tin and Asterix.

SOUTHEAST LONDON

Locals like to joke that this is a separate dimension of retro clothes stores and second-hand bookshops. It's certainly true. The latter aren't even worth listing, because you pass them every few steps. The retro clothing stores are pretty thick on the ground too, and the following represent only a selection.

COMPENDIA Map p463 *Gifts*

☎ 8293 6616; www.compendia.co.uk; Shop 10, Greenwich Market; ⊙ 11am-5.30pm Mon-Fri, 10.30am-5.30pm Sat & Sun; DLR Cutty Sark

It's brilliantly piled high with board and other games from around the world, so discovering this place means you'll never be at a loose end. There's backgammon, chess, Scrabble, solitaire and Carrom (the sit-down Indian version of pool).

EMPORIUM Map p463 *Clothing*

☎ 8305 1670; 332 Creek Rd SE10; ⊙ 10.30am-6pm Wed-Sun; DLR Cutty Sark

A very pleasant vintage shop (unisex), with glass cabinets of paste jewellery and old perfume bottles (under the Shell advertising lamp), straw caps, jackets and blazers.

FLYING DUCK ENTERPRISES

Map p463 *Household*

☎ 8858 1964; 320-322 Creek Rd SE10; ⊙ 11am-6pm Tue-Fri, 10.30am-6pm Sat & Sun; DLR Cutty Sark

A little grotto of kitsch, with two small rooms mainly lit by retro lamps and jam-packed with everything from snow domes and bakelite telephones, to Tretchikoff paintings of exotic women and '70s cocktail kits.

TWINKLED Map p463 *Household*

☎ 8269 0864; www.twinkled.net; 11 Stockwell St SE10; ⊙ 11am-6pm Tue-Fri, 10.30am-6pm Sat & Sun; DLR Cutty Sark

In this disused petrol station you'll find a slightly more serious collection of 1950s, '60s and '70s homewares and clothing than at Flying Duck. Plus, there's a bit more room to move.

Grant & Cutler (Map p450; ☎ 7734 2012; www.grantandcutler.com; 55-57 Great Marlborough St W1; ✚ Oxford Circus) This is London's best-stocked foreign-language bookshop, running the gamut from Arabic to Zulu. However, sometimes staff aren't as knowledgeable as you'd hope in recommending specific books.

Helter Skelter (Map p452; ☎ 7836 1151; www.skelter.demon.co.uk; 4 Denmark St WC2; ✚ Tottenham Court Rd) Literate music fans will be enthralled by this store, which has everything from in-depth band biographies to fanzines.

Housmans (Map pp442-3; ☎ 7837 4473; 5 Caledonian Rd N1; ✚ King's Cross St Pancras) Great radical store, which stocks books you won't find anywhere else. Also has a good stationery section.

Magma (Map pp448-9; ☎ 7242 9503; 117-119 Clerkenwell Rd EC1; ✚ Farringdon) Books, magazines and more on cool, cutting-edge design. There's also a smaller branch in **Covent Garden** (Map p452; ☎ 7240 8498; 8 Earlham St).

Murder One (Map p452; ☎ 7734 3485; 76-78 Charing Cross Rd WC2; ✚ Leicester Sq) Crime fiction from the likes of Harlan Coben, Carl Hiaasen, Elmore Leonard and Alexander McCall Smith join true crime, Sherlock Holmes and romances (including Mills & Boons) in Murder One's relatively new, more spacious premises.

Shipley (Map p452; ☎ 7836 4872; www.artbook.co.uk; 70 Charing Cross Rd; ✚ Leicester Sq) There are three Shipley stores, all in a row. This at No 70 specialises in current and out-of-print arts books, neighbouring **No 72** (☎ 7240 1559) focuses on graphic art, design and architecture, while **No 80** (☎ 7240 4157) covers cinema, photography and journalism.

Sportspages (Map p452; ☎ 7240 9604; www.sportspages.co.uk; 94-96 Charing Cross Rd; ✚ Leicester Sq/Tottenham Court Rd) Get the inside track on sporting heroes, from the Wisden cricket annual to autobiographies from the likes of Lance Armstrong, Kelly Holmes, Michael Shumacher and your whole fantasy football team.

Stanford's (Map p452; ☎ 7836 1321; www.stanfords.co.uk; 12-14 Long Acre WC2; ✚ Leicester Sq/Covent Garden) As a 150-year-old seller of maps, guides and literature, the granddaddy of travel bookstores is a destination in its own right. Ernest Shackleton, David Livingstone, Michael Palin and even Brad Pitt have all popped in here.

Travel Bookshop (Map pp444-5; ☎ 7229 5260; www.travelbookshop.co.uk; 13 Blenheim Cres W11; ✚ Ladbroke Grove) Still known as the bookshop on which Hugh Grant's was modelled in the movie *Notting Hill*, this is crammed with guidebooks, travel literature and antiquarian gems.

Waterstone's (Map p450; ☎ 7851 2400; www.waterstones.co.uk; 203-206 Piccadilly W1; ✚ Piccadilly Circus) The chain's megastore is the biggest bookshop in Europe, boasting knowledgeable staff and regular author readings. Branches throughout the city.

NORTH CENTRAL

Just minutes from Oxford St, but a world away in style and atmosphere, Marylebone High St is fast becoming one of the city's premier strips. A weekly **farmers market** (Map pp448-9; 🕑 10am-2pm Sun) is held in the nearby Cramer St car park, behind Waitrose.

Shopping in Camden is more about cheap, disposable fashion and made-for-tourist trinkets. The area is, of course, dominated by its huge market (p350), although you might be tempted to occasionally pop into one of the many clothes boutiques lining the high street.

CATH KIDSTON Map pp448-9   *Household*

☎ 7935 6555; www.cathkidston.co.uk; 51 Marylebone High St W1; 🕑 10am-7pm Mon-Sat, 11am-5pm Sun; ✚ Baker St

A sort of in-yer-face Laura Ashley for the 21st century, Kidston splashes her homewares and handbags with funky floral designs. Products here also include things like polka-dot picnic tableware and 1950s-style watering cans.

SHOON Map pp448-9   *Fashion & Designer*

☎ 7487 3001; www.shoon.com; 94 Marylebone High St W1; 🕑 10am-6pm Mon-Fri; ✚ Baker St

With its eclectic, upmarket mix of active sportswear, African knick-knacks, travel books and shoes, this spacious store has broad appeal.

NORTH LONDON

The shops in this part of the city cater to a well-heeled crowd, although few of them are going to pull in any outside visitors. In Hampstead, upmarket outlets frequently just mean upmarket chains (although there are a couple of good fashion boutiques uphill from the tube station). Muswell Hill has a wider selection of independent stores, while Crouch End also has some good charity shops.

ROSSLYN DELICATESSEN Map p465 *Food*
☎ 7794 9210; www.delirosslyn.co.uk; 56 Rosslyn Hill NW3; ⏰ 10am-6pm Mon-Fri; ⊖ Hampstead/Belsize Park

Small wonder this fragrant store was voted the best local delicatessen in London by radio station LBC and the *Independent* newspaper. Among the usual pastas, pasta sauces, chutneys, terrines and marinated vegetables at Rosslyn Delicatessen you'll find unusual flavours like caramelised onions, damson jam and mulberry salad dressing. The cakes, chocolates and Union Roasters coffee are delicious, too.

WEST LONDON

Well-heeled Notting Hill and Westbourne Grove have the best shopping here, and most visitors to London will at some stage take a wander down Portobello Rd, with its wall-to-wall antique stores, funky fashion stores, knick-knack shops and weekend market (see p350).

Otherwise, west London shopping is fairly drab. Highlights include the **Shepherd's Bush Market** (⏰ 9.30am-5pm Mon-Wed, Fri & Sat, 9.30am-1pm Thu), running underneath the Hammersmith & City line between Goldhawk Rd and Shepherd's Bush tube stations, and the superb **Troubadour Delicatessen** (Map pp458–9; ☎ 7341 6341; 267 Old Brompton Rd SW5; ⊖ Earl's Court), next to the eatery of the same name.

BALLANTYNE CASHMERE
Map pp444-5   *Fashion & Designer*
☎ 7493 4718; www.ballantyne.it; 303 Westbourne Grove W11; ⏰ 10am-6pm Mon-Sat; ⊖ Notting Hill Gate

The brightly coloured floral wallpaper and the bold designs of its luxury Scottish-cum-Italian knitwear makes Ballantyne the preserve of the thoroughly metrosexual man who's not afraid to get in touch with his fashionista side. Women's jumpers are also on sale.

CERAMICA BLUE Map pp444-5 *Household*
☎ 7727 0288; www.ceramicablue.co.uk; 10 Blenheim Cres W11; ⏰ 11am-5pm Mon, 10am-6.30pm Tue-Sat; ⊖ Ladbroke Grove

Vibrant, eye-catching crockery from more than a dozen countries is found in this friendly china shop. The range runs from Japanese crackleglaze teacups to serving plates with tribal South African designs, and much in between.

COCO RIBBON
Map pp444-5   *Fashion & Designer*
☎ 7229 4904; www.cocoribbon.com; 21 Kensington Park Rd W11; ⏰ 10am-6pm Mon-Sat, 12.30-5.30pm Sun; ⊖ Ladbroke Grove

An award-winning but eminently girlie boutique, Coco Ribbon stocks chiffon dresses and faux-fur gilets but is best for accessories and gifts. Typical offerings might include butterfly patches, Calypso Rose's customisable Clippy Kit handbags, light-hearted words of wisdom for newlyweds or new parents and, for your broken-hearted gal pals, 'boyfriend replacement' kits (sugar pills and chocolate, of course).

Rough Trade record store (opposite)

Music

There's a reason the obsessive novel *High Fidelity* was set in London (unlike the later Chicago-based film). Per head, Britons buy more music than any other nation on earth and, with such great shops as the following, much of that is centred on the capital.

Blackmarket (Map p450; ☎ 7437 0478; www.blackmarket.co.uk; 25 D'Arblay St W1; ✪ Oxford Circus) This is where club DJs flock for the latest international dance music. After all, who can resist a place with a lower-level 'drum and bassment'?

Daddy Kool (Map p450; ☎ 7437 3535; www.daddykoolrecords.com; 12 Berwick St W1; ✪ Oxford Circus) Europe's oldest reggae store, and the best shop in central London for all sorts of Black music, particularly reggae, original ska and classic dub.

Haggle Vinyl (Map pp442-3; ☎ 7354 4666; www.haggle.freeserve.co.uk; 114 Essex Rd N1; ⏲ 9am-7pm Mon-Sat, 10am-5.30pm Sun; ✪ Angel) Vinyl records from as little as £2.50 for the stuff that has spilled over into the boxes on the floor. From 1950s crooners to early hip-hop.

Harold Moores (Map p450; ☎ 7437 1576; www.hmrecords.co.uk; 2 Great Marlborough St W1; ✪ Oxford Circus) London's finest classical-music store stocks an extensive range of vinyl, CDs and videos.

Honest Jon's (Map pp444-5; ☎ 8969 9822; 276-278 Portobello Rd W10; ✪ Ladbroke Grove) Two adjoining shops with jazz, soul and reggae.

HMV (Map p450; ☎ 7631 3423; www.hmv.co.uk; 150 Oxford St W1; ✪ Oxford Circus) Three floors laden with music for all tastes.

Music & Video Exchange (Map pp444–5; ☎ 7243 8573; 38 Notting Hill Gate W11; ✪ Notting Hill Gate) Second-hand store *par excellence*.

Mole Jazz (Map p450; ☎ 7437 8800; 2 Great Marlborough St W1; ✪ Oxford Circus) Great shop for traditional jazz and second-hand CDs.

On the Beat (Map p450; ☎ 7637 8934; 22 Hanway St W1; ✪ Tottenham Court Rd) Mostly '60s and '70s retro, and helpful staff.

Ray's Jazz Shop (Map p452; ☎ 7440 3205; www.foyles.co.uk; 1st fl, Foyles, 113-119 Charing Cross Rd WC2; ✪ Tottenham Court Rd) Quiet and serene with friendly and helpful staff, this is one of the best jazz shops in London.

Reckless Records (Map p450; ☎ 7437 4271; www.reckless.co.uk; 26 & 30 Berwick St W1; ✪ Oxford Circus) New and second-hand records/CDs at these two great stores run the gamut from punk, soul, dance and independent to mainstream.

Tower Records (Map p450; ☎ 7439 2500; www.towerrecords.co.uk; 1 Piccadilly Circus W1; ⏲ to midnight Tue-Fri; ✪ Piccadilly Circus) Though this massive store stocks a lot of everything, the jazz and folk-music sections are particularly extensive.

Rough Trade (Map pp444-5; ☎ 7229 8541; 130 Talbot Rd W11; ✪ Ladbroke Grove) With its underground, alternative and vintage rarities, this home of the eponymous punk-music label remains a haven for vinyl junkies who get misty-eyed about the days before CDs (also on sale) and MP3 players.

Sister Ray (Map p450; ☎ 7287 8385; www.sisterray.co.uk; 94 Berwick St; ✪ Oxford Circus) If you were a fan of the late, great John Peel on the BBC/BBC World Service, this specialist in innovative, experimental and indie music is just right for you.

Virgin Megastore (Map p450; ☎ 7631 1234; www.virgin.com; 14-30 Oxford St W1; ⏲ to 10pm Mon-Sat; ✪ Tottenham Court Rd) The largest of the megastores, with four floors and massive Top 40 displays.

PAUL & JOE Map pp444-5 *Fashion & Designer*
☎ 7243 5510; 39-41 Ledbury Rd W11; ⏲ 10.30am-6pm Mon-Fri, 10.30am-7pm Sat, 1-6pm Sun; ✪ Notting Hill Gate

Both this store's slightly retro clothes and its layout are immensely appealing. Paul & Joe's menswear is sleek and stylish, but it's the female shoppers who are more likely to swoon – over the fabulous frocks (from £200 to £300), the sexy underwear and the make-up you can test while sitting at a vintage dressing table.

Market Forces

Shopping at London's markets isn't just about picking up bargains and rummaging through tonnes of knick-knacks, clothes and all sorts of mystical ephemera and earthly accoutrements – although they give you plenty of opportunity to do that. It's also about taking in the character of this vibrant city, in all its many facets and moods.

For information on farmers markets, see p231.

Borough

Here in some form since the 13th century, **Borough Market** (Map pp454–5; ☎ 7407 1002; www.boroughmarket .org.uk; cnr Borough High & Stoney Sts SE1; 🕙 9am-6pm Fri, 9am-4pm Sat; ⊖ London Bridge) is testament to the British public's increasing interest in good food. Helped by celebrity shopper Jamie Oliver, 'London's Larder' has enjoyed an enormous renaissance in recent years, overflowing with food-lovers, both experienced and wannabe. As well as a section devoted to quality fresh fruit, exotic vegetables and organic meat, there's a fine-foods retail market, with the likes of home-grown honey and homemade bread. Throughout, takeaway stalls allow you to sample a sizzling gourmet sausage or tuck into a quality burger. Shoppers queue at the excellent Monmouth Coffee Company, Neal's Yard Dairy, the Spanish deli Brindisa or butcher Ginger Pig, and generally bleed the local cash machines dry on Saturday. Plans for a new railway link threaten to cut the market in two, but they seem to have been diverted for several years already.

Brixton

This **market** (Reliance Arcade, Market Row, Electric Lane & Electric Ave SW9; 🕙 8am-6pm Mon-Sat, 8am-3pm Wed; ⊖ Brixton) is a heady, cosmopolitan mix, ranging from the silks, wigs, knock-off fashion, Halal butchers and occasional Christian preacher on Electric Ave to the foodstuffs in the covered Brixton Village (formerly Granville Arcade). Tilapia fish, pig's trotters, yams, mangoes, okra, plantains and Jamaican *bullah* cakes (gingerbread) are just some of the exotic products on sale.

Camden Map pp440-1

Although this **market** (www.camdenlock.net/markets; ⊖ Camden Town) remains a top attraction, its heyday is a distant memory. Commercial tat has long taken over from the truly inventive, although you might find some good retro pieces. The place is busiest at weekends, especially Sunday, when the crowds elbow each other all the way north from Camden Town tube station to Chalk Farm Rd. It's composed of several separate markets, which all tend to merge.

Camden Canal Market (cnr Chalk Farm & Castlehaven Rds NW1; 🕙 10am-6pm Sat & Sun) Further north and just over the canal bridge, Camden Canal Market has bric-a-brac from around the world. If you're pushed for time, this is the bit to skip.

Camden Lock Market (Camden Lock Pl NW1; 🕙 10am-6pm Sat & Sun, indoor stalls 10am-6pm daily) Right next to the canal lock, with diverse food, ceramics, furniture, oriental rugs, musical instruments and designer clothes.

Camden Market (cnr Camden High & Buck Sts NW1; 🕙 9am-5.30pm Thu-Sun) This covered market houses stalls for fashion, clothing, jewellery and tourist tat.

Stables (Chalk Farm Rd NW1; 🕙 8am-6pm Sat & Sun) Just beyond the railway arches, opposite Hartland Rd, the Stables is the best part of the market, with antiques, Asian artefacts, rugs and carpets, pine furniture, and '50s and '60s clothing.

Portobello Road

Perhaps because it's less crowded and littered than Camden, Londoners generally prefer this **market** (Map pp444–5; Portobello Rd W10; 🕙 8am-6pm Mon-Wed, 9am-1pm Thu, 7am-7pm Fri & Sat, 9am-4pm Sun; ⊖ Notting Hill Gate/Ladbroke Grove). Though shops and stalls open daily, the busiest days are Friday, Saturday and Sunday. There's an antiques market on Saturday, and a flea market on Portobello Green on Sunday morning. Fruit and veg are sold all week at the Ladbroke Grove end, with an organic market on Thursday. Antiques, jewellery, paintings and ethnic stuff are concentrated at the Notting Hill Gate end of Portobello Rd. Stalls move downmarket as you move north. Beneath the Westway a vast tent covers more stalls selling cheap clothes, shoes and CDs, while the Portobello Green Arcade is home to some cutting-edge clothing and jewellery designers.

Spitalfields

Primarily, **Spitalfields** (Map pp454-5; Commercial St, btwn Brushfield & Lamb Sts E1; ⊗ 9.30am-5.30pm Sun; ⊖ Liverpool St) had been about snaffling the latest street wear at good prices, with young clothes designers joined by jewellers, furniture makers and a variety of fresh-produce stalls. However, at the time of writing a new restaurant and shopping complex was scheduled to open in mid-2006, hogging a good deal of the space and raising fears that the avant-garde, cutting-edge nature of the place is about to be blunted. We hope not.

Other Markets

Bermondsey (Map pp454-5; Bermondsey Sq; ⊗ 5am-1pm Fri; ⊖ Borough/Bermondsey) Reputedly, it's legal to sell stolen goods here before dawn, but late risers will find this market altogether upright and sedate, with cutlery and other old-fashioned silverware, antique porcelain, paintings, and some costume jewellery.

Berwick Street (Map p450; Berwick St W1; ⊗ 8am-6pm Mon-Sat; ⊖ Piccadilly Circus/Oxford Circus) South of Oxford St and running parallel to Wardour St, this fruit-and-vegetable market is a great place to put together a picnic or shop for a prepared meal.

Brick Lane (Brick Lane E2; ⊗ 8am-1pm Sun; ⊖ Aldgate East) Goods on sale range from clothes, fruit and vegetables to household goods, paintings and bric-a-brac.

Camden Passage (Map pp442-3; Camden Passage N1; ⊗ 7am-2pm Wed, 8am-4pm Sat; ⊖ Angel) Not to be confused with Camden Market, this is a series of four arcades selling antiques and curios, located in Islington, at the junction of Upper St and Essex Rd. Stallholders know their stuff, so bargains are rare. Wednesday is busiest, but it's worth visiting on Sunday for the Islington Farmers Market between 10am and 2pm.

Columbia Road Flower Market (Map pp442-3; Columbia Rd E2; ⊗ 7am-1pm Sun; ⊖ Bethnal Green/rail Cambridge Heath/bus 26, 48 or 55) London's most fragrant market shouldn't be missed. Between Gosset St and the Royal Oak pub merchants lay out their blooms, from everyday geraniums to rare pelargoniums.

Covent Garden (Map p452; ⊖ Covent Garden) The shops in the touristy piazza are open daily, while handicrafts and curios are sold in the North Hall. Antiques and collectables are sold in the Jubilee Hall on Monday before 3pm, and general stalls are laid out Tuesday to Friday, while quality crafts are sold on Saturday and Sunday.

Greenwich (Map p463; College Approach SE10; ⊗ 9am-5pm Thu, 9.30am-5.30pm Sat & Sun; DLR Cutty Sark) Greenwich Market is ideally suited for a relaxed few hours' rummaging through its second-hand household objects, glass, rugs, prints and wooden toys. In between, you can snack on speciality foods in the food court. Thursday is the day for antiques, while the general market is open on weekends. Stores around the market open daily, but weekends are best.

Leadenhall Market (Map pp454-5; Whittington Ave EC1; ⊗ 7am-4pm Mon-Fri; ⊖ Bank) As well as being a small attraction in its own right (see p114), this market, off Gracechurch St, has clothes stores and curio shops, a fishmonger, a butcher and a cheesemonger. As it serves a City clientele, prices tend to be high.

Leather Lane (Map pp442-3; Leather Lane EC1; ⊗ 10.30am-2pm Mon-Fri; ⊖ Chancery Lane/Farringdon) This market south of Clerkenwell Rd, running parallel to Hatton Garden, attracts local office workers with its suspiciously cheap videos, tapes and CDs, household goods and clothing sold by archetypal cockney stallholders.

Petticoat Lane (Map pp454-5; Middlesex & Wentworth Sts E1; ⊗ 8am-2pm Sun, Wentworth St only 9am-2pm Mon-Fri; ⊖ Aldgate/Aldgate East/Liverpool St) The famous lane itself has been renamed Middlesex St. The market, however, soldiers on, selling cheap consumer items and clothes.

Ridley Road (Map pp438-9; Ridley Rd E8; ⊗ 8.30am-6pm Mon-Sat; rail Dalston) As colourful and diverse as the Afro-Caribbean community it serves, this market is best for its exotic fruit and vegetables, as well as specialist cuts of meat.

Riverside Walk (Map pp448-9; Riverside Walk SE1; ⊗ 10am-5pm Sat & Sun; ⊖ Waterloo/Embankment) Great for cheap second-hand books long out of print, this is held in all weather outside the National Film Theatre, under the arches of Waterloo Bridge. In summer it helps the South Bank vaguely resemble Paris' Left Bank. Occasionally, individual dealers set up during the week.

Smithfield (Map pp448-9; West Smithfield EC1; ⊗ 4am-noon Mon-Fri; ⊖ Farringdon) London's last surviving meat market is still clinging on, despite nearly getting the chop for an office development in 2005. While cattle were slaughtered here once, today this is the most modern of its kind in Europe and almost bloodless.

SOUTH LONDON

The biggest retail draw in this district is Brixton Market (p350). However, it's always worth popping into unisex clothes and quirky accessory store **Joy** (Map p462; ☎ 7787 9616; 432 Coldharbour Lane SW11; ✛ Brixton).

In Clapham there are several worthwhile stores near the common, including gift shops **Oliver Bonas** (Map p462; ☎ 7720 8272; www .oliverbonas.com; 23 the Pavement SW4; ✛ Clapham Common) and **Zeitgeist** (☎ 7622 5000; 17 the Pavement SW4; ✛ Clapham Common). Shoe store **Bullfrogs** (☎ 7627 4123; 9 the Pavement SW4; ✛ Clapham Common) is also quite interesting.

Northcote Rd in Wandsworth offers some quality food shopping.

Antique Freaks

Portobello might be London's main antique artery, but the following are also worth checking out:

Lassco (Map pp442-3; ☎ 7749 9944; www .lassco.co.uk; St Michael's Church, Mark St EC2; ✛ Old St) This 'architectural salvage' company occupies a disused church. Most stock – slate tiles, oak floorboards, marble fireplaces, garden equipment – is too big to carry on a plane, but there are some small curios.

London Silver Vaults (Map pp448-9; ☎ 7242 3844; 53-63 Chancery Lane WC2; ✛ Chancery Lane) The world's biggest single concentration of silver, from jewellery to tea services.

SOUTHWEST LONDON

The shopping in Fulham and Parson's Green is uninspiring apart from a few designer furniture and fabric shops, one of the best being **Mufti** (☎ 7610 9123; 789 Fulham Rd SW6; ✛ Parson's Green). For antiques head to the northern end of Munster Rd, or try **North End Road Market** (☼ 9am-5pm Mon-Sat) for fruit and veg, cheap clothing and household goods.

Skip Putney (it's full of grim chains) and head to Church Rd and High St in Barnes. Of the many shops lining these adjoining roads, our picks are **Blue Door** (74 Church Rd), with gorgeous Swedish textiles and home furnishings, and **Tom Foolery** (100 Church Rd), selling contemporary jewellery. Anyone wishing to indulge their ankle-biters could try children's toy shops **Farmyard** (63 Barnes High St), **Bradford** (53 Barnes High St) and **Bug Circus** (153 Church Rd), and the paint-your-own-pottery workshop **Brush & Bisque It** (77 Church Rd).

UP RIVER

Richmond High St is full of chains, but there are some independent stores around. There's **YDUK** (Map p464; ☎ 8940 0060; 4 the Square TW9; ✛ Richmond) for street wear or **Fat Face** (Map p464; ☎ 8332 7912; 38 Hill St TW9; ✛ Richmond) for sports gear. In an enclave of cobbled streets you'll find jewellery stores such as **Toko** (Map p464; ☎ 8332 6620; 18 Brewers Lane TW9; ✛ Richmond).

In Chiswick you can pick up delicious foodstuffs at deli **Mortimer & Bennett** (☎ 8995 4145; 33 Turnham Green Tce W4; ✛ Turnham Green) or at the **Chiswick Farmers and Fine Foods Market** (Masonian Bowls Hall, Duke's Meadow W4; ☼ 10am-2pm Sun; ✛ Turnham Green). Antiques are also a local speciality; try **Strand Antiques** (☎ 8994 1912; 46 Devonshire Rd W4; ✛ Turnham Green) or the **Old Cinema** (☎ 8995 4166; 160 Chiswick High Rd W4; ✛ Turnham Green).

Sleeping

Sleeping

Visitors acquainting themselves with the generally small size and big price tags of London hotel rooms might not immediately realise it, but the city's accommodation scene has improved dramatically. Prices have dropped slightly following a few years of lower-than-average demand and there is now something of a miniboom in hotel building, with thousands of new rooms expected before the decade's end. Ten years after Swedish furniture chain Ikea exhorted British households to 'chuck out your chintz', it also seems London's hoteliers have finally got the message. Where *grande dames* such as the Waldorf and Browns have led the way in adopting a more contemporary look, scores of midrange hotels and B&Bs have followed.

At one end of the spectrum, upmarket boutique hotels have brought a real sense of excitement and style to the city's digs. At the other, companies have found a niche in the market providing boringly functional but affordable rooms. However, one of the most heartening recent trends has been the convergence of these two extremes in a new crop of 'budget boutique' hotels, providing a hint of chic at a reasonable price.

None of this is to deny that this is still one of the costliest places on the planet to book a room. Nor should you expect to get anywhere near the same value for your money as in other world cities. But if you choose carefully – looking for online discounts, booking ahead in summer or taking advantage of last-minute offers at other times – you might find the situation far better than the city's reputation would suggest.

Which London?

Where you shelter will have a huge bearing on the image of London you'll take home, so geography should be as important a consideration as comfort, style or expense. Base yourself in the West End and you'll soon get into the throbbing rhythm of London at play. Hoxton, Clerkenwell and Shoreditch are where it's at right now, and there are a few good places to stay here at London's cutting edge. If royal London's your reason for visiting, get close to the Windsors around St James's. For traditional London and the whiff of aristocracy, make Knightsbridge or Mayfair your domain. Newer money and a sense for fashion go together in Chelsea and Notting Hill, while the comfortably well off live quietly around Maida Vale and Primrose Hill. If you want to feel how most Londoners live, you might hang out in Camden or the Northern Heights – if you don't care how Londoners live, you might pause with the travelling circus in Earl's Court and parts of Victoria.

Types of Accommodation

London has a superb range of deluxe hotels (£350-plus per double) and you'll be spoiled for choice with old classics that combine the best in traditional atmosphere and modern comforts. There's also good choice in the 'top end' category (anything from £150 to £350), which offers superior comforts without the prestige. Also in this bracket you'll find many of the boutique and style hotels that have sprung up over the last decade. Below £150 there's a bit of a slide in quality and choice. Although there's an increasing number of terrific places to rest your head without haemorrhaging your hard-earned, it's still not enough. And if you were budgeting to spend less than £100 a night on a double room during the week, let's just say your lodgings won't often provide the most cherished memories of your trip. (On the other hand, you will find some good weekend deals for that price.) In London, cheap means less than £80 per en suite double. This 'cheap sleeps' category includes many formerly residential B&Bs with small rooms, plus a wide range of hostels.

Visit London (☎ 0870 156 6366; www.visitlondon.com) produces a range of free accommodation brochures and also lists options on its website.

APARTMENTS/SERVICED APARTMENTS

If you are visiting for a few weeks or several months, staying in a short-term apartment is the best way to get a sense of living in the city. Many agencies in *Loot* (p413) or other small ads have pretty insalubrious properties; ask to see rooms first. Some better agencies are listed here.

ACCOMMODATION LONDON

☎ 8459 6203; www.acommodationlondon.net; s/d £55/75, cheaper long-stay rates

Has some 300 studio flats and rooms in shared houses for foreign-passport holders (only) in the Willesden Green area. Clean and well-equipped properties, decent prices, popular with younger travellers.

ASTON'S APARTMENTS

☎ 7590 6000; www.astons-apartments.com; s/d/tr/f from £75/105/145/195

The company has three well-located Victorian town houses, divided into serviced apartments of varying sizes.

CITADINES

☎ 0800 376 3898; www.citadines.com; s £75-175, d £140-245

Has apartment blocks throughout the city, some of them slightly older.

FRASER FURNISHED RESIDENCES

☎ 7341 5599; www.fraserhospitality.com; apt sleeping up to 4/6 people £185/320

Luxury serviced apartments in the heart of Canary Wharf. Has longer-stay properties.

UPTOWN RESERVATIONS

☎ 7937 2001; www.uptownres.co.uk; s/d £75/95, apt per week from £550

Offers short-let apartments or B&B accommodation in stylish private homes, most in central or west London.

LONG-TERM RENTALS

Despite gently falling rents over the past few years, most newcomers to the city still find leasing expensive. At the very bottom end, bedsits (£300 to £500 per month) are single furnished rooms, usually with a shared bathroom and kitchen, and they are always pretty grim. A step up is a self-contained studio (£500-plus), which normally has a separate bathroom and kitchen. You'll rarely get a two-bedroom flat for less than £1000. Shared houses and flats generally offer the best value, anywhere from £300 and upwards for a room. Most landlords demand a security deposit (normally one month's rent) plus a month's rent in advance.

To get abreast of current prices, consult the classifieds in publications such as *Loot, TNT, Time Out* and the *Evening Standard*'s Wednesday supplement *Homes & Property*. Capital Flat Share is a free service run by **Capital Radio** (☎ 7484 8000), which collects lists of people willing to share their flats (deadline 6pm Monday) and publishes the list in the *Guide,* an entertainment-listings magazine that comes with Saturday's *Guardian*.

Booking Offices & Other Resources

The London tourist organisation **Visit London** (☎ 0870 156 6366; www.visitlondon.com; ⊙ 9am-5.30pm Mon-Fri, 10am-2pm Sat) offers a free booking service and always has special deals. There's also the **British Hotel Reservation Centre** (☎ 7340 1616; www.bhrconline.com; ⊙ 24hr), which has kiosks at Gatwick Airport, Heathrow Airport and Paddington, Waterloo and Victoria stations. There's also a kiosk on the mezzanine level of the Britain Visitor Centre.

You can book a hostel through the **YHA central reservations system** (☎ 0870 8818; lonres@yha .org.uk). If you want to stay in a B&B or private home, reservations can be made through the following agencies.

AT HOME IN LONDON

☎ 8748 1943; www.athomeinlondon.co.uk; s/d/tr/f from £40/60/80/100

This is worth looking at if you're considering staying two to four weeks, as some properties have weekly rates and minimum stays. However, nightly rentals are more common.

LONDON BED & BREAKFAST AGENCY

☎ 7586 2768; www.londonbb.com; per person £25-45

Offering spare rooms in London homes. You share with the homeowner, many of whom tend to be of a mature age. Properties are concentrated in central, north and southwest London.

LONDON HOMESTEAD SERVICES

☎ 7286 5115; www.lhslondon.com; per person £20-40

Small family-run business offering the usual B&B rooms in Londoners' homes.

Top Five Designer Dens

- **Baglioni** (p364)
- **Hazlitt's** (left)
- **Number 5 Maddox Street** (p363)
- **Soho Hotel** (below)
- **Zetter** (p361)

THE WEST END

You're really at the hub of London life here, where you won't have to worry about running for the last tube home. The city's theatreland, as well some of its best dining and drinking, is right on your doorstep, as are major attractions from the British Museum to the National Gallery.

SOHO

COURTHOUSE HOTEL Map p450   Hotel

☎ 7297 5555; www.courthouse-hotel.com; 19-21 Great Marlborough St W1; r from £295, ste from £590; ⊖ Oxford Circus; ✴

Oscar Wilde, John Lennon, Keith Richards and Mick Jagger all made appearances in this former magistrate's court, which is now a luxury hotel. As well as all the usual features you'd expect, including a spa and pool, it offers the more offbeat opportunity to dine in a magnificently wood-panelled former courtroom. Even weirder, you can sip champagne in the three refurbished Ladies Cells, where the original Victorian lavatories have been transformed into ice-buckets. Even the roof terrace seems like a footnote after this.

HAZLITT'S Map p450   Hotel

☎ 7434 1771; www.hazlittshotel.com; 6 Frith St W1; standard d £250, Baron Willoughby's ste £355; ⊖ Tottenham Court Rd; ✴

This characterful crib is a literature lover's dream. It consists of three 18th-century terraced houses, including one where the great essayist William Hazlitt lived. Since then the likes of Jonathan Swift, Ted Hughes, JK Rowling and Bill Bryson have all rested their heads here. Bedrooms boast a wealth of seductive details, including mahogany four-poster beds, Victorian claw-foot tubs, sumptuous fabrics, winsomely wonky floors and genuine antiques. This is a listed building so there's no lift. Some of the rooms aren't large, but look at the quality!

SOHO HOTEL Map p450   Hotel

☎ 7559 3000; www.firmdale.com; 4 Richmond Mews W1; standard s/d £275/295, ste from £465; ⊖ Tottenham Court Rd; ✴

Talk about going straight to the top of the class! This hotel was just over six months old when *Condé Nast Traveller* magazine declared it one of the world's 60 coolest. It's also the best-looking former car park we've ever seen. All the hallmarks of the eclectically chic Firmdale brand have been writ large over 91 individually designed rooms. Granite bathrooms and patterned dressmakers' dummies make a thematic reappearance, but the black cat sculpture is bigger, the colours are brighter and there are torso-shaped 'body lamps'. In a quiet mews off central Dean St, the Soho has va-va-voom meeting rooms and hi-tech screening cinemas to appeal to surrounding film and advertising companies, and a popular bar/restaurant, Refuel.

COVENT GARDEN, LEICESTER SQUARE & HOLBORN

COVENT GARDEN HOTEL Map p452 Hotel

☎ 7806 1000; www.firmdale.com; 10 Monmouth St WC2; standard s/d from £210/255, loft ste £895; ⊖ Covent Garden/Tottenham Court Rd; ✴

Combining gorgeous graphics, Asian fabrics and English warmth, this hospital-turned-charming-boutique-hotel is still one of the finest places to stay in London. There are also two splendid and charming restaurants, and the Firmdale chain's trademarks of style, comfort and service are all here in spades.

FIELDING HOTEL Map p452 *Hotel*
☎ 7836 8305; www.the-fielding-hotel.co.uk; 4 Broad Ct, Bow St WC2; s/d from £75/100; ⊖ Covent Garden
You can almost feel the pulse of the West End at this hotel, located in a pedestrianised court in the heart of Covent Garden. It was named after the novelist Henry Fielding (1707–54) who lived on the street. Space is at a premium and the décor is shop bought, but it's an excellent location if you want to take in a lot of London in just a few days.

KINGSWAY HALL Map p452 *Hotel*
☎ 7309 0909; www.kingswayhall.co.uk; Great Queen St WC2; standard s/d from £230/255, breakfast extra £12-16, weekend rate incl breakfast £165; ⊖ Holborn; 😵
Tipping its cap fairly determinedly at the professional traveller, Kingsway nonetheless manages to provide smart, comfortable and very central lodgings for anyone with less business and more play on their mind. The atmosphere is more relaxed on the weekend, when rates are considerably cheaper and the fitness centre's not full of barrel-chested types on schedules.

ONE ALDWYCH Map p452 *Hotel*
☎ 7300 1000; www.onealdwych.co.uk; 1 Aldwych WC2; s/d £370/395, ste from £630; ⊖ Covent Garden/Charing Cross; 😵
Luxurious and trendy, One Aldwych has spacious, stylish rooms replete with raw silk curtains, natural tones and modern art, along with bathtubs big enough for two. The highly regarded Axis Restaurant & Bar hosts jazz midweek and is a place to be seen, while the health club and pool are superb for preparing to be seen.

ST MARTIN'S LANE Map p452 *Hotel*
☎ 7300 5500, 0800 634 5500; www.ianschragerhotels.com; 45 St Martin's Lane; standard s/d £230/255, garden r £340, ste from £580; ⊖ Covent Garden/Leicester Sq; 😵
This joint effort between international hotelier Ian Schrager and French designer Philippe Starck is so cool you'd hardly notice it was there. Rooms have floor-to-ceiling windows with sweeping West End views, the public rooms are bustling meeting points, and everything (and everyone) is beautiful. Unquestionably the best place for lift encounters with supermodels.

SAVOY Map p452 *Hotel*
☎ 7836 4343; www.fairmount.com/savoy; Strand WC2; s/d/ste £360/420/560; ⊖ Charing Cross; 😵
Change is afoot at what's now known as 'Savoy, a Fairmount Hotel'. The new management is launching a £26 million nip and tuck

The Savoy (above)

– at the time of writing expected to start in 2006 – which will concentrate on the Thames Foyer, the restaurant overlooking the river and guest bathrooms. However, some things should never be fiddled with here, and fortunately can't really be, including meticulous service and the views from the 'river rooms', celebrated on canvas by one former guest, a certain Monsieur Monet.

TRAFALGAR HILTON Map p452 *Hotel*
☎ 7870 2900; www.hilton.co.uk/trafalgar; 2 Spring Gardens SW1; standard r £200, ste from £375; ⊖ Charing Cross/Embankment; ▣
The demand for designer digs is so strong in London that even Hilton got in on the act a few years back, with this tastefully minimalist hotel near Trafalgar Sq. Large windows offer some of the greatest views over the square and the cityscape, while the cool and spacious Rockwell bar specialises in more than 80 different types of bourbon (in case views aren't your thing).

WALDORF HILTON Map p452 *Hotel*
☎ 7836 2400; www.hilton.co.uk/waldorf; Aldwych WC2; r from £275, breakfast extra £18, weekend rate incl breakfast £210-260; ⊖ Temple/Covent Garden/Charing Cross; ▣
Owners past and present have combined to wave a £30 million magic wand over the interior of the venerable Waldorf, turning Edwardian splendour into cool modernism. So thorough is the break from the past that the 299 rooms are now divided into either just 'contemporary' or 'design'. ('Design' is slightly trendier, with some weird gold and silver dressmakers' dummies.) The lobby now features grey and red chairs plus an illuminated yellow-glass reception desk. Traditionalists will have to console themselves by peering into the heritage-listed Art Deco–style Palm Court.

BLOOMSBURY & FITZROVIA

ACADEMY HOTEL Map pp448-9 *Hotel*
☎ 7631 4115; www.theetoncollection.com; 21 Gower St WC1; s/d £165/195, breakfast extra £11-15, weekend rate r incl breakfast from £130; ⊖ Goodge St; ▣
Orrrfully English, the Academy is set across five Georgian town houses but has a slight Regency feel. Quality rooms have green and pale-red tones, with fluffy duvets, plump cushions and bolster pillows. There's a conservatory overlooking a leafy back garden with fish pond, while the lobby and downstairs bar/breakfast room look more contemporary.

BLOOMS TOWNHOUSE HOTEL
Map pp448-9 *Hotel*
☎ 7323 1717; www.bloomshotel.com; 7 Montague St WC1; s/d from £145/175; ⊖ Tottenham Court Rd/Russell Sq
This elegant and airy 18th-century town house has the feel of a country home, which belies its position in the heart of London (in what used to be the grounds of the British Museum, in fact). Think floral prints, classical music, a delightful garden and staff who 'really, sorry about this, but if you wouldn't mind, awfully sorry, it's just…'

CHARLOTTE STREET HOTEL
Map p450 *Hotel*
☎ 7806 2000; www.firmdale.com; 15 Charlotte St W1; s/d/ste from £195/230/350; ⊖ Tottenham Court Rd; ▣
Where Laura Ashley goes postmodern and comes up smelling of roses, this is a gem from talented hoteliers and gifted interior designers Tim and Kit Kemp, whose Firmdale chain of small hotels has made London a more beautiful place to stay. The bar buzzes by night, while Oscar restaurant is a delightful spot any time of day, but particularly for afternoon tea.

CRESCENT HOTEL Map pp440-1 *Hotel*
☎ 7387 1515; www.crescenthoteloflondon.com; 49-50 Cartwright Gardens WC1; s £55-80, d £95, s with shared bathroom £50; ⊖ Russell Sq
In the middle of academic London, this friendly, family-owned hotel overlooks a private square flanked by student residences. While the rooms range from pokey singles without facilities to relatively spacious doubles with bathrooms, all are clean and comfortable.

HARLINGFORD HOTEL Map pp440-1 *Hotel*
☎ 7387 1551; www.harlingfordhotel.com; 61-63 Cartwright Gardens WC1; s/d/tr/f £80/100/110/115; ⊖ Russell Sq
With its 'H' logo proudly sewn on your bedroom pillows, and a modern interior design with lots

of burgundy and mauve, this revamped Georgian hotel is enjoying a new lease of life. There's still no lift, the green-tiled bathrooms remain small and the Harlingford has a long way to go before it features in *Wallpaper** magazine, but everything's a lot more photogenic here now, especially the guest lounge and breakfast room. Definitely the best on this street.

JENKINS HOTEL Map pp440-1 *Hotel*
☎ 7387 2067; www.jenkinshotel.demon.co.uk; 45 Cartwright Gardens WC1; s £55-75, d £85; ⊖ Russell Sq
Also close to the British Museum, this smoke-free hotel has decent rooms and a friendly welcome. All prices include a full English breakfast, which you are welcome to work off on the tennis courts across the road.

MORGAN HOTEL Map p452 *Hotel*
☎ 7636 3735; 24 & 40 Bloomsbury St WC1; d from £100, ste £130; ⊖ Tottenham Court Rd
In a row of 18th-century Georgian houses alongside the British Museum, this is one of the best midpriced hotels in London, where the warmth and hospitality more than make up for the slightly cramped guest quarters. A recent refurbishment has now been completed and the style is more streamlined. The larger suites are well worth the few extra bob and the double glazing seems to keep out most of the noise from the street.

ST MARGARET'S HOTEL
Map pp448-9 *Hotel*
☎ 7636 4277; www.stmargaretshotel.co.uk; 26 Bedford Pl WC1; s/d £75/95, with shared bathroom £55/65; ⊖ Russell Sq/Holborn
Young and not so young are well catered for at this huge 60-room family-run hotel, which occupies a classic Georgian town house. Rooms are bright and comfortable, and there are relaxing lounges and a lovely rear garden.

SANDERSON Map p450 *Hotel*
☎ 7300 1400; www.ianschragerhotels.com; 50 Berners St W1; standard d from £205, loft ste £500; ⊖ Oxford Circus
Don't be deterred by the nondescript aluminium and glass façade of a 1960s corporate HQ: prolific duo Ian Schrager and Philippe Starck – of St Martin's Lane – are responsible for this 'urban spa', which comes with a lush bamboo-filled garden, artworks and installations, sheets with a 450-thread count and a jumble of personality furniture. It's a little quirky, almost surreal, and gorgeous. Parisian superchef Alain Ducasse continues the theme in Spoon restaurant.

CHEAP SLEEPS

AROSFA Map pp448-9 *Hotel*
☎ 7636 2115; 83 Gower St WC1; s/d £45/66; ⊖ Euston Sq/Goodge St
The rooms might be small and feature prefabricated capsule bathrooms, but Arosfa (Welsh for 'a place to stay') does offer excellent value for such a central location. The place is a breath of fresh air in that smoking is banned. Light sleepers might prefer a room at the back.

ARRAN HOUSE HOTEL Map pp448-9 *Hotel*
☎ 7636 2186; www.arranhotel-london.com; 77-79 Gower St WC1; dm £18.50- 23.50, s/d £55/85, with shared bathroom £45/75; ⊖ Goodge St
This welcoming place in Bloomsbury provides excellent value for the location. Rooms range from basic dormitory-style accommodation to bright well-furnished doubles with bathrooms. The lounge is pleasant, guests can cook for themselves and the atmosphere never feels like anything but a small and welcoming hotel. The rose garden is a bonus in the summer.

HOTEL CAVENDISH Map pp448-9 *Hotel*
☎ 7636 9079; www.hotelcavendish.com; 75 Gower St WC1; s with shared bathroom £42-46, d with shared bathroom £50-70; ⊖ Goodge St
Run by an amiable family, this hotel has simple purple and burgundy rooms, along with a pleasant walled garden and a reasonable English cooked breakfast (included in the price). If the Cavendish is full, you'll be referred to its sister hotel, the Jesmond, nearby, with similar rates and standards.

OXFORD ST YHA Map p450 *Hostel*
☎ 7734 1618; oxfordst@yha.org.uk; 3rd fl, 14 Noel St W1; dm £18.20-22.50; ⊖ Oxford Circus/Tottenham Court Rd
The most central of London's hostels is basic, clean, welcoming and loud. There is a large kitchen but no meals are served apart from a packed breakfast. Most of the 75 beds are in twin rooms.

RIDGEMOUNT HOTEL Map pp448-9 *Hotel*
☎ 7636 1141; www.ridgemounthotel.co.uk; 65-67 Gower St WC1; s/d/tr/f £50/55/80/95, with shared bathroom £40/50/70/85; ⊖ Goodge St
This old-fashioned hotel offers a warmth and consideration that you don't come across very often in the city these days. About half of its 30 utilitarian rooms have bathrooms. Rates include a decent breakfast, and there's a laundry.

EAST CENTRAL

Staying in this area gives you the chance to see London from the other side. While the West End is perpetually overrun with crowds, the city is refreshingly quiet on weekends, yet offers easy access to such attractions as the Tower of London. In Clerkenwell, Hoxton and Shoreditch, you're close to the hip clubs, bars, restaurants and shops of one of London's most happening scenes.

THE CITY

GRANGE CITY HOTEL Map pp454-5 *Hotel*
☎ 7233 7888; www.grangehotels.co.uk; 10 Coopers Row EC3; r from £260; ⊖ Tower Hill; 🖭

Many of the rooms in this classy, five-star city hotel have close-up views of Tower Bridge and the Tower of London, and it's popular with conference guests and tourists alike. Be aware that few restaurants and shops are open in the immediate area on weekends. However, because that's also a quiet period for the hotel, rooms might go for as little £80 on Friday and Saturday nights. Check the website for special deals, or ring the Grange Hotels central reservations number listed here.

THREADNEEDLES Map pp454-5 *Hotel*
☎ 7657 8080; www.theetoncollection.com; 5 Threadneedle St EC2; r from £355, breakfast extra £16-25, weekend rate incl breakfast £195; ⊖ Bank; 🖭

The centrepiece of this discreetly located boutique hotel is its grand circular lobby, which is furnished in a vaguely Art Deco style and covered with a 19th-century hand-painted glass dome. Rooms in this converted bank are just as elegant – richly coloured blankets over duvets and monogrammed pillows are complemented by light, sandy-coloured bathrooms and arty photography. Weekend rates at Threadneedles are more affordable, although there have been some reports about limited staff numbers during those periods.

HOXTON, SHOREDITCH & SPITALFIELDS

GREAT EASTERN HOTEL
Map pp454-5 *Hotel*
☎ 7618 5010; www.great-eastern-hotel.co.uk; Liverpool St EC1; s/d from £265/335; ⊖ /rail Liverpool St; 🖭

While the dark-wood lobby still has a masculine feel, this stylish hotel has been softening the décor in some of its rooms. More whites and blues are in evidence, alongside the older dark wood and red earth tones. The aim is to attract more guests on weekends, when rates (for doubles only, excluding breakfast) drop to £140.

HOTEL SAINT GREGORY
Map pp442-3 *Hotel*
☎ 7613 9800; www.hotelsaintgregory.co.uk; 100 Shoreditch High St EC1; s/d £199/229; ⊖ /rail Liverpool St; 🖭

The modern Hotel Saint Gregory is winning guests over to the not immediately obvious delights of busy Shoreditch High St. A few minutes' bus ride from Liverpool St train station, close to the nightlife of Hoxton and the shopping of Spitalfields, its pale rooms have burnt-sienna blankets and furnishings, plus very stylish bathrooms. Staff can take a while to warm up, though, and it's a much more attractive proposition if you get a cheap online rate (at the time of writing around £80 for a double). Don't forget to pop in to the rooftop Globe Bar and Restaurant for spectacular views.

CLERKENWELL

MALMAISON Map pp448-9 *Hotel*
☎ 7012 3700; Charterhouse Sq EC1; r from £160, weekend rate from £100; ⊖ Farringdon; 🖭

Less than a minute from the hustle and bustle of Charterhouse St (near Smithfield meat market), this contemporary hotel sits on a quiet and leafy square among historic buildings. Public areas are moodily low-lit; rooms are colour-by-numbers hip. The relatively small size of the cheapest rooms proves more tolerable than you first imagine.

ROOKERY Map pp448-9 *Hotel*
☎ 7336 0931; www.rookeryhotel.com; Peter's Lane, Cowcross St EC1; s/d from £275/300, weekend rate r from £150; ⊖ Farringdon

This higgledy-piggledy warren of 33 rooms at the Rookery is kind of Dickens gone designer, with the period charm of its restored

Sleeping – East Central

Victorian bathrooms and furnishings attracting the in set. Two highlights are the small city garden and the two-storey Rook's Nest suite (£465), where the ceiling/floor slides back and forth.

ZETTER Map pp448-9   *Hotel*

☎ 7324 4444; www.thezetter.com; 86-88 Clerkenwell Rd; r from £190, breakfast extra £9-16, weekend rate incl breakfast £130; ✪ Farringdon

Mixing the homely comforts of knitted hot-water bottle covers, blankets decorated with Zzzzs and vintage Penguin books with Internet access via the hi-tech flat screens, this well-positioned establishment is miles more stylish and versatile than you'd expect from the owners of Sainsbury's supermarkets. Zetter's crescent-shaped restaurant is hip and trendy, but we also recommend taking in an intimate afternoon tea (free-range egg and anchovy sandwiches, Aussie lamingtons and more) in the retro, horseshoe-shaped atrium lounge.

CHEAP SLEEPS
CITY OF LONDON YHA

Map pp448-9   *Hostel*

☎ 7236 4965; city@yha.org.uk; 36 Carter Lane EC4; 3-15 bed dm £17-26, s £32, 2-6 bed f £55-150; ✪ St Paul's

Clean, quiet and yet very close to St Paul's Cathedral, the only odd thing about this 193-bed hostel is that some bunk beds are at right angles over each other, so, with your feet covered, you sometimes feel like you're sleeping in a half-open drawer. The whole place is nonsmoking.

LONDON CITY YMCA Map pp442-3   *Hostel*

☎ 7628 8832; www.londoncityy.org; 8 Errol St EC1; s with shared bathroom £34, tw £55; ✪ Barbican

Much nicer than its nearby Barbican counterpart, this has better bathrooms and newer bedrooms with TVs and phones for incoming calls. It's very handy for the Shoreditch and Hoxton areas, but you should book about one month ahead.

The Rookery (opposite)

WEST CENTRAL

This is where London's most splendid deluxe digs are located, hotels so grand that many of them are tourist attractions in their own right. Great views over Hyde Park and opulent rooms offering every luxury, and then some, are there for those wishing to splash out. Accommodation is more modest in Victoria and Pimlico, but you are near major transport links.

MAYFAIR & ST JAMES'S

BROWN'S Map p450 *Hotel*
☎ 0870 458 4050; www.brownshotel.com; 30 Albemarle St W1; s/d from £325; ⊖ Green Park; ⌗

This grand hotel reopened in late 2005 after a £19 million renovation to add new technology (flat-screen TVs, videos on demand, broadband, wi-fi and more) and give the place modern flair. Some traditional features have been retained, however, with stained-glass windows, Edwardian oak panelling, working fireplaces and gilt mirrors remaining in the public areas. The 117 updated rooms have soft colours and works by young English artists. However, each retains one antique.

CHESTERFIELD Map pp448-9 *Hotel*
☎ 7491 2622; www.redcarnationhotels.com; 35 Charles St W1; s/d/ste from £265/350/465, breakfast extra £19; ⊖ Green Park; ⌗

Just a block from Berkeley Sq, the Chesterfield comprises five floors of refinement and lustre hidden behind a fairly plain Georgian town house. It has ceilings with mouldings, marble floors and period-style furnishings as you'd expect from one of the grand dames of London digs. Bonuses are the lush and lovely Conservatory restaurant, themed suites (such as the musical one featuring instruments and other paraphernalia), doggy meals for spoilt pooches and outstanding value for money.

CLARIDGE'S Map pp448-9 *Hotel*
☎ 7629 8860; www.claridges.co.uk; Brook St W1; s/d/ste from £460/495/740, breakfast extra £26; ⊖ Bond St; ⌗

Thankfully the designers who moved in in the late 1990s decided to keep the décor of a bygone era. So this brilliant five-star hotel retains many Art Deco overtones, from the entrance portico right down to the green and white china. The new 800-piece hand-blown glass chandelier by Dale Chihuly in the foyer also blends in. Celebrated chef Gordon Ramsay reigns over the kitchen (p245), while the bar is *the* place to sip martinis whether you're a paying guest or not.

CONNAUGHT Map pp448-9 *Hotel*
☎ 7499 7070; www.theconnaughthotellondon.com; Carlos Pl W1; s/d from £410/465, breakfast extra £18-26; ⊖ Green Park; ⌗

The Connaught steadfastly refuses to cut its clothes to suit this year's fashion and concentrates on its tried-and-tested formula of yesteryear style, coddling comforts and legendary hospitality. Think crystal chandeliers, antiques, gilt frames, mahogany panelling, Wedgwood and guests who never stray far from the lap of comfort. Promotional weekend rates are available, but vary widely.

DORCHESTER Map pp448-9 *Hotel*
☎ 7629 8888; www.dorchesterhotel.com; Park Lane W1; s/d from £375/475, breakfast £20-25, ste incl breakfast from £740; ⊖ Hyde Park Cnr; ⌗

There's no better place to play the recalcitrant rich kid than this most lavish of London foyers, where monumental floral arrangements and faux-marble columns dominate. Elizabeth Taylor and Richard Burton honeymooned at the 'Dorch', but today many guests will be mooning over the technology. With all the modern tools of business and entertainment at your disposal, you can often work your way through the menu from the comfort of your huge four-poster bed. There are even special 'e-butlers' should it all become too difficult.

METROPOLITAN Map pp448-9 *Hotel*
☎ 7447 1000; www.metropolitan.co.uk; 19 Old Park Lane W1; r from £305, breakfast extra £24, ste incl breakfast from £490, weekend rate r incl breakfast £195; ⊖ Hyde Park Cnr; ⌗

In the same stable as the Halkin, the 155-room Metropolitan is another minimalist hotel – 'stripped of nonessentials' (as they say) and decorated in shades of cream and muesli – that attracts a supertrendy, well-heeled crowd (more rock star than royal, really). The hotel's Japanese restaurant **Nobu** (p246) is outstanding. The Met Bar's day as the nocturnal in-scene for the glitterati has passed although it's still difficult to get in without looking the part.

Top Five Grand Hotels

- Claridge's (opposite)
- Dorchester (opposite)
- Lanesborough (p366)
- Ritz (below)
- Savoy (p357)

NUMBER 5 MADDOX STREET

Map p450 *Hotel*

☎ 7647 0200; 5 Maddox St W1; ste £295-730;
✆ Victoria; ⊠

This hotel achieves its stated aim to provide a contemporary, urban sanctuary with considerable élan – they make you feel more like you're 'super styling' in your own rented pad than staying in a hotel. On show are Eastern themes, natural tones and an exquisite eye for detail along with all the technical facilities the contemporary traveller could require, including free broadband Internet connection in every room.

RITZ Map pp448-9 *Hotel*

☎ 7493 8181; www.theritzlondon.com; 150 Piccadilly W1; s/d/ste from £435/620/940; ✆ Green Park; ⊠

Celebrating its 100th birthday in 2006, the original ritzy establishment remains as opulent as ever. Such is its unyielding cred that even the new generation of cultural elite can't get enough of it. The rooms are blue, peach, pink and yellow rococo boudoirs, and the Long Gallery and Palm Court restaurant also have a Louis XVI theme. Book weeks ahead if you want to sample afternoon tea (£34) and, because discreet attendants patrol the lobby to keep out the riff-raff, don't forget to put on your top hat and white tie…(and most importantly a jacket).

SANCTUARY HOUSE HOTEL

Map pp460-1 *Hotel*

☎ 7799 4044; sanctuary@fullers.co.uk; 33 Tothill St SW1; standard/superior d £135/150; ✆ St James's Park

A cut above your average pub hotel, the Sanctuary lives up to its name, although it's just a few minutes' walk from Westminster Abbey and the Houses of Parliament. The style is very much cosy English country cottage and some of the refurbished superior rooms even contain four-poster beds. Rates don't include breakfast, but that can be whisked to your pub table for a mere £5 to £10 extra.

VICTORIA & PIMLICO

CITY INN Map pp460-1 *Hotel*

☎ 7630 1000; www.cityinn.com; 30 John Islip St SW1; r £90-200; ✆ Victoria/Pimlico; ⊠

This large new hotel overlooking the Thames is handy for Labour spin-doctors, spooks from neighbouring MI5 and MI6, and conspiracy theorists. (Are those businesspeople working away on their wi-fi laptops in the opulently red Millbank Lounge government moles? Or perhaps one of the diners in the airy, stylish restaurant is a spy?) The rooms are uncomplicatedly modern, with big, fluffy white duvets and pillows, black armchairs and blond wood. Staff say the 18in-thick concrete walls provide excellent soundproofing, but fail to mention whether they prevent electronic eavesdropping too. Book for a room with a view.

DOLPHIN SQUARE HOTEL

Map pp460-1 *Hotel*

☎ 7798 3800; www.dolphinsquarehotel.co.uk; Chichester St SW1; studio £185, 1-/2-bed ste from £205/260; ✆ Pimlico

With its 400m-long corridors, sunken Art Deco restaurant and subtle maritime themes, this legendary hotel in a 1930s mansion house feels like a cruise ship. Its 'cabins' are slightly old-fashioned but generously sized. All come with kitchenettes, making it popular with longer-stay guests. One of the largest pools in London also attracts families to this quiet location on weekends. And if swimming isn't your thing, pop into the magnificent landscaped square behind the building for a game of croquet.

MORGAN HOUSE Map pp460-1 *Hotel*

☎ 7730 2384; www.morganhouse.co.uk; 120 Ebury St SW1; d/tr/f £86/110/125, s/d with shared bathroom £46/66; ✆ Victoria

The Morgan House might be humble but it knows how to do pretty, with small bunches of fresh flowers placed in rooms using white or blue/mauve tones. The options range from a compact but livable single to a family room with teddy bears placed on the kids' bunk bed. Two doubles with en suites, No 2 and No 8, are at the back and the best in the house.

WINDERMERE HOTEL Map pp460-1 *Hotel*

☎ 7834 5163; www.windermere-hotel.co.uk; 142-144 Warwick Way SW1; s/d from £90/£105, with shared bathroom £70/90; ✆ Victoria

The award-winning Windermere has 22 small, singularly designed and spotless rooms in a

Sleeping – West Central

Brown's hotel (p362)

sparkling, white mid-Victorian town house that offers character and warmth in an area not exactly renowned for such. There's a reliable and reasonably priced restaurant on site.

CHELSEA & BELGRAVIA

41 Map pp460-1 *Hotel*
☎ 7300 0041; www.redcarnationhotels.com; 41 Buckingham Palace Rd SW1; r £290, split-level ste from £405; ✚ Victoria; ⊠
If you're not likely to get a call-up for Buckingham Palace itself, you can console yourself by getting the royal treatment at this nearby club-style hotel, which offers 20 classically designed black-and-white rooms. You have the services of two full-time butlers working around the clock, 24-hour hot and cold buffets, and all the usual business facilities.

B+B BELGRAVIA Map pp460-1 *B&B*
☎ 7730 8513; www.bb-belgravia.com; 64-66 Ebury St SW1; s/d/f £90/95/115; ✚ Victoria
Stunningly remodelled in contemporary style, this place looks even better in real life than it does on the website. There's a chic black-and-white lounge, lots of frosted glass and a breakfast bar, as well as tables, where you can sit comfortably of a morning if you're on your own. The earth-toned rooms aren't enormous, but they're big enough and have flat-screen TVs. One room is equipped for disabled access, all have 24-hour Internet access, and there's a

phonecard system to, refreshingly, keep the price of calls down. As if all this wasn't enough, the welcoming staff really know what they're doing.

LOWNDES HOTEL Map pp444-5 *Hotel*
☎ 7823 1234; www.lowndeshotel.com; 21 Lowndes St SW1; r from £195; ✚ Knightsbridge; ⊠
'Elegant' and 'intimate' are two words constantly used to describe this well-located boutique hotel, which is pretty funny considering the proprietors also own the world's most overblown hotel – Dubai's Jumeriah Beach. Whereas that establishment looks like a giant sail and has cream-cake rich décor, the Lowndes has subtle white and brown tones. It also enjoys a reputation for excellent service and tasty breakfasts.

TOPHAMS BELGRAVIA Map pp460-1 *Hotel*
☎ 7730 8147; www.zolahotels.com; 28 Ebury St SW1; s/d from £115/130; ✚ Victoria
Another traditional English hotel is tossing out its floral bedspreads, as the venerable Tophams gets a makeover during 2006 in favour of more contemporary design. But the hotel will be staying open throughout the refurbishment, during which you could still find yourself in one of the cute granny-like rooms.

KNIGHTSBRIDGE, SOUTH KENSINGTON & HYDE PARK

ASTER HOUSE Map pp444-5 *B&B*
☎ 7581 5888; www.asterhouse.com; 2 Sumner Pl SW7; s £70-100, d & tw £135-180; ✚ South Kensington; ⊠
What's made the Aster House the winner of Visit London's best B&B award not just once but several times? The quintessential English aura, the friendly staff, the comfortable rooms, the reasonable price or the lovely garden with its duck pond? All these put together, plus the leafy 1st-floor conservatory that acts as the breakfast room. The entire place is non-smoking.

BAGLIONI Map pp444-5 *Hotel*
☎ 7368 5700; www.baglionihotellondon.com; 60 Hyde Park Gate W1; r from £335, ste from £590; ✚ South Kensington/High St Kensington; ⊠
This luxury Italian hotel overlooking Kensington Gardens has raised an ostentatiously bejewelled finger to modish minimalism, with its baroque lobby (black chandeliers, gold

ceiling and big flowers) and opulent low-lit rooms. Polished hardwood floors, taupe walls, black lacquered furniture, scarlet-striped sofas, black-and-white prints of Italian film stars and lots of gold tones are complemented by fabulous black, mirrored bathrooms. In the bar downstairs, beautiful young things live *la dolce vita* after an afternoon's shopping in nearby Kensington or Knightsbridge.

BASIL ST HOTEL Map pp444-5 *Hotel*
☎ 7581 3311; www.thebasil.com; Basil St SW3; s/d from £155/230; ⊖ Knightsbridge
This family-owned hotel has been taking care of guests for almost a century. It's a lovely, antique-stuffed hideaway in the heart of Knightsbridge, perfectly placed for carrying heavy bags back from Harrods, Harvey Nicks or Sloane St. It's decidedly low-tech – baths instead of showers, no lifts etc – but it's a delightful vision of little England in big London.

BLAKES Map pp458-9 *Hotel*
☎ 7370 6701; www.blakeshotels.com; 33 Roland Gardens SW7; s/d/ste from £200/325/665, breakfast extra £15-25; ⊖ Gloucester Rd; 🖳
Five Victorian houses were knocked into one to create London's original boutique, opened by designer Anouska Hempel in the 1970s. Rooms are elegantly decked out and individually wrapped with four-poster beds, rich fabrics and antiques. They are gorgeous, if sometimes a little impractical (beds facing away from the TV for example). It's renowned as the stars' hideout from the paparazzi.

CADOGAN HOTEL Map pp444-5 *Hotel*
☎ 7235 7141; 75 Sloane St SW1; r from £290, ste from £425, breakfast extra £15-20; ⊖ Sloane Sq; 🖳
Apart from the Soho Hotel, these were the only other digs in London to be deemed among the world's 60 coolest by *Condé Nast Traveller*. That's thanks to the 2004 makeover that has added fabulously contemporary rooms to this wonderful 65-bedroom town house that's famed for its excellent service.

FIVE SUMNER PLACE Map pp458-9 *Hotel*
☎ 7584 7586; www.sumnerplace.com; 5 Sumner Pl SW7; s/d £100/155; ⊖ South Kensington
Similar to, but not quite as attractive as, its neighbour the Aster, this hotel has 13 well-equipped rooms and a light, airy breakfast room. The singles are quite compact and there are only little showers in most of the bathrooms.

GORE 190 Map pp444-5 *Hotel*
☎ 7584 6601; www.gorehotel.co.uk; 189-190 Queen's Gate SW7; s/d from £185/200, breakfast extra £11-17; ⊖ Gloucester Rd; 🖳
Charismatically kooky, slightly threadbare and irresistibly romantic, this 54-room hotel is a veritable palace of polished mahogany, Turkish carpets, bronze statues, antique-style bathrooms, aspidistras, thousands of portraits and prints, and a great bar. The dark-panelled Tudor Room (£345) is gorgeous, with stained glass and a four-poster bed. The attached Bistrot 190 is a wonderful place for brunch.

HALKIN Map pp448-9 *Hotel*
☎ 7333 1000; www.halkin.co.uk, 5 Halkin St SW1; r from £375, ste from £580, breakfast extra £18-23; ⊖ Hyde Park Cnr; 🖳
The 41-room Halkin is for business travellers of a minimalist bent: lots of burl wood, marble and round glass things. Bedrooms are wood-panelled and stylishly uncluttered; staff strut about in Armani uniforms.

HOTEL 167 Map pp458-9 *Hotel*
☎ 7373 0672; www.hotel167.com; 167 Old Brompton Rd SW5; s £80-95, d £110; ⊖ Gloucester Rd
The new paint job on the outside of this hotel only makes the quirky interior seem more shabby than chic. Likewise, service is reportedly a mixed bag. All said, however, this is a pleasant enough hotel for a short stay. The location is certainly handy, even if the hotel has no lift.

Shameless

London's hotels have witnessed all sorts of rock 'n' roll shenanigans, from tantrums thrown by spoilt guests to TVs thrown from windows. So, just for the record, where did…

- Oscar Wilde get arrested in 1895 for his 'friendship' with Lord Alfred Douglas? Room 118, **Cadogan Hotel** (left).
- Prince Philip hold his stag do before his marriage to the Queen? The **Dorchester** (p362).
- The maid allegedly pull the plug on the champagne bath that Johnny Depp poured for Kate Moss? Room 16, **Portobello Hotel** (p373).
- Boris Becker have a quickie in a broom cupboard with Angela Ermakova that sired a daughter in 1999? The **Metropolitan** (p362).
- Babyshambles and ex-Libertines singer Pete Doherty get arrested for reportedly assaulting a filmmaker in 2005? The **Rookery** (p360).

KNIGHTSBRIDGE HOTEL

Map pp458-9 *Hotel*

☎ 7584 6300; 10 Beaufort Gardens SW3; www.firm dale.com; s/d from £175/215, ste £390, breakfast extra £15; ⊖ Knightsbridge

Another masterpiece from the Kemps, this hotel occupies a 200-year-old house just around the corner from Harrods and has elegant and beautiful interiors done in a sumptuous, subtle and modern English style. Some of the rooms, although beautifully furnished, are too small for the price so you might want to check when booking. There's a self-service 'honesty bar' in a pleasant study and capable staff.

LANESBOROUGH Map pp448-9 *Hotel*

☎ 7259 5599; www.lanesborough.com; Hyde Park Cnr; d from £490; ⊖ Hyde Park Cnr; ⊠

This is where visiting divas doze and Regency opulence meets state-of-the-art technology. The three-bedroom Royal Suite, the most expensive digs in town, comes with a chauffeured Bentley and costs £5875, although you could probably get a couple of quid off if you haggle. The staff, as you might expect, are as helpful as they are impeccably dressed.

L' HOTEL Map pp444-5 *B&B*

☎ 7589 6286; www.capital-london.net/lhotel -lemetro; 28 Basil St SW3; s/d from £185/215; ⊖ Knightsbridge

There seems to be nothing but praise for this small slice of Paris in Knightsbridge, a family-run town-house hotel in a brilliant location that doesn't need to shout about its comforts. There's an old-fashioned lace-iron lift, which leads to rooms decorated in a French country style (patterned wallpaper, pine furniture and window shutters). Breakfast is served in the basement bar. If you arrive late at night you'll have to check in at the Capital Hotel, two doors down.

NUMBER SIXTEEN Map pp458-9 *Hotel*

☎ 7589 5232; www.numbersixteenhotel.co.uk; 16 Sumner Pl SW7; s/d from £115/200, breakfast extra £10-11; ⊖ South Kensington

With cool grey muted colours, tasteful clarity and choice art throughout, this Firmdale gem is a stunning place to repose. And that's even before you see the idyllic back garden set around a fish pond with a few cosy snugs, or have breakfast in the conservatory, or read the newspaper in front of the fire in the drawing room.

SWISS HOUSE HOTEL Map pp458-9 *Hotel*

☎ 7373 2769; www.swiss-hh.demon.co.uk; 171 Old Brompton Rd SW5; s/d £80/95; ⊖ Gloucester Rd

The hushed Swiss House is an outstanding place for the price, set in a Victorian terrace house festooned with flowers. Staff are gracious and welcoming, and the amply sized rooms are cosily shabby chic. Rooms at the rear look out over a pleasant garden and don't get any noise from the street.

VICARAGE HOTEL Map pp444-5 *B&B*

☎ 7229 4030; www.londonvicaragehotel.com; 10 Vicarage Gate W8; d £105, with shared bathroom £85; ⊖ High St Kensington

Gilt mirrors, chandeliers and gold-and-red-striped wallpaper wow guests as they enter this former Victorian home. The rooms are unfortunately a little less lavish, but atmospherically olde-worlde English all the same. Those on the higher floors have shared bathrooms and lower prices.

CHEAP SLEEPS
HOLLAND HOUSE YHA HOSTEL

Map pp444-5 *Hostel*

☎ 0870 770 5866; hollandhouse@yha.org.uk; Holland Walk W8; dm £22; ⊖ High St Kensington

This hostel has 201 beds and is built into the Jacobean wing of Holland House, overlooking Holland Park. It's large, very busy and rather institutional, but the position is unbeatable. There's a café and kitchen, and breakfast is included.

LUNA SIMONE HOTEL Map pp460-1 *Hotel*

☎ 7834 5897; www.lunasimonehotel.com; 47-49 Belgrave Rd SW1; s £50-60, d £65-80 s with shared bathroom £35-45; ⊖ Victoria

If you saw this generic décor in a midrange chain, you'd probably think 'oh, boring'. However, it makes the 35-room Luna Simone look spotless, especially when compared to many other moderate hotels along this central strip. Modern art and slate-tiled new bathrooms provide some focal points, so it's excellent value for the price, really.

VICTORIA HOTEL Map pp460-1 *Hostel*

☎ 7834 3077; www.astorhostels.com; 71 Belgrave Rd SW1; dm £16; ⊖ Pimlico

This hostel has 60 beds so it's busy without being too impersonal. It's staffed by pausing travellers, has Internet and 24-hour reception, and is within easy walking distance of the Tate Britain and Westminster Abbey.

ALONG THE SOUTH BANK

With this once-neglected riverbank now one of the city's most vibrant quarters, the South Bank is an increasingly good base. Restaurant and bar pickings are slimmer than in the West End, but ever on the up. And who wouldn't be tempted by the thought of staying near the Tate Modern, where you can wander among the wonderful epicurean delights of Borough Market of a morning when you pop out for coffee? Further westwards you'll find yourself near the London Eye and well positioned to make a break for the Continent or the English countryside via Waterloo train station.

SOUTH BANK CENTRE & WATERLOO

LONDON MARRIOTT COUNTY HALL

Map pp448-9 · *Hotel*
☎ 7928 5200, 0870 400 7200; www.marriott.co.uk/lonch; Westminster Bridge Rd SE1; r from £285, with river views £320, breakfast extra £20; ⊖ Westminster
This elegant luxury hotel is famed for its fabulous close-up views of the Thames and the Houses of Parliament. It was formerly the headquarters of the Greater London Council and the atmosphere among the traditional rooms is still somewhat stuffy. The sweeping circular driveway seems miles away from the bustle of Westminster Bridge Rd just outside.

BANKSIDE

MAD HATTER Map pp448-9 · *Hotel*
☎ 7401 9222; www.madhatterhotel.com; 3-7 Stamford St SE1; r £115, breakfast extra £6-9, weekend rate incl breakfast £95; ⊖ Southwark
Its rooms are quite generic, but the Mad Hatter feels slightly homier than most chain hotels, thanks to its traditionally styled reception area and the adjacent pub. There's a decent level of comfort, and although the hotel is at a fairly major road junction, inside it doesn't seem too noisy.

SOUTHWARK ROSE HOTEL

Map pp454-5 · *Hotel*
☎ 7015 1480; www.southwarkrosehotel.co.uk; 43-47 Southwark Bridge Rd SW1; d & tw £140, breakfast extra £7-10, weekend rate incl breakfast £85; ⊖ London Bridge; ⊠
Smart enough to please your parents, and hip enough to impress your cool friends, the 'budget boutique' Southwark Rose Hotel is very versatile. Service is good, prices are reasonable and while the rooms are compact, they're stylish in a vaguely minimalist way and have some clever design features. Black-out blinds, fold-away desk compartments with hair dryers, two-way bathroom doors and laptop safes with rechargers all make for a pleasant stay. The location isn't pretty, but it is convenient.

CHEAP SLEEPS

DOVER CASTLE HOSTEL

Map pp454-5 · *Hostel*
☎ 7403 7773; www.dovercastlehostel.co.uk; 6a Great Dover St SE1; 3-12 bed dm £10-16; ⊖ Borough
This 55-bed hostel in a four-storey Victorian terrace house has a Caribbean-theme bar below. It has a TV lounge, kitchen facilities, luggage storage and Internet access.

ST CHRISTOPHER'S VILLAGE

Map pp454-5 · *Hostel*
☎ 7407 1856; www.st-christophers.co.uk; 163 Borough High St SE1; 4-12 bed dm £16-19.50, tw £50; ⊖ Borough/London Bridge
This 164-bed place is the flagship of an excellent hostel chain with basic, but cheap and clean accommodation, and friendly service. There's a roof garden with sauna, solarium, hot tub and excellent views of the Thames. Nearby branches (same contact details) include **St Christopher's Inn** (121 Borough High St SE1), with 48 beds, a pub below the hostel, a small veranda and a chill-out room, and the **Orient Espresso** (59-61 Borough High St SE1), with 36 beds, a laundry and a café. Prices are slightly cheaper in winter and there are sometimes ridiculously cheap Internet deals, so check the website.

Top Five Rooms with a View

- **Grange City Hotel** (p360)
- **London Marriott County Hall** (left)
- **Metropolitan** (p362)
- **Trafalgar Hilton** (p358)
- **Savoy** (p357)

Chains without Frills

Sensing a gap in the market, several discount hotel chains have launched across London offering a consistently clean and modern – if not especially characterful – standard for quite reasonable rates.

Express by Holiday Inn (☎ 7300 4300; www.holidayinn.co.uk) The most upmarket of these three budget chains, Express by Holiday Inn is most notable for its clever locations. Of the 10 or so properties in London, one lies in hotel-poor but nightclub-rich **Hoxton** (Map pp442–3; ☎ 7300 4300); another is located in **Southwark** (Map pp448–9; ☎ 7401 2525) just behind the Tate Modern. Rates start at about £110 for a double during the week.

Premier Travel Inn (☎ 0870 238 3300; www.premiertravelinn.com) London's cheapest chain – at least until **easyHotel** (p374) opens more properties – Premier Travel Inn herds them in and out. Décor is a bit kitsch, beds are soft, the second bed is a pull-out sofa, and public areas often reek of cigarettes, but at £80 to £90 a night per room few complain. The most famous and most recently renovated establishment is at County Hall (Map pp448–9); it's near the London Eye but doesn't have river views. Beware that those at Euston and Tower Bridge are on very busy streets. There's also a Premier Travel Inn at Heathrow.

Travelodge (☎ 0870 085 0950; www.travelodge.co.uk) For roughly the same price as at Premier Travel Inn you get a nicer room, but few public facilities. There's generally no lounge, the reception areas are small and service can leave much to be desired. The hotel near Petticoat Lane (Map pp454–5) is within easy reach of the bars and clubs of Hoxton, but that at King's Cross is on a main street.

SOUTHEAST LONDON

Somewhat insulated from the hustle and bustle across the Thames, you'll feel like you're staying in a village here. It's great for those who fancy getting up early to go for a jog through Greenwich Park, with great river views. Party animals will find it less attractive, because it's difficult to return to late at night.

GREENWICH
HAMILTON HOUSE HOTEL

off Map p463 *Hotel*
☎ 8694 9899; www.hamiltonhousehotel.co.uk;
14 West Grove SE10; s/d £105/125, 4-poster d £155;
⊖ DLR Cutty Sark

About five minutes beyond the Royal Observatory and Greenwich Park, this is a remarkable hilltop Georgian house that has been restored to its original elegance. Once home to two London lord mayors, it now has nine hotel rooms, some of which look over to Canary Wharf, others towards Blackheath. There's a lovely garden and four rooms with four-poster beds. All of this makes it very popular with wedding parties, so book ahead.

HARBOUR MASTER'S HOUSE

Map p463 *Apartment*
☎ 8293 9597; http://website.lineone.net/~harbour
master; 20 Ballast Quay SE10; s or d £85, tr or f £95;
⊖ DLR Cutty Sark

This self-contained basement apartment is right near the river in the Grade II heritage-listed building from where coal-carrying ships

on the Thames used to be controlled. Recently renovated, it combines mod cons such as TV, video, dishwasher and heated towel rails with the charm of arched white-brick ceilings and a vague maritime feel. As it's quite compact, however, it's likely to work better for couples than groups. There's a £10 discount for stays over one week. Book well ahead.

CHEAP SLEEPS
ROTHERHITHE YHA Map pp454-5 *Hostel*
☎ 7232 2114; www.yha.org.uk; 20 Salter Rd SE16;
4-10 bed dm £18-26, d & tw £58; ⊖ Rotherhithe

The facilities at this large, flagship YHA are very good, but the location is a bit remote. There's a bar, a restaurant, kitchen facilities and a laundry, plus four bedrooms adapted for disabled visitors. All rooms have private bathrooms.

ST ALFEGES Map p463 *B&B*
☎ 8353 4337; www.st-alfeges.co.uk; 16 St Alfege's
Passage SE10; s/d from £40/60; ⊖ DLR Cutty Sark

This sweet gay guesthouse situated in the centre of Greenwich has three rooms, individually decorated in shades of blue, green or yellow, and a well-fed, friendly cat decorated in – and simply called – black and white. Owners Robert and Tony do their best to make everyone, gay or straight, feel at home, with chats and cups of tea. For such a central location, the immediate neighbourhood is quiet. Turn the corner into Roan St to find the main door. Discounts are offered for longer stays.

ST CHRISTOPHER'S INN Map p463 *Hostel*
☎ 7407 1856; www.st-christophers.co.uk; 189 Greenwich High Rd SE10; 4-12 bed dm £16-19.50, tw £50; ⊖ DLR Cutty Sark
The Greenwich branch of this well-respected chain of hostels is relatively quieter than some of its more centrally located sisters. There's a coffee shop and pub on site, and frequent promotional deals offering free tickets to performances at the local Greenwich theatre.

NORTH CENTRAL

This area is sandwiched between two of London's biggest green spaces – Hyde Park and Hampstead Heath – and contains another, Regent's Park, at its heart. At the same time it's very central and convenient for shopping and for West End nightlife. So, if you'd rather visit urban London by day and return to leafy 'little England' at night, this is the place for you. By the time you move to Camden or Hampstead you're staying where mainly Londoners live. Camden makes a good base if you're into live music or the weekend market.

MARYLEBONE & REGENT'S PARK

BRYANSTON COURT HOTEL
Map pp444-5 *Hotel*
☎ 7262 3141; www.bryanstonhotel.com; 56-60 Great Cumberland Pl W1; Bryanston s/d/tr/f £95/120/135/150, Concorde s/d/tr/f £70/100/110/120; ⊖ Marble Arch
In a charming village-like enclave just minutes from Hyde Park and Oxford St, this hotel offers reasonable rooms at reasonable prices. The bedroom décor is more dated than that in the spacious lobby – particularly in the cheaper Concorde annexe – but breakfast is generous and the overall atmosphere relaxed and friendly.

CUMBERLAND HOTEL Map pp444-5 *Hotel*
☎ 0870 333 9280; www.thecumberland.co.uk; 56-60 Great Cumberland Pl W1; s/d £315/335; ⊖ Marble Arch; 🖬
You'll wonder whether you've accidentally stumbled into a contemporary art gallery in the hangar-sized lobby of this reinvented hotel; the reception desk is way up the back – yes, keep going – behind the sculptures and mood-lit Perspex columns. Things are more human in scale in the 900 contemporary rooms, some of which have views of nearby Hyde Park. If you don't fancy joining celebrity chef Gary Rhodes in the fine-dining restaurant, there's a tinted-glass bathroom to splash around in and a plasma-screen TV with plenty of films.

DORSET SQUARE HOTEL
Map pp444-5 *Hotel*
☎ 7723 7874; www.dorsetsquare.co.uk; 9-40 Dorset Sq NW1; d from £230; ⊖ Baker St
Two combined Regency town houses contain this enchanting hotel overlooking leafy Dorset Sq, where the very first cricket ground was laid in 1814 (which explains the cricket memorabilia on the walls). Guest quarters are predictably small but almost dreamily decorated with a blend of antiques, sumptuous fabrics, crown-canopied beds, and mahogany/marble bathrooms.

DURRANTS HOTEL Map pp448-9 *Hotel*
☎ 7935 8131; www.durrantshotel.co.uk; George St W1; r from £165, ste £285; ⊖ Bond St
The same family has owned this quintessentially English gem since 1921 and the long-serving and uniformed staff – some have worked here for 40 years – gives it a unique atmosphere. The hotel is luxurious, sprawling, traditional and soothing, and the rooms are charmingly old-fashioned. It's located directly behind the wonderful Wallace Collection and only a shopping bag's swing from Oxford St.

HOTEL LA PLACE Map pp448-9 *Hotel*
☎ 7486 2323; www.hotellaplace.com; 11 Nottingham Pl W1; s £100-125, d £130-140; ⊖ Baker St
The rooms here are very much in the traditional mode, but impeccably cared for, and some have new bathrooms. The friendly family management has installed a 24-hour bar downstairs, with comfy – and stylishly colourful – modern lounge chairs. The place prides itself on being a safe haven for women travelling alone.

CAMDEN

30 KING HENRY'S ROAD Map pp440-1 *B&B*

☎ 7483 2871; 30 King Henry's Rd NW3; s/d £80/100;
⊖ Chalk Farm

This large mid-Victorian family home has one comfortably sized double room, and a great position between loud and lively Camden and dreamy, romantic Primrose Hill. A healthy and delicious Continental-style breakfast (with fruit salad and yogurt) is served in a rather grand kitchen, looking onto a well-tended garden (and a well-groomed greyhound). Book well ahead.

66 CAMDEN SQUARE Map pp440-1 *B&B*

☎ 7485 4622; 66 Camden Sq NW1; B&B per person £45; ⊖ Camden Town

This glass-and-teak B&B combines space, light and comfort in a quiet north London square, not far from Camden Town and Regent's Park. The owners are fans of things Japanese and the whole house is attractively minimalist… apart from the noisy macaw.

PADDINGTON & BAYSWATER

GARDEN COURT HOTEL

Map pp444-5 *Hotel*

☎ 7229 2553; www.gardencourthotel.co.uk; 30-31 Kensington Gardens Sq W2; s/d £65/95, with shared bathroom £40/65; ⊖ Bayswater

Most remarkable for the Beefeater statue in its lobby, the spotless Garden Court is truly a cut above most classic English properties in this price bracket. While the décor retains a few restrained traditional twirls, a total overhaul in 2005 has added a lift, new beds and modern bathrooms. Guests have access not only to the hotel garden, but also to the leafy square across the street.

HEMPEL Map pp444-5 *Hotel*

☎ 7298 9000; www.the-hempel.co.uk; 31-35 Craven Hill Gardens W2; d from £290, studio £425; ⊖ Lancaster Gate/Queensway; 🏢

One of London's most stunning sanctuaries, designer Anouska Hempel's hotel combines Renaissance proportions with Zen-like synchronicity in the public spaces, guest quarters and bathrooms. The monochrome tones, white-on-white spaces and crisp fabrics won't be to everyone's tastes, but high-flying business folk certainly seem to dig it. The superslick I-Thai restaurant continues the minimalist theme, although it's a bit too self-conscious to be fun.

PAVILION HOTEL Map pp444-5 *Hotel*

☎ 7262 0905; www.pavilionhoteluk.com; 34-36 Sussex Gardens W2; s/d £60/100; ⊖ Paddington

'Fashion, Glam & Rock 'n' Roll' is the motto of this place, so if you'd like to cap off your holiday by throwing a TV set out the window, this could be for you. There are 30 individually themed rooms ('Honky Tonky Afro' has a Moorish theme, 'Casablanca' has a 1970s theme). It's fun and good value, although cheesily B-list (especially the service).

ROYAL PARK Map pp444-5 *Hotel*

☎ 7479 6600; www.theroyalpark.com; 3 Westbourne Tce W2; s £195, d from £225, weekend rate s/d incl breakfast from £140/165; ⊖ Lancaster Gate; 🏢 🅿

It is a truth universally acknowledged that a man in possession of a good fortune must be in want of…a classy pad like this. Yes, this is a Jane Austen fantasy come true in the big city, with tasteful Regency furniture throughout the lounge and immaculate bedrooms (plus discreetly placed plasma TVs etc). The hotel, recently renovated to an exacting standard, even maintains a semiperiod look in its sparkling bathrooms. Perfect for modern-day Mr Darcys and Miss Bennetts with a taste for four-star luxury.

VANCOUVER STUDIOS Map pp444-5 *Hotel*

☎ 7243 1270; www.vancouverstudios.co.uk; 30 Prince's Sq W2; s £60-70, d £90-120, f £135; ⊖ Bayswater

Everyone from families to young hipsters should feel at home in this broad church of winning studios, whether just chatting to the down-to-earth staff, sticking a record on the gramophone in the guest lounge or joining the house cat by the fountain in the back garden. Rooms all contain kitchenettes but otherwise differ wildly – ranging from a tiny but well-equipped single (there are larger singles as well) to a generously sized family room, and encompassing all styles of decoration from faux-mink throws to Japanese to gingham. A place with bags of personality.

CHEAP SLEEPS

ASHLEE HOUSE Map pp442-3 *Hostel*

☎ 7833 9400; www.ashleehouse.co.uk; 261-265 Gray's Inn Rd WC1; dm from £13, s £34; ⊖ King's Cross St Pancras

Ashlee House has made a good fist of a central but completely charmless location. The lobby, with a huge Underground map and shaggy-sheepskin sofa backs, looks interesting and although dorms are cramped, they have cheerily striped bed linen and double glazing to keep out noise from busy Gray's Inn Rd. There is a TV lounge in the basement, plus a laundry, decent-sized kitchen, free left-luggage room and Internet access.

GENERATOR Map pp442-3 *Hostel*
☎ 7388 7655; www.the-generator.co.uk; Compton Pl, 37 Tavistock Pl WC1; 14-/8-/6-/4-/2-bed dm per person £12.50/15/16/18/25, weekend extra £2, s weekday/weekend £35/56; ⊖ Russell Sq

You don't have to fight for the right to party at this young and lively budget option, where there's something going on pretty well every evening. The bar stays open until 2am and there are frequent drinking competitions. With its industrial décor, the place looks like an updated set from Terry Gilliam's film *Brazil*. Along with 207 rooms (830 beds), there are pool tables, Internet access, safe-deposit boxes and a large eating area, but no kitchen.

INVERNESS COURT HOTEL
Map pp444-5 *Hotel*
☎ 7229 1444; www.cghotels.com; Inverness Tce W2; s/d £55/80; ⊖ Queensway

This structure was commissioned by Edward VII for his 'confidante' Lillie Langtry, and came with a private theatre that's now a cocktail bar. Panelled walls, stained glass and huge open fires give it a Gothic feel, but most rooms – some overlooking Hyde Park – are pretty ordinary.

LEINSTER INN Map pp444-5 *Hostel*
☎ 7229 9641; www.astorhostels.com; 7-12 Leinster Sq W2; 8-bed dm £14.50-17.50, tr £60; ⊖ Bayswater

In a big, old house close to Bayswater tube station and Portobello Rd Market, this 372-bed hostel is the largest in the Astor stable and has a café, laundry, Internet lounge and bar with a 4am licence and monthly theme parties.

OXFORD HOTEL Map pp444-5 *Hotel*
☎ 7402 6860; www.oxfordhotellondon.co.uk; 13-14 Craven Tce W2; s/d/tr/f from £40/50/65/80; ⊖ Lancaster Gate

For a humble establishment, the Oxford sure tries hard with its sunny yellow walls and new checked bedspreads, although the swirly carpets and wonky stairs are a potent reminder of how much uglier things used to be. There's handy access to Hyde Park and busy Paddington station.

ST CHRISTOPHER'S INN CAMDEN
Map pp440-1 *Hostel*
☎ 7388 1012; www.st-christophers.co.uk; 48-50 Camden High St NW1; dm £16-19.50, tw £25; ⊖ Camden Town

This 54-bed branch of the popular hostel chain is five minutes from Camden tube station

Banner at Generator hostel (above)

along the high street, atop the very busy Belushi's bar, which has a 2am licence. Staff are very friendly, there's no curfew and the lodgings are nice and clean, although some of the private rooms are very small. *july 24-31 '06.*

ST PANCRAS INTERNATIONAL YHA
Map pp440-1 *Hostel*
☎ 0870 770 6044; stpancras@yha.org.uk; 79-81 Euston Rd NW1; dm £25, tw £56-62; ✆ King's Cross St Pancras/Euston
The area isn't great, but this 152-bed hostel is modern, with kitchen, restaurant, lockers, cycle shed and lounge, and it's in the hub of London's transport links.

STYLOTEL Map pp444-5 *Hotel*
☎ 7723 1026; www.stylotel.com; 160-162 Sussex Gardens W2; s/d/tr/q £50/70/90/105; ✆ Paddington
The industrial design here is as predictably self-conscious as the name – particularly the angular-backed chairs in the basement breakfast room, which you wouldn't want to tussle with. However, it is a real joy to get such a comfortable, sleek look at these prices, and

the well-lit lobby lounge is a nice place to chill. Bedrooms have lots of blue, stainless steel and aluminium features, plus capsule bathrooms.

WAKE UP! LONDON Map pp444-5 *Hostel*
☎ 7262 4471; www.wakeuplondon.co.uk; 1 Queen's Gardens W2; dm/s/d/tr from £15/26/45/45, weekly rates available; ✆ Paddington
The famous Sydney establishment comes to London with this 530-bed branch in Bayswater. Aimed at mainly 18- to 40-year-olds, the concept is simple: spacious public areas with loads of facilities and spartan but clean dorms. As well as Internet access, laundry, public phones, laptop safes, a travel agency, a kitchen cleaned four times daily and souvenir underwear of questionable taste, there are even some girls' dorms with vanity mirrors and built-in hairdryers. The bar and sociable atmosphere guarantee you'll have a good time, but – as they don't like to wake up! the neighbours – possibly with fewer exclamation marks than on the website.

NORTH LONDON

North London is not particularly noted for its density of hotels. However, if you wish to base yourself away from the main tourist areas, it does possess a couple of decent options, particularly in Hampstead, one of the city's leafiest and most sought-after residential areas. Here you're really living among Londoners, plus there's easy access to the wonderfully green expanse of Hampstead Heath.

HOUSE HOTEL Map p465 *Hotel*
☎ 7431 8000; www.thehousehotel.co.uk; 2 Rosslyn Hill NW3; d from £100; ✆ Belsize Park; Ⓟ
The entrance hall of this free-standing, light-brick hotel preserves the chandeliers and stained glass of the original house, while the modern rooms have a little more character than usual and all come with bathtubs, too. Among the warren of stairs, there's a surprisingly happy mix of businesspeople, relatives of patients in the nearby Royal Free Hospital and session musicians working in Air Studios across the road. Celebs like Gwen Stefani, George Michael and Claudia Schiffer have been known to drop in to the spacious bar/dining room.

CHEAP SLEEPS
HAMPSTEAD VILLAGE GUEST HOUSE
Map p465 *Guesthouse*
☎ 7435 8679; www.hampsteadguesthouse.com; 2 Kemplay Rd NW3; s/d £65/85, with shared facilities £48/72; ✆ Hampstead
Only 20 minutes by tube from the centre of London, this is a lovely pad with a quirky character, rustic and antique décor and furnishings, comfy beds and a delightful back garden in which you can enjoy a cooked breakfast (if you pay the extra £7). There's also a studio flat, which can accommodate up to five people.

WEST LONDON

From the style hotels of Notting Hill to the budget hostels of Earl's Court, this area has traditionally offered a broad range of accommodation options. In the past few years, however, a gratifying trend has seen the two ends of the spectrum move towards each other to foster a new breed of stylish budget hotel.

NOTTING HILL & WESTBOURNE GROVE

COLONNADE TOWN HOUSE

Map pp444-5   *Hotel*

☎ 7286 1052; www.etontownhouse.com; 2 War-rington Cres W9; s/d from £155/185, breakfast extra £10-15, weekend rate incl breakfast £140/160; ✪ Warwick Ave; ⊠

A charmer in lovely Little Venice, the Colon-nade is the handsome Victorian structure where Sigmund Freud sheltered after he fled Vienna. Apart from two in the basement, rooms are light, spacious and relaxing, and there are nice touches like the provision of slippers and gowns.

GUESTHOUSE WEST Map pp444-5   *Hotel*

☎ 7792 9800; www.guesthousewest.com; 163-165 Westbourne Grove W11; r £155; ✪ Westbourne Park/Royal Oak; ⊠

A fashionable take on the B&B concept, offer-ing four-star chic (ish) at a three-star price, this features grey blankets folded across the bot-tom of white duvets, orchids and muted toffee-coloured bathrooms. The vintage 1950s film posters in the bar are another distinctive touch.

MILLER'S RESIDENCE Map pp444-5   *Hotel*

☎ 7243 1024; www.millersuk.com; 111a Westbourne Grove W2; d from £175; ✪ Bayswater/Notting Hill Gate

More a five-star B&B than a hotel, this '18th-century rooming house' is chock-a-block with curiosities and antique furnishings, and quite literally brimming with personality. Every avail-able surface is plastered with *objets d'art* and the Victorian-style drawing room has to be seen to be believed (preferably by candlelight). Rooms come in all shapes, sizes and shades of antique opulence, but they all offer terrific value and ample opportunity for a romantic sojourn. The hotel entrance is on Hereford Rd.

PEMBRIDGE COURT Map pp444-5   *Hotel*

☎ 7229 9977; 34 Pembridge Gardens W2; s/d from £125/160; ✪ Notting Hill Gate

Behind an elegant neoclassical façade in Not-ting Hill is this sweet and soothing contender for London's best small hotel. A bright and breezy welcome sets the tone, although you'll probably best remember the pet cat, floral dra-pery, Victorian knick-knacks and sumptuous furnishings. The best rooms are up the top and the small singles are *very* small.

PORTOBELLO HOTEL Map pp444-5   *Hotel*

☎ 7727 2777; www.portobello-hotel.co.uk; 22 Stanley Gardens W11; s/d/ste from £130/170/220; ✪ Notting Hill Gate; ⊠

This famous place has been a firm favourite with rock 'n' rollers and movie stars down the years. Rooms and furnishings are eccentric in a funky, haphazard, devil-may-care fashion and there's a 24-hour bar to fuel guests on their merry way.

EARL'S COURT & WEST BROMPTON

MAYFLOWER Map pp458-9   *Hotel*

☎ 7370 0991; www.mayflowerhotel.co.uk; 26-28 Trebovir Rd SW5; s £60-70, d £80-100, tr £110, f £130; ✪ Earl's Court

If the Mayflower is the most celebrated of London's cheaper boutique hotels, it's for its unquestionably impressive look. It's chosen an updated colonial style, with wooden carv-ings from India, ceiling fans and black-tiled bathrooms. There's lots of technology and a juice bar, but the place isn't entirely flawless. The rooms are pretty small, and service can be just a tad ditzy. At least one former guest has complained about poor soundproofing of the back rooms, which adjoin the tube station, so ask for one at the front.

PHILBEACH HOTEL Map pp458-9   *Hotel*

☎ 7373 1244; www.philbeachhotel.freeserve.co .uk; 30/31 Philbeach Gardens SW5; s/d £65/90, with shared bathroom £50/65, student discounts available; ✪ Earl's Court

The Philbeach likes to make the point that it's not just gay-friendly, but a truly gay-run hotel providing guests with a proper introduction to the London queer scene. When you're not lounging around like a buff model in one of the 40 stylish bedrooms, you can cruise the hip new bar or eat in the Thai Princess restaurant.

RUSHMORE Map pp458-9   *Hotel*

☎ 7370 3839; www.rushmore-hotel.co.uk; 11 Trebovir Rd SW5; s £60-70, d £80-90, tr £110-130; ✪ Earl's Court

This modest hotel is a medley of Italian over-tones with Mediterranean wash, faux marble and Roman-style trompe l'oeil in the lobby and a variety of individually decorated rooms that evoke everything from a Tuscan villa to a Venetian palazzo. Ironically, Italian is not spo-ken by the multilingual staff, who are never-theless happy to serve you in Arabic, French, Hindi, Polish, Punjabi or Russian.

TWENTY NEVERN SQUARE

Map pp458-9   *Hotel*

☎ 7565 9555; www.twentynevernsquare.co.uk; 20 Nevern Sq SW5; s £99-120; d £110-140; ⊖ Earl's Court

Staff seem to have their heads a bit more together at this sister establishment of the Mayflower. The same colonial style is replicated here, although with a little less black tile and a lot more carved wood. Several rooms come with four-poster beds and all are reasonably generously sized. The focal point is the charming breakfast room/bar in a conservatory in the rear of the building.

SHEPHERD'S BUSH

K WEST Map pp438-9   *Hotel*

☎ 7674 1000; www.k-west.co.uk; Richmond Way W14; s £120-155, d £120-200, breakfast extra £10-20; ⊖ Shepherd's Bush; Ⓟ

K West is a sleek and stylish place just off Shepherd's Bush Green. The minimalist décor and fleet of staff on duty at reception can be a little disconcerting, but they are friendly and polite. Many people come to stay here to take advantage of the spa alone. (For a fee, all guests can use the extensive spas, saunas and Jacuzzis and enjoy the weird and wonderful natural treatments.) So this is the place to come if you like being covered in mud and then discussing it at length over a £10 cocktail.

CHEAP SLEEPS

BARMY BADGER BACKPACKERS

Map pp458-9   *Hostel*

☎ 7370 5213; barmybadger@hotmail.com; 17 Longridge Rd SW5; 2-/4-/8-bed dm £17/16/15, weekly rates available; ⊖ Earl's Court

This is an old-school hostel in a converted Victorian home and it's the slightly cramped quarters that could drive you barmy here. Still, some guests settle in for the long haul, laying out all their toiletries around the bathroom as if at home. There's a small kitchen, laundry (bizarrely with a toilet should you get caught

short next to the washing machine) and back garden when you need to step out for a breathe of fresh air – or a barbecue.

EARL'S COURT YHA Map pp458-9   *Hostel*

☎ 7373 7083; earlscourt@yha.org.uk; 38 Bolton Gardens SW5; dm £17.20-22.50, tw £54; ⊖ Earl's Court

The Earl's Court Youth Hostel has a great atmosphere and friendly staff, and has been the starting point for many Australians' trips to Britain. The kitchen has been redone in recent years and the whole place is cheerful but basic: most accommodation is in dorms and small but clean four-bedroom rooms with bunks. There is a nice garden out the back for the summer and Internet access from the lounges. Book ahead.

EASYHOTEL Map pp458-9   *Hotel*

www.easyhotel.com; 14 Lexham Gardens SW5; r from £20; ⊖ Gloucester Rd

Using the same pricing model as its sister easyJet airline to get bums on beds, this functional hotel will offer the best deals to early birds. Although the hotel was still being completed at the time of writing, it appeared that garish orange-plastic moulded rooms would contain a bed next to a sink and an apparently see-through capsule shower and toilet unit. No in-room phones are planned, TV is an optional extra and there will be many rooms without windows.

MERLYN COURT HOTEL

Map pp458-9   *Hotel*

☎ 7370 1640; www.merlyncourthotel.com; 2 Barkston Gardens SW5; s/d/tr/f from £45/75/80/85, with shared bathroom £40/60/70/75; ⊖ Earl's Court

The Merlyn Court's humble rooms are unremarkable, but at least they have windows (see preceding entry). The friendly management will generally offer a wake-up call and give you a hand lugging your suitcase or backpack up the stairs.

ST CHRISTOPHER'S Map pp438-9   *Hostel*

☎ 7407 1856; www.st-christophers.co.uk/bush/htm; 13-15 Shepherd's Bush Green; 2-/4-/6-/8-bed dm £25/19.50/18/17, s £50; ⊖ Shepherd's Bush

St Christopher's Shepherd's Bush operation is right in the middle-of the action with no curfew and the tube and a sprawling Australian sports pub right on the doorstep. The accommodation is rather cramped, but special offers can mean beds at under £10 per night. The place to stay if you are a young party animal seeking a base for your debauchery.

Top Five for Style on a Budget

- B+B Belgravia (p364)
- **Mayflower** (p373)
- **Pavilion Hotel** (p370)
- **Southwark Rose Hotel** (p367)
- **Vancouver Studios** (p370)

SOUTHWEST LONDON

Accommodation is fairly limited in this part of town. It's a bit of a trek into town, too, but if you're only here for a short time and want to visit friends – or watch a Chelsea match – it might appeal.

CHELSEA VILLAGE HOTEL

Map pp458-9   *Hotel*

☎ 7565 1400; www.chelseavillage.com; Fulham Rd SW6; r from £160, ste £220, breakfast extra £8-14; ⊖ Fulham Broadway

While definitely not of a standard to keep Chelsea FC's billionaire owner, Roman Abramovich, or his Russian oligarch friends happy, these two interlinked hotels – the Chelsea Village and slightly shabbier Court Hotel -- built into Chelsea's Stamford Bridge stadium are conversely too upmarket for your average football hooligan. None of the rooms overlook the pitch, so you won't see a live game free (that sort of thing only happens in Carling beer adverts). However, while the noise of the crowd can be heard in reception and the bar areas whenever Chelsea play at home, the rooms themselves are well soundproofed. You can also get some fabulously cheap deals out of season.

CHEAP SLEEPS

FULHAM GUESTHOUSE Map pp458-9 *B&B*

☎ 7731 1662; www.fulhamguesthouse.com; 55 Wandsworth Bridge Rd; s/d with shared bathroom £45/65; ⊖ Fulham Broadway/Parson's Green

The Fulham Guesthouse is run by a friendly and welcoming couple in a tastefully renovated Victorian town house. Although none of the rooms have their own bathroom they are all clean and functional.

UP RIVER

Suburban west London is not an obvious place to base yourself for a trip to London – it's quite a slog to the centre and noticeably more expensive than other parts of suburbia. However, anyone wanting to stay in a quieter, more-refined part of London will be right at home here – near greenery and within reach of the river.

RICHMOND

RICHMOND GATE HOTEL

Off Map p464   *Hotel*

☎ 8940 0061; www.corushotels.co.uk/richmond gate; Richmond Hill TW10; s/d £150/180; ⊖ /rail Richmond; Ⓟ

The superb position of the large Richmond Gate Hotel complex is its selling point, overlooking the Thames and just seconds from the wide-open spaces of Richmond Park. The hotel is an amalgamation of Georgian mansions that have been gradually taken over – and both the facilities and decoration are excellent. Rooms are large, light and comfortable, while the facilities include a pool and health club. It's a great place for a pampering getaway within London.

Airport Hotels

London's airports have plenty of hotels to cater for passengers with early morning flights. If you're one of these, the best plan of action is to go to the airport website (see the relevant entry in the Directory chapter, p398) and click on 'book hotels', where you will be taken to www.expedia.co.uk and discount rates.

Otherwise, these easy options are worth considering:

Hilton Gatwick (☎ 01293-518080; www.hilton.co.uk/gatwick; London Gatwick Airport; r £140, breakfast extra £13-17.50) Conveniently connected to the airport building via a short walkway, this hotel is also notable for its two 'relaxation rooms' (£230), with triple glazing, aromatherapy products and tips to help the worst insomniacs get some sleep.

Park Inn Heathrow (☎ 8759 6611; www.rezidorparkinn.com; Bath Rd, Heathrow; r £140) The largest of the Heathrow hotels, and one of the closest to the airport, this is much more luxurious than you'd expect for the money, but is sometimes overrun with customers. Take H2 Hoppa Bus (£3).

Radisson Edwardian Heathrow (☎ 8759 6311; www.radissonedwardian.com; 140 Bath Rd, Hayes UB3; r from £145) This lavish five-star outfit has been voted 'Best airport hotel in the world' for seven years running by the readers of *Business Traveller* magazine.

Radisson SAS Stansted (☎ 01279-661012; www.radissonsas.com; Waltham Close, Stansted Airport; r from £145) A two- to three-minute walk from the main terminal building, this is a new hotel opened in 2004, with a fitness centre and 24-hour reception.

RICHMOND PARK HOTEL Map p464 *Hotel*
☎ 8948 4666; www.therichmondparkhotel.com; 3 Petersham Rd TW10; s/d £70/90; ☻ /rail Richmond

This 22-bedroom hotel at the bottom of Richmond Hill is a pleasant midrange place for anyone wanting to be in the centre of Richmond. All rooms have private facilities and are comfortably furnished with TVs and telephones. While Continental breakfast is included, the owners will do a full calorific English slap-up for a small supplement. This hotel has rate reductions at the weekends.

Excursions

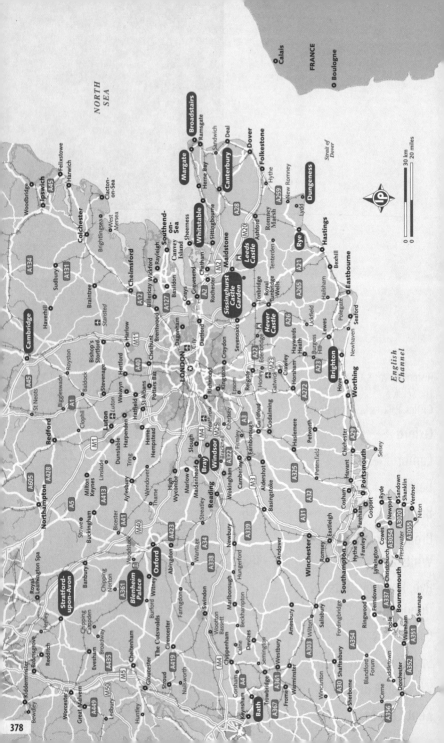

Excursions

London is wildly unrepresentative of the rest of the country, and just outside the capital's staggering ethnic, religious, architectural and social variety, another England suddenly emerges. Picturesque medieval towns, market squares, thatched-roofed cottages and that 'green and pleasant land' referred to in song all still lie within easy reach. You don't have to go far, or stay away long, to find the quaint English countryside eulogised in countless classic books. Or, if you're just looking for a change of scenery, perhaps you might fancy a trip to the sea.

HISTORIC TOWNS & CITIES

If you want a short break from the fast-paced capital, you could start by immersing yourself in **Oxford** (p380) or **Cambridge** (p382). Just over an hour away from London, both have quarters that have remain largely unchanged for eight centuries. Alternatively, there's **Bath** (p384), perhaps the most attractive town in the country – an unfeasibly beautiful West Country city nestled among some wonderful scenery, harking back to – and beyond – the arrival of the Romans in Britain two millennia ago. Commanding **Canterbury Cathedral** (p390) may also take your fancy, while few places have the literary history of **Stratford-upon-Avon** (p392), home of William Shakespeare.

THE SEASIDE

The weather may be unreliable, but that makes English seaside towns try all the harder. **Brighton** (p386) is the most exciting of them all – from piers to shopping to clubbing. During the summer you can even swim at its lovely pebbly beach. Or you might prefer the quieter charms of classic English seaside towns such as nostalgic **Broadstairs**, kitschy **Margate** or relaxed **Whitstable** (see p388). Medieval **Rye** (p389) allows you to combine this with the experience of an old historic town. The **Romney Marsh** and **Dungeness** coastal areas bordering Rye are some of the weirdest you'll ever encounter – in an extremely beguiling way.

CASTLES, PALACES & STATELY HOMES

As if to prove the saying that an Englishman's home is his castle, successive kings, queens, princes, dukes and barons have outdone each other building some of the world's finest country houses over many hundreds of years. **Windsor** (p393), official residence of the Queen, is the oldest inhabited castle in the world (and while you're out this way you can delve into the gastronomic delights of nearby **Bray**). Winston Churchill's birthplace of **Blenheim Palace** (p381) is amazingly opulent, while **Hever Castle** (p395), the childhood home of Henry VIII's second wife, Anne Boleyn, has lovely landscaped gardens. Set on two lakes, fairytale **Leeds Castle** (p395) in Kent has been called 'the loveliest castle in the world'. **Sissinghurst** (p396) is home to one of the planet's most famous contemporary gardens.

Blenheim Palace (p381)

OXFORD
☎ 01865

'That sweet city with her dreaming spires' is how poet Matthew Arnold described Oxford, and they continue to dream today. As England's first university town, it dates back to the early 12th century (having developed from an earlier Saxon village) and in the intervening period has been responsible for educating 26 UK prime ministers. These include Labour leaders Clement Attlee, Tony Blair and Harold Wilson, as well as Tories Anthony Eden, Harold Macmillan, Edward Heath and Margaret Thatcher. Even former US president Bill Clinton briefly studied – and puffed pot – here.

Despite its busy shopping streets, heavy traffic and hordes of summer tourists, Oxford still retains charm. The city's superb architecture and the unique atmosphere of the colleges, quads (quadrangles or courtyards) and gardens remain major attractions. If possible, it's better to visit in term time; the presence of students and professors remind you it's a living city rather than just an academic theme park.

Oxford's 35 colleges and five 'halls' are scattered around the city, but the most important and beautiful are in the centre. A good starting point is the **Carfax Tower**, part of the now-demolished medieval Church of St Martin, at the city's main crossroads. There's a great view from the top (99 steps).

Walk south from the tower along St Aldate's, past the **Museum of Oxford**, which offers an easy introduction to the city's long history, and **Christ Church**, the grandest of the colleges, founded in 1525 and now popular with Harry Potter fans, having appeared in all three movies. The main entrance to Christ Church is below Tom Tower, the top of which was designed by Sir Christopher Wren in 1682. However, the visitors' entrance is further down St Aldate's via the wrought-iron gates of the Memorial Gardens and Broad Walk. The college chapel, **Christ Church Cathedral**, is the smallest in the country.

From Broad Walk continue eastwards then turn left (north) up Merton Grove to Merton St. On your right is **Merton College**, founded in 1264. In the college's 14th-century **Mob Quad** is the oldest medieval library still in use in the UK. JRR Tolkien, the author of *Lord of the Rings*, taught English at Merton from 1945 until his retirement in 1959.

Head north up Magpie Lane to High St. Just opposite, at the corner of High and Catte Sts, is the **University Church of St Mary the Virgin**, whose 14th-century tower can also be climbed. From St Mary's, walk east along High St, with its fascinating mix of architectural styles, to the stunning **Magdalen College** (pronounced *maud*-len) on the River Cherwell. Magdalen has huge grounds, including a deer park – with deer – and Addison's Walk, which meanders through meadows to an island in the Cherwell. On 1 May it's traditional for students to leap off the Magdalen Bridge, although low water levels and fairly severe injuries recently have left question marks over the practice.

Transport

Distance from London 57 miles (92km)

Direction Northwest

Travel time 1½ hours by bus, one to 1½ hours by train

Bus Oxford Tube (☎ 01865-772250; www.stagecoach-oxford.co.uk/oxfordtube) and Oxford Bus Company (☎ 01865-785400; www.oxfordbus.co.uk) run round-the-clock services from Victoria coach station (single £10, return £12 to £15). Megabus (☎ 01738-639095; www.megabus.com) has six departures per day from Gloucester Pl (online returns from £2.50). National Express (☎ 0870 580 8080; www.nationalexpress.com) also has frequent services.

Car The M40 provides access from London, but Oxford has a serious traffic problem and parking is a nightmare. We highly recommend that you don't drive. If you do, use the Park & Ride system – as you approach the city follow the signs for the four car parks.

Train There are two trains (☎ 0845 748 4950; www.nationalrail.co.uk) per hour from London's Paddington train station (adult same-day return from £17)

If you retrace your steps and walk north up Catte St, you'll come to the circular, Palladian-style **Radcliffe Camera** (1749), which is a reading room for the **Bodleian Library**, just to the north across the courtyard (enter via the Great Gate on Catte St).

Continue north along Catte St, passing the **Bridge of Sighs** (a 1914 copy of the famous one in Venice) that spans New College Lane. When you reach Broad St you have two options. Walking north along Parks Rd for about 500m will bring you to the **Oxford University Museum of Natural History**, famous for its dinosaur and dodo skeletons, and the renovated **Pitt Rivers Museum**, crammed to overflowing with things like voodoo dolls and South American shrunken heads.

If you go west along Broad St you'll pass Sir Christopher Wren's first major work, the **Sheldonian Theatre** (1667), on your left. This is where graduations, other important ceremonies and occasional concerts take place. On the right is **Trinity College**, founded in 1555, and next to it, at the corner with Magdalen St, is **Balliol College**. The wooden doors between the inner and outer quadrangles still bear scorch marks from when Protestant martyrs were burned at the stake in the mid-16th century. (Ignore the hokey, multimedia 'Oxford Story' opposite the college.)

A short distance north up Magdalen St to St Giles is the **Ashmolean Museum**. Opened in 1683, this is Britain's oldest museum and houses a stunning collection of European art – from Rembrandts, Michelangelos and Pre-Raphaelite paintings to Turners and Picassos – as well as Middle Eastern antiquities. A little further up St Giles, behind Trinity College, is **St John's**, whose previous students included Tony Blair.

Finally, soak up Oxford's atmosphere by taking to the river Isis in a punt, which can be hired from **Magdalen Bridge Boathouse**. If you don't wish to stand out as a tourist, note that in Oxford the tradition is to punt from the sloping end of the boat.

Around Oxford

If you wish to extend your visit around Oxford, there are two obvious choices. Firstly, **Blenheim Palace** (☎ 0870 060 2080; www.blenheimpalace.com; near Woodstock, Oxfordshire; palace, park & gardens adult/concession/child £11.50/9/6, park only £6/4/2; ☾ palace & gardens 10.30am-4.45pm mid-Feb–Oct, 10.30am-4.45pm Wed-Sun Nov–mid-Dec, park 9am-4.45pm year-round) is the famously over the top Oxfordshire home of the Dukes of Marlborough and the birthplace of Winston Churchill. His bedroom is included on the interesting guided tour of the house, although the tapestries made for the first duke in the aftermath of his incredible military feats at Blenheim against the French are perhaps the highlight. You won't be alone in your journey, however, as the palace is hugely popular, especially in summer.

Oxford also acts as a secondary gateway to the rolling green hills of the **Cotswolds** (the primary gateway is probably Cheltenham). For information on sights and accommodation in the area, try www.oxfordshirecotswolds.org, www.cotswolds.gov.uk/tourism or Lonely Planet's *England* guide.

Sights & Information

The city centre is a 10-minute walk east from the railway station and a few minutes from the bus station at Gloucester Green.

Ashmolean Museum (☎ 278000; www.ashmol.ox.ac.uk; Beaumont St; admission free; ☾ 10am-5pm Tue-Sat, 2-5pm Sun)

Balliol College (☎ 277777; www.balliol.ox.ac.uk)

Bodleian Library & Divinity School (☎ 277000, tours ☎ 277224; tours £4; ☾ 9.30am-4.45pm Mon-Fri, 9.30am-12.30pm Sat; tours 10.30am, 11.30am, 2pm & 3pm Mon-Fri, 10.30am & 11.30am Sat Mar-Oct, 2pm & 3pm Mon-Fri, 10.30am & 11.30am Sat Nov-Feb)

Carfax Tower (☎ 792653; cnr Queen & Cornmarket Sts; adult/6-16yr £1.50/75p; ☾ 9.30am-5pm Apr-Oct, 9.30am-3pm Nov-Mar)

Christ Church (☎ 276150; www.visitchristchurch.net; adult/child £4.50/3.50; ☾ 9am-5pm Mon-Sat, 1-5pm Sun, last entry 4.30pm)

Magdalen Bridge Boathouse (☎ 202643; www.oxford punting.com; Magdalen Bridge; punting per hr £10, on weekends £12, deposit £30 & ID; chauffeured boat max 5 people per ½hr £20; ☾ 10am-8pm Apr-Oct)

Magdalen College (☎ 276000; adult/child £2/1 Apr-Sep, admission free Oct-Mar; ☾ noon-6pm mid-Jun–Sep, 2pm-dusk Oct–mid-Jun)

Merton College (☎ 276310; admission free; ☾ 2-4pm Mon-Fri, 10am-4pm Sat & Sun)

Museum of Oxford (☎ 815559; www.oxford.gov.uk/mus eum; St Aldate's; adult/senior & student/child £2/1.50/50p; ☾ 10am-4pm Tue-Fri, 10am-5pm Sat, noon-4pm Sun)

Oxford University Museum of Natural History (☎ 272950; www.oum.ox.ac.uk; Parks Rd; admission free; ☾ noon-5pm)

Pitt Rivers Museum (☎ 270927; www.prm.ox.ac.uk; Parks Rd; admission free; ☼ noon-4.30pm)

Sheldonian Theatre (☎ 798600; www.sheldon.ox.ac .uk; adult/child £1.50/50p; ☼ 10am-12.30pm & 2-4.30pm Mon-Sat)

Tourist Information Centre (TIC; ☎ 726871; www .visitoxford.org; 15-16 Broad St; ☼ 9.30am-5pm Mon-Sat year-round, plus 10am-3.30pm Sun Apr-Sep) Staff can book accommodation; two-hour guided walking tours of the colleges (adult/child £6.50/3) leave TIC at 11am and 2pm.

Trinity College (☎ 279900; www.trinity.ox.ac.uk; Broad St)

University Church of St Mary the Virgin (☎ 279112; www.university-church.ox.ac.uk; tower admission adult/ child £2/1; ☼ 9am-7pm Jul & Aug, 9am-5pm Sep-Jun)

Eating

In addition to the following, there are plenty of ethnic eateries along Cowley Rd, off High St southeast of Magdalen College.

Branca (☎ 556111; 111 Walton St; mains £5.95-16.95, weekday lunch special £5) In the Jericho district a short walk northwest of the centre, this trendy brasserie serves modern Italian cuisine. Slightly better for veggies than Quod.

Café Coco (☎ 200232; 23 Cowley Rd; mains £6-10) This buzzy place is most famous for loading a traditional English breakfast onto a pizza (£7.95).

Freud Arts Café (☎ 311171; 119 Walton St; mains £5-8) Also in Jericho, this boho hang-out is in a restored church, with pews, stained-glass windows and funky wire figures hanging from the ceiling. Popular with students, it serves sandwiches and pizzas.

Grand Café (☎ 204463; 84 High St; snacks £6-12.50) This museum-piece of a café is on the site of England's first coffee house (1650).

Quod Bar & Grill (☎ 202505; 92-94 High St; pasta £4.95-8.95, mains £9.95-16.95) Perennially popular for its smart surroundings, as well as for its chargrills, fish and pasta. Vegetarian options are very limited.

CAMBRIDGE
☎ 01223

Perhaps even more so than its fierce rival Oxford, Cambridge is the quintessential English university town, where the nation's bright young things ring their bicycle bells in the shadow of gorgeous medieval and neo-Gothic buildings. Whereas Oxford has a solid record in educating political grandees, Cambridge's reputation lies more in the technological sphere. Past names to have worked and studied here range from Isaac Newton and Charles Darwin to the discoverers of DNA, Watson and Crick, and Professor Stephen Hawking. In some senses it's the mother of English scientific ideas. (There have been several of these and someone has to take the blame for them, as writer PJ O'Rourke might have said. Oh yes, Cambridge was also responsible for a strong vein of English humour, nurturing the talents of John Cleese and several others of the Monty Python team.)

Founded in the 13th century, several decades later than Oxford, contemporary Cambridge is less touristy and more manageable than its competitor. However, note that during exam time – mid-April to late June – its colleges are often shut to the public.

The centre of town lies in a wide bend of the River Cam. The best-known section of riverbank is the mile-long Backs, which combines lush scenery with superb views of half a dozen colleges (the other 25 colleges are scattered throughout the city).

Starting at Magdalene Great Bridge to the north, walk southeast along Bridge St until you reach the **Round Church**, built in 1130 to commemorate its namesake in Jerusalem. Turn right down St John's St to **St John's College**. On the other side of the gatehouse (1510) are three beautiful courtyards, two of which date from the 17th century. From the third court, the picturesque **Bridge of Sighs**, named after the one in Venice, spans the Cam. Stand in the centre and watch the punts float by.

Transport

Distance from London 54 miles (87km)

Direction North

Travel time Two hours by bus, 55 minutes by train

Bus National Express (☎ 0870 580 8080; www .nationalexpress.com) runs hourly shuttle buses (day return £9.80)

Car The M11 connects the London Orbital Motorway (M25) to Cambridge. Take Exit 13 onto A1303 (Madingley Rd) and follow it towards the city centre

Train There are trains (☎ 0845 748 4950; www .nationalrail.co.uk) every 30 minutes from King's Cross and Liverpool St stations (day return £17.50)

Just south of St John's, **Trinity College** is one of the largest and most attractive colleges, not to mention the wealthiest. It was established in 1546 by Henry VIII, whose statue peers out from the top niche of the great gateway (he's holding a chair leg instead of the royal sceptre, the result of a student prank). The **Great Court**, the largest in Cambridge or Oxford, incorporates some fine 15th-century buildings. Beyond the Great Court are the cloisters of Nevile's Court and the dignified **Wren Library**, built by Sir Christopher in the 1680s.

Next comes Gonville and Caius (pronounced keys) College and **King's College**, one of the most sublime buildings in Europe and Cambridge's foremost tourist attraction. The **chapel** was begun in 1446 by Henry VI and completed around 1516. Henry VI's successors, notably Henry VIII, added the intricate fan vaulting and elaborate wood-and-stone carvings of the interior. The chapel comes alive when the choir sings and there are services during term time and in July.

Continue south on what is now King's Pde (which becomes Trumpington St) to the **Fitzwilliam Museum**, which houses Greek and Roman art in the lower galleries and has a wonderful new modern courtyard. At the time of writing, its refurbished Egyptian gallery was scheduled to reopen in early 2006.

Taking a punt along the Backs is great fun, but it can also be a wet and hectic experience. The secret to propelling these flat-bottomed boats is to push gently on the pole to get the punt moving and then to use it as a rudder to keep on course. In Cambridge, as opposed to Oxford, the tradition is to punt from the flat, decked end of the boat. **Trinity Punt Hire** and **Scudamore's** have punts for hire and chauffeured rides.

Sights & Information

Fitzwilliam Museum (☎ 332923; www.fitzmuseum.cam .ac.uk; Trumpington St; admission free, tours £3; ✆ 10am-5pm Tue-Sat, noon-5pm Sun, guided tours 2.45pm Sun)

Geoff's Bike Hire (☎ 365629; 65 Devonshire Rd; ✆ 9am-6pm Apr-Sep, 9am-5.30pm Mon-Sat Oct-Mar; bikes per day/week £8/16, deposit £25)

King's College & Chapel (☎ 331212, 331100; www .kings.cam.ac.uk; King's Pde; adult/concession £4.50/3; ✆ 9.30am-3.30pm Mon-Fri, 9.30am-3.15pm Sat, 1.15-2.15pm & 5.30-6pm Sun term time, 9.30am-4.30pm Mon-Sat, 10am-5pm Sun out of term time) Call for choral performance times.

Round Church (Church of the Holy Sepulchre; ☎ 311602; www.christianheritageuk.org.uk; cnr Round Church & Bridge Sts; adult/concession £1/50p; ✆ 10am-5pm Tue-Sat, 1-5pm Sun & Mon)

St John's College (☎ 338676; www.joh.cam.ac.uk; St John St; ✆ 10am-5pm)

Scudamore's (☎ 359750; Grant Pl; per hr £12, deposit £60) Chauffeured rides cost £10 per person.

TIC (☎ 322640; www.visitcambridge.org; the Old Library, Wheeler St; ✆ 10am-5pm Mon-Sat, 11am-4pm Sun Apr-Sep, 10am-5.30pm Mon-Sat Oct-Mar) Just south of Market Sq. TIC staff can arrange accommodation and two-hour walking tours (adult/child £6.50/4 or £8.50/4 including King's College), leaving at 1.30pm year-round, with more during summer.

Trinity College (☎ 332500; www.trin.cam.ac.uk; Trinity Lane; adult/concession £2.20/1.30, check website for free entry periods; ✆ 10am-5pm)

Trinity Punt Hire (☎ 338483; Garret Hostel Lane; per hr £6, deposit £25) Chauffeured tours of the river cost £6 to £10 per person.

Wren Library (✆ noon-2pm Mon-Fri, plus 10.30am-12.30pm Sat in full term time)

Eating

In addition to the places listed below, cheap Indian and Chinese eateries can be found where Lensfield Rd meets Regent St towards the train station.

Fitzbillies (☎ 352500; 52 Trumpington St) While it's also a restaurant at night, this bakery is principally famous for its Chelsea buns and cakes.

Galleria (☎ 362054; 33 Bridge St; mains £5.95-8.95) Noodles, pasta and other Continental fare are served in this café overlooking the Cam river. Try to snag a seat on the balcony.

Light (☎ 308100; 66 Regent St; mains £7.95-12.95) Looking like a trendy, chilled, DJ bar (which it also is), this turns out to be quite welcoming and serves great spicy dishes, alongside down-home burgers and innovative pizza.

Midsummer House (☎ 568336; www.midsummerhouse .co.uk; Midsummer Common; lunch £20, dinner £48.50; ✆ Mon-Sat) Chef Daniel Clifford has been awarded one Michelin star for the fine, mainly French haute cuisine. The formal two-floor restaurant sits on the corner of the common, near the river.

Rainbow (☎ 321551; 9a King's Pde; mains £6.95-7.95) Across the road from King's College, you'll find this old-school vegetarian and vegan restaurant.

River Bar + Kitchen (☎ 307030; Quayside; mains £8.95-12.95) This airy, two-storey riverside brasserie off Bridge St attracts a smart young crowd with its modern Mediterranean cuisine. Freshly made lunchtime sandwiches (£5.95) come with salad or chips.

BATH

☎ 01225

Georgian terraces fronted in honey-coloured stone arranged in wonderful symmetry – these are the elements that make Bath one of England's most graceful towns. But its ancient Roman heritage and hot springs also boost its massive tourist appeal. Surrounded by seven hills, just like Rome, this photogenic city is now a Unesco World Heritage Site. And, after decades without a functioning spa, it now seems on the verge of reclaiming its status as a restorative resort.

The history of bathing in the city's 46°C springs goes back to Celtic times – according to legend, their healing powers were discovered by a leprous swine-herd. The Romans arriving in AD 43 also took to Bath's curative waters, as did the society types, including novelist Jane Austen, who attended the city's amazing Georgian renaissance in the 18th century.

After a public health scare in the 1970s, however, the city's baths were closed. Now a replacement has been built and, at the time of writing, this much-delayed **Thermae Bath Spa** was expected to open in 2006, with an open-air thermal pool on its roof.

As welcome as it is, the new spa is hardly likely to replace the **Roman Baths Museum** as the city's most popular – and most crowded – attraction. Here you can marvel at the Roman-paved **Great Bath**, surrounded by 19th-century arcading, before inspecting a network of smaller baths through which 1.5 million litres of hot water pour every day. The 12th-century **King's Bath** is built around the original sacred spring and you'll also see the ruins of the **Sulis Temple of Minerva** before emerging into the **Pump Room** (stopping for afternoon tea, or a special Bath bun, should you please).

Your next stop should be the stunning **Royal Crescent** built between 1767 and 1771. This hilltop, crescent-shaped row of houses overlooks the city, and the Palladian town house at **No 1 Royal Crescent** has had its interior restored to its late-18th-century appearance. The nearby **Circus** is a circular street, akin to a roundabout only a hell of a lot more aesthetically pleasing.

Bath Abbey was the last great medieval church raised in England. It boasts 640 wall monuments, second only to Westminster Abbey, and hosts the grave of Beau Nash, who masterminded Bath's Georgian makeover. While near the Abbey, take a moment to walk to the River Avon and enjoy the view of **Pulteney Weir**.

Bath always has plenty of visitors, but equally there's plenty to see. If you still have time, consider the **Museum of Costume and Assembly Rooms**, which includes the restored public rooms built by Georgian architectural genius John Wood the Younger, or the **Jane Austen Centre**.

River Avon (above)

Distance from London 106 miles (170km)

Direction Southwest

Travel time 3½ hours by bus, 1½ hours by train

Bus National Express (☎ 0870 580 8080; www
.nationalexpress.com) runs buses from London's
Victoria coach station (£22 return, 10 daily)

Train There are trains (☎ 0845 748 4950; www
.nationalrail.co.uk) every 30 minutes from London's
Paddington station (return £35 to £45)

Sights & Information

Bath Spa railway station is south of the
city centre. A short walk north along Man-
vers St will bring you to the highly visible
Abbey.

Bath Abbey (☎ 422262; requested donation £2;
☺ 9am-6pm Mon-Sat Easter-Oct, 9am-4pm Mon-Sat
Nov-Easter, 1.15-2.45pm Sun year-round) Next to the
Roman Baths entrance.

Jane Austen Centre (☎ 443000; www.janeausten.co.uk;
40 Gay St; adult/child/concession £4.65/2.45/3.95; 10am-
5.30pm Apr-Oct, 11am-4.30pm Nov-Mar)

Museum of Costume and Assembly Rooms
(☎ 477789; www.museumofcostume.co.uk; Bennett St;
adult/child/concession £6.25/4.25/5.25; ☺ 11am-6pm,
last entry 5pm, Mar-Oct, 11am-5pm, last entry 4pm,
Nov-Feb)

No 1 Royal Cres (☎ 428126; www.bath-preservation
-trust.org.uk; adult/concession £4/3.50; ☺ 10.30am-5pm
Tue-Sun Mar-Oct, 10.30am-4pm Tue-Sun Nov)

Roman Baths Museum (☎ 477785; www.roman
baths.co.uk; Stall St; adult/child/senior & student
£8.50/4.80/7.50; ☺ 9am-5pm Mar-Jun, Sep & Oct, 9am-
9pm Jul & Aug, 9.30am-5.30pm Nov-Feb)

Thermae Bath Spa (☎ 477051; www.thermaebathspa
.com; per 2hr/4hr/day £17/23/35; ☺ 9am-10pm) At
the time of writing, the much-anticipated opening was
scheduled for 2006. However, ring just to be sure.

TIC (☎ 0906 711 2000, premium rate; www.visitbath
.co.uk; Abbey Churchyard; ☺ 9.30am-6pm Mon-Sat,
10am-4pm Sun May-Sep, 9.30am-5pm Mon-Sat, 10am-
4pm Sun Oct-Apr) Can help with accommodation and sells
a handy *City Trail* booklet (£1.99).

Eating

Bistro Papillon (☎ 310064; 2 Margaret's Bldg, Brock St;
mains £9-13, set lunch £8; ☺ Mon-Sat) A rustic French/
Polish bistro with candles and checked tablecloths.

Demuth's (☎ 446059; 2 North Pde Passage; mains
£10-13) Serves vegetarian and vegan curries, wraps and
outstanding tapas.

Hop Pole (☎ 446327; 7 Albion Bldg; Upper Bristol Rd;
mains £8-16; ☺ closed lunch Mon) This sociable pub/
restaurant is the sort of place where the proprietors' names –
Barry and Elaine – matter. The Hop Pole serves hearty
cuisine ranging from whitebait and salmon to haggis and
oxtail.

Moody Goose (☎ 466688; 7a Kingsmead Sq; mains
£18-20, set lunch/dinner £18/26) Imaginative use of fresh
local ingredients keeps the modern British cuisine of this
basement restaurant in the highest local regard.

Pimpernel's (☎ 823333; www.royalcrescent.co.uk; 16
Royal Cres; 2-/3-course set lunch £18/25, set dinner £45)
Posh modern British cuisine in a very formal Regency
restaurant in the home of the famous Scarlet Pimpernel –
now Bath's ritziest hotel.

Sleeping

It's best to book ahead at weekends, as Bath
is a popular getaway spot. There are scores
of cheap, chintzy B&Bs as well as the following recommendations:

Athole House (☎ 320009; www.atholehouse.co.uk;
33 Upper Oldfield Park; s/d £48/78) Bright, modern and
without a hint of chintz, this Victorian home is set in
lovely gardens. Pick-ups from the train station can be
arranged.

Bath YMCA (☎ 325900; www.bathymca.co.uk; International House, Broad St; dm/s/d £14/20/32) Central
and modern, if not particularly full of character. There's a
restaurant on site.

Duke's (☎ 787960; wwwdukesbath.co.uk; Great
Pulteney St; d from £125) In a quiet location five minutes
from the centre of Bath, this elegant town house hotel is
renowned for its excellent service and historical ambience.

Harington's Hotel (☎ 466407; Forester Rd; s £70-110,
d £90-130, tw £100-140) Functional is the best word to
describe this straightforward central hotel, which makes a
nice change from all Bath's twee B&Bs.

Queensberry Hotel (☎ 447928; www.thequeensberry
.co.uk; Russell St; d £100-140) Recently refurbished in a
more modern style, this boutique hotel has 29 individually designed rooms and a popular restaurant, the Olive
Tree.

Town House Bath (☎ 422505; www.thetownhouse
bath.co.uk; 7 Bennett St; s £65-95, d £80-100) This
winning B&B uses quality furnishings to create a sense
of luxury (its rooms are neither too traditional nor too
modern, either). Right in the heart of Bath, it serves a
lavish breakfast too.

Excursions – Bath

385

BRIGHTON

☎ 01273

No wonder so many articles about London's favourite seaside resort go for the headline 'Brighton Rocks'. It first became popular when the dissolute Prince Regent (later King George IV) built his outrageous summer palace, the Royal Pavilion, here in the 18th century as a venue for lavish parties. And that charmingly seedy, 'great-place-for-a-dirty-weekend' vibe lasted throughout the gang-ridden 1930s of Graham Greene's novel *Brighton Rock* and the mods v rockers rivalry of the 1960s – think *Quadrophenia*. Today, an easy commute from the capital, it's among the UK's hippest cities. Cate Blanchett, Julie Burchill, Nick Cave, Steve Coogan, Zöe Ball, Norman Cook (aka Fatboy Slim) and other media folk all live here in 'London-on-Sea' (all of them in Hove, actually).

Any visit to Brighton is essentially about life's simple pleasures – shopping in the trendy boutiques in the narrow streets called 'The Lanes' or in the separate 'North Laine', eating, hanging out and perhaps buying a stick of hard 'Brighton rock' candy among the tacky stalls and amusement rides on **Brighton Pier** (only nonlocals call this Palace Pier).

Brighton has a young student population because of its university and language schools, a happening nightlife and, in the Kemp Town area east of Brighton Pier, one of the country's most vibrant gay scenes. However, there's plenty to keep culture vultures occupied, too. The **Royal Pavilion** should be your first port of call in this regard. Originally a farmhouse and converted to a neoclassical villa in 1787, it only began to take its current shape when John Nash, architect of Regent's Park and its surrounding crescents, got his hands on it between 1815 and 1822. As all things Asian were then the rage, he added onion domes and minarets to produce the final Mogul-inspired design.

The interior features giant bamboo staircases and carved wooden palm trees. Don't miss the **Music Room**, with its nine lotus-shaped chandeliers and Chinese murals in vermilion and gold, nor the **Banqueting Room**, with its domed and painted ceiling.

Across from the Pavilion Gardens you'll find the redeveloped **Brighton Museum & Art Gallery**, with three new galleries – Fashion & Style, Body and World Art – joining its ceramics, costume and fine-arts collections from the 15th to 20th centuries.

The historic **West Pier** began to collapse into the sea in December 2002 and, having since caught fire twice, is now a spookily twisted metal skeleton. Ironically, this only appears to have made it seem more interesting to those who flock to see it.

Transport

Distance from London 51 miles (82km)

Direction South

Travel time One hour 50 minutes by bus, 50 minutes by fast train

Bus National Express (☎ 0870 580 8080; www .nationalexpress.com; return £15, day return £9.80, online funfares from £1) and Megabus (www .megabus.com; online fares from £1.50) run hourly services

Car The M23/A23 runs straight into Brighton town centre

Train There are about 40 fast trains (☎ 0845 748 4950; www.nationalrail.co.uk) each day from London's Victoria station (return/day return £23.50/16.80), and slightly slower Thameslink trains from Blackfriars, London Bridge and King's Cross (return/day return £21/13.10)

Sights & Information

Brighton Museum & Art Gallery (☎ 290900; www .brighton.virtualmuseum.info; Church St; admission free; ☼ 10am-7pm Tue, 10am-5pm Wed-Sat & public holidays, 2-5pm Sun)

Brighton Pier (Palace Pier; www.brightonpier.co.uk; Madeira Dr; admission free)

Royal Pavilion (☎ 290900; Pavilion Pde; adult/senior & student/5-15yr £5.80/4/3.40; ☼ 9.30am-5.45pm Apr-Sep, 10am-5.15pm Oct-Mar) Tours of the Royal Pavilion (£1.25)

leave at 11.30am & 2.30pm, with additional departures at 1pm and 1.30pm Saturday and Sunday in summer.

TIC (☎ 0906 711 2255; www.visitbrighton.com; 10 Bartholomew Sq; ☼ 9am-5.30pm Mon-Fri, 10am-5pm Sat, 10am-4pm Sun Mar-Oct, 9am-5pm Mon-Fri, 5pm Sat Nov-Feb)

Eating

Brighton and Hove have more restaurants per head of population than anywhere in the

UK, bar London. Some professional critics complain the local eateries don't match the cosmopolitan nature of the place, but lesser mortals will generally be more than content.

Café/Bar Nia (☎ 671371; 87-88 Trafalgar St; mains £9-14) Even the local celebs love Nia's solid wooden tables and chalkboard menu, but it's a great place for a cappuccino and ciabatta sandwich anyhow.

Donatello (☎ 775477; 1-3 Brighton Pl, the Lanes; mains £4.65-17.95) This huge, well-known Italian restaurant is hard to miss in its section of the Lanes (hence its inclusion here), but the service is usually slow and the food can be variable.

Due South (☎ 821218; 139 Kings Road Arches; mains £11-14) On the seafront, with a wonderfully arched ceiling, this is one of Brighton's most talked-about restaurants. The seasonally changing menu might include things such as local wild rabbit kebabs with spicy peanut sauce or sirloin with garlic and onion butter confit, but always features lots of fish, mussels and oysters.

Real Eating Company (☎ 221444; 86-87 Western Rd, Hove; dishes £4-12.50; ☺ breakfast & lunch daily, dinner Wed & Sat) This hip deli-cum-café is about everyday eating and a top spot for breakfast (eg French toast with bacon and maple syrup).

Regency (☎ 325014; 131 Kings Rd; mains £3-20) All things to everybody is how famed seafood chef Rick Stein has described this beachfront place, which offers everything from fish soup to lobster, as well as pastas and steaks.

Terre à Terre (☎ 729051; 71 East St; mains £12.85-13.25) In 2004 this gourmet vegetarian establishment was named the second best restaurant in England, proving that this is a great place that just happens not to serve meat. Dishes sound overly complicated, but taste simply delicious.

Sleeping

You should book ahead for weekends in summer and during the Brighton Festival in May.

Baggies Backpackers (☎ 733740; 33 Oriental Pl; dm £12-£13, d £35) Clean, relaxed and central, this is the best hostel in town. There's a £5 room-key deposit.

brightonwave (☎ 676794; www.brightonwave.com; 10 Madeira Pl; d £80-190) Combining the cool, muted design you'd expect from an expensive boutique hotel with the warm welcome of the small B&B it really is, this offers great value, service and style. Fantastic breakfasts too.

Drakes (☎ 696394; www.drakesofbrighton.com; 43-44 Marine Pde; s/d from £95/135) It's the 'feature rooms' (£145 to £450) that are most magnificent here, with clawfoot baths in front of curtain windows overlooking the sea. Staff are ever so obliging.

Hotel du Vin (☎ 718588; www.hotelduvin.com; Ship St; d/ste from £130/235) Located in a former wine merchant's Gothic home, this award-winning hotel has an ornate staircase, unusual gargoyles and elegant rooms.

Hotel Pelirocco (☎ 3327055; www.hotelpelirocco.co.uk; s/d from £50/80) Brighton's original rock 'n' roll 'n' fashion hotel is no longer at the cutting edge, but it added new rooms in 2005 and its plush, ironic décor – chandeliers, satin and pictures of stars from Doris Day to Muhammed Ali – is still lots of fun.

Old Ship Hotel (☎ 329001; www.oldshiphotel -brighton.co.uk; Kings Rd; s/d from £60/70) Housed in a heritage-listed building, this larger 152-room hotel isn't particularly trendy, but does have elegant and comfortable rooms.

Royal Pavilion (opposite)

Oriental Hotel (☎ 205050; www.orientalhotel.co.uk; 9 Oriental Pl; s £35-40, standard d £60-£85, deluxe d £85-125) Stylishly decorated in mint and rouge, this groovy boho hotel has fresh flowers, aromatherapy lights and organic breakfasts.

Strawberry Fields (☎ 681576; www.strawberry-fields-hotel.com; 6-7 New Steine; d from £50) Run by a young family and an excellent choice for young families, this Kemp Town B&B even has a play area in the lounge.

White House (☎ 626266; www.whitehousebrighton .com; 6 Bedford St; s £38-55, d £65-130) This well-located place has an updated Regency style, with embossed wallpaper or carved writing desks complemented by the occasional splash of modern colour. Good value for money.

BROADSTAIRS, MARGATE & WHITSTABLE

These three seaside towns have very different characters, so choose whichever takes your fancy. Broadstairs is a nostalgic place with a patina of both Victorian and postwar history. Slightly dilapidated Margate is the archetypal kitsch English seaside resort, now forever associated with homegirl Tracey Emin, the Brit artist. Increasingly gentrified Whitstable is…well, is where you go for fresh oysters. It's been nicknamed 'Islington-on-Sea', as well-heeled Londoners have begun buying up its fishermen's huts as second homes.

People mostly head in this direction to soak up the atmosphere, swim (in good weather) and just hang around. Stroll along the **Broadstairs Promenade**, or take the cliffside walkway from **Viking Bay** to secluded **Louisa Bay**. The **Dickens House Museum** commemorates the writer's love of, and association with, Broadstairs; there's also a Dickens festival in the middle of June.

Alternatively, you could visit Margate's unusual **Shell Grotto**, a mysterious underground temple dating from pagan times that's definitely worth seeing. The 1000-year-old **Margate Caves** have a church, smugglers' refuge, dungeon, cave paintings and some witty (if not 100% proven) historical explanations.

The annual **Whitstable Oyster Festival** is held in the third week in July.

Transport

Distance from London Whitstable 58 miles (93km), Margate 74 miles (118km), Broadstairs 78 miles (125km)

Direction East

Travel time 1¼ hours to 2¾ hours

Bus Five daily departures to Ramsgate stop at all three towns (outward 10.30am to 8.30pm, return 8.05am to 5.55pm). Same-day returns £11 to Whitstable, £11.80 to Broadstairs or Margate.

Car Follow the M2; at Margate/Ramsgate sign, follow the Thanet Way

Train Trains (☎ 0845 748 4950; www.nationalrail .co.uk) from London's Victoria station to Ramsgate leave every 30 minutes (duration 1¼ hours to two hours); day return £17 to Whitstable, £21.40 to Broadstairs or Margate

Sights & Information

Broadstairs TIC (☎ 01843-583333; www.tourism .thanet.gov.uk; 6b High St; ☒ 9.15am-4.45pm Mon-Fri, 10am-4pm Sat & Sun Apr-Sep, 9.15am-4.45pm Mon-Fri, 10am-4.45pm Sat Oct-Mar)

Dickens House Museum (☎ 01843-863453; 2 Victoria Pde, Broadstairs; adult/concession £2/1; ☒ 11am-5pm Mar-Jun & Sep, 11am-9pm Jul & Aug)

Margate Caves (☎ 01843-220139; 1 Northdown Rd, Cliftonville; adult/concession £3/1.50; ☒ 10am-5pm Apr-Oct, 10am-4pm Sat & Sun Nov-Apr)

Margate TIC (☎ 01843-583333; www.tourism.thanet .gov.uk; 12-13 the Parade; ☒ 9.15am-4.45pm Mon-Fri, 10am-4pm Sat & Sun Apr-Sep, 9.15am-4.45pm Mon-Fri, 10am-4.45pm Sat Oct-Mar)

Shell Grotto (☎ 01843-220008; Grotto Hill, Margate; adult/concession/child £2.50/1.50/1; ☒ 10am-5pm Apr-Oct, 11am-4pm Sat & Sun Nov-Apr) Off Northdown Rd.

Whitstable TIC (☎ 01227-275482; www.canterbury .co.uk; 7 Oxford St; ☒ 10am-5pm Mon-Sat Jul & Aug, 10am-4pm Mon-Sat Sep-Jun)

Eating

Both establishments listed here are in Whitstable.

Wheelers Oyster Bar (☎ 01227-273311; 8 High St; mains £6-18; ☒ Thu-Tue) A tiny place that's a favourite with locals – and no, not the Wheelers who founded Lonely Planet.

Whitstable Oyster Fishery Company (☎ 01227-276856; Royal Native Oyster Stores, Horsbridge; mains £13-25; ☒ lunch & dinner Tue-Sat, lunch Sun) Enjoy all kinds of seafood in refurbished company HQ with great sea views.

RYE, ROMNEY MARSH & DUNGENESS

☎ 01797

The impossibly picturesque medieval town of Rye looks like it has been preserved in historical formaldehyde. Not even the most talented Hollywood set designers could have come up with a better representation of Ye Olde English Village: the half-timbered Tudor buildings, Georgian town houses, winding cobbled streets, abundant flowerpots and strong literary associations should be enough to temper even the most hard-bitten cynic's weariness of the made-for-tourism look. (All the same, such cynics should avoid crowded summer weekends.)

The town is easily covered on foot. Around the corner from the TIC, in Strand Quay, are a number of **antique shops** selling all kinds of wonderful junk. From here walk up cobbled **Mermaid St**, with its timber-framed houses dating from the 15th century.

Turn right at the T-junction for the Georgian **Lamb House**, mostly dating from 1722. It was the home of American writer Henry James from 1898 to 1916 (he wrote *The Wings of the Dove* here). Continue around the dogleg until you come out at gorgeous Church Sq. The **Church of St Mary the Virgin** incorporates several styles. The turret clock (1561) is the oldest in England and still works with its original pendulum mechanism. There are great views from the church tower. Turn right at the square's east corner for **Ypres Tower** (variously pronounced yeeps or wipers), part of Rye's former fortifications, and **Castle Museum**.

The town celebrates its medieval heritage with a two-day **festival** each August, and in September there is the two-week **Festival of Music and the Arts**.

East of Rye lies Romney Marsh and Dungeness, England's most otherworldly coast – recorded in Derek Jarman's film *The Garden* and more recently making a guest appearance on the cover of the Thrills' album *So Much for the City*. The vast, flat marsh has a unique ecology, with unusual flora and fauna. Dotted across it, there's also a collection of tiny **medieval churches** – start with **St Augustine's** in Brookland. Desolate, barren Dungeness is the world's largest expanse of shingle and home to an unlikely combination of an **old lighthouse**, a **nuclear power station** and the **Royal Society for the Protection of Birds (RSPB) Nature Reserve**. Derek Jarman's famous garden can still be seen on the road to the old lighthouse, although the new owner of the black cottage has a sign out asking you to respect their privacy, so please do.

Excursions – Rye, Romney Marsh & Dungeness

Transport

Distance from London 54 miles (90km)

Direction Southeast

Travel time One to two hours

Bus To Dungeness, catch the hourly 711 from Rye railway station to the Ship pub at New Romney, from where you can take the Romney, Hythe and Dymchurch Railway (see below)

Car Follow the M2, M20 then A20

Train Trains (☎ 0845 748 4950; www.nationalrail .co.uk) head to Rye from Charing Cross station via Ashford International or Hastings, where you will have to change. Two trains leave every hour, but both leave about the same time (£20 day return). To head directly to Dungeness go from Liverpool St station to Hythe (£17 day return, hourly) then take the toytown-like Romney, Hythe and Dymchurch Railway (☎ 01797-362353; www.rhdr.co.uk; day passes adult/senior/ student £10.50/9/5.25; ⏰ 10.20am-4.20pm Jun-Aug, 10.20am-2.30pm Apr, May & Sep, 9.35am-2.30pm Sat & Sun Oct-Mar), which runs approximately hourly.

Sights & Information

Church of St Mary the Virgin (tower views adult/child £2/1; ⏰ 9am-4pm winter, 9am-6pm rest of the year)

Dungeness RSPB Nature Reserve (☎ 320588; www .rspb.org.uk/reserves/Dungeness; Dungeness Rd, Lydd; adult/concession/child £3/2/1; ⏰ reserve dawn-dusk, visitors centre 10am-5pm Apr-Oct, 10am-4pm Nov-Mar)

Hythe Visitors' Centre (Red Lion Sq; ⏰ 9am-5pm Mon-Sat) Can book accommodation and offer information on Dungeness; open to personal callers only.

Lamb House (☎ 224982; www.nationaltrust.org.uk; West St; adult/child £2.60/1.30; ⏰ 2-6pm Wed & Sat Apr-Oct)

Old Lighthouse (☎ 2321300; tower views adult/child £3/2; ⏰ 10.30am-5pm Jul–mid-Sep, 11am-5pm Sat & Sun mid-Sep–Jun)

Romney Marsh Countryside Project (☎ 367974; www.rmcp.co.uk) This project has a useful website and organises all sorts of interesting guided walks across the marsh.

Rye Hire (☎ 223033; Cyprus Pl; bicycles per day £12, deposit £20) There is a cycle path to Lydd, followed by a road down to Dungeness.

Rye TIC (☎ 226696; www.visitrye.co.uk; Strand Quay; ☯ 10am-5pm Apr-Oct, 10am-4pm Mon-Sat Nov-Mar) Gives out a free guide to the town and offers audio tours (adult/concession/child £2.50/1.50/1). Can also help with basic information on Dungeness.

Ypres Tower and Castle Museum (☎ 226728; 3 East Rye St; admission £1.90; 10.30am-1pm & 2-5pm Thu-Mon Apr-Oct, 10.30-3.30pm Nov-Mar tower only)

Eating

Landgate Bistro (☎ 222327; 1 Tower St; mains £10-13.50, set menu £17.90) By general consensus, this is Rye's best restaurant, serving modern European cuisine with a slightly French flavour in an unpretentious environment.

Mermaid Inn (☎ 223065; Mermaid St) Like the Old Borough Arms, this is typical of the olde-worlde half-timbered English pubs in Rye. There's also a casual restaurant.

Old Borough Arms (☎ 222128; the Strand) This 300-year-old former smugglers' inn is a truly lovely guesthouse with an excellent café.

CANTERBURY

☎ 01227

Canterbury's greatest treasure is its majestic **cathedral**. Yet, despite the impressive 66m **Bell Harry Tower** lording it over the surrounding countryside, it's not the architecture, but the assassination of archbishop Thomas Becket in 1170 inside, that made the building famous. This turned it into the site of one of Europe's most important medieval pilgrimages, as immortalised by Geoffrey Chaucer in *The Canterbury Tales*.

Becket clashed with Henry II over tax and then over the coronation of Henry's son. Hearing Henry mutter 'who will rid me of this turbulent priest?', four knights dispatched themselves to Canterbury, where they scalped the archbishop and amputated his limbs in the late afternoon of 29 December. But the murder caused indignation throughout Europe, and Henry was forced to do penance at Becket's tomb, which was later said to be the site of many miracles.

The traditional approach to the cathedral, which dates from 1070, is along narrow Mercery Lane to Christ Church Gate. The main entrance is through the **southwest porch**, built in 1415 to commemorate the English victory at Agincourt. You'll pass a visitors centre before this, where you can pick up free leaflets, ask for information or book tours.

The perpendicular-style **nave** (1405) into which you enter is famous for its intricate ribbed vaulting – and there's more fabulous vaulting under the Bell Harry Tower. To your right (east) is the pulpitum screen that separates the nave from the quire.

Thomas Becket is believed to have been murdered in the northwest transept before you reach the pulpitum; the modern **Altar of the Sword's Point** marks the spot. On the south side of the nave, you can descend into the Romanesque **crypt**, the main survivor of an earlier cathedral built by St Augustine in 597 to help convert the post-Roman English to Christianity.

Continuing eastwards through the pulpitum into the quire, you'll come to **St Augustine's chair**, the seat of the Archbishop of Canterbury (currently Rowan Williams). Behind this in **Trinity Chapel**, a burning candle and a brass inscription mark the site of the former **Tomb of St Thomas**, which was destroyed on Henry VIII's orders during the Reformation. The chapel's stained glass is mostly 13th century, celebrating the life of St Thomas Becket.

Also in the chapel you'll find the magnificent **Tomb of the Black Prince** (Edward, Prince of Wales, 1330–76), with its famous effigy that includes the prince's shield, gauntlets and

Transport

Distance from London 56 miles (90km)

Direction Southeast

Travel time One hour 50 minutes by bus, 1¾ hours by train

Bus National Express (☎ 0870 580 8080; www.nationalexpress.com) has 16 daily shuttle buses (day return £16.50, funfares from £1)

Train Canterbury East train station is accessible from London's Victoria station, and Canterbury West from Charing Cross and Waterloo stations. Trains (☎ 0845 748 4950; www.nationalrail.co.uk) leave regularly (up to every 10 minutes); same day return is £17.

sword. The **Corona** once contained the slightly macabre relic of the part of Thomas' skull that was sliced off during his assassination.

Outside, walk around the eastern end of the cathedral and turn right into **Green Court**. In the northwestern corner (far left) is the much celebrated **Norman Staircase** (1151).

After the cathedral, Canterbury's other attractions are very much epilogues to the main act.

The **Museum of Canterbury** has been given a thorough revamp, and is particularly aimed at children and families. New hands-on exhibits include a medieval discovery gallery (where you can look at medieval poo under the microscope) and a 'whodunnit' on the mysterious death of playwright Christopher Marlowe (originally a Canterbury lad). Children's cartoon characters Rupert Bear, Bagpuss and the Clangers also appear.

If you're really keen to acquaint or reacquaint yourself with Chaucer's famous stories, head to the **Canterbury Tales**, where, armed with a storytelling audioguide, you pass puppets recreating various scenes. It might be better to just buy the book, though, to read on the train back to London.

Sights & Information

Canterbury Cathedral (☎ 762862; www.canterbury-cath edral.org; Sun St; adult/concession £5/4; 🕙 9am-6pm Mon-Sat, 9am-2pm & 4.30-5.30pm Sun Apr-Oct, 9am-4.30pm Mon-Sat, 10am-2pm & 4.30-5.30pm Sun Nov-Mar, access may be restricted 9am-12.30pm Sun for services) One-hour guided tours (adult/concession £3.50/2.50) leave at 10.30am, noon and 2.30pm Monday to Saturday Easter to September, and noon and 2pm Monday to Saturday October to Easter. A 30-minute audioguide tour costs £2.95/1.95 per adult/child.

Canterbury Tales (☎ 454888, 479227; www.canterbury tales.org.uk; St Margaret's St; adult/senior & student/child £6.95/5.95/5.25; 🕙 9.30am-5.30pm Jul & Aug, 10am-5pm Mar-Jun, Sep & Oct, 10am-4.30pm Nov-Feb)

Museum of Canterbury (☎ 452747; www.canter bury-museums.co.uk; Stour St; adult/child/family £3.25/2.15/8.45; 🕙 10.30am-5pm Mon-Sat, 1.30-5pm Sun Jun-Sep, 10.30am-5pm Mon-Sat Oct-May)

TIC (☎ 766567, 767744; www.canterbury.co.uk; 34 St Margaret's St; 🕙 9.30am-5.30pm Mon-Sat, 10am-4pm Sun Apr-Oct, 9.30am-5pm Mon-Sat, 10am-4pm Sun Nov & Dec, 9.30am-5pm Mon-Sat Jan-Mar)

Eating

Bistro Viêt Nam (☎ 760022; the Old Linen Store, White Horse Lane; mains £5-11) The modern Southeast Asian menu here includes a range of Vietnamese tapas.

Flap Jacques (☎ 781000; 71 Castle St; crepes £4.75-6.50) This is a small French bistro serving Breton-style savoury and sweet pancakes.

Goods Shed (☎ 459153; Station Rd West; mains £8-16; 🕙 lunch & dinner Tue-Sat, lunch Sun) You overlook a farmers market in this fabulous converted railway shed, with its high ceilings, huge windows and exposed brick. The changing French country menu uses that fresh produce inventively.

Christ and Angels gate, Canterbury Cathedral (opposite)

STRATFORD-UPON-AVON

☎ 01789

Stratford is a quiet Norman market town on the river Avon, and its fortunes would have been quite different were it not for William Shakespeare's birth in 1564. While some may find the industry that has grown up around Britain's greatest writer akin to a personality cult, there is plenty of scope for an interesting trip. It's best to avoid the area around Sheep St, a textbook tourist trap full of souvenir shops and overpriced eateries.

The Stratford experience largely consists of five 'Shakespeare houses', with a few ancillary sites in between. Three of the houses are in the town centre. In **Shakespeare's Birthplace** the atmosphere of a well-to-do 16th-century family home has been well preserved. It's not actually certain that Shakespeare was born here, but it's where he spent his early years. The Elizabethan town house of Shakespeare's daughter Susanna, **Hall's Croft**, has a fascinating, and quite gruesome, display devoted to the medical practices in use during Shakespeare's lifetime. **Nash's House & New Place**, on the corner of Chapel St and Chapel Lane, consist of a rather dull house once belonging to Thomas Nash, who married Shakespeare's granddaughter, and the remains of the house (New Place) where Shakespeare is believed to have died in 1616. Legend has it a previous owner destroyed it in 1759, unable to stand all the tourists…

Some 1.5km outside town – reached by regular **City Sightseeing buses** – lies **Anne Hathaway's Cottage**, the home of Shakespeare's wife before the couple was married. The cottage has a traditional thatched roof, as well as lovely gardens. The bus circuit also takes in **Mary Arden's House**, the house of Shakespeare's mother, in the village of Wilmcote. Only a few years ago, fresh evidence showed Mary's family hadn't lived in the medieval hall, as previously thought, but in the smaller cottage next door. This has therefore yet to be returned to its 'original' appearance.

Back in town, next door to Hall's Croft is **Holy Trinity Church**, the resting place of Shakespeare and his wife.

Stratford is home to the **Royal Shakespeare Company**, and there can be no better proof of Shakespeare's endurance than seeing one of the RSC's usually very high-quality performances of his work. In 2006 the RSC is launching its most ambitious programme ever, by performing the bard's complete works in one season. At the same time the company is building a new main theatre and there will be some venue changes over the next few years. In 2006 the small repertory theatre, the Other Place, will be reopened as the new 1000-seat **Courtyard Theatre**. The main **Royal Shakespeare Theatre** and **Swan Theatre** will also remain during this season, but will close in 2007, when the Courtyard will take over as the principal venue until the new Royal Shakespeare Theatre is unveiled in 2009.

Sights & Information

City Sightseeing buses (adult/child £8/6) These leave every half-hour from 9.30am to 3.30pm from outside the TIC, allowing you to hop on and off at any Shakespeare property.

Holy Trinity Church (☎ 266316; www.stratford-upon -avon.org; Old Town; ⏰ 8.30am-6pm Mon-Sat, 12.30-5pm Sun Apr-Sep, 9am-5pm Mon-Sat, 12.30-5pm Sun Mar & Oct, 9am-4pm Mon-Sat, 12.30-5pm Sun Nov-Feb)

Royal Shakespeare Company (☎ 403404, 24hr line ☎ 0870 609 1110; www.rsc.org.uk; ticket prices £5-32; ⏰ box office 9am-8pm Mon-Sat)

Shakespeare's Birthplace (☎ 204016; www.shakespeare .org.uk; Henley St; ⏰ 9am-5.30pm Mon-Sat, 9.30am-5pm Sun Jun-Aug, 10am-5pm Mon-Sat, 9.30am-5pm Sun Apr, May, Sep & Oct, 10am-4pm Mon-Sat, 10.30am-4pm Sun Nov-Mar) A joint ticket for the three houses in town – the

Birthplace, Nash's House and Hall's Croft – costs £6.50; £12 also entitles you to entrance to Ann Hathaway's Cottage and Mary Arden's House outside town.

TIC (☎ 0870 160 7930; www.shakespeare-country.co.uk; ⏰ 9.30am-5.30pm Mon-Sat, 10.30am-4.30pm Sun Apr-Oct, 9.30am-5pm Mon-Sat, 10am-3pm Sun Nov-Mar) Close to the river on Bridgefoot.

Eating

Havilands (☎ 415477; 5 Meer St; cream tea £3.95; ⏰ 9am-5pm Mon-Sat) This is a small, cosy spot for lunch or just for indulging in coffee and homemade cake.

Lamb's (☎ 292554; 12 Sheep St; mains £7.95-15.95; ⏰ lunch & dinner Mon-Sat, lunch Sun) The oak beams here really do date back to Shakespeare's time; the upmarket bistro-style menu is rather more modern and impressive. There's also a fine selection of wines.

Transport

Distance from London 93 miles (150km)

Direction Northwest

Travel time 3½ hours by bus, 2½ hours by train

Bus National Express (☎ 0870 580 8080; www
.nationalexpress.com) buses depart Victoria Central
station three times daily (£18 day return)

Car Take the M40 north, turning off at Junction 15
onto A46 south towards Stratford-upon-Avon

Train Direct trains (☎ 0845 748 4950; www
.nationalrail.co.uk) run hourly from London's
Marylebone station (£25 return)

Sleeping

There is a huge variety of accommodation
on offer in Stratford and the TIC can provide more options. Popular streets for B&Bs
include Evesham Pl, Grove Rd, Broad Walk
and Alcester Rd. In summer you should
book a few weeks ahead.

Moonraker House (☎ 267115; www.moonrakerhouse
.com; 40 Alcester Rd; s/d from £40/55) This luxuriously
comfortable house is done up like an oversized doll's
house, with canopied beds and flowers everywhere, just
five minutes' walk from the train station.

Quilts and Croissants (☎ 2267269; 33 Evesham Pl; s/d
£20/40) The helpful owners help make this humble B&B
feel more comfortable and luxurious than it is.

Shakespeare (☎ 0870 400 8182;
shakespeare@macdonald-hotels.co.uk; Chapel St; s/d
£90/140) Comprised of beautiful historic buildings, and with
a labyrinth of differently shaped historic rooms, this four-
star gets better reports than others of its ilk in town. That
could be partly because its bathrooms are relatively new.

Stratford-upon-Avon YHA (☎ 0870 770 6052;
stratford@yha.org.uk; Hemmingford House, Alveston; dm
£12-17) This 200-bed hostel occupies a Georgian mansion
2 miles out of town. Take bus X18 or 77.

WINDSOR & BRAY
☎ 01753

Gatecrashed by a bearded stand-up comedian wearing a dress and infiltrated by tabloid
journalists delivering a 'bomb', the Queen's weekend home of **Windsor Castle** has been in the
news quite a bit in recent years. That's not to mention the small affair of 'two middle-
aged folk getting married' – the 2005 wedding of Prince Charles and Camilla Parker-
Bowles, who ran into more than a few hitches on their way to the registry office across
the street.

Starting out as a wooden castle erected in 1070 by William the Conqueror, and rebuilt
in stone in 1165, this is one of the world's greatest surviving medieval castles, and its
longevity and easy accessibility from London guarantee its popularity (indeed, it crawls
with tourists all year round). However, it's not the only attraction in the area. Across the
River Thames lies Eton College, while the gastronomic hotspot of Bray is a short bus ride
away.

British monarchs have inhabited Windsor Castle for more than 900 years, and the **State
Apartments** – open to the public at certain times – reverberate with history. Any damage
sustained during a fire in 1992 has long been erased by a £37 million restoration, completed in 1998.

After the **Waterloo Chamber**, created to commemorate the Battle of Waterloo and still used
for formal meals, and the **Garter Throne Room**, you move to the **King's Rooms** and **Queen's Rooms**.
These are lessons in how the other half lives, with opulent furniture, tapestries and paintings by Canaletto, Dürer, Gainsborough, Van Dyck, Hogarth, Holbein, Rembrandt and
Rubens.

Queues form in front of the impossibly intricate **Queen Mary's Dolls' House**, the work of
architect Sir Edwin Lutyens. Built in 1923 on a 1:12 scale, it took 1500 craftsmen three
years to finish and it's complete in every detail, right down to electric lights and flush-
ing toilets.

One of Britain's finest examples of early English architecture, the castle's **St George's Chapel**
(begun in 1475, but not completed until 1528) has a superb nave in perpendicular style,
with gorgeous fan vaulting arching out from the pillars. The chapel contains **royal tombs**,
including those of George V and Queen Mary, George VI, Edward IV and the Queen
Mother.

Have a look at the central columns in Windsor's **Guildhall** on High St beside Castle Hill: the columns don't actually touch the ceiling. The council of the day, in 1686, insisted upon them, but architect Sir Christopher Wren was convinced they weren't necessary and left a few centimetres of clear space to prove his point. Oh yes, the Guildhall is also where the future king of England (probably) was married in a civil ceremony in 2005 (not attended by his mother, the Queen).

Cross the River Thames by the pedestrian Windsor Bridge to reach **Eton College**. This famous public (ie private) school has educated no fewer than 18 prime ministers, and several buildings date from the mid-15th century.

The 1920-hectare **Windsor Great Park**, where in 1999 Queen Elizabeth II's husband, Prince Philip, had an avenue of ancient trees beheaded because they got in the way of his horse and buggy, extends from behind the castle almost as far as Ascot.

The nearby village of Bray is home to 'the world's best restaurant', according to several critics. If you wish to visit Heston Blumenthal's **Fat Duck** you will need to book up to two months ahead, however. The sibling **Riverside Brasserie** is also pretty busy.

Sights & Information

Eton College (☎ 671177; www.etoncollege.com; Baldwins Shore; adult/child £3.80/3; 2-4.30pm term time, 10.30am-4.30pm Easter & summer holidays) One-hour tours are £4.90/4 (adult/child) at 2.15pm and 3.15pm.

French Brothers (☎ 851900; www.boat-trips.co.uk; Clewer Court Rd; adult/concession/child/family £4.50/4.25/2.25/11.25) This company runs a range of cruises, including 35-minute boat trips from Windsor to Boveney lock (hourly 11am to 4pm mid-February to mid-March and Saturday and Sunday November to mid-December, half-hourly 10am to 5pm mid-March to October).

TIC (☎ 743900; www.windsor.gov.uk; 24 High St; 10am-5pm Mon-Sat, 10am-4.30pm Sun Apr-Jun, Sep & Oct, 9.30am-6pm Jul & Aug, 10am-4pm Nov-Mar)

Transport

Distance from London 23 miles (37km)

Direction West

Travel time One hour by bus, 55 minutes by train

Bus Green line buses depart Victoria Central station to Windsor between eight and 12 times per day (day return £10); bus 6 operated by Courtney Coaches (☎ 01344-482200) leaves for Bray outside Barclays Bank on Windsor High St (return £4, 35 minutes, hourly 7am to 6pm)

Train Trains (☎ 0845 748 4950; www.nationalrail .co.uk) from Waterloo station go to Windsor Riverside station every 30 minutes, or hourly on Sunday (£7 day return). Trains from Paddington go via Slough to Eton and Central station (£7.10 day return). Alternatively, to go straight to Bray, catch a Maidenhead train (£7.80 day return) from Paddington station and catch a taxi for the last five minutes of the journey.

Windsor Castle (☎ 831118, 020-7766 7304; www .the-royal-collection.org.uk; adult/senior/5-16yr/family £12.50/10.50/6.50/31.50, when State Apartments are closed £6/5/3.50/15; public areas 9.45am-5.15pm, last entry 4pm, Mar-Oct, 9.45am-4.15pm, last entry 3pm, Nov-Feb)

Windsor Great Park (☎ 860222; admission free; 8am-dusk)

Windsor Guildhall (☎ 743900; High St; admission free; 10am-2pm Mon, except bank holidays)

Eating

In Windsor, Peascod St and its extension, St Leonard's Rd, are full of restaurants, although most are pretty touristy. Bray is where to head for a once-in-a-lifetime gastronomic blow-out.

Fat Duck (☎ 01628-580333; www.fatduck.co.uk; 1 High St, Bray; 3 courses £67.50, tasting menu lunch/dinner £37.50/97.50; lunch Tue-Sun, dinner Tue-Sat) Self-taught chef Heston Blumenthal's fascination with the science of taste has turned this into the best gastropub in the world. The menu includes entirely eclectic combinations – sardine on toast sorbet, oysters and passionfruit, salmon poached with liquorice and pheasant accompanied by rhubarb with popping-candy crumble, smoked bacon and egg ice cream – but it's all delicious, while the atmosphere is refreshingly relaxed.

Riverside Brasserie (☎ 01628-780553; Bray Marina, Monkey Island Lane; mains £13.25-15.95; Tue-Sun) This is Blumenthal's pitch to the less adventurous diner, with a more conventionally British menu. Tuck into pork belly, the most famous dish, while overlooking the river.

Waterside Inn (☎ 01628-620691; Ferry Rd, Bray; mains £21-39; Wed-Sun, plus dinner Tue in summer) Also voted among the world's top 50 restaurants, this Michel Roux establishment serves French haute cuisine in a rustic riverside environment.

KENT CASTLES

Three Kentish castles and stately homes offer particularly pleasant countryside outings. **Leeds Castle** is spectacularly located on two small islands in the middle of a lake, leaving one visitor to declare it 'the loveliest castle in the world'. Surrounded by rolling wooded hills, it was colloquially known as 'Ladies Castle', being home to many queens over the centuries, including Catherine de Valois, Catherine of Aragon and even Elizabeth I, who was imprisoned here before she took the throne. The grounds are particularly striking, from the glorious moat to the gardens and a **maze** with an underground grotto. There is also an **aviary**, with more than 100 endangered bird species, a **museum of dog collars** and interesting, avian-inspired wallpaper and other decorative features in the castle interior.

The gardens at smaller **Hever Castle**, the childhood home of Henry VIII's second wife, Anne Boleyn, are equally spectacular. They include not just roses, bluebells, rhododendrons, topiary, rockeries, Italian sculptures, fountains, lakes and a yew maze; they also manage to combine several of the last two in a **water maze**, which is extremely popular with children. The castle is, however, a little tricky to get to (see below).

Transport

Hever Castle

Distance from London 33 miles (53km)

Direction Southeast

Travel time 40 minutes by car, 40 minutes (weekdays) to 1½ hours (weekends) by train plus 10 minutes by taxi

Car Take the M25, turning off at Junction 5 or 6 and following the signs south to Edenbridge and the castle

Train Catch a train from London Bridge to Edenbridge Town (£9.50 day return), then take a taxi (3 miles). Alternatively, the castle is a 1-mile walk from Hever station. On Sunday services terminate one stop down the line at East Grinstead; a taxi will cost £10.

Leeds Castle

Distance from London 44 miles (70km)

Direction Southeast

Travel time 1½ hours by car, 1½ hours by bus, one hour 10 minutes by train

Bus Both National Express (☎ 0870 580 8080; www.nationalexpress.com; adult/child combined ticket £18/13) and Green Line (☎ 0870 608 7261; www.greenline.co.uk; adult/child combined ticket £15/9) offer combined coach/admission tickets to Leeds Castle, with services leaving Victoria Central station in the morning and returning to Victoria around 5pm or 6pm, Monday to Friday

Car Take the M20 southeast of London, turning off at Junction 8 and following the signs to the nearby castle

Train Trains (☎ 0845 748 4950; www.nationalrail.co.uk) from London's Victoria station go to Bearsted Station (day return £13.40), from where you can catch the connecting coach to Leeds Castle

Sissinghurst Castle Garden

Distance from London 46 miles (74km)

Direction Southeast

Travel time 1½ hours by car, one hour by train plus 15 minutes by castle bus

Bus From Staplehurst train station, there's a special link to Sissinghurst Castle Garden on Tuesday and Sunday May to mid-September, leaving just after noon. Phone ☎ 01580-710700 for exact times.

Car Exit the M20 at Junction 5 or 6 and follow the A229 to the A262

Train Head from Charing Cross station to Staplehurst station (day return £12.40) and catch the special castle bus (see above under Bus) or a taxi (5½ miles)

Sissinghurst Castle Garden is legendary among writers and the green-fingered – it's one of the most famous 20th-century gardens in the world. The creation of poet Vita Sackville-West and her husband Harold Nicolson, it broke new ground by grouping similarly coloured plants to create 10 garden 'rooms' with distinct personalities. The famous **White Garden**, with its many shades of white, grey and green, was a particular source of inspiration for Sackville-West as she gazed upon it in moonlight from her study, which is also open to visitors.

Sights & Information

Hever Castle (☎ 01732-865224; www.hevercastle
.co.uk; Hever, Kent; adult/child/concession castle & gardens
£9.20/5/7.70, gardens only £7.30/4.80/6.30; ☺ gardens
11am-6pm Mar-Oct, 11am-4pm Nov, castle opens 1hr later)

Leeds Castle (☎ 01622-765400, 0870 600 8880; www
.leeds-castle.com; Maidstone, Kent; adult/child/conces-
sion/family castle & gardens £13/9/11/39, gardens only
£10.50/6.50/8.50/33; ☺ 10am-7pm, last admission 5pm,
Mar-Oct, 10am-5pm, last admission 3.30pm, Nov-Feb)

Sissinghurst Castle Garden (☎ 01580-7128500; www
.nationaltrust.org.uk/sissinghurst; Sissinghurst, Cranbrook;
adult/concession/family £7.50/3.50/18; ☺ 11am-6.30pm,
last admission 5.30pm, Mon, Tue & Fri, 10am-6.30pm, last
admission 5.30pm, Sat & Sun mid-Mar–Nov)

Directory

Directory

TRANSPORT

AIRLINES

London is served by nearly every international airline, most with offices in the city. The main airline numbers are listed here.

Aer Lingus (☎ 0845 084 4444; www.aerlingus.com)

Aeroflot (☎ 7355 2233; www.aeroflot.co.uk)

Air Canada (☎ 0871 220 1111; www.aircanada.com)

Air France (☎ 0870 142 4343; www.airfrance.com/uk)

Air New Zealand (☎ 0800 028 4149; www.airnew zealand.co.nz)

Alitalia (☎ 0870 544 8259; www.alitalia.com)

American Airlines (☎ 0845 778 9789; www.aa.com)

BMI (☎ 0870 607 0555; www.flybmi.com)

British Airways (☎ 0870 850 9850; www.ba.com)

Cathay Pacific (☎ 8834 8800; www.cathaypacific.com)

Continental Airlines (☎ 0800 776 464; www.conti nental.com)

Delta Air Lines (☎ 0800 414 767; www.delta.com)

easyJet (☎ 0905 821 0905, 60p per min; www.easyjet.com)

Fly Be (British European; ☎ 0871 700 0123; www.flybe.com)

El Al (☎ 7957 4100; www.elal.com)

Emirates (☎ 0870 243 2222; www.emirates.com/uk)

Iberia (☎ 0845 601 2854; www.iberia.com)

Icelandair (☎ 7874 1000; www.icelandair.net)

KLM (☎ 0870 507 4074; www.klm.com)

Lufthansa Airlines (☎ 0845 773 7747; www.lufthansa .co.uk)

Olympic Airways (☎ 0870 606 0460; www.olympicair ways.com)

Qantas Airways (☎ 0845 774 7767; www.qantas.co.uk)

Ryanair (☎ 0871 246 0000; www.ryanair.com)

Scandinavian Airlines (SAS; ☎ 0870 6072 7727; www .scandinavian.net)

Singapore Airlines (☎ 0870 608 8886; www.singapore air.com)

SN Brussels Airlines (☎ 0870 735 2345; www.flysn.com)

South African Airways (☎ 0870 747 1111; www.flysaa.com)

TAP Air Portugal (☎ 0845 601 0932; www.tap-air portugal.co.uk)

Thai Airways International (☎ 0870 606 0911; www .thaiair.com)

Turkish Airlines (☎ 7766 9300; www.turkishairlines.com)

United Airlines (☎ 0845 844 4777; www.ual.com)

Virgin Atlantic (☎ 0870 574 7747; www.virgin.com/ atlantic)

AIRPORTS

London is served by five major airports: Heathrow (the largest), Gatwick, Stansted, Luton and London City.

Heathrow Airport

Fifteen miles (24km) west of central London, **Heathrow** (LHR; Off Map p437; ☎ 0870 000 0123; www.baa.com/main/airports/ heathrow) is the world's busiest international airport. It has four terminals, with a fifth under construction and due for completion in 2011. Two Piccadilly line tube stations serve the airport: one for Terminals 1, 2 and 3, the other for Terminal 4. (At the time of writing, the station at Terminal 4 was scheduled to be closed until September 2006, with replacement buses making the last, 15-minute leg of the journey from Hatton Cross tube station. Meanwhile, an airport bus does a 40-minute circuit from Terminal 4 to Terminals 1, 2 and 3.)

Each terminal has competitive currency-exchange facilities, information counters and accommodation desks. There are also left-luggage facilities:

Terminal 1 (☎ 8745 5301; 🕑 6am-11pm)

Terminal 2 (☎ 8745 4599; 🕑 5am-11pm)

Terminal 3 (☎ 8759 3344; 🕑 5am-10.30pm)

Terminal 4 (☎ 8745 7460; 🕑 5am-11pm)

The charge is £5.50 per item for 24 hours or part thereof, up to a maximum of 90 days. All branches can forward baggage.

There are some 15 international hotels at or near Heathrow, should you be arriving or leaving particularly early or late. To reach them from Heathrow Terminals 1, 2 or 3, take the Heathrow **Hotel Hoppa bus** (☎ 8400 6659), which departs every 15 minutes 5.30am to 9pm, then every 30 minutes until 11.30pm (£3). The bus does not serve Terminal 4.

Here are options for getting to/from Heathrow Airport:

Underground (☎ 7222 1234; http://tube.tfl.gov.uk) The tube (one way adult/child £3.80/1.40, from central London 50 to 60 minutes, every five to nine minutes) is the cheapest way of getting to Heathrow, though the journey takes a lot longer and is less comfortable than the Express. It runs from approximately 5am (5.50am Sunday) to 11.45pm (10.50pm Sunday). You can buy tickets from machines in the baggage reclaim areas of the Heathrow terminals or in the station.

Heathrow Express (☎ 0845 600 1515; www.heathrow express.com) This ultramodern train (one way/return £14/26, 15 minutes, every 15 minutes) whisks passengers from Heathrow Central station (serving Terminals 1, 2 and 3) and Terminal 4 station to Paddington station. The Heathrow Central train runs approximately from 5.10am (in both directions) to between 11.30pm (from Paddington) and midnight (from the airport). To Terminal 4 takes an extra eight minutes.

Heathrow Connect (☎ 0845 678 6975; www.heathrow connect.com) Also travelling between Heathrow and Paddington station, this modern passenger service (one way/return £9.50/19, 25 minutes, every 30 minutes) makes several stops en route, in places such as Ealing and Southall. The first trains leave Heathrow at about 5.30am (6.15am Sunday) and the last service is around midnight. From Paddington, services leave between approximately 4.45am (6.15am Sunday) and 11pm.

National Express (☎ 0870 580 8080; www.national express.com) Buses 032, 035, 403, 412 and 501 (one way/ return from £10/15, tickets valid three months, 45 minutes to one hour 10 minutes, every 30 minutes to one hour) link Heathrow with Victoria coach station (☎ 7730 3466; 164 Buckingham Palace Rd SW1) about 50 times per day. The first bus leaves the Heathrow Central Bus station (at Terminals 1, 2 and 3) at 5.35am with the last departure at 9.35pm. The first bus leaves Victoria at 7.15am, the last at 11.30pm.

Black cabs A metered trip to/from central London (Oxford St) will cost £45 to £55.

Gatwick Airport

Located some 30 miles (48km) south of central London, **Gatwick** (LGW; Off Map p437; ☎ 0870 000 2468; www.baa.com/ main/airports/gatwick) is smaller and better organised than Heathrow. The North and South Terminals are linked by an efficient monorail service, with the journey time about two minutes. Gatwick also has left-luggage facilities:

North Terminal (☎ 01293-502 013; ⏱ 5am-9pm)

South Terminal (☎ 01293-502 014; ⏱ 24hr)

The charge is £5.50 per item for 24 hours or part thereof, up to a maximum of 90 days.

Here are options for getting to/from Gatwick Airport:

Gatwick Express (☎ 0845 850 1530; www.gatwick express.com) Trains (one way/return £12/23.50, 30 minutes, every 15 minutes) link the station near the South Terminal with Victoria station. From the airport, there are regular services between 5.50am and 12.35am. From Victoria, they leave between 5am and 11.45pm. In both directions, there are four less-regular overnight services.

Southern Trains (☎ 0845 748 4950; www.southernrail way.com) This service (one way/return £8/16, 45 minutes, every 15 to 30 minutes, every hour from midnight to 4am) runs from Victoria station to both terminals.

Thameslink service (national rail enquiries ☎ 0845 748 4950; www.thameslink.co.uk) This service (one way/return £10/15, one hour 10 minutes) runs through King's Cross, Farringdon and London Bridge train stations.

National Express (☎ 0870 580 8080; www.national express.com) Bus 025 (one way/return £6.20/11.40, tickets valid three months, one hour five minutes to one hour 25 minutes) runs from Brighton to Victoria coach station via Gatwick nearly 20 times per day. Services leave Gatwick approximately hourly between 5.15am and 10.15pm and operate from Victoria between 7am and 11.30pm, with one very early service at 3.30am).

Black cabs A metered trip to/from central London costs £80 to £85.

Stansted Airport

London's third-busiest international gateway, **Stansted** (STN; ☎ 0870 000 0303; www .baa.com/main/airports/stansted) is 35 miles (56km) northeast of central London, heading towards Cambridge. It's become Europe's fastest-growing airport thanks to no-frills carriers Ryanair and easyJet, which use it as a hub. With many services to central and eastern Europe, it was also boosted by the expansion of the EU in 2004.

Here are options for getting to/from Stansted Airport:

Stansted Express (☎ 0845 850 0150; www.standsted express.com) This service (one way/return £14.50/24, 45 minutes, every 15 to 30 minutes) links the airport and Liverpool St station. From the airport the first train leaves at 5.30am (6am Saturday and Sunday), the last just before midnight. Trains depart Liverpool St station from 4.30am (5am Saturday and Sunday) to 11.30pm. If you need to connect with the tube, change at Tottenham Hale for the Victoria line or stay on to Liverpool St station for the Central line. Some early services do not stop at Tottenham Hale. Stansted Express also operates a night coach service (one way/return £14.50/24, one hour, every 30 minutes) between the last train and the next morning's first service. Services depart Liverpool St between 2.30am and 4.30am. From the airport, they leave between midnight and 4am. They do not stop at Tottenham Hale.

National Express (☎ 0870 580 8080; www.national express.com) Coaches run around the clock, offering some 120 services per day. The A6 runs to Victoria coach station (one way/return £10/15, one hour 45 minutes, every 15 to 20 minutes), via north London (£8/13, one hour). The A9 runs to Stratford (£7/12, 45 minutes, every half-hour), from where you can catch a Jubilee line tube (20 minutes) into central London. The A7 runs via Stratford to Victoria between approximately midnight and 5am.

Black cabs A metered trip to/from central London costs £100 to £105.

London City Airport

Its close proximity to central London, 6 miles (10km) to its west, and to the commercial district of the Docklands, means **London City Airport** (LCY; Map p437; ☎ 7646 0000; www.londoncityairport.com) is predominantly a business airport, although it does also serve holiday travellers with its 22 Continental European and eight national destinations.

Here are options for getting to/from London City Airport:

Docklands Light Railway (DLR; ☎ 7363 9700; www.tfl.gov .uk/dlr) At the time of writing, the DLR was expected to run all the way to London City Airport from 2006, connecting to the pre-existing transport network at Canning Town. Trains run every seven to 10 minutes, between 5.30am and 12.30am Monday to Saturday and 7am and 11.30pm Sunday. Journey time is 15 minutes to Canary Wharf and 22 minutes to Bank.

Blue airport shuttlebus (☎ 7646 0088; www.london cityairport.com/shuttlebus) Connects the airport with Canary Wharf (£3.50, 10 minutes) and Liverpool St (£6.50, 30 minutes), running every 10 minutes Monday to Friday and every 15 minutes Saturday and Sunday between 6.55am (11.55am Sunday) and 9.20pm (1.15pm Saturday). The first bus leaves Liverpool St at 6.10am (11.55am Sunday); the last departs 8.45pm weekdays (12.40pm Saturday).

Black cabs A metered trip to/from central London costs about £25 to £30.

Luton Airport

A smallish airport some 35 miles north of London, **Luton** (LTN; Off Map p437; ☎ 01582-405100; www.london-luton.co .uk) caters mainly for cheap charter flights, though the discount airline easyJet operates scheduled services from here.

Here are options for getting to/from Luton Airport:

Thameslink (national rail enquiries ☎ 0845 748 4950; www.thameslink.co.uk) Trains (off-peak one way/return £10.70/10.90, 30 to 40 minutes, every six to 15 minutes 7am to 10pm) run from King's Cross and other central London stations to Luton Airport Parkway station, from where an airport shuttle bus will take you to the airport in eight minutes.

Green Line bus 757 (☎ 0870 608 7261; www.greenline .co.uk) Buses to Luton (one way/return £8.50/12, one hour) run from Buckingham Palace Rd south of Victoria station, leaving approximately every half-hour from 9.30am to 8pm, with hourly services between 8pm and midnight and one or two staggered services before 9.30am.

Black cabs A metered trip to/from central London costs £95 to £100.

Websites

As well as airline websites (p398), there are efficient online resources for buying good-value plane tickets. Some of the best include www.cheapflights.co.uk, www .ebookers.com, www.lastminute.com and www.opodo.co.uk.

BICYCLE

Cycling along London's canals or along the South Bank is delightful, but heading through the heavy traffic and fumes of central streets is pretty grim. So not only should you always wear a helmet, you might also want to join the many Londoners who also wear facemasks to filter out pollution.

The **London Cycling Campaign** (LCC; ☎ 7928 7220; www.lcc.org.uk) is working towards improving conditions throughout the city, campaigning to establish a comprehensive London cycle network.

In conjunction with the LCC, Transport for London publishes a series of 19 London Cycle Guides. These can be ordered via www.lcc.org.uk or www.tfl.gov.uk/tfl/ cycle_guide.shtml, or by calling ☎ 7222 1234. Online maps of cycle routes are also available at www.londoncyclenetwork.org.

Hire

London Bicycle Tour Company (Map pp448–9; ☎ 7928 6838; www.londonbicycle.com; 1a Gabriel's Wharf, 56 Upper Ground SE1; ◆ Blackfriars) Rentals cost £3 per hour or £16 for the first day, £8 for subsequent days, £48 for the first week and £30 per week after that. It also offers three-hour bike tours of London (2pm Saturday and Sunday) for £17 including the bike. (Those with their own bikes get a discount of about 20%.) Routes are on its website. You will need to provide credit card details as a deposit and must show ID.

On Your Bike (Map pp454–5; ☎ 7378 6669; www .onyourbike.net; 52-54 Tooley St SE1; ✆ London Bridge) Rentals cost £12 for the first day, £8 for subsequent days, £30 for a weekend and £60 per week. Prices include hire of a helmet. A deposit of £200 (via credit card) is necessary and you will be required to show ID.

Bicycles on Public Transport

Bicycles can be taken only on the District, Circle, Hammersmith & City and Metropolitan tube lines outside the rush hour – ie 10am to 4pm and after 7pm Monday to Friday. Folding bikes can be taken on any line, however. Bicycles can also travel on the above-ground sections of some other tube lines and the Silverlink line. But on the DLR, bicycles are banned.

Restrictions on taking a bike on suburban and mainline trains vary from company to company so you need to check before setting out. For details call ☎ 0845 748 4950.

Pedicabs

Three-wheeled cycle rickshaws, seating two or three passengers, have been a regular, if much-cursed, part of the Soho scene since the late 1990s. They're less a mode of transport than a nice gimmick for tourists and other pleasure-trippers. Prices start at £3 for a quick trip across Soho.

BOAT

With the drive to make use of London's often overlooked 'liquid artery', companies running boats on the river have been sprouting up in recent years. Only the Thames Clippers really offers commuter services, however. For sightseeing tours, see p94.

Thames Clippers (☎ 0870 781 5049, 7977 6892; www .thamesclippers.com; adult single £2.50-4.25, return £4-6.75, child half-price; ☽ 6.20am-8pm, roughly every 20-40min) Serving more as commuter boats than tourist boats, these are cheap and fast, giving you access to lots of the river sights. They run from Savoy Pier at Embankment to Masthouse Tce in Docklands, passing Tower Bridge, Tate Modern, Shakespeare's Globe and Canary Wharf.

BUS

With the demise of London's iconic double-decker Routemaster (see p96), bus travel has lost some of its charm. But even on modern double-deckers and single-decker 'bendy' buses, you see more of the city than while underground on the tube. Just beware that the going can be slow, thanks to traffic jams and the nearly four million commuters that get on and off the buses every day. See below for information on buying your ticket.

Information

There are numerous free bus guides available to areas as far-flung as Harrow, Romford and Hounslow. Most visitors, however, will find the central London bus guide/map sufficient. Maps are available from most transport travel information centres, via the **Transport for London Order Line** (☎ 7371 0247) or from www.tfl.gov.uk/buses. For general information on London buses, and on how services are running, call ☎ 7222 1234 (24 hours).

Night Buses

More than 60 night bus routes (which are prefixed with the letter 'N') run from midnight to 4.30am, when the tube shuts down and the daytime buses return to the barn. Oxford Circus, Tottenham Court Rd and Trafalgar Sq are the main hubs, but check bus-stop information boards to familiarise yourself with routes. Night buses can be infrequent and stop only on request, meaning you must signal clearly to the driver to stop.

Buy Before You Board

In central London, at stops where signs have a yellow background, drivers no longer sell tickets and you must buy before you board, using the machines provided. Annoyingly, even when these work they do not give change, so you'll need exact money. However, they do sell daily bus passes (see p402). If a machine is broken, drivers are supposed to take you to the next stop with a working ticket machine and wait for you to make a purchase – although this is very frustrating for all involved, including your fellow passengers.

Fares

Any single-journey adult bus ticket within London costs £1.20; children under 16 travel free. At the time of writing, it was proposed that from September 2006 under-18s in full-time education will be entitled to free bus travel, too. Travelcards are valid on all buses, including night buses.

TRAVEL PASSES & DISCOUNT FARES

A Saver ticket (£6) is a book of six bus tickets valid on all buses, including those in central London and night buses. They are transferable but valid for one journey only.

If you plan to use only buses during your stay in London, you can buy a one-day bus pass valid throughout London for £3/1 (adult/child). Unlike Travelcards (p405), these are valid before 9.30am. Weekly or monthly bus passes cost £11/4 (adult/child) or £42.30/15.40.

Everyone should consider an Oyster card (see p405). Using these on buses you only pay 80p per single journey, or £1 between 6.30am and 9.30am Monday to Friday.

Within the UK & to Europe

National Express (☎ 0870 580 8080; www.nationalexpress.com) and low-cost Megabus (☎ 0900 160 0900, 60p per min; www.megabus.com) are the main national operators. Megabus operates a no-frills airline style of seat pricing, where some tickets go for as little as £1. National Express has dropped its fares to compete. Smaller competitors on main UK routes include Green Line (☎ 0870 608 7261; www.greenline.co.uk).

Eurolines (☎ 0870 514 3219; www.eurolines.com; 52 Grosvenor Gardens SW1) has buses to Continental Europe, operated via National Express and leaving from Victoria coach station (☎ 7730 3466; 164 Buckingham Palace Rd SW1).

CAR & MOTORCYCLE

To drive in London is to learn the true meaning of road rage: traffic jams are common, parking space is at a premium and the congestion charge (right) adds to the general expense, including the high price of petrol. Traffic wardens and wheel clampers operate with extreme efficiency and if your vehicle is clamped it will cost you at least £215 to have it released. If this happens call the number on the ticket; this varies across different London boroughs. If the car has been removed, ring the 24-hour Tracing Section (☎ 7747 4747). It will cost you at least £200 to get your vehicle back.

Driving

ROAD RULES

We don't recommend driving in London. However, if you insist, you should first obtain the *Highway Code*, which is available at AA and RAC outlets as well as some bookshops and Tourist Information Centres (TICs). A foreign driving licence is valid in Britain for up to 12 months from the time of your last entry into the country. If you bring a car from Europe make sure you're adequately insured. All drivers and passengers must wear seatbelts and motorcyclists must wear a helmet.

THE CONGESTION CHARGE

London was the world's first major city to introduce a congestion charge to reduce the flow of traffic into its centre from Monday to Friday. While the traffic entering the 'congestion zone' has fallen as a result, driving in London can still be very slow work.

As a rough guide, the charge zone is south of the Euston Rd, west of Commercial St, north of Kennington Lane and east of Park Lane. As you enter the zone, you will see a large letter 'C' in a red circle. If you enter the zone between 7am and 6.30pm Monday to Friday (excluding public holidays), you must pay the £8 charge before 10pm the same day (or £10 between 10pm and midnight the same day) to avoid receiving a £100 fine. Those living within the congestion zone receive a 90% discount on the charge, although you must be a registered resident to qualify. You can pay online, at newsagents, petrol stations or any shop displaying the 'C' sign, by telephone on ☎ 0845 900 1234 and even by text message once you've registered online. For full details log on to www.cclondon.com.

Plans have been mooted to extend the zone west, but at the time of writing it was expected that won't take effect until at least 2007. Transport for London has said that, despite press reports to the contrary, it has no intention of levying the charge against motorbikes or scooters.

Rental

Although driving in London is expensive and often slow, there is no shortage of rental agencies. Competition is fierce, with easycar.com having significantly undersold many of the other more traditional companies over the past few years, forcing down prices. Compare prices, models and agency locations at one of the following websites: www.easycar.com; www.hertz.com; www.avis.com.

TAXI
Black Cabs

The black London taxicab (www.london blackcabs.co.uk) is as much a feature of the cityscape as the red bus, although these days it comes in several colours, sometimes with advertising. Licensed black-cab drivers have 'the knowledge' – ie they undergo rigorous training and exams, and are supposed to know every central London street.

Cabs are available for hire when the yellow sign above the windscreen is lit; just stick your arm out to signal one. Fares are metered, with a minimum charge of £2.20 (covering the first 336m during a weekday), rising by increments of 20p for each subsequent 168m. Fares are more expensive in the evenings and overnight. You can tip taxi drivers up to 10% but most people round up to the nearest pound.

Do not expect to hail a taxi in popular nightlife areas of London such as Soho late at night (and especially after pub closing time at 11pm). If you do find yourself in any of those areas, signal all taxis – even those with their lights off – and try to look sober. Many drivers are very choosy about their fares at this time of night. To order a cab by phone try Computer Cabs (☎ 7908 0207); it charges a £2 booking fee, plus what it costs to get to you, up to £3.80, as well as your actual fare. You can only prebook using a credit card; if you're paying cash you must ring when you need the cab. (For cash prebookings, see Minicabs, right.)

Zingo Taxi (☎ 0870 070 0700; www.zingo taxi.com) uses GPS to connect your mobile phone to that of the nearest free black-cab driver – after which you can explain to the cabbie exactly where you are. This service costs only £1.60, which is included in the final price of the taxi. It's a good idea late at night, when it's notoriously difficult to find a free cab. The service has only 1,000 vehicles and it will find you a (more expensive) Computer Cab, if none of these are available.

Minicabs

Minicabs, some of which are now licensed, are cheaper, freelance competitors of black cabs. However, minicab drivers are often untrained and less sure of the way than black-cab drivers and may not be properly insured. Minicabs cannot legally be hailed on the street – they must be hired by phone or directly from one of the minicab offices (every high street has at least one). Minicab drivers seeking fares might approach you; it's best to decline their offer, as there have been allegations of rape made against some unlicensed cab drivers.

The cabs don't have meters, so it's essential to fix a price before you start (it's therefore not usual to tip minicab drivers). Most drivers start higher than the fare they're prepared to accept.

Ask a local for the name of a reputable minicab company, or phone a large 24-hour operator (☎ 7387 8888, 7272 2222, 7272 3322, 8888 4444). Women travelling alone at night can choose Ladycabs (☎ 7272 3300), which has women drivers. Liberty Cars (☎ 7734 1313) caters for the gay and lesbian market, although gay couples are extremely unlikely to experience open homophobia from drivers of black cabs.

TRAIN
Docklands Light Railway

Looking a bit like an urban ski train, the driverless Docklands Light Railway (DLR; ☎ 7363 9700; www.tfl.gov.uk/dlr) is basically an adjunct to the Underground. It links the City at Bank and Tower Hill with Beckton and Stratford to the east and northeast and the Docklands (as far as Island Gardens at the southern end of the Isle of Dogs), Greenwich and Lewisham to the south. The DLR runs from 5.30am to 12.30am Monday to Saturday and from 7am to 11.30pm Sunday. Fares are the same as those on the tube, although there are some group discounts and a Rail & River Rover ticket (in conjunction with boat operator City Cruises; see p94) unique to the DLR.

For news of how services are running, call ☎ 7222 1234.

Suburban Trains

Several rail companies operate passenger trains in London, including the **Silverlink** (North London; ☎ 0845 601 4867; www .silverlink-trains.com) line and the crowded **Thameslink** (☎ 0845 748 4950; www.thames link.co.uk). Silverlink links Richmond in the southwest with North Woolwich in the southeast via Kew, West Hampstead, Camden Rd, Highbury & Islington and Stratford stations. Thameslink goes from Elephant & Castle and London Bridge in the south through the City to King's Cross and as far north as Luton. Most lines connect with the Underground system, and Travelcards can be used on them. Note, however, that Oyster prepay cannot yet be used at all train stations.

If you're staying long term in southeast London, where suburban trains are usually much more useful than the tube, it's worth buying a one-year Network Railcard. This card offers one-third off most rail fares in southeast England and on one-day Travelcards for all six zones. Travel is permitted only after 10am Monday to Friday and at any time on Saturday and Sunday. The card costs £20 and is available at most stations.

Most of the large mainline London stations have left-luggage facilities available, although due to the perceived terrorist threat, baggage lockers no longer exist. **Excess Baggage** (☎ 0800 783 1085; www.excess baggage.co.uk) has services costing £6 per bag per 24 hours or part thereof. These services operate from Paddington, Euston, Waterloo, King's Cross, Liverpool St and Charing Cross stations.

Within the UK & to Europe

Main national rail routes are served by InterCity trains, which can travel up to 140mph (225km/h). However, with the privatised service known for its inefficiency, don't be surprised by delays. Same-day returns and one-week advance purchase are the cheapest tickets for those without rail passes (which are available from mainline train stations). **National Rail Enquiries** (☎ 0845 748 4950; www.nationalrail.co.uk) has time-tables and fares.

The high-speed passenger rail service **Eurostar** (☎ 0870 518 6186; www.eurostar .com) links London's Waterloo station with the Channel Tunnel with Paris' Gare du Nord (three hours, up to 25 per day) and Brussels (two hours 40 minutes, up to 12 per day); some trains also stop at Lille and Calais in France. Fares vary enormously. To Paris/Brussels, for example, costs between £59 for a cheap APEX return (booked at least 21 days in advance, staying a Saturday night) and £300. In 2007, when the Channel Tunnel extension is expected to be complete, services are scheduled to begin running all the way through to King's Cross.

Le Shuttle (☎ 0870 535 3535; www.euro tunnel.com) transports motor vehicles and bicycles between Folkestone in England and Coquelles (near Calais) in France. Services run up to every 15 minutes (hourly 1am to 6am). Booking online is cheapest, where a two- to five-day excursion fare costs from £105, day/overnight fares cost from £40 and same-day returns (travelling out and back on the same day you book) cost from £100. All prices include a car and passengers. At the time of writing, the company Eurotunnel was suffering dire financial difficulties, so if the listed number doesn't work, you can always ask for information at Waterloo station.

For other European train enquiries contact **Rail Europe** (☎ 0870 584 8848; www.rail europe.co.uk).

TRAM

A small London tram network, Tramlink, exists in South London. There are three routes, one running from Wimbledon through Croydon to Elmers End, one running from Croydon to Beckenham and one running from Croydon to New Addington. Single tickets cost £1.20/40p per adult/child. Oyster cards (see opposite) and bus passes (see p402) are also valid on trams. See www.tfl .gov.uk/trams for more details.

UNDERGROUND

Despite the nervousness in using the tube that some Londoners have felt since the 2005 bombings, and despite much-needed renovations and the frequent threat of strikes, the London Underground, or 'the tube', is overall the quickest and easiest way of getting around the city. It is expensive, however: compare the cheapest one-way fare in central London (£2) with those charged on the Paris metro and New York subway and Londoners clearly pay over the odds.

Information

Underground travel information centres sell tickets and provide free maps. There are centres at all Heathrow terminals and at Euston, King's Cross St Pancras, Liverpool St, Oxford Circus, Piccadilly Circus, St James's Park and Victoria tube and mainline train stations. There is also an information office at Hammersmith bus station. For general information on the tube, buses, the DLR or trains within London ring ☎ 7222 1234 or visit www.tfl.gov.uk.

Network

Greater London is served by 12 tube lines, along with the independent (though linked) and privately owned DLR and an interconnected rail network (see the map, p466). The first tube train operates around 5.30am Mondays to Saturdays and 7am Sundays; the last train leaves between 11.30pm and 12.30am depending on the day, the station and the line. Plans are underway to run services an hour later on Friday and Saturday nights, starting an hour later on Saturday and Sunday mornings.

Tube lines vary in their reliability, and the Circle Line, which links most of the mainline stations and is therefore much used by tourists, has one of the worst track records. However, when it works, this line is very fast. Other lines low in the league tables are the Northern line (though improving) and the Hammersmith & City (often referred to as the 'Hammersmith & Shitty') line. The Piccadilly line to/from Heathrow is usually pretty good, as are the Victoria line, linking the station with Oxford Circus and King's Cross, and the Jubilee line, linking London Bridge, Southwark and Waterloo with Baker St.

Remember that, although a design icon (see p34), the London Underground map is a graphical representation of the actual tunnels. Some stations, most famously Leicester Sq and Covent Garden, are much closer in real life than they appear on the map. Often, as between those two stations, it's quicker to walk the distance.

Fares

The Underground divides London into six concentric zones. Fares for the more central zones are more expensive than for those zones further out. One-way basic adult/child fares, as of March 2005, are listed here:

Zone 1 £2/60p

Zones 1 and 2 £2.30/80p

Zone 2, 3, 4, 5 or 6 only £1.30/50p

Zones 2 and 3, 3 and 4, 4 or 5 or 5 and 6 £1.30/50p

Zones 2 to 4, 2 to 5, 2 to 6, 3 to 5, 3 to 6 or 4 to 6 £2.10/80p

Zones 1 to 3 or 1 to 4 £2.80/1.10

Zones 1 to 5 or 1 to 6 £3.80/1.40

If you're travelling several times in one day or through a couple of zones, you should consider a Travelcard or some other discounted fare (see below).

If you're caught on the Underground without a valid ticket (and that includes crossing into a zone that your ticket doesn't cover) you're liable for an on-the-spot fine of £20.

TRAVEL PASSES & DISCOUNT FARES

Travelcards make getting around London cheaper. Many visitors opt for an off-peak, one-day Travelcard (£4.70 for zones 1 and 2), which can be used after 9.30am Monday

Oyster Card

The credit-card style Oyster card is the London commuter's new best friend, and tannoy reminders to 'touch in and touch out' have become as common as the warning to 'mind the gap' at stations. You're required to fill out a form and pay a £3 refundable deposit for the card, but this takes minimal effort and soon pays for itself handsomely.

The Oyster card is a smart card, on which you can store either credit towards so-called 'prepay' fares, a Travelcard or both. When entering the tube or boarding a bus, you need to touch your card on a reader at the tube gates or near the driver to register your journey. The system will then deduct the appropriate amount of credit from your card as necessary. The benefit lies in the fact that fares for Oyster users are lower than the norm – eg £1.70 for a zone 1 single as opposed to the usual £2, and 80p instead of £1.20 on buses. If you are making many journeys during the day, you will never pay more than the appropriate Travelcard (peak or off-peak).

When leaving tube stations, you must also touch the card on a reader, so the system knows your journey was only, say, a zone 1 and 2 journey. Regular commuters can also store weekly or monthly Travelcards on their Oyster card.

to Friday and all day Saturday, Sunday and public holidays on all forms of transport in London: the tube, suburban trains, the DLR and buses. However, the longer the validity of the Travelcard, the proportionally cheaper it usually is. So choose a weekly (adult/child £21.40/8.60 for zones 1 and 2) or monthly (£82.20/33.10) Travelcard if you're here this long. An exception is the three-day Travelcard, which really only offers savings over the one-day Travelcard if you're travelling during peak times (£15/7.50 adult/child for zones 1 and 2) or journeying across all six zones (peak £36/18, off-peak £18/6).

Other Travelcards are available for other zones. A one-day Travelcard for children aged five to 15 costs £2 regardless of how many zones it covers, but those aged 14 and 15 need a Child Photocard to travel on this fare. You can buy Travelcards from stations several days ahead. For monthly tickets or longer, you will need a Photocard.

If you will be making many tube journeys exclusively within zone 1, you can buy a carnet of 10 tickets for £17/5 (adult/child) – a useful saving – although remember that if you cross over into zone 2 (eg from King's Cross St Pancras to Camden Town) you'll be travelling on an invalid ticket and therefore liable for a penalty.

PRACTICALITIES

ACCOMMODATION

The accommodation options in this guide are listed alphabetically by area for mid- and top-range hotels, followed by a separate cheap-sleeps section. When budgeting for your trip remember that hotel rates often rise in the summer, while there are frequent bargains during winter.

Paying for accommodation in London will usually swallow a very significant chunk of your budget, however much money you have to spend. The average hotel rate is £80 to £150-plus per night, while hostels average about £30 to £40. See the boxed text, p358, for more information on accommodation prices. The choice is enormous, but the lower end is consistently oversubscribed, so if your budget is limited it's a good idea to book well ahead. See p354 for further information.

Good resources for finding and booking hotels include www.hotelsoflondon .co.uk, www.londonlodging.co.uk and www .frontdesk.co.uk.

BABY-SITTING

All the top-range hotels offer in-house baby-sitting services. Prices vary enormously from hotel to hotel, so enquire with the concierges. You might also like to try **Childminders** (day bookings ☎ 7935 2049, evenings ☎ 7935 3000; www.babysitter.co.uk). Membership costs from £12.75 plus VAT for three months and prices start at £5.20 per hour. Two other recommended baby-sitting services are **Top Notch Nannies** (☎ 7565 2640; www.topnotchnannies.com) and, in West London only, **Nick's Babysitting** (☎ 0798 652 1955; www.nicksbabysittingservice .co.uk).

BUSINESS

London is a world business hub, and doing business here (not including the media and new-technology industries) is as formal as you would expect from the English. Looking smart at all times is still seen as a key indicator of professionalism, along with punctuality and politeness. Business cards are commonplace.

Business Hours

While the City of London continues to work a very traditional Monday to Friday 9am to 5pm routine (the Square Mile is deserted at weekends), business hours elsewhere in the city are extremely flexible. Larger shops and chain stores are usually open until 7pm Monday to Friday, as well as until at least 5pm Saturday and Sunday. Thursday, or sometimes Wednesday, there's late-night shopping (for more details, see p334).

Banks in central London are open until 5pm, although counter transactions after 3.30pm are usually not processed until the next working day. Post offices vary in their opening times, but most are open from 9am to 5.30pm Monday to Saturday.

Traditionally, pubs and bars have been open from midday until 11pm. The licensing laws were changed in 2005 to allow pubs and bars to apply for licences to stay open 24 hours. However, amid concerns about binge drinking, antisocial behaviour and fears of complaints from local residents, at the time of writing few pubs and bars had yet to ask to even slightly extend their opening hours.

Restaurants are usually open for lunch from noon until 2.30pm, and dinner from

7pm until 10pm. Those hours are for 'food served' rather than 'restaurant open'.

CHILDREN

London offers a wealth of sights and museums that appeal to children; see p144. It's a city with many green spaces, often including safe areas for children to play, and swings and slides.

There is nearly always a special child's entry rate to paying attractions, although ages of eligibility may vary. Children also travel more cheaply on public transport (and bus travel is free for under 16s).

The only places where children are traditionally not accepted are pubs, although many now have a family area, a garden or a restaurant where kids are welcome.

CLIMATE

Many who live in London would swear that global warming has added a twist to the city's unpredictable climatic conditions. While locals used to complain about the frequent, but still somehow always unforeseen, arrival of rain, now they find themselves faced with sudden outbreaks of sunshine and dry heat instead. Recent summers have seen record temperatures, approaching 40°C. As the tube turns into the Black Hole of Calcutta and traffic fumes become choking, London is particularly ill-equipped to cope with such heat.

However, meteorologists point out that recent statistics don't represent anything terribly out of the ordinary yet for such a naturally variable climate. The average maximum temperature for July, the hottest month, is still only about 23°C. In spring and autumn temperatures drop to between 13° and 17°C. In winter the average daily maximum is 8°C, the overnight minimum 2°C. Despite the appearance of snow in the past few years, it still rarely freezes in London.

What weather forecasters do predict in the long term, as a result of climate change in London, is drier summers, wetter and stormier winters and more flash floods. Meanwhile, for more immediately useful reports on actual and imminent conditions in Greater London, ring **Weathercall** (☎ 0906 654 3268, 60p per min) or visit www.bbc.london.co.uk/weather for a five-day forecast.

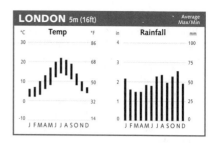

COURSES

London is a centre of learning, and boasts countless colleges, universities and other educational institutions. The jewel in its crown is the University of London, whose world-renowned colleges include King's, University and Imperial Colleges as well as the London School of Economics.

Many people come to London to study English as a foreign language, and on a walk down Oxford St you're likely to be handed a flyer on the subject. The **British Council** (☎ 7930 8466; www.britishcouncil.org; 10 Spring Gardens SW1; ⊖ Charing Cross) publishes a free list of accredited colleges whose facilities and teaching reach the required standards, and it can also advise foreign students on educational opportunities in the UK.

Thousands of London courses, from needlework to Nietzsche, photography to politics, are listed in the annual **Floodlight** (www.floodlight.co.uk; £3.95) and the quarterly **Hotcourses** (www.hotcourses.com; £1.95), both available from larger newsagents and bookshops. For more vocational courses, try the free **Learndirect** (☎ 0800 100 900; www.learndirect-advice.co.uk).

CUSTOMS

Like other nations belonging to the EU, the UK has a two-tier customs system: one for goods bought duty-free and one for goods bought in another EU country where taxes and duties have already been paid.

Duty-Free

For goods purchased at airports or on ferries outside the EU, you are allowed to import 200 cigarettes, 50 cigars or 250g of tobacco; 2L of still wine plus 1L of spirits over 22% or another 2L of wine (sparkling or otherwise); 50g of perfume and 250cc of toilet water; and other duty-free goods to the value of £145.

Tax & Duty Paid

Although you can no longer bring in duty-free goods from another EU country, you can bring in duty-paid goods that cost less than you'd pay for the same items in your destination country. The items are supposed to be for individual consumption but a thriving business has developed, with many Londoners making day trips to France to load up their cars with cheap grog and smokes.

If you purchase from a normal retail outlet on the Continent, customs uses the following maximum quantities as a guide to distinguish personal imports from those on a commercial scale: 800 cigarettes, 200 cigars, 1kg of tobacco, 10L of spirits, 20L of fortified wine, 90L of wine (of which not more than 60L is sparkling) and 110L of beer.

DISABLED TRAVELLERS

For disabled travellers London is an odd mix of user-friendliness and downright disinterest. New hotels and modern tourist attractions are usually accessible by people in wheelchairs, but many B&Bs and guesthouses are in older buildings, which are hard (if not impossible) to adapt. This means that travellers who have mobility problems may end up paying more for accommodation.

It's a similar story with public transport. Access to the tube is limited. However, some of the newer trains and buses have steps that lower for easier access and there are two dedicated bus services with automatic ramps offering disabled access: the 205 and the 705. The 205 runs from Paddington to Whitechapel every 10 to 12 minutes. The 705 runs between Victoria, Waterloo and London Bridge half-hourly. Both services operate approximately from 6am to midnight.

Transport for London's **Access & Mobility for Disabled Passengers** (☎ 7222 1234, textphone ☎ 7918 3015; Windsor House, 42/50 Victoria St, London SW1 9TN) can give you detailed advice and it publishes *Access to the Underground*, which indicates which tube stations have ramps and lifts (all DLR stations do).

The **Royal Association for Disability and Rehabilitation** (Radar; ☎ 7250 3222; www.radar.org .uk; Unit 12, City Forum, 250 City Rd, London EC1V 8AF) is an umbrella organisation for voluntary groups for people with disabilities. Many disabled-user toilets can be opened only with a special key, which can be obtained from tourist offices or for £3.50 (plus a brief statement of your disability) via the Radar website. The organisation also has an accommodation website, www .radarsearch.org, listing hotels with appropriate facilities.

The **Royal National Institute for the Blind** (☎ 7388 1266; www.rnib.org.uk; 105 Judd St, London WC1) can also be contacted via its confidential **helpline** (☎ 0845 766 9999; ☻ 9am-5pm Mon-Fri) and is the best point of initial contact for sight-impaired visitors to London. The **Royal National Institute for Deaf People** (freephone ☎ 0808 808 0123, freephone/textphone ☎ 0808 808 9000; www .rnid.org.uk; 19-23 Featherstone St, London EC1) is a similar organisation for the deaf and hard of hearing. Many ticket offices and banks are fitted with hearing loops to help the hearing-impaired; look for the ear symbol.

DISCOUNT CARDS

Students studying full-time in London are eligible for discounted travel on all London public transport. However, it takes some time to receive your discount card, as it needs to be sent by post for processing – ask for a form to fill out at any tube station.

For details on Travelcards offering discounts on public transport, see p405.

Possibly of most interest to visitors who want to take in lots of sights and attractions is **London Pass** (www.londonpass.com). Passes start at £12 per day, although they can be altered to include use of the Underground and buses. They offer free entry and queue-jumping to all major attractions – check the website for details.

ELECTRICITY

The standard voltage throughout the UK is 230/240V AC, 50Hz. Plugs have three square pins and can look rather curious to non-Brits. Adapters for European, Australasian and American electrical items are available at any electrical store.

EMBASSIES

It's important to realise what your own embassy – the embassy of the country of which you are a citizen – can and cannot do to help you if you get into trouble.

Generally, it won't be much help if the trouble you're in is remotely your own fault. Remember that while in London you are bound by British law. Your embassy will not be sympathetic if you end up in prison after committing a crime locally, even if such actions are legal in your own country.

In genuine emergencies you might get some assistance, but only if other channels have been exhausted. For example, if you need to get home urgently, a free ticket is highly unlikely – the embassy would expect you to have insurance. If you have all your money and documents stolen, it might assist with getting a new passport but a loan for onward travel is almost always out of the question.

The following is a list of selected foreign representative offices in London. Embassies are designed to help their own nationals but they often also contain a consulate section where visas are issued to other nationals wishing to visit this country. Where consulates have a separate address, these are listed. For a more complete list check under 'Embassies & Consulates' in the central London **Yellow Pages** (www.yell.co.uk).

Australia High Commission (Map pp448-9; ☎ 7379 4334; www.australia.org.uk; Australia House, Strand WC2; ✪ Holborn/Temple)

Belgium (Map pp460-1; ☎ 7470 3700, for visa appointments ☎ 0906 550 8963, per min £1; www.diplobel .org/uk; 103 Eaton Sq SW1; ✪ Victoria) Appointments are necessary to obtain a visa.

Canada Embassy (Map p452; ☎ 7258 6600; www .canada.org.uk; Canada House, Trafalgar Sq SW1; ✪ Charing Cross); Consulate (Map pp448–9; ☎ 7258 6600; www.canada.org.uk; 38 Grosvenor Sq W1; ✪ Bond St)

France (Map pp458-9; ☎ 7073 1200, for visas ☎ 0906 554 0700, per min £1; www.ambafrance-uk.org; 21 Cromwell Rd SW7; ✪ South Kensington)

Germany (Map pp460-1; ☎ 7824 1300, for visa appointments ☎ 09065 540 740, per min £1; www.german -embassy.org.uk; 23 Belgrave Sq SW1; ✪ Hyde Park Cnr) Appointments are necessary to obtain a visa.

Ireland Embassy (Map pp448-9; ☎ 0870 005 6725; http://ireland.embassyhomepage.com; 17 Grosvenor Pl SW1; ✪ Hyde Park Cnr); Consulate (☎ 0870 005 6725, 7255 7700; Montpelier House, 106 Brompton Rd SW3; ✪ South Kensington)

Netherlands (Map pp444-5; ☎ 7590 3200; www .netherlands-embassy.org.uk; 38 Hyde Park Gate SW7; ✪ High St Kensington)

New Zealand (Map p450; ☎ 7930 8422; www.nz embassy.com; New Zealand House, 80 Haymarket SW1; ✪ Piccadilly Circus)

South Africa (Map p452; ☎ 7451 7299; www.south africahouse.com; South Africa House, Trafalgar Sq WC2; ✪ Charing Cross)

Spain Embassy (Map pp460-1; ☎ 7235 5555; 39 Chesham Pl SW1; ✪ Hyde Park Cnr); Consulate (Map pp458-9; ☎ 7589 8989; 20 Draycott Pl SW3; ✪ South Kensington)

USA (Map pp448-9; ☎ 7499 9000, 0906 820 0290; www .usembassy.org.uk; 5 Upper Grosvenor St W1; ✪ Bond St)

EMERGENCIES

Dial ☎ 999 to call the police, fire brigade or ambulance in an emergency. For hospitals with 24-hour accident and emergency departments see p411.

GAY & LESBIAN TRAVELLERS

London is a mecca for gay travellers, who come here for the nightlife and relaxed atmosphere of its cafés and bars – centred on Soho's Old Compton St. It is rare to encounter any problems with couples sharing rooms or holding hands in public. However, outside central London, discretion is often the best policy. In the event of an incident, the Metropolitan Police take homophobic crime very seriously, ranking it as a 'hate crime' alongside racial harassment.

The tabloids **Boyz** (www.boyz.co.uk) and **QX** (http://qxmagazine.com), as well as the more serious **Pink Paper** (www.pinkpaper .com), are all available free in most gay bars and cafés. They include weekly listings for clubs, bars and other events, and often contain flyers for discounted entry to various venues. Magazines including **Gay Times** (www.gaytimes.co.uk; £3.25), *Diva* and **Attitude** (www.attitude.co.uk) are all available in newsagents throughout London, although some less enlightened proprietors still place them on the top shelf next to the pornography.

Check out the following websites:

Gay Britain (www.gaybritain.co.uk)

Gay Britain Network (www.gaypride.co.uk)

London Gay Accommodation (www.londongay.co.uk)

Rainbow Network (www.rainbownetwork.com)

For information on gay-friendly taxis, see p403.

HOLIDAYS

With typically four to five weeks' annual leave, Britons get fewer holidays than their European compatriots, but more than their American friends.

Public Holidays

Most attractions and businesses close for a couple of days over Christmas, and those places that normally shut on Sundays will probably also do so on Bank Holiday Mondays.

New Year's Day 1 January

Good Friday/Easter Monday Late March/April

May Day Holiday First Monday in May

Spring Bank Holiday Last Monday in May

Summer Bank Holiday Last Monday in August

Christmas Day 25 December

Boxing Day 26 December

For details of the many festivals London hosts throughout the year, see p10.

School Holidays

These change from year to year and often from school to school. Moreover, public (ie private) school holidays tend to differ from those of state schools. As a general rule, however:

Summer holiday Late July to early September

Autumn half term Last week of October

Christmas holidays 20 December to 6 January

Spring half term One week in mid-February

Easter holidays Two weeks either side of Easter Sunday

Summer half term One week end of May/early June

INTERNET ACCESS

Logging onto the Internet shouldn't be a problem – if you have your own laptop you can go online with ease from your hotel room, and if you don't you can drop into any Internet café throughout the capital. The most important thing as a traveller with your own laptop is to buy an adapter that slots onto the standard telephone cord to fit to the wider, thinner UK phone line. These are available in any hardware or electrical store for about £4 or £5. Some of the better-known and centrally located Internet

cafés are listed here, but these are a fraction of those available.

BTR (Map pp448–9; ☎ 7681 4223; www.be-the-reds .com; 39 Whitfield St W1; per 30min £1; ☺ 10am-10pm Mon-Fri, 11am-7pm Sat & Sun; ➍ Goodge St) Formerly Cyberia, the UK's first Internet café, this offers most services apart from wi-fi and serves yummy Asian snacks.

Buzz Bar (Map pp444–5; ☎ 7460 4910; www.portobello gold.com/Internet.html; 95 Portobello Rd W11; per hr £2 (minimum charge); ☺ 10am-11pm; ➍ Notting Hill Gate) This might be 'the most relaxed Internet café in London', but perhaps not after 9pm, when only two terminals are left available. Upstairs from the Portobello Gold Hotel, the bar also offers wi-fi Internet access for enabled laptops and CD burning.

Cyberg@te (Map pp442–3; ☎ 7387 3810; www.c-gate .com; 3 Leigh St WC1; per 30min £1; ☺ 9am-9pm Mon-Sat, noon-8pm Sun; ➍ Russell Sq) Cyberg@te's 20 or so terminals are complemented by wired and wireless laptop connection, CD burning, printing and so on. Plans are to keep the store open until 11pm in summer.

easyEverything (Map pp460–1; ☎ 7938 1841; www .easyeverything.com; 12-14 Wilton Rd SW1; per 20min-1hr (depending on time of day) £1; ☺ 24hr; ➍ Victoria) This cybercafé chain is a division of the airline easyJet and is similarly no-frills. Seventeen London branches include: **Tottenham Court Road** (Map p450; 9-16 Tottenham Court Rd W1; ➍ Tottenham Court Rd); **Kensington** (Map pp444–5; 160-166 Kensington High St W8; ➍ Kensington High St); **Oxford Circus** (Map pp448–9; 358 Oxford St W1; ➍ Oxford Circus); **Trafalgar Square** (Map p452; 7 Strand WC2; ➍ Charing Cross); **Baker Street** (Map pp444–5; 122 Baker St, inside McDonald's; ➍ Baker St); **Piccadilly Circus** (Map p450; 46 Regent St, inside Burger King; ➍ Piccadilly Circus) and **King's Road** (Map pp458–9; Unit G1, King's Walk, 120 King's Rd; ➍ Sloane Sq).

Vibe Bar (Map pp454–5; ☎ 7377 2899; www.vibe-bar .co.uk; Truman Brewery, 91-95 Brick Lane E1; usage free; ☺ 11am-11.30pm Sun-Thu, to 1am Fri & Sat; ➍ Aldgate East) Seven terminals are available at no charge to customers.

Virgin Megastore (Map p450; ☎ 7631 1234; 14-30 Oxford St W1; per 30min £1 (minimum charge); ☺ 9am-9pm Mon-Sat, 11am-6pm Sun; ➍ Tottenham Court Rd) This huge record store has access on 20 terminals.

LEGAL MATTERS

Should you face any legal difficulties while in London, visit any one of the **Citizens Advice Bureaux** (www.citizensadvice.org.uk) listed under 'Counselling & Advice' in the Yellow Pages, or contact the **Community Legal Services Directory** (☎ 0845 345 4345; www.clsdirect .org.uk).

Driving Offences

The laws against drink-driving have become tougher and are treated more seriously than they used to be. Currently you're allowed to have a blood-alcohol level of 35mg/100mL but there's talk of reducing the limit. The safest approach is not to drink anything at all if you're planning to drive.

Drugs

Illegal drugs of every type are widely available in London, especially in clubs. Nonetheless, all the usual drug warnings apply. Cannabis was reclassified as a Class C drug in 2004, removing the risk of arrest for the possession of small quantities. In 2005, however, new studies prompted a government re-think, so the drug might be reclassified as Class B, warranting stiff penalties. Possession of harder drugs, including heroin and cocaine, is always treated seriously.

Fines

In general you rarely have to cough up on the spot for an offence. The exceptions are trains, the tube and buses, where people who can't produce a valid ticket for the journey when asked to by an inspector can be fined £20 there and then. No excuses are accepted.

Britain has introduced new 'Anti-Social Behaviour Orders', allowing police to issue fixed penalty notices for antisocial behaviour. These run from £50 for minors attempting to buy alcohol to £80 for being drunk and disorderly, making false 999 calls or wasting police time.

MAPS

The *London A-Z* series produces a range of excellent maps and handheld street atlases. All areas of London mapped on this system can be accessed at www.streetmap.co.uk, one of London's most invaluable websites.

Lonely Planet also publishes a *London City Map*.

Bookshops with a wide selection of maps include Stanford's, Foyles, Waterstone's and Daunt (for details, see p346).

MEDICAL SERVICES

Reciprocal arrangements with the UK allow Australian residents, New Zealand nationals, and residents and nationals of several other countries to receive free emergency medical treatment and subsidised dental care through the **National Health Service** (NHS; ☎ 0845 4647; www.nhsdirect.nhs.uk). They can use hospital emergency departments, GPs and dentists (check the Yellow Pages). Visitors staying 12 months or longer, with the proper documentation, will receive care under the NHS by registering with a specific practice near their residence.

EU nationals can obtain free emergency treatment on presentation of an E111 form that has been validated in their home country. In 2004 a European Health Insurance card was introduced, which will gradually replace the E111.

Travel insurance, however, is advisable as it offers greater flexibility over where and how you're treated and covers expenses for an ambulance and repatriation that won't be picked up by the NHS.

Hospitals

The following hospitals have 24-hour accident and emergency departments:

Charing Cross Hospital (Map pp438–9; ☎ 8846 1234; Fulham Palace Rd W6; ✆ Hammersmith)

Chelsea & Westminster Hospital (Map pp458–9; ☎ 8746 8000; 369 Fulham Rd SW10; ✆ South Kensington, then bus 14 or 211)

Guy's Hospital (Map pp454–5; ☎ 7955 5000; St Thomas St SE1; ✆ London Bridge)

Homerton Hospital (Map pp438–9; ☎ 8919 5555; Homerton Row E9; rail Homerton)

Royal Free Hospital (Map pp465; ☎ 7794 0500; Pond St NW3; ✆ Belsize Park)

Royal London Hospital (Map pp454–5; ☎ 7377 7000; Whitechapel Rd E1; ✆ Whitechapel)

University College Hospital (Map pp440–1; ☎ 7380 9300; 253 Euston Rd NW1; ✆ Euston Sq)

Dental Services

For emergency dental care, call into **Eastman Dental Hospital** (☎ 7915 1000; 256 Gray's Inn Rd WC1; ✆ King's Cross).

METRIC SYSTEM

People in London use both the metric and imperial systems interchangeably. Some older people will not readily comprehend metric measurements and, similarly, some younger people will not readily understand imperial. See the inside front cover for conversions.

MONEY

Despite being a member of the EU, the UK has not signed up to the euro and has retained the pound sterling as its unit of currency. One pound sterling is made up of 100 pence (pronounced 'pee', colloquially). Notes come in denominations of £5, £10, £20 and £50, while coins are 1p, 2p, 5p, 10p, 20p, 50p, £1 and £2. Unless otherwise noted, all prices in this book are in pounds sterling. See p28 for an idea of the cost of living in London.

ATMs

ATMs are a way of life in London, as the huge queues by them on Saturday nights in the West End attest. There is no area in London unserved by them, and they accept cards from any bank in the world that is tied into the Visa, MasterCard, Cirrus or Maestro systems, as well as some other more obscure ones. After a national campaign, most banks now allow their cardholders to withdraw money from other banks' ATMs without charge, and vice versa. However, those without UK high-street bankcards should be warned that there is nearly always a transaction surcharge for cash withdrawals. You should contact your bank to find out how much this is before using ATMs too freely.

Also, always beware of suspicious-looking devices attached to ATMs. Many London ATMs have now been made tamper-proof, but certain fraudsters' devices are capable of sucking your card into the machine, allowing the fraudsters to release it when you have given up and left.

Changing Money

You can change money in most high-street banks and some travel-agent chains, as well as at the numerous bureaux de change throughout the city. Compare rates and watch for the commission that is not always mentioned. The trick is to ask how many pounds you'll receive in all before committing – you'll lose nothing by shopping around.

Credit & Debit Cards

Credit and debit cards are accepted almost universally in London, from restaurants and bars to shops and even some taxis. American Express and Diner's Club are less widely used than Visa and MasterCard, while most Londoners simply live off their Switch debit cards, which can also be used to get 'cash back' from supermarkets, saving a trip to an ATM if you are low on cash.

NEWSPAPERS & MAGAZINES

Newspapers

For a good selection of foreign-language newspapers, try the newsstands in the Victoria Pl shopping centre at Victoria train station, along Charing Cross Rd, in Old Compton St and along Queensway. See p409 for details of gay and lesbian publications.

DAILY PAPERS

Daily Express Middle-level tabloid.

Daily Mail This is often called the voice of middle England – the rabid voice of middle England, we reckon, given its regular anti-immigration campaigns.

Daily Star Tabloid with wacky tales that often beggar belief.

Daily Telegraph Ownership worries and job losses have left the 'Torygraph' – once the UK's biggest-circulation broadsheet – in even worse condition than its beloved Conservative party.

Evening Standard London's main daily paper has introduced a free *Evening Standard Lite* to compete with the giveaway *Metro*. Most useful on Thursdays for its listings magazine *Metro Life*.

Financial Times Heavyweight business paper with a great travel section in its weekend edition.

Guardian Middle class and mildly left-wing, the *Guardian* is increasingly obsessed with fashion and celebrity, and relaunched itself in Autumn 2005 in a 'Berliner' size (a halfway house between broadsheet and tabloid). An entertainment supplement, the *Guide*, comes with Saturday's paper.

Independent The politically nonaligned *Independent* sparked a revolution when it went from a struggling broadsheet to 'newspaper of the year' by converting to a serious-minded tabloid.

Metro This free morning paper from the *Daily Mail* stable litters tube stations and seats, giving you an extra excuse to ignore your fellow passengers. It's as lightweight as it is thin.

Mirror New Labour PM Tony Blair briefly rediscovered this working-class tabloid bastion of Old Labour support during the 2005 election, when his front-page handwritten letter to readers explained why they should vote for him.

Sun The UK's bestseller, this gossip-loving tabloid is owner Rupert Murdoch's entrée to power here. Legendary for its clever (and sometimes offensive) headlines, it supported the Tories during their 1980s glory years, before switching to New Labour.

Times The first to follow the *Independent* in downsizing to a smaller format, this stalwart of the British press is now a tabloid, too. It's also part of the Murdoch stable.

SUNDAY PAPERS

News of the World Sister to the *Sun*, this is the ultimate scandal mag, with an enormous readership. It has a passion for kiss-and-tell stories, famously including one involving David Beckham and Rebecca Loos.

Observer Sunday-only paper similar in tone and style to the *Guardian*, which owns it.

Sunday Telegraph As serious as its weekly sister.

Sunday Times Full of scandal and fashion. Probably destroys at least one rainforest per issue, but most of it can be arguably tossed in the recycling bin upon purchase.

Magazines

London is pretty much the world's publishing capital. Although seminal style magazines like the *Face* have bitten the dust, a whole new generation of celebrity rags have arisen to keep newsagents' shelves overflowing. International publications such as *Condé Nast Traveller, Cosmopolitan, Elle, Esquire, FHM, Glamour, Newsweek, Marie Claire, Time* and *Vogue* naturally have British or European editions – indeed several even originated here.

There are a couple of film titles on the market, such as *Empire* and *Total Film*, while music magazines include the weekly *NME* newspaper and the middle-aged *Mojo*. Other titles include:

Dazed and Confused The heady days when Rankin made his name as a photographer are long gone, but Jefferson Hack (father of Kate Moss' daughter) has managed to keep his style magazine going many years.

Economist In-depth global news stories come with an unsurprising but unobtrusive financial bent in this quietly successful weekly magazine (or, as the proprietors insist, 'newspaper'). The one people say they read to create an aura of substance.

Heat This phenomenally successful celebrity mag created a whole new genre, as rivals raced to imitate its weekly dose of iconoclasm and sycophancy.

i-D This über-cool London fashion/music gospel is possibly too hip for its own good, but it's still turning out its trademark winking covers every month.

Loaded The original lads mag (as opposed to a men's magazine like the market-leading *FHM*), *Loaded* has recently relaunched itself as a 'new lads' mag, throwing some investigative journalism, real-life stories and an 'arty' black-and-white centrefold section into the mix.

London Review of Books Shunning the general trend for lifestyle journalism, this literary criticism magazine sticks to academic-style essays.

Loot (www.loot.com) This paper appears five times per week and is made up of classified ads placed free by sellers. You can find everything from kitchen sinks to cars, as well as an extensive selection of flat- and house-share ads.

New Statesman This left-wing intellectual news magazine was going through a bad patch, with dull articles and convoluted writing. Then new editor John Kampfner was appointed in 2005 to turn things around.

Nuts Just when you thought lads mags couldn't get any lower than *Loaded,* along comes this weekly tits 'n' sports special, and its rival *Zoo,* to prove you dead wrong.

Private Eye (see p25) Satirical weekly, established by comedian Peter Cook and edited by Ian Hislop, that provides a refreshing perspective on the news. Might be largely incomprehensible to a non-British readership, but is worth a shot for the front page alone.

Spectator This right-wing weekly's funny, thought-provoking writing has even left-wingers loving it despite themselves. Has made big news in the past few years – when editor and Tory MP Boris Johnson made a gaffe over Liverpool and home secretary David Blunkett was found to have had an affair with publisher Kimberley Quinn.

Time Out (www.timeout.com) The London going-out bible is published every Tuesday, providing a complete listing of what's on and where.

TNT Magazine; Southern Cross; SA Times These weekly freebies have Australasian and South African news and sports results for homesick travellers and are also useful for their entertainment listings, travel sections and classified ads for jobs, cheap tickets, shipping services and accommodation. They can be found outside most tube stations.

Wallpaper* The style magazine that defined the aspirant lifestyle of the late 1990s, Wallpaper* has faded since Tyler Brûlé, its unlikely sounding but visionary founder, moved on to pastures new.

PHARMACIES

There's always one neighbourhood chemist that's open 24 hours; check the Yellow Pages for one near you.

Most people will be instantly struck by the almost total monopoly enjoyed by Boots the Chemist, which has a store at **Piccadilly Circus** (Map p450; ☎ 7734 6126; 44-46 Regent St; ☽ 9am-8pm Mon-Sat, noon-6pm Sun; ✪ Piccadilly Circus). The Superdrug chain is the only potential rival. Both chains are extremely well supplied.

POST

Once the pride of Britain, the Royal Mail has a somewhat poorer reputation since privatisation. It's still generally very reliable, but it's no longer possible to take for granted the speed and accuracy that once was its hallmark.

For general postal enquiries ring ☎ 0845 722 3344, or visit www.royalmail.co.uk.

Postal Rates

Domestic 1st-class mail is quicker (next working day) but more expensive (30/46p per letter up to 60/100g) than 2nd class (21/35p taking three working days).

Postcards and letters up to 20g cost 42p to anywhere in Europe; to almost everywhere else, including the Americas and Australasia, it's 47/68p up to 10/20g. Parcels up to 100/200g cost £1.14/1.34 to Europe and £2.16/2.35 elsewhere. They must be taken to the post office for weighing.

Airmail letters to the USA or Canada generally take three to five days; to Australia or New Zealand, allow five days to a week (although mail to Australia might get through in two to three days!).

Poste Restante

Unless you (or the person writing to you) specify otherwise, poste restante mail sent to London ends up at the Trafalgar Square post office (Map p452; 24-28 William IV St WC2; ☯ 8.30am-6.30pm Mon-Fri, 9am-5.30pm Sat; ⊖ Charing Cross). Mail will be held for four weeks; ID is required.

Postcodes

The unusual London postal code system dates back to WW1. The whole city is divided up into districts denoted by a letter (or letters) and a number; see the map, p464. For example, W1, the Mayfair and Soho postcode, stands for 'West London, district 1'. EC1, on the other hand, stands for 'East Central London, district 1'. The numbers are assigned alphabetically throughout the districts and make little logical sense, but help differentiate London streets with identical names. For example, Harrow Rd exists in E6, E11, NW10, W2, W10 and W9! The sets of three or four digits and letters following the main postcode allow every building in London to have a different postcode.

RADIO

For a taste of London on the airwaves, tune into the following stations:

BBC London Live (94.9 FM) Talk station with a London bias.

Capital FM (95.8 FM) The commercial equivalent of the BBC's national Radio 1 and the most popular pop station in the city.

Capital Gold (1548AM) Plays oldies from the '60s, '70s and '80s.

Choice FM (96.9 FM) Soul station.

Classic FM (100.9 FM) Yes, it's classical music.

Jazz FM (102.2 FM) For middle-of-the-road jazz and blues aficionados.

Kiss 100 (100 FM) Dance station.

LBC (1152AM) A talkback channel.

Magic FM (105.4 FM) Plays mainstream oldies.

News Direct (97.3 FM) An all-news station with full reports every 20 minutes.

Talk Sport (1089AM) Self-explanatory!

Virgin (105.8 FM) Pop station.

Xfm (104.9 FM) An alternative radio station playing indie music.

TAXES & REFUNDS

Value-added tax (VAT) is a 17.5% sales tax levied on most goods and services except food, books and children's clothing. Restaurants must, by law, include VAT in their menu prices.

It's sometimes possible for visitors to claim a refund of VAT paid on goods, resulting in considerable savings. You're eligible if you have spent fewer than 365 days out of the two years prior to making the purchase living in the UK, and if you're leaving the EU within three months of making the purchase.

Not all shops participate in the VAT refund scheme, called the Retail Export Scheme or Tax-Free Shopping, and different shops will have different minimum purchase conditions (normally around £75 in any one shop). On request, participating shops will give you a special form (VAT 407). This must be presented with the goods and receipts to customs when you depart (VAT-free goods can't be posted or shipped home). After customs has certified the form, it should be returned to the shop for a refund (minus an administration or handling fee), which takes about eight to 10 weeks to come through.

TELEPHONE

British Telecom's (BT's) famous red phone boxes survive in conservation areas only (notably Westminster), and in the mobile-phone age the company is even lobbying to get rid of its more modern glass cubicles.

Some phones still accept coins, but most take phonecards or credit cards. BT's £3, £5, £10 and £20 phonecards are widely available from retailers including most post offices and newsagents. A digital display on the telephone indicates how much credit is left on the card.

The following are some important telephone numbers and codes (some numbers are charged calls):

International dialling code (☎ 00)

Local and national directory enquiries (☎ 118 118/118 500)

International directory enquiries (☎ 118 661/118 505)

Local and national operator (☎ 100)

International operator (☎ 155)

Reverse-charge/collect calls (☎ 155)

Time (☎ 123)

Weathercall (Greater London) (☎ 0906 654 3268)

Following are some special phone codes worth knowing:

Toll-free (☎ 0500/0800)

Local call rate applies (☎ 0845)

National call rate applies (☎ 0870/0871)

Premium rate applies (from 60p per minute) (☎ 09)

Calling London

London's area code is 020, followed by an eight-digit number beginning with 7, 8 or, more recently, 3. You only need to dial the 020 when you are calling London from elsewhere in the UK.

To call London from abroad, dial your country's international access code, then 44 (the UK's country code), then 20 (dropping the initial 0) followed by the eight-digit phone number.

Local & National Call Rates

Local calls are charged by time alone; regional and national calls are charged by both time and distance. Daytime rates apply from 6am to 6pm Monday to Friday; the cheap rate applies from 6pm to 6am Monday to Friday; and the cheap weekend rate applies from midnight Friday to midnight Sunday. There is a minimum call charge of 5p.

Calls to local and national directory enquiries cost 11p per minute from public phones (minimum deposit of 20p) and 15p per minute from private phones, plus an initial 40p connection charge.

International Calls & Rates

International direct dialling (IDD) calls to almost anywhere can be made from nearly all public telephones. To call someone outside the UK dial 00, then the country code, then the area code (you usually drop the initial zero if there is one) and then the number. For example, to ring Melbourne, where the area code is 03 and the code for Australia is 61, you would dial ☎ 00-61-3-1234 5678. To reach Boston, where the area code is 617 and the code for the USA is 1, dial ☎ 00-1-617-123 4567.

Direct dialling is cheaper than making a reverse-charge (collect) call through the international operator (☎ 155). International directory enquiries (☎ 118 505, 118 661) cost a whopping £1.50 per minute from private phones.

Some private firms offer cheaper international calls than BT. In such shops you phone from a metered booth and then pay the bill. There will be at least one such call centre on most high streets. Some cyber-cafés and Internet access shops also offer cheap rates for international calls.

It's also possible to undercut BT international call rates by buying a special card (usually denominated £5, £10 or £20) with a PIN that you use from any phone, even a home phone, by dialling a special access number. There are dozens of cards – with bizarre names such as Alpha, Omega, Banana Call, First National and Swiftlink – available from newsagents and grocers. To decide which is best you really have to compare the rate each offers for the particular country you want – posters with the rates of the various companies are often displayed on shop doors or windows.

Mobile Phones

The UK uses the GSM 900 network, which covers Europe, Australia and New Zealand, but is not compatible with the North American GSM 1900 or the totally different system in Japan (though many North Americans have GSM 1900/900 phones that do work here). If you have a GSM phone, check with your service provider about using it in the UK, and beware of calls being routed internationally. It's usually most convenient to buy a local SIM card from the nearest branch of the **Link** (☎ 0870 154 5540; www .thelink.co.uk) or **Carphone Warehouse** (☎ 0870 168 2002; www.carphonewarehouse.com). You can also rent phones, including from **Mobell** (☎ 0800 243 524; www.mobell.com) and **Cellhire** (☎ 0870 561 0610; www.cellhire .com).

TELEVISION

Digital TV has come to the UK, with dozens of digital channels, as well as satellite and cable channels such as BSkyB. However, still just five free-to-air analogue stations exist. They, and some of their leading programmes, are:

BBC1 *EastEnders, Strictly Come Dancing, Doctor Who, Panorama*

BBC2 *University Challenge, Newsnight, The Apprentice*

ITV *Pop Idol, Who Wants to be a Millionaire, I'm a Celebrity, Get Me Out of Here, Coronation Street, The Bill, Ant & Dec*

C4 *Hollyoaks, Channel 4 News, Big Brother, Desperate Housewives, The Simpsons*

C5 *Mainly reruns of '80s B-movies*

TIME

Wherever you are in the world, the time on your watch is measured in relation to the time at Greenwich in London – Greenwich Mean Time (GMT). British Summer Time, the UK's form of daylight-saving time, muddies the water so that even London is ahead of GMT from late March to late October. To give you an idea, San Francisco is usually eight hours and New York five hours behind GMT, while Sydney is 10 hours ahead of GMT. Phone the international operator on ☎ 155 to find out the exact difference.

TIPPING

Many restaurants now add a 'discretionary' service charge to your bill, but in places that don't you are expected to leave a 10% to 15% tip unless the service was unsatisfactory. Waiting staff are often paid poorly.

It's legal for restaurants to include a service charge in the bill but this should be clearly advertised. You needn't add a further tip (for more information on tipping in restaurants, see p230). You never tip to have your pint pulled in a pub but staff at bars now often return change in a little metal dish, expecting some of the coins to glue themselves to the bottom.

If you take a boat trip on the Thames you'll find some guides and/or drivers importuning for a tip in return for their commentary. Whether you pay is up to you. See p403 for information on tipping taxi drivers.

TOILETS

Although many toilets in central London are still pretty grim, those at main train stations, bus terminals and attractions are generally good and usually have facilities for people with disabilities and those with young children. At train and bus stations you usually have to pay 20p to use the facilities. You also have to pay to use the self-cleaning concrete pods in places such as Leicester Sq (and yes, they do open automatically after a set amount of time, so no hanky-panky – or at least make it snappy).

It's an offence to urinate in the streets, although arrests are rare. However, with the streets of Soho so frequently stinking of urine, Westminster council has pioneered an excellent scheme whereby public urinals are set up on the streets at weekends for those who can't make it to the next bar without relieving themselves. These can be found on Soho Sq, Wardour St and the Strand, among other locations.

For information on toilets for the disabled, see p408.

TOURIST INFORMATION

London is a major travel centre, so along with information on London, tourist offices can help with England, Scotland, Wales, Ireland and most countries worldwide.

Tourist Information Centres

Visit London (formerly the London Tourist Board; ☎ 7234 5800, 0870 156 6366; www .visitlondon.com) can fill you in on everything from tourist attractions and events (such as the Changing of the Guard) to river trips and tours, accommodation, eating, theatre, shopping, children's London and gay and lesbian venues. Its **London Line** (☎ 0906 866 3344, per min 60p) has recorded information.

London's main tourist office is the **Britain Visitor Centre** (Map p450; 1 Regent St SW1; ☼ 9.30am-6.30pm Mon, 9am-6.30pm Tue-Fri, 10am-4pm Sat & Sun, to 5pm Sat Jun-Sep; ♦ Piccadilly Circus). It has comprehensive information in eight languages, not just on London, but on Wales, Scotland, Northern Ireland, the Irish Republic and Jersey too. It can arrange accommodation, tours and train, air and car travel. It also has a theatre ticket agency, a bureau de change, international telephones and a few computer terminals for accessing tourist information on the Web. The centre deals with walk-in enquiries only, so if you're not in the area, contact the **British Tourist Authority** (☎ 8846 9000; www .visitbritain.com).

Other useful tourist offices include the **London Visitor Centre** (Map pp448–9; Arrivals Hall, Waterloo International Terminal; ☼ 8.30am-10.30pm), **Heathrow Airport TIC** (Terminal 1, 2 & 3 Underground station; ☼ 8am-6pm) and **Liverpool Street TIC** (Map pp454–5; Liverpool St Underground station; ☼ 8am-6pm). Hotel booking offices are also found at in the halls of Paddington train station, **Victoria train station** (☼ 8am-8pm Mon-Sat, 8am-6pm Sun Apr-Oct, 8am-6pm Mon-Sat, 9am-4pm Sun Nov-Mar; ♦ Victoria) and Victoria coach station. There are also accommodation booking services at other London airports.

A few London boroughs and neighbourhoods have their own TICs. These include:

City Information Centre (Map pp454-5; ☎ 7332 1456; www.cityoflondon.gov.uk; St Paul's Churchyard EC4; ☼ 9.30am-5pm Apr-Sep, 9.30am-5pm Mon-Fri, 9.30am-12.30pm Sat Oct-Mar; ♦ St Paul's) Opposite St Paul's Cathedral.

Greenwich (Map p463; ☎ 0870 608 2000; www.green wich.gov.uk; Pepys House, 2 Cutty Sark Gardens SW10; ☼ 10am-5pm; DLR Cutty Sark)

Richmond (Map p464; ☎ 8940 9125; www.visitrichmond .co.uk; Old Town Hall, Whittaker Ave, Richmond, Surrey TW9 1TP; ☼ 9am-5pm Mon-Sat, plus 10.30am-1pm Sun May-Sep; rail Richmond)

Southwark (Map pp454-5; ☎ 7357 9168; www.south wark.gov.uk; Vinopolis, 1 Bank End SE1; ☼ 10am-6pm Tue-Sun; ♦ London Bridge)

VISAS

Citizens of Australia, Canada, New Zealand, South Africa and the USA are given, at their point of arrival, 'leave to enter' the UK for up to six months but are prohibited from working without a work permit. If you're a citizen of the EU, you don't need a visa to enter the country and may live and work here freely for as long as you like.

Visa regulations are always subject to change, so check at www.ukvisas.gov.uk or with your local British embassy before leaving home.

Immigration authorities in the UK are tough – dress neatly and be able to prove that you have sufficient funds to support yourself. A credit card and/or an onward ticket will help.

Visa Extensions

Tourist visas can only be extended in clear emergencies (eg an accident, death of a relative). Otherwise you'll have to leave the UK (perhaps going to Ireland or France) and apply for a fresh one, although this tactic will arouse suspicion after the second or third visa. To extend (or attempt to extend) your stay in the UK, ring the **Visa & Passport Information Line** (☎ 0870 606 7766, 8649 7878; the Home Office's Immigration & Nationality Directorate, Lunar House, 40 Wellesley Rd, Croydon CR9 2BY; ☼ 10am-noon & 2-4pm Mon-Fri; rail East Croydon) before your current visa expires. The process takes a few days in France/Ireland. Trying to extend within the UK takes a lot longer (no time scale).

Student Visas

Nationals of EU countries can enter the country to study without formalities. Otherwise you need to be enrolled in a full-time course of at least 15 hours per week of weekday, daytime study at a single educational institution to be allowed to remain as a student. For more details, consult the British embassy, high commission or consulate in your own country.

WOMEN TRAVELLERS

In general, London is a fairly laid-back place, and you're unlikely to have too many problems provided you take the usual city precautions. Apart from the occasional wolf whistle and unwelcome body contact on the tube, women will find male Londoners reasonably enlightened. There's nothing to stop women going into pubs alone, though this is not necessarily a comfortable experience even in central London. For details of the women-only taxi service, see p403.

Safety Precautions

Solo women travellers should have few problems, although common-sense caution should be observed, especially at night. It's particularly unwise to get into an Underground carriage with no-one else in it or with just one or two men, and there are a few tube stations, especially on the far reaches of the Northern line, where you won't feel comfortable late at night. The same goes for some of the mainline stations in the south (such as Lambeth) and southeast (such as Bromley), which may be unstaffed and look pretty grim. In such cases you should hang the expense and take a taxi.

Information & Organisations

Marie Stopes International (Map pp448-9; ☎ 0845 300 8090; 108 Whitfield St W1; ⊖ Warren St; ⏱ 9am-5pm Thu-Mon, 9am-8pm Tue & Wed) Provides contraception, sexual health checks and abortions.

Rape & Sexual Abuse Helpline (☎ 8239 1122; ⏱ noon-2.30pm & 7-9.30pm Mon-Fri, 2.30-5pm Sat & Sun)

WORK

Even if you're unskilled you'll almost certainly find work in London, but you will have to be prepared to work long hours at menial jobs for low pay. Without skills it's difficult to find a job that pays well enough to save money. Mostly, you'll just break even.

Traditionally, unskilled visitors have worked in pubs and restaurants and as nannies. Both jobs often provide live-in accommodation, but the hours are long, the work exhausting and the pay not so good. A minimum wage (£5.05 per hour; £4.25 for those aged 18 to 21) exists, but if you're working under the table no-one's obliged to pay you even that.

Accountants, health professionals, journalists, computer programmers, lawyers, teachers, bankers and clerical workers with computer experience stand a better chance of finding well-paid work. Even so, you'll probably need to have saved some money to tide you over while you search. Don't forget copies of your qualifications, references (which will probably be checked) and a CV (résumé).

Teachers should contact the individual London borough councils, which have separate education departments, although some schools recruit directly.

To work as a trained nurse or midwife you have to apply (£140) to the UK Nursing & Midwifery Council; the registration process that follows can take up to nine months and it will cost another £160 to register. Write to the Overseas Registration Department, UKNMC, 23 Portland Pl, London W1N 4JT, or phone ☎ 7333 9333. If you aren't registered then you can still work as an auxiliary nurse.

The free *TNT Magazine* is a good starting point for jobs and agencies aimed at travellers. For au pair and nanny work buy the quaintly titled *The Lady*. Also check the *Evening Standard*, the national newspapers and government-operated Jobcentres, which are scattered throughout London and listed under 'Employment Services' in the phone directory. Whatever your skills, it's worth registering with a few temporary agencies.

If you play a musical instrument or have other artistic talents, busking will make you some pocket money. However, to perform in Underground stations, you have to go through a rigorous process taking several months. After signing up at www .tfl.gov.uk, you will have to go through an audition and get police security clearance (£10) before being granted a licence to perform and then getting yourself on a rota of marked pitches. Buskers also need to have a permit to work at top tourist attractions and popular areas such as Covent Garden and Leicester Sq. Contact the local borough council for details.

Tax

As an official employee, you'll find income tax and National Insurance are automatically deducted from your weekly pay packet. However, the deductions will be calculated on the assumption that you're working for the entire financial year (which runs from 6 April to 5 April). If you don't work as long as that, you may be eligible for a refund. Visit the website of the **Inland Revenue** (www.inlandrevenue .org.uk) to locate your nearest tax office, or use one of the agencies that advertise in *TNT Magazine* (but check their fee or percentage charge first).

Work Permits

EU and Swiss nationals don't need a work permit to work in London but everyone else does.

If you're a citizen of a Commonwealth country and aged between 17 and 30, you may apply for a Working Holiday Entry Certificate, which allows you to spend up to two years in the UK and take 12 months' work 'incidental' to your holiday. You're not allowed to set up your own business or work as a professional sportsperson. You must apply to your country's British consulate or high commission before departure – Working Holiday Entry Certificates are not granted on arrival in Britain. It is not possible to switch from being a visitor to a working holidaymaker, nor can you claim back any time spent out of the UK during the two-year period. When you apply, you must satisfy the authorities that you have the means to pay for a return or onward journey and that you will be able to maintain yourself without recourse to public funds.

If you're a Commonwealth citizen and have a parent born in the UK, you may be eligible for a Certificate of Entitlement to the Right of Abode (or indeed a British passport), which means you can live and work in Britain free of immigration control.

If you're a Commonwealth citizen with a grandparent born in the UK, or if the grandparent was born before 31 March 1922 in what is now the Republic of Ireland, you may qualify for a UK Ancestry Employment Certificate, which means you can work in the UK full time for up to four years.

Students from the US who are at least 18 years old and studying full time at a college or university can get a Blue Card permit for US$250, allowing them to work in the UK for six months. It's available through the **British Universities North America Club** (Bunac; ☎ 203 264 0901; wib@bunacusa.com; PO Box 430, Southbury CT 06488). Once in the UK, Bunac can help Blue Card holders find jobs and accommodation; it also runs programmes for Australians, Canadians and New Zealanders but you must apply before leaving home. For more details visit www.bunac.org.

Most other travellers wishing to work and not fitting into any of the above categories will need a work permit and to be sponsored by a British company. See www .ukvisas.gov.uk for more details.

If you have any queries once you're in the UK, contact the **Home Office** (☎ 0870 000 1585).

Behind the Scenes

THE LONELY PLANET STORY

The story begins with a classic travel adventure: Tony and Maureen Wheeler's 1972 journey across Europe and Asia to Australia. There was no useful information about the overland trail then, so Tony and Maureen published the first Lonely Planet guidebook to meet a growing need.

From a kitchen table, Lonely Planet has grown to become the largest independent travel publisher in the world, with offices in Melbourne (Australia), Oakland (USA) and London (UK). Today Lonely Planet guidebooks cover the globe. There is an ever-growing list of books and information in a variety of media. Some things haven't changed. The main aim is still to make it possible for adventurous travellers to get out there – to explore and better understand the world.

At Lonely Planet we believe travellers can make a positive contribution to the countries they visit – if they respect their host communities and spend their money wisely. Every year 5% of company profit is donated to charities around the world.

THIS BOOK

This 5th edition of *London* was researched and written by Sarah Johnstone and Tom Masters. Martin Hughes, Sarah Johnston and Tom Masters wrote the 4th edition. Steve Fallon wrote the 3rd edition. Pat Yale wrote the 1st and 2nd editions. The guide was commissioned in Lonely Planet's London office and produced in Melbourne.

Commissioning Editors Amanda Canning, Sam Trafford
Coordinating Editor Andrea Dobbin
Coordinating Cartographer Amanda Sierp
Coordinating Layout Designer Laura Jane
Assisting Editors & Proofreaders Sarah Bailey, Yvonne Byron, Margedd Heliosz
Cover Designer Pepi Bluck
Managing Cartographer Mark Griffiths
Managing Editor Bruce Evans
Project Manager Chris Love

Thanks to Piotr Czajkowski, Stephanie Pearson, Sally Darmody, Celia Wood, Jolyon Philcox, Imogen Hall

Cover photographs London Eye, Howard Kingsnorth/Getty Images (top); Guardsmen, Steve Vidler/eStock Photo (bottom); St Paul's Cathedral from Millennium Bridge, Jonathan Smith/Lonely Planet Images (back).

Internal photographs by Lonely Planet Images and Neil Setchfield except for the following: p67 (#2), p71 (#4), p167 (#4) Juliet Coombe; p68 (#2), p170 (#2), p220, p245, p258, p266, p270, p287, p315 (#1), p316 (#3), p317 (#1, 2, 4), p318 (#4), p322 (#1), p371 Jonathan Smith; p71 (#3) Simon Bracken; p73 (#3) Elliot Gerard Daniel; p74 (#1) Ian Connellan; p74 (#2), p164 (#3), p167 (#2) Richard I'Anson; p74 (#3), p384, p391 Dennis Johnson; p155 (#3), p167 (#1) Christer Fredriksson; p155 (#4), p170 (#1) Charlotte Hindle; p156 (#2) Adina Tovy Amsel; p160 (#4), p165 (#1), p166 (#3) Doug McKinlay; p161 (#1), p162 (#1) Lawrence Worcester; p161 (#2), p320 (#2) Martin Moos; p162 (#2) Rocco Fasano; p163 (#3) Mark Daffey; p169 (#2) Conor Caffrey; p379 Veronica Garbutt; p387 David Tomlinson. All images are the copyright of the photographers unless otherwise indicated. Many of the images in this guide are available for licensing from Lonely Planet Images: www.lonelyplanetimages.com.

ACKNOWLEDGMENTS

Many thanks to the following for the use of their content:
London Underground Map © Transport for London 2005

SEND US YOUR FEEDBACK

We love to hear from travellers – your comments keep us on our toes and help make our books better. Our well-travelled team reads every word on what you loved or loathed about this book. Although we cannot reply individually to postal submissions, we always guarantee that your feedback goes straight to the appropriate authors, in time for the next edition. Each person who sends us information is thanked in the next edition – and the most useful submissions are rewarded with a free book.

To send us your updates – and find out about Lonely Planet events, newsletters and travel news – visit our award-winning website: www.lonelyplanet.com/feedback.

Note: We may edit, reproduce and incorporate your comments in Lonely Planet products such as guidebooks, websites and digital products, so let us know if you don't want your comments reproduced or your name acknowledged. For a copy of our privacy policy visit www.lonelyplanet.com/privacy.

THANKS

SARAH

I'm a little bit burnt out on this one, so I'm just going to say one big 'thank you' to all those who helped me get this beast out, in whatever way, as friends, contacts and colleagues. You know who you are...and I'm sure that none of you read this far into the book anyway!

TOM

Thanks first of all to James, who has inspired me to love London more than anyone else I've ever known. Thanks to everyone who helped me with my research: Gray Jordan, Zeeba Sadiq, Leila Rejali, Chris Mackay, Rosemary Masters and Zurab Zaalishvili. Special thanks to Gabriel Gatehouse for his jazz advice and great nights out and to Max Schaefer for his eating tips and suggestions. Huge additional thanks to Sarah Johnstone for her tireless hard work as my co-author and co-ordinating author of this book and to Amanda Canning and Sam Trafford in the London office for all their efforts. Finally, much gratitude to the production team at Lonely Planet in Melbourne for all their huge input to this vast project!

OUR READERS

Many thanks to the travellers who used the last edition and wrote to us with helpful hints, useful advice and interesting anecdotes:

Carrie Anderson, Fiona Anderson, Kaare Arkteg, Peter Barnett, Rebecca Bourne Jones, M Ter Brugge, Mark Burbidge, Eugenia Bursey, John Bush, Helen Cardrick, Kirsti Collins, Mario Commeyne, Marino del Prete, Judith Edwards, Anneliese Frank, Christina Gellura, Christopher P Getz, Ronalie Green, Lora Hish, Victoria Hughes, Amy Jackson, Magnus Jansson, Noa Kamrat, Nina Kessing, Monique Kloosterman, Mackenzie Klubnik, Julia Kowalle, Jo Lloyd-Rogers, Sarah McDonald, Angel Marcos, Howard Mathers, Trevor Mazzucchelli, Martin Meiland, Nick Merry, Paul Mitchell, Jani Moliis, Gertraude Molloy, Audrey Moran, Julie Myers, Shalom S Paul, Dave Perrin, Lance Perryman, Stefan Private, David Ramsey, William Reeves, Stephane Reynolds, Stan Rolfe, Stephanie Schiest'L, Geoffrey Shelley, Melanie Simunovic, Rob Smallwood, Paul Stephenson, Jill Stokes, Jenny Storti, Ondrej Tejnecky, Nienke Ten, James Thomas, Sarah Torma, Susanne Ueberhuber, Robert van de Water, Ken Westmoreland, Dave Wollman, Tina Wu, Andrew Young

Notes

Notes

Index

See also separate indexes for Eating (p431), Drinking (p432), Shopping (p433) and Sleeping (p434).

Index

428

000 map pages
000 photographs

000 map pages
000 photographs

Index

434

MAP LEGEND

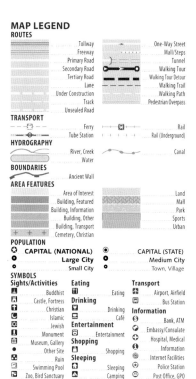

ROUTES

Tollway	One-Way Street
Freeway	Mall/Steps
Primary Road	Tunnel
Secondary Road	Walking Tour
Tertiary Road	Walking Tour Detour
Lane	Walking Trail
Under Construction	Walking Path
Track	Pedestrian Overpass
Unsealed Road	

TRANSPORT

Ferry	Rail
Tube Station	Rail (Underground)

HYDROGRAPHY

River, Creek	Canal
Water	

BOUNDARIES

Ancient Wall

AREA FEATURES

Area of Interest	Land
Building, Featured	Mall
Building, Information	Park
Building, Other	Sports
Building, Transport	Urban
Cemetery, Christian	

POPULATION

CAPITAL (NATIONAL)	CAPITAL (STATE)
Large City	Medium City
Small City	Town, Village

SYMBOLS

Sights/Activities
- Buddhist
- Castle, Fortress
- Christian
- Islamic
- Jewish
- Monument
- Museum, Gallery
- Other Site
- Ruin
- Swimming Pool
- Zoo, Bird Sanctuary

Eating
- Eating

Drinking
- Drinking
- Café

Entertainment
- Entertainment

Shopping
- Shopping

Sleeping
- Sleeping
- Camping

Transport
- Airport, Airfield
- Bus Station

Information
- Bank, ATM
- Embassy/Consulate
- Hospital, Medical
- Information
- Internet Facilities
- Police Station
- Post Office, GPO

Map Section

GREATER LONDON

0 — 10 km
0 — 6 miles

437

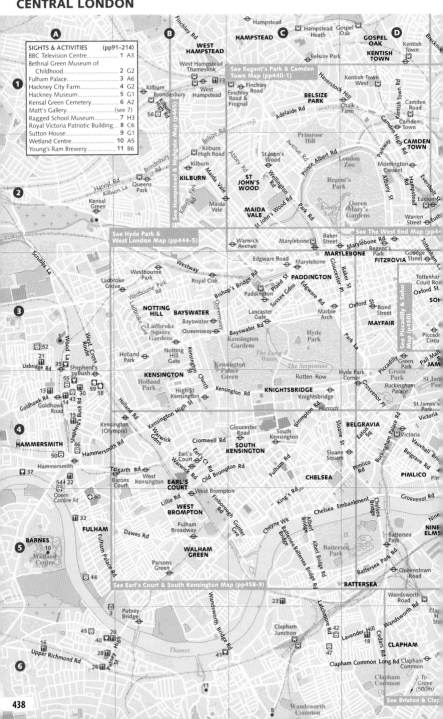

SIGHTS & ACTIVITIES (pp91–214)

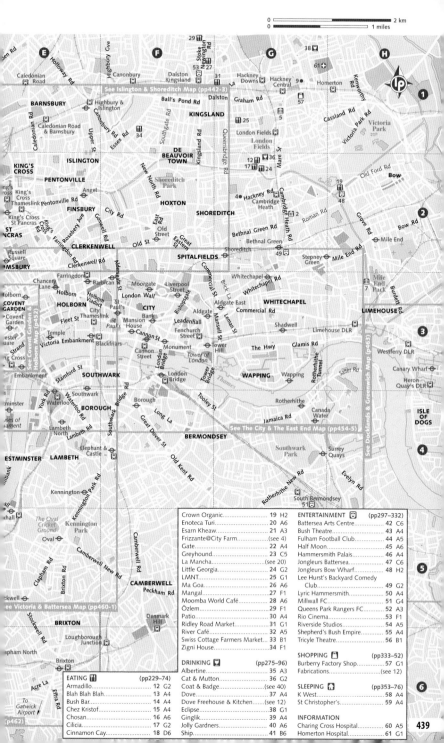

EATING 🍽 (pp229–74)
Armadillo....................... 12 G2
Blah Blah Blah................ 13 A4
Bush Bar....................... 14 A4
Chez Kristof................... 15 A4
Chosan........................ 16 A6
Cilicia......................... 17 A4
Cinnamon Cay................ 18 D6

Crown Organic................ 19 H2
Enoteca Turi................... 20 A6
Esarn Kheaw.................. 21 A3
Frizzante@City Farm.......(see 4)
Gate........................... 22 A4
Greyhound.................... 23 C5
La Mancha.................(see 20)
Little Georgia................. 24 G1
LMNT......................... 25 G1
Ma Goa....................... 26 A6
Mangal........................ 27 F1
Moomba World Café......... 28 A6
Özlem......................... 29 F1
Patio.......................... 30 A4
Ridley Road Market.......... 31 G1
River Café.................... 32 A5
Swiss Cottage Farmers Market.. 33 B1
Zigni House................... 34 F1

DRINKING 🍷 (pp275–96)
Albertine...................... 35 A3
Cat & Mutton................. 36 G2
Coat & Badge..............(see 40)
Dove.......................... 37 A4
Dove Freehouse & Kitchen..(see 12)
Eclipse........................ 38 G1
Ginglik........................ 39 A4
Jolly Gardners................ 40 A6
Ship........................... 41 B6

ENTERTAINMENT 🎭 (pp297–332)
Battersea Arts Centre......... 42 C6
Bush Theatre.................. 43 A4
Fulham Football Club......... 44 A5
Half Moon..................... 45 A6
Hammersmith Palais.......... 46 A4
Jongleurs Battersea........... 47 C6
Jongleurs Bow Wharf......... 48 H2
Lee Hurst's Backyard Comedy
  Club....................... 49 G2
Lyric Hammersmith........... 50 A4
Millwall FC................... 51 G4
Queens Park Rangers FC...... 52 A3
Rio Cinema.................... 53 F1
Riverside Studios.............. 54 A5
Shepherd's Bush Empire....... 55 A4
Tricyle Theatre................ 56 B1

SHOPPING 🛍 (pp333–52)
Burberry Factory Shop........ 57 G1
Fabrications...............(see 12)

SLEEPING 🛏 (pp353–76)
K West........................ 58 A4
St Christopher's............... 59 A4

INFORMATION
Charing Cross Hospital........ 60 A5
Homerton Hospital............ 61 G1

439

SIGHTS & ACTIVITIES (pp91–214)
Abbey Rd Zebra
Crossing.................................1 B4
British Library............................2 H5
Camden Market........................3 F3
Freud Museum...........................4 B1
Isokon Apartments....................5 D1
Jewish Museum..........................6 F3
London Central Islamic Centre &
Mosque.................................7 C5
London Zoo Entrance.................8 D4
Percival David Foundation of
Chinese Art............................9 H6
Petrie Museum of Egyptian
Archaeology.........................10 G6
St Pancras New Church............11 H5

EATING (pp229–74)
Asakusa...................................12 G4
Bar Gansa................................13 F3
Café Corfu...............................14 F3
Café Delancey..........................15 F3
Castle's....................................16 G2

Cottons Rhum Shop, Bar &
Restaurant...........................17 E2
Diwana Bhel Poori House..........18 G5
El Parador................................19 G4
Engineer..................................20 E3
Jamón Jamón...........................21 F3
Mango Room............................22 F3
Manna....................................23 D2
Terra Brasil...............................24 H5
Trojka.....................................25 D2

DRINKING (pp275–96)
Bar Vinyl.................................26 F3
Bartok.....................................27 E2
Crown & Goose........................28 F3
Edinboro Castle........................29 F3
Queen's...................................30 D3
Warrington Hotel.....................31 A5
World's End.............................32 F3

ENTERTAINMENT (pp297–332)
Barfly@the Monarch.................33 E2
Cecil Sharp House....................34 E3

Dingwalls...............................(see 39)
Dublin Castle...........................35 F3
Enterprise................................36 E2
Hampstead Theatre...................37 B2
Jazz Café..................................38 F3
Jongleurs.................................39 F2
Koko.......................................40 G4
Lord's......................................41 B5
Place.......................................42 H5
Underworld............................(see 32)

SLEEPING (pp353–76)
30 King Henry's Road................43 C2
66 Camden Square....................44 G1
Crescent Hotel.........................45 H5
Harlingford Hotel.....................46 H5
Jenkins Hotel...........................47 H5
St Christopher's Inn
Camden...............................48 F3
St Pancras International YHA.....49 H5

INFORMATION
University College Hospital........50 G6

SIGHTS & ACTIVITIES (pp91–214)
Clerk's Well	1 D6
Coram's Fields	2 B6
Dickens House Museum	3 B6
Estorick Collection of Modern Italian Art	4 D2
Geffrye Museum	5 G4
Karl Marx Memorial Library	6 D6
London Canal Museum	7 B4
St Pancras Chambers	8 A4
White Cube	9 G5

EATING (pp229–74)
Addis	10 B4
Afghan Kitchen	11 D3
Almeida	12 D2
Brick Lane Beigel Bake	13 H6
Cicada	14 D6
Duke of Cambridge	15 E4
Eagle	16 C6
Eyre Brothers	17 G6
Fifteen	18 F5
Frederick's	19 D3
Gallipoli	20 D3
Gallipoli Again	21 D3
House	22 D2
Islington Farmer's Market	23 D3
Konstam	24 B5
Le Mercury	25 D3
Les Trois Garçons	26 H6
Medcalf Bar	27 C5
Metrogusto	28 D3
Moro	29 C5
North Sea Fish Restaurant	30 A5
Ottolenghi	31 D2
Pasha	32 D3

Quality Chop House	33 C6
Real Greek	34 G5
Social	35 E3
Souvlaki Bar	36 D6
Sông Quê	37 G4

DRINKING (pp275–96)
1001	38 H6
Albion	39 C2
Bar Kick	40 G5
Bluu	41 G5
Bricklayers Arms	42 G5
Café Kick	43 C5
Cantaloupe	44 G5
Cargo	45 G5
Dragon Bar	46 F5
Dreambagsjaguarshoes	47 G5
Elbow Room	48 C4
Elk in the Woods	49 D3
Embassy	50 E2
Foundry	51 G5
George & Dragon	52 G5
Joiners Arms	53 H4
King's Bar	54 A6
Kinky Mambo	55 D2
Lord John Russell	56 A5
Loungelover	57 H6
Lush Bar	58 D1
Medicine Bar	59 D2
Medicine Bar	60 G5
Mother Bar	(see 65)
Old Blue Last	61 G6
Ruby Lounge	62 B4
Smersh	63 F5
T Bar	64 G6

ENTERTAINMENT (pp297–332)
333	65 G5
Almeida Theatre	66 D3
Aquarium	67 F5
Carling Islington Academy	68 D3
Comedy Café	69 G5
Cross	70 A3

Egg	71 A2
Garage	72 D1
Herbal	73 G5
Ironmonger Baths	74 E5
Plastic People	75 G5
Renoir	76 A6
Sadler's Wells	77 D5
Scala	78 B4
Screen on the Green	79 D3

SHOPPING (pp333–52)
Antoni & Alison	80 C6
Aria	81 D2
Camden Passage Market	82 D3
Clerkenwell Green Association	83 D6
Columbia Road Flower Market	84 H5
Diverse	(see 31)
EC One	85 C5
Gay's the Word	86 A6
Haggle Vinyl	87 E3
Housmans	88 B4
Hoxton Boutique	89 G5
Lassco	90 G6
Leather Lane Mambo	91 C6
Lesley Craze Gallery	92 D6
Mathmos	93 E6
No-one	94 G5
Past Caring	95 D3
Start	96 G5
Start	97 G5
Tatty Devine	98 G5

SLEEPING (pp353–76)
Ashlee House	99 B5
Express by Holiday Inn	100 G5
Generator	101 A5
Hotel Saint Gregory	102 G5
London City YMCA	103 F6

INFORMATION
Cyberg@te	104 A5
Eastman Dental Hospital	105 B5

443

Harrow Rd

A **B** **C** **D**

Warrington Cres

1

79

Goldney Rd

Marylands Rd

Sutherland Ave

Shirland Rd

88

49

Harrow Rd

Wa
Ave

Woodfield Rd

Wornington Rd

Elkstone Rd

St Ervan's Rd

Colborne Rd

Bevington Rd

Portobello Rd

Ladbroke Gve

Clifton

30

28

Delamere Tce

Senior St

Bourne Tce

Grand Union Canal

Westbourne Park

Westway

Alfred Rd

2

74

61

Tavistock Cres

Great Western Rd

Aldridge Rd Villas

Shrewsbury Rd

55

24

Westbourne Park Villas

Royal
Oak

Lord Hills Rd

57

All Saints Rd

St Luke's Rd

St Stephen's Gdns

Porchester Rd

Ladbroke Grove

47

Lancaster Rd

Westbourne Park Rd

Powis
Gdns

Talbot Rd

Colville Tce

Chepstow Rd

Hereford Rd

Kildare Tce

Alexander St

Newtown

Bishop's Bridge Rd

65

21

Inverness Tce

3

43

25

82

70

81

69

71

59

52

Elgin Cres

Blenheim Cres

Colville Tce

Ledbury Rd

Lonsdale
Rd

Artesian Rd

**NOTTING
HILL**

46

38

94

76

35

29

101

Westbourne Gve

99

Leinster
Sq

Garway Rd

Prince's
Sq

41

Kensington
Gdns Sq

91

Porchester
Gdns

23

Queensway

Clarendon Rd

77

Arundel Gdns

68

111

45

78

Chepstow Villas

Chepstow Villas

Pembridge Villas

Pembridge Pl

Dawson Pl

108

Ilchester Gdns

Chester Gdns

Moscow Rd

Bayswater

Inverness Tce

Ladbroke
Gdns

Stanley Gdns

105

Ladbroke Sq

Kensington Park Rd

Ladbroke Square Gardens

Portobello Rd

Pembridge Rd

Pembridge Cres

Pembridge Sq

Ossington St

Palace Ct

St Petersburgh Pl

97

39

34

BAYSWATER

Queensway

Lansdowne Rd

Lansdowne
Cres

St John's Gdns

Kensington Park

Ladbroke Gve

Ladbroke Tce

104

92

53

36

80

Pembridge
Gdns

Linden Gdns

Clanricarde Gdns

75

4

Portland Rd

Lansdowne Wk

Aubrey Rd

Hinde St

Holland Park

Notting Hill
Gate

63

60

22

Kramer Mews

26

37

62

Notting Hill Gate

Kensington Pl

Palace Gdns Tce

Palace Gardens
Mews

Brunswick Gdns

3

8

Holland Park Ave

Holland Park Mws

Holland Park

Campden Hill

Peel St

56

Campden St

Bedford Gdns

Sheffield Tce

Vicarage Gate

109

Kensington Church St

Kensington
Palace

4

**Kensington
Palace
Green**

Palace Ave

Palace
Green

The Broad Wk

5

KENSINGTON

Campden Hill

Holland
Park

96

64

Duchess of Bedford's
Walk

Camden Great

Hornton St

Holland St

83

44

84

Holland Park Ave

Addison Rd

Abbotsbury Rd

Phillimore Gdns

Melbury Rd

Allen St

Wright's La

High Street
Kensington

Gate

See Earl's Court & South Kensington Map (pp458-9)

Oakwood Ct

5

112

2

St Alban's
Gve

Victoria Gve

6

Kensington
(Olympia)

Holland Rd

Holland Park Rd

Edwardes Sq

Kensington High St

Earl's Ct Rd

Marloes Rd

Scarsdale Villas

Stanford Rd

Launceston Pl

Cornwall
Gdns

Kensington
(Olympia)

Olympia

THE WEST END

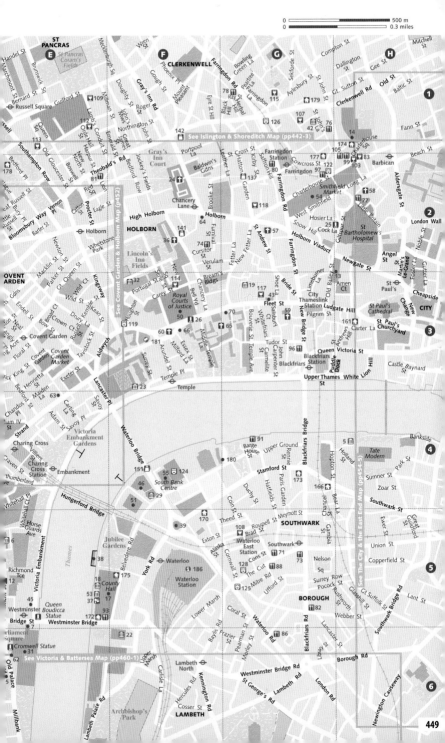

PICCADILLY & SOHO

PICCADILLY & SOHO

COVENT GARDEN & HOLBORN

COVENT GARDEN & HOLBORN

A   B   Bunhill Fields   C   Great Eastern St   Holywell St   D   Sclater St

Gee St   Clere St   Luke St   Scrutton St   Shoreditch

Clerkenwell Rd   Baltic St   Garett St   Banner St   Epworth St   SPITALFIELDS

Chequer St   Dufferin St   Worship St   Quaker St   102

Whitcross St   Errol St   Bunhill Row   88   44

Fann St   Fortune St   Golden La   St Paul St   Clifton St   Sun St   96   100   27   Hanb

Charterhouse St   Chiswell St   Milton St   Earl St   Appold St   81   24   69   Princ

Charterhouse Sq   Beach St   Ropemaker St   Lackington St   Wilson St   105   Lamb St   Fournier St   16

Barbican   Finsbury Pave   Spital   Steward   104   Fashion St

Long La   Aldersgate St   91   Silk St   Finsbury   South Pl   Eldon St   Liverpool Street Station   Spitalfields Market   Brushfield St   8   106

Barbican Centre   Moor La   Moorgate   Finsbury Circus   Liverpool Street   121   Artillery La   White's Row   Brune

Bartholomew's Hospital   25   London Wall   Moorgate   Blomfield St   108   Petticoat Lane Market   103

Angel   Basinghall Ave   Copthall Ave   Great Winchester St   New St   117   Wentworth St   Coulston St   Aldgate East

Newgate St   St Martin's Le-Grand   Guildhall   17   Basinghall St   Coleman St   Old Broad St   Houndsditch   Camomile St   Aldgate   Aldgate High St   Whitechapel High St   Braham St

St Paul's   Gresham St   Lothbury   Bank of England   Threadneedle St   Bishopsgate   Bevis Marks   1   Mansell St   Alie St

68   Cheapside   Bow La   Princes St   3   116   Leadenhall St   Goodmans Yard

St Paul's Cathedral   49   36   New Change   Poultry   Bank   Cornhill   82   19   Leadenhall St   20   Billiter St   Minories   Prescot

St Paul's Churchyard   119   Watling St   22   39   37   34   Lombard St   Birchin La   Gracechurch St   Lime St   Fenchurch St   Fenchurch Street Station

Carter La   CITY   Mansion House   73   King William St   Cannon St   Monument   Eastcheap   Great Tower St   Mark La   Seething La   Pepys St   107   Tower Hill   Byward St   2   St   Tower Hill

Queen Victoria St   Cloak La   Cannon Street Station   23   Monument   Lower Thames St   Old Billingsgate Market   East Smithfie

Castle Baynard St   Upper Thames St   Arthur St   Tower of London   41   Tower Bridge Approach   St Katharine Dock   64

White Lion Hill   Millennium Bridge   Thames   London Bridge   18   Tower Bridge

Bankside   New Globe Walk   92   71   Southwark Bridge   Park St   Battle Br   60   9   52   63   Shad Thames

38   28   74   78   10   Clink St   15   Tooley St   118   Tooley St   6   Gainsford St   Curlew St   12

SOUTHWARK   Sumner St   110   45   48   30   21   London Br Ar   26   London Bridge   Magdalen St   Horsleydown   Elizabeth St

Southwark St   Zoar St   113   101   70   55   89   83   51   111   London Bridge Station   Tooley St

Lavington St   95   Thrale St   66   5   79   St Thomas St   54   99   Fair St   Druid St

Copperfield St   Union St   75   114   120   Snowsfields   56   White's Grounds

Ayres St   Newcomen St   115   Crosby Row   Guy St   98   14   77   58   Tanner St   Tooley St

Gt Suffolk St   Sawyer St   Mint St   57   Borough   Kipling St   Weston St   Leathermarket St   Bermondsey St

Otashill St   Redcross Way   Lant St   Borough   Great Dover Hostel   86   Tabard St   50   Tower Bridge Rd   Riley Rd   Abbey St   Enid St

BOROUGH   Southwark Bridge Rd   Great Dover St   Swan St   Staple St   97   BERMONDSEY   Neckinger St

Borough Rd   93   Newington Causeway   Harper Rd   Trinity St   109   Law St   Wild's Rents   D Bermondsey   Thomas St   65   59

Great Dover St   Long La

A
B
C
D

1

Kensington (Olympia)

Kensington (Olympia)

7

Oakwood Ct.

Ilchester

Melbury Rd

Holland Park Rd

Holland High St

Kensington High St

Phillimore Gdns

Edwardes Sq

Allen St

Phillimore Wk

Wright's La

High St Kensington

St Alban's Gve

Stanford Rd

Victoria Rd

Abingdon Villas

Scarsdale Villas

Markes Rd

Cornwall Gdn

Olympia

Hammersmith Rd

Avonmore Rd

Warwick Gdns

Warwick Rd

Holland Rd

Pembroke Sq

Pembroke Gdns

Pembroke Rd

Earl's Court Rd

Logan Pl

Cromwell Cres

Stratford Rd

Lexham Gdns

Cromwell Hospital

Cromwell Rd

57

2

West Cromwell Rd

Longridge Rd

Templeton Pl

Nevern Sq

Redfield La.

Kenway Rd

Hogarth Rd

54

42

66

69

63

Earl's Ct Gdns

Collingham Pl

Collingham Gdns

Courtfield Gdns

Courtfield

Harring

Edith Rd

Gunterstone Rd

68

Trebovir

62

Earl's Court

Barkston Gdns

Collingham Gdns

Bramham Gdns

Bolton Gdns

EARL'S COURT

Earl's Court

Penywern Rd

Earl's Ct Sq

Barons Court

Talgarth Rd

West Kensington

Philbeach Gdns

65

West Kensington

56

29

26

Old Brompton Rd

The Little Boltor

3

45

Eardley Cres

28

Redcliffe Gdns

36

Coleherne Rd

Wetgate Tce

Harcourt Tce

West Brompton

WEST BROMPTON

16

Lillie Rd

Sedlescombe Rd

Onbar Rd

Tamworth St

Racton Rd

Seagrave Rd

Brompton Cemetery

Ifield Rd

4

Anselm Rd

Halford Rd

1

Walham Gve

Farm La

Dawes Rd

40

Vanston Pl

23

Fulham Broadway

44

North End Rd

15

17

Fulham Bdwy

Fulham Rd

Holmead Rd

18

41

Barclay Rd

Effie Rd

Harwood Rd

Waterford Rd

Moore Park Rd

Maxwell Rd

Britannia Rd

King's Rd

Michael Rd

5

38

WALHAM GREEN

Musgrave

Eel Brook Common

Harwood Tce

Fulham Rd

Novello St

Acre Rd

Basuto Rd

Favart Rd

New King's Rd

Wandsworth Bridge Rd

59

Imperial R

6

Parsons Green

43

Crondace Rd

Condace Rd

Parsons Green

Fulham Palace Rd

VICTORIA & BATTERSEA

Chapel St
Grosvenor Pl
Buckingham Palace Gardens

A
19 Motcomb St
L W Halkin St
Belgrave
42
43
Belgrave Pl

Chester St
Wilton Mws
Wilton St
Upper Belgrave St

B
Royal Mews
Lower Grosvenor
11
28
Bressenden Pl
Grosvenor
Eaton
La
Allington St

Catherine Pl
Petty France
St James's Park
Castle La
Buckingham Gate
Caxton St
Palace St

C
Tothill St
Broadway
34
Broad Sanctuary

D
Strutton Ground
Old Pye St
Great Peter St
Great Smith St
Dartmouth St

See Hyde Park & West London Map (pp444-5)

Eccleston Mws
40
Hobart Pl
Lower Belgrave St

Victoria St
Howick Pl

1

Sloane St
Cadogan Pl
Chesham Pl
Cadogan La

Eaton Pl
Eaton Mws North

BELGRAVIA
Eaton Sq
35
Chester Mws

Ebury Mws
29
13
12
15

24
Victoria Bus Station
Terminus Pl
Victoria St
Victoria Station
41
Wilton Rd

Ashley Pl
Morpeth Tce
Carlisle Pl
Francis St
Greencoat Pl

10
Greycoat St
Artillery Row
Rochester Row

18
Elverton St
Maunsel St

Monck St
Medway St
Horseferry Rd
Marsham St

WESTMINSTER
Page St
Vincent St

2

Ellis St
27
Sloane Tce
Cliveden Pl
Sloane Sq
Sloane Square
Sloane Gdns

South Eaton Pl
Elizabeth St
33
Eccleston St

Eccleston Bridge
VICTORIA

Bridge Pl
39
Gillingham St
Guildhouse St
25
37

Vincent Sq
Willow Pl

Westminster School Playing Field

Regency St
Causton St

Erasmus St
Herrick St
John Islip St

Lower Sloane St
Bourne St
Graham Tce
Cundy St

Victoria Coach Station
Elizabeth Bridge
Buckingham Palace Rd

Hugh St
Eccleston Sq

Churton St
32

Vauxhall Bridge Rd

Chapter St

3

Frank's Row
Royal Hospital Rd
Holbein Pl
14
16
Pimlico Rd
Bloomfield Tce
Ranelagh Gve
St Barnabas St
Ebury Bridge

38
PIMLICO
Winchester St
Clarendon St
Cumberland St
Gloucester St
Sutherland St
Westmoreland Tce
Turpentine La
Peabody Ave

Alderney St
Cambridge St
Denbigh St
Charlwood St
Lupus St

St George's Dr
Warwick Sq
Moreton Tce
Moreton St
36
Belgrave Rd
Tachbrook St
Pimlico
Bessborough St

4

Ebury Bridge Rd
Gatliff Rd

Ranelagh Gardens

Johnson's St
Clarendon St

Chichester St
31
St George's Sq
Dolphin Sq
Aylesford St

Pimlico Gardens

Churchill Gdns Rd
Grosvenor Rd

Charles II Statue
Chelsea Embankment

Chelsea Bridge Rd

Chelsea Bridge

See Earl's Court & South Kensington Map (pp458-9)

Nine Elms La
Ponton Rd

Carriage Dr North

Tennis Courts

Battersea Power Station
2

Cringle St

NINE ELMS

Children's Zoo

BATTERSEA
Battersea Park

Carriage Dr East
Queenstown Rd

Duck Pond

6
Ladies Pond

Boating Lake

5

Havelock Tce
1

Wandsworth

Carriage Dr South

Battersea Park
Lurline Gdns

Prince of Wales Dr
Warriner Gdns
Battersea Park Rd

Queenstown Road

Stewarts Rd

6

20
Charlotte Despard Ave

See Brixton & Clapham Map (p462)

460

SIGHTS & ACTIVITIES	(pp91–214)
Battersea Dogs Home	1 B5
Battersea Power Station	2 B4
Imperial War Museum	3 G1
Lambeth Palace	4 F1
Museum of Garden History	5 F2
Pump House	6 A5
St John's Smith Square	7 E1
Tate Britain	8 E2
Vincent van Gogh's Home	9 F6
Westminster Cathedral	10 C1

EATING 🍴	(pp229–74)
Goring	11 B1
Jenny Lo's Tea House	12 B2
Ken Lo's Memories of China	13 B2
La Poule au Pot	14 A2
Olivo	15 B2
Pimlico Road Farmers Market	16 A3
Rebato's	17 E5
Vincent Rooms	18 D2
Zafferano	19 A1

DRINKING 🍷	(pp275–96)
Dusk	20 A6

ENTERTAINMENT 🎭	(pp297–332)
Crash	21 E3
Fire	22 E6
Oval	23 F4
Pacha	24 B1
Queen Mother Sports Centre	25 C2
Vauxhall Tavern	26 E3

SHOPPING 🛍	(pp333–52)
Lulu Guinness	27 A2

SLEEPING 🛏	(pp353–76)
41	28 C1
B+B Belgravia	29 B2
City Inn	30 E2
Dolphin Square Hotel	31 C3
Luna Simone Hotel	32 C2
Morgan House	33 B2
Sanctuary House Hotel	34 D1
Tophams Belgravia	35 B2
Victoria Hotel	36 C3
Wellington Hall	37 C2
Windermere Hotel	38 B3

TRANSPORT	(pp398–407)
Green Line Bus Station	39 B2

INFORMATION	
Belgian Embassy	40 B1
easyEverything	41 C2
German Embassy	42 A1
Spanish Embassy	43 A1

BRIXTON & CLAPHAM

SIGHTS & ACTIVITIES	(pp91–214)	Prince of Wales	16 B3
Holy Trinity	1 B3	Sand	17 C4
		So.uk	18 B3
EATING	(pp229–74)	Tim Bobbin	(see 16)
Abbeville	2 B4	White Horse	19 D4
Asmara	3 E3		
Bamboula	4 E3	**ENTERTAINMENT**	(pp297–332)
Brixton Bar & Grill	5 E3	Brixton Academy	20 E2
Bruno	6 E3	Brockwell Park Lido	21 F4
Bug	7 E3	Clapham Picture House	22 B3
Fujiyama	8 E3	Efra Hall Tavern	23 E3
Neon	9 E3	Fridge	24 E3
Pepper Tree	10 B3	MASS	25 E3
Verso	11 B3	Ritzy Cinema	26 E3
White House	12 B3		
		SHOPPING	(pp333–52)
DRINKING	(pp275–96)	Brixton Village	27 E3
Brixtonian Havana Club	13 E2	Joy	28 E3
Dogstar	14 E3	Oliver Bonas	29 B3
Plan B	15 E3		

Scale

| 0 | | 500 m |
| 0 | | 0.3 miles |

DOCKLANDS & GREENWICH

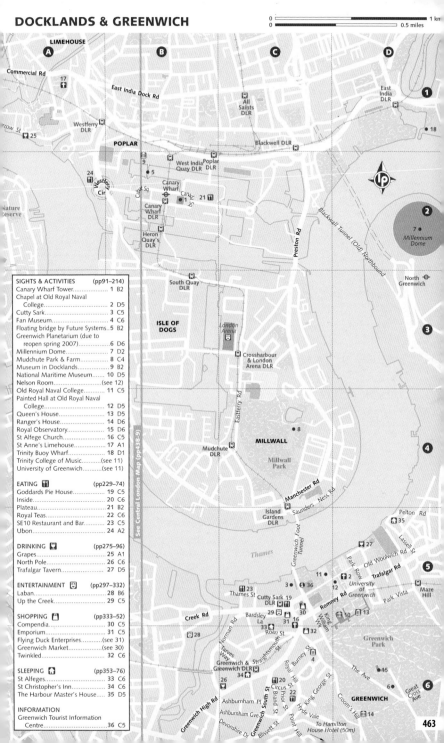

SIGHTS & ACTIVITIES	(pp91–214)	
Canary Wharf Tower	1	B2
Chapel at Old Royal Naval College	2	D5
Cutty Sark	3	C5
Fan Museum	4	C6
Floating bridge by Future Systems	5	B2
Greenwich Planetarium (due to reopen spring 2007)	6	D6
Millennium Dome	7	D2
Mudchute Park & Farm	8	C4
Museum in Docklands	9	B2
National Maritime Museum	10	D5
Nelson Room	(see 12)	
Old Royal Naval College	11	C5
Painted Hall at Old Royal Naval College	12	D5
Queen's House	13	D5
Ranger's House	14	D6
Royal Observatory	15	D6
St Alfege Church	16	C5
St Anne's Limehouse	17	A1
Trinity Buoy Wharf	18	D1
Trinity College of Music	(see 11)	
University of Greenwich	(see 11)	

EATING 🍴	(pp229–74)	
Goddards Pie House	19	C6
Inside	20	C6
Plateau	21	B2
Royal Teas	22	C6
SE10 Restaurant and Bar	23	C5
Ubon	24	A2

DRINKING 🍷	(pp275–96)	
Grapes	25	A1
North Pole	26	C6
Trafalgar Tavern	27	D5

ENTERTAINMENT 🎭	(pp297–332)	
Laban	28	B6
Up the Creek	29	C5

SHOPPING 🛍️	(pp333–52)	
Compendia	30	C5
Emporium	31	C5
Flying Duck Enterprises	(see 31)	
Greenwich Market	(see 30)	
Twinkled	32	C6

SLEEPING 🛏️	(pp353–76)	
St Alfeges	33	C6
St Christopher's Inn	34	C6
The Harbour Master's House	35	D5

INFORMATION		
Greenwich Tourist Information Centre	36	C5

463

RICHMOND

| 0 | 300 m |
| 0 | 0.2 mile |

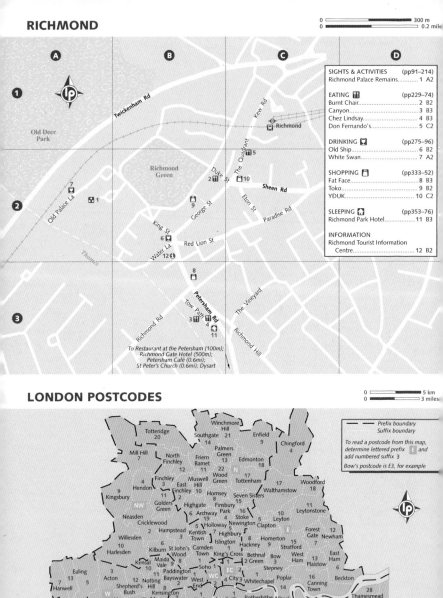

SIGHTS & ACTIVITIES	(pp91–214)	
Richmond Palace Remains	1	A2
EATING 🍴	(pp229–74)	
Burnt Chair	2	B2
Canyon	3	B3
Chez Lindsay	4	B3
Don Fernando's	5	C2
DRINKING 🍷	(pp275–96)	
Old Ship	6	B2
White Swan	7	A2
SHOPPING 🛍	(pp333–52)	
Fat Face	8	B3
Toko	9	B2
YDUK	10	C2
SLEEPING 🛏	(pp353–76)	
Richmond Park Hotel	11	B3
INFORMATION		
Richmond Tourist Information Centre	12	B2

Old Deer Park

Twickenham Rd

Richmond Green

Kew Rd

Richmond

The Quadrant

Duke St

Sheen Rd

Old Palace La

George St

Eton St

Paradise Rd

King St

Red Lion St

Water La

Thames

Petersham Rd

Tow Path

The Vineyard

Richmond Rd

Richmond Hill

To Restaurant at the Petersham (100m);
Richmond Gate Hotel (500m);
Petersham Café (0.6mi);
St Peter's Church (0.6mi); Dysart

LONDON POSTCODES

| 0 | 5 km |
| 0 | 3 miles |

– – – Prefix boundary
——— Suffix boundary

To read a postcode from this map, determine lettered prefix **E** and add numbered suffix 3

Bow's postcode is E3, for example

Winchmore Hill 21
Totteridge 20
Southgate 14
Enfield 9
Chingford 4
Mill Hill 7
North Finchley
Friern Barnet 11
Palmers Green 13
Edmonton 18
Finchley 3
Wood Green 22
Tottenham 17
Muswell Hill 10
East Finchley 2
Hornsey 8
Woodford 18
Hendon 4
Seven Sisters 15
Walthamstow 17
Kingsbury 9
Golders Green 11
Highgate 6
Finsbury Park 4
Stoke Newington 16
Leyton 10
Leytonstone 11
Neasden
Cricklewood 2
Hampstead 3
Archway 19
Holloway 7
Highbury 5
Clapton 5
Forest Gate 7
Newham 12
Willesden 10
Kentish Town 5
Islington 1
Homerton 9
Stratford 15
East Ham 6
Harlesden
Kilburn 6
Maida Vale 9
St John's Wood 8
Camden Town 1
King's Cross
Hackney 8
Bow 3
West Ham 13
Plaistow
Kensal
Paddington 2
Soho 1
Bethnal Green 2
Stepney 1
Canning Town 16
Beckton 6
Ealing
Acton 3
Notting Hill 11
Bayswater 2
West End
City 3
Poplar 14
Hanwell 13
Shepherd's Bush 12
Kensington 8
Pimlico 1
Whitechapel 1
Docklands 14
Charlton 7
Woolwich 18
Thamesmead 28
Chiswick 4
Earl's Ct 5
Chelsea 3
Lambeth
Vauxhall
Rotherhithe 16
Greenwich 10
Plumstead 18
Abbey Wood 2
Sheen 14
Hammersmith 6
Fulham 10
Battersea 11
Camberwell 5
Deptford 8
New Cross
Blackheath 3
Eltham 9
Barnes 13
Putney 15
Clapham 4
Stockwell 9
Peckham 15
Lewisham 13
Grove Park 12
Wandsworth 18
Brixton 2
Herne Hill 24
Brockley 4
Catford 6
Wimbledon 19
Balham 12
Dulwich 21
Honor Oak 23
Sydenham 26
Raynes Park 20
Tooting 17
Streatham 16
Crystal Palace 20
Penge
Norwood 25

NW N E EC WC W SW SE

Thames

HAMPSTEAD & HIGHGATE

| 0 | | 1 km |
| 0 | | 0.5 miles |

See Central London Map (pp438–9)

See Regent's Park & Camden Town Map (pp440–1)

LONDON UNDERGROUND MAP

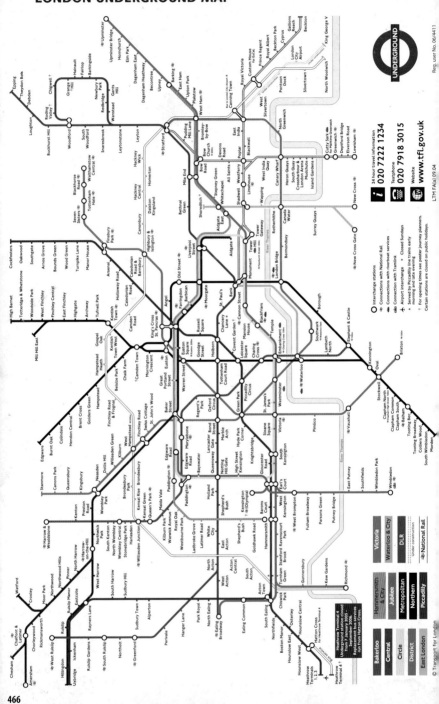